Falconer Madan

The early Oxford Press

A Bibliography of Printing and Publishing at Oxford, '1468'-1640

Falconer Madan

The early Oxford Press
A Bibliography of Printing and Publishing at Oxford, '1468'-1640

ISBN/EAN: 9783337252755

Printed in Europe, USA, Canada, Australia, Japan

Cover: Foto ©ninafisch / pixelio.de

More available books at **www.hansebooks.com**

EARLY OXFORD PRESS

MADAN

London
HENRY FROWDE
OXFORD UNIVERSITY PRESS WAREHOUSE
AMEN CORNER, E.C.

New York
MACMILLAN & CO., 66 FIFTH AVENUE

AN OXFORD TITLE-PAGE, 1640

The

Early Oxford Press

A BIBLIOGRAPHY OF
PRINTING AND PUBLISHING AT OXFORD

'1468'—1640

WITH NOTES, APPENDIXES AND ILLUSTRATIONS

BY

FALCONER MADAN, M.A.

FELLOW OF BRASENOSE COLLEGE, OXFORD

Oxford
AT THE CLARENDON PRESS
1895

Oxford
PRINTED AT THE CLARENDON PRESS
BY HORACE HART, PRINTER TO THE UNIVERSITY

PREFACE

THE present work was undertaken early in 1889, and is an attempt to describe in detail the products and working of the Oxford Press in its early days. Though eclipsed by the glories of the later University Press, the first period, included in this book, has a natural importance of its own. The Fifteenth and early Sixteenth Century presses [1] are necessarily of interest, and when printing became firmly established in 1585 it began to reflect faithfully the current tendencies of thought and study in the University. Theology is predominant. animated on its controversial side with fierce opposition to the Church of Rome, but the quieter fields of classical work are well represented, and side by side is seen an increasing study of English literature. Of lighter books there are few, and of chapbooks perhaps only one (1603, no. 5).

The most important works produced at Oxford between 1585 and 1640 were Richard de Bury's Philobiblon (1599), Wycliff's treatises (1608), capt. John Smith's Map of Virginia (1612). Burton's Anatomy of Melancholy (1621, &c.), Field on the Church (1628, &c.), Sandys' translations of Ovid's Metamorphoses (1633), the University Statutes (1634), Chaucer's Troilus and Cressida in English and Latin (1635), Chillingworth's Religion of Protestants (1638), and Bacon's Advancement and Proficience of Learning, in English (1640: see frontispiece). There are of course many books on logic, philosophy and the like, intended for the University curriculum, and many collections

---

[1] See Appendixes A, B.

of the rhetorical poems by which the University was expected
to condole or rejoice with every change in the royal estate. 180
pages of mechanical grief at Elizabeth's death in 1603 are at once
followed by 200 pages of equally mechanical congratulations to
James I : and the metrical tears dropped in turn on the grave of
the latter monarch in March 1625, are in May succeeded with
indecorous haste by songs of joy on the marriage of his successor.
Some volumes of English poems and plays occur. by Skelton,
Nicholas Breton, Churchyard, Fitz-Geffrey, Randolph, Cartwright, Fletcher, and others, and a few still lighter pieces, such
as a Masque at Richmond, partly in Wiltshire dialect, and
" Bushell's Rock," both in 1636. There are traces of the study
of Spanish, French and Welsh, as well as of Latin and Greek ;
and an attempt to introduce phonetic writing and spelling was
made by Charles Butler in 1633 and 1634. Even theological
disputes are lightened by the solemn account of certain Jesuits
in the East, who dressed up a carcase as that of a queen recently
deceased, obtained much glory from the miracles it wrought,
until the real corpse arrived and the priests vacated the vicinity
(1633, Gregorius). There is something surprising in Oxford
being chosen as the printing-place of a book to persuade mothers
to nurse their own children (1622, Clinton) ; and an episcopal
alchemist is not often to be met with in real life (1621, Thornborough). It is less to be wondered at that a college which had
leased land to Queen Elizabeth for a quiet five thousand years,
should try to be relieved of its agreement within fifty (1623,
Oxford).

There is no need of a general history of the University Press
at this time, as distinguished from the annals which the Appendixes of this work present. The printers were privileged
members of the University, and occasionally printed "cum
privilegio," but there is little to invest their personal proceedings
with importance. Though it is true that money was advanced
in 1585 by the Earl of Leicester, Chancellor of the University, to
set up Joseph Barnes with a new press, and that the charter of
privileges in 1632 gave the University direct control of the
printing, there are as yet few signs of actual academical patronage or interference, and the failures and successes of the printers
and publishers, which can be traced in detail in Appendixes C

and F, are the ordinary fluctuations of trade. Nor can the Oxford press at this time claim much connexion with the greater world of the English Court or Church. After it was placed on a permanent footing by the Earl of Leicester, its one great patron and protector within our period was Archbishop Laud, who occupied a similar position to that of Bishop Fell at a later period in the same century.

The year 1640 has been chosen as the inferior limit of this bibliography, partly because both the British Museum Catalogue of early English books and Arber's Transcript of the Registers of the Stationers' Company stop at that point, partly because the interest in the products of the press as such was found to be rapidly diminishing, and partly in consequence of the break-up of all quiet progress during the convulsions of the Rebellion, combined with the dismal prospect of that trackless wilderness— the literature of the Civil War.

The present bibliography presents, it is believed, four features of novelty :—the better representation of the titlepage by the use of Roman and Italic capitals as well as ordinary type; the mention of the chief type used in each book; the furnishing of the first words of certain pages, to facilitate the identification of imperfect copies; and the insertion of actual pages[1] of books printed at Oxford, selected from works which are cheap and common. These points are explained and discussed in a paper on *Method in Bibliography*, printed at pp. 91–106 of vol. 1 of the Transactions of the Bibliographical Society (1893), to which the reader is referred, if he wishes to see a fuller account of the whole aim and method of the present book.

The best thanks of the writer are due for general help to Mr. E. Gordon Duff, Librarian of the John Rylands (late Spencer) Library at Manchester, to Mr. F. J. H. Jenkinson, Librarian of the Cambridge University Library, and to Mr. W. H. Allnutt of the Bodleian : but especially to the Delegates of the Clarendon Press both for undertaking on liberal terms a work which can scarcely prove remunerative, and for enabling the Oxford Historical Society to supply copies to its members, as

---

[1] Separate leaves from rare and costly books are given in G. E. Klemming's *Sveriges äldre liturgiska literatur* 'Stockholm, 1879 —a practice which cannot be approved— but no local press has as yet been similarly illustrated.

vol. xxix, at a price far below its actual cost [1]. Mr. Horace Hart, the Controller of the Press, has taken a warm personal interest in the printing. and any merits of form which may be found are due to his experience and to the co-operation of his compositors. Nothing, however, can relieve the writer of responsibility for the errors and shortcomings which will be detected ; and he can only plead that it is better to bring out an imperfect book, if it is a useful one and the result of hard work, than, by straining after an unattainable completeness, to delay indefinitely its publication.

F. MADAN.

OXFORD, *Dec.,* 1894.

[1] Separate copies can *only* be obtained by ordering them from the Clarendon Press. and are not supplied by the Society.

MINOR POINTS.

Dates. The books classed under a given year, such as 1615, are necessarily such as were issued between 25 March 1615 and 24 March 1616, since no means exist for dividing them according to the historical year. In recording a date between Jan. 1 and March 24, the form used is invariably the double one, such as 23 Feb. 161$\frac{5}{6}$, by which is implied what we understand by 23 Feb. 1616.

Numbers of books. Some notes on the number of books printed at Oxford will be found on p. 291, and of books printed or published at Oxford on p. 292, among the Notanda.

References. The usual style of reference throughout the book (including index) is to the *year* followed by the *initial letter* of the particular heading ; as 1634 C, when the reference is to no. 9 on p. 177 (Cosin). A few references will be found in the earlier pages to years beyond 1640. made before it was decided to close the work at that year.

Titles. The heading usually presents the author's name in the form by which he is generally known to posterity, as " James ii, king," although at the time of the book referred to he was prince James.

LIST OF CONTENTS

LIST OF ILLUSTRATIONS AND TABLES

OXFORD PRINTING, 1585–1640.

Each of the first seven hundred copies of this work contains three specimens of actual pages from old Oxford books, copies of which are both common and cheap. Thus nos. 1–200 contain pages from (1) Ursinus's Summe of Christian Religion, 1587, (2) N. Fuller's Miscellanea Sacra, 1616, (3) Carpenter's Philosophia Libera, 1636: nos. 201–322 (1) Ursinus, (2) Fuller, (3) Reusner's Symbola, 1638: nos. 323–500 (1) Ursinus, (2) Sanderson's Logica, 1618, (3) Reusner: nos. 501–700 (1) Ursinus's Summe of Christian Religion, 1589, (2) Du Moulin's Accomplishment of the prophecies, 1613, (3) Grotius's Defensio fidei catholicæ, 1636.

After no. 700, at least one actual page will be given, and its provenance will be indicated by a note of the form "38.20," implying a page from the 20th book of 1638 (Reusner).

LIST OF TABLES.

PLAN OF THE BIBLIOGRAPHY

15th and early 16th century.

The books of these periods are in some respects exceptionally treated, but the general plan is similar to that of the later press. Pages 1-7 (printed off in 1889) must be taken in close connexion with Appendixes A and B, which correct and supplement those pages in important points.

1585-1640.

1. After the heading (which in all cases is the author or a body representing the author, if known; otherwise the catch-title) comes the title, reproduced faithfully so far as was possible with the employment of four types. A fifth minute type indicates letters represented by contractions in the original. The occurrence of a "motto" (whether a text or quotation), a device (see p. 289) or woodcuts (see p. 290) is noted in square brackets. A * before the heading implies "undated": a † "no place of printing mentioned."

2. Next follows the technical description, comprising :—

a. The number of the imprint (see pp. 292-310 : it would have been better to add the names of the printer and publisher to the bare reference).

b. The date.

c. The apparent size of a page of an ordinary uncut copy, according to the scale,

for narrow sizes		*for broad sizes*	
in.		in.	
12-18	folio	12-18	large 4°
9-12	large 8°	9-12	4°
7-9	8°	7-9	small 4°
6-7	12°	6-7	square 12°
5-6	16°		&c.
4-5	24°		

The number of leaves in a section (quire or gathering) precedes, within round brackets, when different from what is suggested by the apparent size : as "(eights) small 4°." When it has been desirable to indicate further the way in which the original sheets of paper have been folded, the words *single, double,* or *treble* (for once, twice, or thrice folded) are used on p. 238.

d. The number of pages of a perfect copy, in square brackets when there is no printed pagination, as " pp. [16] + 121 + [9]." When printed pagination does not occur in the book at all, the signatures are also given.

e. The first words of the 11th page, and of later ones in the case of a large work, always in italics.

f. The common type of the body of the work, followed by the terms Roman, Italic, or English (i. e. Black-letter): see pp. 291-2.

g. The contents. *Every page not mentioned is blank,* without exception.

3. Notes on the book. A reference to Wood's *Athenæ* and *Fasti Oxonienses,* as edited by Bliss (1813-20), has been considered as superseding in most instances any biographical account of the author. And the limitation of the present work to a bibliography of a press, not of books connected with the University, has been borne in mind.

THE OXFORD PRESS.

Ʈhe Fifteenth Century Press[1].

"1468."

[**Rufinus**, of Aquileia].   [Sign. a 1ʳ:—] Incipit exposicio sancti Ieronimi in | simbolum apostolorum ad papam laurentium. [Sign. e 9ᵛ:—] Explicit exposicio sancti Ieronimi in | simbolo apostolorum ad papam lauren|cium Impressa Oxonie Et finita An'no domini . M . cccc . lxviij . xvij . die | decembris.

Impr. as above, Oxford, "1468": 8º: | *tali generacione.* Contents:—pp. (1–82) pp. [84], signn. a–d⁸ e¹ᵃ: sign. b 1ʳ beg. | the treatise.

The work here ascribed to St. Jerome is in reality by Tyrannius Rufinus of Aquileia, *d.* 610.

1479.

1. **Aegidius** de Columna, of Rome.   [Sign. a 2ʳ:—] Incipit tractatus solennis fratris Egi|dij de ordine fratrum Augustinensium de | peccato originali [Sign. c 7ᵛ:—] Explicit tractatus breue [altered by hand to *breuis*] et vtilis de | originali peccato Editus a fratre Egidio | Romano ordinis fratrum heremitarum san'cti augustini. Impresso [altered by hand to *impressus*] et finito [*finitus*, as before] Oxonie. | A natiuitate domini . M . cccc . lxxix . xiiij . die | mensis marcij

Impr. as above, Oxford, probably 14⁷⁸⁄₉: | *quod contrahamus.* Contents:—pp. (3–46) 8º: pp. [48], signn. a–c⁸: sign. b 1ʳ beg. | the treatise.

The *editio princeps* of this work by bp. Aegidius de Columna, of Rome.

2. **Aristotle.**   [Sign. y 6ʳ:—] Explicit textus ethicorum Aristotelis | per leonardum arretinum lucidissime transla.tus correctissimeque. Imp ressus Oxoniis | Anno domini . M . cccc . lxxix.

Impr. as above, Oxford, 1479: 8º: pp. | facio leonardi arretini in libros ethico-[348], signn. a–x⁸ y⁶: sign. b 1ʳ beg. | rum ": (5–15) " prologus " by the same : *Mnis ars.* Contents:—pp. (3–4) " pre- | 17–347) the treatise.

A Latin translation of the Nicomachean Ethics of Aristotle by Leonardus Brunus of Arezzo (Arretium).

---

[1] For a discussion of special points connected with the Fifteenth Century Oxford Press, see Appendix A.

B

1480.

***¹Cicero**, Marcus Tullius.   [M. Tulli Ciceronis Oratio pro T. Annio Milone.]

[Oxford, about 1480]: 6°: probably 60 pages, signn. a–e⁶. Contents:—pp. (probably 3–60) the oration.

Only known from fragments containing signn. b 3, b 4, e 3, e 4, in the Bodleian Library at Oxford. It is still not absolutely certain that this book was printed at Oxford. If it was, this, and not the Andria of Terence printed by Pynson in 1497, was the first English edition of any part of a classic author in the original language.

1481.

1. **Alexander** de Hales, the *doctor irrefragabilis*.   [Sign. g 5ᵛ :—] Explicit expositio venerabilis | Alexandri super primum librum de anima. [Sign. y 7ᵛ :—] Explicit elucidantissima exposi=tio egregij Alexandri super secundum | librum de anima. [Sign. ʜ 8ʳ :—] Explicit sentenciosa atque studio | digna expositio venerabilis Alexan᷄dri super tercium librum de anima. Im=᷄pressum per me Theodericum rood de | Colonia in alma vniuersitate Oxoñ. | Anno incarnacionis dominice . M . cccc . | lxxxi . xi . die mensis Octobris.

Impr. as above, Oxford, 1481: la. 8°, perhaps eights' fol.: pp. [480], signn. a–f⁸. g⁶, h–s⁸. t–x⁶, y–z and A 11⁸: sign. b 1ʳ beg. *vel non sit*, ʙ 1ʳ beg. *vna natura*. Contents:—signn. a 2ʳ g 5ᵛ, bk. 1, with short preface : h 1ʳ y 7ᵛ, bk. 2 : z 1ʳ–11 8ʳ, bk. 3.

The *editio princeps* et unica of the Latin Commentary on the De Anima (περὶ ψυχῆς) of Aristotle, made by Alexander de Hales (i. e. probably Hailes near Winchcombe) the *doctor irrefragabilis* (d. 1245 , to be distinguished from Alexander de Ales or Alesius. Of this book there are two issues, the earlier with no border, the later with an elaborate woodcut border, the first ever found in an English printed book. surrounding the entire printed text of sign. a 2ʳ. There are two similar issues of the Lathbury, 1482.

2. ***¹Latin Grammar.**   [A Latin Grammar in English with examples, only known from two leaves in the British Museum, signn. b 2 and (presumably) b 5 : b 2 beg. "case As I muste", ends "adyectyuys and voy": b 5 beg. "Also when y haue", ends "quem queris". Date probably 1481 : probably sm. 4° (but in eights), the chain lines being across the page.]

1482.

¹**Lathbury**, John.   [Sign. b 8ᵛ :—] Explicit prologus Sequitur li=|ber moralium super trenis Iheremie pro=|phete &c̄. [Sign. z 8ᵛ :—] Et sic est finis huius operis mo=|ralium super ca . 1 . trenorum ihere. prophete In | cipit trenorum Capitulum secundum. [A similar colophon follows chapter 2 on sign. K ("k k") 7ᵛ.] [Sign. L 7ᵛ :—] Explicit exposicio ac morali-sacio | tercij capituli trenorum Iheremie pro|phete . Anno domini M . cccc . lxxxij vlti=| ma die mensis Iulij | [Sign. O5ᵛ :—] Explicit tabula

super opus trenorum | compilatum per Iohannem Lattebu. | rij ordinis minorum.

Impr. as above, [Oxford] 1482: la. 8º, perhaps (eights) fol.: pp. [384], signn. a–z, A–I, kk. I–M⁸, N–O⁶: sign. b 1ʳ beg. *strennuitatem*, н 1ʳ beg. *didit &c.* Con-tents:—signn. a 2ʳ–b 8ʳ, prologue: c 1ʳ–l. 7ᵛ, the work in 3 chapters: M 1ʳ o 5ᵛ, alphabetical index.

The *editio princeps* et unica of the Latin Commentary on the Lamentations of Jeremiah, made by John Lathbury. Of this book there are two issues, with and without the woodcut border mentioned under the Alexander de Hales, 1481.

1483.

1. [*†**Anwykyll**, John].   [Compendium totius grammaticae]. [Sign. n 1ʳ:—] Vulgaria quedam abs Terentio in Anglicam ling|uam traducta.

No doubt printed at Oxford, probably in 1483: sm. 4º: pp. [256?], signn. a–q (?). Contents:—signn. a–m, the work (?), n 1ʳ–q 8ʳ, Vulgaria Terentii.

A Latin Grammar in Latin believed to be by John Anwykyll, of which this edition is only known from fragments, but which was reprinted at Deventer in 1489. The Vulgaria Terentii (sentences from Terence with English translation) was sold as a separate part, and still exists complete in itself. There are two issues of the Grammar, not at present clearly distinguished.

2. *†**Hampole**, Richard Rolle of.   [Sign. a 2ʳ:—] Explanationes notabiles deuotissimi viri Ricardi | Hampole heremite super lectiones illas beati Iob que solent | in exequijs defunctorum legi que non minus historiam quam tropo | logiam & anagogiam ad studentium vtilitatem exactissi=|me annotauit. [Sign. k 6ᵛ:—] Sermo beati Augustini de misericordia | et pia oracione pro defunctis. |

[Oxford, probably 1483]: (sixes) 12º: pp. [128], signn. a–k [" lr "]⁶ l⁴: sign. b 1ʳ beg. *visitat ad.* Contents:—sign. a 2ʳ–k 6ʳ, Hampole on Job: k 6ᵛ–l 3ᵛ, Augustine.

3. * **Logic.**   [Sign. A 2ʳ:—] Uoniam ex terminis fiunt proposiciones ... [19 Latin treatises on logical subjects].

No place or date [Oxf., about 1483]: (sixes) 8º: pp. [328], signn. A–Z, Aa Cc⁶ dd⁸: sign. B 1ʳ beg. *nulla proposicio,* bb 1ʳ *illis superfluum.* Contents: — signn. A 2ʳ–dd 5 nineteen logical treatises, the last ending "Explicit tractatus de motu velocitatis. Sequitur tabula": dd 6ʳ–8ᵛ, a table in Latin giving the heads of the parts of each treatise, each group preceded by "Tractatus": dd 8ᵛ "Ad lectores carmen" and "Registrum cartarum".

These nineteen logical treatises are strung together to form a systematic work on Logic: at the end of the 17th, on sign. bb 3ᵛ, is "Et sic finiuntur insolubilia swynishede.", i. e. Roger Swineshede (Suinesheved, Swincet &c.), but he was probably only the author of that part. The last treatise is physical rather than logical.

4. * **Lyndewoode**, William.   [Sign. S 9ᵛ:—] Explicit opus magistri wil|helmi lyndewoode Super con=|stituciones prouinciales laus deo. [Sign. dd 7ᵛ:—] Explicit tabula compendiosa super librum | qui intitulatur prouincialis compilata per wil=|helmum de Tylia nemore com-pleta In festo | conuersacionis Sancti Pauli . Anno domini | Millesimo . CCCC . xxxiij.

No imprint, but Oxford about 1483: (eights) fol. : pp. [732], signn. a-c⁸, d⁶, e-i⁸, k⁶, l-o⁸, p⁴, q-s⁸, t⁶, v-y⁸, z⁶, A-D⁸, E⁶, F-N⁸, O⁶, P-R⁸. s¹⁰, aa-cc⁸, dd¹⁰: sign. b 1ʳ beg. *de hijs habes*, u 1ʳ beg. *supra c. proxi.*, bb 1ʳ beg. *eas delinquat.* Contents:—sign. a 1ᵛ, woodcut of a doctor at his desk : a 2ʳ, "Prologus": a 2ᵛ-s 9ᵛ, the work in five books: aa 2ʳ-aa 2ᵛ "tabula constitucionum prouincialium" : aa 3ʳ-dd 7ᵛ, an index: dd 8ʳ-10ʳ, table of Constitutions according to author.

The *editio princeps* of the Provincial Constitutions of England, in Latin, with a Latin Commentary on them by William Lyndewoode (*d.* 1446). See 1664 L, 1679 L.

1485.

1. ***Alexander** de Villa Dei.   [Textus Alexandri cum sententiis].

[Oxford, about 1485]: sm. 4°.

Only known from two leaves (signn. c³-c³) in the Library of St. John's College, Cambridge.   A grammatical work, of which other editions were printed in London by Wynkin de Worde (sine anno) and Pynson (1516), and elsewhere.

2. Phalaris.   [Sign. a 2ʳ :—] Francisci Aretini Oratoris preclarissimi in eloquentissimas Phala|ridis tyranni epistolas per ipsum | e greco in latinum versas. Prohe|mium foeliciter incipit [Sign. m 6ʳ :—] Hoc oposculum in alma vniuersi|tate Oxonie. A Natali christiano | Ducentesima & nonagesima septima. | Olimpiade foeliciter impressum est.

Oxford, 1485, printed by Theodoric Rood and Thomas Hunte : (eights) squ. 12° : pp. [176], signn. a-d⁸, e⁶, f⁴, g⁸, h⁴, i⁸, k-l⁸, m⁶ : sign. b 1ʳ beg. *Udio vos.* Contents: —sign. a 1ᵛ "Carmeliani Brixiensis Poete ad lectorem Carmen," 12 elegiac lines : a 2ʳ-m 6ʳ, the work : on m 6ᵛ after the colophon "Hoc Teodericus rood quem collonia misit | Sanguine germanus nobile pressit opus | Atque sibi socius thomas fuit anglicus hunte. | Dij dent vt venetos exuperare queant | Quam ienson venetos decuit vir gallicus artem | Ingenio didicit terra britanna suo. | Celatos veneti nobis transmittere libros | Cedite nos alijs vendimus o veneti | Que fuerat vobis ars primum no ta latini | Est eadem nobis ipsa reperta patres. | Quamuis semotos toto canit orbe britannos | Uirgilius. placet his lingua latina tamen.

A Latin translation of the spurious Letters of Phalaris.

1486.

['**Mirk,** John].   [Sign. ( ) 2ʳ :—] Incipit liber qui | vocatur festialis [Sign. z 3ʳ :—] Here endith the boke | that is callid festiuall. | the yere of oure lord M | cccc . lxxxvi . the day aftir | seint Edward the kyng.

Imprint as above, n. pl., but Oxford 1486 (probably 19 Mar. 1489) : la. 8° : pp. [348], signn. ( )⁸, a-b⁸, c⁶, d⁸, d.⁸, e⁶, f⁸, g⁴, h⁸, i⁶, k-l⁸, m⁶, n-o⁸, p⁶, q⁴, r⁶, s⁸, t-v⁶, x⁸, y⁶, z⁴ : sign. b 1ʳ beg. *diuerse skylles.* Contents :—sign. ( ) 1ʳ, woodcut of Crucifixion : ( ) 1ᵛ-z 3ʳ, the work.

English sermons on the holy days and a few of the Sundays of the year : written or collected by John Mirk, canon of Lilleshall. Other early English printed editions exist, beginning with one by Caxton in about 1483. Variations are found in the setting up of signn. h and i.   The first two leaves are not at present known to exist.

ᏰᏂᴇ Ꮧarly Ꮪixteenth Ꮯentury Ꮲress[1].

1517.

Burley, Walter. ⁌ Tractatus expositorius / super libros poste-|
riorum Arestotilis: preclarissimi philisophi | Walteri Burlei artium liber-
alium | et trium philosophiarum magi-|stri meritissimi : ac in sacra | theo-
logia doctoris perspi|cacissimi planissimique | suis posteris Oxoniensibus
admodum vtilis incipit feli-|citer cum summa diligentia. | recognitus.
[Then *woodcut*]. [Sign. B 6ᵛ :—] Explicit scriptum planissimi doctoris
Walteri | Burlei super libros posteriorum Impressum | in academia Oxonie
anno dominice in carnationis . M . CCCCC . xvii . | Die vero decembris
quar|to ad laudem dei | & profectum | studentium. [Then *woodcut*: then]
Fata regunt finem : spero dij cepta secundent. |

Impr. as above, Oxford 1517 : sm. 4° : | arms of University : A 1ᵛ–B 5ᵛ, the work :
pp. [20], signn. A⁴, B⁶ : sign. B 1ʳ beg. *Sed* | B 6ʳ, royal arms : B 6ᵛ, colophon with
quia. Contents :— sign. A 1ʳ, title, with | arms of University repeated.

A Latin Commentary by Walter Burley on the Posterior Analytics of Aristotle.

1518.

1. **Burley,** Walter. ⁌ Tractatus perbreuis de materia & forma :|
Magis|ri Walteri Burlei doctoris planissimi. [Then *woodcut*: then] ⁌ Aliud
perbreue compendium de relatiuis e-|iusdem doctoris vtile tamen admodum
| nouellis logicis. [Sign. B 3ʳ :—] ⁌ Finit tractatus duorum principio-|
rum et de relatiuis. Magis|ri Walte|ri Burley Oxoniensis. | ⁌ Finis.
[Sign. B 4ᵛ :—] ⁌ Impositus est finis tractatui doctoris planissimi | de
duobus principijs . s.[iue] mater ia et forma et de rela-|tiuis cum speciali
priuilegio per septennium ex edicto dig|nissimi cancellarii Oxonie. [Then
woodcut: then] ⁌ Impressum est presens opusculum in celeberima |
vniuersitate Oxoniensi per me Ioannem Scolar in | viculo diui Ioannis
baptiste moram trahentem An-|no domini . M . CCCCC . decimooctauo.
Mensis vero Iu-|nij die septimo.

Impr. as above, Oxford, 1518 : sm. 4" : | B 3ʳ, the work in two parts : B 3ᵛ, wood-
pp. [16], signn. A–B⁴ : sign. B 1ʳ beg. *est* | cut of royal arms : B 4ᵛ, colophon.
dare. Contents : - sign. A 1ʳ, title : A 2ʳ—|

[1] For a general discussion of the circumstances of the Early Sixteenth Century
Oxford Press, see Appendix B.

2. **Dedicus,** Joannes.   Questiones | moralissime super li=|bros Ethicorum eruditissimi | viri Ioannis Dedicus artium libe=|ralium triumque philosophiarum magistri | optime meriti / et in moralibus pre ceteris satis pe=|riti feliciter incipiunt subtilissimis Oxoniensibus in philo=|sophia morali lucubrare cupientibus non magis | vtiles quam necessarie. | [Then *engraving of the University arms*]. [Sign. N 4ᵛ :—] ℭ Explicitum est Ioannis Dedici Oxoniensis in | morali philosophia eruditissimi preclarum opus-culum | questionum / subtilissimediscucientium (licet sparsim cum | quadam tamen dependentia) singulas materias in decem | libris ethicorum Arestotilis inuestigatas / vti summa | industria lucubranti patebit. Impressumque in cele=|berima vniuersitate Oxoniensi per me Iohannem | Scolar in viculo sancti Ioannis Baptiste moram tra=|hentem . Anno domini . M . CCCCC . decimooctauo . Men=|sis vero Maij die decimoquinto . [*ornament*] | ℭ Cum priuilegio . | ℭ Uetitum est per edictum sub sigillo cancellariatus | ne quis in septennio hoc insigne opus imprimat | vel aliorum ductu impensis venditet in vni=|uersitate Oxonie : aut infra precinctum | ciusdem : sub pena amissionis omnium | librorum et quinque librarum ster=|lingorum pro singulis sic ven|ditis ubiubi impressi fue=|rint preter penam pretax=| atam in decreto. | ℭ Cornicum oculos configere noli.

Impr. as above, Oxf. 1518: (eights & fours) sm. 4ᵒ: pp. [152], foll. 75 + [1], signn. A⁸, B⁴, C⁸, D⁴, E⁸, F⁴, G⁸, H⁴, I⁸, K⁴, L⁸, M–N⁴: sign. B 1ʳ beg. *pertinet ad.* Contents:—p. (1) Title and large wood-cut : (2) large woodcut of the royal arms with supporters &c. : (3–152) the work : (152) colophon, &c.

Of Johannes Dedicus (perhaps, as has been suggested by prof. H. W. Chandler, Dethick) nothing is known. The Quaestiones extend to the end of the 5th book of the Ethics, and the last paragraph is a summary of the 6th.

3. *****Laet,** Jaspar.   [at end:—] FIniunt prenostica exerpta a prenosticis egregii viri magistri Iasparis | Laet angligenis cognitu maxime vtilia. Et in celebe=|rima oxoniensi academia | [*woodcuts*] impressa [*woodcuts*]. |

Imprint as above, Oxford, [probably 1518]: 4ᵒ [?]: broadside. Contents:— on 1st page, the Praenostica.

Only known from the lower half of the sheet preserved in the Cambridge University Library, where the upper half is also believed to be.

4. **Lux.**   ℭ Compendium questionum de luce et lumine [followed by a small woodcut and the four quaestiones]. | Sign. B 4ᵛ :—] ℭ Cum priuilegio dignissi=mi Cancellarij vniuer=|sitatis Oxonie. [Then a large woodcut : then] ℭ Finit compendium questiuncularum de luce & de | lumine nouiter recognitum. Impressumque in celiberi=|ma vniuersitate Oxoniensi per me Ioannem Sco=|lar in viculo diui Ioannis baptiste moram trahentem | Anno domini . M . CCCCC . decimooctauo . Mensis vero | Iunij die quinto.

Impr. as above, Oxford, 1518 : sm. 4ᵒ: pp. [16], signn. A–B⁸: sign. B 1ʳ beg. *re* | *intentio.* Contents :—A 1ʳ, title : A 1ᵛ–B 4ʳ, the work : B 4ᵛ, the colophon.

5. **Whittington,** Robert. ❡ De heteroclitis nominibus. | ❡ Editio Roberti Whittintoni lichfeldien|sis Grammatice magistri : et protouatis | anglie in florentissima Oxoniensi achade'mia Laureati / de heteroclitis nominibus | et gradibus comparationis. ['Then *woodcut*: then a "tetrastichon" and a "distichon." | Sign. B 4ᵛ :—] [Roberti] whittintoni lichfeldiensis de heteroclitis no|[minibus & de] gradibus comparationis Oxonie impressa per|[me Ioannem] Scolar in viculo diui Ioannis baptiste mo|[ram tra]hentem Anno domini . M . CCCCC . decimooctauo | [M]ensis vero Iunij . die vicesimoseptimo.

Impr. as above, Oxford, 1518 : sm. 4″ : pp. [16], signn. A⁶, B¹ : sign. B 1ᵉ beg. *Hic tapes.* Contents :—A 1ᵉ, title &c. as   above : A 2ᵉ–B 4ᵛ, the work (on B 4ᵛ also occur a woodcut of the arms of the University and the colophon).

Only known from an imperfect copy in the Bodleian rescued from the binding of a book.

1519.

Compotus. ❡ Compotus manualis | ad vsum Oxoniensium. | [*device*]. [sign. B 4ᵛ :—] ❡ Impressum est presens opusculum in ce|leberrima vniuersitate Oxoniensi per | me Carolum Kyrfoth. In vico | diui Joannis baptiste moram | trahentem Anno domini . M . D . xix. Mensis | vero Februarij . die V. |

Imprint as above, Oxford, 1519 : sm. 4° : pp. [16], signn. A–B⁴ : sign. B 1ᵉ beg.   ❡ *Februarius.* Contents :—A 1ᵉ, title, and woodcut : A 1ᵛ–B 4ᵉ, the Compotus : B 4ᵛ, University arms and colophon.

A system of arithmetic illustrated by wood engravings of the open hand, values being attached to each part. Panzer after Maittaire mentions a Paris ed. of 1498 "cum commento."

FICTITIOUS OR LOST OXFORD BOOKS.

1459–1584.

1459.

A small sheet of paper printed on the ice-bound Thames at London 18 Jan. 1716 ascribes to Oxford the first printing in England, in the year 1459. Most of the information on the sheet is derived from Atkyns's *Original and Growth of Printing* (Lond. 1664).

1461.

Printing was "practised in Oxford in 1461," according to Randle Holmes's *Academy of Armory* (Chester, 1688), quoted in Bigmore, i. 337.

1469–70.

In Herbert's Ames, iii. 1393 we read:—"In the late Tho. Osborne's catalogue of books for sale in June 1756, No. 1343 'Plinii Secundi Epistolarum, Liber primus. Exemplar elegans, literis initial. colorat. corio turcico, fol. deaur. lineis rubris & auro elegans ornat. 15l. 15s. Oxon. apud F. Corsellis. 1469.' To which is added this note, 'Hocce unicum est exemplar notum, a variis allegatum, et vix uni visum adeo ut Phoenix librorum dici mereretur [*sic*], certe primus est ex libris a Corcellis impressis, cui nomen suum adjunxerit, secundus vero ordine omnium quos unquam ille impressit, priorem scilicet scimus fuisse, Jeronymi Expositionem in Symbol. Apostol. Oxoniae 1468. Anno 1470, varia idem typographus impressit Opuscula, addito in fine nomine, sed nec unicum eorum reperitur hodie integrum. Possident quidam amatores fragmenta aliqua poematum Latinorum, ut Gerardi Lystrii Rhenensis, &c. Carmen Listrii lividorum hominum venenosas linguas, &c.' This raised the curiosity of the book collectors, who considered this article as a confirmation of what R. Atkins had asserted about printing at Oxford. They all flocked to Osborne's shop, who instead of the book, produced a letter from a man at Amsterdam, filled with frivolous excuses for not sending them to him. They were disappointed, and looked on the whole as a Hvm; however the Plinii Epistolæ, and Ger. Listrii Oratio, &c. afterwards appeared at an auction at Amsterdam, and were bought for the late Dr. Ant. Askew; and were sold again at an auction of his books, by Baker and Leigh, in Feb. 1775. Lot 2064, and

2622, to which articles are annexed, viz. to Lot 2064, 'Ad finem hæc verba, *Impr. Oxon. apud F. Corsellis,* 1470, Manu recentiore exarata sunt.' Also to lot 2622, 'Hæc verba, *Imprim. Oxon. ap. Corsellis,* 1469, Manu recentiore exarata sunt.' To those who are at all conversant in early printing, the dates will appear at first sight a bungling forgery." So far Herbert's Ames, cf. Bowyer and Nichols's *Origin of Printing,* 2nd ed. (Lond. 1776), p. 171. The full entry of art. 2064 is " Listrii (Ger.) Oratio habita in Enarrationem Dionysii Halicarnassii ; Dionysii Orbis expositio e Greco tralata Prisciano interprete ; Ejusdem Carmen in venenosas Linguas Hominum, & Epicedium doctissimi Adoloscentis Ingenisissimique Petri Thessaliensis ": sold to Mr. Dent for £2 3s. : art. 2622 has 1569 for 1469, and was sold to Capt. Smith for £1 6s.

In the Auction Catalogue of the Library of Dr. Abr. de Vries of Haarlem (Amsterdam, Frederick Muller, 1864) art. 181 was :—" COR-CELLIS.—Collection de lettres, copies authentiques, déclarations et notices en 1756 et 57 sur l'imposture fameuse du falsaire G. SMITH, à Amsterdam et la Haye, qui fabriqua une édition de *Plinii epistolæ,* avec souscription : *Oxoniæ, Corcellis.* 1469. *Hedwigii liber* 16. ibidem. 1470, etc. et trompa Mr. P. v. Damme et autres en Angleterre.— Recueillie et con-servée pour prouver son innocence à la falsification et annotée par Mr. v. Damme. 12 pc. MS. Collection très-curieuse, contenant e. a. 7 lettres de Smith à v. Damme, une lettre forgée ou falsifié du Comte de Pembroke, une lettre de P. Burman Sec., copie d'une déclaration de Meerman, etc. etc." It is to be hoped that this interesting collection will be brought to light again.

In the *Monthly Miscellany, or Memoirs for the Curious* (June 1708), p. 177 it is stated that in the Bishop of Ely's Library (now at Cambridge) are books " of the first printing in England at Oxford in 1469."

1480.

" Guido de Columnia de historia Trojana, per T. R. (*Theodore Rood*). Quarto. 1480." So Herbert's Ames, p. 1393. The source of the error was discovered by Cotton to be a forgery in a copy of Guido sine anno et loco preserved in the Earl of Pembroke's Library at Wilton (*Typ. Gaz.,* 1st ser., 2nd ed., p. 209.)

Before 1487.

" Books from the Oxford Press.... 208*. The Chronicles of England. Folio. Lent by the Earl of Jersey." So in the Catalogue of the Caxton Celebration, 1877, p. 28. Some error. The reference is no doubt to Caxton's Chronicle of England, printed in 1482.

1489.

When Cotton printed his *Typographical Gazetteer,* 2nd series. (Oxf. 1866) he believed that an Indulgence of 1489 (altered to 1499), in the

Library of Trinity College, Dublin, was printed at Oxford. It is "a small broadside on vellum, consisting of 24 lines only, printed very closely and occupying a space of about nine inches by six." The Indulgence is from Johannes de Gigliis alias de Liliis Apostolicus Subdiaconus, granted by Pope Innocent iii: and is dated 1499, there being no name of place or date of printing. There is no doubt that Cotton was mistaken in attributing this piece to the Oxford press.

1498.

1. Bagford, in his inaccurate way, gives the title of an edition of the Greek text of the Ethics of Aristotle by Aretinus "Oxon. 1498" (Brit. Mus. MS. Harl. 5901, fol. 3). He mentions the 1479 edition of the Latin text separately, but the former date can only be due to some confusion with the latter.

2. The Rufinus of 1468 appears as dated 1498 in Panzer, who quotes Schoenemann i. 585, and also in Migne's *Patrologia Latina*, xxi. col. 17.

1499.

Indulgence: see 1489.

1500.

1. Buridanus: see next article.

2. "Gualtheri Burley Tractatus de materia et forma ac de relativis. Oxonii 1500. 4." So in Panzer ii (1794) p. 244, quoting Maittaire p. 739, ex Bibl. Bodl. p. 117 (an allusion to an error in the Bodleian Catalogue of 1674, repeated in the 1738 Catalogue p. 206). Bagford makes the same mistake, twisting the author's name into Johannes Buridanus (Brit. Mus. MS. Harl. 5901, fol. 3). Even Hain (no. 4142) has copied from Panzer. The colophon of 1518. B shows how the error arose, as Cotton points out (*Typ. Gaz.*, 1st ser., 2nd ed., p. 209).

3, 4. Bagford is responsible for two more fictitious Oxford books of 1500, a *Quaestiones de lumine et luce* (Brit. Mus. MS. Harl. 5901, fol. 3, Bodl. MS. Rawl. D. 375, fol. 103: a confusion with 1518. L.) and a Whitinton *de heteroclytis nominibus* printed at Oxford by Peter Treveris (!) (Bodl. MS. Rawl. D. 375, fol. 103: see 1518. W).

1506.

The following book though not printed at Oxford supplies information about an Oxford bookseller:—[sign. a 1ʳ:—] "Principia seu introductiones *fratris* peregrini ytalici de lugo in via doctoris subtilis : adipisci eiusdem doctoris doctrinam cupientibus. [at foot :—] Uenundantur autem in alma ac florentissima vniuersitate Oxoniense. in intacte virginis ac immaculate / vico: sancti iohannis euangeliste / ad intersignium. [Then follow 4 tractatus : then on sign. g 4ᵣ :—] Expliciunt principia seu introductiones (pro iuuenibus) fratris peregrini de lugo ... Inpressa autem Londini. per Richardum pynson. cum solerti cura ac diligentia Honestissimi Iuuenis ac prudentissimi Hugonis Meslier. Expensis autem georgii castellani / oxonii morantis / ad intersignium sancti Iohannis euangeliste : in quo venundatur opus hoc. Finis. ..." Then follows a 5th treatise, ending with a letter from Peregrinus de Lugo dated "Tholose quarto Kalendas Februarij . M . cccc . vj." Herbert's Ames (iii. 1396) refers this book to Oxford, although at i. 252 it is referred rightly to Pynson's press at London.

1510.

References to a *Compendium quaestiuncularum de luce et lumine*, Oxford 1510, will be found in Bagford (Brit. Mus. MS. Harl. 5901, fol. 22ᵛ, Bodl. MS. Rawl. D. 375, p. 104), no doubt from the *Catalogus librorum MSSᵣᵤₘ Angliæ et Hiberniæ* (Oxf. 1697, fol.), tom. 2, p. 280, col. 1, among the printed books of John Moore bp. of Norwich. An error for 1518.

1511.

The 1481 Alexander de Hales appears in Bagford (Brit. Mus. MS. Harl. 5901, fol. 23, Bodl. MS. Rawl. D. 375, p. 104) as of 1511, printed at Oxford.

1512.

"Walterus Burleius. super libros Posteriorum. 1512. 4⁰." So in Cotton's *Typ. Gaz.*, 2nd ser., p. 169, and in a longer form in Herbert's Ames iii. 1396, and Panzer vii. p. 494, quoting Brüggemann i. 172. The source of the mistake is easily found in the colophon of 1517. B, a "v" having been overlooked. The error is repeated in the *Bookworm* (1868) p. 126.

Before 1519.

According to Cotton (*Typ. Gaz.*, 2nd ser., p. 169) an edition of "Jo. Duns Scotus, Scriptum Oxoniense super primum Sententiarum" (Paris 1519) professes to be "impressa juxta editionem Oxoniensem." This cannot be correct, unless *editio* refers only to some traditional method of exposition or arrangement at Oxford.

About 1519.

"The following book printed at the charge of Cardinal Wolsey, with the King's arms on one side, and the cardinal's on the other; though it has neither date nor printer's name, was probably performed about this time [1519] at this place [Oxford]." 'Libellus prim. epistol. M. Tullii Cicer. Decus Oxoniensium, finitum universitate Oxoniensi. Quarto.' So in Herbert's Ames, iii. 1398, and substantially in Bagford's account (Brit. Mus. MS. Harl. 5901, fol. 24ᵛ, Bodl. MS. Rawl. D. 375, fol. 103): see Cotton's *Typ. Gaz.*, 2nd ser., p. 169. Clearly a blunder. The book which is said to be at Trinity College, Dublin, could not be found there in 1885.

1519.

" Roberti Whitintoni Lichfeldiensis Protovatis Angliæ in Florentissimâ Oxoniensi Academiâ Laureati, Opusculum de Concinnitate Grammatices & Constructione recognitum Anno Domini xix supra Sesquimillesimum, in 4to." So Bagford (Brit. Mus. MS. Harl. 5901, fol. 23ᵛ, cf. Bodl. MS. Rawl. D. 375, p. 103). Probably not printed at Oxford.

Before 1520.

John Dorne, bookseller in Oxford, sold in 1520 several copies of a small book described in his day-book as " Bene fundatum," " Bene fundatum Oxonie" or " Bene fundatum uosgraf." This seems to be a trace of a real Oxford book now lost, but no such printer as Vosgraf or Foxgrave (Dorne was from the Low Countries) is known. It would probably belong to the 1517-19 press. See Dorne's book edited in the *Collectanea* vol. i of the Oxford Historical Society, 1885. Cotton erroneously reads the title as " Bene sum datum."

1542.

Shepery's *Hippolytus*: see under 1586. S.

1549.

" P. Martyr de Sacramento Eucharistiæ, disputatio hab. in acad., 1549," 4°. So in the *Catalogus librorum R. Davisii*, pt. 4 (1692), p. 7; cf. p. 10. Some error.

1564.

" Analysis libri Aristotelis de Sophisticis Elenchis, opera et studio Griff. Poweli." So in the *Catalogus librorum R. Davisii*, pt. 2 (1686), p. 72. Error for 1594, which see.

1565.

" Ἰωάννου τοῦ Χρυσοστόμου Ὁμιλίαι. Oxonii 1565 in forma minore." So in the *Bibliotheca Gudiana* (Hamb. 1706), p. 75 : thence in Brüggeman, p. 422. An error for 1586, which see.

1569.

1. Guild's *Throne of David or an Exposition of the 2nd of Samuel.* Error in the *Catalogus librorum R. Davisii*, pt. 1 (1686). p. 164, for 1659, which see.

2. " 1569. An account of the Lithuanian translation of the Bible is in the Brit. Museum. Quarto." So Herbert's Ames, iii. p. 1398. For 1659, which see under *Chylinski,* Samuel B.

1576.

Fabricius, J. S.: " Meditationes Sacræ de unitate Ecclesiæ Britannicæ. 1576," 8vo. So *twice* in the *Catalogus librorum R. Davisii*, pt. 2 (1686) p. 20, pt. 3 (1688) p. 11. For 1676, which see.

1578.

" Thesaurus œconomiæ . . . Johanne Caso Authore. 1597 . . . Again 1578." So Herbert's Ames, iii. 1407. Perhaps for 1598, which see, but even that is perhaps an error for 1597 !

1584.

Shepery's *Hippolytus :* see under 1586. S.

The Oxford University Press.

1585.

1. **Bilson**, Thomas.　　THE TRVE DIFFE-|RENCE BETWEENE CHRI-| STIAN SVBIECTION AND | VNCHRISTIAN REBELLION : | WHEREIN THE PRINCES LAWFVLL | power to commaund for trueth, and inde|priuable | right to beare the sword are defended against the | Popes censures and the Iesuits sophismes vt-|tered in their APOLOGIE and DE-|FENCE OF ENGLISH CATHOLIKES : | *With a demonstration that the thinges refourmed in the Church of England by the | Lawes of this Realme are truely Catholike, notwithstanding the vaine shew | made to the contrary in their late* Rhemish Testament : *by* | THOMAS BILSON Warden of Winchester. | Perused and allowed by publike authoritie. | [*Device* : then *two mottos*].

Impr. 2 : 1585 (CIↃIↃXXCV) : (eights) sm. 4° : pp. [24] + 820 + [10] : p. 11 beg. *woe bee farre*, p. 111 *be not Iudges* : chiefly Pica English. Contents :— p. (1) title : (3–12) Epistle dedicatorie to queen Elizabeth : (13) "the generall contents of euerie part" : (14–22) "To the Christian Reader" : 1–820 the work, in 4 parts : (1–9) "the speciall contents of euery part" : (9) "Faultes escaped", i.e. errata.

For the author &c. see Wood's *Ath. Oxon.* ii. 169 : where it is pointed out that the book has a curious history. Its ostensible purpose is to uphold the doctrine afterwards called "passive obedience" by refuting two books which were regarded as subversive of the Queen's temporal power, (1) *An apologie and true declaration of the institution . . . of the tvvo English colleges . . . in Rome . . . (and) in Rhemes*, 1581 (ascribed to card. Will. Allen, (2) *A true, sincere and modest defence of English catholiques that suffer for their faith*, n. d. (asserted by Antony à Wood to be also by card. Allen). But Wood declares that the Queen "conceiving it convenient for her worldly designs to take on her the protection of the Low-Countries against the King of Spain, did employ our author . . . to write the said book " to *justify* the Netherland revolt. And certain it is that in consequence of the temperance and fairness with which Bp. Bilson treats his subject, the parliamentary party in Charles I's time used this book to *oppose* "passive obedience."

Probably issued about the end of November, 1585. Greek type is used on p. 263 and perhaps elsewhere. Another ed. appeared at London in 1586 : au extract from pp. 520–21 was reprinted in 1641 and again in Somers's Tracts, 2nd ed., iv. 29 (Lond. 1810).

2. **Case**, John.　　[*Ornament*] SPECVLVM MORALIVM | QVAESTIONVM IN VNIVERSAM ETHICEN | Aristotelis, Authore Magistro IOHANNE CASO | Oxoniensi, olim Collegij Diui Io-|hannis Præcursoris | Socio. | [then the University Arms : then a *motto* from Seneca].

Impr. 1, so also colophon: 1585: (eights) sm. 4°: pp. [28] + 401 + [19]: p. 11 beg. *Off. Iuuenes,* p. 111, *Distinctio:* chiefly Pica Roman. Contents:—p. (1) Title: (3-7) Epistola nuncupatoria to Robert Dudley, earl of Leicester, chancellor of the University, signed "Iohannes Casus": (8-10) "Ad studiosos iuuenes vtriusque academiae": (10) "Prosopopœia Libri Ad Lectorem": (11) "Hono- ratissimo suo domino et patrono Comiti Leicestrensi &c. Iosephus Barnesius Typographus Oxoniensis": (12-23) Complimentary Latin verses to the author: between (24) and (25) "Tabula virtutum et vitiorum omnium", a folio leaf printed on one side only: (25-28) Præfatio: 1- 401 the work in 6 books: (1-2) "Peroratio ad lectorem": (4-17) Index: (17) Errata and colophon.

The first book printed at the new Oxford press. The allusions to this and kindred facts are (1) in the "Epistola Nuncupatoria." Case says of the reasons for dedicating the work to the Earl of Leicester "Unum est nouum hoc præli beneficium, quod te authore nostra Academia nuper recepit ... Prælum hoc nouum (cuius author existis) hunc nouum de moribus libellum pressit. Ne ergo author libelli præli authori videatur ingratus, tibi primùm eiusdem fructum ex animo propinauit ..." (2) the printer himself writes "Admirabilem hanc artem typographicam Mecenas amplissime, primum Iohannes Faustus Moguntiæ fauste genuit [the marg. supplies "Anno 1450"], eandem Guilielmus Caxtonus ciuis Londinensis probè aluit & perpoliuit: Laus summa debetur authori qui invenit, laus magna debetur mercatori qui primùm ad nos transuexit ... Londinum diù in hac arte floruit, & non inuideo: Cantabrigia eandem nunc didicit, Oxonia recepit, & certè gaudeo. Nam si characteres typographi sint vera insignia & arma Mineruæ; vbi terrarum potius floreret hæc nobilis scientia, quàm vbi vera publicè docetur sapientia? vt enim à fonte in riuum dulcis aqua, ita hic quidem à mente in prælum dulcissima Musa fluet. Non nugæ, non aniles fabulæ, non Aristarchi dentata opera hic excudentur: ea solùm ex his prælis in lucem venient quę sapientum calculis approbentur, & Sybillę foliis sint veriora. Hoc vnum nunc restat (vir inclytissime vt hunc librum opus alterius ingenij & pignus laboris mei tuo honori offeram ... Vt ergo Thomas Thomasius collega meus [Cantabrigiensis] suo, ita ego Iosephus Barnesius tibi (vir summe) meo patrono dominoque gratulor: nos ambo & publico pro multis, & priuato nomine pro magnis in nos meritis vobis vtriusque Academiæ patronis deuincti sumus, gratias immortales vterque agimus, maiores in posterum pollicemur": (3) the Vice-chancellor, J. Underhill, writes "Non dedit hoc seclo prælum Oxoniense priorem [librum] | Doctrinâque dabunt secula nulla parem." (4) Laurence Humfrey says "Hoc Speculum vobis nunc Oxoniensis alumnus | Porrigit, en præli dat quoque primitias."

It is clear that neither the Vice-chancellor nor the printer of this volume had any suspicion that there had been printing in Oxford previous to the publication of the present volume, unless "recepit" be a vague allusion to it.

The work is a companion one to the same author's *Summa veterum interpretum in universam dialecticam Aristotelis,* Lond., Tho. Vautrollerius, 1584, see 1592. C, 1598. C: and there is even a typographical connexion between the two.

For an account of the author, see Wood's *Ath. Oxon.,* i. 685. The method adopted by Case is by *quaestiones, oppositiones* and *responsiones* in the manner of the disputations in the schools at the time. Other editions were issued at Oxford in 1596, and at Frankfurt in 1589, 1610 and 1625. See 1596. C.

3. **Corro, Antonio de.** Sermons on Ecclesiastes: see 1586. E.

4. **Dudley,** Robert, earl of Leicester. [*ornament*] IN | ADVENTVM ILLVSTRIS-|*SIMI LECESTRENSIS COMITIS AD* | *Collegium Lincolniense.* |

Impr. 3: "tertio idus Iannarij" 1585: (one) 8°: pp. [2]: chiefly Pica Roman. Contents:—p. (1) title as above: large device of University arms: then "Carmen gratulatorium" of 8 elegiac lines, *beg.* "Comiter hoc factum est": then imprint.

Very rare. The visit appears from Wood's *Annals* ii. 223 to have been in Jan. 158⅘. and the date of printing 11 Jan. 158⅘. The difficulties in the way of regarding this sheet as the first printing of the new Oxford Press are the form of the date, which usually implies Jan. 158⅘, the assertion of Barnes that the Case was the first production, and the improbability that the Committee of Convocation appointed to consider "de libris imprimendis" on 23 Dec. 1584 would proceed to action so soon as 11 Jan

158¾. But the fitness of the earlier date is too obvious to be gainsaid. This piece is probably the first printed sheet issued by Barnes.

5. **Parsons**, Robert.   A | BOOKE OF | CHRISTIAN EX- ERCISE APPERTAI-|ning to RESOLVTI-'ON. that is, shewing | how that we should re-,solue our selues to be- come Christians in-|deede. *By R. P.* | *Perused, and accompanied* | *nowe with a treatise ten-|ding to pacificati-|on. By* | EDMVND BVNNY. [Then a *motto* from Hebr. xiii. 8: the whole title and imprint is within a border of ornament.]

Impr. 2a (colophon 4): 15°5: sm. 12°: pp. [28] + 494 + [2] + 140: p. 11 beg. *ons, or if*, 111 *confidence*, 2nd p. 11 *helpes whatsoeuer*, 111 *hel should*: chiefly Long Primer Roman. Contents:—p. (1) title: (3-8 Bunny's Epistle dedicatorie to Edwin Sandys, archbp. of York (9-18) Bunny's "Preface to the reader": (19-28) "The contents of . . . this booke": 1-493 [misprinted 439]. the work, in 2 parts: (1) title of Bunny's treatise: 1-140, the treatise: before p. 1 of the treatise is an oblong sheet 5 × 11 in., folded, containing on one side in two divisions "A table . . . of the treatise following": on p. 140 is also a colophon.

Of this book also there is a curious history. Gaspare Loarte, a Spanish Jesuit who spent most of his life at Rome, wrote an "Essercitio della vita christiana" some time before 1569. In 1579 J. Sancer, a friend of Robert Parsons the Jesuit, published a translation into English of one of the three parts of the work. In 1582 Parsons himself published "The firste booke of the Christian Exercise, appertayning to resolution" in two parts, which is practically a new work based on part of the original "Essercitio." Loarte is mentioned in the preface, but the author only signs his name by the initials, R. P. This was again issued without Parsons' knowledge in 1584.

In 1585 (or according to Wood and Ames, copied by Herbert and Dibdin, in 1584) Edmund Bunny printed and published the first edition of an adaptation of Parsons' book fitted for Protestant readers "at London, by N. Newton, for John Wight," 8°. The dedication is to the archbp. of York and the preface dated 9 July 1584 at Bolton-Percy. The book was entered at Stationers' Hall on 28 Aug. 1584. The Oxford edition before us is a reprint of this London edition with no intentional variation, except the omission of the arms of the archbishop of York on the *verso* of the title of the London issue. Some of the woodcut ornaments and capitals of the two issues are identical.

In "1585, Aug. 30" Parsons again put out his book in a revised and largely augmented form with a new title "A Christian Directorie" which when complete was to consist of three books, the first of which, treating of Resolution, is alone contained in this edition. The preface contains a criticism of the London issue of Bunny's adaptation, which provoked "A briefe answer vnto those idle and friuolous quarrels of R. P. against the late edition of the Resolution: By Edmund Bunny." Lond., 1589, 8°.

Other editions of Bunny's adaptation of Parsons' "Christian exercise" are 1586 (Lond., "by I. Iackson and Ed. Bollifant for John Wight," 12°; in Herbert's possession), 1589 (Lond., 12°: Bohn), 1594 (Lond., 24°: Bohn), 1609 (Lond., 12°: Bohn), 1615 (Lond., 12°). See also next art. Parsons' own work was several times reprinted: and in 1591 appeared an edition of his "Christian Directorie," anonymously adapted, as the former work, for the use of Protestants, and with the deceptive title "The second part of the booke of Christian Exercise, appertayning to Resolution, or a Christian directorie . . . written by the former authour R. P." (Lond., 12°). This was several times reprinted, as in 1592, 1594, 1598, 1615. See also Wood's *Ath. Oxon.*, ii. 221: and the next art.

6. **Parsons**, Robert.   A | BOOKE OF | CHRISTIAN EX-|ERCISE APPERTAI-|NING TO RESOLVTION, | that is, shewing how that | wee shoulde resolue our selues to become Christi-|ans indeede, *By R. P.* | *Perused, and accompanied now* | *with a treatise tending to* | *Pacification, By* | EDMVND BVNNY. | [*motto*. The whole title is within a border.]

Impr. 2a (colophon 4): 1585: sm. 12°: pp. [30] + 492 + [2] + 140: p. 11 beg. *what man,* 111 *Gospell, which*: also p. 11 *nounce all,* 111 *it they should*: chiefly Long Primer Roman. Contents:—as preceding article, without the folded "Table" to Bunny's treatise, viz. :—p. (1) title: (3-9) epistle: (10-19) preface: (20-29) contents: 1-491, the treatise: (1) title: 1-140 Bunny's treatise, with colophon.

This volume is apparently identical in text (not spelling or punctuation) with the preceding art., but is entirely reset : from p. 252 of this edition (= 254 of the other) the two correspond page for page in Parsons' treatise.

7. Prime, John. A SERMON BRIEF-|LY COMPARING THE E-|STATE OF KING SALOMON AND | his Subiectes togither with the condi-|tion of Queene ELIZABETH | and her people. | PREACHED IN SAINCT MA-|*ries in Oxford the* 17. *of Nouember, and* | *now printed with some small alteration,* | *by* IOHN PRIME, | 1585. | [*ornament.*]

Impr. 4: 1585: sm. 8°: pp. [32], sign. A-B⁴: sign. B 1ʳ beg. *passion, that*: chiefly Pica English. Contents :—p. (1) title : (3-5) Epistle "to the Christian reader": (6-30) the sermon, on 1 Kings x. 9: (31-32) "A praier in consideration of the former respects."

See Wood's *Ath. Oxon.*, i. 653. The Epistle is dated 27 Nov. 1585, and alludes to Bilson's book as "euen now comming foorth."

8. Shepery, John. See 1586. S.

9. Sparke, Thomas. "'A Sermon preached at Cheanies the 14. of September, 1585, at the burial of the right Honorable the Earle of Bedford, by Thomas Sparke Doctor of Diuinitie.' The university's arms. 'Imprinted at Oxford by *him* Printer to that famous Vniuersitie.' My copy is cut so close at bottom that it is uncertain whether there was any date added. Dedicated 'To — Arthur Lord Gray of Wilton, Knight of — the Garter.—At Bletchley the 25 of September, 1585.—Thomas Sparke.' The text, 'Apocal. 14. 13. I heard a voice from heauen' &c. At the end of the sermon 'September 22. An. Do. 1585.' Besides; 110 pages. W. H. 16°."

The above is the account of the book in Herbert's Ames, iii. 1399, in the account of Joseph Barnes's press at Oxford in 1585. The copy sold in the Heber sale, 9 April 1825, Catal. pt. vi, p. 248, art. 3559 for 8*s.* was probably Herbert's. Ames in his *Typographical Antiquities* (Lond. 1749) gives a shorter title and describes the book as a quarto. Other edd. are Lond. 1585, in eights (pp. [10] + 106), and Oxf. 1594 (with 25 *December* at end of dedication, pp. [10] + 110): but both are different from the present book, if Herbert's description may be trusted.

1586.

1. Case, John. "'Reflexus speculi moralis, seu commentarius in magna moralia Aristotelis. Authore Johanne Caso.' Again 1596. Octavo."

The above is from Herbert's Ames, iii. 1401, slightly altered from Ames, p. 453: but both are probably errors for 1596 : see 1596. C.

2. Catilinariae proditiones.   "'In Catilinarias proditiones, ac proditores domesticos. Odæ 6.' The university arms. 'Oxoniæ, ex Officina Typographica Josephi Barnesii, & veneunt in cœmeterio Paulino sub signo capitis Tygurini. Anno 1586.' On the back. in a lozenge form, 'Odæ sex ornatissimis viris D. Doctori Jameso Ædis Christi Oxon. decano, et doctori Hetono prodecano, cæterisque clarissimis atque optimis viris eiusdem ecclesiæ præbendariis, & privatæ observantiæ, et publicæ pietatis ergò dicatæ.' 8 leaves, the first has only signature A. Brit. Museum. Octavo."

The above is from Herbert's Ames, iii. p. 1401. In May 1886 the officials of the British Museum were unable to find the book. A copy was sold at the Bliss sale in 1858 (Catal. pt. 2, art. 7) to Stenson a bookseller for £4 4s.

3. Chardon, John.   A SERMON | VPON PART OF | THE NINTH CHAP-TER | OF THE HOLY GOSPEL | OF IESVS CHRIST | *ACCORDING TO* | S. IOHN : | Preached at S. Maries in | Oxford by *Iohn Chardon* | Doctor of Diuinitie. | [*motto.*]

Impr. 2b: 1586: (eights) 16°: pp. [48], signn. A–C⁸: sign. B 1ʳ beg. *streight waie*: chiefly Pica English. Contents:— p. (1) title: (3–10) Epistle dedicatory to Ambrose earl of Warwick, Oxf. 6 Oct. 1586: (11–44) the sermon, on John ix. 1–3: (45–47) "The prayer."

See Wood's *Ath. Oxon.,* i. 716.

4. Chardon, bp. John.   "'A comfortable sermon for all such as thirst and desire to be ioined with their head Jesus Christ. &c. Preached at the funerals of Syr Gawen Carewe, very worshipfully buried in the Cathedral Church of Exeter, 22d April, 1584, By John Charden bachelor of Divinity.' The text, 1 Thes. 4; 13–18. Octavo."

So in Herbert's Ames, iii. 1400 : see Wood's *Ath. Oxon.,* i. 716, Maunsell i. 97.

5. Chrysostom, St.   D. IOANNIS CHRY-|SOSTOMI ARCHIE- PISCOPI CON-STANTI- NOPOLITANI, | *Homiliæ sex,* | Ex manuscriptis Codicibus Noui Collegij ; | IOANNIS HARMARI, eiusdem Col-|legij socij. & Græcarum literarum in | inclyta OXONIENSI Academia | Professoris Regij, opera & | industria nunc primùm | græcè in lucem | editæ. | [*device.*]

Impr. 5 : 1586 (CIↃIↃXXXCVI) : (eights) 16°: pp. [12]+138: p. 11 beg. οἷον αὐτοῦ, ἢ πάντες συμφωνοῦσιν: chiefly Long Primer Greek. Contents :—p. (1, title : (3–12) Epistola dedicatoria to sir Thomas Bromley, lord chancellor of Eng-land, Oxf. 28 Dec. [1585] : 1–138, the six Homilies. in Greek.

"Primitiæ typographici nostri in græcis literis preli," as the dedication says. The first Greek book printed in England was also a Chrysostom (Two Homilies, Lond., Reg. Wolfe, 1543), but separate Greek words occur in the first book printed at Cam-bridge (Cujusdam .. Christiani Epistola, 1521), and single words cut in wood still earlier. The six homilies are 1. Κατὰ τῶν παρατηρούντων τὰς νεομηνίας Migne, *Patrol. Gr.,*Chrysost., i. 953 . 2–5. Εἰς τὸν Λάζαρον, α΄, β΄, γ΄, δ΄ (ibid. 963. 981, 991, 1005). 6. Εἰς τὸ Περὶ δὲ τῶν κεκοιμημένων ibid. 1017). See p. 12 1565 .Wood's *Ath. Oxon.,* ii. 138. An imperfect book, ('signn. A 2-D 7', containing Isocrates Πρὸς Δημόνικον. Πρὸς Νικοκλέα, Νικόκλης ἢ συμβουλευτικὸς λόγος τρίτος, Plutarch Περὶ παίδων ἀγωγῆς and "Luciani Cupido," all in Greek, once owned by Thomas Hearne and now in the Bodleian Library, is in similar type to this Chrysostom and is accordingly assigned by Hearne to Barnes's Press. But minute inspection shows that some of the wood-cuts of the book are not identical with any used at Oxford. It is probably London printing (not Bynneman 1581 nor 1621: perhaps Bishop 1599: see Brüggemann, p. 128.)

6. Ecclesiastes. SOLOMONS SERMON: | OF MANS CHIEF | FELICITIE : CALLED | IN HEBREW KOHELETH, | IN GREEKE AND LATIN | ECCLESIASTES. | With a learned, godly, and familiar pa-'raphrase vppon the same : gathe- red out of the Lectures of A. | C. & now englished for | the benefit of the | vnlearned. | [*motto & device.*]

Impr. 4 : 1586: (eights) 16° : pp. [16] + 219 + [1] : p. 11 beg. *that is brought,* 111 *and this meditation* : Pica Roman. Contents :—p. (1) title : (3–7) Epistle dedicatorie to the "lady Marie Dudley."

Oxford. 8 Mar. 1586, signed "T. P.": '8–16 "To the Christian reader . . ." with the writer's name, Th. Pie : 1–219, the paraphrase, the text of Ecclesiastes occurring in the margin.

This book is a translation into English of "Sapientissimi regis Salomonis concio de summo hominis bono quam . . . Latini Ecclesiasten vocant, in Latinam linguam ab Antonio Corrano . . . versa et ex eiusdem prœlectionibus paraphrasi illustrata : accesserunt & notæ quædam " (Lond., 1579) with the omission of the notes. For Ant. de Corro see Wood's *Ath. Oxon.,* i. 578 : and for Thomas Pye, *ibid.* ii. 59. Wood was not acquainted with this earliest work of Pye, but alludes to the book (as above, i. 581) as Corro's " Sermons on Ecclesiastes. Abridged by Thomas Pitt. Oxon. 1585, oct., which is called by some Pitt's Paraphrase on Ecclesiastes "! The name Pitt, but not the error of date, may be taken from Maunsell, who three times i. 38, 81, 104 alludes to the book as by Tho. Pitt. Pye in his Epistle states with respect to the original Latin edition, " which treatise, as it came first to the print, myselfe by occasion being charged with som o/erseeing of the presse, at the earnest request aswel of the author himself, as of other many, I translated into English : being the rather a greate deale moued thereunto, because there was no comment or like exposition then extant in our vulgar tongue vpon this part of Scripture." This latter statement is not strictly true, since " An exposition of Salomon's booke called Ecclesiastes" was printed in London in 1573. In 1585 Serranus's commentary translated into English by T. Wilcocke was printed in London.

7. Hutchins, Edward. A SERMON | PREACHED IN S. | PETERS CHURCH AT | WEST-CHESTER THE XXV | OF *SEPTEMBER,* 1586. | CONTAINING MATTER | *FIT FOR THE TIME* : | By Edward Hutchins Maister | of Arts, and Fellowe of Bra- zennose College. |

Impr. 6 : (1586) : (eights) 16° : pp. [32] : sign. B 2ʳ beg. *the fould* : chiefly Pica English. Contents :—p. (1) title :

(3–4) dedication to Roger Puleston : (5–30) the sermon, on Gal. 5. 12.

Rare. See Wood's *Ath. Oxon.,* ii. 453. The only copy seen, that in the British Museum, wants the last leaf, presumably blank.

8. Hutchins, Edward. A | SERMON PREA-'CHED IN WEST- CHESTER THE VIII. | OF OCTOBER, 1586. | *BEFORE THE IVD-'GES AND CERTAIN* | *RECVSANTES:* | Wherein the conditions of al he-.retiques, but especiallie of stub- born and peruerting Papists, | are discouered, & the duty | of al magistrats concer- ning such persons, ap- plied & opened ' *By* EDWARD HVTCHINS, *Ma- ster of Artes, & Fellowe of* BRA-'SENNOSE Colledge. | . . .

Impr. 6 : (1586) : (eights) 16° : pp. [32]. signn. A–B': sign. B 2ʳ beg. *are they* : chiefly Pica English. Contents :—p. (1)

title : (3–4) dedication to Thomas Egerton : (5–32, the sermon, on Canticles ii. 15.

See Wood's *Ath. Oxon.,* ii. 452.

9. Massie, William.   A | SERMON PREA-|CHED AT TRAFFORD | IN LANCASHIRE AT | *THE MARIAGE OF A* | DAVGHTER OF THE | right Worshipfull Sir Ed-mond TRAFFORDE | Knight, the 6. of Sep-*tember Anno,* 1586. | By WILLIAM MASSIE bacheler in di-uinity, and fellow of Brasennose Col-ledge in Oxforde. | [*motto.*]

Impr. 6: 1586: (eights) 16º: pp. [32], signn. A–B⁸: sign. B 1ʳ beg. *of body, sor-row:* chiefly Pica English. Contents :—   p. (1) title : (3–4) dedication to sir E. Trafford : (5–32) the sermon, on Ps. cxxviii.

See Wood's *Fasti Oxon..* i. 237. The marriage was between Margaret Trafford and Sir Urian Legh, kt., of Adlington, a member of the same College as the preacher.

10. Music.   THE PRAISE | OF MVSICKE : | Wherein besides the antiquitie, | dignitie, delectation, & vse there- of in ciuill matters, is also decla-red the sober and lawfull vse of the | same in the congregation and | Church of God. | [*device, then motto.*]

Impr. 6: 1586: (eights) 16º: pp. [8] + 152 : p. 11 beg. *Mu-sicke of.* in *proper place:* Pica English. Contents :—p. (1) title : (3–4) dedication by the printer to "sir Walter Rawley": (5–8) "The preface to the Reader": 1–152, the work in 12 chapters, with the sub-title "The antiquitie and original of Musicke . . ."

This work has been constantly attributed to John Case, the author of the *Apologia Musices,* Oxf. 1588. but the present writer believes that from internal evidence it cannot be regarded as his. See Appendix C, and Wood's *Ath. Oxon.,* i. 686. It was reprinted in the *Choir and Musical Record* 1864, by dr. Rimbault, who contributed an introduction.

11. Overton, John.   IACOBS | TROVBLE-|SOME IOVR-|NEY TO BE-|THEL : Conteining a briefe ex-|position, or excellent | Treatise of the four first | verses of the 33. Chapter | of GENESIS : | *Set foorth by* IOHN OVER-TON, *Maister of Arts.* | [*motto.*]

Impr. 7: 1586: (eights) 16º: pp. [8] + 75 + [5]: p. 11 beg. *many wise:* Pica English. Contents :—p. (1) title : (3–7) Epistle dedicatory to William Brent, | Welsborne, 1 Apr. 1586: (8 Gen. xxxiii. 1–3: 1–75, the treatise: (1 5) "A prayer against the enimies of the Church of Christ . . ."

This book was the "first fruits" of the author's study.

12. *†Philosophy.   DE | PHILOSO- PHIA. | PANATHENA-|ICAE DVAE : | IN COMITIIS OXONII HABITAE. | [*woodcuts and motto.* The whole title is within a border.]

N. pl. : n. d. (1586?): (eights) 12º: pp. [32], signn. A B⁸: sign. B 1ʳ beg. *tem, Demosthenem:* Pica Roman. Contents :— p. (1–2) unknown : (3) title : (5) three | Quaestiones: 6–18 "Panathenaica prima, v. Id. Iulii 1585. habita" : (19–20 three Quaestiones : (20–31) "Panathenaica secunda, iii Id. Iulii 1586. habita."

The Bodleian Catalogue suggests that these speeches are perhaps by Thomas Savile (see Wood's *Ath. Oxon.,* i. 591), brother of sir Henry Savile, both of Merton. There is no place of imprint, but probably it is Oxford printing. Wood did not know the book.

13. Rainolds, John.   A SERMON | VPON PART | OF THE EIGH-|TEENTH PSALM : | Preached to the publik assem-|blie of Scholers in the

Vniuer-|sitie of Oxford the last day | of August, 1586. by | IOHN RAINOLDS: | Vpon occasion of their meeting to giue | thankes to God for the late detection | *and apprehension of Traitours, who* | wickedlie conspired against the *Queenes Maiestie and the* | state of the Realme. | [*motto.*]

Impr. 2: 1586: (eights) 16°: pp. [40]. signn. A–B⁴ C¹: sign. B 1ʳ beg. *But al this*: Pica English.   Contents :⁻ sign. A 1ʳ "Aj.": A 2ʳ, title: A 3ʳ–A 4ʳ, " Iohn Rainoldes, to the Reader," Oxford, 24 Oct. 1586: A 4ᵛ, Ps. xviii. 47–51: A 5ʳ–C 4ᵛ, the sermon, on Ps. xviii. 47–51: C 4ᵛ, Ps xxi. 7–9.

See Wood's *Ath. Oxon.*, ii. 15.   Reprinted at Oxford in 1613.   Occasioned by "Babington's conspiracy": there are several references to current events.

14. *Shepery, John.   HYPPOLITVS OVIDIANÆ | PHAEDRAE RES- PONDENS, PER IOAN-|NEM SCHEPREVVM SOMA- TO CHRISTIANVM. | [*device.*]

Impr. 8: [1586]: (eights) 12°: pp. [80], signn. * A–D³: sign. B 1ʳ beg. *Scilicet expectas*: Pica Italic.   Contents :—sign. *1ᵛ, title: *2ʳ–*7ᵛ, " Ioannis Schepreui præfatio, in epistolam Hyppoliti sui ad Phædram, ad M. Guadum dedicatam," in Latin elegiacs: *8ʳ–*8ᵛ, "Candido lectori Georgius Edrychus medicus S. P. D.," a Latin preface: A 1ʳ–D 8ʳ, the poem.

See Wood's *Ath. Oxon.*, i. 135.   This work is an imaginary reply of Hippolytus to the temptations of Phaedra, in Ovidian elegiacs.   The author, John Shepery, of Corpus Christi College ("Somatochristianus"), tells us in the preface that it was composed as a return for kindness shown him by one Guadus (Wade ?, whom the editor describes as a chaplain to Henry viii), but delayed for some years.   Shepery died in 1542, aged 32 years.   George Etheridge (" Edrychus ") was a pupil of Shepery, fellow of Corpus, and a Roman Catholic.

The date is fixed at 1586 by two passages: Etheridge in his preface states that for about 53 years he had been a member of the University: he was admitted scholar of Corpus in Nov. 1534.   Also Dr. Humphrey in his introduction to the *Summa et synopsis* (see below) alludes to the *Hippolytus* as "nuperrime impressum."   Wood places the date at about 1584, and the Bodleian catalogue of 1843 assigns the book to 1542, owing to the date of Shepery's death, which happens to occur prominently at the end of Etheridge's preface.

15. Shepery, John.   SVMMA | ET SYNOPSIS | NOVI TESTAMEN-|TI DISTICHIS DV- CENTIS SEXAGIN-|TA, QVAE TOTI- DEM CAPITIBVS | RESPONDENT, | *comprehensa*: | Prior a IOANNE SCHEPREVO | Oxoniensi olim conscripta: Posterior ex ERASMI | ROTERODAMI *Editione decerpta: Tyrunculis & om-*| nibus pietatis & Theologiæ candidatis non inutilis, à | LAVRENTIO HVMFREDO *recognita, & iu-* uandæ memoriæ causâ, edita : | Cui præmissa est eiusdem | *De Scholis & studijs Christianorum piè & metho-*|*dicè institu-endis breuis Admonitio.* | [*motto* by L. H.(umfrey).]

Impr. 5: 1586: (eights) 16°: pp. [62], signn. A–B⁸ C⁹ (see below) D⁶: sign. B 1ʳ beg. *disticha Ioannis*: Pica Italic.   Contents :—sign. A 1ʳ, title : A 2ʳ–A 8ᵛ " Admonitio Laurentii Humfredi ad Studio- sos ": A 8ᵛ, " Librorum Novi Testamenti elenchus & ordo per Cor. Graphæ. . . . ": B 1ʳ–C 3ᵛ " Disticha Ioannis Schepreui . . . ": verso of leaf after C 3–D 6ʳ, " Disticha . . . in Editione Erasmi Roterodami inserta."

The " Summa Ioannis Scheprevi " is a set of elegiac stanzas, each stanza describing the contents of a chapter in the New Testament, and beginning successively with the letters of the alphabet, written by John Shepery, of Corpus Christi College, Reader of the Hebrew Lecture from about 1537 to his death in 1542.   The *Summa* is stated by Wood to have been first published at Strasburg in about 1556 by John Parkhurst bp. of Norwich, next in Lond. 1560 (Wood), and from Humfrey's ed. in " Gemma Fabri," Lond. 1598, and " Biblii (or Bibliorum) summula," Lond. 1621, etc.   The first distich is " A priscis oritur Christus, turbatur Ioseph, ' Angelus hunc retinet, virgo beata parit." MS. C. C. C. (Oxf.) 266 contains these verses.

The "Synopsis" is a similar set of elegiac stanzas, without the alphabetical succession of first letters, first inserted in the Latin editions of Erasmus's New Testament, from that of 1542 on. The author appears to be unknown : the first distich is " Angelus in somnis iustum solatur Ioseph, | Prototoco Mariæ nomen Iesus erit."

In the preface Dr. Humfrey states that his object in editing the book was to recall young students to the study of the text of the Bible, and that he had collated a MS. copy of the *Summa* with bp. Parkhurst's edition, and had compared different editions of the *Synopsis* : he alludes also to the Hippolytus of Shepery as "nuperrime impressum."

See Wood's *Ath. Oxon.*, i. 135, 360. Dr. Philip Bliss noted in his copy " Whoever wants to write a history of the Oxford press should first get together all the little vols printed by Jo. Barnes, of which this is one of the rarest."

16. Spanish.   REGLAS GRAM- MATICALES PARA A | PRENDER LA LENGVA ESPA-ñola y Francesa, confiriendo la | vna con la otra, segun el or- den de las partes de la o- ration Latinas. | *** | [*woodcuts.*]

Impr. 9* : 1586 : 12° in size.

Only known from a title-page in the British Museum (Bagford Collection, 463. h. 8, no. 456). Mentioned in Ames and Herbert's Ames, but not in such terms as to prove that either editor had seen the book complete. For the reference to the British Museum and a transcript of the title I am indebted to Mr. E. G. Duff, of Wadham College, Oxford.

17. Westfaling, Herbert.   " ' Articles Ecclesiasticall to be inquired of by the Church-wardens and the Sworne-men within the dioces of Hereford in the first visitation of the reuerend father in God, Harbart Bishop of the said dioces : this present yeare M . D . lxxxvi and the xxviii. yeare of the raigne of our most gracious soueraigne Lady Queene Elizabeth, &c. And so hereafter, till the next visitation, and from time to time to be presented.' B, in fours : 70 articles. W. H. Quarto."

So in Herbert's Ames, iii. 1401.

1587.

1. [Bailey, Walter.]   A briefe discours of certain Bathes . . . neare vnto . . . Newnam Regis, 1587.

Probably not printed at Oxford, but at London, though ascribed to the former place in the British Museum Catalogue.

2. Beza, Theodorus.   MASTER BEZAES SER- MONS VPON THE THREE | FIRST CHAPTERS OF THE | CANTICLE OF CANTICLES : | WHEREIN ARE HANDLED THE | CHIEFEST POINTS OF RELIGION | *CONTROVERSED AND DEBATED BE- TWEENE VS AND THE ADVERSA-* RIE AT THIS DAY, ESPECIALLY TOV- *CHING THE TRVE IESVS CHRIST AND* | THE TRVE CHVRCH, AND THE CER- TAINE & INFALLIBLE MARKS | BOTH OF THE ONE AND | OF THE OTHER. | *TRANSLATED OVT OF FRENCH INTO* | ENGLISH BY IOHN HARMAR, HER HIGHNES | *PRO- FESSOR IN THE GREEKE TOVNG* | IN THE VNIVERSITIE OF OXFORD, | AND FELOWE OF THE NEWE | COLLEGE THERE. | [*woodcut.*]

Impr. 6a : 1587 : (fours) 8° : pp. [12] +435 + [1] : p. 11 beg. *and because no, | III with all rigor* : Pica Roman. Contents :—p. (1) title : (3–6) epistle dedicatory to the earl of Leicester : (7–12, " The Argument of the xlv. Psalme, seruing for an Argument of . . . the Canticle of Canticles . . ." : 1–435, the sermons (thirty-one) on the Song of Solomon chapp. 1–3.

See Wood's *Ath. Oxon.*, ii. 138. The best account of this work will be extracts from the Epistle dedicatory. John Harmar the translator was in this year Proctor, Regius professor of Greek and Fellow of New College. He says, " I was requested, right honorable, by manie of my friends to emploie the time of this last vacation of mine from my publique readinges in the Vniuersitie, in the translating of Master Bezaes Sermons vpon the Canticle of Canticles, which I had a little before receaued from the Francfurt mart in French, into our vulgare and Mother tongue." The patronage of Lord Dudley is acknowledged and details of the translator's life are given, as that he attended Beza's lectures and sermons at Geneva. The work translated was no doubt Beza's " Sermons sur les trois premiers chapitres du Cantique des cantiques de Salomon," *Genève, Jehan le Preux*, 1586, 8º (Brunet).

3. **Case,** John.   "'Thesaurus oeconomiae, seu commentarius oeconomica Aristotelis.   Authore Johanne Caso.'   Again 1598.   Quarto."

So Herbert's Ames, iii. 1402, after Ames : but perhaps an error for 1597.

4. **Legatus.**   DE LEGATO ET ABSOLV-|TO PRINCIPE PERDV-|ELLIONIS REO. | [*device.*]

Impr. 10 : 1587 : (eight) 12º : pp. [16],   Italic. Contents :—p. (1) title : (3-16) sign. A⁸ : p. (11) beg. *in fortuito* : Pica   the treatise.

This anonymous treatise is a formal and precise legal argument on the question " Utrum legatus alicuius principis absoluti vel ipse princeps absolutus morte sit afficiendus, si in aliena republica, contra vitam principis vel salutem totius reipublicae, nefariam coniurationem fuerint machinati." It was intended to support Queen Elizabeth in her resolution to execute Mary Queen of Scots, and seems to have been written after 4 Dec. 1586 (p. 13) and before the execution 8 Feb. 1587 : but there is no clue to the author.

5. **[Penry,** John.]   A TREATISE | CONTAINING | THE AEQVITY OF | AN HVMBLE SVPPLI- CATION WHICH IS TO BE *EXHIBITED VNTO HIR* GRACIOVS MAIESTY AND | this high Court of Parliament | *in the behalfe of the Countrey of* | Wales, that some order may | *be taken for the preaching of* | the Gospell among those | people. | Wherein also is set downe as much of the | estate of our people as without offence | could be made known, to the end that | our case (if it please God) may be piti- ed by them who are not of this assem-|bly, and so they also may be driuen to | labour on our behalfe. |

Impr. 6 : 1587 : (eights) 16º : pp. 62 | 3-10, " To al that mourn in Sion . . ." : + [2] : p. 11 beg. *The Necessity* : Long | 11-62, the work : (1) " To the reader " Primer Roman. Contents :—p. 1, title : | explanation and erratum.

The author's name nowhere occurs, but there can be but little doubt that the volume was written by John Penry of St. Alban hall, Oxford (B.A. 1586), who is conspicuous in the Marprelate controversy and who published *An exhortation vnto the Gouernours and people of Wales, to labour earnestly to haue the preaching of the Gospell planted among them* (n. pl. or d., and n. pl. 1588 : and also *A View of . . . publike wants & disorders . . . in the service of God . . . within Wales*, n. pl. 1588. The author says, p. 63, " Some rumor of the speedy dissolution of the Parliament enforced me from the 32 Pag. or there abouts (so much being already vnder the presse) to cut off more of the booke by two parts than is now in the whole." Parliament sat in 1586 from 28 Oct. to 2 Dec. and not during 1587. At pp. 53-4 Penry alludes to the state of the Universities. Wood does not know of this work, and the best account of the author is in Cooper's *Athenæ Cantabr.*, ii. 154.

6. Prime, John. AN | EXPOSITION, | AND OBSERVATI-ONS VPON SAINT | PAVL TO THE GALA- THIANS, TOGETHER | with incident Qæstions de-*bated, and Motives re-* moued, by | IOHN PRIME. | [*woodcut.*]

Impr. 6: 1587: (eights) 16°: pp. [8] + 317 + [3]: p. 11 beg. *moment,* 111 *dangerous:* Pica English. Contents:— p. (1) title: (3-7) dedication to John

Pierce bishop of Salisbury, Oxford, 30 Jan. "1587": 1-317, the work: (2-3) unknown.

See Wood's *Ath. Oxon.*, i. 653. Compiled from notes of fortnightly discourses at Abingdon.

7. Rainolds, John. IOHANNIS RAINOLDI | ORATIONES DVÆ: | Ex ijs quas habuit in Collegio | Corporis Christi, quum | linguam Graecam | profiteretur. | HABITÆ, QVVM STVDIA, DE | more per ferias intermissa, | repeterentur: | *Prior, quæ duodecima, post vaca-tionem Natalitiam; Posterior, decima tertia, post va- cationem Paschalem;* | Anno 1576. | [*woodcut.*]

Impr. 5: 1587: (eights) 16°: pp. [88]: p. 11 beg. *ignorantiam:* Pica Roman. Contents:—p. 1 "A": 3, title: 5-8,

"Iohannes Rainoldus Academicis Oxoni-ensibus S. P. D.." with preface following, Oxf. 2 Feb.: 9 85. the two Orations.

These are general exhortations to study, selected out of twenty orations of the kind. They are reprinted in the various editions of Rainolds's Orations. See Wood's *Ath. Oxon.*, ii. 15.

8. Sidney, sir Philip. EXEQVLE | ILLVSTRISSIMI | EQVITIS, D. PHILIP- PI SIDNÆI, GRATISSI- MAE MEMORIAE AC NO- *MINI IMPENSÆ.* | [*device:* then *motto.*]

Impr. 5: 1587: sm. 4°: pp. [96], signn. *, A L⁴: sign. B 1ʳ beg. *Et verò:* Pica Roman and Italic. Contents:— sign. *1ʳ, title: *2ʳ-3ᵛ, Epistola dedica-toria to the earl of Leicester, signed

"Guilielmus Gagerus," Oxf., 22 Oct. 1587: *4ᵛ, Latin poem by Laurence Humfrey: A 1ʳ-L 4ᵛ, the poems, in Latin: L 4ᵛ, an erratum.

Sir Philip Sidney died at Arnheim 7 Oct. 1586. Dr. William James, dean of Christ Church, urged W. Gager to collect and edit poems which had been privately made at the time of Sidney's death: the editor found it necessary from considerations of space to reject Hebrew, Greek, French and Italian poems, but it may be doubted whether the printer possessed Hebrew type. See next art.

9. Sidney, sir Philip. PEPLVS | ILLVSTRISSIMI | VIRI D. PHILIPPI | SIDNÆI SVPRE- MIS HONORIBVS | DICATVS. | [*woodcut,* then two *mottos.*]

Impr. 11: 1587: sm. 4°: pp. 54 + [2]: p. 11 beg. *Cur temet:* Pica Roman and Italic. Contents:—p. 1, title: 3-4, dedi-cation to Henry Herbert earl of Pem-

broke, in Latin, by "Ioannes Luidus," New college, Oxford, 26 Aug. 1587: 5-54, the work: 54, two errata.

The title is an allusion to the spurious Peplus of Aristotle, a commemoration of the heroes who fell before Troy. The editor was John Lhuyd, and the poems (almost all Latin) are all by New College men, among whom the earl of Pembroke, Sidney's brother-in-law, had been educated. See preceding art., and Wood's *Ath. Oxon.*, i. 523.

10. Sprint, John.   AD | ILLVSTRIS-|SIMOS COMI-|TES WARWICENSEM | ET LEICESTRENSEM ORA- *TIO GRATVLATORIA* | BRISTOLLLE HABITA   *APRIL.* *ANNO* | 1587. | [*woodcut.*]

Impr. 5: (1587) : (eight) 16° : pp. [16], sign. A⁸ : p. 11 beg. *Atque hic* : Pica Italic. Contents :—sign. A 1 unknown : A 2ʳ, title : A 2ᵛ, introduction to the speech, in Latin : A 3ʳ, dedication to lord Leicester by " Ioh. Sprint " dean of Bristol : A 3ʳ–A 7ᵛ, the speech, 16 Apr. | 1587 : A 8ʳ, " In aduentum Illustrissimi Comitis Leicestrensis cùm primùm Cancellarius Oxoniensis Academiam accederet " 29 Aug. 1566 ?, a poem of 13 hexameters, the initial letters of the words forming a complimentary wish.

Extremely rare : see Wood's *Ath. Oxon.*, ii. 333, where the poem &c. is reprinted.

11. Ursinus, Zacharias.   THE SVMME OF CHRISTIAN | *RELIGION* : Deliuered by ZACHA- RIAS VRSINVS in his Le-|*ctures vpon the Catechism* *auto-* rised by the noble Prince FREDE- RICK, throughout his dominions : | *Wherein are debated and re-*|*solued the Questions of whatsoe- uer new* *ioints of moment, which haue be ne | or are contro-*|*uersed in Diuinitie.* | *Translated into English by* HEN- RIE PARRIE, *out of the last & best | Latin* *Editions, together with some sup-*|*plie of wants out of his Discourses of* *Di-*|*uinitie, and with correction of sundrie | faults & imperfections, which* *ar as yet | remaining in the best corrected Latine.*

Impr. 6 : 1587 : (eights, 12° : pp. [16] + 1047 + [9] : p. 11 beg. *alone is it,* 111 *iecting it of,* 1001 *Now we haue* : Long Primer Roman. Contents :—p. 1 title, within a border : (3-8) Epistle dedica-torie to the earl of Pembroke, signed by Parry : (9-15 " To the Christian readers," by Parry : 1-1047, the work : (2-9 " A table . . ." of contents.

Other editions were printed at Oxford in 1589, 1591, 1595, 1601. The work, which is a commentary on the Heidelberg Catechism, appears to be a cento from the Tractationes Theologicae of Ursinus vol. 1, 1587, fol. . See Wood's *Ath. Oxon.*, ii. 192. Parry's Prefaces are reprinted in 1600. U.

1588.

1. Ca[se], Jo[hn].   APOLOGIA MV-|SICES TAM VO-|CALIS QVAM | INSTRUMEN-|*TALIS ET* | MINT.E. | [four *mottos.*]

Impr. 11 : 1588 : (eights, 16° : pp. [6] + 78 (" 77 ") : p. 11 beg. *am, Lydiam* : Pica Italic. Contents : — p. (1 title : (3-6) dedication " Henrico Vntono et Guilielmo Hattono . . . Io. Ca. S. P. D.," with preface signed " I. C.," Oxf. 30 Nov. 1588 : 1-" 77 " the work.

Rare. By John Case, cf. 1586. M. Wood's *Ath. Oxon.*, i. 686. The dedication is to two persons for their fathers' interest in music. Sign. F consists of F 1 & F 3 only, paged 74-77 instead of 75-78. Copies usually have a border, &c. of red ink lines, throughout.

2. Case, John.   SPHÆRA CIVITATIS, | AVTHORE MAGISTRO | IOHANNE CASO OXONI-|ENSI, OLIM COLLEGII DIVI | Iohannis Præcursoris socio. | [*device, then motto.*]

Impr. 11 : 1588 : (eights) sm. 4° : pp. [36] + 740 + [12] : p. 11 beg. *regni plus- quam*, 111 *Communitas* : Pica Roman. Contents :—p. (1 title : 2 4 verses to the author from the "Sphæra Civitatis" : with a curious engraving of the sphere surmounted by the head and shoulders of the queen : (3) Latin poem to the author signed "Richardus Late-War" pres. of St. John's college : (5-9) Epi- stola dedicatoria to Christopher lord Hat- ton : 10-25 "Ad Christianum lectorem," 11 May 1588 : 26-28, complimentary poems : (29-36) "Quæstiones et dubia quæ in octo libris Politicorum continen- tur," a table of contents : 36, two com- plimentary poems : 1-740, the work : 1-4 "Peroratio operis," 11 May, 1588 : (5-11) "Rerum contentarum index."

See Wood's *Ath. Oxon.*, i. 686. A commentary on the Politics of Aristotle, made into a general political treatise. On 16 July 1590 Barnes petitioned for a decree of Convocation that every determining bachelor should purchase this work, but it does not appear that any action was taken on the petition. Reprinted at Frankfurt in 1616.

3. **Catechism.**

A CATECHISME, | OR SHORT KIND OF IN- STRVCTION, WHEREBY | TO TEACH CHILDREN AND | THE IGNORAVNTER SORT, THE | *CHRIS- TIAN RELIGION. | Whereunto is prefixed a learned Treatise of the necessity and vse of | Catechising : together with Godly praiers most fit for al estates at al | times. | [device.]*

Impr. 6 : 1588 : sm. 4° : pp. [10] + 212 + [2] : p. 11 beg. *God, committed*. 111 *lowest partes* : Pica Roman. Contents :— (1) title : (3-9) Epistle dedicatory by Thomas Sparke and John Seddon to Arthur lord Grey of Wilton, Bletchley, 30 Jan. 1587 : 1-61, the treatise on cate- chising, signed by Sparke : 62, a prayer : 63-194, the catechism : 195-211, prayers, with a confession of the faith : 212 "Causes why men doe not vnderstand the holie Scriptures," &c.

Rare. See Wood's *Ath. Oxon.*, ii. 190 (bis). This is the Heidelberg Catechism translated into English by Thomas Sparke and John Seddon, with scriptural proofs annexed to each paragraph, and a long treatise on catechising. See next art.

4. **Catechism.**

A CATECHISME, OR SHORT | KIND OF INSTRVCTION, WHEREBY, | *TO TEACH CHILDREN, AND* | THE IGNORAVNTER SORT, THE | *CHRISTIAN RELIGION | Whereunto, is prefixed, a learned Treatise, of the necessity, & vse of Ca- techising : together, with Godly praiers, most fit, for al estates, at al times. | [device.]*

Impr. 6 : 1588 : (eights) 12° : pp. [12] + 274 (?) : p. 11 beg. *the greatnes*, 111 *I beleeue* : Pica Roman. Contents : -(1) title : (3-11) Epistle, as before : 1 80, the treatise, as before : 81, "The causes ..." &c. as before at end : 82, a prayer : 83-254, the catechism : 255-274, prayers &c. as above.

This is a reprint of the preceding quarto edition, with slight varieties of spelling, arrangement, &c. : the type is newly set up throughout.

5. **Humfrey,** Laurence.

A VIEW | OF THE ROMISH | HYDRA AND MON- STER TREASON A- GAINST THE LORDS | *ANNOINTED: CON-*DEMNED BY DAVID | 1. *SAM.* 26 *AND NOWE* CONFVTED IN SE- VEN SERMONS To perswade Obedience to Prin- ces, Concord among ourselues, and a | *generall Refor- mation and Repen-*taunce in all states | By L. H. | [*two mottos.*]

Impr. 6 : 1588 : (eights) 16° : pp. [24] + 192 : p. 11 beg. *as K. Holcot*, 111 *Kent, Roger* : Pica English. Contents:— p. (1) title : (2) "The Dialogue and talk of Dauid..." (1 Sam. xxvi. 8-12) : (3-17) Epistle dedicatory to the earl of Leicester,

Oxf., " Decemb. 28 " [1587], furnishing | (24) ' Faultes escaped correct thus," six :
the author's full name : 18-24 ' ".A table | 1–192, the seven sermons, on 1 Sam. xxvi.
of the special points and common places ": | 8–12.

Very rare. Wood's *Ath. Oxon.* (i. 560) represents this as a London book, but
Maunsell (i. 100) and Herbert (iii. 1403) testify to this Oxford edition. The
Bodleian copy wants the title and all after p. 186, the account of which is from a very
accurate description obligingly supplied from a copy in the Peterborough Cathedral
Library by the Bishop of Leicester in Dec. 1888.

6. Prime, John. [*woodcut.* | THE CONSO-'LATIONS OF DAVID, ' BREEFLY
APPLIED TO | QVEENE ELIZABETH : IN A | Sermon preached in Ox-ford
the 17. of Nouember. | By IOHN PRIME, | 1588. | [*motto* : then *woodcut.*]

Impr. 6*b* : 1588 : (eights) 16° : pp. | the bp. of Winchester, Oxf. 7 Dec. 1588 :
[32], signn. A-B² : sign. B 1ʳ beg. *wentereth* | A 4ʳ-B 7ʳ, the sermon, on Ps. xxiii. 4 : B 7ᵛ,
his : Pica English. Contents :—sign. A 1ʳ, | 2 Kings vi. 15-16.
title : A 2ᵛ-A 3ᵛ, Epistle dedicatorie to |

See Wood's *Ath. Oxon.*, i. 653. The Mar-prelate controversy and the defeat of the
Armada are mentioned.

7. Sparke, Thomas. " Treatise to prove that Ministers publicly,
and Householders privately, are bound to catechise their Parishioners and
Families &c. Oxon. 1588. oct."

So Wood (*Ath. Oxon.*, ii. 190) : the treatise is part of the Catechism above, and is
unlikely to have been separately issued.

8. Theocritus. SIXE IDILLIA | THAT IS *SIXE SMALL, OR PETTY* |
POEMS, OR ÆGLOGVES, CHO-*sen out of the right famous Sicilian* | Poet
THEOCRITVS, and tran-*slated into English verse.* | [*motto* : then *woodcut.*]

Impr. 7*a* : 1588 : (eight 12° : pp. [16], | *benter hic & omnis exantlabitur* | *Labor,*
sign. A⁸ : p. (11) beg. *The heauens* : Long | *in tue spem gratia.*" [Hor, Epod. i. 23-4],
Primer Italic. Contents :—sign. A 1ʳ, | within a border : " H " 2ʳ-A 8ᵛ, Idylls 8,
title, within a border : A 1ᵛ "E. D. *Li-* | 11, 16, 18, 21, 31 of Theocritus.

The only copy known is in the Bodleian. It was reprinted in 1883 at the private
press of Mr. C. H. Daniel of Worcester College, Oxford. Each idyll is preceded by
an " argument " and followed by an " embleme " or motto. It has been suggested
that E. D. to whom the dedication is addressed, may be Edward Dyer. This is the
first Oxford *édition de luxe*, except perhaps the xvth. cent. issues on vellum.

1589.

1. Hermaica gymnasmata. HERMAICA GYM-NASMATA. | Lite-
rarum nobilitas, & gloria. | LITERAE ORTV CAELESTES, | genere divinæ,
authoritate & gratia illustres, | *studijs sapientum præclaræ, fructu saluta-*
res, iucunditate præstantes. | [*woodcut.*]

Impr. 1*a* : 1589 : (eights) 12° : pp. | Exercises : A 2ᵛ, " Philologo " : A 3ʳ
[88], signn. A-E⁸, F⁴ : sign. B 1ʳ beg. | F 3 (" A 3 " ᵛ, the exercises : F 3ᵛ, note
luat : *aut* : Pica Italic. Contents :—sign. | that the 3rd Exercise is out of its place :
A 1ʳ, title : A 1ᵛ, " Tituli " of the 22 | F 4, unknown.

Very rare. Twenty-two short anonymous exercises in Latin prose, such as would serve for College or University disputations. By a Magdalen man, the " Epitaphius " being on William of Waynfleet, cf. the Phasma, &c.

2. **Hutchins,** Edward.   A SERMON | PREACHED AT | S. MARIES IN OXFORD VPON THE FEAST OF EPI-*PHANY CONCERNING* THE TRVE COMFORT OF | *GOD HIS CHVRCH TRVLY* | MILLITANT AND APOLO-*gie of the same.* | Ianuary 6. 1589. | By Edwarde Hutchins Maister | of Arts, and fellow of Brazen- nose College in Oxford. | [*woodcut.*]

Impr. 6*b*: 1589`: (eights) 12°: pp. [32]. signn. A-B`: sign. B 1ʳ beg. *blessing*: *no*: Pica English. Contents:—sign. A 1ʳ, | title: A 2ʳ-A 2ᵛ, dedication to Thomas Egerton: A 3ʳ B 8ʳ, the sermon, on Cant. iv. 7.

See Wood's *Ath. Oxon.*, ii. 452, where the book is divided into two, without cause.

3. **Rider,** John.   BIBLIOTHECA | SCHOLASTICA. | A DOVBLE DICTION-ARIE. | Penned for all those that would haue within short | space the vse of the Latin tongue, either to speake, or write. | *Verie profitable and necessarie for Scholers, Courtiers, Lawyers and their* | Clarkes, Apprentices of London, Travellers, Factors for Marchants, : and briefly for all Dis-continuers within her Majesties realmes | of England and Ireland. | *Compiled by* Iohn Rider, *Master of Arts, and preacher of Gods word.* | [*device.*] | { First reade / With others c . . . / Then censure | *Read the Preface, &c . . .* | [*imprint*] Cum privile . . . |

Impr. 12: 1589: (eights) sm. 4°: pp. [12] + 1820 columns, 3 in a page + ? : col. 111 beg. *Belching*, 1001. *Notched*: Minion. Contents:—p. (1, title: (3 4) dedication to sir Francis Walsingham, signed " Iohannes Riderus," Oxford, 1 Oct. [1589], in Latin: (5) "To the Reader," signed " Ioh. Ridir," 30 Sept.: (6) " Directions for the Reader": (7) "Rideri gratitudinis carmen, ad suum prænobilem Mecænatem,"acrostics" Comiti Sussexio" and " VVilielmo VVaddo": 8-12` complimentary Latin verses to the author: coll. 1-1800, the work, English-Latin: (?)

Very rare. See Wood's *Ath. Oxon.*, ii. 457. *Notes and Queries.* 6th S. iv. 274. The above description is from a copy of the first part, with damaged title, in the Bodleian. Rider claims that the Dictionarie is the first " that hath the English before the Latine, with a ful Index of al such latine words as are in any one common Dictionarie " and that it has 4000 more words than any other. He acknowledges the pecuniary help of the earl of Sussex and Will. Waade. The book is a " retort courteous " to the Cambridge dictionary by Tho. Thomas of 1588. Several edd. were subsequently issued (see 1627. 11), and Thomas Holyoke refashioned it.

4. **Skelton,** John.   " A Skeltonicall salutation, | or condigne gratulation | and iust vexation | of the Spanish nation, | that in a bravado | spent many a crusado | in setting forth an armado | England to invado | 4to, Oxf. J. Barnes, 1589."

So in the *Catalogue of the . . . library of . . . Benjamin Heywood Bright . . . which will be sold by auction . . .* 1845, art. 5276, p. 331. Extremely rare. J. Payne Collier once saw a copy (*Notes and Queries*, 1st S. i. 18, 1849), the imprint being nearly as No. 5 *b*. There were copies in the Farmer sale (1798, sold to lord Spencer) and Inglis sale (1826). In *Notes and Queries, ibid.,* p. 12 is printed a letter from John Aylmer bp. of London to the Lord Treasurer about " this foolish rime." The London reprint, which contains a Latin version said not to be in the Oxford edition (but query?) "imprinted at London for Toby Cooke, 1589" (sm. 4°, 8 leaves', is not uncommon. See also Brydges, *Censura Literaria*, 2nd ed., p. 18, Ames and Herbert's Ames.

5. Ursinus, Zacharias. THE SVMME | OF CHRISTIAN | RELIGION : | Delivered by ZACHARIAS VRSINVS in | his Lectures vpon the Catechisme, authori- *sed by the noble Prince* FREDERICKE | throughout his Dominions: | Wherein are debated and resolved the Questions | *of whatsoeuer points of moment, which haue beene,* | or are controversed in Divinity. | *Translated into English by* HENRY PARRY, *out of the last and* | best Latine Editions, together with some supplie of | *wants out of his Discourses of Divinity, and with correction* | of sundry faults & imperfections, which are | as yet remaining in the best corrected Latine. | [*woodcut.*]

Impr. 6 : 1589 : (eights) 12° : pp. [16] +966 + [10] : p. 11 beg. *nister comfort,* 111 *might fal?,* 501 *father al* : Long Primer Roman. Contents :—p. (1) title : (3-8) Epistle dedicatorie to the earl of Pembroke, signed by Parry : (9-15) "To the Christian readers" by Parry : 1-966, the work : (1-9) "A Table ..." of contents.

See 1587. U. It is noteworthy that the change from u consonantal to v can be traced in progress by a comparison of this title with that of the first edition.

1590.

1. Bacon, Roger. LIBELLVS ROGERII BA-|CONI ANGLI, DOCTISSIMI MA- thematici & medici, De retardandis senectu- *tis accidentibus, & de sensibus* conservandis. | Item, | LIBELLVS VRSONIS | MEDICI, DE PRIMARVM QVALI-|tatum arcanis & effectibus. Vterque affixis ad *marginem notulis* illustratus, & emendatus, | in lucem prodijt, operâ Iohannis Willi- *ams Oxoniensis, cuius* | sequitur | Tractatus Philosophicus, de humo-|rum numero & natura, complexionis, morbi, | *perturbationum origine, caloris & humidi nati-*|vi virtute & munere in humano corpore, & de | *aëris infec-|tione, vnde non rarò humores* | & spiritus coinquinantur. |

Impr. 5 : 1590 : (eights) 12° : pp. [8] + 31 + [1] + 134 + [2]. (signatures continuous : p. 11 beg. *cana rerum,* also *tur, Sed potest,* 111 *li. tendones* : Brevier Roman (1st part), Pica Italic 2nd and 3rd parts. Contents :—p. (1) title : (3-5) epistola dedicatoria to Christopher lord Hatton by J. Williams : (6-7) "Ad lectorem," a preface, mentioning some errata : (8) title of Bacon's treatise, and a poetical Latin "R. Baconi Vita" : 1-31, Bacon's treatise : 1-29. Urso's treatise : 33-134, Williams's treatise, signed at end by the author.

The preface contains curious critical principles. See Wood's *Ath. Oxon.,* ii. 132.

2. Gentilis, Albericus. ALBERICI GEN- TILIS I. C. PROFES- SORIS REGII | DE INIVSTITIA BELLICA | ROMANORVM ACTIO. | [*device.*]

Impr. 13 : 1590 : sm. 4° : pp. [8] + 23 + [1] : p. 11 beg. *rum vos non* : Pica Roman. Contents :—p. 1 "◦ j" : 3 title : (5-8) dedication "Roberto Devo-raxio . . . comiti Essexio," Oxford, 24 Dec. 1590 : 1-23, the treatise.

Rare. See Wood's *Ath. Oxon.,* ii. 91. The author says that he has a treatise ready prepared defending the precise opposite of the present argument.

3. Josephus.   ΦΛΑΒΙΟΥ ΙΩΣΗΠΟΥ ΕΙΣ ΜΑΚΚΑ-βαίους λόγος· ἢ περὶ αὐτοκράτορος λογισμοῦ. | Flavij Iosephi de Maccabæ-*is ; seu de Rationis imperio liber.* | MANVSCRIPTI CODICIS *OPE. LONGE, QVAM* antehac, & emendatior, & au-*ctior : cum Latina interpreta-tione ac notis Ioannis Luidi.* | [*woodcut.*]

Impr. 11 : 1590 : (eights) 16° : pp. [8] + 33 + [4] + 39 + [4], signn. ¶', A E': p. 11 beg. οὐχ οὕτως, also *ramo Moses* or *sim tt* : Long Primer Greek and Latin. Contents : — p. 1 title : (3-7 dedication to Roger Gifford physician to the King | by Ioannes Luidus, in Latin. Oxford, 29 Sept. 1590 : 1-33, & 1', text of Josephus : (2-4) "Veterum de hocce Iosephi libello elogia" : 1 ("6") 39, Latin tr. of Josephus : (1 3) "Adversaria" including various readings : (3-4. "Castigationes."

See Wood's *Ath. Oxon.,* i. 738 for John Lhuyd or Lloyd. The paging of the second part is very irregular up to p. 12.

4. Trigge, Francis.   "Comment. in cap. 12. ad Rom. Ox. 1590."

So in Bliss's ed. of Wood's *Ath. Oxon.,* i. 759.

5. Trigge, Francis.   "Noctes sacræ seu lucubrationes in primam partem apocalypseos in quibus perspicue docetur quænam sit vera ecclesia, et quæ falsa, quod hoc seculo tam multos in religione et fide suspensos tenet, &c. Oxon. 1590, 4to.   RAWLINSON."

So in Bliss's ed. of Wood's *Ath. Oxon.,* i. 760.   A copy was sold in the Davis sale at Oxford in 1686 (Catal. pt. 1, p. 26).

1591.

1. Barne, Thomas.   A | SERMON PREA-CHED AT PAVLS CROSSE | THE THIRTEENTH OF IVNE, THE SE-cond Sunday in Trinitie tearme 1591. by | THOMAS BARNE *student in Diuinity.* | [*three mottos,* then a *metal engraving* (arms of the University &c.)].

Impr. 4 : 1591 : 8° in size.

Extremely rare.   Only known from a titlepage preserved in the Bodleian Library. Probably this is the source of Herbert's description (iii. 1405).   He calls the book a quarto : the size of the close-cut titlepage is $6\frac{1}{8}$ in. × $3\frac{1}{4}$ in.   The metal engraving is curious : see 1591. T.

2. Hacket, Roger.   "Roger Hacket, his sermon at Paules Crosse on 1 Sam. xi ; 5, 6, 7 . . . Octavo."

So Herbert's Ames, p. 1404, from Maunsell, i. 100.   See Wood's *Ath. Oxon,* ii. 317.

3. Herodotus.   ἩΡΟΔΟΤΟΥ ἉΛΙΚΑΡΝΑΣΣΕΩΣ ἹΣΤΟΡΙ-ΩΝ ΠΡΩΤΗ, ΚΛΕΙΩ'. | HERODOTI HALICAR-NASSENSIS HISTORIARVM | liber primus, Clio. | [*device.*]

Impr. 15 : 1591 : sm. 4° : pp. 69 + [3] : p. 11 beg. Βιώτατον : Pica Greek. Contents :—p. 1, title : 2, "Herodoti vita ex Suida," &c. : 3-69, Herodotus. bk. 1 : 69, "Errata graviora sic corrigenda."

---

4. Sparke, Thomas. AN ANSWERE TO MA-|STER IOHN DE ALBINES, | NOTABLE DISCOVRSE AGAINST | heresies (as his frendes call his booke) | *Compiled by* THOMAS SPARK *pastor* | of Blechley in the county of Buck. | [two *mottos,* then *device.*]

Impr. 4 : 1591 : 8° : pp. [76] + 426 + [6] : p. 11 beg. *you are quite,* 111 *thing which it* : Pica English. Contents :— p. (1) Title : 3-14, Epistle dedicatorie to Arthur lord Grey of Wilton, signed "Thomas Sparke" : 15-76 "The preface to the Reader," including (27-76) an answer to the preface to Albines' book : 1-407, the treatise : 408-426, "A short answere to a new offer ... an enumeration of six ... signes of Antichristians ...": (1-4) "A Table" : (5) "Faults escaped in printing, through the absence of the author, the hardnes and smalnes of the hand, wherein the copy was offered to the presse, and the vnacquaintance of the overseers with the same."

In answer to Jean de Albin's treatise against heresies printed in English at Douai in 1575 : the text of which appears to be entirely reprinted in this edition. See Wood's *Ath. Oxon.,* ii. 190.

---

5. Tacitus. THE | ENDE OF NERO | AND BEGINNING OF | GALBA. | FOWER BOOKES OF THE HISTO-|RIES OF CORNELIVS TACITVS. | THE LIFE OF AGRICOLA. |

[Colophon on sign. H 2ʳ :—] impr. 14 : [on titlepage :— M. D. LXXXXI] 1591 : (sixes) la. 8° : pp. [6] + 17 + [1] + 267 + (1) + 80 + [4] : p. 11 beg. *so good a,* and *another Prince,* 111 *xxix. The setting,* 11 *ted to all* : 1st pt. Great Primer. 2nd pt. Pica, Roman. Contents :—p. (1) title : (3-4) dedication to the Queen, signed "Henry Savile" : (5 6) "A. B. To the Reader" : 1-17, the Ende of Nero, &c. : 1-267, the translation of Tacitus's Histories bks. 1-4, and (p. 237) his Life of Agricola : 1-48, Annotations upon the four books and the Life : 49-75, "A view of certain militar matters," with plan of Roman camp at p. 59 : 75-77, "The explication of a place in Polybius" about Greek money : 78-80, "Translations of the marginall Greeke" : (1) "A note of the editions vsed in such authors as are cited by page" : (2) "Errours of the printe, or changes" : (3) colophon.

See Wood's *Ath. Oxon.,* ii. 312. The A. B. of the preface was believed to be lord Essex Edm. Bolton's *Hypercritica* ad fin., Oxf. 1722). There is something peculiar about this edition, for bibliographers describe it as London, and the woodcut in the dedication is not otherwise known to belong to Barnes. The titlepage and form are rather of London than Oxford. A metal engraving in the text is perhaps Barnes's : see 1591. B.

---

6. Trigge, Francis. ANALYSIS CAPI-|TIS VICESIMI QVARTI | EVAN-|GELII SECVNDVM MATTHÆVM, | in qua Prophetiæ omnes, & quæ ad Sinagogam, | *& quæ ad Antichristum seductorem illum, & quæ ad nostra | tempora spectant, clarè explicantur, nec non ministerium ec-*|*clesiasticum cum omnibus suis adiunctis declaratur | ac delineatur.* | Authore FRANCISCO TRIGGO. | [*device.*]

Impr. 1*a* : 1591 : sm. 4° : pp. [4] + 128 : p. 11 beg. *loquutus est,* 111 *ti ora vult* : Pica Roman. Contents :—p. (1) title : (3-4) dedication to Will. James, dean of Christ Church, vice-chancellor, "ex Welburnia mea" 19 Apr. 1591 : 1-128, the Analysis.

See Wood's *Ath. Oxon.,* i. 759.

7. **Ursinus**, Zacharias.　　THE SVMME | OF CHRISTIAN | RELIGION : |
[&c. as 1589. U, except in l. 7 : for ., l. 9 comma added after *beene*, l. 15
is in italic, in imprint "*Tygres head. 1591*" for "Tygres | *head.
1589* "].

Impr. 6 : 1591 : (eights) 12° : pp. [16]
+966+[10] : p. 11 beg. *mister comfort*,
111 *might fall?*, 501 *father al* : Long　Primer Roman. Contents :—p. (1) title:
(3-16), as 1589. U : 1-966, the cate-
chism : (1-9) " A table . . ." of contents.

See 1587. U.

1592.

1. **Barlaamus**.　　ΤΟΥ͂ ΣΟΦΩΤΑ΄ΤΟΥ ΒΑΡΛΑΑ΄Μ ΛΟ΄ΓΟΣ ΠΕΡΙ΄ |
ΤΗ͂Σ ΤΟΥ͂ ΠΑ΄ΠΑ ΄ΑΡΧΗ͂Σ. | BARLAAMI DE PAPAE PRINCI- PATV LIBELLVS. |
Nunc primùm Græcé & Latiné editus opera ΙΟΑΝΝΙS | LVIDI *Procuratoris
Academiæ Oxoniensis.* | Ad | Illustrissimum Dominum Bucchurstium |
eiusdem Academiæ Cancellarium | Amplissimum. | [*device.*]

Impr. 11 : 1592 : sm. 4° : pp. [40],
signn. ¶, A D⁴ : sign. B 1ʳ beg. ἀξιοῦσθαι
χειροτονίας : Pica Greek and Roman.
Contents :—¶ 1ʳ, "¶ j" : ¶ 2ʳ, title : ¶ 2ʳ,
arms of Buckhurst engraved on metal :　¶ 3ʳ-¶ 4ʳ, epistle dedicatory to Thomas
Sackville lord Buckhurst, afterwards earl of
Dorset, 1 Jan. "1592," i.e. 159½ : A 1ʳ-
B 3ʳ, the Greek text : B 4ʳ-D 3ᵛ, the Latin
text.

See Wood's *Ath. Oxon.*, i. 739. This is the editio princeps of the work of bp.
Barlaamus. A copy presented by the author to John Selden, now in the Bodleian, is
without the device on the titlepage.

2. **Brasbridge**, Thomas.　　Quæstiones in Officia M. T. Ciceronis,
compendiariam totius Opusculi Epitomen continentes. 16° : (Impr. 5).

From notes of a copy belonging to lord Robartes, seen by me in Dec. 1879. The
dedication is dated 1586, of which date there is a copy of the book in Christ Church
Library, Oxford : see 1615. B, an edition noticed in Wood's *Ath. Oxon.*, i. 526.

3. **Breton**, Nicholas.　　THE PILGRIMAGE TO PARA-|DISE, IOYNED
WITH THE | Countesse of Pembrookes loue, compiled | *in verse by*
NICHOLAS BRETON | *Gentleman.* | [*motto*, then *device.*]

Impr. 6 : 1592 : sm. 4° : pp. [8] + 102
+ [2] : p. 11 beg. *But. waking* : Primer
(Great Primer?) Roman. Contents :—
p. (1) title : (3-4) epistle dedicatory to
Mary Countess of Pembroke : (5) " To
the Gentlemen students and Scholers of
Oxforde," 12 Apr. 1592, with a note dis-
claiming an edition " of late printed in
london by one Richarde Ioanes . . . en-　tituled *Bretons bower of delight*," as unauthorized and to a large extent not his
own poems : (6) " To my honest true
friende Master Nicholas Breton," signed
" Iohn Case " : (7 8) poems by Will.
Gager and Henry Price to Breton : 1-65,
the pilgrimage : 66-102, the countess of
Pembroke's love, both poems in 6-line
stanzas : (1) 7 " Errata."

Very rare. See Hazlitt's *Handbook*, p. 56.

4. **Case**, John.　　SVMMA | VETERVM INTER- PRETVM IN VNIVER- SAM
DIALECTICAM ARISTO- *TELIS; QVAM VERE FALSO*- ue Ramus in Aristotelem
inueha-|tur, ostendens. | *Auctore.* | IOANNE CASE OXONIENSI, | olim Collegii
D. Ioannis Præcurso-|ris socio. | *Omnibus Socraticæ Peripateticæque*

philosophiæ studiosis in | *primis vtilis ac necessaria.* | *Recognita & emen-data.* | Cum INDICE rerum & verborum locupletiss. | [*device.*]

Impr. 11 : 1592 : (eights) 12° : pp. [8] + 201 + [7] : p. 11 beg. *Resp. Definitio, III Opponens Aliquid* : Brevier Roman. Contents :—p. (1) title : (2) "Ioannis Readi carmen, in dialecticam Ioannis Casi" : (3-5) Epistola nuncupatoria to Rob. Dudley earl of Leicester : (6-8 "Ad benevolum lectorem," dated "Idibus August." : 1-201, the work : (1-6) Index.

The first edition of this book was issued at London by Thomas Vautrollier in 1584. The text of the treatise appears to be an inaccurate reprint of the 1584 edition, but most of the complimentary verses, with Nicholas Maurice's preface dated Sept. 1582, are here omitted : and there are other slight alterations. See 1598. C. See Wood's *Ath. Oxon.,* i. 686.

5. **Churchyard,** Thomas.   A | HANDEFVL OF | GLADSOME VERSES, | giuen to the Queenes Maiesty | *at Woodstocke this Prograce.* | 1592. | By | THOMAS CHVRCHYARDE. | [*device.*]

Impr. 2 : 1592 : sm. 4° (perhaps [fours] 8°) : pp. [20], signn. A B¹ C² : sign. B 2ᵛ beg. *That pleaseth* : Pica English. Contents :—sign. A 1ʳ title, within border : A 2ʳ–A 2ᵛ, dedication to the Queen : A 3ʳ– A 4ᵛ, "A few volu ntary verses to the general readers " : B 1ʳ C 2ʳ, the Handful of Verses : C 2ᵛ " [A V]erse of variety to all those that honors the onely Phœnix of the world " i. e. the Queen.

Extremely rare : a copy is in the British Museum. Reprinted in H. Huth's *Fugitive Tracts in Verse,* 1st Ser., no. xxxi (privately printed, Lond. 1875).

6. **Elizabeth,** queen.   [Speeches delivered | to Her Majesty this last Progress | at the Rt. Hon. the Lady Russels, at | Bissam ; the Lord Chandos | at Sudeley ; the Lord | Norris, at Ricott.]

[Impr. 7a : 1592] : sm. 4° : pp. [24], signn. A–C⁴ : sign. B 2ʳ beg. *Daphnes mischance* : Pica Roman. Contents :— [A 1ʳ, title ?] : A 2ʳ C 4ʳ, the speeches, &c.

Very rare. In the British Museum copy, the only one at present known (?), the titlepage (A 1) is lost, a transcript being supplied apparently from some other copy : also B 1 is lost. The text is reprinted in John Nichols' *Progresses . . . of Queen Elizabeth,* new edition, iii. (London. 1823), p. 130, but the source is not stated. A copy was sold in the Heber sale (Catal. pt. ii, p. 198, lot 3800) in 1834. Herbert's Ames in the Additions iii. 1813 mentions the book.

7. **Gager,** William.   MELEAGER. | Tragœdia noua. | BIS PVBLICE ACTA IN | *ÆDE CHRISTI* | Oxoniæ.   [*device.*]

Impr. 11 : 1592 : (eights) 16° : pp. [96], signn. A–F⁴ : sign. B 1ʳ beg. *Non lenior* : Pica Italic. Contents :—sign. A 1ʳ title : A 2ʳ–A 3ʳ, letter dedicatory to Robert earl of Essex, 1 Jan. "1592" (1593 ?), signed " Guilielmus Gagerus " : A 3ᵛ–A 4ʳ, Complimentary poems to the author, one by Albericus Gentilis : A 4ᵛ– A 5ʳ, short poetical and prose account of the play by the author : A 5ᵛ "Personae " : A 6ʳ–E 7ᵛ, the play with prologues, argu- ment and epilogues : E 8ʳ F 5ᵛ, " Panni- culus Hippolyto Senecæ Tragœdiæ as- sutus 1591," a short play : F 6ʳ " Apollo προλογίζει ad Serenissimam Reginam Eli- zabetham 1592," a poem : F 6ᵛ–F 7ᵛ, Pro- logue and Epilogue to " Bellum Gram- maticale." [F 8 not seen].

For the controversy caused by the publication of this play (which had been acted according to the letter dedicatory in 1581 or 1582 and 1584 or 1585), see Wood's *Ath. Oxon.,* ii. 88.

8. Gager, William. VLYSSES REDVX | TRAGOEDIA NOVA. | IN AEDE CHRISTI OXONIAE | *PVBLICE ACADEMICIS RE-|CITATA, OCTAVO IDVS FEBRVARII.* 1591. | [*device.*]

Impr. 11 : 1591 : (eights) 12° : pp. [96], signn. A-F⁸ : sign. B 1ʳ beg. *Itaque jessum* : Pica Italic. Contents :— sign. A 1ʳ, title : A 2ʳ–A 2ᵛ, " Prologus ad Academicos " in verse : A 3ʳ-A 4ᵛ, epistle dedicatory to lord Buckhurst, Ch. Ch., 10 May 1592, signed " Guilielmus Ga- gerus " : A 4ᵛ–A 7ʳ, complimentary poems, &c., one by Albericus Gentilis : A 7ᵛ, " Personæ " : A 8ʳ–F 1ʳ, the play : F 2ʳ– F 6ᵛ, five Latin pieces by Gager, includ- ing a " Prologus in Rivales, Comœdiam." [F 8 not seen]

See Wood's *Ath. Oxon.*, ii. 89.

9. Lycophron. ΛΥΚΟΦΡΟΝΟΣ ΤΟΥ | ΧΑΛΚΙΔΕΩΣ | Ἀλεξάνδρα. LYCOPHRONIS CHAL-|cidensis Alexandra. | *In vsum Academiæ Oxoniensis.* | [*device.*]

Impr. 13a : 1592 : (fours) 12° : pp. [2] + 44 + [2] : p. 11 beg. ὠνητὸς διθαλω : Pica Greek. Contents :—p. (1 title, within a border : 1-44, the work : (1-2 (not seen.)

The poem is better known as the *Cassandra*, which is the running title throughout. Some various readings are printed in the margin.

10. Sanford, John. APOLLINIS ET MVSARVM | 'ΕΥΚΤΙΚΑ' 'ΕΙΔΥΛΛΙΑ, | *IN SERENISSIMÆ REGINÆ* ELIZABETHAE | auspicatissimum Oxoniam ad- uentum, de-|*cimo die Calend. Octobris, An*: *M.D.LXXXXII.* | [*device.*]

Impr. 11 : (1592) : sm. 4° : pp. [24], signn. A-C¹ : sign. B 1ʳ beg. *Cernis et* : Great Primer Roman. Contents :—sign. A 1ʳ, title : A 1ᵛ, Latin poetical dedica- tion to dr. Nicholas Bond, vice-chancellor and president of Magdalen college, signed " Ioannes Sanfordus " : A 2ʳ-C 4ᵛ, the Idylls.

Very rare, unknown even to Wood and Nichols (*Progresses of Qu. Elizabeth*). Two copies are in the British Museum, and lord Robartes has an imperfect one, seen in 1881. Reprinted literatim in the Oxford Historical Society's viii[th] volume, (Oxf., 1887. 8vᵒ), where see notes by the editor, the rev. Charles Plummer. The poems are 'in honour of the Queen's Visit, and especially in connection with a banquet given by the President and Fellows of Magdalen to the nobles and Privy Councillors of the Queen's retinue,' 22 Sept. 1592.

11. Thorne, William. DVCENTE DEO. | WILLELMI THORNI | TVLLIVS, SEV ΡΉΤΩΡ IN TRIA | *STROMATA DIVISVS.* | [*motto.*] E NOVO BEATÆ MARIÆ | WINTON IN OXON COLLEGIO. | [*woodcuts.*]

Impr. 16 : 1592 : (eights) 12° : pp. [32] + 253 + [3] : p. 11 beg. *Primi Stro- matis*, III 'Πρόληψις : Long Primer Ro- man. Contents :—p. (1) title : (2, En- graved arms and motto of lord Pembroke, with verses : (3-8) epistle dedicatory to William Herbert heir of lord Pembroke : (9-25) " Eidem Willelmi Thorni paræ- nesis ad Rhetoricam ἐγκωμιαστική " : (26-30) complimentary verses to Thorn : (31-32 address to the reader, in Latin : (32 3 lines of errata : 1-253, the work, in three Stromata and an appendix : (1) " Errata sic corrigenda."

See Wood's *Ath. Oxon.*, ii. 480. A treatise on Rhetoric. A poem on p. (30) shows that John Sanford of Magdalen was ' Corrector Typograph.'

1593.

1. Aristophanes. ΑΡΙΣΤΟΦΑΝΟΥΣ | ΙΠΠΕΙΣ. | *,* | ARISTO- PHANIS | EQVITES | [*device.*]

Impr. 11: 1593: sm. 4°: pp. [56], signn. A G¹: sign. B 1ʳ beg. Κλέπτων τὸν οἶνον: Pica Greek. Contents:—sign. A 1ʳ, title within border: A 2ʳ, Ὑπόθεσις and Δράματος πρόσωπα: A 3ʳ G 4ʳ, the play.

The first separate edition of this comedy.

2. Demosthenes. "'Demosthenis Orationes 15, cum interpretatione Nicolai Carri; 3 Olynthiacarum, 4 Philippicarum.' Quarto."

So in Herbert's Ames, iii. 1405. Possibly a mistake for 1597.

3. Gentilis, Albericus. "'Albericus Gentilis Commentarii de Malificis & Mathemat. & aliis similibus.' Quarto."

So in Herbert's Ames, iii. 1405. In the reprint (*Hanover*, 1604) the title is ' Alberici Gentilis, I. C., Professoris Regii, Ad Tit. C. de Maleficis et Math. & ceter. similibus commentarius . . .;' the preface is dated Oxford 26 June 1593, and addressed to dr. Toby Matthew.

4. G[winne], M[atthew], and Henry Price. EPICEDIVM | IN OBITVM ILLVS- TRISSIMI HEROIS HEN- RICI COMITIS DER- BEIENSIS. &C. | [*device*: then *motto*.]

Impr. 11: 1593: sm. 4°: pp. [16], signn. A–B¹: sign. B 1ʳ beg. *Epitaphium*: Great Primer Roman. Contents:—sign. A 1ʳ, title: A 2ʳ–A 2ᵛ, epistle dedicatory to Ferdinand Stanley ("Sanleio") earl of Derby, signed M[atthew] G[winne], H[enry] P[rice]: A 3ʳ–B 4ᵛ, seven Latin poems or epitaphs, the last signed in full "Henricus Priceus."

See Wood's *Ath. Oxon.*, i. 702, ii. 415.

5. Parry, Henry. "Concio de Victoria Christianâ, in Apoc. 3. 21. Oxon. 1593–94. Lond. 1606."

See Wood's *Ath. Oxon.*, ii. 193: see 1594. P.

6. Sparke, Thomas. A | SERMON PREA- *CHED AT WHADDON* in Buckinghamshyre the 22. of | *November* 1593. *at the buriall of* | the Right Honorable, ARTHUR | *Lorde* GREY *of Wilton*, *Knight of the* | most Honorable order of the Garter, | *by* | THOMAS SPARKE Pastor of | *Blechley.* | [*woodcut.*]

Impr. 2: 1593: (eights) 16°: pp. [8] + 87 + [1]: p. 11 beg. *talkes of*: Pica English. Contents:— 1, title, within border: 3 7 Epistle dedicatorie to the countess of Bedford, her daughter lady Grey and Thomas lord Grey of Wilton, Bletchley, 1 Dec. 1593: (8) "In obitum clarissimi Herois, Domini Arthuri Greij. θρηνῳδία," a Latin hexameter poem by "Ioannes Sanfordus": 1–87, the sermon, on Is. lvii. 1–2: 87, "Faultes escaped," eight errata.

See Wood's *Ath. Oxon.*, ii. 190.

1. **Beacon**, Richard.   SOLON HIS FOLLIE, | OR | A POLITIQVE DIS-|COVRSE, TOVCHING THE | Reformation of common-weales conque-|red, declined or corrupted. | BY RICHARD BEACON GENT. STV-*DENT OF GRAVES INNE, AND SOME-*|times her Maiesties Attorney of the province | *of Mounster in Irelande.* | *_** | [*device.*]

Impr. 2 : 1594 : sm. 4° : pp. [12] + 114 + [2] : p. 11 beg. *nius. Sol* :, 111, *the thirde matter* : Pica English. Contents :— pp. (1-2) (not seen, but presumably blank) : (3) title : (5-8) Epistle dedi-catorie to the queen : (9) "The Authour to the Reader," (10) "The booke vnto the Reader" : 1-114, the treatise : (1-2) (not seen, but presumably blank).

2. **[Lewes**, Richard.]   [*woodcuts*] APOLOGIA | INNOCENTIAE ET | INTEGRITATIS R. L. | *SACRÆ THEOLOGIÆ BAC-*calaurei adversus inquissi-mas | E. Osb. transfugæ sacrifi-culi calumnias ad Acade-|micos Oxonienses. | [*woodcuts.*]

Impr. 11 : 1594 : (eights) 12° : pp. [48], sign. A-c⁸ : sign. B 1ʳ beg. *& Apo-stolus* : Pica Roman. Contents :— sign. A 1ʳ title : A 2ʳ-A 7ᵛ, the Apologia : A 8ʳ- c 8ʳ, "Concio habita Oxoniæ festo cineri-tio, A. D. 1594 per R. L. B. S. Th. Textus ex 3. cap. Ep. D. Pau. ad Philipp. Ver. 1."

Very rare. A diatribe against Edward Osberne's *Palinodia*, printed in the *Concer-tatio ecclesiae catholicae in Anglia* by Johannes Aquepontanus (Bridgwater), *Augsburg* 1594, p. 240, in which Osberne who had been twice converted to the Roman Catholic religion had made reflexions on Lewes a Protestant. The clue to the author's name is sign. A 5' compared with p. 241 of the Concertatio. Some account of the author is in Wood's *Ath. Oxon.*, i. 227.

3. **Lewes**, R[ichard].   A | SERMON PREA-|*CHED AT PAVLES* | Crosse, by R. LEWES, Bacche-|ler of Divinitie, concerning *Isaac* | his Testament, disposed by the | Lord to *Iacobs* comfort, though it | were intended to *Esau* by his fa-|ther; shewing, that the counsel of | God shal stand, albeit the whole | worlde withstande it. | [*device.*]

Impr. 2a : 1594 : (eights) 12° : pp. [48], signn. A-c⁸ : sign. B 1ʳ beg. *Isaac, see* : Pica English. Contents :— sign. A 1ʳ, title, within a border : A 2ʳ-A 3ʳ, Epistle dedicatory to sir Henry Unton, dated "This xviij of June" : A 4ʳ-c 8ᵛ, the sermon, on Gen. xxvii. 1-10.

See Wood's *Fasti Oxon.*, i. 227.

4. **Parry**, Henry.   VICTORIA CHRISTIANA. | CONCIO AD | CLERVM : HABITA | OXONIAE ANNO | Domini. 1591. | *H. Parry Auctore.* | [*woodcuts.*]

Impr. 11 : 1594 : (eights) 16° : pp. [48], signn. A-c⁸ : sign. B 1ʳ beg. *culco suo* : Pica Roman. Contents :— sign. A 1ʳ, title : A 2ʳ-A 4ᵛ, epistle dedicatory to William Herbert, lord Cardiff : sign. A 5ʳ-c 7ʳ ?: c 7 not seen), the sermon, on Rev. iii. 21 : c 8 (not seen, probably blank.)

See Wood's *Ath. Oxon.*, ii. 193, where an edition of 1593 is mentioned, perhaps by error.

5. **Powel**, Griffith.   ANALYSIS | ANALYTICO-|RVM POSTERIORVM |

SIVE LIBRORVM ARISTO- telis de Demonstratione, in | qua singula capita per quæ-'stiones & responsiones | perspicuè exponuntur : | *adhibitis* | QVIBVSDAM SCHOLIIS, | ex optimis quibusque interpretibus | *desumptis, opera & studio G. P. Oxoniensis | confecta & edita in vsum iuniorum.* | [*wood-cuts.*]

Impr. 11 : 1594 : eights) 16º : pp. [16] + " 344 " [really 333] + [3] : p. 11 beg. *mia magnitudinem,* " 111 " *singularis* : Long Primer Roman. Contents :—p. (1) title : (3–6) epistle dedicatory to Robert earl of Essex, signed " Griffinus Powel," Jesus coll. Oxford, Feb. 27 : (7–10) " Ad Lectorem Academicum " : (11–15) " Prolegomena " : 1–" 344," the Analysis.

See Wood's *Ath. Oxon.,* ii. 283. In the preface the author promises a similar analysis of the Topica, Sophistici Elenchi (see 1598. P) and Physica, and says that his method is derived from that of Ursinus. The paging is very wild ; the signatures are *, A – X² = 352 pages. See 1564. Diagrams occur in the text and margins.

6. Powel, Griffith.   " Analysis libri Aristot. de Sophisticis Elenchis. Ox. 1594." A mistake in Wood's *Ath. Oxon.,* ed. Bliss, ii. 283 for 1598 : see 1598. P.

7. **Sparke,**   A | SERMON | *PREACHED AT* | Cheanies the 14. of *September,* 1585, *at the bu-'*riall of the Right Honora-*ble the Earle of* BEDFORDE, | *by* | THOMAS SPARKE Do-*ctor of Divinitie.* | *Newly perused and corrected by* | *the Authour.* | [*woodcuts.*]

Impr. 2 : 1594 : (eights) 16º : pp. [10] + 110 : p. 11 beg. *as good* : Pica English. Contents :—p. (1) title, within border : (3–10) Epistle dedicatorie to Arthur lord Grey of Wilton, dated Bletchley, 25 Dec. 1585 : 1–110, the sermon, dated at end 22 Sept. 1594.

See Wood's *Ath. Oxon.,* ii. 193. A new ed. of 1585. S.

8. **Trigge,** Francis.   A | GODLY AND FRVIT-FVLL SERMON PREA-| *CHED AT GRANTHAM.* | Anno. Dom. 1592. | by | FRANCIS TRIGGE. | Wherein as in a glasse, every de-'gree may plainely see their spots and staines : | *and may bee thereby made in deede beautifull* | (if they doe not hate to be reformed) | *against the appearance of* | *Jesus Christ.* | [*woodcuts.*]

Impr. 7 : 1594 : (eights) 16º : pp. [96], signn. A·F⁴ : sign. B 1ʳ beg. *state of Christes* : Pica English. Contents :—sign. A 1ʳ, title : A 2ʳ–A 4ᵛ, address " To the Christian Reader " : A 5ʳ–F 8ʳ, the sermon, on Is. xxiv. 1–3.

See Wood's *Ath. Oxon.,* i. 759 : and 1595. T.

1595.

1. **Moore,** Robert.   DIARIVM HISTORICOPOETICVM, | IN QVO | PRAETER CONSTELLATIO- NVM VTRIVSQVE HEMISPHAE- RII, ET ZODIACI, ORTVS, ET OCCA-|sus, numerum stellarum causarum- que, ad poesin spectantium, vari-|etatem, *declarantur* | CVIVSQVE MENSIS DIES FERE | *SINGVLI, REGVM, IMPERATORVM,* | Principum, Pontificum, virorumque doctorum, na- *talibus,*

nuptiis, inaugurationibus, morte desnique, aut re alia quacunque insig-'niore. celebriores, | sic, | VT NIHIL PAENE DESIDERARI POSSIT, | ad perfectam rerum gestarum Chronolo-'giam, cum, ex auctoribus probatissimis, accu-'*rata quoque annorum ratio margini* | *ascribatur.* | [*motto*] | Suasu, & permissu superiorum. |

Impr. 11 : 1595 : sm. 4" : pp. [8] + 102 + [6] : p. 11 beg. *Sic respiraram* : Pica Roman. Contents :– p. (1) title : (3-5) Epistola Dedicatoria to sir ?, John Wolley and his wife Elizabeth, signed "Robertus Moore," New college, Oxford, 6 July 1595: (7-8) address "Ad Lectorem Benevolum": 8, "Auctoris ad libellum parænesis." a short poem : 1-102, the work : (1-6) Index : (6) five errata.

See Wood's *Ath. Oxon.,* ii. 654. The book is a long hexameter poem, divided into twelve books, one for each month, in which historical events are successively alluded to.

2. **Trigge,** Francis. "Trigge (F.) Godly and Fruitfull Sermon, at Grantham, 1592, *black letter, Oxford,* 1593."

So in the Pyne Auction sale catalogue at Sotheby's, art. 1058, sold on 8 July 1886. Quaritch ascertained that the date was correct. Probably a reissue of 1594. T.

3. **Ursinus,** Zacharias. THE SVMME | OF CHRISTIAN | RELIGION : Delivered by ZACHARIAS VRSINVS in | his Lectures vpon the Catechisme, authori-'*sed by the noble Prince* FREDERICKE | throughout his dominions. Wherein are debated and resolved the Questions | *of whatsoever pointes of moment, which have beene* | or are controversed in Divinity. | *Translated into English by* HENRY PARRY, *out of the last and* | best Latine Editions, together with some supply of | *wantes out of his Discourses of Divinity, and with correction* | of sundry faults & imperfections. which are | *as yet remaining in the best corrected Latine.* | [*woodcut.*]

Impr. 6 : 1595 : (eights) 12° : pp. [16] + 966 + [10] : p. 11 beg. *nister comfort,* 111 *might fall,* 801 *he that hath* : Long Primer Roman. Contents :—p. (1) title : (3-8) Epistle dedicatorie to the earl of Pembroke : 9-15 "To the Christian readers" : 1-966, the treatise : (1-9) "A table . . .".

See 1587. U.

4. **Wermueller,** Otto. PERL MEWN ADFYD | neu, | Perl paprydawl, gwprtßfawrocaf, | *yn dyscu i bôb dyn garu, a chofleidio y groes,* | *meis peth hyfryd angenrheidiawl ir enaid, pa gonffordd sy yw gael o honi,* *ple, ac ym ha fodd,* | *y dylid ceisiaw diddanwch, a chymorth ym hob* *adfyd : a thrachefn, pa wedd y dyle bawb i ym-ddwyn i hunain mewn blinder, yn ol gair duw,* | *a escrifannwyd yn gyntaf mewn Dwitch* | *gann bregethwr dyscedig* Otho Wer- | mulerus, *ac a droed ir Saesonaeg gann* D. Miles Cowrdal, | *ac yrawrhon yn hwyr ir* | Gambraeg *gann.* | H L. | [Welsh *motto,* then *woodcuts.*]

Impr. 17 : 1595 : 12° : pp. [24] + 246 + [6] : pp. 11 beg. *mal i llefarod',* 111 *dwaw, er* : Pica English. Contents :—p. (1) title : (3-11) dedication to dr. Richard Vychan (Vaughan), archdn. of Middlesex, signed "Huw Lewys" : (12-13) poem "At yr vnrhyw wr" by Lewys : (15-23) "Ir darlennydd Christnogaidd rhad a thangneddyf Ynghrist" : 1-246 the work : (1-4) poem "Cowydd ir Iesu" by Lewys : (5) "Gweddi ferr yw duedyd mewn adfyd."

A translation into Welsh by Hugh Lewis of Wermueller's *Spiritual and most precious Pearl*, a religious treatise, translated from the German into English by Miles Coverdale (*Lond.* 1550). See M. Williams's *Cofrestr o'r holl Lyfrau printjedig ... yn y Faith Gymraeg ...* (Lond. 1717), *Cambrian Bibliography* by the rev. William Rowlands, ed. by the rev. D. S. Evans (*Llandidloes*, 1869, 8vo), p. 71. This is the first Welsh book printed at Oxford and the first occurrence of Rhydychen (Oxen-ford) in Oxford imprints. The translator begs the reader to excuse the absence of *y* in some places before *u* and *r*, the printer's stock being too small. For the same reason *dd* is usually *d*, and *ll l*. If a word is here and there omitted it should be remembered that the printing is done by Englishmen!

1596.

1. **Case**, John.   REFLEXVS | SPECVLI MORALIS | QVI COMMENTARII VICE | esse poterit in Magna Moralia Aristo-telis: auctore JOHANNE CASO, | in Medicina Doctore, Collegij | Divi Iohannis Præcursoris | Oxon. olim socio. | [*five mottos*, then *woodcuts*.]

Impr. 5*a*: 1596: (eights) 12°: pp. [16] + 271 + [1] : p. 11 beg. *one ab*, 111 *Quest.* 3: Pica Roman. Contents :—p. 1 title : (3-5) Epistola dedicatoria to Richardus Phetiplacius, Oxf. 20 Sept. 1596: (7-11) address "Ad Lectorem. Benevolum" 26 Nov. 1596: (13-15) 5 Latin poems on the book : 1-198, the work : 199-200, "Peroratio operis, ad lectorem" 20 Sept. 1596 : 201-206, "Quæstionum ... ordo ...": 207-208, "Index Capitum": 209-268, "A B Cedarium moralis philosophiæ Johanni Phetipacio Richardi Phetiplacii filiolo : omnibusque Tyronibus virtutum studiosis, scriptum & commendatum," by question and answer: 269-271, "Peroratio ad adolescentem studiosum lectorem," 30 Nov. (1596).

See Wood's *Ath. Oxon.*, i. 687. The first address shows that for a time the printer refused to produce the work, which is related to the *Speculum* of 1585, for fear that it might be reprinted at once elsewhere, and he suffer loss as in the case of the *Sphæra Civitatis* of 1588. See 1586. C. A presentation copy has red lines round the page, on three sides double. This book is strictly the second part of the next art., Case's *Speculum*.

2. **Case**, John.   SPECVLVM | QVÆSTIONVM | MORALIVM, IN VNI-|VERSAM ARISTOTELIS | Philosophi summi Ethicen, cui ad-|ditur brevis commentarius in magna | Moralia Aristotelis, qui ab Autho-|re Reflexus speculi Moralis | nominatur, | IOHANNE CASO OXONIENSI | Doctore in Medicina olim Collegii præ-|cursoris socio Authore, | *NVNC DENVO RECOGNITVM,* | *& à mendis plerisque repurgatum.* | CVM INDICE VERBORVM ET RERVM | præcipuè memorabilium locuplete. | [*woodcuts.*]

Impr. 20 : 1596 : (eights) 12° : pp. [32] + folded sheet + 533 + [27] : p. 11 beg. *empli causa*, 111 *tur : quod* : Pica Roman. Contents : p. (1) title : (3-9) epistola nuncupatoria to the earl of Leicester, dated 7 Mar. "1585" : (11-15) address "ad studiosos iuvenes utriusque academiæ," with a short poem : (17-31) complimentary Latin verses : a "Tabula virtutum et vitiorum omnium," folio sheet printed on one side only : 1-531, the work : 532-533, "Peroratio ad lectorem" : 1-26, Index.

A reprint of 1585. C. The above title covers the preceding article, Case's *Reflexus Speculi*, but for convenience they are separately treated.

3. **Fitz-Geffrey**, Charles.   SIR | FRANCIS DRAKE | *His* | Honorable

lifes com-,mendation, and his | Tragicall Deathes lamentation. *** | [*motto*, then *woodcuts*.]

Impr. 19: 1596: (eights) 12°: pp. [106], signn. A², one leaf, B–G²: sign. B2ʳ beg. *See how Apollo*: Long Primer English. Contents:—sign. A1ʳ title, within border: A2ʳ poetical dedication to lady Elizabeth widow of sir F. Drake, signed by the author of the book "Charles Fitz-geffrey": A3ʳ "To the Authour," poem, beg. *Once dead*, signed "Richard Rous": A3ᵛ "To C. F.," poem, beg. *When to*, signed "Francis Rous": A4ʳ "To the Authour," poem, beg. *Englands Ulysses*, signed "D. W.": 5th leaf ʳ "In Dracum redivivum; Carmen," beg. *Quis vostrûm*, signed "Thomas Michelborne": B1ʳ–G8ᵛ, the poem.

Very rare. See Wood's *Ath. Oxon.*, ii. 607. The book was reprinted in the same year with small differences in the text chiefly of spelling, but with considerable changes in the prefatory matter: see below. It was also reprinted in 1819 at the Lee Priory Press, and edited by dr. Grosart in 1881. The poem is in 7-line stanzas, rhyming ABABBCC. Woodcut ornaments occur at the top and bottom of almost every page, and the book has the appearance of an *édition de luxe*.

4. **Fitz-Geffrey,** Charles.   SIR | FRANCIS DRAKE | *his* | Honorable lifes com-mendation, and his | Tragicall Deathes | lamentation. | *** | [*motto*.] | Newly Printed with additions. | [*woodcuts*.]

Impr. 19: 1596: (eights) 12°: pp. [112], signn. A–G²: sign. B2ʳ beg. *See how Apollo*: Long Primer English. Contents:—sign. A1ʳ title, within border: A2ʳ poetical dedication to lady Elizabeth Drake, signed "Charles Fitz-geffrey": A2ᵛ "To C. F.," poem, beg. *Once dead*, signed "Richard Rous": A3ʳ "To C. F.," poem, beg. *When to*, signed "Francis Rous": A3ᵛ "To C. F.," poem, beg. *Many greate*, signed "Thomas Mychelborne": A4ʳ "To the Author," poem, beg. *Englands Ulysses*, signed "Diag. Vvh.," i.e. Degory Whear: A4ᵛ "Ad Dracum," English poem, beg. *Weepe not*, signed "Ty. Co.": A5ʳ–A6ᵛ, address "To the Reader" signed "C. F." Broadgates (Oxford), 17 Nov. 1596: A7ʳ–A8ᵛ, quotations ending "Hæc ferè sunt quæ de Draco nostro apud exoticos poetas legimus": B1ʳ–G8ᵛ, the poem.

See preceding article.
Very rare. This issue is almost identical with the first, but the whole text appears to be newly set up, with minute differences.

5. **Morlet,** Pierre.   IANITRIX | siue | *INSTITVTIO AD PER-*fectam linguæ Gallicæ | cognitionem ac-*quirendam*. | Authore PETRO MORLETO | GALLO. | [*motto*: then *device*.]

Impr. 11: 1596: (eights) 16°: pp. [8]+92+[4]: p. 11 beg. *Antequam vero*: Pica Italic. Contents:—p. (1) title, within a border: (3–7) Epistola dedicatoria to sir Robert Beal, dated Broadgates Hall, "15 Mar. 1596": (9–13) complimentary poems in Latin and Greek: (14) "Errata": 1–92 the treatise.

Very rare: a French grammar, in Latin, by Pierre Morlet (?). The dedication states that the author was tutor to sir Robert Beal, having been introduced by David Chytræus.

6. **Perrot,** sir James.   "A Discovery of Discontented Minds wherein their several sorts & purposes are described especially such as are gone beyond ÿ Seas. Dedicated to ÿ Earl of Essex by James Perrot & printed at Oxford in 4ᵗᵒ by Joseph Barnes Printer to the University—1596."

Very rare. The above is from Brit. Mus. MS. Harl. 5904 (Bigford's Collections), foll. 20 & 171. See Wood's *Ath. Oxon.*, ii. 606, Herbert's Ames, p. 1406, both notices derived from Oldys's *Catalogue of pamphlets in the Harleian Library* (Harleian Miscellany, vol. x. (1813), p. 358, where ' Quarto, in thirty-four pages ' is added).

7. **Pinner,** Charles.   [Sermon by Charles Pinner at Marlborough, on 1 Tim. iv. 16.]

(Impr. ? : 1596?): (eights) 16° : pp. 53 + [3] : p. 11 beg. *through knowledge* : Pica English. Contents :—p. 1 title : 3-4, Epistle dedicatory to " master Iohn Bailife " of Marlborough, dated from Wotton Basset, 20 Oct. 1596 : 5-53, the sermon.

Very rare : see Wood's *Ath. Oxon.*, i. 667. In the Bodleian copy, the only one known, the title is lost, so that the date is uncertain. But the book was certainly printed at Oxford, the woodcut on p. 3 being decisive.

8. **Rainolds,** John.   JOHANNIS RAINOLDI, | DE ROMANÆ ECCLE- SIÆ IDOLOLATRIA, IN | CVLTV SANCTORVM, RE- liquiarum, imaginum, aquæ, salis, olei, | alarumque rerum consecratarum, & | sacramenti Eucharistiæ, | OPERIS INCHOATI | LIBRI DVO. | *IN QVIBUS CUM ALIA MVLTA* | *VARIORVM PAPISMI PATRONO- rum errata patefiunt: tùm inprimis Bellarmini,* | *Gregoriique de Valentia, calumniæ in Calvi- num ac ceteros Protestantes, argutiæque* | pro Papistico idolorum cultu | discutiuntur & ven- tilantur. | [*motto* : then *woodcuts.*]

Impr. 18 : 1596 : eights, sm. 4° : pp. [16] + 646 : p. 11 beg. *cisse tantùm*, 111 *am secundum*, 501 *bus Gentium* : English Roman.   Contents :—p. (1) " ¶ 1 " alone : (3) title : 5-12, dedicatory epistle to the earl of Essex, in Latin, Queen's coll. Oxford, 7 July 1596 : (13-15) " Index tractatuum, librorum, et capitum " : 1-609, the work in two books, preceded by an " Epistola ad Anglicorum Seminariorum alumnos Romæ & Rhemis " and preface, and followed by an " Admonitio ad lectorem " : 609-627, " Index locorum Sacræ Scripturæ " : 628-646, " Index rerum præcipuarum."

See Wood's *Ath. Oxon.*, ii. 15.   Hebrew Pica type occurs on p. 497 and elsewhere, both pointed and without points : and unpointed Long Primer on pp. 169, 451, 603, &c.

9. **Unton,** sir Henry.   FVNEBRIA | NOBILISSIMI AC | PRÆSTANTISSIMI | EQVITIS, | D. HENRICI VNTONI, | *AD GALLOS BIS LEGATI* | Regij, ibique nuper fato functi, | CHARISSIMÆ MEMORIÆ, | *ac desiderio, à Musis Oxoniensi- bus Apparata.* | [*woodcuts.*]

Impr. 11 : 1596 : sm. 4° : pp. [68], signn. ¶, A G⁴, H² : sign. B 1ʳ beg. *Virtutis movere* : Pica Italic.   Contents :— sign. ¶ 1ʳ title : ¶ 1ᵛ " Liber ad Lectorem," Latin poem : ¶ 2ʳ-¶ 2ᵛ, address " Benevolo lectori," signed " Robertus Wright," Trinity college, Oxford, 13 June 1596 : ¶ 3ʳ-H 2ᵛ, poems in memory of Unton, the only two not Latin being on sign. A 1ʳ in Greek and Hebrew : see below.

See Wood's *Ath. Oxon.*, i. 648. The first (unpointed) Hebrew type used at Oxford appears in the poem alluded to above, a Pica fount. Some (probably early) copies omit the preface, the ' Liber ad Lectorem ' occurring on sign. ¶ 2ʳ, the page preceding and following being blank.

1. **Agatharchides.** AGATHAR- CHIDIS ET MEM- NONIS HISTORI- | corum, quæ supersunt, | *omnia, è Græco iam recèns in* | *Latinum traducta*: | per | RICH. BRETTVM, Oxonien- sem, è Collegio Lincoln. | [*woodcuts.*]

Impr. 5 : 1597 : (eights 16° : pp. [16] + 128 + " 140 " (really 142) + [2] : p. 11 beg. *ἐπιβουλευθῆναι*, 111 *ῥεῦσεν. ἐκεῖθεν*, also 11 *bus coctum*, 111 *actarum* : Pica Greek and Roman. Contents :—p. (1) " *j " only : (3) title : (5-13) Epistola dedicatoria to sir Thomas Egerton, dated 20 Aug. 1597 : 1-62, Ἐκ τῶν τοῦ Ἀγα- θαρχίδου περὶ τῆς ἐρυθρᾶς θαλάσσης ἐκλο- γαί : 63-128, Ἐκ τῶν τοῦ Μέμνονος : 1-71, " Excerpta quaedam ex Agathar- chide de rubro mari " : 72-140, " Ex Memnone excerpta quaedam " de statu Heraclææ Ponticæ.

See Wood's *Ath. Oxon.*, ii. 611. The excerpts of both authors are from Photius's *Bibliotheca.*

2. **Case,** John. THESAVRVS OECONO- MIÆ, SEV COMMENTA- RIVS IN OECONOMICA A- ristotelis ; in quo veræ divitiæ fami- liarum, earumque leges, partes, & | *officia describuntur*: | JOHANNE CASO Authore. | [*device*, then *motto*.]

Impr. 20 : 1597 : (eights) sm. 4° : pp. [12] + folded sheet + 277 + [13] : p. 11 beg. *prætoriam*, 111 *admittantur* : Pica Roman. Contents :—p. (1) title : (3-8) epistola dedicatoria to lord Buckhurst : (9-11) epistola ad lectorem : (12) two compli- mentary poems : then a small folio sheet containing an analysis of the work : 1-245, the work, in two books : 246-277, " Appendix Thesauri Oeconomici " : (1) " Peroratio operis ad Lectorem " : (2-12), " Index rerum . . .".

See Wood's *Ath. Oxon.*, i. 687 : also 1578, 1587. C, 1598. C. In the Epistola Case gives some account of his works, printed and manuscript. A reference in the Bowman Catalogue Oxf. 1687 p. 14 to Case's *Cursus Philosophicus* in 3 volumes (Oxf. 1597 can only refer to a set of Case's books of various years.

3. **Demosthenes.** ΔΗΜΟΣΘΕΝΟΥΣ | ΛΟΓΟΙ ΙΕ. | [*woodcuts*] | Ὀλυνθιακοὶ. γ. | κατὰ Φιλίππου. δ. | Περὶ εἰρήνης. | Περὶ τῶν ἐν Χεῤῥονήσῳ. | Επιστολὴ Φιλίππου. | Πρὸς τὴν Φιλίππου ἐπιστολήν. | Περί συνταξέων. | Περὶ συμμοριῶν. | Περὶ Ῥοδίων ἐλευθερίας. | Ὑπὲρ Μεγαλοπολιτῶν. | [*woodcuts.*]

Impr. 20 : 1597 : sm. 4° : pp. [96] : p. 11 beg. τῆς καὶ πολλῶν : Pica Greek. Contents :—p. 1, title, within border : 3-96, the orations &c. some with ὑποθέ- σεις.

See 1593. D.

4. **King,** John. LECTVRES | VPON IONAS, | DELIVERED AT | YORKE | In the yeare of our Lorde 1594. | By JOHN KINGE. | [*device.*]

Impr. 19a : 1597 : (eights) 4° : pp. [12] + 706, not including two unpaged title- leaves, see below. + [2] : p. 11 beg. *Who hath instructed*, 111 *their former labours*, 671 *& these (in* : Pica Roman. Con- tents :—p. (3) title : (5-11) Epistle dedi- catorie to the lord keeper sir Thomas Egerton : 1-660, the 48 lectures : after 660 " A | SERMON PREACHED AT THE FVNERALLES OF | THE MOST REVEREND | FATHER, JOHN, late | Arch-bishoppe of Yorke, No- vemb. the 17. *in the yeare* of | *our Lorde,* 1594." | [*device* : then impr. 7a, 1597 : then a blank page] : 661-683, the sermon, on Ps. cxlvi. 3-4 : after 683 a blank page (684), then " A | SERMON PREACHED | IN YORKE THE SEVEN- TEENTH DAY OF NO- VEMBER IN THE YEARE OF | our Lorde 1595. being the | *Queenes day*." | [*device*, then impr. 7a, 1597 : then a blank page] : 685-706, the sermon, on 2 Kings xxiii. 25 : 706, " Faultes escaped in Printing . . .".

See 1599. K, 1600. K : other edd. were printed at London.   For King, see Wood's *Ath. Oxon.*, ii. 294.

5. **Pinner**, Charles.   A | SERMON, VPON | the wordes of Paul the Apostle | vnto Timothie, Epist. 1. Chap. 4. | *vers.* 8. | *PREACHED AT LITLE-*cot, in the Chappel of the Right Ho-|nourable Sir IOHN POMP-HAM, | Knight, Lord chiefe Iustice, of En-|gland, before his honourable Lordeshippe, and to the as-|semblie there, the 17. of | *Iulie.* 1597. | By CHARLES PINNER, Minister of | *the Church of Wotton Basset, in* | *North-Wiltshire.* ¦ [*motto,* then *woodcuts.*]

Impr. 19*a* : 1597 : (eights) 12° : pp. 40 : p. 11 beg. *haue or doe* : Pica English.   Contents :—p. 1, title : 3 5, epistle dedicatorie to John Sims, dated Wotton Basset, 23 July 1597 : 7-40, the sermon.

Very rare.   See Wood's *Ath. Oxon.*, i. 667.

6. **Pinner**, Charles.   "Sermon . . . *Honour all Men, love brotherly Fellowship,* on 1 *Pet.* 2. 17. Oxon 1597, in oct."

So Wood's *Ath. Oxon.*, i. 667.

7. **Williams**, rev. John.   "*De Christi Justitia & in Regno spirituali Ecclesie Pastorum Officio, Concio ad Clerum, Oxon. in cap.* 10. *Rev. vers.* 1. Oxon. 1597. qu[arto]."

So Wood's *Ath. Oxon.*, ii. 132, copied by Herbert.

8. **Presse**, Symon.   "'A sermon preached at Eggington, in the County of Darby, concerning the right vse of things indifferent, the 8. Day of August, 1596.   By Symon Presse Minister there.   Feare God, honour the Kinge.   1 Pet. 2 ; 17.   Printed at Oxford —, and are to bee solde in Paules Church-yard at the signe of the Bible. 1597.'   Dedicated 'To his loving Parishioners Mr. F. Cooke,' &c.   The text, 1 Cor. 8 ; 10–13.   Pages 28, including the title.   W. H.   Sixteens."

So in Herbert's Ames, iii. 1406 : see Wood's *Fasti Oxon.*, i. 220.   Impr. 19*a*.

9. **Symeon**, Metaphrastes.   VITÆ SANC-TORVM EVAN-GELIST. IOHAN-|NIS, & LVCÆ, à SY-MEONE METAPHRASTE *olim con-|cinnate, iam recens* | *traducte à* | RICH. BRETTO. | [*woodcuts.*]

Impr. 20 : 1597 : eights) 16° : pp. [16] + 95 + [1] : p. 11 beg. *Montem Tabor* : Pica Greek and Roman.   Contents :—p. (1) "Ai" only : (3) title, within border : (5-14) Epistola dedicatoria to judge Thomas Owen (Ovvinus), dated Lincoln college, Oxford, 23 Dec. 1596 : 1-95. Οἱ Βίοι τῶν ἁγίων Εὐαγγελιστῶν Ἰωάννου καὶ Λουκᾶ ὑπὸ Συμεὼν τοῦ Μεταφράστου πάλαι ἀναταχθέντες" in Greek and Latin.

See Wood's *Ath. Oxon.*, ii. 611.   The editor has practically made the Latin translation a commentary by expanding where his author was obscure, and the like.

1598.

1. **Abbot**, George, archbp. of Canterbury.   QVÆSTIO-NES SEX, TOTI-DEM PRÆLECTIO-|NIBVS, IN SCHOLA | THEOLOGICA, OXONIÆ, | PRO

FORMA, HABITIS, | DISCVSS.E, ET | DISCEPTATÆ. | ANNO. 1597. | IN QVIBVS, E
SACRA SCRIP- TVRA, ET PATRIBVS AN- tiquissimis, quid statuendum | sit,
definitur : | PER GEORGIVM ABBATEM | tunc Collegij Baliolensis | socium. |
[*mottos*, then *woodcuts.*]

Impr. 5 *b* : 1598 : sm. 4° : pp. [12] +
214 ("224" the next p. to 24 being
"35 ") + [18] : p. 11 beg. *verè est*, 111
secretiique: English Roman. Contents:—
p. (1) "A" between woodcuts: 3. title :
5-10, Epistola dedicatoria to lord Buckhurst, dated University college, Oxford.
16 May 1598 : (11) List of contents :
1-21, Præfatio ad lectorem : 23 "224."
the six lectures : (1-15) "Index rerum
præcipuarum."

See Wood's *Ath. Oxon.*, ii. 562. Reprinted at Frankfurt in 1616, with the title
' Georgii Abbatti . . . Explicatio sex illustrium quæstionum . . .'

    2. **Case**, John.   SVMMA | VETERVM INTER- PRETVM IN VNIVERSAM |
DIALECTICAM ARISTOTELIS; | *QVAM VERE FALSOVE RAMVS* | in Aristotelem
inuehatur, | ostendens. | *Auctore.* | IOANNE CASE OXONIENSI, | olim Collegij
D. Ioannis Præcur-'soris socio. | *Omnibus Socraticæ Peripateticæque philo-
sophiæ* | *studiosis in primis vtilis ac necessaria.* | *Recognita & emendata.* |
Cum INDICE rerum & verborum locupletiss. | [*device.*]

Impr. 11 : 1598 : (eights) 12° : pp. [8]
+ 201 + [7] : p. 11 beg. *Respondens. Definitio* : 111 *Oppon. Aliquid* : Brevier
Roman. Contents :—p. (1) title : (3-8)
as 1592. C : 1-201, the work : (1-6)
Index.

See Wood's *Ath. Oxon.*, i. 686. A reprint of 1592. C, almost *literatim.*

    3. Case, John.   " 1587. 'Thesaurus oeconomiae, seu commen-
tarius oeconomica Aristotelis. Authore Johanne Caso.' Again 1598.
Quarto."

So Herbert's Ames, p. 1402 : see 1587. C. Error for 1597?.

    4. **Ingmethorp**, Thomas.   A | SERMON VPON | PART OF THE
SE-'cond chapter of the first e-'pistle of S. Iohn : | *Preached by* THOMAS
INGMETHORP. | The summe whereof is briefly compri- sed in this Hexa-
meter : | *Omne tulit punctum qui* πρᾶξω *miscuit arti* : | He beares the bell
awaie, | that liues, as he doth saie. | [*motto*, then *woodcuts.*]

Impr. 2 : 1598 : (eights) 16° : pp. [8]
+ 45 + [3] : p. 11 beg. *of Christ. This* :
Pica English. Contents :—p. (1 title :
(3-5) dedication to "master Thomas
Flit" of the city of Worcester, the author's
godfather, dated Stainton-in-the-Street,
1 Mar. "1597": (7-8) "To the Reader":
1 45, the sermon, on 1 John ii. 3-6.

See Wood's *Ath. Oxon.*, ii. 592.

    5. **Powell**, Griffith.   *ANALYSIS* | LIB. ARISTOTELIS | DE SOPHIS-
TICIS ELEN- chis, in qua singula capita per | quæstiones & responsiones |
perspicuè & dilucidè ex-|ponuntur, | *Adhibitis* | Quibusdam scholiis ex
optimis quibusque in-'terpretibus desumptis, in quibus natura | & modi
Fallaciarum plenè | explicantur, | *Necnon* | Exemplis, partim Sophistarum
Paralogismis, partim Hæreticorum Elenchis | illustrantur, | *operâ & studio*
G. P. *Oxoniensis confecta & edita* | *in vsum iuniorum.* | [*woodcuts.*]

Impr. 5a : 1598 : (eights) 16° : pp. [16] + 396 + [4] : p. 11 beg. *hostias quas, 111 tariam &* : Long Primer Roman and Pica Italic. Contents :—p. 1 title : (3-6) dedication to the earl of Essex, signed " Griffinus Powel," Jesus coll.,

Oxford. 3 Apr. 1598 : 7-8 "Ad lectorem Acamedicum" : 8 "Liber ad Lectorem," a Latin poem : 9-16 Prolegomena : 1-396, the Analysis of the two books.

See Wood's *Ath. Oxon.*, ii. 283 : and 1594. P. (*bis*), 1664. P.

6. Richard de Bury.   Philobiblon : see 1599. R.

1599.

1. **Case**, John.   ANCILLA | PHILOSOPHIÆ. SEV | EPITOME IN OCTO LIBROS PHYSICORUM ARISTOTELIS, | *Authore,* | Jo. Caso Oxon. | [*device.*]

Impr. 11 : 1599 : sm. 4° : pp. [4] + 73 + [7] : p. 11 beg. *De genere* : Pica Roman. Contents :—p. (1) title : (3-4) dedication to the young John Egerton :

"ab ędibus meis Oxon.", 26 Oct. 1599 : 1-4. "Ad lectorem benignum" : 5-73, the work : (2-7) Index : (7) "Corrigenda."

See Wood's *Ath. Oxon.*, i. 687. Connected with the *Lapis philosophicus*, see below : but issued (apparently) slightly later. In the preface Case alludes to his approaching end, and his unpublished work on Philosophy.

2. **Case**, John.   LAPIS | PHILOSOPHICVS SEV | commentarius in 8° lib: | *phys: Aristot: in quo* | arcana | *Physiologiæ exa*-minantur AVCTORE Io: CASO | *in Medicina Doctore* | Oxoniensi |

Impr. 11a : (1599) : (eights) sm. 4° : pp. [32] + 871 ["869," for 109-112 are omitted and 274-279 doubled, in the pagination] + [17] : p. 11 beg. *magnum pondus,* 113 *si materia,* 501 *tatur si ergo* : Pica Italic and Roman. Contents :—p. (1) title, engraved, see below : (3-8) dedication to sir Thomas Egerton : (9-17) "Epistola ad lectorem." 31 Oct.

1599 : (18) " In primæ paginæ decem Imagines Decastichon" : (19-25) complimentary verses, in Latin and Greek : (26-32) " Quæstiones & dubia quæ in octo libris Physicorum continentur " : 1-30. " Prolegomena " : 31-" 869." the work : (1) " Lectori benevolo," 31 Oct. 1599 : (2-15) Index : (16) " Lectori ingenuo et philosopho " (errata).

See Wood's *Ath. Oxon.*, i. 687. The titlepage is an elaborate engraving on metal, the title within 10 squares arranged
$$\begin{matrix} 4. & 5. & 6 \\ 3 & & 7 \\ 2 & & 8 \\ 1. & 10. & 9 \end{matrix}$$
, representing Chaos, Nature, Fortune, the Fates. Time, Phaethon and Arctos, Sky, Space, Infinity and Terminus, Effigy of Case. The last compartment represents the author in effigy on a tomb with the words " Casus in occasum vergit vivitque sepultus." The whole tone of the prefaces is pathetic, Case feeling that he was close to his end, which actually came on 23 Jan. 1599. At p. (7) is a reference to the new Bodleian : at p. (11) it is stated that some German friends with those at Oxford offered to pay the expense of printing the book rather than that it should not be printed at all, and that the author carefully revised and pruned it five times before publication. In an epilogue to the first book p. 170, dated 25 June 1597. Case apologises to a friend for not giving the *text* of each book and for not printing his discourse on Philosophy in general. See the *Ancilla philosophiae,* above.

3. **Holland**, Thomas.   ORATIO | SA- RISBVRIE HABITA | *viii. Id. Iun.* | CVM REVERENDVS IN CHRIS- to Pater HENRICVS permissione divinâ | Episcopus Sarisburiensis gradum | Docto- ratus in Theologiâ susciperet,

ex de-|*creto Convocationis Oxoniensis.* | *Authore* T. HOLLAND *Theol. Doct.* | *& Profess. Regio.* | [*woodcuts.*]

Impr. 11 : 1599 : sm. 4° : pp. [12], signn. A¹, B² : sign. B 1ʳ beg. *tutis, erudi-* | *tionis* : Pica Roman. Contents :—p. (1) title : (3-12) the Oration.

See Wood's *Ath. Oxon.*, ii. 111 : *Reg. Univ. Oxon.*, vol. 2 ed. Clark, pt. i, p. 145. The Commission to confer the degree on bp. Henry Cotton (of Magdalen) is dated 2 June 1599. The oration gives an interesting account of the ceremony of conferment 6 June and its symbolism.

4. **James, Thomas.** (Bagford's statement that James's " Catalogue of the Oxford and Cambridge Manuscripts " appeared in this year (Brit. Mus. MS. Harl. 5901. fol. 65), is due to the title of the Appendix of Richard de Bury's *Philobiblon*, see below. The Catalogue came out in 1600.)

5. **Kinge,** John, bp. of London. ARTICLES MINISTRED | IN THE VISITATION OF | THE RIGHT WORSHIPFVLL | Maister JOHN KING Archdeacon | *of Nottingham, in the yeare of our* | *Lord God.* 1599. | [*device.*]

Impr. 4 : (1599) : sm. 4° : pp. [12], signn. A⁴, B² : sign. B 1ʳ beg. 29. *Whether they* : Pica English. Contents :—p. 1) title : (3-10) the 43 questions : (11) " The oath of the Church-wardens and side-men."

6. **King,** John. LECTVRES | VPON IONAS. | DELIVERED AT | YORKE In the yeare of our Lorde 1594. | By JOHN KINGE : | *Newlie corrected and amended.* | [*device.*]

Impr. 19*a* : 1599 : (eights) sm. 4° : pp. [12] + 706 + [2]. not counting two extra title-leaves, see below : p. 11 beg. *Who hath instructed.* 111 *their former, 671 & these in* : Pica Roman. Contents :—precisely as 1597, K, except LATE not " late," *No-*|*vem.*, not *No- vemb.*. 1494 (by error) not 1594. and 1599 on both extra titles. not 1597 : there is no list of Errata. The first and last leaves have not been seen.

See Wood's *Ath. Oxon.*, ii. 295. A reprint of 1597. K.

7. **Lomazzo,** Giovanni Paolo (Lomatius). [*engraved title :—*] A | TRACTE CONTAI-|NING THE ARTES | of curious Paintinge Caruinge & | Buildinge | written first in Italian by Jo: | Paul Lomatius painter of Milan | AND ENGLISHED BY | R. H. student in Physik | [*motto.*]

Impr. 21. as colophon : 1598 : (sixes) la. 8° : pp. [24] + 119 + [1] + 218 + [2] : p. 11 beg. *hardly bee able.* 111 *wise a master* : English Roman. Contents :— p. 1) engraved title. see below : (3 4) dedication to sir Thomas Bodley, signed " Richard Haydocke." New coll., Oxford, 24 Aug. 1598 : 5 12) the Translator to the ingenuous Reader : 13-14) " Iohn Case D. of Physicke to his friende R. H. of New Colledge " : 15) " The titles of the bookes," five in all : (17-23) " A table of the Chapters . . ." : 1-7, " The preface to the worke " by Lomazzo : 9-11, " The division of the worke " : 13-119. and 1-218, the work : 1, Device and colophon.

See Wood's *Ath. Oxon.*, i. 678. Lomazzo's *Trattato dell' arte de la pittura* was published at Milan in 1584, and Haydocke's Preface gives an account of its rarity in England. Only five out of the seven books of the original are here published. In the dedication the translator alludes to Bodley's design of " erecting and restoring of this worthie Panbiblion or Temple of all the Muses," the Bodleian.

The title is an elaborate engraving on metal, the words on an oval in the centre : at top " JO: PAOLO LOMAZZO : " surrounding his bust : on either side Juno and

Apollo ? : on either side the oval, the arms of the University and of New College :
below, in the centre a bust of the translator surmounted by his arms, between figures
derived from classical mythology.   In the book are thirteen full-page engravings
marked A—I, K—N, and a profusion of woodcut ornaments.   On the last page but
one occurs the large device of the University arms, within a border : then the colophon :
then a woodcut of the arms of New College between two Ws (William of Wykeham).
By some confusion this book is dated 1605 by Bagford (Brit. Mus. MS. Harl. 5901,
fol. 66).

8. Richard de Bury, bp. of Durham, *d.* 1345.   PHILOBIBLON |
RICHARDI | DUNELMENSIS | *sive* | DE AMORE LIBRORVM, ET INSTI- *TVTIONE*
BIBLIOTHECÆ, | *tractatus pulcherrimus.* | Ex collatione cum varijs manu-
scriptis edi-|*tio jam secunda;* | cui | *Accessit appendix de manuscriptis*
Oxoniensibus. | Omnia hæc. | *Opera & studio T. I. Novi Coll. in alma*
Academia | *Oxoniensi Socij.* [*motto*, preceded by "B. P. N.," then
woodcuts.]

Impr. 11 : 1599 : sm. 4° : pp. [8] + 62
+ [10] : p. 11 beg. *tiqui pro* : Pica Roman.   Contents :—p. 1 title : (3 6)
Epistola dedicatoria to sir Thomas Bodley. " ex Musæo meo in Collegio Novo.
Iulij. 6. 1599," signed "Thomas James" :
(7) " Vita ex Balæo " : 1–4. " Præfatio
auctoris ad lectorem " : 5. " Capitula
libri sequentis " : 7–62. the work in 20
chapters : (3–10) " Appendix de manuscriptis Oxoniensibus."

Rare.   See Wood's *Ath. Oxon.,* ii. 466.   This is the first English edition of the
first book on the love of books.   The *editio princeps* is that of 1473 printed at Cologne :
the next Spires, 1483 and Paris 1500.   An account of these editions and of the known
MSS. of the *Philobiblon* will be found in E. C. Thomas's edition (Lond., 1888).   The
mysterious " *B. P. N.*" on the titlepage (followed by " Non quæro quod mihi vtile est,
sed quod multis"), is explained by him as perhaps " Bibliothecae Praefectus Novae "
or " Nostrae " or rather " Bono Publico Natus: " it has been suggested that they may
stand for " Beati Pauli Norma," alluding to 1 Cor. x. 33.   The Editor explains that
it was intended that the work should be followed by an Appendix containing a catalogue of all MSS. at Oxford, a purpose which seriously delayed the issue of the book.
In fact the whole of the text of the *Philobiblon* was printed off in 1598, as is proved
by a single copy still preserved in the Bodleian dated in that year but containing only
the titlepage, (identical in type with the published one, except in one figure of the
date) and pp. 1 to 62 + [2 blank].   As it is, the Appendix only contains an alphabetical list, without references, of the authors of which manuscripts were preserved at
Oxford : the intended catalogue appears in the *Ecloga Oxonio-Cantabrigiensis,* Lond.,
1600.   The preface alludes to the founding of the Bodleian, but dr. James had not yet
been appointed Librarian.   There is no sufficient ground for supposing with mr.
Thomas *ut supra,* p. lv) and mr. Macray (*Annals of the Bodleian,* 2nd ed., p. 25)
that the single advance copy of 1598 implies an issue or edition of that year.

9. Roche, Robert.   EVSTATHIA | *or the* | CONSTANCIE OF SVSANNA |
CONTAINING THE PRESER-|vation of the Godly, subversion of the wic- ked,
precepts for the aged, instructi-|*ons for youth, pleasure* | *with profitte.* |
Penned by R. R. G.   [*motto,* then *woodcuts.*]

Impr. 19*a* : 1599 : eights 12° : pp.
[128], signn. A–H° : sign. B 1ʳ beg. *Then*
elims : Pica Roman.   Contents :—sign.
A 1ʳ, title : A 2ʳ–A 2ᵛ, dedication to " Mistris M.B. wife to . . . D.B. Esquier,"
signed Robert Roche : A 3ʳ–A 4ʳ "To the
Reader," a poem : A 4ᵛ–A 5ᵛ, " Coricæus
to the Author," a poem signed "C. A. R.":
A 5ᵛ–B 1ᵛ, " An induction to the story " :
H 2ʳ–H 7ʳ, the poem : H 7ʳ, " Faultes
escaped."

The Bodleian copy, which belonged to Robert Burton, is perhaps unique.   See
Wood's *Ath. Oxon.,* i. 682, where extracts are given from this poem, which is chiefly
in a peculiar 7-line stanza, ABABBCC.   G. on the titlepage is no doubt *Gentleman.*

10. **Ubaldini, Petruccio.** (The edition of "La Vita di Carlo Magno Imperadore. Di nuevo corretta" by P. Ubaldini, doubtfully ascribed in the Catalogue of the Printed Books in the British Museum to the Oxford Press, was certainly not printed there.)

1600.

1. **Butler,** Charles. "'Rhetoricæ libri duo, quorum Prior de Tropis & Figuris, Posterior de Voce & Gestu, Præcipiti [*sic*] in vsum scholarum accuratiùs editi. Oxoniæ, Excudebat—1600. . . . Viro virtutis & honoris nomine nobilissimo, Thomæ Egertono, Equiti, Domino Custodi magni sigilli Angliæ, Carolus Butler Magdalenensis, S. D.—Basingstochiæ, 5 Jdus Martii. 1600.' . . . Some commendatory verses; Lat. & Gr. . . . Ad lectorem.' I3, in eights, besides the prefixes. W. H. Sixteens."

So in Herbert's Ames, iii. 1409. For the author, see Wood's *Ath. Oxon.*, iii. 209, Bloxam's *Magd. Reg.*, i. 20. See 1618. B, 1629 B.

2. **Holland,** Robert. "'Darmerth, neu Arlwy Gweddi, a ddychymygwyd er mawr dderchafiad Duwioldeb, ac i chwanegu Gwybodaeth ac Awydd yr annysgedig ewyllysgar i iawn wasanaethu'r gwir Dduw. Gan Robert Holland, gweinidog gair Duw, a Pherson Llan Ddeferowg, yn sir Gaerfyrddin' [Rhydychain, 4plyg."]

So in W. Rowland's *Cambrian Bibliography*, ed. by D. S. Evans (Llanidloes, 1869) p. 72. It is ascribed also to Oxford in M. Williams's *Cofrestr* (Lond. 1717): but the evidence is at present not sufficient to establish a connexion with Barnes's press : nor is the present place of any copy known to the editor of Rowlands.

3. Holland, Thomas. Panegyris : see 1601. II.

4. **King,** John. LECTVRES | VPON IONAS | DELIVERED AT | YORKE | In the yeare of our Lorde 1594. | By JOHN KINGE : | *Newly corrected and amended.* | [*device.*]

Impr. 19*a* : 1600 : (eights) sm. 4° : pp. [12]+706+[2] : p. 11 beg. *Who hath instructed, &c. their former,* 671 *& these in* : Pica Roman. Contents :—exactly as 1599. K, except (in 2nd title) "Lord" not "Lorde," 1594 not 1494, (in 3rd title) NOVEM-BER not NO-VEMBER, *daie* not *day* : and dates on titles 1600 not 1599. The first and last leaves have not been seen.

A reprint of 1599. K.

5. **Perrot,** sir James. [*woodcut.*] THE | FIRST PART | OF THE CONSIDE-RATION OF HV-|mane Condition : | *WHERIN IS CONTAINED* | *the Morall Consideration of a mans selfe :* | *as what, who, and what manner* | *of man he is.* | Written by I. P. Esquier. | | *motto :* then *woodcuts.*]

Impr. 19 : 1600 : sm. 4° : pp. [8]+60 : p. 11 beg. *of the earth* : Pica Roman. Contents :—p. 3 title : 5-6) dedication to lord Buckhurst, dated Haroldston 16 Nov. 1600. signed "I. P." : 7-8) "To the indifferent and friendly Reader," signed "Iames Perrott" : 1-60, the work, in three sections.

See Wood's *Ath. Oxon.* ii. 605. The second part was to be the Political consideration of things under us, the third the Natural Consideration of things about us, the last the Metaphysical Consideration of things above us: but they were never published.

---

5. **Roberts,** Hugh.   THE | DAY OF HEARING: | *Or,* | SIX LECTVRES VPON THE | latter part of the thirde Chapter of the Epi-|stle to the Hebrewes: of the time and | meanes that God hath appointed for | *men to come to the knowledge of his | truth, that they may be sa-ved from his wrath.* | The summary pointes of every one of which Lectures are set | downe immediatly after the Epistle dedicatory. | Herevnto is adioyned a Sermon against | *fleshly lusts, & against certaine mischie-vous May-games which are the | fruit thereof.* | By H. R. Master of Artes, and now | *Minister of the word.* | [*motto,* then *woodcuts.*]

Impr. 19*a* : 1600 : 'eights' 16° : pp. [12] + 116 + [32] : p. 11 beg. *which he wrought,* lll *now for the* : Pica Roman. Contents :—p. 1 title : '3-10' dedication to sir Thomas Egerton, signed "Hugh Roberts" : (11-12) "The Contents or briefe summe of the Lectures . . ." : 1-116, the six lectures on Heb. iii. 7-11, 12-13, 14, 15, 16-17, 18-19 : 1' title of sermon "A GODLY AND | NECES-SARY SERMON | against fleshly lustes ; and against cer-taine mischievous May-games, which | are the fruite thereof. Preached | *vpon the first Sabbath day in Maie,* | *in the yeere.* 1598. | By H. R. Master of Artes, and now | Minister of the word. | [*Motto,* then *woodcuts*]." Impr. 19*a.* 1600 : '3-5' "To the Reader" : (7-32) the sermon, on 1 Pet. ii. 11.

In the preface to the sermon it is hinted that the publication of the sermon was prevented when it was first delivered "now more then a yeere and a halfe agone." Wood (*Ath. Oxon.* i. 703) describes this book as "*Lond.* 1600, *quarto,*" wrongly.

---

6. **Terry,** John.   [*woodcut.*] | THE | TRIAL OF TRVTH : | *Containing* | A PLAINE AND SHORT DISCOVE-|ry of the chiefest pointes of the Doctrine of the | great Antichrist, and of his adherentes the | false Teachers and Heretikes of these | last times. | [*mottos :* then *woodcuts.*]

Impr. 19 : 1600 : sm. 4° : pp. [24] + 160 : p. 11 beg. *a faithfull brother,* lll *are remitted* : Pica Roman. Contents :— p. 1 title : (3-7) Epistle dedicatorie to bp. Henry Cotton, signed "Iohn Terry" : (9-22) "To the Christian Reader," also signed : (23-24) "The principall vses of this Treatise" : 1-160, the work (first part.)

See Wood's *Ath. Oxon.* ii. 410. For the second and third parts, see 1602. T, (which contains on the last page "Faultes escaped in printing the first part", 1625 T.

---

7. **Ursinus,** Zacharias.   A | COLLECTION OF CERTAINE | LEARNED DISCOVRSES, | *WRITTEN* | BY THAT FAMOVS MAN OF MEMORY | ZACHARY VRSINE ; Doctor and Pro-*fessor of Divinitie in the noble and flou-*|rishing Schoole of NEVSTAD. | *For explication of divers difficult points,* | laide downe by that Author in his | CATECHISME. | Lately put in Print in Latin by the last | labour of D. DAVID PARRY : and | *now newlie translated into English* | *by* I. H. *for the benefit and | behoofe of our Christian | countrymen.* | [*woodcuts.*]

Impr. 19 : 1600 : 'eights' 12° : pp. [8] + "341" really 327, for 180-191 and 236-237 are omitted in the pagination) + [1] : p. 11 beg. *vnto it certaine,* lll *ble that it is* : Pica Roman. Contents : | p. (1 title : (3-5) "To the Reader" : 7)

"A table of the several discourses": 1-341, the nine discourses (1 is Parry's prefaces to the 3rd and 4th parts of Ursinus's Catechism in the first edition (see 1587. U); 5, 6 are translated by Parry; 3 is a passage out of Vigilius about the Incarnation; 9 a funeral oration on Ursinus (who died "6 Mar. 1583") by Francis Junius: (1) "Faultes escaped."

Rare. The editor apologizes in the preface for this "three weekes worke," due to the importunity of the printer, after the editor had given over the task when only begun.

1601.

1. **Fitz-Geoffrey,** Charles.   CAROLI | FITZGEOFRIDI | AFFANIAE: | sive | EPIGRAMMATVM | *Libri tres*: | Ejusdem | CENOTAPHIA. | [*motto*, then *woodcuts*.]

Impr. 11: 1601: (eights) 12°: pp. [200], signn. A-M⁸ N⁴: sign. B1ʳ beg. *Vel si quid*, M1ʳ *Si non immemor*: Pica Roman. Contents:—sign. A1ʳ title: A2ʳ-A2ᵛ poetical Latin dedication to Edw. Michelborne: A3ʳ, Michelborne's reply in Latin verse: A3ᵛ, poetical Latin dedication to William Raleigh barrister: A4ʳ-M1ᵛ the Affaniae in 3 books: M2ʳ [*woodcuts*] | CENOTAPHIA. | A | CAROLO FITZGEOFRIDO | *Posita & sacrata* | D. M. & piæ Memoriæ | nonnullorum, | *Quos nunc emeritæ permensos tempora vitæ* | *Secreti sinus orbis habet mundusque piorum.* | [*woodcuts*]: then impr. 11, 1061 [*sic*]: M3ʳ-N4ᵛ, the epitaphs.

Rare. See Wood's *Ath. Oxon.* ii. 607. The epigrams and epitaphs are of much interest, and some are translated and printed in Dr. Grosart's *Poems of Charles Fitzgeoffrey*, 1881.

2. **Holland,** Thomas.   Πανηγυρὶς | *D. Elizabethæ, Dei gratiá Angliæ, Franciæ, & Hiberniæ Reginæ.* | A | SERMON PREACHED AT PAVLS | in London the 17. of November Ann. Dom. 1599. the | one and fortieth yeare of her Maiesties raigne, and aug- mented in those places wherein, for the shortnes of the | time, it could not there be then delivered. | *Thereunto is adioyned an Apologeticall discourse,* | *whereby all such sclanderous Accusations are fully* | *and faithfully confuted, wherewith the Honour of* | *this Realme hath beene vncharitably traduced by* | *some of our adversaries in forraine nations, and at* | *home, for observing the* 17. *of November yeerely in* | *the forme of an Holy-day, and for the ioifull exerci-* | *ses, and Courtly triumphes on that day in the honour* | *of her Maiestie exhibited.* | By THOMAS HOLLAND, Doctor of Divinity, | & her Highnes Professor thereof in her Vni- versity of Oxford. | [*woodcuts*.]

Impr. 19: 1601: sm. 4°: pp. [166], signn. *a-c*, A-R⁴, S², and one folded leaf, see below: sign. B1ʳ beg. *Moses, who,* O1ʳ *shall be safe*: Pica Roman. Contents:—sign. *a*1ʳ title: *a*1ᵛ Latin poem on the Queen's arms: then a folded leaf, see below: *a*2ʳ-*c*2ᵛ "To al faithful Christians . . .": *c*3ʳ-*c*3ᵛ dedication to Richard Bancroft, bp. of London, dated "Oxoniæ, è Collegio Exon." 1 Oct. 1599: *c*4ʳ "Faultes escaped, and certaine observations": A1ʳ-H1ʳ, the sermon, on Matt. xii. 42: H1ʳ-S2ᵛ, the Apology.

See Wood's *Ath. Oxon.* ii. 111, and 1602. H. At sign. L3ʳ begins a long dissertation on St. Hugh of Lincoln, and at sign. N3ʳ the author claims for the University of Oxford the first celebration of Nov. 17 as the Queen's Day. in 1569? The Stonor Press and Edm. Campian's *Decem Rationes* are alluded to in sign. B4. The folding leaf contains a woodcut of the royal arms between two pillars connected by a scroll bearing the words VIVAT·RE· On the base of the columns are "I" "D" (the engraver's initials ?).   The woodcut, which is of a rough character, is $5\frac{7}{8}$ in. × $6\frac{1}{2}$ in. A curious usage has been pointed out to me: on sign. D 4ʳ, E 2ʳ, P 4ʳ, Q 1ʳ and perhaps elsewhere Hebrew words are transliterated, but in *b* 2ʳ, O 3ʳ, O 4ʳ, P 1ʳ unpointed Hebrew type is used.   In the Laing Sale ii. 3709 (15 Apr. 1880) there is mention of a 1600 edition of this book.

3. **Ursinus,** Zacharias.   [*woodcuts.*] | THE SVMME | OF CHRISTIAN | RELIGION : | DELIVERED BY ZACHARIAS VRSINVS IN HIS | Lectures vpon the Catechisme, authorised by the noble | *Prince* FREDERICKE *throughout his dominions.* | Wherein are debated and resolved the Questions of what-| *soeuer pointes of moment, which haue beene or are* | *controuersed in Diuinitie.* | Translated into English first by D. Henrie Parry, and late-|ly conferred with the last and best Latine Edition of | D. DAVID PAREVS *Professor of Diuinity* | *in Heidelberge.* | [*woodcuts.*]

Impr. 19 : 1601 : (eights) sm. 4ᵒ : pp. [8] + 1139 + [13] : p. 11 beg. *authors, we,* III 4. *VVhat are,* IIII *euer of the elect* : English Roman.   Contents:— p. (1) title : (3–6) " To the Christian Readers Henry Parry . . ." : (7–8) " To the same Christ-ian Readers Richard Crosse . . ." : 1–1139, the catechism : (1–10) " A Table . . .", a short analysis of the book : (10) " Faults escaped" : pp. (11–12) have not been seen.

See 1587. U.   Richard Crosse edited this edition with some slight additions.

1602.

1. [**Bailey,** dr. Walter.]   [*woodcuts.*] | A | BRIEFE | TREATISE TOV= ching the preservation of | *the eie sight, consisting partly* | in good order of diet, and partly | in vse of medicines. | *The sixte Edition.* | [*woodcuts.*]

Impr. 24 : 1602 : (eights) 16ᵒ : pp. [6] + 25 + [1] : p. 11 beg. *recited by the* : Pica Roman.   Contents :— p. (1) title : (3–5) a preface : 1–17, 19–25, the treatise.

Rare.   For author see Wood's *Ath. Oxon.* i. 586 : the first edition with the author's name is that of 1616.   An edition of 1586 (London) is in the British Museum, but the other four preceding the present one appear to be unknown.   See 1616. B, 1654. B, 1673. B : other editions were issued, not at Oxford.

2. **Budden,** dr. John.   [*woodcut.*] | GVLIELMI | PATTENI, CVI | VVAYN-FLETI AGNOMEN | FVIT, WINTONIENSIS ECCLE-|*SIÆ PRÆSULIS QVONDAM* | pientissimi, Summi Angliæ Cancellarij, | Collegijque Beatæ Mariæ Magdalenæ | apud Oxonienses fundato=|*ris celeberrimi, vi=|ta obitusque.* | [*motto* : then *woodcuts.*]

Impr. 11 : 1602 : sm. 4ᵒ : pp. [12] + 84 : p. 11 beg. *centis pend* : Great Primer Roman.   Contents :– p. (1) title : (3–6) Epistola nuncupatoria to dr. Nicholas Bond president of Magdalen college, Ox-ford, signed " Johannes Buddenvs" : (7–11) complimentary verses, in Latin, except one Italian sonnet by Alberico Gentile : 1–84, the work.

See Wood's *Ath. Oxon.* ii. 282.   Budden was philosophy reader at Magdalen (afterwards principal of New Inn hall and Broadgates hall), and this biography was entrusted to him by the college.   The running title is " Waynfleti παλιγγενεσία." Several original documents are printed in the work : which was reprinted in [Bates's] *Vitæ selectorum aliquot virorum,* Lond. 1681, p. 49.   Rhetoric is more prominent than historical treatment.

E 2

3. **Chrysostom,** st.   ΘΕΩΡΒΕΜΩΝ: | *or,* | THE ANCIENT AND
MOST | comfortable Goldenmouth'd Father, | S^t. CHRYSOSTOME Arch-
bishop of | Constantinople, treating on severall places | of holy scripture:
selected, and tran- slated faithfully according to | the Greeke Copies: |
by | JOHN WILLOVGHBIE. | [3 *mottos,* then *woodcuts.*]

Impr. 24: 1602: (eights) 16°: pp. [24] + 287 + [1]: p. 11 beg. *saultes of humane,* 111 *beleegs much time* : English Roman. Contents :—p. (1) title : (3–15) Epistle dedicatorie to a kinsman of the author lately deceased: (16–21) "To the Christian Reader," dated from "Brode- gats hall," Oxford, 2 Sept. 1602: (22–23) "Τοῖς περὶ τῶν λόγων τουτωνὶ Ἑλληνο- Ἀγγλοικῶν ἰσγνωμόνως ἔχουσιν," a Greek preface : (24) "The names of the [seven] Tractes contained in this Booke," and a quotation : 1–287, the treatises.

See Wood's *Ath. Oxon.* ii. 28.   Wood did not know Willoughby as an author, and
Bliss could find no trace of his academical career.   But a John Willoughby certainly
matriculated at Exeter College in 1585 (B.A. 1589, M.A. 1593).   The treatises are on the
Pharisee and the Publican (Luke xviii), on Ps. xlix. 16, on Ps. xxxix. 6, on the Sick
of the Palsy (John v), on 2 Cor. xii. 9, on the Shepherd and Sheep, &c. (John xx)
and "A Tracte of *Vertue* and *Vice.*"   Unpointed English and Long Primer Hebrew is
used on pp. 1, 26, 67, 107.

4. **Higins,** John.   [*woodcuts*] | AN | ANSVVERE TO | MASTER
WILLIAM | PERKINS, CONCER- ning Christs Descen- *sion into Hell:* | *By* |
JOHN HIGINS. | [*woodcuts.*]

Impr. 24: 1602: (eights) 16° : pp. [4] + 52 : p. 11 beg. *to it they* : Eng-lish Roman.   Contents :—p. (1) title : (3–4) preface "To the Christian Reader," Winsam, 22 June 1602 : 1–51, the trea-tise : 52. "Faultes escaped in the print-ing ... Finis."

Rare.   See Wood's *Ath. Oxon.* i. 734, and following art.

5. Higins, John.   AN | ANSWERE | TO MASTER WILLI- am Perkins,
concerning | *Christs Descension in-* to hell. | By JOHN HIGINS. | [*device.*]

Impr. 24: 1602: (eights) 16° : pp. [4] + 51 + [1] : p. 11 beg. *it they must* : Small Pica Roman.   Contents :—p. (1) title : (3–4) preface "To the Christian Reader," Winsam, 22 June 1602 : 1–51, the treatise.

Rare.   See preceding art.   Like the Powel below this book was certainly not printed
at Oxford, and the imprint is fictitious, the type and woodcuts being unknown at
Oxford.   These falsifications can hardly be unconnected with the fact that John Barnes,
the son of Joseph Barnes, in this year set up business for himself in London.   The text
is a reprint of no. 4 above.

6. **Howson,** dr. John.   A | SERMON | PREACHED AT S^t. | MARIES
IN OXFORD, | THE 17. DAY OF NO- 'vember, 1602. in defence of | *the Festi-*
vities of the Church | of *England, and namely* | *that of her Maiesties* |
Coronation. | By JOHN HOWSON DOCTOR OF | *Divinitie, one of her Highnes*
Chaplaines, and | *Vicechancellour of the Vniversitie* | *of Oxforde.* | [*wood-*
cuts.]

Impr. 23: 1602: sm. 4° : pp. [36], sign. ( )² A–D⁴ : sign. B 1ʳ beg. *ship or honor* : English Roman.   Contents :— sign. ( ) 1ʳ title : ( ) 2ʳ–2ᵛ, dedication to lord Buckhurst, dated from Christ Church, Oxford, 29 Nov. 1602 : A 1ʳ D 3ᵛ, the sermon, on Ps. cxviii. 24.

See 1603. II, and Wood's *Ath. Oxon.* ii. 518.   On a kindred subject with Holland's
speech printed in 1601 : the priority of the University in celebrating the Queen's day
is again mentioned.   Reprinted in Somers' *Tracts.*

7. Howson, dr. John.　　　[*woodcuts*] | VXORE | DIMISSA PROPTER fornicationem aliam non | *licet superinducere.* | TERTIA THESIS | IOANNIS HOVSONI | Inceptoris in Sacra Theolo-|gia, proposita & disputata in *Vesperijs Oxonij.* | 1602. | [*woodcuts.*]

Impr. 11 : 1602 : (eights) 16° : [2] + 61 + [1] : p. 11 beg. *dij, & quæ* : English | Roman. Contents :—p. (1) title : 1–61, the essay.

See 1606. 11, and Wood's *Ath. Oxon.* ii. 60, 518, iii. 18, where a bibliography is given of the controversy excited by Dr. Howson's Thesis. The actual day of disputation was 10 July 1602. There are two issues of this book, one in which the title is a separate leaf, independent of the four sections (A–D) which follow, D 8 being blank : the other where the title is A 1, D 8 being the last leaf of the *text.*

8. †Oxford, Trinity College.　　　Decretum de Gratiis Collegio rependendis. | [the text of the decree.]

No imprint, but probably printed at Oxford : (1602 ?) : (one) fol. : pp. [2] : l. 11 beg. I. *Imprimis* : English Roman. | Contents :—p. (1) title and text of the decree.

A Latin decree passed by the President and Fellows of Trinity college on 12 Dec. 1602, compelling all who have been or are on the foundation of the college to show their gratitude by a proportionate gift of money, and enjoining on all future scholars an oath that they will fulfil this decree. Signed by the President and Fellows. There is another issue similar in form but apparently printed in London, which can readily be distinguished by having a headline of woodcuts, and 43 (instead of 52) lines of print.

9. *†Oxford, University.　　　[Orders for the Market of the City of Oxford, issued by the Chancellor of the University : beg. "Thomas Baron of Buckurst," ends "transgressor of this commaundement. God save the Queene."]

No impr. : [not later than 1602] : (one) fol. : pp. [4] : English Roman. | Contents :—pp. (1, 3) the orders (probably 30 in number).

The only copy known was rescued from a binding in Brasenose College Library at Oxford, where it now is. The titles of Lord Buckhurst are given, and show that the earliest possible date is 15 May 1598 when he became Lord High Treasurer : the latest being 24 March 160¾, when the Queen died. No doubt the sheets were fastened together forming one long notice. The Brasenose copy has lost a few lines at the end of the first column (67 lines left), the second is complete (62 lines).

10. Powel, Gabriel.　　　PRODROMVS. | A LOGICALL | RESOLVTION OF THE | 1. Chap. of the Epistle of | *the Apostle* PAVLE | *vnto the Romans.* | TOGITHER WITH SVCH | severall Jnstructions, Notes, Ob-|*servations, and Vses, as naturally* | *arise out of every particular* | *Verse. By* | *Gabriel Powel.* | [*motto, then asterisks.*]

Impr. 22 : 1602 : (eights) 16° : pp. [16] + 267 + [5] : p. 11 beg. *sumption is, III profit al, wisdom* : English Roman. Contents :—p. (3) title : (5–12) Epistle dedicatorie to John Whitgift archbp. of Canterbury and William Morgan bp. of | St. Asaph, dated from St. Mary hall, Oxford, 5 July 1602 : (13 15) "To the Christian Reader," dated similarly : 1–267, the work : (1) "Faults escaped in the Printing."

See 1615. P : Wood's *Ath. Oxon.* ii. 25. The dedications are due to his patrons' favour to his father David as well as to himself.

11. **Powel, Gabriel.** *Theologicall and Scholasticall* | Positions, concerning | Vsurie. | Set forth, by *Definitions* and *Partitions*, | framed according to the rules of | a naturall Method. | [*asterisks, then woodcut.*]

Impr. 23: 1602: (eights) 16°: pp. [16] + 71 + [1]: p. 11 beg. *and quantitie*: English Roman. Contents:—p. (1) "A": (3) title: (5-13) Epistle dedicatorie to | Ralph Hockenhul and Hugh Hurlston, dated from St. Mary hall, Oxford, 1 Apr. 1602: (14) "The Contents of this Treatise": 1-71, the treatise.

See Wood's *Ath. Oxon.* ii. 25. In spite of the imprint this book, like the Higins (No. 5) above, was not printed at Oxford, the type but especially the woodcuts (with one exception) being entirely unknown at Oxford. It was printed no doubt in London, and the imprint falsified, perhaps in order to escape the necessity of registration at the office of the Stationers' Company.

12. **Rawlinson, John.** See under 1612. R.

13. **Sanderson, dr. John.** INSTITVTI-ONVM DIALEC-TICARVM LI-|*bri Quatuor*, | *A* IOANNE SANDERSONO, | Lancastrensi, Anglo, Liberalium | artium Magistro, & sacræ Theologiæ | *Doctore, Metropolitanæ Ec-|clesiæ Cameracensis Ca-nonico, conscripti.* | *Editio tertia.* | [*woodcuts.*]

Impr. 11: 1602: 8°: pp. [4] + 228 + [4]: p. 11 beg. *Vox singularis*, III *vltus, habitus*: Long Primer Roman. Contents:—p. (1) title: (3-4) "Auctoris | Præfatio ad inuentutem bonarum artium studiosam": 1-228, the work: (pp. (3-4) not seen.)

Rare. This John Sanderson of Lancashire, doctor of Theology, canon of Cambrai, seems to have escaped the notice of biographers. The better known bp. Robert Sanderson also wrote on Logic, see 1615. s. The preface throws no light on the life of the author. For the 4th ed., see 1609. s. The first edition was printed by Plantin at Antwerp in 1589, the dedication to cardinal Allen being dated from Antwerp 1 Jan. "1589," but neither in the dedication nor in the congratulatory poems which follow in this first edition is there any biographical matter.

14. **Smith, bp. Miles.** [*woodcuts*] | A | LEARNED AND | GODLY SERMON, | preached at Worcester, [*at an Assise:* | *By* | THE REVEREND | and learned, MILES SMITH. *Doctor of Diuinitie.* [*woodcuts.*]

Impr. 23: 1602: (eights) 16°: pp. [16] + 64: p. 11 beg. *him, and so*: English Roman. Contents:—p. (1) title: (3-13) Epistle dedicatorie to Gervase Babington, bp. of Worcester. dated from | C. C. C., Oxford, Nov. 12. 1602, signed "Robert Burhil" who issued the sermon: (15) "The chiefe points of matter ... in the sermon ...": 1-63, the sermon, on Jer. ix. 23-24.

Rare. See Wood's *Ath. Oxon.* ii. 360. The preface states that the sermon was issued without the knowledge of the author, he being too modest to publish his works.

15. **Terry, John.** [*woodcut*] THE SECOND PART | OF | THE TRIAL OF TRVTH: | WHEREIN IS SET DOWNE THE | proper fountaine or foundation of all good | *works. & the fowre principal motiues which the spi-rit of God so often vseth in the sacred scriptures to perswade* | therevnto: | togither with the contrariety of the doctrine of | the Church of Rome to the same: wherein also are ope-ned not only the causes of all true piety and godli-ness, but also of all heresie and Idolatry, which is | and hath beene among Gentiles and Iewes, | and vs likewise that are called | Christians. | By JOHN TERRY. | [two *mottos.*]

Impr. 23: 1602: sm. 4°: pp. [38] +
125 + [1]: p. 11 beg. *venemous drops*, 111
mande the carefull: Pica Roman. Contents:—p. (1) title: (3–14) Epistle dedicatorie to dr. George Rives, Warden, and
all other students of New College, Oxford: (15–37) "To the Christian Reader":
(37) a short prayer: 1–125, the work:
(1) "Faultes escaped" in parts one and
two.

See 1600. T, Wood's *Ath. Oxon.* ii. 410.

1603.

1. Brett, Richard. ICONVM SA-CRARVM DECAS, IN | QVA E SVBIECTIS
TYPIS | compluscula sanæ doctrinæ | *capita eruuntur.* | Autore *R. B.*
Sacræ Theol. Baccalaureo. | [*device.*]

Impr. 11: 1603: sm. 4°: pp. [8] + 72:
p. 11 beg. *divini vultus*: Pica Roman.
Contents:—p. (1) title: (3–8) Latin dedication to the King, signed "Richardus
Brett," 12 Aug. 1603: 1–72, the work, in
ten essays.

See Wood's *Ath. Oxon.* ii. 611. The preface explains ' Icones inscripsi prςsens
opusculum, quia sub typis varia fidei & morum adumbrat documenta. Nam . . . est
aliquando sub cute literæ, suavis quædam & interior medulla."

2. Burhill, Robert. Invitatorius panegyricus : see under *Oxford*
(no. 9, below).

3. Carleton, George. HEROICI CHARACTERES. | AD | ILLVSTRISSI-|
MVM EQVITEM, | *Henricum Nevillum.* | AVTORE, | *Georgio Carltono.* |
[*device.*]

Impr. 11: 1603: sm. 4°: pp. [6] + 48
+ [2]: p. 11 beg. *Numine tanta*: Pica
Roman. Contents:—p. (1) title: (3–5)
Latin poetical dedication to sir Henry
Nevill: 1–48, the work.

See Wood's *Ath. Oxon.* ii. 423, 425. The pieces are "Ad . . . Elizabetham . . .
Carmen Panegyricum," "Ad . . . Iacobum . . . Carmen Panegyricum," "Devor-
axeis," on the earl of Essex, "P. Sidnæi funus," all Latin hexameter poems.

4. Davies, John, of Hereford. *MICROCOSMOS.* | THE DISCOVERY |
OF THE LITTLE | World, with the government | thereof. | [*motto*] | By
IOHN DAVIES. | [*woodcuts.*]

Impr. 23: 1603: sm. 4°: pp. [16] +
254 + [30]: p. 11 beg. *The Day, 111 And^e
Providence* : English Roman. Contents:—p. (1) title, within a border: (3)
poetical dedication to king James: (4)
Do. to the queen: (5–8) short poems by
Davies : (8–16) complimentary verses to
the author or book: 1–28, "A Preface
. . ." to the king: (29–38) "Cambria to
the . . . Prince of Wales," both poems:
29–232, the work: 233–254, " An ex-
tasie," a poem: (1–20) short poems by
Davies, including two to Magdalen college, p. (17): (20–29) complimentary
verses to the author or book.

Rare. See Wood's *Ath. Oxon.* ii. 262, and 1603. D. The poem describes the whole
state of man, his condition, qualities and surroundings, in a discursive manner which
allows a short history of England to come in (at p. 131). The stanzas are 9-line,
rhyming ABABBCBCC. The author was a professional calligrapher in Oxford, not a
member of the University. Davies's *Works* were edited by dr. Grosart in 1878. An
ed. of 1611 is perhaps only due to a misprint in a 17th cent. bookseller's catalogue.

5. †**Godwin**, Francis, bp. of Hereford.　　　[*woodcut*] | TO THE PARSON, VICAR | or Cur ate, of　　　| and to everie of them. | [letter-press of the articles.]

No imprint: (1603): (two) sm. 4º: pp. 4: p. 3 beg. *or M. Doctor Trevor*: Pica English. Contents:— p. 1, head title, as above: 1-4, the orders: signed at end "Matherne. Sept. 30. 1603. *Fr. Landaven.*," i.e. F. Godwin, then bp. of Llandaff.

Very rare. Orders of the bishop of Llandaff for the reformation of abuses in his diocese. The woodcuts are sufficient to prove by their particular imperfections that this is a product of the Oxford press.

6. **Howson**, dr. John.　　　A | SERMON | [&c. precisely as 1602. H, except that a line "The second Impression." is added after "of Oxforde" before the woodcuts.]

Impr. 23: 1603: sm. 4º: pp. [4] + 30 + [2]: sign. B 1ʳ beg. *ship or honor*, p. 11 *& hyems erat*: English Roman. Contents:—(exactly as 1602. II.)

See Wood's *Ath. Oxon.* ii. 318. This is a verbatim but not literatim reprint of 1602. II, except as noted above.

7. **Oxford**, University.　　　ACADEMIÆ OXONIENSIS | *PIETAS* | ERGA SERENISSI-|MVM ET POTEN- TISSIMVM IACOBVM AN-|*GLIÆ SCOTJÆ FRANCIÆ* | *& Hiberniæ Regem, fidei defenso- rem, Beatissimæ Elisabethæ nu-| per Reginæ legitimè & au-|spicatissimè succedentem.* | **.* *.** | **.** | [*device.*]

Impr. 13*h*: 1603: (eights) sm. 4º: pp. [4] + 207 + 1: p. 11 beg. *Virginis atque*: 111 *Votum pro*: Pica Roman. Contents:—p. (1, title: (3-4) dedication to the King in Latin, by the university: 1-207, the poems: (1) "Votum Typographi ad . . . Regem," a poem.

More than 470 Latin poems, with a few in Greek, Italian, and French. On p. 17 there is a complaint of the lack of Hebrew type. There is an earlier and less common issue without the "Votum typographi," the page being left blank.

8. **Oxford**, University.　　　THE | ANSVVERE | OF THE VICECHAN-|CELOVR, THE DOCTORS, | both the Proctors, and other the | Heads of Houses in the Vniversi-|*tie of Oxford*: | (*Agreeable, vndoubtedly, to the ioint and Vniforme | opinion, of all the Deanes and Chapters, and all o-|ther the learned and obedient Cleargy,* | *in the Church of England.*) | To the humble Petition of the Ministers of the | Church of England, desiring Reformation of cer- taine Ceremonies and Abuses of the Church. | [two *mottos*: then *woodcuts*.]

Impr. 2: 1603: sm. 4º: pp. [16] + 32, signn. ¶, *¶, A-D¹: sign. *¶ 1ʳ beg. *you hartely*, p. 11 beg. *Concerning the*: English Roman. Contents:—p. (1) title: (3-13) "Epistle dedicatorie" to the arch- bp. of Canterbury and the Chancellors of the Universities of Oxford and Cambridge, beg. "Many and excellent": 1-5, "The humble petition of the Ministers . . .": 6-32, "The Answer . . .".

Three other issues are known:—(*a*), title identical except that the imprint is no. 25: after p. (13) comes (14-16, a letter from the University of Cambridge to that of Oxford in Latin, 7 Oct. 1603, introduced by a few sentences "to the reader": the rest identical: (*b*) with title identical till the 9th line which runs:—"*opinion, of all the Deanes and Chapters, and all other | the learned & obedient Cleargy, in the Church of Eng*: | And confirmed by the expresse consent of the | *Vniversitie of Cambridge.*) | To the humble Petition" [&c. as before]: with the same imprint as (*a*), but in small roman type. Four new leaves follow the title, *2ʳ–*4ʳ containing a dedication to the king, and ¶1ʳ the arms of the University with woodcuts above and below. Then follows "the Præface," the title only being re-set, and the headline being no longer "The Epistle | dedicatorie" but "The Præface | to the L.L.", while on **4ᵛ a passage from Gregory Nazianzen is inserted: all the rest is identical with the other issues: *c* identical with (*b*) throughout except that the imprint is no. 2 and is without date. Of these four editions or issues, the first is very rare, being perhaps stopped in the course of issue: *a* is common, *b* less so, *c* rare.

See Wood's *Ath. Oxon.* i. 3 (where a doubtful 1641 edition is referred to): 1604. o.

9. **Oxford,** University.　OXONIENSIS ACADEMIÆ | Funebre Officium | *IN* | MEMORIAM | HONORATISSIMAM | SERENISSIMÆ ET BEATIS: SIMÆ ELISABETHÆ, NVPER | *Angliæ, Franciæ, & Hiberniæ* | *Reginæ.* | [*device.*]

Impr. 13*b*: 1603: sm. 4°: pp. [4] + 182 + [2]: p. 11 beg. *Lugentem, III Sævit, &*: Pica Roman. Contents:—p. (1) | title: (3–4) Poetical Latin dedication to the king: 1–182, the poems.

Chiefly Latin poems in memory of queen Elizabeth: a few Greek occur, one Hebrew (p. 5, cf. 97, 171), one French (p. 64), one Italian p. 171). The longest poem is one by Robert Burhill entitled "Invitatorius Panegyricus . . . de . . . Reginæ posteriore ad Oxoniam adventu," which Wood mentions (*Ath. Oxon.* iii. 18) as a separate publication.

10. **Storre,** William.　THE | MANNER OF | THE CRVELL OVT-| RAGIOVS MVRTHER OF | WILLIAM STORRE *Mast. of Art, Mi-*nister, and Preacher at Market Raisin in | the County of Lincolne: | COMMITTED | *By Francis Cartwright one of his parishioners,* | *the* 30. *day of August Anno.* 1602. | [*device.*]

Impr. 7: 1603: sm. 4°: pp. [12 ?], | *for*: Pica Roman. Contents:—p. (1) signn. A⁴ B² ?): sign. A 3ʳ beg. *thirsted* | title: (3–11 ?) the work.

Extremely rare. The only known copy, in the Bodleian, has sign. A 4 imperfect, and has lost all after that leaf. The pamphlet was reprinted with slight changes at London in 1613 with the title "Three bloodie Murders . . ." of which this is the first. "The Life, confession, and heartie repentance of Francis Cartwright, gentleman; for his bloodie sinne in killing of one Master Storr, Master of Arts . . . written with his owne hand" was published at London in 1621. Storre was a Fellow of Corpus Christi College at Oxford.

11. **Thornborough,** bp. John.　[*woodcut.*] | ARTICLES | TO BE MINISTRED | AND TO BE ENQVIRED | OF, AND ANSWERED IN the first generall visitation of | *the reverend father in God, John,* | *by Gods permission, Bishop* | *of Bristoll.* | *⁎* | [*device.*]

Impr. 2*c*: 1603: sm. 4°: pp. [2] + 18: p. 11 beg. *or keep*: Pica English. Contents:—p. (1) title: (2) "The Tenor of the oath ministred to the Church-wardens, and sworne men": 1–18, the articles, 37 + 41 in number.

12. **Willoughby,** John.　"*A Treatise for the Preparation of the Lord's Supper.* Oxon. 1603, ded. to K. James I. at which time the author was living in Oxon."

So in Wood's *Ath. Oxon.* i. 744: very rare: a copy is mentioned in "A catalogue of choice English books . . . which will be sold by Auction, 6 Aug. 1688" (Lond. 1688, 4°) Appendix p. 7.

1604.

1. Abbot, archbp. George.   THE | REASONS | VVHICH DOCTOVR
HILL | HATH BROVGHT, FOR THE | vpholding of Papistry, which is false-*lie
termed the Catholike Religion* : | *Vnmasked, and shewed to be very weake,
and vpon exa*-*mination most insufficient for that purpose* : | By GEORGE
ABBOT Doctor of Divinity & Deane | of the Cathedrall *Church_in
Winchester.* | The first Part. | [two *mottos* : then *woodcuts*] |

Impr. 25 : 1604 : (eights) sm. 4° : pp.
[8] + "438" (really 436 for 384-5 are
omitted in the pagination) + [8] : p. 11
beg. *is both*, 111 G. *Abbot* : Pica Roman.
Contents :—p. (1) large device of the
University arms between woodcuts : (3,
title : (5-7) Epistle dedicatorie to lord
Buckhurst, dated from University college
Oxford, 4 Jan. "1604" : 1-438, the
work : (1-6) "To the Christian Reader."

See Wood's *Ath. Oxon.* ii. 562. The book is in answer to dr. Thomas Hill's
"Quartron of reasons of Catholike Religion," Antw. 1600 : but contains only ten out
of sixteen answers which the author had prepared.

2. Bridges, John, bp. of Oxford.   ARTICLES TO | BE ENQVIRED OF
WITHIN THE | Dioces of Oxford, giuen by the Reuerende | *Father in God*
IOHN *by Gods permission now* | Bishop of Oxford in his Visitation begun |
the second day of October. 1604. | [*device.*]

Impr. 7 : 1604 : sm. 4° : pp. [12],
signn. A¹-B²: sign. B 1ʳ beg. *your Parish* :
Pica English. Contents :—sign. A 1ʳ, title :
A 2ʳ-B 2ʳ, the 55 articles : B 2ʳ "the oath
of the Church-wardens and Sidemen."

3. Corderoy, Jeremy.   A | SHORT DIA-'LOGVE, WHEREIN | is
proved, that no man can | be saved without good | vvorkes. | Edit. 2.
With some Additions | [*motto*, then *woodcuts.*]

Impr. 25 : 1604 : (twelves) 16° : pp.
[22] + 2 + 110 + [2] : p. 11 beg. *which no
doubt*, 101 *workes he may* : Pica Roman.
Contents :—p. (1) title : (3-6) Epistle
dedicatorie to sir Robert Vernon, signed
"Ieremy Corderoy" : (7-21) "To the
Christian Reader," also signed : 1-2, 1-
110, the work, the half title being "A
short dialogue between a Gallant, a
Scholler of Oxforde, and a Church-
Papist . . .".

Rare. See Wood's *Ath. Oxon.* ii. 47. The first edition may be the one of *Lond.*
1604 recorded by Watt in the *Bibliotheca Britannica.*

4. Hubbocke, William.   AN ORATI-'ON GRATVLATORY TO | the
High and Mighty IAMES of *England*, | *Scotland, France and Ireland,
King, Defendor of the* | faith, &c. On the twelft day of February last
pre-|*sented, when his Maiesty entred the Tower of* | London to performe
the residue of the solemni-*ties of his Coronation thorough the citie of
London* | differred by reason of the plague : and publi-*shed by his High-
nesse speciall allowance.* | *Wherein both the description of the Tower of* |
London and the vnion of the kingdomes is | *compendiously touched* : | By |
WILLIAM HVBBOCKE. | [*woodcuts.*]

Impr. 25 : 1604 : sm. 4° : pp. [16],
signn. A 1.¹: sign. B 1ʳ beg. *I will giue* :
English Roman. Contents :—sign. A 1ʳ
title : A 1ᵛ, Latin dedication to the king :
A 2ʳ-A 4ᵛ, the speech, in Latin : B 1ʳ-B 4ᵛ,
the same in English.

Extremely rare: the only copy at present known is in the Bodleian, but there was a copy among the Harleian Pamphlets. See Wood's *Ath. Oxon.* i. 753. The speech was really delivered on *March* 12, not February, 1603, Hubbocke being Chaplain at the Tower. The speech describes the Tower as mint, armoury, jewel-house, &c. It is reprinted in Nichols's *Progresses of king James I.*

5. **Oxford.**   THE | ANSVVERE | OF THE VICECHAN- CELOVR . . . [&c. exactly as 1603, *Oxford* Answer, variation *b*.]

Impr. 25: 1604: sm. 4°: pp. [46], signn. A–E¹ F² ( )¹: sign. B 1ʳ beg. *But these*: Pica Roman. Contents:—p. (1) title: (3–6) dedication to the king: (7–15) "The Præface": (16–17) Letter from Cambridge, 7 Oct. 1603, introduced by a short note: (18) quotation from Gregory Nazianzen: 19–22) "The humble petition of the Ministers . . .": (23–44) "The Answere . . . to the Petition . . ."

See Wood's *Ath. Oxon.* i. 3, and 1603. o. This is a reprint of variation *b*.

6. **Panke,** John.   A | SHORT ADMONI- tion by way of Dialogue, to all | those who hitherto vpon pretence of | of their vnworthines haue dangerously, | *in respect of their saluation, with held them-* selues from comming to the Lordes Table: | *Exhorting them without any longer delay | to present themselues hereunto. | VVherein is shewed that there is an* vns worthy receiving of baptisme, an vnworthy | *hearing of the worde, and an vnworthy pre-* senting our selues to prayer aswell as an vnworthy receiving of the supper, which | yet these vnworthies worthi- ly thinke not of. | *By* IOHN PANKE. | [*motto,* then *woodcuts.*]

Impr. 25: 1604: (eights) 12°: pp. [72], signn. A–Dᵉ E⁴: sign. B 1ʳ beg. *adding to*: Pica Roman. Contents:— sign. A 1ʳ, title: A 2ʳ–A 3ᵛ, epistle dedicatorie to lady Katherine Wroughton, dated from Broad Hinton, 25 Mar. "1604": A 4ʳ–A 6ᵛ, "To the Christian and Godly Reader": A 7ʳ– F. 4ᵛ, the dialogue, between "Romannus the scholler" and "Tuberius the gentleman."

See Wood's *Ath. Oxon.* ii. 274.

7. **[Parkes,** Richard.]   A | BRIEFE | AN- SVVERE VNTO CER- TAINE OBIECTIONS AND | Reasons against the descension of Christ | *into hell, lately sent in writing vnto a Gen- tleman in the Countrey.* | [*motto,* then *woodcuts.*]

Impr. 25: 1604: sm. 4°: pp. [8] + 58 + [2]: p. 11 beg. *tweene Death*: Pica Roman. Contents:—p. (1) title: (3–7) "To the Christian Reader": 1–58, the work: (1) "A note for the Readers Instruction," bibliographical, on the meaning of certain references to books.

See 1613. A. This controversy about the Descent into Hell began with the manuscript (?) objections referred to in the title: then came this book which is anonymous, but confessed by the author in his *Apologie,* see below), followed by (1 [Andrew Willett's] *Limbo-mastix, that is a Cannise of Limbus Patrum* published without the author's knowledge), with a reply to the *Brief answere* (Lond. 1604): then (2) by an interminable rejoinder by Richard Parkes (*An Apologie,* Lond. 1607, of which the first part is a revised issue of the *Brief Answer,*) answered by Willett's *Loidoromastix: that is a scourge for a rayler* (Cambr. 1607). The *Brief Answer* holds the orthodox opinion of the "local descension of Christ's soul to Hell."

8. **Powel,** Gabriel.   A | CONSIDERATION OF the Papists Reasons of State and Reli- gion, for toleration of Poperie in England, | INTI-

MATED IN THEIR | *Supplication vnto the Kings Maie-*|*stie, & the States of the Pre-*|*sent Parliament.* | [*motto,* then *woodcuts.*]

Impr. 25: 1604: sm. 4°: pp. [4]+ 128: p. ii beg. *Priest: or,* iii *and was the*: Pica Roman. Contents:—p. (1) title: (3-4) "To the Christian Reader," signed " Oxford, from S*. Marie Hall. 13. of Aprill. 1604. . . . Gabriel Powel ": 1-125, the work: 126-128. "The Auctors Teares and humble Petition vnto Almightie God."

See Wood's *Ath. Oxon.* ii. 25.

9. **Sanford,** John.   GODS ARROWE | *Of the* | *PESTILENCE.* | *By* | JOHN SANFORD Master of Artes, and Chapleine of Magdalen | *Colledge in Oxford.* | [*motto*: then *woodcut.*]

Impr. 25: 1604: (eights) 16°: pp. [8] +55+[1]: p. ii beg. *that verse of*: Pica English. Contents:—p. (1) title: (3-8) Epistle dedicatorie to the University of Oxford, dated from Magdalen college 13 Mar. 160?: 1-55, the discourse, on Ps. xxxviii. 2.

See Wood's *Ath. Oxon.* ii. 472. Intended as a sermon, but the author found himself disabled in speech, and could not deliver it.

10. **Sanford,** J[ohn].   [*woodcut.*] | Le | *Guichet François.* | SIVE *JANICULA ET BREVIS INTRO-*|*ductio ad Linguam Gallicam.* | [three *mottos*: then *woodcuts.*]

Impr. 11: 1604: sm. 4°: pp. [40 + inserted leaf], signn. A E¹, and one leaf after D1: sign. B1ʳ beg. *ta aliaq*:: Long Primer Roman. Contents:— sign. A1ʳ, title: A2ʳ A3ᵛ, Latin dedication to dr. Bond president of Magdalen college Oxford, signed " I. Sanfordus ": A4ʳ-B1ᵛ " Ad Gallicæ Linguæ Studiosum Lectorem ": B2ʳ-E4ʳ, the work.

Rare. See Wood's *Ath. Oxon.* ii. 472. This is a French grammar and syntax written in Latin. After sign. D1 is a folio folded leaf, printed on one side only, a " Tabula coniugationum." See 1605. s.

1605.

1. **Davies,** John, of Hereford.   *MICROCOSMOS.* | THE DISCOVERY OF THE LITTLE | World, with the governe-|ment thereof. | [*motto*] | By Iohn Davies. | [*woodcuts.*]

Impr. 27: 1605: &c. as 1603. D. Contents:—exactly as 1603. D.

Very rare. See 1603. D, of which this is a reissue, with no alteration whatever except a new titlepage.

2. **Hutten,** Leonard.   AN | ANSVVERE TO A CER-|TAINE TREATISE OF THE | CROSSE IN BAPTISME. | *Intituled* | A Short Treatise of the Crosse in Baptisme, con-|tracted into this Syllogisme. | [*the syllogism follows in six lines*] | VVherein not only the weaknesse of the Syllogisme it|selfe, but also of the grounds and proofes there-|of, are plainely discovered. | *By L. H. Doct. of Divinitie.* | [two *mottos,* then *woodcuts.*]

Impr. 25 a: 1605: sm. 4°: pp. [8] + 139+[1]: p. ii beg. *tions were,* iii *needed to set*: English Roman. Contents:—p. (1) title: (3-7) Epistle dedicatory to the archbp. of Canterbury, signed " Leon. Hutten ": 1-139, the answer.

See Wood's *Ath. Oxon.* ii. 533. The book to which this is a reply is [William Bradshaw's] *Short treatise of the crosse in Baptisme, n. p.* 1604, in which the unlawfulness of the use of the cross was insisted on.

3. **Hutton,** Thomas. REASONS FOR REFVSAL | OF SVBSCRIPTION TO THE | booke of Common praier, vnder the | hands of certaine Ministers of Devon, and | Cornwall word for word as they were ex- hibited by them to the Right Reverend | Father in God WILLIAM CO-TON Doctor of Divinitie | *L. Bishop of Exeter.* | *WITH AN ANSWERE AT SE-*verall times returned them in publike conference | *and in diverse sermons vpon occasion prea-*|ched in the Cathedrall Church of *Exeter,* | by THOMAS HVTTON, Bachi-|ler of Divinitie & fellow of | St. Iohns Coll. in Oxon. | AND NOW PVBLISHED AT | *the very earnest intreatie of some especiall* | friends for a farther contentment of o-|ther the Kings Maiesties good | and loyall subiects. | [*motto,* then *woodcuts.*]

Impr. 25 a : 1605 : sm. 4° : pp. 200 : p. II beg. *are, wherein,* III *times haue thought* : English Roman. Contents :— p. I title : 3 6, Epistle dedicatorie to the bp. of Exeter : 7–10, "To my fellow brethren the ministers of Devon and Cornwall . . .": 10–17, "To the Christian Reader": 18 34, the Reasons : 35–200, the Answer to the Reasons.

See Wood's *Ath. Oxon.* ii. 646. A "Second and last part of Reasons for Refusall . . ." was published in London in 1606, and "The Remoonall of certaine imputations laid vpon the Ministers of Deuon : and Cornwall by one M. T. H. . . .," printed abroad in 1606 : and other books on the controversy later.

4. **James,** Thomas. CATALOGVS LIBRORVM | BIBLIOTHECÆ PVB-|LICÆ QVAM VIR ORNATIS-'simus THOMAS BODLEIVS Eques | Auratus in Academia Oxoniensi nuper in-'stituit ; continet autem Libros Alphabeti-| cè dispositos secundum quatuor | Facultates : | CVM | QVADRVPLICI ELENCHO | Expositorum S. Scripturæ, Aristotelis, Iuris | *vtriusque &* *Principum Medicinæ, ad vsum* | Almæ Academiæ Oxoniensis, | *Auctore* | THOMA JAMES | Ibidem Bibliothecario. | [*woodcuts*]

Impr. 18 : 1605 : sm. 4° : pp. [8] + "655" (really 651) + [67] : p. II beg. *A.* II. 1. *Chron..* III *P.* 1. 1. *Philon.,* p. 501 *V ¶ Hug. de* : English Roman. Contents :— p. (1) title : (2) "Observanda in hoc catalogo" : (3–4) Epistola dedicatoria to Henry Frederick prince of Wales : (5–8) "Præfatio ad Benevolum Lectorem," dated "E Bibliotheca publica Oxoniæ Iunij 27. Anno. 1605." : 1–162, catalogue of "Libri Theologici" : 163–179, "Catalogus Expositorum S. Scripturæ iuxta ordinem Voluminum vtriusque Testamenti dispositus" : 180, "Ad Lectorem" : 181–218, "Libri Medici" : 219–274. "Libri Iuris" : 275–415, "Libri Artium" : 417–425. "Interpretes libro-rum Aristotelis" : 427–640, "Appendix" to each of the four faculties : 641–646, "Appendix ad Expositores S. Scripturæ" : 646–648, "Appendix ad Interpretes Lib. Arist." : 648 651, "Interpretes Juris Civilis" : 651–652, "Interpretes Juris Canonici" : 652–653. "In omnia vel pleraque Scripta Hippocrat." : 653 655, "Scriptores in Cl. Galenum" : 655, "Scriptores in Dioscoridem" : (2 67) "Index Auctorum in hoc volumine" : 68) "Nomina Hebraica quæ corruptè imprimuntur : & quia defuerunt characteres Hebraici. Latinè hic omnia exprimimus" : 68) "Errata in Latinis nominibus."

Rare. See Wood's *Ath. Oxon.* ii. 466, and 1620.). The catalogue includes also the MSS. then in the Library. In the dedication the "Bibliotheca Bodleiana" is stated to be not yet four years old, having been formally opened on 8 Nov. 1602. The preface gives an interesting account of the early history of the Library. In the pagination a leaf is omitted after p. 426, but "457" follows "450" : the total number of pages is no doubt 726 (signn. ⸿ A–Y[1] 2[2], Aa–Zz, Aaa–Zzz, Aaaa–Xxxx[1] ( )[1]), so that Upcott *English Topography*, iii. p. 1122, Lond. 1818) is wrong. Other editions of the complete catalogue of Bodleian printed books were issued at Oxford in 1620, 1674, 1738 and 1843, and one of the MSS. in 1697.

5. King, John, bp. of London.   ARTICLES MINISTRED | IN THE VISITATION OF | THE RIGHT WORSHIPFVL. MAI-|ster IOHN KING, Doctor of divinitie, Arch-|deacon of Nottingham, in the yeare of | *our Lord God.* 1605. | [*device.*]

Impr. 7 *a*: 1605: sm. 4°: pp. [8 +?]: | Pica English.   Contents:—sign. A 1ʳ. signn. A[1] +?: sign. A 4ʳ beg. *Visiting of*: | title: A 2ʳ–?, the articles.

Very rare.   The only recorded copy, in the Bodleian, contains only sign. A.   For the issuer see Wood's *Ath. Oxon.* ii. 294.

6. Kingsmill, Thomas.   CLASSICVM | POENITENTIALE, | THOMA KINGESMILLO, auctore, | *olim Socio Coll. Magdalenensis & non ita* | *pridem Hebraicæ Linguæ in alma Aca-|demia Oxon: professore regio.* | [*device.*]

Impr. 26: 1605: sm. 4°: pp. [56] + 130 + [2] + 65 + [3]: p. 11 be. *resipis-|centiam,* 111 *mitto cætera,* 2nd p. 11 beg. *suluerunt. vos*: English and (2nd part) Pica Roman.   Contents:—p. (1) title: (3–47) dedication to the king: (49–56) | "Ad Lectorem": 1–130, the treatise: (1) a title:—" [*woodcut*] | TRACTATVS DE SCANDALO | EODEM AVCTORE. | [*de-|vice.*]."   Impr. 11, 1605: 1–65, the second treatise.

See Wood's *Ath. Oxon.* i. 758.   These two treatises on the moral state of England are printed without list of contents, index or even division into paragraphs.   No one but the author and compositor can have ever read them, and the former had been insane, though according to Wood he recovered his powers.

7. Oxford, Christ Church.   MVSA HOSPITALIS | ECCLESIÆ CHRISTI OXON. | *In adventum Fœlicissimum Sereniss.* IACOBI | *Regis,* ANNÆ *Reginæ,* & HENRICI *Prin-|cipis ad eandem Ecclesiam.* | [*device.*]

Impr. 18: 1605: sm. 4°: pp. [48].   signn. A–F[4]: English Roman. Con-|tents:—sign. A 1ʳ, title: A 2ʳ–F 4ʳ, the poems.

Christ Church poems to commemorate the visit of the King, Queen, and Prince Henry to Oxford and Christ Church, 27–30 Aug. 1605.   All but one (Greek) are in Latin.

8. Oxford, New College.   ENCOMION | RODOLPHI VVARCOP-|PI ORNA-|TISSIMI, QVEM | habuit Anglia, Armigeri, qui commu- ni totius patriæ luctu extinctus est | *Die Iovis Kalend. Aug.* 1605. | [*motto*: then *device.*]

Impr. 18: 1605: sm. 4°: pp. [32], signn. A E[4]: sign. B1ʳ beg. *Magne Deus*: English Roman.   Contents:—sign. A 1ʳ, title: A 2ʳ A 2ᵛ, dedication to Will. lord Knollys de Grays, unsigned: A 3ʳ E 3ᵛ, | poems to the memory of Warcop, the first signed "W. Kingesmillus," the editor of the volume, "Oxonij e Coll. Novo die 25. Octob."

See Wood's *Ath. Oxon.* i. 754, *Fasti Oxon.* i. 366.   The poems, which are all except one (Greek) in Latin, are by New College men and edited by William Kingsmill of New College, a nephew of Warcop, who was himself at Ch. Ch.   The device on the titlepage bears the arms of New College, between W. W. (William of Wykeham).

9. Sanford, John.   *A* | BRIEFE EX-|TRACT OF THE FOR-|MER LATIN

GRAMMER, | DONE INTO ENGLISH, FOR | the easier instruction of | *the Learner.* | [*motto*, then *woodcuts.*]

Impr. 25 : 1605 : sm. 4° : pp. [16], signn. A–B⁴ : sign. B 1ʳ beg. *I. in the middest* : Pica Roman. Contents :—sign. A1ʳ, title : A 2ʳ–A 3ᵛ, dedication to William Grey son of Arthur lord Grey of Wilton, signed " John Sanford ": A 4ʳ B 4ᵛ, the extracts.

Rare. See Wood's *Ath. Oxon.* ii. 472. The word "Latin" on the title seems to be a mistake for " French," see 1604. s, to which this is a sort of appendix.

10. **Sanford**, John. *A* | GRAMMER | OR INTRODVCTION | TO THE ITALIAN | *TONGVE.* | §§§ | [*motto*, then *woodcuts.*]

Impr. 25 : 1605 : sm. 4° : pp. [8] + 44 + [4?] : p. II beg. *as i Soldati* : Pica Roman. Contents :—p. (1) title : (2) motto from Dante : (3–6) dedication to Magdalen college, Oxford, signed " Joan- nes Sanford " : (7) " To the reader " : (8) poem " Sur l'Autheur " in French, by Jean More : 1–44, the grammar : perhaps two blank leaves follow.

Very rare. See Wood's *Ath. Oxon.* ii. 472. The grammar includes a short syntax.

11. *****Thornborough**, John, bp. of Bristol. THE IOIE- FVLL AND BLESSED REV-'niting the two mighty & famous King-'domes, England & Scotland into their an-|*cient name of great Brittaine.* | By JOHN BRISTOLL. [*device.*]

Impr. 25 *a* : [1605 ?] : sm. 4° : pp. [8] + 80 : p. II beg. *Therefore the wise* : Pica Roman. Contents :—p. (1) title : (3–6) dedication to king James : 1–80, the treatise.

The preface alludes to "my two bookes," the other being " A discourse plainely proving the euident vtilitie and vrgent necessitie of the . . . Vnion of . . . England and Scotland . . . " (Lond., 1604, sm. 4° , which latter was the subject of a remon- strance of the House of Commons to the House of Lords, 26 May 1604, ending in an apology on the part of the author. There is nothing but Wood's express statement (*Ath. Oxon.* iii. 5) to settle whether this book was published at the close of 1604 or in 1605 : so that statement has been accepted. Otherwise it would seem that the two books were not long separated in point of time. Both were reprinted at London in 1641.

12. **Wakeman**, Robert. THE | CHRISTIAN | PRACTISE. | *A* Sermon preached on the Act-Sun-*day in S*. *Maries Church in* | *Oxford, Iul.* 8. 1604. | By ROB. WAKEMAN Bachelor | of Divinity and fellow of Baliol | Colledge in Oxford. | [*motto*, then *woodcuts.*]

Impr. 25 *a* : 1605 : (eights) 16° : pp. 92 + [4] : p. II beg. *ple but serued* : Eng- lish Roman. Contents :—p. 1, title : 2, " Points handled in this Sermon ": 3 92, the sermon, on Acts ii. 46.

See Wood's *Ath. Oxon.* ii. 471, and 1612. W.

13. **Wakeman**, Robert. SALOMONS EXALTATION. | *A* | SERMON PREA- CHED BEFORE THE | KINGS Maiestie at None- *Such, April.* 30. 1605. By ROB. WAKEMAN Bachelor | of Divinity and fellow of Baliol | Colledge in Oxford. [*motto*, then *woodcuts.*]

Impr. 25 *a* : 1605 : (eights) 16° : pp. [2] + 68 + [2] : p. II beg. *halt goe* : Eng- lish Roman. Contents :—p. (1) title : 1–68, the sermon, on 2 Chron. ix. 8.

See Wood's *Ath. Oxon.* ii. 471.

1606.

1. **[Burhill, Robert.]**   IN CONTRO- VERSIAM INTER IO- HANNEM HOWSONVM | & *Thomam Pyum* S. T. Doctores de | *novis post divortium ob adulteri- um nuptijs.* | TRACTATVS MODESTVS ET | Christianus in sex commentationes, & | *Elenchum monitorium distinctus.* | VBI ET AD EX- CVSAM D. PYI AD | D. Howsonum Epistolam, quâ libri Howsoni- *ani refutationem molitur, & ad ejusdem* | *alteram manuscriptam Epistolam e- iusdem argumenti, quâ contra* Al- bericum Gentilem *iurispruden- tiæ apud Oxonienses professorem* | *regium disputat, diligenter* | *respondetur.* | *[woodcuts.]*

Impr. 11: 1606: sm. 4°: pp. [12]+ 206+[20]: p. 1¹ beg. *non licuisse,* ut *polluatur? Ita:* Pica Roman. Con- tents:—p. 1) title: 2) "Auctoris pro- testatio de calumniâ": (3) "Admoni- tiones ad Lectorem": (4) 17 lines of errata, not found in all copies, & some- times pasted on: 5-6) Latin poem to Rich. Bancroft archbp. of Canterbury: (7-11) "Dispositio totius operis": 1- 176, the work in six parts: 177-206, the Elenchus: 1) "Ad Lectorem," a preface to what follows: (2 10) "To Master Doctor Pye," a letter in English from dr. "John Rainold's," dated 27 Feb. [160?]: (13) "Ad Lectorem," introduc- tory: (15-20) Latin letter from Albericus Gentilis to dr. Howson, dated from Lon- don, 12 Aug. 1603.

See Wood's *Ath. Oxon.* iii. 18, also ii. 15 and 60. Thomas Pye's work against Howson's Thesis is entitled "Epistola ad . . . D. Johannem Housonum, quâ Dogma ejus . . . refutatur . . ." Lond. 1603. The signatures show that this work (which is strictly anonymous) is part of the art. *Howson* below, and was indeed printed before it, and written before there was any intention of reprinting the *Thesis.*

2. **Howson,** dr. John.   VXORE DI- MISSA PROPTER FOR- nicationem aliam non licet | *superinducere.* | TERTIA THESIS | IOANNIS HOWSONI IN- ceptoris in Sacra Theologia, propo- sita & disputata in Vesperijs | *Oxonij.* 1602. | *ACCESSIT EIVSDEM THESEOS* | *defensio contra reprehensiones T. Pyi* | *S. T. Doctoris.* | *[woodcuts.]*

Impr. 28: 1606: sm. 4°: pp. [2]+36 +[2]: p. 1¹ beg. *tis impetum:* English Roman. Contents:—p. (1) title: (2) "Ad Lectorem," a note that the pages of the 1602 edition are noted in the margin, because the "Defensio" refers to them: 1-36, the thesis.

See Wood's *Ath. Oxon.* ii. 518, and 1602. 11, of which this is a verbatim reprint. The entry above under *Burhill* is really part of this work, but treated separately for convenience.

3. **King,** John.   THE | FOVRTH | SERMON PREACHED AT | HAMPTON COVRT ON | *Tuesday the last of Sept.* 1606. | *[line]* | BY | *[line]* | JOHN KINGE Doctor of Divinity, and | *Deane of Christ-Church in Oxon.* | *[device, then line.]*

Impr. 2: 1606: sm. 4°: pp. [2]+49 + 1]: p. 1¹ beg. *stration of the:* Eng- lish Roman. Contents:—p. (1) title, within lines: 1-49, the sermon, on Cant. viii. 11: 49, "Faults escaped in the printing . . ."

See Wood's *Ath. Oxon.* ii. 295: and 1607. K.

.4 **Oxford,** Magdalen college. BEATÆ MAR- RIAE MAGDALENAE
LACHRYMÆ, IN OBITVM | NOBILISSIMI IVVENIS GV- LIELMI GREY, Domini
ARTHVRI | GREY *Baronis de l'Vilton, aureæ* | *Periscelidis Equitis Claris-
simi,* | *Filij natu minoris.* | [*device.*]

Impr. 11: 1606: sm. 4°: pp. [4] +
42: p. 11 beg. *Perpetuos:* English Roman. Contents:—p. (1) title: (3–4) dedication to lady Joanna Sybil Grey, dowager
lady Grey, mother of William Grey, signed
"Rob. Barnes," dated Magd. coll. Oxford,
11 March (160⅚): 1 42, the poems.

Poems by members of Magdalen college, Oxford, in memory of William Grey, who
matriculated at Magdalen, 18 May 1604 and died 18 Feb. 160⅚. The editor of the
volume was a son of the printer of the book and a Fellow of Magdalen. The poems
are Latin except four Greek, one Spanish (?) and one Italian.

5. *†**Oxford,** University. [Orders for the Market of the City of
Oxford, issued by the Chancellor of the University: beg. "Thomas
Earle of Dorset," ends "transgressor of this commaudement. God
saue the King."]

No impr.: [1606]: (one) obl. fol.:
pp. [2]: English Roman. Contents:—
p. (1) the orders (31 in number).

"Proclaimed July 2°, 1606. Dr. Abbotts Vice-Chancellor," according to a MS.
note on the copy in the Oxford University Archives.

6. **Rawlinson,** rev. John. THE | FOVRE SVM- MONS OF THE |
SHVLAMITE. | A | *Sermon preached at Pauls Crosse vpon* | *Rogation
Sunday, the 5. of* | May. 1605. | By JOHN RAWLINSON, Bache- lor of
Divinitie, and fellow of | Saint Iohns Colledge in | Oxford. | [*motto*: then
woodcuts.]

Impr. 25 a: 1606: (eights) 16°: pp.
[10] + 82 + [4]: p. 11 beg. *and commeth*:
English Roman. Contents:—p. (1) title:
(3–9) "To the Reader," dated from St.
John's College in Oxon, 10 Jan [160⅚]:
1–82 the sermon, on Cant. vi. 13: [3–4)
have not been seen.]

Rare. See Wood's *Ath. Oxon.,* ii. 506. The author states that the sermon occupied
two hours in delivery.

7. **Trelcatius,** Lucas. SCHOLASTICA, | ET METHODICA, | Locorum
Communium, | *S. Theologiæ Institutio,* | Didacticè, & Elencticè in Epitome
explicata: | IN QVA, | *Veritas Locorum Communium, definitionis eu- iusque
Loci, per Causas suas Analysi asseritur:* | *Contraria verò Argumenta,
imprimis* | *Bellarmini, Generalium* | *Solutionum appendice* | *refutantur:*
Auctore, LVCA TRELCATIO, L. F. | *Pastore, & Professore,* | [*woodcuts.*]

Impr. 11: 1606: (eights?) 12°?.

Only known at present from a titlepage in the Bagford collections at the British
Museum, but no doubt other copies exist. Probably a reprint of the first edition,
Lugd. Bat. 1604, 4°.

8. **Wakeman,** Robert. IONAHS SERMON, | AND | *Niniuehs repent-
ance.* | A | SERMON PREACHED AT | Pauls Crosse Jun. 20. 1602. and now |
thought fit to be published for | our meditations in | these times. | *By*

Ro. Wakeman *Master of Arts,* | *and fellow of Balioll Colledge* | *in
Oxford.* | The second Impression. | [*motto,* then *woodcuts.*]

Impr. 25 a: 1606: (eights) 16°: pp. | from "Balioll Colledg in Oxford October.
[8] + 102 + [2]: p. 11 beg. *to send his*: | 10. 1603.": (7) "Ionah. 3. 4. 5. The
English Roman. Contents:—p. (1) title: | Analysis of the Text.": 1–102, the ser-
(3–5) "To the Christian Reader," dated | mon, on Jonah iii. 4–5.

Rare. See Wood's *Ath. Oxon.,* ii. 471. No copy of the first impression, which may
have been printed at Oxford in 1603 or 1604, has yet been seen. There is no allusion
to this being a second edition, in the preface.

1607.

1. **Bunny,** Francis.   AN | ANSVVERE TO A | POPISH LIBELL IN-|
tituled *A Petition to the Bishops,* | *Preachers, and Gospellers,* | lately
spread abroad in | the North partes. | By Francis Bvnny *Prebenda-'ry
of Durham ; sometimes fel-low of Magdalen Col-ledge in Oxford.* |
[*motto,* then *woodcuts.*]

Impr. 2: 1607: (eights) 12°: pp. [16] | tents:— pp. (1–2) [not seen]: (3) title:
+ 159 + [1]: p. 11 beg. *who would,* 111 | (5–15) "To all Popish Recusants . . .":
receive some: English Roman. Con- | 1–159, the work.

See Wood's *Ath. Oxon.,* ii. 201. The "Petition" came out in "September last"
(1606 ?).

2. **Cleland,** James.   ΗΡΩ-ΠΑΙΔΕΙΑ, | OR | THE INSTITVTION OF A |
YOVNG NOBLE MAN, | BY | JAMES CLELAND. | [*device.*]

Impr. 7: 1607: sm. 4°: pp. [16] + | Subiect and Order of these six Bookes":
"271" (really 269, for 249–50 are omitted | (15) some errata, with introductory note:
in the pagination) + [3]: p. 11 beg. *the* | (16) dedication of the preface and book
first booke, 111 *fained voice*: English Ro- | 1 to lord Hay: 1–10 the preface: 11–271,
man. Contents:—p. (1) title, within lines: | the work in six books each with a dedi-
(3–4) dedication to prince Charles: 5–8) | cation, see below.
"To the Noble Reader": (9) "The |

See 1612 C., which is simply a reissue with new titlepage. The author recommends
a nobleman to go to no University, but to Prince Henry's Court or Academy at
Nonsuch. The 2nd book is dedicated to Thomas Mourray, tutor to prince Charles:
the 3rd to George earl of Essex, son of the marquess of Huntly : the 4th to sir John
Harington, son of lord Harington : the 5th to mr. Francis Stewart Master of Mourray,
and to mr. John Stewart son of the duke of Lennox : the 6th to Robert earl of Essex.
The author was not an Oxford man, nor, apparently, connected with the place in any
way.

3. **Cooper,** Thomas.   NONÆ NOVEMBRIS | *Æternitati Consecratæ* |
IN | *Memoriam admirandæ illius liberationis* Principis, | *& Populi Angli-
cani à Proditione* | *Sulphurea.* | [*motto,* then *woodcuts.*]

Impr. 11: 1607: sm. 4°: pp. [24] + | orem . . . ," signed "Thomas Cooper":
124: p. 11 beg. *Num laqueus,* 111 *mus* | (8–23) "Praeludia ad Nonas," short poems
Deum: English Roman. Contents:—p. | by Cooper: (23) "Errata . . .": 1–124,
(1) title: (3) dedication to the king and | the work.
parliament: (4–7) "Praefatio ad Lect- |

See Wood's *Ath. Oxon.,* i. 612, *Fasti* i. 285, but the identity of the author appears to be still quite uncertain. The work is a rhetorical commentary, almost a sermon, on the Gunpowder Plot of 5 Nov. 1605 : but seems to afford no clue to the connexion of the author with Oxford.

4. D[unster], I[ohn]. A | PROTESTATION A-|GAINST POPERY BY | *way of a Confession of Christian* | *Religion collected for the benefit* | *of private friends.* | [*two mottos* : then *woodcut.*]

Impr. 2 : 1607 : eights, 12° : pp. [2] +38 : p. 11 beg. *of his transgression* : English Roman. Contents :—p. (1) title : 1–38, the treatise, signed on last page "I. D.", followed by a short poem "To the reader " signed " Roger Knight."

See 1609 D, and for the author Wood's *Ath. Oxon.*, ii. 142. The poem on p. 38 explains that the work was written "some time agoe" "for priuate vse." The Bodleian Catalogue (perhaps following Draudius's *Bibliotheca Exotica*, Frankf. 1625, p. 293) ascribes this book to John Dunster, but Wood did not know the author.

5. James, dr. Thomas. [*woodcut*] | CONCORDANTIÆ | SANC-TORVM | PATRVM HOC EST VERA ET | PIA LIBRI CANTICORVM PER | Patres vniversos tam Græcos quam Lati-|*nos expositio.* | *Auctore Thoma Iames* *in Alma Academia Oxo-*|*niensi Proto-Bibliothecario* & | *olim Socio Coll. Novi.* | [*woodcuts.*]

Impr. 11 : 1607 : sm. 4° : pp. [4]+18 +[2] : p. 11 beg. 930. *Hieron.* : English Roman. Contents :—p. (1) title : (2) motto : (3) "Lectori pio doctoque . . .", dated 30 July 1607 : (4) List of Com-mentators on the Song of Solomon : 1–18, the work, a catena of references to printed expositions of the Song : (1–2) biblio-graphical list of editions cited.

See Wood's *Ath. Oxon.*, ii. 467. One of the Bodleian copies (4° A. 64 Th.) has a MS. list by James of 26 presentation copies, out of 78 copies "receaued of Mr. Joseph [Barnes?] . . . 30 Jul", and some private opinions and suggestions about the book. The preface explains that if this instalment was well received, the author intended to proceed to similar publications for the rest of the Bible.

6. King, bp. John. " John King's Five Sermons preached before the King. Oxf. 1607."

So in "Catalogi variorum . . . librorum Richardi Davis . . . Pars Tertia" (1688), p. 83, cf. " . . . Pars secunda" (1686), p. 125. Rare. See next art.

7. King, bp. John. THE | FOVRTH | SERMON PREACHED AT | *HAMPTON COVRT ON* | *Tuesday the last of Sept.* 1606. | [*line*] | BY | [*line*] | JOHN KINGE Doctor of Divinity, and | *Deane of Christ-Church in Oxon.* | [*device*, then *line.*]

Impr. 2 : 1607 : sm. 4° : pp. [2]+49+ [1] : p. 11 beg. *stration of the* : English Roman. Contents :—p. (1) title, within lines : 3–49, the sermon, on Cant. viii. 11.

A reprint of 1606 K. This is perhaps part of the preceding article.

8. King, John. A | SERMON | PREACHED IN OXO^N : | the 5. of November. 1607. | [*line*] | BY | [*line*] | JOHN KINGE Doctor of Divinity, Deane | *of Christ Church, and Vicechancellor* | of the Vniversity. | [*device.*]

Impr. 7: 1607: sm. 4°: pp. [4]+35
+[1]: p. 11 beg. *causes and*: English
1–35 the sermon, on Ps. xlvi. 7–11.
See Wood's *Ath. Oxon.*, ii. 295.

Roman. Contents:—(3) title, within lines:

9. **Prideaux**, John.   TABVLÆ | AD GRAM-MATICA GRÆCA | INTRO-DVCTORIÆ. | IN QVIBVS | *Succinctè compingitur, brevissima, sed tamen ex-|pedita, singularum partium orationis decli=nabilium, Variandi ratio. | Accessit* | Vestibuli vice, ad eandem linguam παραίνεσις, in gratiam | tyronum, quibus vt convenit explicatiora evol- vere, ita necesse est haec | ipsa | ad vnguem tenere. [*motto, then woodcuts.*]

Impr. 11: 1607: sm. 4°: pp. [34], sign. A b¹, ( )¹: sign. b 1ʳ beg. *profero clarâ*: English Roman. Contents:—sign. A 1ʳ title: A 2ʳ–A 2ᵛ, dedication to dr. Tho. Holland, signed " Jo. Prideaux ": A 3ʳ-b 3ᵛ "In Isocratis Busiridem de Græcæ linguæ studio. Præfatio": b 4ʳ-b 4ᵛ "Grammatices Græcæ, Σχεδάρια.", the work in six sections: ( )1ʳ "Con-clusio ad Lectorem," and short epigram.

See Wood's *Ath. Oxon.*, iii. 267 where the date 1608 may be an error for 1607 : and 1629 p, 1639 p, both of which edd. supply the date of the dedication as "1 Jan. 1607 = 160⅞." but are otherwise apparently simply reprints. The dedication declares that the work was due to the suggestion of dr. Holland, and done in the last Whitsun-tide holidays (1606).

10. **Wake**, Isaac.   REX PLATONICVS: | SIVE, | DE POTEN-TISSIMI PRINCIPIS | IACOBI BRITANNIARVM | Regis, ad illustrissimam Academiam | *Oxoniensem, adventu, Aug. 27.* | Anno. 1605. | *NARRATIO* | *AB ISAACO VVAKE, PVBLICO A-cademiæ ejusdem Oratore, tum temporis | conscripta, nunc verò in lucem | edita, non sine authoritate | Superiorum.* | [*woodcuts.*]

Impr. 11: 1607: sm. 4°: pp. [8]+140+[4]: p. 11 beg. *cademiæ, III Ro-manas*: English Roman. Contents:— p. (3) title: (5–8) dedication to Henry prince of Wales, dated " Oxoniæ, e Col-legio Mertonensi ", 19 June (1607): 1–140. the work, with the running title " Rex Platonicus, Sive Musæ Regnantes": (1–2) Latin letter from the Chancellor of the University to the Vice-Chancellor, about the royal visit, with a preface by Wake.

See Wood's *Ath. Oxon.*, ii. 540. For other edd., which are only slightly altered, but add a funeral oration, see next art., and 1615 w, 1627 w, 1635 w, 1663 w. The visit of the King was from 27 to 30 Aug. 1605. The author says he wrote the account at the actual time of the visit. The oration was also printed at Oxford in 1608, and in English in Fuller's *Abel Redivivus.*

11. ———.   REX PLATONICVS: | SIVE, | DE POTENTIS-SIMI PRINCIPIS IA-COBI BRITANNIARVM | Regis, ad illustrissimam Aca-demiam Oxoniensem, | *adventu, Aug. 27.* | Anno. 1605. | *NARRATIO* | AB ISAACO WAKE, PVBLI-CO Academiæ ejusdem Oratore, | *tunc temporis conscripta, nunc i-terum in lucem edita, multis | in locis auctior & emen-datior.* | Editio Secunda. | [*woodcuts.*]

Impr. 11: 1607: (twelves) 16°: pp. [8]+224+[18]: p. 11 beg. *minum me-moriam. III cumano irruunt*: Long Primer Roman. Contents:—p. (1) title : (3–7) dedication to prince Henry, dated as 1st ed.: 1–224. the work: (1–3) the Chancellor's letter, with preface: (4) device: (5) ORATIO | FVNEBRIS HA-bita in Templo be-atæ Mariæ Oxon. | Ab ISAACO WAKE, | PVBLICO ACADE-mic Oratore, *Maij* 25. *An.* | 1607. quum mœsti | *Oxonienses, pijs mani-bus* Io-HANNIS | RAINOLDI | *parentarent.* | [wood-cuts, then Impr. 11, 1607.]: (6–18) the oration.

Rare : see preceding art. : for edd. of the Oration, see also preceding art.

1608.

1. **Chetwind,** Edward. CONCIO AD | CLERVM PRO GRA- dû habita Oxoniæ. 9. die | *Decembris.* 1607. | Per EDOARDVM CHETWIND è Coll. *Exoniensi sacræ Theologiæ* | *Bacchalaureum.* | *Matri Academiæ Sacra.* [*device.*]

Impr. 11 : 1608 : (eights) 16º : pp. [4] + 40 + [4] : p. 11 beg. *vt vobis* : Long Primer Roman. Contents :—p. (1) title : (3-4) " Methodus, brevisque summa to- tius concionis " : 1-40, the sermon, on Acts xx. 24 : (1) " Ad Lectores . . . amicos."

See Wood's *Ath. Oxon.*, ii. 641.

2. **Cooke,** James. IVRIDICA TRIVM QVÆSTI- onum ad *Maiestatem pertinentium deter-* minatio ; | IN QVARVM PRIMA ET VLTIMA | Processus Iudicialis contra *H. Garnetum* institutus, ex Iure Civili & Canonico defenditur : | IN SECVNDA SVPREMA ET VNI- versalis Principum potestas explicatur, & ex eisdem | *principijs succinctè asseritur* ; | OPPOSITA PRAECIPVE EPISTOLAE CVI- dam Dedicatoriæ Ad clarissimum virum. D. E. C. | militem, advocatum fiscalem Generalem à Ca- tholico, (vt ipse subscribit) Theo- logo conscriptæ ; | *Habita Oxoniæ in vesperijs Comitiorum Anno Do- mini* 1608. *à* JACOBO COOKE *Novi* | *Collegij Socio Inceptore in* | *Iure Civili.* [*motto,* in Greek : then *device.*]

Impr. 11 : 1608 : sm. 4º : pp. [4] + 49 + [3] : p. 11 beg. *intelligitur?* : Great Primer Roman. Contents :—p. (1) title : (3) dedication to Tho. Bilson bp. of Winchester : 1-49, the three theses and their determination.

See Wood's *Ath. Oxon.*, ii. 95. The theses were for the degree of D.C.L., chosen by the candidate himself.

3. **Hakewill,** George. THE | VANITIE OF | the eie. | First beganne for the Comfort of a | Gentlewoman bereaved of | her sight, and since vpon | occasion inlarged & | published for the | Common | good, BY | GEORGE HAKEWILL *Master* | *of Arts, and fellow of Exe-* ter Coll. in Oxford. [*motto* : then *woodcuts.*]

Impr. 7 : 1608 : (twelves) 16º : pp. [6] + 161 + [1] : p. 11 beg. *and by conse- quence, III gers may not* : Pica Roman. Contents :—p. (1) title : (3-6) " The Contents . . . " : pp. 1-161, the work, in 31 chapters.

See Wood's *Ath. Oxon.*, iii. 255 : and next art., 1615 11, 1633 11. The treatise contains all that can be said on physical and moral grounds against the Eye.

4. ——. [exactly as above, except that after " *Oxford.*" is added " *The second Edition augmented by the* | *Authour.* "]

Impr. 7 : 1608 : (twelves) 16º : pp. [6] + 170 + [4] : p. 11 beg. *and by con- sequence, III maker ; 1* : Pica Roman. Contents :—(1-6) as 1st ed. : 1-170, the work, in 31 chapters.

See preceding art., of which this is a reprint with additions, except that the titlepage is not reprinted but only re-set.

5. **James**, Thomas.　　　AN | APOLOGIE FOR IOHN | WICKLIFFE, shewing his conformitie | with the new Church of England; with an- swere to such slaunderous obiections, | as haue beene lately vrged against him | by Father Parsons, the Apolo-|gists, and others. | *COLLECTED CHIEFLY OVT OF* | diuerse works of his in written hand, by Gods e-|speciall providence remaining in the Publike | Library at Oxford, of the Honorable foun- dation of Sʳ. THOMAS BODLEY Knight : | BY | THOMAS JAMES keeper of the same.　[*motto*, then *woodcuts.*]

Impr. 2 : 1608 : sm. 4° : pp. [8] + 75 + [5] : p. II beg. *providence, which* : English Roman. Contents :—p. (1) title : (3-7) dedication to sir Edw. Cooke, lord chief justice of the Common Pleas. dated " From the Library in Oxford *Feb.* 10. 1608" : (8) " Faults escaped in the print-ing . . .": 1-3. "the Preface vnto all true Catholicks, and Christian Readers": 5-75, the Apology : 2-5, " Iohn VVickliffs life collected out of diuerse Auctors."

See Wood's *Ath. Oxon.*, ii. 467. This is closely connected with the Wycliff art., below : and on p. 60 marg. the other is said to be " printed with this Apologie": the form of the signatures also indicates connexion. The Bodleian MSS. quoted seem to be MSS. Bodl. 288 and 647, perhaps with others.

6. **King**, John.　　　A | SERMON | PREACHED AT WHITE-HALL THE 5. DAY OF NO.vember. ann. 1608. | [*line*] | BY | [*line*] | JOHN KING Doctor of Divinity, Deane of | *Christ=Church in Oxon : and Vicechauncel- lor of the Vniversity.* | *Published by commandement.* | [*device.*]

Impr. 2 : 1608 : sm. 4° : pp. [2] + 40 + [2] : p. II beg. *Seldome shal* : English Roman. Contents :—p. (1) title, within | lines : 1-40, the sermon, ou Ps. xi. 2-4, within lines.

See Wood's *Ath. Oxen.*, ii. 295.

7. ——.　　　A | SERMON | PREACHED IN Sᵗ. MARIES | at Oxford the 24. of March being the | day of his sacred Maiesties inauguration | *and Maundie thursday.* | [*line*] | BY | [*line*] | JOHN KINGE Doctor of Divinity, Deane | *of Christ Church, and Vicechancellor* | *of the Vniversitie.* | [*device.*]

Impr. 7 : 1608 : sm. 4° : pp. [2] + 30 : p. II beg. *dome, hee* : English Roman. Contents:—p. (1) title, within lines : 1-30, the sermon, on 1 Chron. xxix. 26-28, within lines.

See Wood's *Ath. Oxen.*, ii. 295.

8. **Panke**, John.　　　THE FAL OF BABEL. | *By the confusion of tongues, directly proving against the* | Papists of this, and former ages ; *that a view of their wri- tings, and bookes being taken, it cannot be discerned by any man* | *living, what they would say, or how be vnderstoode, in the* | *question of the sacrifice of the Masse, the Reall pre- sence or transubstanti- ation ; but in explaning* | *their mindes, they fall vpon such termes,* | *as the Protestants vse and allow.* | FVRTHER | In the question of the Popes supre-macy is shewed, how they | abuse an authority of the auncient father Sᵗ. Cyprian, A Canon of | the 1. Niceene counsell, And the Ecclesiasticall historie of Socra- tes, and Sozomen. And lastly is set downe a briefe of the suc-|cession of Popes in the sea of Rome for these 1600. yeeres |

togither ; what diversity there is in their accompt, what here- sies, schismes, and intrusions there hath bin in that seat, ' *deliuered in opposition against their tables, where- with now adaies they are very busie ; and o- ther things discovered against them.* | *By* | IOHN PANKE. | [*motto, then woodcuts.*]

Impr. 7 *a* : 1608 : sm. 4° : pp. [34] + 147 + [3]: p. 11 beg. *fence & proofe,* in *shop of Rome*: Pica Roman. Contents:— p. (1) title : (3–7) general Epistle dedicatorie to Protestants at Oxford, Cambridge and elsewhere, dated "From Tydworth the 1. of Nouember, 1607": (9–29) "To al . . . Recusants . . .", dated as before: (31–2) "The names of the Popish Writers, out of which this booke hath beene gathered.": 1–147, the work, in the form of a dialogue between "Tiberius the Gent." and "Romannus the Scholler": (2–3) "The names of the Bishops or Popes of Rome for these 1600. yeeres . . .".

See Wood's *Ath. Oxon.*, ii. 274. The work has no divisions, index or table of contents.

9. **Price**, Daniel.   THE MARCHANT. | A | SERMON | PREACHED AT PAVLES | Crosse on Sunday the 24. of Au- gust, being the day before Bar- tholomew faire. 1607. | [*line*] | BY | [*line*] | DANIELL PRICE *Master of Arts, of Exeter* | *Colledge in Oxford.* | [*device.*] |

Impr. 7 : 1608 : sm. 4° : pp. [4] + 38 : p. 11 beg. *of many who* : English Roman. Contents:—p. (1) title, within lines: (3–4) dedication "to the honorable Companie of Merchants of the Cittie of London", dated from Exeter Coll., Oxford, 20 Apr. 1608 : 1–38, the sermon, on Matt. xiii. 45–46 : every page of the book is within lines.

See Wood's *Ath. Oxon.*, ii. 511.

10. ——.   *Prælium & præmium.* | THE CHRISTIANS WARRE | and rewarde. | A | SERMON PREACHED | before the Kings Maiestie at VVhitehall the 3. of May. 1608. | [*line*] | BY | [*line*] | DANIELL PRICE *Master of Arts of Exeter* | *Colledge, and Chapleyn in ordinarie* | *to the* PRINCE. [*motto, then device.*]

Impr. 7 *b* : 1608 : sm. 4° : pp. [4] + 34 + [2] : p. 11 beg. *guler, effectnal* : English Roman. Contents :—p. (1) title, within lines : (3–4) dedication to the archbp. of Canterbury, dated from Exeter coll., Oxford, 19 June 1608 : 1–34, the sermon on Rev. ii. 26 : every page of the book has a border of lines.

See Wood's *Ath. Oxon.*, ii. 511. The dedication implies that the book took four days to print (?), and claims to be the first from the University Press since the archbishop (Richard Bancroft) became Chancellor (23 Apr. 1608).

11. ——.   RECVSANTS | CONVERSION : | A | SERMON PREACHED AT S^t. JAMES, before the PRINCE on the 25. | *of Februarie.* 1608. | [*line*] | BY | [*line*] | DANIELL PRICE *Master of Arts, of Exeter* | *Colledge in Oxford.* | [*device.*]

Impr. 7 : 1608 : sm. 4° : pp. [2] + 35 + [3]: p. 11 beg. *ctions and* : English Roman. Contents :—p. (1) title, within lines : 1–2, dedication to prince Henry : 3–35, the sermon, on Is. ii. 3, within lines : (2–3) [not seen].

See Wood's *Ath. Oxon.*, ii. 511.

12. **Prideaux, John.**   [The *Tabulae ad Grammatica Graeca,*

assigned by Wood (*Ath. Oxon.*, iii. 267) to this date, is probably the 1607 edition, which see.]

13. **Rainolds,** John.   IOHANNIS RAI-ˈNOLDI ORATI-|ones duæ, | Ex ijs quas habuit in Collegio Cor-ˈporis Christi, quum linguam | Græcam profiteretur. | HABITAE, QVVM STVDIA, DE | more per ferias intermissa, | repeterentur : | *Prior, quæ duodecima, post vaca-ˈtionem Natalitiam ; | Posterior, decima tertia, post vaca-ˈtionem Paschalem ; | Anno.* 1576. [*woodcuts.*]

Impr. 5 : 1608 : (twelves) 16° : pp. [8] + 106 + [6] : p. 11 beg. *non exhorter*, 101 *& in* : Pica English. Contents :—p. (1) title : (3–8) "Iohannes Rainoldus Aca- | demicis Oxoniensibus . . .", dated "è Colleg. Corp. Christ. Februar. 2 :" 1–52, the first oration : 53–106, the second oration.

The only copy at present met with is one in Worcester College Library at Oxford, but there is no special reason why the book should be scarce.

14. **S[ansbury],** I[ohn].   [*woodcuts*] | *ILIVM IN ITALIAM.* OXONIA AD | PROTECTIONEM *Regis sui omnium opti- mi filia, pedisequa.* | [*woodcuts.*]

Impr. 11 : 1608 : (eights) 16° : pp. [48], signn. A–C² : sign. B 1ʳ beg. *Flos regum* : Long Primer Italic. Contents : —sign. A 1ʳ, title : A 1ᵛ, dedication to | the king, signed " I. S.", i. e. John Sansbury : A 2ʳ–C 7ʳ, the work, the verso of every leaf being blank.

Rare and valuable. See Wood's *Ath. Oxon.*, ii. 58, where some extracts are given. Each leaf bears an engraving of the arms of the University or a College, and a short Latin poem following. The title appears to indicate the struggle of king James and England against Italian wiles, the words being from Virg. Aen. i. 72, where the context bears a different meaning. The dedication shows that the poems were written in 1606. The arms are in some respects peculiar, and were probably engraved at Oxford.

15. **Twyne,** Brian.   ANTIQVI-ˈTATIS ACADEMIÆ OXO- NIENSIS APO-|LOGIA. | *In tres libros divisa.* | AVTHORE | BRIANO TWYNO *in facultate Artium Ma-gistro, & Collegij Corporis Christi in eâdem* | *Academia Socio.* | [*device.*]

Impr. 11 : 1608 : sm. 4° : pp. [8] + 384 + [72] : p. 11 beg. *perit quod nemo,* 111 *xilo;, sed etiam* : Pica Roman. Contents :—p. (1) title : (3 6) dedication to Robert Sackvill earl of Dorset, dated from Corpus Christi college, Oxford, 3 June 1608 : 1–384, the work, in three books : (1–10) "Index rerum et verborum . . .": (11–21) "Catalogus authorum . . . quibus Author . . . vsus est": (21) "Errata . . .": (23–54) "Miscellanea quædam de antiquis aulis et studentium collegiis . . .", according to parishes : (55–72) "Summorum Oxoniensis Academiæ Magistratuum [Chancellors, Vice-Chancellors, Proctors] . . . catalogus."

See Wood's *Ath. Oxon.*, iii. 109 (where there is much about the fate of the MS., Twyne's intentions. &c. ii. 358. This is the first history of Oxford, but to some extent thrown into a controversial form, to prove the prior antiquity of Oxford to that of Cambridge. For a man of 28 it is, as Wood says, a wonderful performance. Almost all Twyne's Oxford collections are still preserved in the University Archives and the Library of Corpus Christi college, Oxford. See 1620 T.

16. **Wake,** Isaac.   ORATIO FV- NEBRIS HABI-ta in Templo beatæ | *Mariæ Oxon.* | Ab ISAACO WAKE | [&c. precisely as in 1607 W.] | [*woodcuts.*]

Impr. 11 : 1608 : (twelve) 16⁰ : pp. [24], sign. A¹² ; sign. A 4ʳ beg. *occasionis ratione*: Pica English. Contents :—sign. | A 2ʳ title: A 3ʳ–A 9ʳ, the oration : A 1 and A 12 not seen).

A reprint of 1607 W (speech in 2nd ed.), which see.

17. [Wells, William.] Epistola ad authorem anonymum Libelli . . . cui titulus Stricturæ Breves in Epistolas D.D. Genevensium & Oxoniensium.

Oxonii, e Theatro Sheldoniano, . . . MDCVIII, 4⁰.

An error for 1708.

18. **Wycliff,** John. [*woodcut.*] | TVVO SHORT TREA-‖TISES, AGAINST THE | *Orders of the Begging Friars,* | *compiled by* | THAT | *FAMOVS DOCTOVR OF THE CHVRCH,* | *and Preacher of Gods word* JOHN WICKLIFFE, *sometime fellow of Merton, and Master of* | *Balliol Coll. in Oxford, and afterwards* | Parson of Lutterworth in Lece- *stershire.* | Faithfully Printed according to two ancient | Manuscript Copies, extant, the one in | Benet Colledge in Cambridge, the o- ther remaining in the Publike Li-‖brarie at Oxford. | [*motto.*]

Impr. 2 : 1608 : sm. 4⁰: pp. [8] + 62 + [2] : p. 11 beg. *thow shalt haue*: English Roman. Contents :—p. (1) title: (2) "Faults escaped in the printing . . .": (3–8) Epistle dedicatorie to sir Thomas Flemynge, lord chief justice of England : signed "Tho: Iames." "from the Pub- like Librarie in Oxford. Feb. 10, 1608 ": 1–17, "A complaint of Iohn VVickliffe, exhibited to the King and Parliament": 19–62, "A Treatise of Iohn VVickliffe against the orders of Friars": (1–2) "An exposition of the hardest words," a gloss- ary.

See Wood's *Ath. Oxon.*, ii. 468. This is still the only printed edition of these two works of Wyclif, edited by dr. James. The usual titles of the treatises are "Four Articles" and "Objections of Freres." This book is usually found with the James volume above, which is alluded to in the dedication. Dr. James does not specify the MSS. from which these treatises are printed, but MS. C.C.C. (Cambr.) 296 seems to have both, while MS. Bodley 647 only contains the latter of the two.

1609.

1. **Butler,** Charles. THE | *FEMININE MONARCHIE* | OR | A TREATISE CONCERNING. BEES, | AND THE DVE ORDERING OF THEM : | *Wherein* | The truth, found out by experience and diligent | observation, discovereth the idle and fond | conceipts, which many haue writ- ten anent this subiect. | *By* | CHAR: BVTLER Magd. | [*device.*] |

Impr. 7 : 1609: (eights) 12⁰: pp. [240], sign. a⁴ b, A–N⁸ O⁴ : sign. B 1ʳ beg. *animum, artem,* I. 1ʳ *In Aquarius*: Pica Roman. Contents:—sign. a 1ʳ, title: a 2ʳ– a 4ʳ, "The preface to the Reader", dated from Wotton (St. Lawrence) 11 July 1609: a 4ᵛ–b 1ʳ, three commendatory poems, by Warner South (Latin) and A. Crosley: b 1ᵛ b 8ᵛ, "The contents of this Booke ": A 1ʳ–O 4ᵛ, the treatise.

See Wood's *Ath. Oxon.*, iii. 209, and 1633 B, 1634 B, 1682 B (in Latin) : there are also edd. at Lond. 1623 and (in Latin) 1673. This is a remarkable book, from the style and evident practical experience of its author. Rude engravings occur on sign. c 7ʳ, c 7ᵛ and (the first music printed at Oxford) F 1ʳ. The author mentions incident- ally in the preface that a book on bees by T. H. of London (presumably Thomas

Hill's *Profitable instructions for the ordering of bees*, Lond. 1579 and 1593) is really a plagiarism from Georgius Pictorius.

2. **Du Moulin,** Pierre (*d.* 1658).   HERACLITVS: | OR | MEDITATIONS VPON THE | vanity & misery of humane life, first | written in French by that excel-|lent Scholler & admirable di-vine *Peter Du Moulin* Mi-nister of the sacred | word in the refor- med Church | of Paris: | *And translated into English by* | R. S. Gentleman. | [*woodcuts.*]

Impr. 7 *a*: 1609: (twelves) 16°: pp. [14 + 121 + [1]: p. 11 beg. *time is,* I will say: English Roman. Contents:— p. (1) title: [3–6 Epistle dedicatorie "to his much honored Father: S. F. S.":

(7–13) "The authors epistle dedicatory to the Lady Ann of Rohan, Sister to the Duke of Rohan", signed "Peter du Moulin": 1–121, the work.

See 1634 D.   The original edition of Pierre Du Moulin's Héraclite, ou de la Vanité et Misère de la vie humaine was printed in 1609.   The present translator was probably Robert Stafford of Exeter college, who matr. on 15 Mar. 160⅘ at the age of 16, his father being sir Francis (?) Stafford, see Wood's *Ath. Oxon.*, ii. 291. and especially Bliss's MS. additions in his own copy of the *Athenæ* in the Bodleian.   The coincidence of initials with Richard Smith in the 1634 edition seems to be accidental.   See next art.

3. ——.   [Another issue, almost identical in appearance, but entirely reprinted: easy tests of the two issues are such as (1) on the titlepage of this second issue, if it be the second, the fourth line begins immediately under the beginning of the third line, whereas in the first issue it begins an *em* to the right: (2) the O of the imprint is upside down in the first issue: (3) in the title of the author's Epistle the second issue has "Anne", the first "Ann": (4) p. 41 l. 6 of text, the first issue has "Enuy", the second "Envy": (5) p. 121 l. 1 of text, the first issue ends with "God", the second with "God is." But it is difficult to say which is a reprint of the other: the second issue is more modern in spelling and type, and the woodcut ornaments are possibly less worn in the first.   In fact it is conceivable that the second issue is in reality a few years later.]

4. **D[unster],** J[ohn].   A | CONFESSION OF | CHRISTIAN RELIGION. [four *mottos,* then *woodcuts.*]

Impr. 7: 1609: (eights) 12°: pp. 52 + [4]: p. 11 beg. *and punishment*: English Roman.   Contents:—p. 1, title: 3–

48, the treatise: on p. 48 "Etiam sic sentio, sic credo. I. D.".

For the author see Wood's *Ath. Oxon.*, ii. 42.   This is a reprint, omitting the poem at the end, of 1607 D.   The paging is wild.

5. **H[eale],** W[illiam].   AN | APOLOGIE | FOR VVOMEN. | OR | AN OPPOSITION TO Mr. | Dr. G. his assertion. Who held | in the Act at Oxforde. | *Anno.* 1608. | *That it was lawfull for husbands to beate* | *their wiues.* | By W. H. of Ex. in Ox. | [*motto*: then *device.*]

Impr. 2: 1609: sm. 4°: pp. [6] + 66: p. 11 beg. *temnize marriage*: English Roman.   Contents:—p. (1) title: (3–4) dedication " to the honourable and right-

vertuous Ladie, the Ladie M. H. . . . .": (5) "The contents of this Apologie": (6) the arms of the University: 1–66, the work.

See Wood's *Ath. Oxon.*, ii. 89. where Wood states that the author was William Heale and the person opposed dr. William Gager, D.C.L. in 1589. The question "An liceat marito uxorem verberare" was one of those selected for the degree of D.C.L., 11 July 1608, but Gager was neither inceptor nor respondent. The lady M. H. seems from the dedication to have commanded Heale to undertake the task of replying and to have allowed him scant time in which to do it.

6. Reuter, Adam. EX L. VT | VIM 3. D. IVST : | ET JVRE. *QVÆSTIONES* | Iuris controversi | 12. | *Auctore* | ADAMO REVTER. Cotbusio L. | Siles. | [*woodcuts.*]

Impr. 11 : 1609 : sm. 4°: pp. [56], signn. A-G¹: sign. B 1ʳ beg. *pi patitur* : Pica Roman. Contents :—p. (1) title : 3-4) dedication to New College, dated "Cursim ex Musæo. Oxon." 1 Jan. "1609": (5-56) the 12 quaestiones.

See Wood's *Ath. Oxon.*, ii. 420. Wood is mistaken in calling Reuter a Welshman. He was a Silesian from Cottbus, as he testifies above and in the admission register of the Bodleian, 3 Sept. 1608. L probably stands for Licentiatus utriusque juris. He was never matriculated.

7. Sanderson, John. INSTITVTIONVM | DIALECTICARVM | *Libri Quatuor,* | *A* | IOANNE SANDERSONO, | Lancastrensi, Anglo, Liberalium | *artium Magistro, et sacræ Theologiæ* | *Doctore, Metropolitanæ Ec-* clesiæ Cameracensis Ca-|nonico, conscripti. | *Editio quarta.* | [*woodcuts.*]

Impr. 11 : 1609: 8°: pp. [4] + 91 + [1]: beg. ᵇ*Propriũ est*: Brevier Roman. Contents :—p. (1) title : (3-4) " Auctoris praefatio. Ad iuventutem bonarum artium studiosam": 5-91, the work.

A reprint of 1602 s, which see.

1610.

1. Benefield, Sebastian. DOCTRINÆ CHRISTIANÆ | SEX CAPITA, | *TOTIDEM PRÆLECTIONIBVS* | *in Schola Theologica Oxoniæ pro forma* *habilis discussa, &* | *disceptata.* | ACCESSIT APPENDIX AD CA- put secundum, de Consiliis Evangelicis, in | quâ ad omnes SS. PATRVM autorita- tes, ab HVMPHREDO LEECHIO | pro iisdem asserendis citatas, | respondetur. AVTORE | SEBASTIANO BENEFIELD. | SS. THEOLOGIÆ D. COLLEGII | Corporis Christi Socio. | [*motto*: then *woodcuts.*]

Impr. 11 : 1610: sm. 4°: pp. [20] + 208 + [12]: p. 11 beg. *& Sacerdotes,* 111 *ci me dedet*: English Roman. Contents :— p. (1) title : (3-6) dedication to bp. George Abbot, dated "Oxon. è Collegio Corporis Christi. Junii 7. 1610": (7) " Catalogus eorum quæ hoc opere continentur": (9-20) praefatio ad Academicos Oxonienses, 10 June 1610: 1-208, the work : p. 145 is a titlepage:—"APPENDIX | AD CAPVT. SECVNDVM, DE | CONSILIIS EVANGELI-| cis, in quâ ad omnes S. S. PA-|TRVM autoritates, ab HVM- PHREDO LEECHIO pro *iisdem asserendis cita- tas, respondetur.* AVTORE | SEBASTIANO BENEFIELD. | SS. THEOLOGIÆ D. COLLEGII | Corporis Christi Oxon. Socio. | [2 *mottos,* then *wood- cuts,* then impr. 7 and date]: 1-4 " Index locorum Sacræ Scripturæ . . .": (5-12) " Index rerum ": (12) " Ad lectorem . . . Errata typographica . . ." corrected in some copies.

See Wood's *Ath. Oxon.*, ii. 488. This work is a reply to a challenge from Leech.

2. Bunny, Edmund. OF DIVORCE | FOR ADVLTERIE, AND | Marrying againe: that there is | *no sufficient warrant so to do.* | WITH A

NOTE IN THE END, | *that* R. P. *many yeeres since was answered.* | By
EDM. BVNNY Bachelour of Divinitie. | [*device.*]

Impr. 7 *a*: 1610: sm. 4°: pp. [22] +
171 + [9]: p. 11 beg. *ees, which,* 111 *they
had not*: English Roman. Contents:—
p. (1 title: (3-5) Dedication to archbp.
Bancroft, dated Oxford, 3 July 1610: (6-
11) the preface, dated Bolton Percy, 13
Dec. 1595: (12-18) " An Advertisement
to the Reader," dated Oxford 4 June
1610: (19-20) " The Contents of the
Treatice . . .": (21-22) " The Table of
Method " an inserted quarto leaf folded,
printed on the recto only, a logical plan
of the argument: 1-171, the treatise:
(1-3) " Another note for the Reader "
against R. P. and Radford, dated Oxford,
22 June 1610: (4-9) " The Alphabet
Table . . . ," an index.

See Wood's *Ath. Oxon.,* ii. 222. The dedication states that the treatise was completed many years before (1595 ?) and that archbp. Whitgift had it in his hands and
approved it. The advertisement gives further details of the occasion and history of the
treatise. The note alludes to Bunny's connexion with Robert Parsons' *Resolution* or
Directory, see 1585 P, and J. Radford's *Directory.* See 1613 B.

3. **Dunster,** John. CÆSARS PENNY, | *OR* | A SERMON OF | OBEDI-
ENCE, PROVING | by the practise of all ages, that all per-*sons ought to be
subiect to the* | *King, as to the Su-*periour. | PREACHED AT St MARIES | in
Oxford at the Assises the 24 | of Iuly 1610. | By | JOHN DVNSTER
*Master of Arts and Fel-*low *of Magdal. Colledge.* | [*motto,* then *wood-
cuts.*]

Impr. 7: 1610: (eights) 12°: pp. [6]
+ 38 + [4]: p. 11 beg. *effendere no*: English Roman. Contents: p. (1) title: (3-6)
dedication to George Abbot bp. of London: 1-38, the sermon, on 1 Pet. ii. 13-
14.

See Wood's *Ath. Oxon.,* ii. 142.

4. **Holyoke,** Francis. A | SERMON OF OBEDIENCE | ESPECIALLY
VNTO AVTHORITIE | Ecclesiasticall wherein the principall controver-isies
of our church are handled, and many of | their obiections which are
refractorie to | the government established, answered | *though briefly as
time and space could* | *permit; being preached at a Visita-*tion *of the
Right Worsh:* | *M*r D. HINTON, | *in Coventree.* | *By* | FRAN: HOLYOKE.
[*woodcuts.*]

Impr. 7: 1610: sm. 4°: pp. [4] + 32:
p. 11 beg. *readeth, receiueth*: English
Roman. Contents:—p. (1) title: (2)
short dedication to sir Clement Throck-
merton: (3-4) preface to the author signed
I. D. H.: 1-32, the sermon, on Hebr.
xiii. 17: 32, "To the Reader ", an apology
for the rude style.

See Wood's *Ath. Oxon.,* iii. 346: and 1613 H. The author is the wellknown writer
of the Latin and English Dictionary. From the preface it is clear that the sermon,
which is written in an uncompromising tone, caused great opposition in Coventry, of
which town some curious details of the puritanical feeling are given: it is now published "not altogether against " the author's mind. See 1613 H.

5. **James,** Thomas. BELLVM GREGORIANVM | SIVE | CORRVPTI-
ONIS ROMANÆ IN OPE-RIBVS D. GREGORII M. JVS- su Pontificum Rom.
recognitis atque | editis, ex Typographia Vaticana, | *Loca insigniora,
observata à* | *Theologis ad hoc offici-*um *deputatis.* [three *stars*: then
device.]

Impr. 11: 1610: sm. 4°: pp. [8], sign. A⁴: p. 7 beg. *Rome* 1591: Long Primer Roman. Contents:—p. (1) title: (2) dedication to English theologians by "Tho. Iames" in Latin: (3-4 preface "benevolo lectori": (5-7) the list of passages: (7-8) conclusion: (8) list of MSS. used.

A table of passages corrupted in the Rome edition of 1591 and the Bâle ed. of 1564, of the Epistolae, Moralia and Pastoralia of Gregory the Great, compared with the readings of MSS. in the Bodleian, New, Oriel, Merton, Corpus and St. John's colleges, and belonging to Richard Bancroft, archbishop of Canterbury, Thomas Allen, and Rich. Hooker, the task being undertaken by 12 theologians.

6. **Price**, Daniel.   [*line*] | THE | [*line*] | DEFENCE | OF TRVTH AGAINST A | *booke falsely called* | THE TRIVMPH OF TRVTH | sent over from Arras A. D. 1609. | BY | HVMFREY LEECH late Minister. | *Which booke in all particulars is answered,* | *and the adioining Motiues of his* | *revolt confuted*: | BY | DANIELL PRICE, of Exeter Colledge in | Oxford, Chaplaine in ordinary to the most high | and mighty, the *Prince* of *Wales*. | [*motto,* then *device.*]

Impr. 7: 1610: sm. 4°: pp. [4] + 379 + [1]: p. II beg. *ving to vindicate,* III *your soule*: English Roman. Contents:— p. (1) title: (3-4) dedication to the Prince of Wales: 1-379. the work: (1) a postscript: then "Errata."

See Wood's *Ath. Oxon.,* ii. 511. The book is an answer to Leech's *A triumph of truth. Or declaration of the doctrine concerning Evangelicall counsayles; lately delivered in Oxford . . . n. pl.* 1609, 8°: and appears to reprint the whole of the latter work.

7. **Rainolds**, John.   SVMMA COLLO-|QVII JOHANNIS RAINOLDI | CVM JOHANNE HARTO | *De Capite & Fide Ecclesiæ* | VBI VARIÆ OBITER TRAC-TANTVR QVÆSTI-ones, de *Sufficientia,* & *orthodoxa expositione Scripturarum, Ministerio* | *Ecclesiæ, Functione Sacerdotali, Sacrificio Missæ,* unà cum aliis, | quę in religione agitantur controversiis; pręcipuè | verò, & ex instituto. quæstio de *Ecclesiæ regi-mine,* explicata in iis quę de Christi su-premâ Monarchiâ, de Petri pre-tensâ, Papę usurpatâ, Princi-pis *legitimâ supremitate* | disputantur. | A JOHANNE RAINOLDO CONSCRIPTA, CONVENIENTER COM-pendiis illis quæ uterque scripto man-dârat: examinata demum, à JOHAN-NE HARTO, atque (post addita quædam, quædam mutata ut ipsi | commodum videbatur) pro fideli narratione eorum, quæ | inter ipsos in Colloquio disserebantur, | habita & comprobata. | ANTE QVATVOR ET VIGINTI ANNOS EX AN-glico *sermone in Latinum versa, nunc autem primùm jussu, curáque Reverendis-simi atque vigilantissimi Præsulis,* RICHARDI BANCROFTI, | *Cantuariensis Archi-episcopi (qui non domesticarum modò,* | *quibus præest, sed etiam extrarum Ecclesiarum* | *bono impensè studet,) è situ & pulvere evo-cata, & in lucem emissa.* | HENRICO PARRAEO, *Gloucestrensi Episcopo, interprete.* | [*line.*] | [*device.*] | [*line.*]

Impr. 11: 1610: (sixes) la. 8° or perhaps fol.: pp. [16] + 402 + [14]: p. II beg. *bras; neque,* III *tit, & pre*: English Roman. Contents:—p. (3) title: (5-7) dedication to Christian iv, king of Denmark brother of the Queen, by Parry: (9-10) "Iohannes Hartus candido Lectori," dated "ex Arce Londinensi, Julii 7": (11-16) "Johaunes Rainoldus alumnis anglicorum Seminariorum Romæ & Rhemis": 1-402. the work: (3-11) "Index rerum . . .": (12-14) "Index locorum Sacræ Scripturæ": (14) "Errata typographica quorum quædam in omnibus, quædam in quibusdam exemplaribus tantùm." Every page is within a border of lines.

See Wood's *Ath. Oxon.*, ii. 15. The original *Summe of the Conference* was published at London in 1584 &c. The conference itself was at the Tower of London in about 1583, see Gillow's *English Catholics* iii (1888?). 155.

1611.

1. **Benefield,** Sebastian.　　A | SERMON | PREACHED IN St MARIES | Church in Oxford, March xxiv. MDCX. | at the solemnizing of the happy in-|*auguration of our gracious sove-*raigne KING IAMES. | WHEREIN IS PROVED THAT KINGS DOE | hold their kingdomes immediately from God. | *By* | SEBASTIAN BENEFIELD D. of Divinitie | *Fellow of Corpus Christi College.* | [*device.*]

Impr. 7 : 1611 : sm. 4°: pp. [4]+18 +[2]: p. II beg. *v/, is avowed* : English Roman. Contents:—p. (1) title: (3–4) dedication to John King, bp. of London, dated "from my study in Corpus Christi College. Septemb. 9. 1611 ": 1–18, the sermon, on Ps. xxi. 6.

See Wood's *Ath. Oxon.*, ii. 488. The Bp. of London had only been consecrated the day before this dedication.

2. Davies, John.　　Microcosmos : see 1603 D.

3. **Jesuit's Pater Noster.**　　THE | IESVITES PATER | NOSTER | *Giuen* | TO PHILIP III KING | of SPAINE for his new | *yeares gift this present* | yea e. 1611. | *Together with the Ave Maria.* | Written first in French : Engli-shed by *W. I.* | [*woodcuts.*]

Impr. 7 *a* : (four) 16° or 12° : pp. [8], sign. A^4 : sign. A 3^r beg. *There are:* Pica Roman. Contents:—sign. A 1^r, title, within a border : A 2^r–A 3^v, "The Jesuits Pater Noster," beg. "O Mighty Phillip King Of men" : A 4^r–A 4^v, "The Ave Maria to the Queene of France", beg. "WHen Iudas with a kisse betraid his Lord."

The only copy known is in the British Museum. A bitter satire against the Jesuits. In each piece the stanzas consist of four English lines and a Latin clause of the Pater Noster or Ave Maria (24 and 8 respectively). This piece was probably not printed at Oxford, two of the woodcuts being not otherwise found there.

4. **Reinolds,** John.　　EPIGRAMMATA, | AVCTORE IOAN-NE REINOLDO IN I.I. | Baccalaureo. Novi Colle-gij socio. | [*motto* : then *device.*]

Impr. 11 : 1611 : (eight) 12°: pp. [16], sign. A^8 : sign. A 4^r beg. 21. *Guiderius* : Long Primer Roman. Contents:—sign. A 1^r title : A 1^v divisions of "Prima Chilias complectens disticha tantùm an-thropina in decem centurias divisa " (Reges, Episcopi, Barones, Doctores, Equites, Graduati, Armigeri. Scholares, Generosi, Generalia) : A 2^r "Prima centuria reges Britannici & Anglici in Honorem regis Jacobi," with a motto : A 2^v "Elenchum personarum tibi lector exhiberemus, nisi libellus ipse esset pro Elencho": A 2^r– A 8^v the prima Centuria, 111 Latin distiches : A 8^v "Ad Lectorem," promising 10 Centuriae.

See Wood's *Ath. Oxon.*, ii. 148, and 1612 R. This is a first instalment of 111 distiches on Kings and Queens of Britain : only the second part (Episcopi) seems to have subsequently seen the light, in 1612.

1612.

1. Cleland, James.   The Instruction of | a young Noble-man. BY | JAMES CLELAND. | [*woodcut: the whole title is within a border of ornament.*]

Impr. 7 : 1612 : in every other point identical with 1607 C.

This is a reissue of the sheets of 1607 C, errata and all, with a new titlepage sewn in, the old one being torn off. The new titlepage was not printed at Oxford, as is shown by the woodcut ornaments and general style, but probably by W. Stansby for John Barnes in London.

2. Day, John, of Oriel college, Oxford.   CONCIO AD CLERVM. Habita in Templo *B. Mariæ* Oxon. | *Iunij* 25 *Ann. Dom.* 1612. JOANNES C. 9. V. 1. [*error for* 4] | *Donec* DIES *est.* | [*University arms.*]

Impr. 11 : 1612 : sm. 4° : pp. [4] + 25 + [3] : p. 11 beg. *Magistratus indicat* : English Roman. Contents :—p. (1) title : (2–3) Latin dedication to the heads of Colleges and Halls at Oxford, signed " Joannes Dayus," with a list of the — Heads : (4) text of the sermon, 2 Kings vi. 1–4 : 1 25, the sermon : (2–3) Latin letter from Day to dr. Thomas Clayton, dated from Oriel coll. Oxford, 11 July (1612).

See Wood's *Ath. Oxon.*, ii. 412, and 1615 D. The dedication gives a complete list of the Heads of Houses, and two official orders of the Colleges, in dignity, and in antiquity. The letter gives details of possible future publications by Day and personal points about dr. Clayton, who advised the printing of this sermon. At p. 21 is a list of Founders of Colleges.

3. Day, John.   Concio ad Clerum " In Joh. 9. 4. Oxon. 1612. qu[arto]."

So in Wood's *Ath. Oxon.*, ii. 412, after the notice of the preceding art., and no doubt due to confusion with it.

4. Day, John. DAVIDS DESIRE | TO GO TO CHVRCH : | as it was published in two | Sermons in St *Maries* | in Oxford. | The *One* the *fift* of *November* in the After- noone to the Vniversity 1609. The | *Other* on Christmas Day fo llow-'ing to the Parishioners | of that place. | *By* | IOHN DAY Bachelour of Divinity, and one of the *Fellowes* of | *Oriell Colledge.* | [*motto* : then *woodcuts.*]

Impr. 7 : 1612 : (eights) 16° : pp. [16] + 104 : p. 11 beg. *Even that* : English Roman. Contents :—pp. (1–2 [not seen]: (3) title : (5) dedication to Oriel college — and St. Mary's parish, Oxford : (7–15) " The Epistle dedicatorie " : 1–57 the 1st sermon, on Ps. xxvii. 4 : 57, an Erratum : 59–104. the 2nd sermon, on the same.

See Wood's *Ath. Oxon.*, ii. 412, and 1615 D. The second sermon is stated by the author to have been his first preached as Vicar of St. Mary's, succeeding mr. Wharton. At p. 40 he mentions Tuesday as a proverbially fatal day to the Irish.

5. Du Moulin, Pierre, the elder.   THE WATERS OF SILOE. | TO QVENCH | THE FIRE OF PVRGATORY | and to drowne the traditions, Lim- boes, mans satisfactions and all Popish | Indulgences, against the rea-

sons and allegations of a Portu-|*gall Frier of the order of* | St. Frances, *suppor-*|*ted by three* | *treatises.* | The one written by the same Franciscan and | entituled *The fierie torrent, &c.* | The other two by two Doctors of Sorbon. | The one intituled *The burning furnasse.* The | other *The fire of Helie.* | BY | PETER DV MOVLIN Minister of | Gods word. | [*motto*] | Faithfully translated out of French by *I. B.* |

Impr. 30: 1612: (eights) 12°: pp. [34]+406: p. 11 beg. *assured of*, 111 *one part of*: English Roman. Contents:— p. (3) title: (5 7) Epistle dedicatory to "sir Dudley Digs," signed "I. B.": (9-32) "The Preface to the Reader": (33-34) "The Contents of this booke": 1 406, the work, entitled "A Confutation of Purgatory."

The Friar against whom this book was written was Jacques (sign. A 4r) i. e. Jacques Suares, and the two Doctors were P. V. Palma Cayer and A. Duval (sign. A 3v). The first French edition was printed in 1603, entitled *Accroissement des eaux de Siloé* . . . The work is one of Du Moulin's less known productions.

6. **Henry,** prince, *d.* 1612. [*woodcuts*] | EIDYLLIA | IN OBITVM FVLGENTISSIMI | HENRICI | Walliæ Principis duodecimi, Romæque ruentis Terroris maximi, | *Quo nihil maius meliúsve terris* | *Fata donavere,* *boníque Divi* | *Nec dabunt, quamvis redeant in aurum* | *Tempora priscum.* | [*device.*]

Impr. 11: 1612: sm. 4°: pp. [36], sign. A-D' E²: sign. B 1r beg. *Amyntas*: English Roman. Contents:—sign. A 1v, title: A 2r, short dedication to the memory of prince Henry, in Latin: A 3r-E 2r, the poems: E 2v "Lectori ξυναποθνήσκοντι," an epilogue.

The writers and editor of these poems on the death of Prince Henry are more disguised than usual. The editor was undoubtedly "Jacobus Aretius," i. e. James Martin, of Broadgates hall. There is one poem in Chaldee (Hebrew type), one in Syriac, one in Arabic, one in Turkish (all three in Roman type) and a few in Greek. There are three Idylls, "Amyntas," "Tityrus," and "Daphnis," in Latin hexameter verse, presumably by the Editor.

7. ——. LVCTVS POSTHVMVS | SIVE | ERGA DEFVN-|CTVM ILLVSTRIS-|SIMVM HENRICVM WAL-|LIÆ PRINCIPEM, COL-|legij Beatæ Mariæ Magdalenæ | apud Oxonienses Mecænatem | longè indulgentissimum, | *Magdalenen-*|*sium of-*|ficiosa Pietas. | [*motto*: then *device.*]

Impr. 11: 1612: sm. 4°: pp. [2]+ 62+[8]:p. 11 leg. *Multáque Myrrhâ*: English Roman. Contents:—p. (1) title: (2) distich, within a border: 1-62, the poems: 1-7, ". . . Oratio funebris habita apud Magdalenenses tempore Prandij exequialis. 7° Decemb. quo die desideratiss. Principis Henrici funeri iusta persoluta fuere," signed "Accep. Frewen."

Poems, chiefly in Latin (a few in Greek and one Spanish), by members of Magdalen College, on the death of Prince Henry (*d.* 6 Nov. 1612), who was connected with the College through his tutor John Wilkinson.

8. **Hooker,** dr. Richard. [*woodcut.*] | THE | ANSVVERE | OF | Mr. RICHARD HOOKER TO A | *SVPPLICATION PREFERRED* | by Mr. WALTER TRAVERS to | the H H. Lords of the Pri-*vie* Counsell. | [*University arms.*]

Impr. 29: 1612: sm. 4°: pp. [2]+32 +[2]: p. 11 beg. *ver heard that*: English Roman. Contents:—p. (1) title: 1-32, the Answer.

See Wood's *Ath. Oxon.*, i. 697, and under *Travers*, below: both treatises have often been reprinted. This and the following treatises by Hooker seem to have been edited by Henry Jackson, see Wood's *Ath. Oxon.*, iii. 577.

9. ———. A | LEARNED | AND COMFORTA-|BLE SERMON OF THE | certaintie and perpetuitie of | *faith in the Elect; especially* | *of the Prophet Habak-*|*kuks faith.* | BY | RICHARD HOOKER, SOME- times fellow of Corpus Christi | *College in Oxford.* | [*University arms.*]

Impr. 29 : 1612 : sm. 4° : pp. [2] + 17 + [1] : p. 11 beg. *ly enimy is* : English　　Roman. Contents :—p. (1) title : 1-17, the sermon, on Hab. i. 4.

See Wood's *Ath. Oxon.*, i. 697.

10. ———. A | LEARNED | DISCOVRSE OF IV-|STIFICATION, WOKKES, | and how the foundation of faith | *is overthrowne.* | *By* | RICHARD HOOKER, sometimes Fellow | of Corpus Christi College | *in Oxford.* | **** [*University arms.*]

Impr. 29 : 1612 : sm. 4° : pp. [4] + 69 + [3] : p. 11 beg. *should make vs.* 61, *men, how many* : English Roman. Contents : p. (1) title : (3 4) "To the　　Christian reader" signed "from Corpus Christi College in Oxford" "Henry Iackson" : 1 69, the Sermon (on Hab. i. 4 : (2 3) (not seen).

See Wood's *Ath. Oxon.*, i. 697. This is the first edition, and apparently the first of Jackson's issues of Hooker's sermons.

11. ———. [*woodcut.*] | A | LEARNED | SERMON OF | THE NATVRE | OF PRIDE, | BY | RICHARD HOOKER, SOME-|times fellow of Corpus Christi | *College in Oxford.* | [*University arms.*]

Impr. 29 : 1612 : sm. 4° : pp. [2] + 17 + [1] : p. 11 beg. *dome as my* : English　　Roman. Contents :—p. (1) title : 1 17, the sermon, on Hab. ii. 4.

See Wood's *Ath. Oxon.*, i. 697.

12. ———. [*woodcut*] | A | REMEDIE | AGAINST SOR-|ROW AND FEARE, | delivered in a funerall | *Sermon,* | BY | RICHARD HOOKER, SOME-|times fellow of Corpus Christi | *College in Oxford.* | [*University arms.*]

Impr. 29 : 1612 : sm. 4° : pp. [2] + 14 : p. 11 beg. *full and faintharted* : English　　Roman. Contents :—p. (1) title : 1-14, the sermon, on John xiv. 27.

See Wood's *Ath. Oxon.*, i. 697.

13. **James**, dr. Thomas. *The Iesuits Downefall,* | THREATNED AGAINST THEM | BY THE SECVLAR | Priests for their wicked liues, accur-|*sed manners, Hereticall doctrine, and more then Matchiavil- lian Policie.* | TOGETHER | WITH THE LIFE OF FATHER | PARSONS *AN ENGLISH* | *IESVITE.* | [*motto,* then *woodcuts.*]

Impr. 29 : 1612 : sm. 4° : pp. [12] + 72 : p. 11 beg. *by a secular* : English Roman. Contents :—p. (1) title : (3-9) Epistle dedicatory to the "Iudges and Iustices of Peace for the Countie of Oxon.", dated "From the Publique Li-　　brary in Oxford, Sept. 16. 1612", signed "Tho. James" : (10-12) "The Propositions" : 1-51, 100 propositions against Jesuits stated and commented on : 52 72, the Life of Parsons.

Rare. See Wood's *Ath. Oxon.*, ii. 467. A story is told at p. 53 of Parsons dis-furnishing the Balliol College Library of "many ancient bookes and rare Manuscripts", and of his expulsion at a later period from the College.

14. [**Mornay**, Philippe de, seigneur Du Plessis.]   [*woodcuts.*] | TWO | HOMILIES | CONCERNING | the meanes how to re-|*solue the controver-sies of this time.* | *.*.* | *Translated out of French.* | [*woodcuts.*]

Impr. 7 : 1612 : (twelves) 16° : pp. [4] + 138 : p. 11 beg. *it be*, 111 *the one* : Pica English. Contents :—p. (1) title : (3-4) "To the Reader" : 1-71, homily on Matt. xvii. 5 (*Hunc audite*) : 72-138, homily on Matt. xix. 8 (*Non sic fuit ab initio*) : 138, "Errata."

Rare. There is another issue of this book in the same year, identical in every respect, even to the Errata, except that on the title after the asterisks and before the woodcuts come the words " *First written in French by* Ph. | Mornay, *and now trans-lated into English*", instead of the single line of the first issue. The second issue appears to be less rare. In each sign. A 1 is almost entirely gone, which consisted of the titlepage in some early form before a preface was decided on. The preface even in the second issue pretends that the author is unknown to the translator : who *may* be identical with the " I. V." of 1615 M.

15. **Panke**, John.   *ECLOGARIVS*, | OR BRIEFE SVMME | OF THE TRVTH OF THAT | Title of Supreame Governour, given | to his Maiestie in causes Spirituall, | and Ecclesiasticall, from the Kings of Israell, | in the old Testament ; the Christian Em-|perours in the Primitiue Church ; | confirmed by 40. Epistles of Leo the Bishop of Rome, vnto | the Emperours, Theo-|dosius, Martianus, | and Leo. | *Not published before.* | BY | IOHN PANKE. [*motto* : then *woodcut.*]

Impr. 7 : 1612 : (eights) 12° : pp. [2] + (82 + ?) : p. 11 beg. *may take an oath* : Pica Roman. Contents :—p. (1) title : 1-(82-?, the treatise.

Very rare. The running title is " The truth of the oath | of Supremacie." All after p. 82 (sign. F 2) is at present unknown, the British Museum copy being imperfect : but probably other copies exist.

16. **Sclater**, William, of King's college, Cambridge.   [*woodcut.*] | THE | CHRISTIANS | STRENGTH. | BY | WILLIAM SCLATER. | BATCHELAR OF DIVINITY | *and Minister of the word of God at* PIT-MISTER *in Somerset.* | [*University arms.*]

Impr. 7 : 1612 : sm. 4° : pp. [4] + 17 + [3] : p. 11 beg. **Be warmed* : English Roman. Contents :—p. (1) title : (3-4) dedication to William Hill of Pitmi[n]s-ter : 1-17, the sermon, on Phil. iv. 13.

See Wood's *Ath. Oxon.*, iii. 228.

17. ——.   [*woodcut.*] | THE | MINISTERS | PORTION. | BY | WILLIAM SCLATER. | BATCHELAR OF DIVINITY | *and Minister of the word of God at* PIT-|MISTER *in Somerset.* | [*University arms.*]

Impr. 7 : 1612 : sm. 4° : pp. [4] + 49 + [3] : p. 11 beg. *Christs priesthood* : English Roman. Contents :—p. (1) title : (3-4) dedication to Thomas Southcot of Moones-Ottery in Devon : 1-49, the ser-mon, on 1 Cor. ix. 13-14.

See Wood's *Ath. Oxon.*, iii. 228.

18. ——. [*woodcut.*] | THE | SICK SOVLS | SALVE. | BY | WILLIAM SCLATER. | BATCHELAR OF DIVINITY | *and Minister of the word of God at* PIT- MISTER *in Somerset.* | [*University arms.*]

Impr. 7 : 1612 : sm. 4° : pp. [4] + 36 : p. 11 beg. *wish? The* : English Roman. Contents :— p. (1) title : (3-4) dedication to John and Anna Horner of Melles in Somerset : 1-36, the sermon, on Prov. xviii. 14.

See Wood's *Ath. Oxon.*, iii. 228.

19. **Smith,** capt. John. *A MAP OF VIRGINIA* | VVITH A DE-SCRIPTI- ON OF THE COVNTREY, THE | Commodities, People, Govern-| ment and Religion. | *VVritten by Captaine* SMITH, *sometimes Go-'vernour of the Countrey.* | WHEREVNTO IS ANNEXED THE | proceedings of those Colonies, since their first | departure from England, with the dis-courses, | Orations, and relations of the Salvages, | and the accidents that befell | them in all their Iournies | and discoveries. | *TAKEN FAITHFVLLY AS THEY* | *were written out of the writings of* | DOCTOR RVSSELL. RICHARD WIEFIN. | THO. STVDLEY. WILL. PRETTIPLACE. | ANAS TODKILL. NATHANIEL POVVELL. | IEFFRA ABOT RICHARD POTS. | And the relations of divers other diligent observers there | *present then, and now many of them in England.* | *By VV. S.* | [*woodcuts.*]

Impr. 7 : 1612 : sm. 4° : pp. [8] + map + 39 + [5] + 110 + [2] : p. 11 beg. *some neere*, also *Such actions*, 101 *those humors* : English Roman. Contents :— p. (1) title : (3) dedication "To the hand" (explained by " I found it only dedicated to a Hand, and to that hand I addresse it "), signed "T. A." : (5-7) glossary of Indian words, with a few sentences &c. : after p. (8) a map, see below : 1-39, "The description of Virginia by captaine Smith" : (2) title. "The proceedings of the English colonie" &c. as next art. : (4-5) "To the Reader", signed "T. Abbay" : 1-110, the Pro-ceedings.

Very rare : priced in Quaritch's Rough List 88, (1888), no. 174 (cf. 181), at £125 : the map alone at £40. See Wood's *Ath. Oxon.*, i. 650. The map of Virginia which follows p. 8 is about 12⅜ in. high × 16¾ in. broad, taking the extreme limits of the copperplate (the inner bounding line is 12⅜ × 15¾ in.) : the title " Virginia " is on a scroll, and below the Scale of Leagues is " Discovered and Discribed by Captain Iohn Smith | Grauen by William Hole " : at the top left corner (to the reader) is a picture of Powhatan in state, and at the top right corner a figure of a "Sasquesahanoug" man. This first state of the map ought *not* to have "1607" below the inscription about Powhatan, *nor* "1606" below the word "Smith" in the words below the Scale, *nor* " Page 41 | Smith " in the lower right corner. *nor* the latitude and longitude marks on any side except the base ; all of which additions are on the reissue of the map in Smith's *General Historie of Virginia* . . . (Lond. 1624, fol.), and also in the reissue in *Purchas his Pilgrimes*, 4th part, Lond. 1625, except that instead of " Page 41 Smith " there is in the upper right (?) corner "1690," a reference to the page.

The W. S. of the first part is the rev. William Simmonds, D.D. of Magd. Coll. Oxford, for some time a resident in Virginia, see Wood's *Ath. Oxon.*, ii. 142, while the publisher of both parts was Thomas Abbay. The whole of the first part with trifling changes is reprinted in Smith's *Generall Historie of Virginia* (London. 1624, fol.) bk. 2, p. 21 : in *Purchas his Pilgrimes* (Lond. 1625, fol.) Lib. ix, ch. 3, p. 1691 : and the second part, slightly abridged, in the same books. bk. 3. p. 41, where the glossary and map occur, but the 12th chap. is considerably altered : and ch. 4. p. 1705, respectively . The whole is carefully reprinted from the 1612 ed. by Edw. Arber in his *English Scholar's Library. Capt. John Smith . . . Works.* (Birmingham, 1884), from whose notes the following words are taken :—

[Preface to part 1].

" The first part of this Work is evidently an expanded and revised text of that " Mappe of the Bay and Rivers, with an annexed Relation of the Countries and Nations that inhabit them " (p. 444), which President JOHN SMITH sent home, about November 1608, to the Council in London, as the result of his explorations in Chesapeake Bay in the previous summer.

That this book of travels &c. should have been printed at the Oxford University Press is a most singular fact. . . .

The hand printing presses in England were jealously registered, and locked up every night, to prevent surrepti'tilous printing; all through the lifetime of our Author: and the Company of Stationers of London especially watched with a keen jealousy the printing operations of the two Universities of Cambridge and Oxford, who each possessed a single hand press. See W. HERBERT's edition of J. AMES's *Typographical Antiquities*, iii, 1398, Ed. 1790, 4to.

This solitary hand printing press at Oxford, usually produced sermons, theological and learned Works, &c.; in the midst of which, this book of travels crops up in a startling manner.

Why could not, or would not SMITH get it printed in London? Had the revision of its second Part by the Rev. DR. SIMMONDS anything to do with the printing at Oxford? These nuts we must leave for others to crack.

Of course, being printed at Oxford, this book was not registered at Stationer's Hall, London . . .

It is sometimes misnamed the Oxford *tract*; but it is rather a book than a tract.

[Preface to part 2].

T. ABBAY states, . . . [in his preface] respecting this second Part,

Neither am I the author, for they are many, whose particular discourses are signed by their names. This solid treatise, first was compiled by Richard Pots, *since passing the hands of many to peruse, chancing into my hands, for that I know them honest men, and can partly well witness their relations true, I could do no lesse in charity to the world then reveale; nor in conscience, but approve.*

This Part is therefore the Vindication or Manifesto of the thirty or forty Gentlemen and Soldiers, who, under SMITH, saved the Colony . . .

This second Part of the *Map of Virginia*, compiled, and perhaps added to, by RICHARD POTS, . . . tested and revised by the Rev. WILLIAM SIMMONDS, D.D., . . . and published by T. ABBAY; is a condensed summary of the sayings and writings of the following seven Virginian Colonists:

GENTLEMEN.

Original Planters, 1607.

NATHANIEL POWELL (killed in the Massacre, 22 March 1622) . . .

THOMAS STUDLEY, Cape Merchant or Colonial Storekeeper (who died 28 August 1607) . . .

First Supply, 1608.

WILLIAM PHETTIPLACE, ...
Dr. WALTER RUSSELL, . . .
RICHARD WIFFIN, . . .

Second Supply, 1609.

THOMAS ABBAY . . .

SOLDIER.

Original Planter, 1607.

ANAS TODKILL . . .

In the revision of this text in the *General History*, Lib. 3, in 1624; the testimonies of eight other Gentlemen were incorporated (not *invented* as some would think) . . .

It is to be especially noted that, while he would endorse it all, Captain SMITH is not named as an author of *any portion* of this Second Part, either in the title in the previous page or in the text itself: therefore no allusion to the POCAHONTAS deliverance should be expected in it ; and there is none."

20. **Smith**, capt. John, of Virginia.   THE | PROCEEDINGS OF | THE ENGLISH COLONIE IN | Virginia since their first beginning from | England in the yeare of our Lord 1606, | *till this present 1612, with all their | accidents that befell them in their | Iournies and Discoveries. |* Also the Salvages discourses, orations and relations | of the Bordering neighbours, and how they be-|came subiect to the English. | *Vnfolding even the fundamentall causes from whence haue sprang so many mise-|ries to the vndertakers, and scandals to the businesse: taken faith-|fully as they were written out of the writings of Thomas | Studley the first provant maister, Anas Todkill, Walter | Russell Doctor of Phisicke, Nathaniell Powell, | William Phettyplace, Richard Wyffin, Tho-|mas Abbay, Tho: Hope, Rich. Potts and | the labours of divers other dili-|gent observers, that were | residents in Virginia. | And pervsed and confirmed by diverse now resident in | England that were actors in this busines. |* By W. S. | [*woodcuts.*]

Impr. 7 : 1612 : strictly speaking part of the preceding art., which see.

21. **Smyth**, rev. Richard, of Barnstaple.   MVNITION A-|GAINST MANS | *MISERY AND | MORTALITY. | A |* TREATICE CONTAI-|ning the most effectuall remedies | against the miserable state of | man in this life, selected | out of the chiefest | both humane | and divine | authors; | BY | RICHARD SMYTH *preacher of | Gods word in Barstaple in | Devon-shire.* | The second Edition. | [*woodcuts.*]

Impr. 7: 1612: (twelves) 16°: pp. [18] + 136 + [2] : p. 11 beg. *ved with the,* III *ry bosomes* : Long Primer Roman. Contents :—p. (1) title : (3-10) Epistle dedicatorie to lady Elizabeth Basset, dated from Barnstaple, 1 Jan. "1609" : (11-13) "The contents of the severall chapters" : (14-17) "The sinners counsell to his soule. A Sonnet of the Authors," 18 quatrains, beg. "Awake ô Soule, and looke abroad" : 1-136, the treatise.

Nothing seems to be known of the author, nor can I find mention of the 1st edition, presumably issued in 1609 or 1610. See 1634 s.

22. **Rawlinson**, rev. John.   MERCY TO A BEAST. | *A |* SERMON | PREACHED AT SAINT | MARIES SPITTLE IN | London on Tuseday in *Easter weeke.* 1612. | BY | IOHN RAWLINSON DOCTOR | *OF DIVINITIE.* [*University arms.*]

Impr. 7: 1612: sm. 4°: pp. [6] + 52 + [2]: p. 11 beg. *sort, that of* : English Roman. Contents :—p. (1) title : (3-6) epistle dedicatorie to Thomas lord Elles-mere, chancellor of the University of Oxford : 1-52, the sermon, on Prov. xii. 10.

See Wood's *Ath. Oxon.,* ii. 506 (where 1612 is misprinted 1602). The author was chaplain to lord Ellesmere.

23. **Reinolds**, John.   (Antony Wood asserts, in his *Ath. Oxon.,* ii. 149, that the second part of John Reinolds' Epigrammata (in

Episcopos) was printed at Oxford in 1612 in 8º.   No copy appears now
to be known.)

24. Travers, Walter.   [*woodcut*] | A | SVPPLICATI-|ON MADE TO
THE | PRIVY COVNSEL | BY | Mr WALTER TRAVERS. | [*University arms.*]

Impr. 29: 1612: sm. 4º: pp. [2]+25 | Roman. Contents:—p (1) title: 1-25,
+[1]: p. 11 beg. *there were*: English | the treatise.

This is an appeal made by Travers, who was afternoon preacher at the Temple in
London when Hooker was Master (about 1585-91), against the inhibition from
preaching issued against him by the Privy Council. Travers was ordained at Antwerp,
and had imbibed Genevan doctrine with which he opposed Hooker. See Hooker's
Answer above.   Both treatises have been frequently reprinted. in Hooker's *Works*, &c.
This issue does not seem to have been published by Travers himself, but only in order
to accompany Hooker's posthumously printed *Answer*.

25. Twofold treatise.   [*woodcut*] | A | TVVO-FOLD | TREATISE, |
THE ONE | *DECYPHERING THE* | *worth of* SPECVLATION, | *and of a retired*
life. | THE OTHER | CONTAINING A | discoverie of YOUTH | and OLD AGE. |
[*woodcut.*]

Impr. 7: 1612: (twelves) 16º: pp. [2] | Contents:—p. (1) title: 1-45, the first
+45+[1]+35+[1]: pp. 11 beg. *vn-* | treatise: 1-35, the second treatise.
willing to, and *her behalfe*: Pica Roman. |

26. Wakeman, Robert.   THE | CHRISTIAN | PRACTISE. | *A* | Sermon
preached on the Act-Sun-*day in S. Maries Church in* | *Oxford. Iul.*
8. 1604. | By Rob. WAKEMAN Bachelor | *of Divinity & fellow of*
Balliol | *Colledge in Oxford.* [*motto.*] | The second Impression. | [*wood-*
cuts.]

Impr. 29: 1612: (eights) 12º: pp. 92 | "Points handled in this Sermon": 3-92,
+[4]: p. 11 beg. *ple, but served*: Pica | the sermon, on Acts ii. 46.
Roman. Contents:—p. 1, title: 2, |

See 1605 W, of which this is a verbatim reprint.

27. Wakeman, Robert.   "Jonah's Sermon and Ninivehs repentance (*J. Barnes*) 1612 . . . 16*mo*."

So in the *Catalogue of the Second . . . portion of the . . . library formed by . . . Philip
Bliss*, Lond. (1858), p. 6, corroborated by a MS. note in a Bodleian copy (once the
editor's) of Bliss's Wood's *Athenæ*, which states that this is a third edition.

28. Wyclif, John.   WICKLIFFES WICKET, | OR | A LEARNED AND |
GODLY TREATISE OF | *THE SACRAMENT,* | *made by* | JOHN WICKLIFFE. |
Set forth according to an ancient | *Printed Copie.* | *⁎* | [*University*
arms.]

Impr. 29: 1612: sm. 4º: pp. [8]+18 | about Wyclif: dated "from Corpus
+[2]: p. 11 beg. *comprehend either*: | Christi College in Oxford, Iuly 6.
English Roman. Contents:—p. (1) title: | MDCXII," signed "Henry Iackson":
(3-7) preface "To the Christian Reader" | 1-18, the sermon, on Rom. xv. 30.

For the editor see Wood's *Ath. Oxon.*, iii. 577. The "ancient printed copie" was neither of the two issues dated Nuremberg 1546, but the undated one (probably 1546) "overseen" by M[iles] C[overdale], though Coverdale's preface is omitted. This was reprinted at Cambr. in 1851, and one of the others at Oxford in 1828.

1613.

1. Answer.   A | BRIEFE AN-|SWERE VNTO | Certaine Obiections | and Reasons against the Descen-|tion of Christ into Hell, late-|ly sent in writing vnto a | Gentleman in the | Countrey. | [*motto*, then *wood-cut.*] |

Impr. 32 : 1613 : the rest precisely as 1604 A.

A reissue of the sheets of 1604 A, with a new titlepage not printed at Oxford, the woodcut on title being unknown there.

2. Basse, William.   GREAT BRITTAINES | SVNNES-SET, | *BEWAILED WITH A SHOW-|ER OF TEARES.* | BY | WILLIAM BASSE.

Impr. 7 (not at foot of page, but, with date, close to rest of title) : 1613 : (eight & four) 16° : pp. [2] + 22 : Long Primer Roman.   Contents :—p. (1) title : (2) short dedication "to his honourable mas-ter Sʳ Richard Wenman Knight" : 1–19, the poem in 8-line stanzas, one on each page. ending with "finis." : 21–22, "A morning after mourning," 2 more stanzas, ending with "finis."

Extremely rare. This book has never been found except in fragments. and usually in the bindings of books. The Bodleian copy is complete : Merton college, Oxford, has nearly a complete one from its bindings : the British Museum copy was dr. Bandinel's (Sale Catal., Aug. 1861, no. 44), and contains the first 16 (?) pages. Other fragments are known to exist. chiefly in Oxford college library bindings. The poem was reproduced in facsimile in 1872 by W. H. Allnutt (100 copies).

It seems on the whole probable that this William Basse, who was a retainer in sir R. Wenman's house (Thame Park), is identical with the William Bas who wrote *Sword and Buckler* (Lond. 1602, 4°), which is a poetical defence of Serving-men against the scorn of their superiors. In Stanza 2 of the present poem is a clear reference to Bas's *Three Pastoral Elegies* (Lond. 1602, 4°) in the following terms :—" Not 'like as when some triviall discontents | First taught my raw and lucklesse youth to rue | Doe I to Flockes, now vtter my laments . . .". On the other hand the author of the *Sword and Buckler* had two sons, whereas here he speaks of his " young Muse." Other poems by "William Basse" (Bas) prepared for the press in 1653 were printed by J. P. Collier in 1870; and contributions to the *Annalia Dubrensia* (1636) and Walton's *Angler*, as well as an "Epitaph upon Shakespeare" are mentioned.

See J. Payne Collier's *Bibliographical account* (1865) p. 54, W. C. Hazlitt's *Hand-book* (1867) and (*Bibliographical*) *Collections*. 1st series (1876). The author is mentioned as living at Moreton near Thame, in Wood's *Ath. Oxon.*, iv. 222.

The subject of the first poem is Prince Henry's death, and of the " Morning " the wedding of the princess Elizabeth.

3. Benefield, Sebastian.   [*woodcut.*] | A | COMMENTARIE | OR EXPOSITION VPON THE FIRST | Chapter of the Prophecy of AMOS. de-livered | in xxi. Sermons in the Parish Church of | MEISEY HAMPTON *in the Di-|ocesse of Gloucester,* | BY | SEBASTIAN BENEFIELD DOCTOR | of Divinity and fellow of Corpus Christi | *College in Oxford.* | HEREVNTO IS ADDED A SERMON | *vpon* 1. *Cor.* 9. 19. *wherein is touched the law-*full vse of things indifferent. | [*motto*, then *woodcuts.*]

Impr. 29 *a* : 1613: sm. 4° : pp. [8] + 280 + [8] : p. 11 beg. *the* numbring, 111 *Which truth* : Pica Roman. Contents:— p (1) title : (3–4) dedication to bp. King, dated " from my study in Corpus Christi College in Oxford, Iuly 5. 1613 " : (5–7) "The Preface to the Christian Reader" : 1–264, the 21 "lectures": 265, a title:— "*[woodcut]* | A | SERMON | PREACHED AT WOTTON | VNDER EDGE in the Diocesse of | *Gloucester before the Clergy* there assem-'bled at the Episcopall Visitation of | THOMAS RAVIS, *late Bishop* | of *Gloucester*. 1605. | BY SEBASTIAN BENEFIELD. | [*motto*, then *woodcuts*]," impr. 7 *a*, 1613: 267–280, the sermon, on 1 Cor. ix. 19. with the head title " The Christians Libertie ": 280, Errata, corrected in many copies: (1–7) "A Table of such particulars as are contained in this Commentarie," alphabetical.

See Wood's *Ath. Oxon.*, ii. 488. A Latin translation of the lectures (without the sermon) was made by Benefield's pupil Henry Jackson (*ibid.* iii. 578) and published at Oppenheim in 1615, the preface being dated 21 May 1614 and addressed to Abraham Scultetus who had visited Oxford and made a friendship with Benefield. Benefield printed a commentary in 21 sermons on Amos chap. 2 at London in 1620, and in 17 sermons on Amos chap. 3 (together with a separate reprint of the present commentary) at London in 1629.

4. **Benefield**, Sebastian. THE | HAVEN OF THE AFFLICTED. | A SERMON | PREACHED IN THE | CATHEDRAL CHVRCH | OF GLOVCESTER | *Aug.* 10. 1613. | BY | SEBASTIAN BENEFIELD Doctor of Divinity | and fellow of C. C. C. | *in Oxford.* | [*motto*, then *woodcuts.*]

Impr. 7 : 1613: sm. 4° : pp. [6] + 20 + [2] : p. 11 beg. *wife, rebellious* : English Roman. Contents :—p. (1) title : (3–5) Epistle dedicatorie to bp. Miles Smyth, dated " from my study in Corpus Christi College in Oxford, August 27, 1613 " : (6) A quotation from Augustine with English translation : 1–20, the sermon, on Amos iii. 6.

See Wood's *Ath. Oxon.*, ii. 488.

5. **Bible**, Psalms. [*woodcut.*] | A | MEDITATI-'ON ON PART OF | THE SEAVENTH | PSALME. | [*motto*, then *device.*]

Impr. 7 *a* : 1613: sm. 4° : pp. [4] + 31 + [1] : p. 11 beg. *not Henry* : English Roman. Contents :—p. (1) title : (3) dedication " to the worshipfull his loving Cousen Mʳ E. N. and his virtuous wife Mistris K. N. . . .", dated " from Cote," 7 Nov. 1605 : 1–31, the meditation, on Ps. vii. 9.

Very rare.

6. **Bunny**, Edmund. OF | DIVORCE | For Adulterie, and | Marrying againe : that there | is no sufficient warrant | so to doe. | With a note in the end, that *R. P.* many | yeares since was answered. | By *Edm. Bunny* Batchelour of Deuinitie. | [*woodcut.*] [The whole title is within a border of woodcut ornaments.]

Impr. 32 : 1613 : &c. precisely as 1610 B.

This is a rare reissue of 1610 B with a new titlepage printed (not at Oxford, for the woodcut in the title is unknown there, but at London, perhaps by W. Stansby. The old titlepage was simply cut off, and the new one pasted in.

7. **Burhill**, Robert. DE POTESTATE | REGIA, ET VSVR-|*patione Papali*, | PRO TORTVRA TORTI, | Contra Parallelum ANDREÆ EVDÆ-|

MONIOANNIS Cydonij Iesuitæ, | *Responsio* | ROBERTI BVRHILLI | ANGLI. | [*motto*: then *woodcut.*]

Impr. 11 : 1613 : (eights) 12° : pp. [8] + 291 + [1]: p. 11 beg. *piscopi Romani, 111 quod contra vos*: Pica Roman. Contents:—p. (1) title: (3-4) Latin poem to prince Charles: (5) " Summa Tractatuum " : (6-8) " Index Responsionum iuxta ordinem apud Adversarium ": 1– 280, the treatise, in three " tractatus ": 280, " Lectori ", a note : 281–291, " Appendix, ubi Auctoris ante biennium edita Responsio, ad Martini Becani Refutationem (quam vocat) Torturæ Torti defenditur . . .".

See Wood's *Ath. Oxon.*, iii. 18. The bibliography of the controversy excited by the fresh oath of Allegiance imposed after the Gunpowder Plot is too intricate to be here treated. It was begun by card. Bellarmine (" Matthaeus Tortus ") and James I, and followed by bp. Andrewes' *Tortura Torti*, Andreas Eudaemon-johannes (André L'Heureux's) *Parallelus Torti ac Tortoris* (Colon. 1611), Martinus Becanus's *Refutatio Torturae Torti* (Mogunt. 1610), and many others. See *Du Moulin*, below.

8. **Byrd**, Josias.　　LOVES PEERELES PARAGON, | OR | *THE ATTRIBVTES, AND PROGRESSE* | OF THE CHVRCH. | A | SERMON | PREACHED IN st. MARIES IN | Oxford, and at HARFIELD in Middle-sex. 1613. | BY JOSIAS BYRD. | [Latin *motto*, and *translation* : then *woodcuts.*]

Impr. 7 *a* : 1613 : sm. 4° : pp. [6] + 27 + [3]: p. 11 beg. *The Church is*: Pica Roman. Contents :—p. (1) title : (3-5) dedication to Alice " dowager of Derby, wife to the . . . Baron of Elsemere ", dated from " Oxford, Alsoules. September the 3. 1613 " : 1–27, the sermon, on Cant. ii. 10 : (1) " Faults escaped ", at end " Delay is dangerous | and hast erroneous ", all between woodcuts.

The author took his B.A. degree at Cambridge, and incorporated at All Souls on 4 May 1609; M.A., 1610.

9. **Colmore**, Matthew.　　*ORATIO FVNEBRIS* | IN OBITVM | clarissimi viri et mvni-|FICENTISSIMI COLLEGII COR-|PORIS CHRISTI Oxon. benefactoris | GEORGII SANCTPAVL. Equitis | Aurati, habita in medijs epulis | Decembris 9. 1613. | *A* | MATTHÆO COLMORE | Somatochristiano. | [*motto*, then *device.*]

Impr. 11 : 1613 : sm. 4° : pp. [12], signn. A⁴ B²: sign. B 1ʳ beg. *mentis luxuriæ*: English Roman. Contents:—sign. A 1ʳ, title : A 2ʳ, Latin preface to the reader : A 3ʳ–B 2ʳ, the oration.

Rare. Little seems to be known of the subject of this Oration. Sir George St. Paul of Snarford never matriculated or took a degree, though according to the oration a commoner of Corpus for two years. His work at Lincoln and Stamford is described, and his munificence to the College and the new Schools at Oxford.

10. **Du Moulin**, Pierre.　　THE | ACCOMPLISHMENT | OF THE PROPHECIES; | OR THE THIRD BOOKE IN | defense of the Catholicke faith, con-|tained in the booke of the high | & mighty KING IAMES . I. | by the grace of God King | of Great Brittaine | and Ireland. | *AGAINST THE ALLEGATIONS* | *of* R. Bellarmine; *and* F. N. Coëffeteau *& other Doctors of the Romish Church*: | BY | PETER DV MOVLIN Minister of the | *word of God in the Church of Paris.* | *Translated out of French by* I. HEATH, *Fellow of* | *New College in Oxford.* | [*woodcuts.*]

Impr. 29 *a* : 1613 : (eights) 16° : pp. [18] + 484 + [2] : p. 11 beg. *Innocent in his, 111 of this, but this* : Pica Roman. Contents :—p. (1) title : (3-16) "The preface to the Reader" : (17-18) "A table of the matters contained in this third booke." : 1-484, the work.

See Wood's *Ath. Oxon.*, ii. 169. The title of the complete work is "Defense de la foy catholique contenue au livre de . . . Iaques I Roy de la grãd' Bretagne . . . contenue en trois liures. Contre la Response de F. N. Coeffeteau . . . Par Pierre du Moulin . . . 1612." The 3rd book was subsequently printed separately in French also, with the title "Accomplissement des propheties . . . Par Pierre du Moulin . . .". The original work by King James I is "Triplici nodo, triplex cuneus. Or an apologie for the oath of allegiance . . ." (anon., Lond. 1607, and with author's name Lond. 1609 &c. : in Latin *Apologia pro iuramento fidelitatis*, Lond. 1609, &c.). Coeffeteau's book was "Responce a l'Advertissement . . . par le . . . Roy de la grande Bretagne . . ." (Par. 1610). See *Burhill*, above.

11. **Gamage**, William. LINSI-WOOLSIE. | OR | TWO CENTVRIES OF | *EPIGRAMMES.* | *Written by* WILLIAM GAMAGE *Batche-|lour in the Artes.* | [*motto* : then *device.*]

Impr. 29 : 1613 : (eights) 12° : pp. [80], signn. A-E⁸ : sign. B 1ʳ beg. *Which vptvard's* : Pica Roman. Contents :— sign. A 1ʳ, title : A 2ʳ-A 2ᵛ, dedication to Katherine lady Mansell, daughter of lord Lisle : A 3ʳ-A 5ʳ, complimentary verses to the author : A 5ᵛ, "The Author to the Praisers of his booke", a short poem : A 6ʳ-E 8ᵛ, the 200 epigrams.

Very rare : see Wood's *Ath. Oxon.*, ii. 350. This author escaped Wood's notice altogether, and his claim to be an Oxford man eluded even dr. Bliss when he edited Wood in 1815 : but he subsequently writes in a MS. note, "I have now no doubt but that the author of *Linsi-Woolsie* was of Jesus, matriculated May 18. 1604, a native of Glamorgan, pleb. fil., æt. 20 : B.A. Dec. 17. 1607." The verses are extremely poor. The only copy at present known is that in the British Museum, which was the Heber copy (Heber sale, 1834, pt. 1, p. 141, no. 2734.)

12. **Glanville**, John. ARTICVLI | CHRISTIANÆ | FIDEI, QVAM EC-| CLESIA PROFITETVR | ANGLICANA, | VERSV | (*QVOAD EIVS FIERI POTVIT*) | *EXPRESSI FACILLIMO.* | [*device*, then two *mottos*.]

Impr. 11 : 1613 : sm. 4° : pp. [6] + 39 + [3] : p. 11 beg. *Articulus* 13 : English Roman. Contents :—p. (1) title : (3-4) dedication to John King, bp. of London, signed "Johannes Glanvillus" : (5) "Ad Carmen meum", a poem in Latin : (6) "Ad lectorem benevolum", a distich : 1-39, the 40 Articles, in elegiac verse, the 40th being "De Articulorum ratificatione" : (1-2) "De numero & nominibus Articulorum", a list : (2) "Ad lectorem", a Latin poem.

See Wood's *Fasti Oxon.*, i. 343. The verses are a paraphrase, with short additional poems of a meditative kind, written during an illness.

13. Godwin, Thomas. "*Romanæ Historiæ Anthologia. An English Exposition of the Roman Antiquities* . . . Oxon. 1613 . . . &c. qu."

So in Wood's *Ath. Oxon.*, iii. 52, but probably a misprint for 1614, which see, though Wood's apparent error is copied by Watt, Bohn's Lowndes, &c.

14. **Hinde**, William. A | *PATH TO PIETIE.* | LEADING TO THE | WAY, THE TRVTH, | AND THE LIFE | CHRIST IESVS. | *DRAWNE VPON THE* | Ground *and according to* | *the* Rule *of Faith,* | BY | WILLIAM HINDE |

Sometimes Fellow of Queenes | College in Oxford, and now | Preacher
of Gods word | at BVNBVRY in | Cheshire. | *Published for the benfit of
his owne* | *Flocke and Family.* | [*woodcut.*]

Impr. 7 : 1613 : (eights) 16°? : pp. [8] | Master, and to the 4 Wardens, of the
+56 : p. 11 beg. *Q. VVhat learne* : Pica | Haberdashers' Company in London, dated
Roman & Italic. Contents :—(1) title : | Bunbury, 19 July 1613 : 1–56, the treatise,
(3–7) dedication to sir Thomas Lowe, | in question and answer.

Rare. For the author see Wood's *Ath. Oxon.*, ii. 461, where *Banbury* is twice a
misprint for *Bunbury.*

15. **Holyoke**, Francis.   A | Sermon of Obedience, | Especially
vnto Authoritie Ecclesiasticall, | wherein the principall controuersies of
our | *Church are handled, and many of their* | Obiections which are
refractorie to | *the gouernment established, answered,* | though briefly as
time and | place could permit : | Being preached at a Visitation of the
right | Worshipfull M.D. *Hinton*, in *Couentry.* | *By* | FRAN: HOLYOKE. |
[*woodcut.*]

Impr. 29 : 1613 : (rest as 1610 II.)

A re-issue of the sheets of 1610 H, with a new titlepage printed in London, within
a border of woodcuts. The woodcut on the titlepage is unknown at Oxford.

16. **Hooker**, dr. Richard.   (A learned discourse of Iustification,
&c., a reprint of the title of 1612 II, adding after the word "Oxford
**** " :—*The second edition, corrected, and amended.* |

Impr. 7 : 1613 : sm. 4° : pp. [4] + 68 : | Reader ", signed as before, but dated
p. 11 beg. *should make vs,* 61 *man should* | "from Corpus Christi College in Oxford
hope : English Roman. Contents :—p. | the 6. of July. 1612." : 1–68, the dis-
(1) title : (3–4) "To the Christian | course, on Hab. i. 4.

A second edition of 1612 II : the alterations are chiefly literal and verbal.

17. **Kilbie**, Richard.   A | SERMON | PREACHED IN SAINT MA-|RIES
CHVRCH IN OXFORD | March 26. 1612. at the funerall of | THOMAS
HOLLAND, Do·ctor of the Chaire in Divini-|tie, and Rector of Exce-|ter
College, | BY | RICHARD KILBIE *Doctor of Divinity, Rector* | *of Lincolne
College.* | [*device.*]

Impr. 29 *a* : 1613 : sm. 4" : pp. [2] + | English Roman. Contents :—p. (1) title :
20 + [2] : p. 11 beg. *ken away euen* : | 1–20, the sermon, on 1 Cor. xv. 55–57.

See Wood's *Ath. Oxon.*, ii. 287 & 112. There is some little biographical matter
about dr. Holland.

18. **Oxford**, Exeter College.   *THRENI EXONIENSIVM* | IN OBITVM |
ILLVSTRISSIMI VIRI D. Ios|HANNIS PETREI, BARONIS DE | Writtle, Filij
honoratissimi viri D. | GVILIELMI PETREI ordinis au-|ree Periscelidis
Equitis clarissimi, | & quatuor Principibus à con-|silijs secretioribus. |
Qui Exoniense Collegium octo Socijs, amplis reditibus, | *plurimis priui-
legijs, auxerunt liberaliter & orna-|runt, Benefactores, Macenates, &*

Patroni | *munificentissimi.* | Per ejusdem Collegij Alumnos & ceteros studiosos. | [*device.*]

Impr. 11 : 1613 : sm. 4° : pp. [4] + 48 : p. 11 beg. Δεύτερος : English Roman. Contents :—p. (1) title : (3) dedication, partly in Latin verse, to lord William Petrie son of lord Petre of Writtle : 1–48, the poems.

Most of the poems are Latin, but 4 Greek, 2 Hebrew, and one French. John lord Petre died on 11 Oct. 1613.

19. —— Merton College.   [*woodcut.*] | BODLEIO-MNEMA. | [*device.*]

Impr. 11 : 1613 : sm. 4° : pp. [4] + 84 + [20] : p. 11 beg. *Ad sanam* : English Roman. Contents :—p. (1) title : (3) Latin dedication to the memory of sir Thomas Bodley, by Merton college : (4) Latin poem by the editor : 1–84, the poems, chiefly Latin : (1–18) "Oratio funebris habita in Collegio Mertonensi à Johanne Halesio ... anno 1613 Martij 29"; quo die Clarissimo Equiti D. Thomæ Bodleio funus ducebatur."

This book consists of about 80 poems (four in Greek, the rest in Latin) in memory of sir Thomas Bodley by members of Merton college, of which society Bodley was a fellow. The editor's name does not appear. Bodley died in London on Jan. 28. 161⅔, but both the dedication of this volume and p. 117 of the *Justa Funebria* (see below) state that it was on Jan. 29 : see Wood's *Ath. Oxon.*, ii. 126.

20. **Oxford**, University.   [*woodcut*] | EPITHALAMIA. | SIVE | LVSVS PALA-tini in nvptias celsissi-|mi principis domini fride-rici comitis pala-tini ad | *RHENVM,&C.ET SERENISSI-*|MÆ ELISABETHÆ IACOBI | *POTENTISSIMI* *BRI-*|*TANNIÆ REGIS* | *FILIÆ* PRIMO-*GENITÆ* | [*device.*]

Impr. 31 : 1613 : sm. 4° : pp. [128], signn. ( )² A-P⁴ Q² : sign. B 1ʳ beg. *Cur* *Atalanta*, M 1ʳ Impar nulla : English Roman. Contents :—sign. ( ) 1ʳ title : ( ) 2ʳ "Oxonia Heydelbergæ", a short poem : A 1ʳ-Q 2ᵛ, the verses.

Poems by Oxford men on the marriage of Frederick v, elector Palatine, with the princess Elizabeth of England on 14 Feb. 161⅔. All are Latin except five Greek, two Italian and one Hebrew (unpointed, Pica and Brevier).

21. —— University.   IVSTA FVNEBRIA | PTOLEMÆI | OXONI-ENSIS THO-|MÆ BODLEII EQVITIS | AVRATI CELEBRATA | in Academiâ Oxoniensi | *Mensis Martij* 29. | 1613. | [*device.*]

Impr. 31 : 1613 : sm. 4° : pp. [4] + 134 + [14] : p. 11 beg. *Sed calcanda*, III *Non famam.* Contents :—p. (1) title : (3) short Latin poems as by the University : 1–134, the poems : (1) a titlepage :—"ORATIO FVNEBRIS | HABITA IN | SCHOLA THEO-|LOGICA AB | ORATORE PVBLICO, IN OBI-|TV CLARISSIMI EQVITIS |*THOMÆ BODLEII.*| *⁕⁕⁕⁕* | [*device*]", impr. 11 : (3) "Ad lectorem " a preface by the orator (Isaac Wake) : (5–12) the oration.

About 270 poems, chiefly Latin, but two Hebrew (unpointed, Pica), four Greek, two Italian, one English : in memory of sir Thomas Bodley, see preceding art. The oration by Wake (see Wood's *Ath. Oxon.*, ii. 540) was reprinted in W. Bates's *Vitæ selectorum virorum* (1681), p. 416. The British Museum printed Catalogue, and the Catalogue of English Books in the Museum up to 1640, attribute this speech to Richard Corbet, by error.

22. **Petrucci**, Lodovico.   [*woodcuts*] | RACCOLTA, | D' ALCVNE RIME, DEL CAVA-|liere LODOVICO PETRVCCI, Nobile Toscano, in | più

luoghi, e tempi composte, & à diversi Pren-|cipi dedicate ; con la selua delle sue | Persecutioni. | *FARRAGO POEMATVM, EQVITIS LVDO-|VICI PETRVCCI, Nobilis Tuscani, diversis lo-|cis et temporibus conscriptorum. & ad diversos | Principes dedicatorum ; vnà cum syluá, sua-|rum Persecu-|tionum.* | * * * * | * * * | [*woodcuts.*]

Impr. 11 : 1613 : sm. 4º : pp. [130], signn. A–P¹, Q 1–3, one leaf, Q 4 : sign. II 1ʳ beg. *Quod signis* : English Roman. Contents :—sign. A 1ʳ, title : A 1ᵛ, A 2ᵛ, Italian dedication to James i signed "L'infelice Lodovico Petrucci Cavaliere" : A 2ʳ, A 3ʳ, the same in Latin : A 3ᵛ–Q 3ᵛ, the poems in Italian and Latin : (one leaf,⸱ "I principali errori commessi nell' Italiano di questo libro", a long list, beginning with the titlepage ("Caval-liere"), followed by some Errata in the Latin : the references oddly are to *pages*.

See Wood's *Ath. Oxon.*, ii. 293. This is a singular and uncommon book. The author was a soldier of fortune, who was admitted as a reader in the Bodleian as from St. Edmund hall on 27 Apr. 1611, but did not matriculate till 5 Sept. 1612. The verso of each leaf is in general Italian poems, and the recto of the next leaf a Latin version of them. On signn. F 2ᵛ and L 3ᵛ–M 2ᵛ are letters and testimonials about him : at II 1ᵛ is a poem in Italian and Latin on sir Thomas Bodley's death : at II 2ᵛ begins his *Selua* or *Sylva* in two parts, and at N 4ᵛ a long and curious account in Italian and Latin verse of his stay in England and particularly Oxford and New College, which he was forced to leave (in 1614 ?) by the puritanical party. On M 3ᵛ is an oration delivered in Italy, and on Q 2ᵛ is a poem in both languages on the death of dr. Rives, which is repeated on Q 3ʳ. The whole book was intended to be produced at the wedding of Frederick elector Palatine with the princess Elizabeth 14 Feb. 1614, but by the printer's delay was too late.

23. **Potter**, bp. Barnabas.　　　*THE BARONETS BVRIALL,* | OR | A FVNERALL | SERMON PREACHED | at the solemnitie of that honou- rable Baronet Sʳ EDVVARD | SEYMOURS buriall. | * * * | BY | BARNABY POTTER | *Bachelor in Divinitie, Fellow of Queenes Col-lege in Oxford, and Preacher to the | Towne of Tottnes in Devon.* | [*motto,* then *woodcuts.*]

Impr. 7 a : 1613 : sm. 4º : pp. [6] + 37 + [1] : p. 11 beg. *the divell* : English Roman. Contents :—p. (1) title : (3–5) dedication to sir Edw. and lady Mary Giles, dated "from your house at Bow-don, Aug. 24. 1613." : 1–37, the sermon, on Deut. xxxiv. 5.

See Wood's *Ath. Oxon.*, iii. 22. The author seems to have been private chaplain to sir E. Giles. He quotes against himself in the dedication a thesis disputed at the Act in Oxford 1613 "Doctior quisque fuit in scribendo parcissimus."

24. **Powell**, Thomas, of Brasenose college, Oxford.　　　[*woodcut*] | A | SERMON | PREACHED IN SAINT MA-|RIES IN OXFORD, | BY THOMAS POWELL. | 1613. | [*device.*]

Impr. 7 : 1613 : sm. 4º : pp. [4] + 17 + [3] : p. 11 beg. *vpon the text* : English Roman. Contents :—p. (1) title : (3–4) Latin dedication to dr. Thomas Singleton, principal of Brasenose : 1–17, the sermon, on Ex. xxviii. 34.

25. **Price**, Daniel.　　　DAVID HIS OATH OF | ALLEGEANCE TO | IERVSALEM. | THE | SERMON PREACHED ON ACT | SVNDAY LAST IN THE MORNING, | *IN Sᵗ. MARIES IN OXFORD.* | BY | DANIEL PRICE *Doctor in Divinity.* | [*motto,* then *device.*]

Impr. 7 : 1613 : sm. 4° : pp. [4] + 40 : p. 11 beg. *the blood of Ahab* : English Roman. Contents :—p. (1) title : (3-4) dedication to Charles i, dated from Exeter college Oxford, July 27 (1613) : 1-40, the sermon, on Ps. cxxxvii. 5.

See Wood's *Ath. Oxon.*, ii. 512. Every printed page has lines bounding the text, head-line and margin.

26. ——. PRINCE HENRY | HIS | FIRST ANNIVERSARY. | [*motto.*] | BY | DANIEL PRICE *Doctor in Divinity, one of* | *his Highnesse Chaplaines.* | [*device.*]

Impr. 7 : 1613 : sm. 4° : pp. [4] + 32 : p. 11 beg. *himselfe with* : English Roman. Contents :—p. (1) title : (3-4) dedication to Will. Cotton bp. of Exeter : 1-32, the "meditation."

See Wood's *Ath. Oxon.*, ii. 512, and 1614 P. The essay, which contains some personal matter about prince Henry of historical interest, was written for 6 Nov. 1613. The text, head-line and margin of each printed page are within bounding lines.

27. ——. SPIRITVALL | ODOVRS TO THE | MEMORY OF PRINCE | *HENRY* | IN FOVRE OF THE LAST SER-|mons preached in St JAMES after his High-'nesse death, the last being the Sermon be- fore the body, the day before | the Funerall. | BY | DANIEL PRICE *then Chaplaine in Attendance.* | [*motto,* then *device.*]

Impr. 29 : 1613 : sm. 4° : pp. [4] + 52 + [4] + 29 + [5] + 26 : p. 11 beg. (1) *the Manna,* (2) *ccs, the furies,* (3) *Lastly to close* : English Roman. Contents :—p. (1) title : (3) short dedication to Charles i : 1-26, sermon on Ps. xc. 15 : 27 52, sermon on 2 Sam. xii. 23, with running title to both " Meditations of Consolation in our Lamentations" : (1) a title :— "SORROVV | FOR THE SINNES OF | *THE TIME.* | *A* | SERMON PREACHED AT St. | JAMES on the third Sunday after | *the* PRINCE *his death.* | BY | DANIEL PRICE *then Chaplaine in Attendance.* | [*motto,* then *device,* then *impr.* 29. 1613.]" : (3-4) dedication to lady (Robert) Carey : 1-29, the sermon, on Ezek. ix. 4 : (2) title :—" TEARES | SHED OVER ABNER. | *THE* | SERMON PREACHED ON THE | Sunday before the PRINCE his fu-|nerall in St. JAMES Chappell | *before the body.* | BY | DANIELL PRICE *then Chaplaine in Attendance.* | [*motto,* then *device,* then *impr.* 29. 1613.]" : (4-5) dedication to sir David Murray : the sermon, on 2 Sam. iii. 31.

See Wood's *Ath. Oxon.*, ii. 511. Every printed page is within lines bounding the text, head-line and margin. The signatures are continuous, ( )² A-O¹ I¹². There is very little of historical interest in the sermons.

28. **Rainolds,** dr. John. D. IOHANNIS | RAINOLDI | OLIM GRÆCÆ LIN-'guæ Prælectoris in Col-|legio CORPORIS | CHRISTI apud | *Oxoni-enses,* | *ORATIONES 5. CVM* | *aliis quibusdam opusculis.* | OMNIA NVNC PRI-|*MVM EDITA.* | [*woodcuts.*]

Impr. 11 : 1613 : 16°.

At present this book is only known to me from a titlepage at the end of the 1614 edition of Rainolds's *Orationes* (which see), and notices in Thomas Bowman's *Catalogus librorum* (Oxf. 1687) [sign. I¹ :—" 146. Rainoldi (Joan) Orationes. Oxon. 1613 "] and Brit. Mus. MS. Harl. 5901, fol. 70 (Bagford). But the book is not likely to be really rare, unless the 1614 edition caused its recall or destruction.

29. ——. THE | PROPHECIE | OF OBADIAH | OPENED AND APPLYED IN | SVNDRY LEARNED AND GRA-|CIOVS SERMONS PREACHED | at ALL-HALLOWES

and S^t | Maries in Oxford, | By | that famovs and ivdici-|ous Divine
Iohn Rainolds D. | of Divinity and late President of | Corp. Chr. Coll. |
Published for the honour and vse of that famous Vni-|versity, and for
the benefit of the Churches of | Christ abroad in the Country, | by w. h. |
[*device.*]

Impr. 7 : 1613 : sm. 4° : pp. [8] + 136
+ [4] + 20 : p. 11 beg. (1) *promised to
consume,* (2) *had of the Philistines* : English Roman.   Contents :—p. (1) title :
(3–8) epistle dedicatory to D. Airay provost of Queen's college, Oxford, dated
" Bunbury in Cheshire, July 19. 1613 ",
signed " W. Hinde " : 1–136, the com-
mentary : (1) a title :—" A | SERMON |
VPON PART OF THE | eighteenth Psalme. |
PREACHED TO THE PVBLIKE | assembly
of Scholers in the Vniversity of | Oxford
the last day of August, 1586. | by | John
Rainoldes | *Vpon occasion of their meet-
ing to giue thankes to God* | *for the detec-
tion and apprehension of Trai-|tours, who
wickedly conspired against* | *the* Queenes
Maiestie and | the state of the Realme. |
[*motto,* then *woodcuts*] ", impr. 7 a, 1613 :
(3–4) " Iohn Rainolds, to the Reader
. . .", dated " At Corpus Christi College
in Oxford, Octob. 24. 1586." : 1–20, the
sermon, on Ps. xviii. 47–51.

See Wood's *Ath. Oxon.*, ii. 16 & 19, and 1586 R.   The commentary has special
reference to the 1st Epistle of St. Peter, and is in 10 divisions or sermons.   The editor,
William Hinde of Queen's college, seems to have long posses-ed the MS. of the
lectures.   The sermon is a reprint of 1586 R, and an integral part of the whole
volume, as the signatures show, which for the sermon begin at T 1.   Every printed
page has bounding lines to the text, margin and head-line.

30. S[mith], S[amuel].   Aditus ad logicam. In usum eorum qui
primò Academiam salutant. Autore S. S. Artium Magistro.   Imprint :—
" Anno Domini 1613 ", (eights) 12°.

This book is attributed to the Oxford Press by Wood (*Ath. Oxon.*, ii. 283), but was
not printed there, the woodcuts being unknown in Oxford.   See 1684 s.

1614.

1. **Andrewes**, John.   " Christ his Crosse, or the most comfortable Doctrine of Christ Crucified & joyfull Tidings of his Passion,
teaching us to Love & Embrace his Crosse, as the most Sweete &
Celestiall Doctrine unto the Soule, and how We should behave our-
selves therein according to the Word of God. Newly Published by
John Andrewes, Minister & Preacher of the Word of God at Barricke
Basset in the County of Wiltes."

So in manuscript in the Bagford collections (Brit. Mus. MS. Harl. 5901, fol. 71) :
see Wood's *Ath. Oxon.*, ii. 493, where the book is described as quarto in two parts.
The existence of a copy does not seem to be at present known, nor is one noticed in
the ordinary bibliographical works.

2. **Benefield**, Sebastian.   EIGHT SER-|MONS PVBLIKELY | PREACHED
IN THE V-NIVERSITY OF OXFORD, | the second at St *Peters* in the *East.* |
the rest at St *Maries* Church . Be-|gunne in the yeare 1595. | *Decemb.*
XIII. | *NOW FIRST PVBLISHED BY SEBAS-TIAN* BENEFIELD Doctor, and
Professour of | Divinity for the Lady MARGARET. | [*motto* : then *device.*]

Impr. 7 : 1613 : sm. 4° : pp. [4] + 153 + [7] : p. 11 beg. *It may be,* 111 *what they thinke :* Pica Roman. Contents :—p. (1) title : (3-4) dedication to lord Ellesmere, Chancellor of the University of Oxford, dated "from my Study in Corpus Christi College in Oxford, July 2. 1614 " : 1-57, three sermons on Luke ix. 23 : 58-153, five sermons on James iv. 10 : (2-6) "The table containing in alphabeticall order the particulars of this booke."

See Wood's *Ath. Oxon.,* ii. 488.

3. **Dawes,** Lancelot.　　　"*Two Sermons preached at the Assize holden at Carlisle, touching sundry Corruptions of these times.* Oxon. 1614. oct."

Impr. — : 1614 ? : (eights) 16° : pp. [8] + 146 + [2 ?] : p. 11 beg. *turall disposi-tion,* 111 *his brother, and :* Pica Roman. Contents :—p. (1) title : (3-7 dedication to dr. Robinson bp. of Carlisle, signed "Lancelot Dawes " : 1-75, a sermon, on Matt. xxvi. 15 : 77-146, a sermon, on Ps. lxxxii. 6-7 : (1-2) (*not seen.*)

Rare. See Wood's *Ath. Oxon.,* iii. 349, where the above title is given. The only copy readily traceable is that in the Bodleian which has lost the title and following leaf, beginning on ¶ 3, as well as a blank leaf there must have been after p. 146 sign. K 1.) The sermons and dedication, but not title, were reprinted in *Sermons . . . by Lancelot Dawes . . .* (Lond., 1653), pp. 49, 105. At present the date (1614) depends on Wood's accuracy.

4. **Day,** John.　　　DAY'S DYALL | OR, | HIS TWELVE HOWRES | THAT IS, | TWELVE SEVERALL LECTVRES | BY WAY OF CATECHISME. AS | they were delivered by him in the Chappel of | ORIELL COLLEDGE in Ox-|ford, in the yeeres of our Lord | God 1612, and 1613. | [*device,* then two *mottos.*]

Impr. 7 : 1614 : sm. 4° : pp. [8] + 329 + [3] : p. 11 beg. *which our Master,* 111 *speakes: The :* Pica Roman. Contents :—p. (1) title : (3-7) dedication to Oriel college, Oxford, dated "from my Study in that Colledge . . . Octob. 17. 1614 ", signed "John Day " : (8) "The severall arguments with the severall Texts of Scripture, of every severall Lecture in this Booke ", with a quotation : 1-329, the twelve lectures, with a page occasion-ally blank : (1-2) "To the Reader ", including a few errata.

See Wood's *Ath. Oxon.,* ii. 412. The author in the Preface says that he was appointed "Catechisme Reader " in Oriel for a year in 1612, when these lectures were delivered. In a footnote he alludes to his father John Day the printer. The general subjects are those of the Catechism, but carried further.

5. **Godwin,** Thomas.　　　ROMANÆ HISTORIÆ ANTHOLOGIA. | AN | ENGLISH EX-|POSITION OF | THE ROMANE AN-|TIQVITIES, WHEREIN | many Romane and English | offices are paralleld and di-|vers obscure phrases | *explained.* | BY | THOMAS GODWYN *Master of Arts.* | For the vse of ABINGDON *Schoole.* | [*device.*]

Impr. 7 : 1614 : sm. 4° : pp. [8] + 193 + [19] : p. 11 beg. *ved in the treasury,* 111 *cense the people :* Pica Roman. Contents :—p. (1) title : (3-4) dedication in Latin to dr. Francis James, dated "Abing-doniæ decimo calend. Aprilis, Anno 1613." [i. e. 23 Mar. 1613], signed "Thomas Godwinus " : (5-6) "Benevolo Lectori ": (7) Latin poems on the book by dr. Laurence Humphrey and John Sanford : (8) "A short table shewing the argument of every Booke and Section " : 1-193, the work : (2-18) "Index rerum et verborum maxime insignium."

See Wood's *Ath. Oxon.,* iii. 52. This was a popular work, see 1616 G, 1620 G, 1623 G, 1625 G, 1628 G, 1631 G, 1633 G, 1638 G, 1642 G, 1655 G, 1658 G.

Other edd. were printed at London in 1661, 1668, 1674, 1680, 1685 (14th), 1689 (15th), 1696 (16th). For the supposed 1613 ed., see 1613 G. Godwin's *Synopsis Antiquitatum Hebraicarum* (see 1616 G) and Francis Rous's *Archæologia Attica* (see 1637 R) may be regarded as companion works to the present volume, and are often found bound with it. The author apologizes for an English treatise on such a subject, and states that one of his main objects was to illustrate Cicero.

6. **Goodwin,** dr. William. A | SERMON | PREACHED BEFORE THE KINGS MOST | EXCELLENT MAIES-|TIE AT WOODSTOCKE, | AVG. 28. 1614. | BY | WILLIAM GOODWIN, *Deane . of Christ's | Church and Vice-Chancellor of the Vni-versity of Oxon.* | Published by Commandement. [*device.*]

Impr. 7 : 1614 : sm. 4° : pp. [2] + 38 : p. 11 beg. *à Peccato ; delicta* : English Roman. Contents :—p. (1) title : 1–38, the sermon, on Jer. i. 10.

See Wood's *Fasti Oxon.,* i. 297. The sermon is directed against the jurisdiction of the Roman Church over temporal sovereigns.

7. **Hooker,** dr. Richard. [*woodcut.*] | | TVVO | SERMONS | VPON PART OF | S. JVDES EPISTLE, | BY | RICHARD HOOKER *sometimes Fellow of Corpus Christi College in Oxford.* | [*device.*]

Impr. 7 *a*: 1614: sm. 4°: pp. [8] + 56: p. 11 beg. *Iesus with* : English Roman. Contents :—p. (1) title : (3–7) dedication to George Summaster, principal of "Broad-Gates Hall in Oxford," by "Henry Iackson," dated "Oxon. from Corp. Christ. College, this 13. of Ianuary, 1613" (161¾): 1–29, the first sermon: 31–56, the second, both on Jude 17–21.

Rare. See Wood's *Ath. Oxon.,* i. 698, and for the editor iii. 577. This and other Sermons of Hooker were reprinted with editions of the *Ecclesiastical Polity,* in 1622, &c.

8. **Jewell,** bp. John. ΑΠΟΛΟΓΙΑ ΤΗΣ ΑΓΓΛΩΝ | Εκκλησίας Ελληνιστὶ μετα-'φρασθεῖσα. | APOLOGIA ECCLE-siæ Anglicanæ Graecè versa. | *Interprete* I. S. *Bacc. in Art.* | Πρωτοπείρῳ συγγνώμη. | [*woodcuts.*]

Impr. 11: 1614: (twelves) 24°: pp. [24] + 214 + [2] : p. 11 beg. ὁ Ἱερώνυμος), ΙΙΙ θολικῆς πίστεως: Pica Greek. Contents :—p. (3) title : (5–13) dedication to dr. William Langton, pres. of Magdalen college, Oxford, dated 22 July 1613, signed "Joh. Smith": (15–20, "Lectori φιλέλληνι": 1 214, the Apologia : (1) "Errata sic corrigenda."

See Wood's *Ath. Oxon.,* i. 393, and 1639 J, 1671 J. The original edition of this celebrated *Apologia* was published in 1562, an English translation in the same year, and a German in 1589. This is the first Greek edition, as 1671 J is the first Welsh one. The translator, John Smith of Magdalen, explains that the task was meant as a College exercise merely, at first : and apologizes for using such words as Ἰουβιλαῖα, Βούλλαι, Ἰνδουλγεντίαι, for νὴ Δία in a Christian work, and for having only a month and a half to spare for the work.

9. **N., S.** "*Papistogelastes, or Apologues by which are pleasantly discovered the Abuses, Follies, Superstitions, Idolatries, and Impieties, of the Synagogue of the Pope, and especially of the Priests and Monks thereof,* written first in Ital. by N. S. and thence translated into French by S. J. and now out of French into English by R. W. ut supr. Oxon, 1614, in tw[elves]."

So in an account of Rowland Willet in Wood's *Fasti Oxon.*, i. 362: but I find no other reference to a copy.

10. Price, dr. Daniel.   PRINCE HENRY | HIS | SECOND | ANNIVER-SARY. | [*motto*.] | BY | DANIEL PRICE Doctor in Divinity, one of | his Highnesse chaplaines. | [*device*.]

Impr. 33: 1614: sm. 4°: pp. [4]+ 44: p. 11 beg. *wherein they might*: English Roman. Contents:—p. (1) title: (3-4) dedication to king Charles i, dated

" Ex. Coll. Novemb. 6. [1614] the fatall day of Prince Henries decease": 1-44, the discourse.

See 1613 P, and for the author Wood's *Ath. Oxon.*, ii. 511: there is some historical matter in the essay. Every printed page has its text, margin and headline within bounding lines.

11. Price, Sampson.   A | HEAVENLY | PROCLAMATION TO | FLY ROMISH BABYLON. | *A* | SERMON PREACHED AT OX-|ford in St MARIES *Nov. 21. 1613.* | BY | SAMPSON PRICE *Master of Arts of Exe-|ter Colledge and Preacher to the Citty* | *of Oxford.* | [*motto*, then *device*.]

Impr. 7: 1614: sm. 4°: pp. [4]+34 +[2]: p. 11 beg. *ing. drunkennesse*: English Roman. Contents:—p. (1) title: 3 4) dedication to sir Roger Owen, dated

" from my study at Exeter Colledge, Oct. 28. 1614.": 1-34, the sermon, on Rev. xviii. 4.

See Wood's *Ath. Oxon.*, ii. 489, where it is related that Price earned the name of " the Mawle of Heretics" for his violence against Roman Catholicism. The preface gives some biographical details of Price, incidentally.

12. Prideaux, dr. John.   CASTIGATIO | CVIVSDAM CIR-|CVLATORIS, QVI R. P. | ANDREAM EVDÆMON-|IOHANNEM CYDONI-|VM E SOCIETATE IE-|su seipsum nuncupat. | *OPPOSITA IPSIVS CA-lumnijs in Epistolam* ISAACI | CASAVBONI *ad Fronto- nem Ducæum.* | Per IOHANNEM PRIDEAVX SS. The-|ologiæ Doctorem & Collegij | *Exoniensis Rectorem.* | [*motto*, then *wood-cuts*.]

Impr. 11: 1614: (eights) 12°: pp. [16]+242: p. 11 beg. *apud regiam*, ill *us, qui opus*: Pica Roman. Contents:—p. (1) title: (3-7) dedication to archbp. Abbot, dated " Oxon. è Collegio Exoni-

ensi 9. Cal. Ianuarij": (9-13) " Ad Lectorem": (14-15 " Index capitum ...": 1-242, the work, p. 20 being blank.

See Wood's *Ath. Oxon.*, iii. 267. The circumstances of this book will be found in Mark Pattison's *Isaac Casaubon* (Lond., 1875: a work without an index), pp. 332, 347, 353, 410, esp. 438-443. Briefly, Casaubon's " . . . ad Frontonem Ducæum [Fronto Le Duc] . . . Epistola . . . (Lond. 1611) was a defence of the execution of Henry Garnett in 1606, against some Jesuit books ; a reply was published at Cologne in 1613 by Andreas Eudaemon-Johannes (L'Heureux) " . . . Epistola ad Amicum Gallum . . . item Responsio ad Epistolam Isaaci Casauboni ", the Responsio being dated 1612 on a separate titlepage. Then Prideaux was selected to answer the *Responsio*, in order to relieve Casaubon of the task: at p. 224 he quotes Casaubon's account of his father's last days. There is no real ground for Pattison's remark that " few copies of Prideaux's pamphlet survive " (*ut supra*, p. 443).

13. ——.   EPHESVS BACKSLIDING | CONSIDE- RED AND APPLY-|ED TO THESE | times, in a Sermon preached at | Oxford, in St MARIES, the | tenth of Iuly, being the Act | *Sunday*. 1614. | BY | IOHN PRIDEAVX,

Doctor of Divinity, | and Rector of Exceter College. | [*motto*, then *device*.]

Impr. 7: 1614: sm. 4°: pp. [8]+37 +[3]: p. 11 beg. *worthie comming*: English Roman. Contents:— p. (1) title: (3-6) dedication to dr. Bodley, "canon of Exeter, and parson of Shobrooke in Devon," dated "from Exeter College in Oxford, August 5.", 1614: 1-37, the sermon, on Rev. ii. 4.

For the author see Wood's *Ath. Oxon.*, iii. 265. This sermon was reprinted in 1621 (London) and 1636, see 1636 v. The dedication mentions dr. Bodley's favours towards Prideaux, and mr. (sir William?) Periam's to one Orford of Exeter Coll., Oxford.

14. **R[ainolds]**, J[ohn]. THE | DISCOVERY | OF THE MAN OF SINNE: | WHEREIN IS SET FORTH THE | CHANGES OF GODS CHURCH, | *In her* { *Afflictions by his Raigne.* | *Consolations by his Raine.* } First preached in divers Sermons to the Vniver-|sitie and Cittie of Oxon, by a Reverend & Iu-|dicious Divine IR. D. of Divinity and some-|times of Queenes College. | *And now published for the farther vse of both, and* | *comfort of all that hate Antichrist and loue* | *the Lord Iesus Christ wheresoever:* | *By W. H.* | [*motto*, then *woodcuts*.]

Impr. 7: 1614: sm. 4°: pp. [6]+50: p. 11 beg. *gather that seeing*: Pica Roman Contents:—p. (1) title: (3-4) dedication to dr. Airay provost of Queen's college, Oxford, dated "Bunbury in Cheshire, Iuly 8. 1614" signed "W. Hinde": (5-6) "Advertisement to the Reader," dated as before, with "William Hinde": 1-50, one sermon, on 2 Thess. ii. 3.

See Wood's *Ath. Oxon.*, ii. 16,462. Dr. John Raynolds was Scholar, Fellow, and President of Corpus Christi College, Oxford, but at one time or another was connected with Queen's, Merton, New College, University, and Oriel (*Register of the Univ. of Oxford*, vol. 2, ed. A. Clark, pt. 1, p. 4). There is no clear reference to the author being dr. Raynolds anywhere in the volume, but the fact is undoubted. The "Advertisement," as a matter of printing, follows the Sermon, but was probably intended to be torn off at that place and pasted in where it is described above.

15. **Rainolds**, dr. John. V. CL. | D. IOANNIS | *RAINOLDI,* | OLIM GRÆCÆ LIN-|guæ Prælectoris in *Collegio* | *Corporis Christi* apud | Oxonienses, | *Orationes Duodecim ; cum alijs* | quibusdam opusculis. | ADIECTA EST ORATIO | Funebris, in obitu eiusdem habi-|ta à M. Isaaco WAKE | Oratore Publico. | [*woodcuts*.]

Impr. 11: 1614: (twelves) 16°: pp. [6]+77+[17]+201+[111]: p. 11 beg. (1) *mi sint Antonii.* (2) *ponant laborioso,* (3) *speramus. Veruntamen*: Pica English. Contents:—p. (1) title: (3-6) "Iohannes Rainoldus Academicis Oxoniensibus ...", the Latin preface of 1587. R reprinted, date and all, "è Colleg. Corp. Christ. Februar. 2.": 1-36 (i) "Oratio post vacationem Natalitiam. 1576.", beg. *Epaminondam*: 37-77 (ii) "Oratio post vacationem Paschalem, Anno. 1576.", beg. *Etsi Vestros*: (2) (iii) a titlepage:—"ORATIO FV-|NEBRIS HABI-|ta in Templo Beatæ | *Mariæ* Oxon. | Ab Isaaco WAKE, | PVBLICO ACADE-|miæ Oratore, *Maij 25. An.* | 1607. quum mœsti | *Oxonienses, pijs mani-|bus* IOHANNIS | RAINOLDI | *parentarent.* |". woodcuts, then impr. 11: 4-12, the oration, beg. *Quam fragilis*: 1-45 (iv) "Oratio post festum Paschatis. 1574.", beg. *Pythagoram*: 46-66 (v) "Oratio post festum Nat. Chr. 1575. . . .", beg. *Cicero cum*: 67-111 (vi "Oratio post festum Paschatis, 1576.", beg. *Consideranti*: 112-142 (vii "Oratio post festum Michael. 1575.", beg. *Non modo*: 143-164 (viii) "Oratio post festum Michael. 1576.", beg. *Frequentia*: 165-196 (ix)

"" D. Iohannes Rainoldus Gulielmo Rain-oldo fratri suo . . .", a Latin epistle on the Church, beg. *Neque meus*, dated "Oxoniæ 4. Non. Septemb.": 197-199 (x) "D. Iohannes Rainoldus D. Gulielmo VVhitakero . . .", an epistle urging Whit-aker to answer Possevinus, dated "Oxon. 14 Kaleud. Novemb.", beg. "Facit amor": 200-201 (xi) the dedication to the Queen of Rainolds's *De Romanæ Ecclesiæ Idolo-latria*, dated "Iul. vii. MDXCVI," beg. *Quod olim*: (2) (xii) a titlepage:— "PLVTARCHI | CHÆRONENSIS | LIB. II. | 1 *De vtilitate ex hostibus | capienda.* | 2 *De morbis animi & cor-|poris.* | D. IOHANNE RAINOLDO | Interprete. |", woodcuts, then impr. 11: (4-12) Dedi-cation in Latin to Queen Elizabeth, dated "Oxon. è Coll. Corp. Christi.", (13-41, 42-50) the two treatises: (52) (xiii) a titlepage:—"MAXIMI TYRII | PHILO-SOPHI PLATONICI | Disputationes Tres, | 1 *Vitam activam contem-|plativâ,* | 2 *Contemplativam activâ | meliorem esse.* | 3 *Qui morbi graviores, ani-|mi, an cor-poris.* | D. IOHANNE RAINOLDO | Inter-prete. |," woodcuts, then impr. 11: (54-60 Latin dedication to Thomas Wilson "Regiæ Majestati à libellis supplicibus": 61-78, 79-94, 95-109) the three dispu-tations: (110) (xiv) the titlepage noticed in 1613. R.

See Wood's *Ath. Oxon.*, ii. 16, where he mentions that Henry Jackson was editor of all the Orations except the first two which had been published before, see 1587 R. The funeral oration was first printed in 1607, see 1607 (Wake, 2nd ed.). From a biblio-graphical point of view there is great confusion in this and the two subsequent editions of Rainolds's Orations (*Lond.* 1610, and *Lond.* 1628). For instance Wood himself in his remarks about Henry Jackson has confused the London edd. (B. C.) with the Oxford one (A).

In A (the present volume) it is impossible to reckon twelve Orations, and the book falls into three parts *a*) pp. [6] + 77 + [17], signn. A-D¹², sectt. i-iii. above: (*b*) pp. 201 + [1], signn. A-H¹², 1 I-5, sectt. iv-xi.: (*c*) pp. [110], signn. I 6-12, K-N¹², scctt. xii-xiv. In B (Lond. 1619) *a* is as before occupying pp. [12] + 1-106: then follows ". . . Rainoldi . . . Orationes quinque . . ." with a separate titlepage and preface by H. Jackson, occupying pp. 107-348 [the Orations beg. *Si quis* (1573). *Redit agricolis* (1574), *Si quantum vel, cum in isto* (1577). *Si quantum ad* (1573)]: then *b*, pp. 349-528: then *c*, the Plutarch and Maximus Tyrius, with separate titlepages, occupying pp. 529-624: there is no extra titlepage at end. In C (Lond. 1628) the same four sections occupy pp. [6] + 1-92, 93-302, 303-460, 461-548, corresponding closely with B in contents.

16. **St. Paul,** sir George.   "2591. Oxford. Carmina Funebria in Obitum Clarissimi Viri Georgii de Sancto Paulo Equitis Aurati C.C.C. Oxon. olim Convictoris et *ejusdem Benefactoris munifici,*   *Oxoniæ*, Jos. Barnesius, 1614" quarto.

So in the *Bibliotheca Heberiana* (Auction catalogue of Richard Heber's Library), part 6 (Lond. 1835), p. 185: the book sold for 9*s.* See 1613 C.

17. Smith, Samuel.   "262. Smith (Sam.) & Brerewoodi Logica— Oxon. 1614."

So in "Catalogi Librorum Richardi Davis bibliopolæ. Pars secunda" Lond. 1686, p. 77. No Oxford edition of Smith's *Aditus ad Logicam* is at present known, see 1613. S, 1617. S (reff. there), but as the latter is a 3rd edition, there may well have been one printed at Oxford in this year, of which no copy has yet found its way into bibliography. Of Brerewood's *Logica* there is a London 1614 ed., probably alluded to in Davis's Catalogue above.

1615.

1. **Anyan,** Thomas.   A | SERMON | PREACHED AT SAINT | MARIE SPITTLE | *April. 10. 1615.* | BY | THOMAS ANYAN Doctour of Divinity, and | *President of Corpus Christi College* | *in Oxon.* | [*device.*]

Impr. 2: (1615): sm. 4°: pp. [2] + 42 + [2]: p. 11 beg. *like Vessels*: English Roman.   Contents:—p. (1) title: (3) dedication to Thomas Egerton lord Ellesmere, chancellor of the University: 1–42, the sermon, on Acts x. 34 35.

See Wood's *Fasti Oxon.*, i. 359.

2. **Benefield**, Sebastian.   THE | SINNE | AGAINST THE HOLY GHOST DISCOVERED: | AND OTHER CHRISTI-|an doctrines delivered: | IN | TWELVE SERMONS VPON PART | of the tenth Chapter of the Epistle to | the Hebrewes. | *By* | SEBASTIAN BENEFIELD *Doctor of Divinity* | *and Professour for the Lady Margaret,* | *in the Vniversitie of* OXFORD. | [*motto,* then *device.*]

Impr. 2: 1615: sm. 4°: pp. [4] + 181 + [3]: p. 11 beg. *hold on their,* 111 *The writer of*: Pica Roman.   Contents:—p. (1) title: (3–4) dedication to William lord Paget, "From my Study in Corpus Christi College in Oxford, March 25. 1615": 1–181, the 12 sermons, on Heb. x. 26 31: (1–3) "The Table containing the particulers of this booke," an alphabetical index.

See Wood's *Ath. Oxon.*, ii. 488. The dedication states that the Sermons were written "many years" before, and existed in several MS. copies, and thanks lord Paget for benefactions to the Margaret Professor. The Sin is discovered to be a malicious denial of Christianity.

3. **Brasbridge**, Thomas.   "*Questiones in Officia M. T. Ciceronis, compendiariam totius opusculi Epitomen continentes.* Oxon. 1615, oct. Dedicated to Dr. Laur. Humphrey president of Magd. coll. an. 1586."

So in Wood's *Ath. Oxon.*, i. 526, cf. Wood's *Historia et Antiquitates Universitatis Oxoniensis* Oxon. 1674 lib. 2, p. 197. See 1592 B.

4. **Case**, John.   "292 Casus (Joan.) de Sphæra Civitatis — — Oxon. 1615"

A doubtful entry in Tho. Bowman's *Catalogus librorum* (Oxf. 1687) sign. 11 1ᵛ.

5. **Day**, John.   CONCIO AD CLERVM | IN SECVNDI, VEL QVARTI, RE-GVM, CAPITIS SEXTI, VER-|SVM PRIMVM, SECVNDVM, | TERTIVM, ET QVARTVM. | Habita in Templo *B. Mariæ* Oxon. | Iunij 25°. *Ann. Dom.* 1612. | PER IOANNEM DAYVM BACCALAV-|reum in Theologia, et Collegij ORIELEN-SIS apud Oxonienses Socium. | EDITIO SECVNDA. | [*device,* then *motto.*]

Impr. 11: 1615: sm. 4°: pp. [4] + 26 + [2]: p. 11 beg. *dimento minimè*: English Roman.   Contents:—p. (1) title: (3) Latin dedication, nearly as 1st ed.: (4) "Thema," the text: 1–26, the sermon: (1–2) letter, as 1st ed.

See Wood's *Ath. Oxon.*, ii. 412. This is a reprint with a few changes of 1612 D.

6. ——.   DAVID'S DESIRE | TO GOE TO CHVRCH: AS IT | was published in two Sermons | in S⸵ MARIES in | OXFORD. | The *One,* the *Fift* of *November,* in the Afternoone | to the Vniversitie, in the Yeare of our Lord | God 1609. the *Other,* on *Christmas* | *Day* next following, to the Pa-|rishioners of that | place. | [*device,* then 2 *mottos.*]

Impr. 7 *a*: 1615: sm. 4°: pp. [8] + 48: p. 11 beg. *waies but often*: Pica Roman. Contents:—p. (1) title: (3-8) epistle dedicatory to Oriel college and St. Mary's parish, Oxford, signed " Iohn Day": 1-25. the first sermon: 26, quotation from Camden's Annales about queen Elizabeth: 27-48, the second sermon.

See Wood's *Ath. Oxon.*, ii. 411. This is a reprint of 1612 D, but neither is that fact mentioned, nor is the author's name on the title.

7. ——.   DAY'S FESTIVALS | *OR,* | *TWELVE OF HIS SERMONS*: | DELIVERED BY HIM AT SEVERAL | times to the PARISHIONERS of St MARYES | in OXFORD, on the three Chiefe FESTI-|VALS of the Yeere, CHRISTMAS, | EASTER, and WHIT-SONTIDE. | *THREE OF VVHICH SERMONS,* | *are touching* our SAVIOUR; ONE, *the* HO-LY GHOST; TWO, *the* TWO SA-|CRAMENTS; *The other* SIX, *such* | *severall* DVTIES *as belong to* | *the severall sorts of all* | CHRISTIANS. | [*device, then two mottos.*]

Impr. 7 *a*: 1615: sm. 4°: pp. [8] + 352: p. 11 beg. *the Nations of. 111 selfe same Steps*: Pica Roman. Contents:— p. (1) title: (3-7) dedication to Oriel college, Oxford: 8 " The Severall Arguments, with the Severall Texts.. ", with a note: 1-160, six sermons: 161-188, short pieces on the Lord's Supper, containing a letter to " Ea." of St. Mary's parish dated " Oriel. Coll. March. 2.", " Sacred Fragments" (on both Sacraments) and prayers: 189-352, the six last sermons.

See Wood's *Ath. Oxon.*, ii. 411. The dedication alludes to the circumstances of preaching " David's Desire to go to Church,' see 1612 D, and foreg. art.

8. **Evans,** Edward.   VERBA DIERVM, | OR, | *THE DAYES REPORT,* | OF GODS GLORY. | *As it hath beene delivered some yeeres since, at Foure Ser-mons, or Lectures vpon one Text, in the Famous V-niversity of* OXFORD; *And since that time* | *somewhat Augmented; And is now com-mended vnto All Times to be Aug-mented and Amended.* | *By* | EDWARD EVANS, Preacher and Minister | *of Gods word.* | [3 *mottos, then wood-cuts.*]

Impr. 7: 1615: sm. 4°: pp. [4] + 181 + [3]: p. 11 beg. *tie? And,* 111 *to come. By*: English Roman. Contents:—p. (1) title: (3) dedication to the honour of God: (4) " Faults of Omission and Commission . . ." beg. " Pag. 5. for ὀλὴν Read, ὅλην ": 1-181, the four sermons, on Ps. xix. 2: (1) 3 mottos.

See Wood's *Ath. Oxon.*, ii. 168, where a MS. note by Bliss in his own copy shows that the author *was* the Fellow of New College, and that Wood was in error in supposing otherwise. See next art.

9. ——.   VERBA DIERVM, | [&c. precisely as foreg. art.]

Impr. 7: 1615: sm. 4°: pp. [4] + 181 + [3]: p. 11 beg. *tie? And,* 111 *to come. By*: English Roman. Contents: - p. (1) title: (2-3) dedication to the honour of God, with words in italic inserted between the two parts of the original dedication: (4) " Faults of Omission and Commission," beg. " Pag. 31. lin. 1 For *tations* ": rest as foreg. art., except 4 mottos, not 3.

This is a second issue, with some of the text re-set, with additions and alterations, as for instance on p. 144 in which the paginal misprint " 134 " is corrected, and which begins " newes of His Glory," instead of " of Speech more warrantable."

10. **Hakewill,** George.   THE | VANITIE OF | *THE EYE,* | First

beganne [&c. exactly as 1608 II, second edition, except "*third*" for "*second*," "*Author*" for "*Authour*," and different woodcuts on title.]

Impr. 2: 1615: (twelves) 16°: pp. [8] + 170 + [24]: p. 11 beg. *and by conse-quence,* III *maker; I*: Pica Roman. Contents :—p. (3) title: 5 8, "The Con-tents …": 1-170, the work: (1-18) additional quotations and notes for the third edition, preceded by an explanatory paragraph.

See 1608 II. This is a reprint throughout, with the addition of some quotations on an extra sheet.

11. Haven. "The hauen of the afflicted / *Oxon.* 1615.".

A doubtful entry in the *Bibliotheca classica … authore M. Georgio Draudio* (Francof. 1625), 2nd part, p. 269: probably referring to Sebastian Benefield's Sermon, 1613, which see.

12. **Mornay**, Philippe de, seigneur Du Plessis.   AN | HOMILY VPON | THESE WORDS | of Saint Matthew, | Chap. 16, v. 18. | *Tu es Petrus.* | WRITTEN FIRST | in French by that Hono-*rable and learned perso-* nage, Monsieur Du PLES-SIS MORNAY. | AND TRANSLATED | into English by I. V. | [*woodcuts.*]

Impr. 2: 1615: (twelve & six) 16°: pp. [8] + 28: p. 11 beg. *ceaued of God*: Long Primer Roman. Contents :—p. (3) title: (5-7) epistle dedicatory to Dr Prideaux rector of Exeter college Oxford "my most respected good Master," signed "I. V": 1-28, the homily.

The "I. V." is supposed to be John Verneuil sublibrarian of the Bodleian, who was a Frenchman by birth: but he was of Magdalen and so not very likely to dedicate his first work to the head of another college. The collocation of this work and another translation of Mornay (1612 M) in a Bodleian volume suggest the possibility of the same person being translator of both.

13. Powell, Gabriel.   "*Prodromus. A Logical Resolution of the first Chapter of the Epist. of St. Paul to the Rom.* Lond. 1600. Ox. 1602. oc. … Printed there again in Lat. 1615. oct. *Theological and Scho-lastical Positions concerning Usury.*—Pr. with *Prodromus.*"

So in Wood's *Ath. Oxon.*, ii. 25, perhaps dubious.

14. **Prayer**, book of Common.   LIBER | PRECVM | PVBLICARVM IN VSVM ECCLE- siæ Chathedralis Chri-*sti Oxon.* | [*woodcuts.*]

Impr. 11: 1615: (eights) 16°: pp. [40] + 240 + [16]: p. 11 beg. *filiæ Sion,* III 12. *Nam liberabit*: Pica Roman. Contents :—p. (1) title: (3-40) Matutinæ preces, Vespertinæ preces, Letania, not in full: 1-240, the Psalms, in Latin: (1-6) Special prayers, "Pro officio totius Ecclesiæ in Communi," "Pro Rege," "Tempore Pestilentiæ," "Pro docili-tate." "Gratiæ. Ante cibum" and "Post cibum": (7) the versicle and response still used at Ch. Ch. after the Anthem, a prayer for the King and a commemora-tion of Henry viii, founder of Ch. Ch., all in Latin: (9-16) Psalms 43, 114, 117, 119 (part), 133, 150, in Latin rhyming verse, perhaps a separate piece of print-ing.

See 1639 P, 1660, 1676, 1689, 1726, all which editions differ in the details of contents, and the 1639 ed. is entitled "Liber Psalmorum et precum …" It may be noted that the signatures and paging constitute the Psalms a separate book, whereas the Stationers' Company had obtained in 1603 a monopoly of printing the Psalms, confirmed in 1615.

15. **Prideaux,** dr. John.   [*woodcut*] | CHRISTS | COVNSELL FOR EX-|DING LAW CASES. | *AS IT HATH BEENE DELIVE-*|red in two Sermons vpon the 25th | Verse of the 5th of Matthew. | By | JOHN PRIDEAUX *Doctor of Divinity and* | *Rector* of Exceter Colledge. | [*motto,* then *device.*]

Impr. 2 : 1615 : sm. 4°: pp. [2]+58 : | Roman.   Contents :—p. (1) title : 1-26, p. 11 beg. *Tremelius notes :* English | 27-58, the sermons.

See 1636 P.

16. [**Sanderson,** Robert].   LOGICÆ AR-|*TIS COMPENDIVM.* | *In quo* | Vniversæ artis Synopsis, methodo ac for-|mâ ad Scholarum vsum, quàm fieri | potuit, accommodatissi-|mâ breviter pro-|ponitur. | *In privatam nonnullorum gratiam* | *& vtilitatem tantisper edi-*|*tum, dùm ad pleniora* | *maturuerint.* | [*woodcuts.*]

Impr. 11 : 1615 : (eights) 16°: pp. [8] +230 + [Appendixes, see below] 124 + [4] : p. 11 beg. *possunt. Individua :* 111 *tur auferendo :* Pica Roman.   Con- | tents :—p. (1) title : (3-6) "Elenchus capitum" : (7-8) "Admonitio ad Lectorem" : 1-230, the Compendium, in three parts.

Very rare. See Wood's *Ath. Oxon.,* iii. 626. See 1618 s (2nd. ed., reprinted in Sanderson's Works, vol. 6), 1631 s (3rd), 1640 s (4th), 1657 (5th), 1664 (6th), (7th), 1672 (8th), 1680 (9th), *no date* (10th, according to dr. Jacobson, Sanderson's editor), and 1707, 1741, 1841, 1854 (in Sanderson's Works, Oxf. 1854, vol. 6). Cf. 1602 s. The *Admonitio* declares that the Appendixes are not ready and must be omitted. There is no clue to the author in the book. The only copy I have seen (in Queen's College Library, Oxford) has the Appendixes of the second edition bound with it, so possibly they were printed in time to be issued with some copies.

17. **Sharpe,** Lionel, archdeacon of Berkshire.   ARTICLES MIN-ISTRED IN | the Visitation of the Right Worshipfull | Mr. DOCTOR SHARPE Arch-|*deacon of Barkeshire, in the yeare* | *of our Lord God.   1615.* | [*device.*]

Impr. 4 : 1615 : sm. 4°: pp. [12], signn. A⁴ B²: sign. B 1ʳ beg. *at morning :* Pica English.   Contents :—sign. A 1ʳ, | title : A 2ʳ-B 2ʳ, 51 articles : B 2ᵛ, "The oath of the Church-wardens."

18. **Wake,** Isaac.   REX PLATONICVS : | [&c. exactly as 1607 w, 2nd ed., except "Aug." for "Aug", "An." for "Anno.", "*NARRATIO,*" "AB ISAACO WAKE", "*e-*|*mendatior,*" and "Tertia" for "Secunda."]

Impr. 13 c : 1615 : (twelves) 16°: pp. [8] +224 +[20] : p. 11 beg. *minum me-moriam,* 111 *cunano irruunt :* Long Primer Roman.   Contents :—as 1607 w., 2nd ed., except "13 Cal. Jul." in dedi- | cation, and in 2nd titlepage "HABI-|ta," "beatæ | ," "ACADE-|miæ," "*piis,*" "*parenta-*rent.", and the Oration is (6-19), and dated 1615.

This is a reprint verbatim but not literatim. Cf. 1607 w., 2nd ed.

1616.

1. **Advice.**   [*woodcut*] | THE | ADVISE OF | A SONNE, NOVV PRO-|FESSING THE RELIGI-|ON ESTABLISHED IN | the present Church of England, | *to his deare Mother, yet a Ro-*|man Catholike. | [*device.*]

Impr. 2 : 1616: sm. 4º: pp. [2] + 38 : p. 11 beg. *answere, that* : English Ro- man. Contents :— p. (1) title : 1–38, the work.

A controversial discourse against Roman Catholicism.

2. **Bailey,** Walter. *TWO* | TREATISES | CONCERNING | the Preser- uation of | EIE-SIGHT. | The first written by Do- ctor BAILY sometimes of Ox-|ford : the other collected | *out of those two famous* | Physicions FERNELIVS | and RIOLANVS. | [*device.*]

Impr. 34 : 1616: (eights) 12º: pp. [8] + 64: p. 11 beg. *yeeld into*: Pica Roman. Contents :—p. (3) title : (5–7) “To the Reader,” a preface by I[ohn] B[arnes]: 1–24, “A broefe Treatise concerning the preseruation of the eye sight”: 25-62, “A Treatise of the principall diseases of the eyes, gathered *out of* Fernelius *and* Iohn Riolamus *Doctors of Phisicke.*”

See Wood's *Ath. Oxon.,* i. 586 and 1602 n, for the first treatise. Johannes Fernelius and Johannes Riolanus the elder, both French physicians, died in 1558 and 1609 re- spectively, but neither wrote a special treatise on eyesight. The preface is no doubt by John Barnes and alludes to the worth and undeserved obscurity of Bailey's work. The whole book with the possible exception of the titlepage, was printed in London, the woodcuts being quite unknown at Oxford. Even the arms of the University on the titlepage are re-cut on wood. The first treatise is only a reprint, Dr. Bailey having died in 1592, and the whole book, preface and all, was reprinted at London in 1626.

3. **Fuller,** Nicholas. *MISCELLANEORVM* | *Theologicorum,* | QVIBVS NON | MODO SCRIPTVRÆ DIVINÆ, | SED ET ALIORVM CLASSICO- rum Auctorum plurima monumenta explican-|tur atque illustrantur; | LIBRI TRES, | *Plu- rimarum observationum, in hac Editione, insigni* | auctario Locupletati : | *His insuper accessit, consimilis argumenti,* Liber | item Quartus, *antehac nunquam pervulgatus.* | *AVCTORE* | Nicolao Fullero antiquæ & inclytæ Ecclesiæ Cathedralis | SARISBVRIENSIS | *Canonico.* | [*woodcuts.*]

Impr. 11 : 1616: sm. 4º: pp. [16] + “452” (440–443 are omitted in the num- bers of pages) + [8] + “453”—“645” + [3]: p. 11 beg. *mi, quibus ait,* 111 *Astro- logum,* 501 *sum est illud*: English Ro- man. Contents :—p. (1) title : (3–8) Epistola dedicatoria to sir Henry Wallop, dated “Ex Musæo nostro Aldingtonæ” 25 Jan. 1615 i. e. 161⅚: (9–10) “Ad lec- torem”: (11–16) list of chapters in books 1–3: 1–452, the work, bks. 1–3: (1–5) dedication of bk. 4 to dr. Arthur Lake warden of New College, Oxford, dated “Ex Musæo nostro Aldingtonæ 1 Feb. 1615” i. e. 161⅚: (6–8) list of chapters in bk. 4: 453–645, the work, bk. 4: (1) “Errata . . . & prætermissa . . . .”.

See Wood's *Ath. Oxon.,* ii. 327, the biography in which appears to be largely founded on the preface to this book. The first edition of bks. 1–3 is *Heidelberg* 1612, the pre- face dated 1609. There is a reissue of the sheets of the present edition (Errata and all) “Londini, apud Johannem Billium. Anno 1617,” the titlepage alone being newly printed and the old one torn off. The 4th and 5th books were published at Leyden in 1622, and all reprinted in the 9th volume of the *Critici Sacri* (Lond. 1660).

4. **Godwin,** Thomas. ROMANÆ HISTORIÆ ANTHOLOGIA | [&c. exactly as 1614 G, except “Eng-|lish,” “and | divers,” “For the use of” (not italic) : and after “Schoole” is added | “Editio Secunda.” |]

Impr. 2 : 1616: sm. 4º: pp. [8] + 193 + [19]: p. 11 beg. *ved in the treasurie,* 111 *ense the people*: Pica Roman. Con- tents :—exactly as 1614 G, except “Ca- lend.” and “Godwinus.”

See 1614 G., of which this is a verbatim and almost paginatim, but not literatim, reprint.

5. **Godwin,** Thomas. SYNOPSIS | ANTIQVITATVM HE-|braicarum, ad explicationem vtri-|usque Testamenti valde | necessaria. | *AD FACILI-OREM INTELLE-|CTVM, PLVRIMA SVNT COL-|LATA CVM REBVS HO-|DIE IN vsv.* | *Authore* | THOMA GODWINO | in *Art. Magistro.* | [*device.*]

Impr. 11 : 1616: sm. 4°: pp. [8] + 190 + [10]: p. 11 beg. *illic loci.* 111 *& inter semen*: English Roman. Contents:—p. (1) title: (3–4) dedication to James Montague bp. of Bath & Wells, dated "Oxon. pridie Iduum Januarij": (5–6) " Lectori ...": (7) a table of the divisions: 1 190. the work: (1) Comparative table of Hebrew and English Coins: (3–9) " Index rerum et verborum maxime insignium."

See Wood's *Ath. Oxon.*, iii. 52, and 1613 G note. The author was chaplain to the bp. of Bath and Wells. The *Moses et Aaron* of the same author (Lond. 1625 and often) covers some of the same ground, but is a distinct work and in English.

6. [**Nixon,** Anthony.] THE | DIGNITIE | OF MAN, | Both | IN THE PERFECTIONS | OF HIS SOVLE AND BODIE. | [*line*] | *SHEWING AS WELL THE* | faculties in the disposition of the one: as the | Senses and Organs, in the composi-|tion of the other. | By *N. A* | [*line*, then *device* with *woodcuts*, then *line*]

Impr. 35: 1616: sm. 4°: pp. [8] + 125 + [3]: p. 11 beg. *Q. How are*, 111 *Q. What is the*: English Roman. Contents:—pp. (1–2) [not seen]: (3) title : (5–7) dedication to William Redman of Great Shelford, signed N. A.: 1–125, the work: (1–3) [not seen.]

Very rare. This book is questions and answers on almost every subject concerned with man's body and mind. Not a line of it was printed at Oxford, the woodcuts and type differ from Oxford ones, and even the device, which is like the smaller Oxford Arms of the University, is from a different block. The British Museum catalogue supplies the author's name.

7. **Persius.** AVLVS PERSIVS FLACCVS | *HIS* | SATIRES TRANSLA-*TED INTO ENGLISH*, | BY | BARTEN HOLYDAY M^r of Arts, | and Student of Christ-Church | *in Oxford.* | [*motto*] | The second Impression. | [*device.*]

Impr. 2 : 1616: (eights) 12°: pp. [72], signn. A-D⁴ E⁴: sign. B 4ʳ beg. *Dissolu'd vnto*: Long Primer Roman. Contents:— sign. A 1ʳ title: A 2ʳ–A 5ʳ, "To the Reader": A 5ʳ B 1ʳ, Complimentary letter from John Ley, and verses by John Wall and others: B 1ᵛ–E 2ʳ, the translation, with a few notes: E 2ᵛ–E 3ʳ, " An apostrophe of the translatour to his Authour *Persius*," &c.

See Wood's *Ath. Oxon.*, iii. 523. The first edition seems to be unrecorded. There are London editions of 1617, 1635, and 1650: and Oxf. 1673. Some edition of this book was entered at Stationers' Hall by John Barnes on 14 Nov. 1616, and another by William Arundel, by John Barnes's consent on 29 Mar. 1617.

8. **Robinson,** Hugh. "*Preces.* Written for the use of the children of Winchester school in Lat. and Engl. *Grammaticalia quædam*, in Lat. and Engl. *Antiquæ Historiæ Synopsis.* All which were printed at Oxon. 1616. in a large oct."

So Wood's *Ath. Oxon.*, iii. 395.

1617.

1. **Angelus,** Christophorus.　　　[*woodcut.*] | Πόνημα Χριστοφόρου τοῦ
Ἀγγέλου, Ἕλληνος τοῦ πολλῶν πλη- γῶν, καὶ Μαστίγων γευσαμένου ἀδίκως παρὰ
τῶν | Τουρκῶν διὰ τὴν εἰς Χριστὸν Πίστιν. | [*device.*]

Impr. 36: 1617: sm. 4°: pp. [16], signn. A⁴ B⁴: sign. B 1ʳ beg. σφόδρα· καὶ ὅτι: Pica Greek. Contents :—sign. A 1ʳ | title : A 2ʳ, dedication to English people in Greek : A 2ʳ–B 2ʳ, the work : B 2ᵛ, a woodcut, see below.

Rare. See Wood's *Ath. Oxon.*, ii. 633, and the next art. Two very rude wood engravings illustrate the text, one on sign. A 4ʳ depicting the tortures inflicted on Angelus by the Turks, the other sig. B 4ᵛ) possibly an emblematic figure representing England.

2. ——.　　　[*woodcut*] | CHRISTOPHER ANGELL,—a Grecian, who
tasted of many | stripes and torments inflicted by the | Turkes for
the faith which he | had in Christ Iesus. | *₊*₊* | [*line*] | [*woodcut*] |
[*line.*]

Impr. 36: 1617: sm. 4°: pp. [16], signn. A B⁴: sign. B 1ʳ beg. *much in debt*: Pica Roman. Contents:—sign. A 1ʳ title: | A 2ʳ, dedication to England: A 2ʳ–B 3ʳ, the work: B 4ʳ, a woodcut, see below.

Rare. See Wood's *Ath. Oxon.*, ii. 633, 1618 A, and preceding art., of which this is a translation, in good English. The same two engravings occur as in the Greek text, on sign. A 4ʳ and B 4ʳ.

3. **Duck,** Arthur.　　　[*woodcut.*] | VITA | HENRICI | CHICHELE | ARCHI-
EPISCOPI | *CANTVARIENSIS* | SVB REGIBVS HENRIC: V. ET VI. | DESCRIPTA AB
ARTHVRO DVCK: | *LL. D.* | [*woodcuts.*]

Impr. 11: 1617: sm. 4°: pp. [2]+ 108+[4]: p. 11 beg. *licentur etiam*: English Roman. Contents:—p. (1) title: | 1–108, the Life: (1) account of the sources of the Life: (3) " Errata."

See Wood's *Ath. Oxon.*, iii. 258. The Life was reprinted in [Bates's] *Vitæ Selec- torum . . . virorum,* Lond. 1681, p. 1: and an English translation was published at London in 1699. This Life of the founder of All Souls contains some solid historical matter, with a few documents. Some copies want the Errata.

4. **Hales,** John.　　　A | SERMON | PREACHED AT Sᵗ MA-|RIES IN OXFORD
VPON | TVESDAY IN EASTER | *VVEEKE,* 1617. | *CONCERNING THE ABVSES* |
of obscure and difficult places of holy | *Scripture, and remedies a- gainst*
them. | By IOHN HALES, | FELLOW OF ETON COLLEDGE, | and *Regius Pro-*
fessour of the Greeke | tongue in the Vniversitie | of Oxford. | [*line :*
then *device :* then *line.*]

Impr. 36: 1617: sm. 4°: pp. [2]+41 +[1]: p. 11 beg. *monly they*: English | Roman. Contents :—p. (1) title : 1–41, the sermon, on 2 Pet. iii. 16.

For the author see Wood's *Ath. Oxon.*, iii. 409. This sermon was reprinted in Hales's *Golden Remains* (Lond. 1659 &c.), with others. The text, outer margin and headlines of every page are within bounding lines.

5. **Hutchins,** Robert.　　　Stationers' Register, ed. Arber, iii. 654
" 7° Augusti 1619. John Barnes. Entred for his copie by order of a

Court *A short Catechisme* made by ROBERT HUTCHINS which was the copie of **Joseph Barnes** his ffathers . . . vj^d^," assigned to John Wright the same day. This Catechism cannot be later than 1617, in which year Joseph Barnes ceased printing, nor before 1605 when John Wright began to publish: but I find no other notice of the book or author.

6. **Jackson,** Thomas. NAZARETH AND BETHLEHEM, | OR, | ISRAEL'S PORTION IN THE SONNE | OF IESSE. | AND, | MANKINDS COMFORT | *FROM THE WEAKER SENE.* | *TVVO SERMONS PREACHED IN* | St Maryes Church in Oxford. | BY | THOMAS IACKSON, Bachelour of Divinitie, and | Fellow of Corpus Christi College | *in Oxford.* | [*motto*, then *woodcuts.*]

Impr. 38: 1617: sm. 4°: pp. [4] + 75 + [1]: p. 11 beg. *returne to*: English Roman. Contents:—p. (1) title: (3-4) dedication to James Montague bp. of Winchester, dated "from my study in Corpus Christi College . . . Septemb. 6. 1617": 1-37, the first sermon, on Jer. xxxi. 21-22: 38-75, the second, on Gal. iv. 4-5.

See Wood's *Ath. Oxon.,* ii. 668. The text, outer margins and headlines are within bounding lines.

7. **M[orrice?],** T[homas?] DIGESTA | SCHOLASTICA, IN GRATIAM PVE-|RORVM EDITA: | IN DVAS DIVISA PAR-*tes: quarum prior Prosaica,* | *posterior Metrica* | *continet.* | Per T. M. | [*device.*]

Impr. 37: 1617: (eights) 12°: pp. [4] + 52 + 127 + [1]: pp. 11 beg. *impetu* and *Ipse Perilleo,* 111 *Vt plus:* Long Primer Roman. Contents:— p. (1) title: (3) "ad lectorem": (4) the contents: 1-52, the first part: 1 127, the second part.

See Wood's *Fasti Oxon.,* i. 272. The book consists of adages and extracts suitable for school use.

8. **Oxford,** University. IACOBI ARA | [*engraving*] | CEV, IN IACOBI MAG- NÆ BRITANNIÆ FRANCIÆ | ET HIBERNIÆ REGIS SERENIS-|SIMI, &c: AVSPICATISSIMVM | REDITVM E SCOTIA IN | ANGLIAM, ACADEMIÆ | *OXONIENSIS* GRA-|TVLATORIA. |

Impr. 37: 1617: sm. 4°: pp. [80], sigu. A K¹: sign. B 1^r beg. *Vis restituta:* English Roman. Contents:— sign. A 1^r title: A 1^v "Iacobi patriarchæ cum Iacobo rege . . . comparatio," a poem: A 2^r K 4^r, the poems: K 4^v, "Conclusio," a poem.

Congratulatory poems by members of the University of Oxford, on the occasion of the return of James I from a short visit to Scotland. All are in Latin except two Greek and two French: one is acrostic, and one in the shape of an altar. On the title is a rough wood engraving of an altar with fire, bearing the words DEO REDVCI:.

9. **Smith,** Samuel. ADITVS | AD | LOGICAM. | In vsum eorum qui pri-|mò ACADEMIAM | Salutant. | [*line*] | *Autore* SAMVELE SMITH | *Artium Magistro.* | [*line*] | Editio Tertia. | [*woodcuts.*]

Impr. 13^c: 1617: (twelves) 16°: [2] + 204 + [2] + 2 unpaged tables, see be-low: p. 11 beg. *Tertio Ge*-, 111 *ctiram habet*: Long Primer Roman. Contents:—p. (1) title: 1-204, the work, in 3 books, with two sm. 4° leaves unpaged inserted at pp. 32-3 and 42-3, printed on one side only with logical divisions of Substantia and Qualitas respectively: (1) "Lectoribus . . .", a deprecation of criticism.

For the author see Wood's *Ath. Oxon.*, ii. 283. This is the first known Oxford edition: see 1613 s., 1614 s., 1618 s., 1627 s., 1633 s., 1639 s., 1684. There is also a London ed. of 1621.

10. **Terry,** John. *THE* | REASONA-|BLENESSE OF WISE AND | holy truth : and the absurditie | *of foolish and wicked* | *Errour.* | [*two texts,* then *device.*]

Impr. 36 : 1617 : sm. 4° : pp. [4] + 38 + [2] : p. 11 beg. *able so* : Pica Roman. Contents :—p. (1) title : (3-4) dedication to Arthur Lake, bp. of Bath and Wells : 1-38, the sermon, on John xvii. 17.

See Wood's *Ath. Oxon.*, ii. 410.

11. **W.,** R., of Hart Hall, Oxford. "*Merry Jests concerning Popes, Monkes and ffryers* translated out of Ffrench by R. W. Bachelour of Arts of H[arts]. H[all]. in Oxon."

So in Arber's *Transcript of the Stationers' Register*, as a book of Joseph Barnes's, entered at Stationers' Hall 26 Feb. 1628 by John Barnes. It must have been printed between 1585 and 1617 inclusive, probably after 1610.

<h2 style="text-align:center">1618.</h2>

1. **Angelus,** Christophorus. [*woodcut*] | CHRISTO-|PHER ANGELL, A GRECIAN, WHO TA-sted of many stripes and tor-ments inflicted by the *Turkes for the faith* | *which he had in* | *Christ Iesus.* | **** | [*device*].

Impr. 39 : 1618 : sm. 4° : pp. [16], signn. A–B⁴ : sign. B1ʳ beg. *much in debt* : Pica Roman. Contents :—sign. A 1ʳ title : A 2ʳ, dedication to England : A 2ᵛ–B 3ʳ, the work : B 4ʳ, a woodcut, see below.

Very rare : for the author see Wood's *Ath. Oxon.*, ii. 633. Dr. Bliss in his copy of Angelus, now in the Bodleian, suggests that this edition was worked off without the Greek when Angelus betook himself to travel about the country. It is a reprint almost literatim of 1617 A. Angelus was in Oxford, according to Dr. Bliss, from Whitsuntide 1610 to about Easter 1618, and died 1 Feb. 1638. The second woodcut is a new and rather more elaborate one than in the 1617 issue, but not more intelligible, and is enclosed in an oval frame : the first (on sign. A 4ʳ) is unchanged.

2.*† ————. [Letters testimonial to the good behaviour of Christopher Angell, (1) & (3) from the University of Oxford, 10 May 1610 and 20 Mar. 1617 (161⅞), and (2) from the bp. of Salisbury 15 Aug. 1616, all in English.

Probably printed at Oxford in 1618 : (one) la. 8° : pp. [2] : p. 1 beg. " [wood-cuts] *The bearer hereof, Christopher An-* *gell*" : Pica Roman. Contents :—p. (1) the testimonials.

Very rare.

3. **Butler,** Charles. "*Rhetoricæ Libri duo, 'quorum prior de Tropis & Figuris, posterior de Voce & Gestu præcipit,* &c.' Oxon. 1618, the 4th edit. . . . qu."

So Wood's *Ath. Oxon.*, iii. 210 : see Supplement 1598 B ; and 1600 B.

4. **Farrear**, Robert.   "'*A brief Direction to the French Tongue, &c.*' Oxon. 1618. oct. in the title of which book he wrote himself M.A."

So Wood's *Ath. Oxon.*, ii. 278.

5. **Panke**, John.   *COLLECTANEA.* | Ovt Of | st GREGORY | THE GREAT, | AND | St *BERNARD THE* | *Devout, against the Papists who ad-here to the doctrine of the present* | *Church of Rome, in the most* | *funda-mentall points* | *betweene them* | *and vs.* | [*motto*, then *woodcuts*.]

Impr. 39: 1618: (eights) 12°: pp. [22] + 113 + [1] : p. ii beg. *which by Sathans, iii quod accepistis*: Pica Ro-man. Contents :— p. (1) title : (3-21) Epistle dedicatorie to George Churchowse, | mayor of "New Sarum" and the cor-poration, dated "from the Close at Sarum this 24 *Iunij. 1618*," signed "John Panke."

See Wood's *Ath. Oxon.*, ii. 274. This tract was reprinted at Salisbury in 1835, in 8vo, with the title "Romanism condemned by the Church of Rome, or Popery con-victed ... By the Rev. John Panke ...," with the spelling modernized.

6. **Sanderson**, Robert.   LOGICÆ . ARTIS COMPEN-|*DIVM.* | SECVNDA HAC EDI-tione recognitum, duplici | *Appendice auctum, & pub-lici iuris factum* | à ROB. SANDERSON Col-legij Lincolniensis in al-*ma Oxoniensi Socio.* | [*device*.]

Impr. 40: 1618: (eights) 12°: pp. [8] + 232 + 124 + [4] : pp. ii beg. *possunt. Individua* and *sed ij ferè*: iii *tur aufe-rendo* and *margine peculiari*: Pica Ro-man. Contents :— p. (1) title : 3-7) | "Elenchus capitum": 1-232, the work, in three parts: 1-87, the first Appendix, De usu Logicæ: 89-124, the second Ap-pendix, Miscella : 1) Errata typogra-phica.

See Wood's *Ath. Oxon.*, ii. 626, and 1615 s.

7. **Smith**, Samuel.   ADITVS AD | LOGICAM. | In vsum eorum qui pri = mo ACADEMIAM | Salutant. | [*line*] *Autore* SAMVELE SMITH | *Artium Magistro.* | [*line*] | Editio quarta à multis mendis | quæ per incuriam Typo-graphi irrepserunt, | repurgata. | [*woodcuts*.]

Impr. 41: 1618: (twelves) 16°: pp. [2] + 205 + [1] + 2 unpaged tables, see below: p. ii beg. *Tertiò Ge-*, iii *ctivam habet*: Long Primer Roman. Contents :— | p. (1) title : 1-205, the work, with two sm. 4° leaves, as in the 3rd ed. : (1 "Lectoribus ...".

See 1617 s of which this is a slightly corrected reprint.

1619.

1. **Bedé**, Jean.   *THE* | MASSE DIS-PLAYED. WRITTEN IN FRENCH | by Mr JOHN BEDE, advocate to | *the Parliament of* Paris, *and* | *now translated into* | *English.* | [*motto*, then *device*].

Impr. 39: 1619: sm. 4°: pp. [16] + 112: p. ii beg. *signifieth to, iii bin no small*: Pica Roman. Contents :— p. (3 | title : (5-16) "The Preface to the Reader", signed "E. C." : 1-112, the work.

This is a translation of " La Messe en François, exposée par M. Iean Bedé Angevin
. . .", Geneva, 1610, 8º. The translator may be Edward Chaloner, as suggested in the
Bliss Sale Catalogue, for whom see Wood's *Ath. Oxon.*, ii. 377.

2. **Bernard,** Richard.   *THE* | FABVLOVS | FOVNDATION OF | THE
POPEDOME: | *OR* | A FAMILIAR CONFERENCE BE-|tween two friends to the
truth PHILALETHES, | and ORTHOLOGVS, shewing that it can-|not be
proued, *That Peter was | ever at Rome. | VVHEREVNTO IS ADDED A
CHRONOGRAPHICALL DESCRIP-tion of* Pauls *peregrination with* Peters
*travells, | and the reasons why he could not be at | Rome, that so the truth
in one | view may be more fully and ea- sily be scene of e-very one.* | [two
mottos, then *woodcuts.*]

Impr. 43: 1619: sm. 4º: pp. [10] +
68 + 1 unpaged sheet. see below + [2]: p.
11 beg. *Christs Vicar*: Pica Roman.
Contents:—p. (3) title: (5-6) dedication
to drs. Goodwin. Prideaux and Benefield,
dated " Batcombe April 1. 1619," signed
" Richard Bernard": (7-8) " To the
Reader", same date signed " R. B. B ":
(9-10) " A summarie of the reasons.
proning Peter neuer to haue beene at
Rome ": 1-68, the work: after p. 68 a
large folded folio printed sheet, printed on
one side only, " A short chronographicall
description . . .", signed R. B. B, and with
impr. 43. Pp. (1-2) (7-8) are an addition, wanting in some copies.

3. **Crakanthorp,** Richard.   *INTRODVCTIO* | IN | METAPHYSICAM.
AVTHORE | RI. CRAKANTHORP | olim Collegij Reginæ | Oxon. Socio.
[*motto,* then *woodcuts.*]

Impr. 40: 1619: (eights) 12º: pp.
[16] + 96: p. 11 beg. *di modum*: Long
Primer Roman. Contents:—p. 3) title,
within a border: (5-8) " Ad studiosos
Academiæ Oxoniensis alumnos," dated
" Oxon. è Collegio Reginæ. Decemb. 7.
1619", signed " Guiliel. Richardson ":
(9-12) " Lectori benevolo," signed " R.
C[rakanthorp]": (13-16) " Index capitum et rerum . . .": 1-96, the work.

See Wood's *Ath. Oxon.*, ii. 362. The author seems to have allowed Richardson to
take the book through the press, but to have revised and prepared it himself.

4. **Flavel,** John.   TRACTA-'TVS DE DE-'MONSTRATIONE | METHODI-
CVS & | POLEMICVS, quatuor | libris absolutus: | *antehæc in usum Iuven-
tutis* | in Collegio WADHAMI | apud Oxonienses privatis | prælectionibus
traditus, | à | IOANNE FLAVEL | Art. Mag. & ejusdem | Collegii Socio. |
[*device.*]

Impr. 42: 1619: (eights) 12": pp.
[12] + 1 unpaged sheet + 144 + [12]: p.
11 beg. *Tractatus de.* III *rantiæ suæ*:
Long Primer English. Contents:—p.
1) title: (3-4) dedication to bp. Arthur
Lake, dated " Oxonij è Coll. Wad. Kal.
Martij. 1618 [1 Mar. 161⅞]", signed
" Alexander Huish": (5-6) " Lectori . . ."
by Huish: (7-10) " Index capitum . . .":
after p. (12) is a folded obl. sm. 4º sheet
containing a conspectus of the work,
printed on one side only: 1 " Prooemium ": 2-144. the work, in 4 bks.:
(1-12) " Index rerum et verborum."

See Wood's *Ath. Oxon.*, ii. 207, and 1624 F, 1651 F. Flavel died in Nov. 1617, a
Huish a co-collegian issued this volume from notes of Flavel's pupils, preparing and
editing them as he thought best.

5. **Howson,** bp. John.   ARTICLES | TO BE ENQVIRED | OF VVITHIN
THE DIO-'ces of Oxford, in the first Visitation | of the Right Reverend
Father | in God, *Iohn* Bishop | of *Oxford.* | *HELD* | In the yeare of our

Lord God 1619. in the seuen-'teenth yeare of the Raigne of our most
gratious Sove-'raigne Lord, *Iames*, by the grace of God, King | of Great
Brittaine, *France*, and *Ireland.* Defender of the | Faith: &c. and of
Scotland | the three & fiftieth. | [*deuice.*]

Impr. 44: 1619: sm. 4°: pp. [16].
signn. A B⁴: sign. B 1ʳ beg. *Parents*
dwell: Pica English. Contents:—sign.
A 1ʳ, title: A 1ᵛ, "The . . . Oath ministred
to the Churchwardens . . .", and "The
Charge of the Churchwardens . . .":
A 2ʳ B 3ʳ, the articles: B 3ᵛ, a further
charge.

6. **Mandevill,** Robert.
TIMOTHIES | TASKE: | *OR* | *A CHRISTIAN
SEA-CARD,* | *guiding through the coastes of a peaceable con-'science to a peace
constant, and a* | *Crowne immortall.* | Wherein I. Pastors are put in minde
of their | double dutie, and how to discharge it. 1. Personall, | as
watchful men. 2. Pastorall, as faithful watch-|men. II. True doctrine is
advanced. III. Tradi-|tions discountenanced, & their rancour discovered. |
In two Synodoll assemblies at Carliell, *out of two seuerall, but* | *sutable
Scriptures. This of* 1 Timoth. 4. 16. *and* | *that of Actes* 20. 28. | Since
concorporate, and couched with augmentation vnder their prime Head: |
BY | ROBERT MANDEVILL, *sometimes of Queenes Colledge* | *in Oxford, and
Preacher of Gods word at* | *Abbey-holme in Cumberland.* | [*text,* then
woodcut.]

Impr. 45: 1619: sm. 4°: pp. [8] + 64:
p. 11 beg. *but Nusquam*: Pica Roman.
Contents:— p. (1) title: (3) dedication to
the University, signed "Rob. Magnade-
villa": (5-7) dedicatory Epistle to dr.
William Goodwin, dated "In Coll:
Regin: . . . 8 Idus Iulij . . , MDCXIX,"
signed "Tho: Vicars": 8) two laudatory
Latin poems: 1-64. the discourse, on
1 Tim. iv. 16, ending with a chronogram.

See Wood's *Ath. Oxon.,* ii. 251. Vicars published the book, the author having died
in 1618.

7. **Oxford,** University.
Academiæ Oxoniensis | FVNEBRIA | SACRA. |
ÆTERNÆ MEMORIÆ SERENISSIMÆ REGINÆ | ANNÆ | *POTENTISSIMI MON-
ARCHÆ* | IACOBI Magnæ Britanniæ, Fran-|ciæ, & Hiberniæ Regis &c.
De- sideratissimæ Sponsæ, | DICATA. | [*deuice.*]

Impr. 42: 1619: sm. 4°: pp. [144],
signn. A S¹: sign. B 4ʳ beg. *Quæ solita,*
R 1ʳ *Et obruemus*: English Roman.
Contents:—sign. A 1ʳ title: A 2ʳ, dedicatory Latin poem to King James 1: A 2ᵛ-
S 1ᵛ, the poems: S 2ʳ-S 3ʳ, "Ad . . . regem . . . conclusio", a poem.

Poems on the death of queen Anne of Denmark, 1 Mar. 161⅔: all in Latin except
8 Greek and 3 Hebrew: there are also chronograms, anagrams and an acrostic.

8. **Rainolds,** John.
"The sum of a conference" &c. Oxon.
1619, fol. So in Wood's *Ath. Oxon.,* ii. 193, 1619 being an error for
1610.

9. **Rawlinson,** John.
VIVAT REX. | *A* | SERMON PREACHED | AT
PAVLS CROSSE ON THE | day of his Maiesties happie inau-'guration,
March 24°. | *1614.* | *And now newly published, by occasion of His* | *late
(no lesse happy) recovery.* | By | JOHN RAWLINSON Dʳ of Divinity, and | one
of his Maiesties Chaplaines | in Ordinary. | [*line, motto, line, woodcuts.*]

Impr. 39 : 1619 : sm. 4° : pp. [6] + 40 + [2] : p. 11 beg. *But let him* : Pica Roman. Contents :—p. (1) title : (3-5) dedication to the King : (6) University arms : 1-40, the sermon, on 1 Sam. x. 24.

See Wood's *Ath. Oxon.*, ii. 506. Page 1 shows that the ordinary length of a Paul's Cross sermon was two hours.

1620.

1. Day, John. DAY'S DESCANT | *ON* | DAVIDS PSALMES : | *OR* | A *Commentary* vpon the *Psalter*, as it is vsually | read throughout the Yeere, at *Mor-|ning*, and *Euening* Prayer. | And First, | Of the First *Eight Psalmes*, appointed to be read, | the *First* Day of the *Moneth*. | [*device*, then 3 *mottos*.]

Impr. 39 : 1620 : sm. 4° : pp. [40] + 222 : p. 11 beg. *not in these*, 111 11 *Destroy thou* : Pica Roman. Contents :—p. (1) title : (3-8) Epistle dedicatory to archbp. Abbot, signed "John Day" : (9-40) "To the reader" : 1-220, the work, on Ps. 1-8 : 221-222, "To the reader", on the author's orthography, with Errata.

See Wood's *Ath. Oxon.*, ii. 412. The introduction contains some auto-biographical matter, and treats of "Our Lady's Psalter."

2. Du Moulin, Pierre. A | SERMON | PREACHED | BEFORE THE KINGS | MAIESTY at *Greenwich* the | 15. of Iune. 1615. | *BY* | Master PETER du MOVLIN, one of the Preachers | of Gods Word in the Church of Paris, and | newly translated out of French into | English, by I. V. | *According to the Copy printed at* Charenton | *by* Paris. 1620. | [*device*].

Impr. 46 : 1620 : sm. 4° : pp. [4] + 35 + [1] : p. 11 beg. *to certaine fishes* : English Roman. Contents :—p. (1) title : (3) dedication to the Curators of the Bodleian, signed "Iohannes Vernulius, Bodleianæ Bibliothecæ hypobibliothecarius" the translator : 1-35, the sermon, on Rom. i. 16.

See Wood's *Ath. Oxon.*, iii. 221. The text, margin and headline of each page are within bounding lines.

3. Godwin, Thomas. ROMANÆ HISTORIÆ | *ANTHOLOGIA.* | AN | ENGLISH EXPO-|SITION OF THE RO-MANE ANTIQVITIES, | WHEREIN MANY RO-|MANE AND ENGLISH | Offices are parallel'd, and | divers obscure Phrases | Explained. | BY | THOMAS GODWIN *Master of Arts*. | For the vse of ABINGDON Schoole. | Editio Tertia. | [*device*.]

Impr. 48 : 1620 : 12°?

For the author see Wood's *Ath. Oxon.*, iii. 51 : see 1614 G. Only known at present from references in 17th cent. catalogues and from a titlepage in the Bagford Collections at the British Museum (463. h. 3, no. 546), but it is not likely to be really rare.

4. Goffe, Thomas. ORATIO | FVNEBRIS | HABITA IN ECCLESIA | Cathedrali Christi Oxon | in Obitum viri omni ævo dig-*nissimi* | GVLIELMI | GOODVVIN *istius* | *Ecclesiæ Decani, S.* | Theol. Doctoris. | A THO. GOFFE *Artium Ma-|gistro ex Æde Christi.* | [*device*].

Impr. 40 : 1620 : sm. 4° : pp. [12], signn. A¹ B² : sign. B 1ʳ beg. *fecit opera-tiones* : English Roman. Contents :— | sign. A 1ʳ title : A 2ʳ "Ad Lectorem" : A 3ʳ–B 2ʳ the oration.

See Wood's *Ath. Oxon.*, ii. 463. Goodwin died 11 June 1620. A second edition of this year is simply a reissue of the sheets with an identical titlepage adding only "Editio Secunda," in a separate line after " Æde Christi."

5. **James,** Thomas.   CATALOGVS | VNIVERSALIS LIBRO-ʳRVM IN BIBLIOTHECA | BODLEIANA omnium Librorum. ' Linguarum & Scientiarum genere | refertissimâ, sic compositus ; | Vt | *Non solum Publicis per Europam Vniversam Bibliothe- cis, sed etiam Privatis Musæis, aliisque ad Catalogum Librorum conficiendum vsui esse possit.* | Accessit Appendix Librorum, qui vel ex munificentiâ aliorum, | vel ex censibus Bibliothecæ recens allati sunt, | Auctore THOMA IAMES S. Th. | Doctore, ac nuper Proto-'Bibliothecario | *Oxoniensi.* | *Operis vsum ac vtilitatem, Præfatio* | *ad Lectorem indicabit.* | [*device*].

Impr. 42, adding "Impensis Bodlei-anis" : 1620 : (eights) sm. 4° : pp. [16] +539+[1]+36 : p. 11 beg. *Albertus Dux, III Somnium magni* : Long Primer Roman. Contents :—p. (1) title : (3-4) | dedication to the King, prince Charles, &c. : (5-14) "Prooemium . . . ," dated 30 June 1620 : 1-539, the catalogue in alphabetical order : 1-36, "Appendix ad catalogum priorem."

This is a new edition of 1605 J, arranged in one alphabetical order of authors' names. The *Prooemium* contains much information about the Library. The MSS. and printed books are treated alike in this catalogue, each with its pressmark. Dr. James had resigned the office of Librarian in May 1620 from illness. The Hebrew MSS. are not all entered in the Catalogue, and "propter typorum defectum" are de-scribed in Latin, not Hebrew type. A second edition of the Appendix was issued in 1635. The expense of printing the volume was £112 10*s*., (Reg. Convoc. N. 23, fol. 93, quoted by Macray *Annals of the Bodleian*, 2nd ed. p. 58 *n*.)

6. **Twyne,** Brian.   ANTIQVI-|TATIS ACADEMIÆ OXO-'NIENSIS APO-LOGIA. | *In tres Libros divisa.* | AVTHORE | BRIANO TWYNO *in facultate Artium Ma-'gistro, & Collegij Corporis Christi in eâdem* | *Academia Socio.* | Vltima Editio. | [*device*].

Impr. 47 : 1620 : the rest as 1608 T.

This is a simple reissue of the sheets of the 1608 edition, with a new titlepage, but is extremely rare.

1621.

1. **Broad,** Thomas.   THREE | QVESTIONS | ANSVVERED. | I. QVES-TION. | *What should our meaning be, when after the reading of* | *the fourth Commandement, we pray ; Lord incline our* | *hearts to keepe this law?* | II. QVESTION. | *How shall the fourth Commandement, being deliuered in* | *such forme of words, binde vs to sanctifie any day, but onely* | *the seauenth, the day wherein God rested, & which the Iewes* | *sanctified?* | III. QVES-TION. | *How shall it appeare to be the Law of Nature to sancti-*|*fie one day in every weeke?* | [*motto,* then *device.*]

Impr. 39 : 1621 : sm. 4° : pp. [4]+38 +[2] : p. 11 ('10') beg. *which is the* : | English Roman. Contents :—p. (1) title : (3 4) "To the Reader", signed "Th.

Broad ": 1–26, the work : 27–33 " A DIALOGVE | BETVVEENE A IEVV and a CHRISTI-|AN of the Common | Opinion." | 33–38. "*A note touching the Lords Day*": (1) " Errata."

See Wood's *Ath. Oxon.*, ii. 594. A treatise against too strict observance of Sunday, answered by George Abbot, M.P. for Guildford, in his *Vindiciæ Sabbathi*, Lond. 1641.

2. **[Burton, Robert.]** *THE* | ANATOMY OF | MELANCHOLY, | *I'THAT IT IS.* | VVITH ALL THE KINDES, | CAVSES, SYMPTOMES, PROG-*NOSTICKES, AND SEVE. RALL CVRES OF IT.* | IN THREE MAINE PARTITIONS | with their seuerall SECTIONS, MEM-|BERS, and SVBSEC-|TIONS. | *PHILOSOPHICALLY, MEDICI-|NALLY, HISTORICALLY, OPE-|NED AND CVT VP.* | BY | DEMOCRITVS *Iunior.* | With a Satyricall PREFACE, conducing to | *the following Discourse.* | [*motto.*]

Impr. 48: 1621: (eights) sm. 4°: pp. [4] + 72 + [8] + 783 + [9]: pp. 11 beg. *sed and busied* and *Lethargye*, 111 *Mutavere viros*, 611 *" Mille habet*: Pica Roman. Contents :—p. (1) title : (3) dedication to lord Berkeley : 1–72, "Democritus Iunior to the Reader": (1–8) "The Synopsis of the first partition": 1–783, the work : (1) 3 mottos : (2–7) "The Conclusion of the Author to the Reader", signed "Robert Burton. From my Studie in *Christchurch Oxon.* Decemb. 5. 1620": (8) " Errata."

See Wood's *Ath. Oxon.*, ii. 653. For subsequent Oxford editions see 1624 B, 1628 B, 1632 B, 1638 B, 1651. Other editions are Lond. 1660 (7th), 1676 (8th), 1800 (9th), (10th), 1806 (11th), 1845, 188-, as well as epitomes. This celebrated work is replete with erudition, humour, and acuteness. The recondite sources of the numberless quotations are perhaps only to be found in the Bodleian, to which Burton bequeathed his printed books, of which a catalogue is among the Bodleian MSS. This first edition, which is anonymous except for one signature on p. (7) of the Conclusion, is accounted rare, but copies not infrequently appear for sale. Each successive edition during the author's lifetime (he died in Jan. 1639⁄40) shows alterations.

3. **Denison,** John. DE | CONFESSIONIS | AVRICVLARIS | VANITATE. AD-|VERSVS CARDINALIS | BELLARMINI | *Sophismata,* | ET DE | *SIGILLI CON-FESSIONIS IMPIE-late, contra Scholasticorum, & Neoterico-|rum quorundam dogmata* | *Disputatio.* | *AVTHORE* | IOANNE DENISONO Oxoniensi | Sacræ Theologiæ Doctore. [*motto, then woodcuts.*]

Impr. 39: 1621: sm. 4°: pp. [10] + 126: p. 11 beg. *catione, tum*, 111 *Cap. 2. Argumenta*: Pica Roman. Contents :— p. (1) title : (3–6) dedicatory epistle to the king: (7–8) "Ad Lectorem": (9–10) "Elenchus Capitum . . .": 1–126, the work, in two parts : 126 " Errata ".

See Wood's *Ath. Oxon.*, ii. 439.

4. **Heylyn,** Peter. MICROCOSMVS. | OR | A LITTLE DE-|SCRIPTION OF | THE GREAT WORLD. | A Treatise Historicall, Geographicall, Politicall, Theologicall. | [*line*] | By P. H. | [*line, then motto, then device.*]

Impr. 39: 1621: sm. 4°: pp. [16] + 417 (" 317 ") + [3]: p. 11 beg. *pearance of diuers*, 111 *of Florence*: Pica Roman. Contents :—p. (1) title : (3–5) Epistle dedicatory to prince Charles, signed " Pet. Heylyn ": (7–11) "The Preface": (12– 13) "To my brother the Author" an English poem by Edw. Heylyn: (14–15) "The Table" of contents, in alphabetical order : (16) "A computation of the forraine Coynes herein mentioned with ours": 1–417, (1–2) the work : (3) " Errata."

See Wood's *Ath. Oxon.*, iii. 557, where 1622 is a misprint for 1621 and 1624 for 1625. For other Oxford editions of this well-known and popular manual of Geography see 1625 H, 1627 H, 1629 H, 1631 H, 1633 H, 1636 H, 1639 H: there are also London editions (entitled *Cosmographie*) of 1652, 1657, 1664?, 1666, 1670, 1674?, 1677, 1682, 1703.

5. Savile, sir Henry.   [two *lines*] | PRAELE-|CTIONES TRES-|DECIM IN PRIN-|CIPIVM ELEMENTO-|RVM EVCLIDIS, | *OXONII HABITÆ.* | M.DC.XX. | [*device*, see below.]

Impr. 40: 1621: sm. 4°: pp. [4] + 260: p. II beg. *ma. Quid*, III *trag; à centro*: Great Primer Roman. Contents:—p. (1) title: (2) "Errata . . .": (3) "Henricus Savilius lectori": 1–260, the work.

See Wood's *Ath. Oxon.*, ii. 314. This was Savile's last publication, for he died 19 Feb. 162½. There are many woodcuts of figures of propositions. Most copies have a device on the titlepage, but a presentation copy from the author to the Bodleian and the copy in the Savile Library omit it. The absence of a dedication is unusual.

6. Thornborough, bp. John.   ΛΙΘΟΘΕΩΡΙΚΟΣ, | *SIVE,* | *NIHIL,* *ALIQVID, OMNIA,* | ANTIQVORVM | SAPIENTVM VI-|vis coloribus depicta, Philo-*sophicostheologicè,* | In gratiam eorum qui Artem auriferam Physico-chymicè & piè profitentur. | *AVTHORE* | IOHANNE THORNBVRGH, EPISCOPO | *VVIGORNIENSI.* | [2 *mottos.*]

Impr. 40: 1621: sm. 4°: pp. [12] + plate + 152: p. II beg. *tur potiùs*, III *lestium corporum*: English Roman. Contents:—p. (1) title: (3–6) dedication to the duke of Lennox: (7–11) "Ad Lec-torem benevolum": (12) "Παραμυάδες sic restituantur . . .": folded quarto leaf, see below: 1–152, the work in three divisions.

See Wood's *Ath. Oxon.*, iii. 5. The Episcopal Alchemist endeavours to find the Philosopher's stone through Sulphurous Magnesia (Nil), water (Aliquid) and gold (Omnia). Vitriol is regarded as of vital importance. Much Theology is introduced. The woodcut plate represents the concord and discord of the four elements in various relations, in a circular table.

1622.

1. Abbot, George.   [*woodcut*] | THE COPPIE | OF A LETTER SENT | from my Lords Grace of Can-|terburie shewing the graue and | *weighty reasons which induced* | *the Kings Maiestie to pre-|scribe those former* | *directions for* | *Preachers.* | [*device.*]

Impr. 45: 1622: sm. 4°: pp. [16]. sign. A, *¹: sign. A 3ʳ beg. *damentall grounds*, * 3ʳ *or of the Vniversalitie*: English Roman. Contents:—sign. A 1ʳ, title: A 2ʳ–3ᵛ. the letter, to the bp. of Oxford: dated "from Croydon Sept. 4th *1622*": A 4 [not seen, probably blank]: * 1ʳ–4ʳ, "To the minister, churchwardens and parishioners of   in the Diocesse of Oxon.", 31 Aug. 1622, as under *Howson*, John, below.

See Wood's *Ath. Oxon.*, ii. 564. The latter part of this piece seems to have been issued separately, see Howson, John, below.

2. Carpenter, Nathanael.   PHILOSOPHIA | LIBERA, | *TRIPLICI EXERCITA-|tionum Decade proposita.* | *IN QVA,* | ADVERSVS HVIVS TEM-|poris Philosophos, dogmata | quædam noua discu-|tiuntur. | AVTHORE | NA-THANAELE CARPNETARIO, | *Exoniensis Collegij, in florentissimâ* | *Academiâ*

Oxoniensi, Socio. | EDITIO SECVNDA, VNA | Decade auctior, & emendatior. [*motto.*]

Impr. 42 *a* : 1622 : (eights) 16° : pp. [24] + 395 + [5] : p. 11 beg. *tute ab alio,* 111 *ali : At nullam* : Pica Roman. Contents :—p. (3) title : (5–14) dedication to James Hamilton duke of Hamilton (*d.* 1649) : (15–21) "Ad florentissimam Oxoniensis Academiæ Iuventutem Præfatio" : (22–23) "Elenchus Exercitationum . . ." : 1–395, the work : (2) "Errata Typographica."

See Wood's *Ath. Oxon.*, ii. 421, where *Lond.* is a misprint for *Oxon.* The first edition was issued at Frankfort in 1621 "authore N. C. Cosmopolitano," with different prefatory matter, only two Decads, and variations in text and arrangement. See 1636 c, 1637 c, 1675. Some woodcuts of diagrams occur in the text.

3. **Clinton,** Elizabeth, countess of Lincoln. [*woodcuts*] | THE | COVNTESSE | OF LINCOLNES | NVRSERIE· | [*device.*]

Impr. 39 : 1622 : sm. 4° : pp. [8] + 21 + [3] : p. 11 beg. *own natural* : Great Primer English. Contents :—p. (1) title : (3–5) dedication to lady Briget countesse of Lincolne, signed "Elizabeth Lincolne" : (7–8) "To the . . . Reader," signed "T. L.", i.e. Thomas Lodge : 1–21, the work : (2–3) not seen.

Rare. The object of this small treatise, "the first worke of" the authoress "that ever came in Print," is to persuade mothers to nurse their own children. The author appears to dedicate it to her daughter-in-law, not mother-in-law as Bliss states (Wood's *Ath. Oxon.*, ii. 384 *n.*). The authorship has been ascribed to Thomas Lodge (Wood, as above), but there is every internal mark that he only wrote the address to the Reader, and possibly revised the whole.

4. **Gardiner,** Richard. A | SERMON | PREACHED AT | St MARIES IN OX-FORD ON ACT SVN-|*DAY LAST IN THE AF-*|TER-NOONE 1622. | BY | RICHARD GARDINER Student | *of Christ-Church.* | [*device.*]

Impr. 49 : 1622 : sm. 4° : pp. [8] + 30 + [2] : p. 11 beg. *and crabbed* : English Roman. Contents :—p. (3) title : (5–8) dedication to Richard earl of Dorset : 1–30, the sermon, on Gen. xlv. 8.

See Wood's *Ath. Oxon.*, iii. 921.

5. Heylyn, Peter. Microcosmus: see 1621 H.

6. *†**Howson,** John, bp. of Oxford. [*woodcut*] TO THE MINISTER | CHVRCHWARDENS | and parishioners of | *in the Diocesse of Oxon.* | [text begins on same page.]

No impr. or date, but 1622 : sm. 4° : pp. [8], sign. *¹ : sign. * 2ʳ beg. *By this you see* : English Roman. Contents :— sign. * 1ʳ, heading as above : * 1ʳ–4*ʳ, the directions.

These are Directions to preachers in the Diocese of Oxford, to restrict their choice of subjects and treatment of them within the bounds of the XXXIX Articles. The Directions are dated 31 Aug. 1622, and quote mandates from the King (4 Aug. 1622) and the archbp. of Canterbury (12 Aug. 1622). It is perhaps doubtful whether this is genuinely a separate book from *Abbot's* Letter, above.

7. **Oxford,** University. DECRETVM | VNIVERSITATIS | OXONIENSIS DAMNANS | PROPOSITIONES NEOTERI-|CORVM INFRA-SCRIPTAS, | SIVE *IESVITA-RVM,* | SIVE | *PVRITANORVM,* SIVE | aliorum cuiuscunque gene-|*ris Scrip-torum.* | [*device.*]

Impr. 40: 1622: sm. 4°: pp. [12], signn. A¹ B²: sign. B 1ʳ beg. *Vniversitas*: Great Primer Roman. Contents:—sign. A 2ʳ title: A 3ʳ–B 2ʳ, the propositions.

See Wood's *Ath. Oxon.*, i. 3 and *Hist. and Antiqq. of the University of Oxford*, sub anno 1622. The propositions condemned were those delivered by William Knight of Broadgates Hall in a University sermon on Apr. 15, 1622, founded on principles of David Pareus, to the effect that subjects may take up arms against their sovereign. The propositions and censures were considered in a Convocation 25 June 1622. The form of oath to be taken by all future graduates is appended, and a note that Pareus's book was burnt on 6 June 1622.

8. **Oxford,** University. [*woodcut*] | VLTIMA LINEA | SAVILII | SIVE IN OBITVM CLARISSI-|mi Domini HENRICI SAVILII E-|quitis Aurati, Mathe-maticorum facilè Principis, nuperri- mè Collegij MERTONENSIS Custodis Vigi- *lantissimi,* ETONENSIS *iuxta Windsore Præ-*|*positi dignissimi, & *BENEFACTORIS | *de Vniversitate Oxoniensi* | *optimè meriti.* | *Iusta Aca-demica.* | [*device.*]

Impr. 40: sm. 4°: pp. [58] signn. ( ), *¹, **¹, A-F¹: sign. B 1ʳ beg. *Heronm vulgus*: Pica Roman. Contents:—sign.) 2ʳ title: ( ) 3ʳ "Munificentia Savilii in celeberrimam Vniversitatem Oxoniensem": ( ) 4ʳ, dedication to the Earl of Pembroke by the "Genius Scholarum": ( ) 4ᵛ, see below: * 1ʳ–**1ᵛ "Oratio funebris habita in scholâ Theologiæ Oxon. in obitum celeberrimi viri, Henrici Savilii, Equitis Aurati. A Tho. Goffe . . . publico Academiæ Oratore tunc temporis deputato": ( ) 4ᵛ, A 1ʳ–F 3ᵛ, the poems.

See Wood's *Ath. Oxon.*, ii. 315, 463. The poems are nearly all in Latin, but 5 are Greek, 2 Hebrew, one French, and one English: there is one chronogram. The "Oratio funebris" is clearly an added piece.

9. **Rawlinson,** John. "*The Bridegroom and Bride*: On Cant. 4. 8. Ib. [i. e. Oxon.] 1622, &c. qu."

So in Wood's list of Rawlinson's sermons (*Ath. Oxon.*, ii. 506). It was preached in 1662 and re-printed at Oxford in 1625, but Wood's statement is explicit, and there may have been a separate issue in 1622, though I have not met with a copy or other reference to it.

10. **Spark.** A | SPARKE | OF CHRISTS | BEAVTY. | [*device.*]

Impr. 44 *a*: 1622: sm. 4°: pp. [8] + 39 + [1]: p. 11 beg. *wrought our*: English Roman. Contents:—p. (1–2) [not seen]: (3) title: (4–7) "To the Reader . . .": 1–39, the work, a discourse on Is. ix. 6.

Very rare.

1623.

1. **Cotta,** John. COTTA | CONTRA | ANTONIVM: | *OR* | AN ANT-ANTONY: | *OR* | AN ANT-APOLOGY, | manifesting Doctor *Antony* his Apo-|logie for *Aurum potabile,* in true and e-|quall ballance of right Reason, to | be false and counterfait. | *By* IOHN COTTA Doctor in Physicke. | [*woodcuts.*]

Impr. 48: 1623: sm. 4°: pp. [12] + 108: p. 11 beg. *may be one*: Pica Roman. Contents:—p. (1) title: (2) Advertise-ment to the reader about the prefaces: (3–7) Epistle dedicatory to the resident Doctors in Physic in the University of Oxford: (8) "Errata . . .": (9–12) "To the Reader": 1–108, the work.

This is a reply by a Cambridge man to Francis Anthony's supposed discovery of a medicine called Aurum Potabile, in his *Apologia veritatis illucescentis, pro auro potabili,* Lond. 1616. For the controversy see Wood's *Ath. Oxon.,* ii. 416. This work was sent to press at Oxford in 1616, but recalled before printing.

2. **France.** ARTICLES | AGREED ON | IN THE | NATIONALL SYNODE | of the Reformed Churches of | FRANCE, | Held at *Charenton* neere *Paris,* in the Moneth | *of September,* 1623. | Which the same ordaineth to be inuiolably kept | in all the CHVRCHES and VNIVERSI-|TIES of that REALME. | [*device.*]

Impr. 39: 1623: sm. 4°: pp. [2]+ 34: p. 11 beg. *Who teach, That*: Pica | Roman. Contents:—p. (1) title: 1-34, the Articles in 4 chapters.

See 1624 F.

3. **Godwin,** Thomas. ROMANAE | HISTORIAE | ANTHOLOGIA | RECOGNITA ET | AVCTA. | *AN* | ENGLISH EXPOSITION OF | THE ROMANE ANTI-QVITIES, | wherein many Romane and English | offices are paralleld, and divers | obscure Phrases | *explained.* | *For the vse of* ABINGDON *Schoole.* | [*line*] | Revised and enlarged by the Author | [*line*: then *device.*]

Impr. 47: 1623: sm. 4°: pp. [8]+ 277+[27]: p. 11 beg. *a malefactor,* III *ther, sometimes*: Pica Roman. Contents:—p. (1) title: (3-4) dedication to dr. John Young dean of Winchester, | dated "Abindoniæ 14. Calend. Decemb. ... 1622," signed "Tho. Godwyn": (5) "Benevolo lectori": (7) "A short Table ..." of contents: 1-277, the work: (2-24) "Index Rerum et Verborum ..."

See 1614 G.

4. *°*¹**Oxford,** Merton College. Merton Colledge Case. | [the text follows.]

No place or date, but probably printed at Oxford in about 1623: folio: pp. [4], sign. ( )²: sign. ( ) 2ʳ beg. 3 *What* | *Baron Althams*: Pica Roman. Contents:—pp. (2-3), the Case.

Merton College let the manor of Maldon to the Queen in 21 Eliz. (1578-79), for 5000 years. The lease was disputed by the College in 1621 ("about two yeares since"), and again in this Case, which sets out the reasons for annulling the same.

5. **Oxford,** University. CAROLVS | REDVX. | [*device,* with AC. on one side and OX. on the other.]

Impr. 42: 1623: sm. 4°: pp. [92], signn. ( )² ¶¹ ¶¶² A-I⁴ K²: sign. B 1ʳ beg. *Pierides nuper*: Pica Roman. Contents:—sign. ( ) 1ʳ title; 2ʳ-2ᵛ, dedications to king James and prince Charles, Latin poems by the vice-chancellor: ¶ 1ʳ- | ¶¶ 2ᵛ "ΠΑΝΑΚΑΔΗΜΙΚΟΣ. sive, gratulatio pro Carolo reduce, Oxoniensium nomine recitata, à Iohanne King publico Acad. Oratore": A 1ʳ-K 1ʳ, the poems: K 2ʳ "Epilogus typographorum ad Principem," two short Latin poems.

Poems by members of the University of Oxford to congratulate prince Charles on his return from Madrid to England 5 Oct. 1623. Most are in Latin, but 4 in Greek and 2 in Hebrew: there are also 4 chronograms, 1 acrostich and 1 anagram. For King's speech see Wood's *Ath. Oxon.,* ii. 632.

6. Panke, John. See 1613 P.

1. **A, J.**   The younger brother his apologie: see 1634 A.

2. **'A[yton, sir] R[obert].**   [*woodcut*] | IN | OBITVM | THOMÆ RHÆDI, | *VIRI VNDEQVAQVE* | *MERITISSIMI,* | ET | *SERENISSIMO REGI* | *AB* | *EPIS-TOLIS LATINIS* | EPICEDIVM. | [*device.*]

No imprint : 1624: sm. 4° : pp. [8] : ( ) 3ʳ beg. *Consilium extorsit:* Great Primer Roman. Contents :—( ) 1ʳ, title : 2ʳ-4ʳ, the Latin poem, at end " *Faciebat R.A.*"

A Latin hexameter poem on the death of sir Thomas Reid, of whom I do not readily find any account. No part of this was printed in Oxford, the woodcuts and type being unknown there : even the small device of the Arms of the University on the titlepage (which has caused this work to be ascribed to the Oxford Press) differs from the genuine one. No doubt the book was printed in London.

3. **[Burton, Robert].**   THE | ANATOMY OF | MELANCHOLY: | *VVHAT IT IS.* | VVITH ALL THE KINDES, CAV-|SES, SYMPTOMES, PROGNOSTICKS, | AND SEVERALL CVRES OF IT. | *IN THREE MAINE PARTITIONS,* | with their seuerall SECTIONS, MEM-|BERS, AND SVBSECTIONS. | *PHILOSOPHICALLY,* *MEDICI-* | *NALLY, HISTORICALLY* | *opened and cut vp,* | BY | DEMOCRITVS *Iunior.* | With a Satyricall PREFACE, conducing to | the following Dis-course. | *The second Edition, corrected and aug-|mented by the Author.* | [*motto,* then *device.*]

Impr. 48 : 1624: (fours) folio : pp. [4] + 64 + [4] + " 1 "-" 188 " + [4] + " 189 "-" 332 " + [2] + " 333 "-" 557 " + [7]: pp. 11 beg. *make sport,* and *uing borne in,* 401 *Da mihi basia* : English Roman. Contents :—p. (1) title : (3) dedication to George lord Berkeley : 1-64. " Demo-critus Iunior to the Reader ": 64, Errata : (1-4) " The Synopsis of the first par-tition ": 1-188, the first part : (1-4) " The Synopsis of the second partition ": 189-332, the second part : (1-2) "Analy-sis of the third partition": 333-557, the third part : (1-7) " the table."

See Wood's *Ath. Oxon.,* ii. 653, and 1621 B. The author's name does not seem to occur anywhere in the book.

4. **C[arleton], G[eorge],** bishop of Chichester.   ΑΣΤΡΟΛΟΓΟ-MANIA : | The Madnesse of ASTROLOGERS. | OR | An Examination of Sir | Christopher Heydons | Booke, | *INTITULED* | A DEFENCE OF | Iudiciarie Astrologie. | *Written neere vpon twenty yeares ago, by* G. C. *And* | by permission of the Author set forth for the Vse of | *such as might happily be misled by the* | *Knights booke.* | Published by T. V. B. of D. | [*motto.*]

Impr. 51 : 1624: sm. 4°: pp. [24] + 123 + [1]: p. 11 beg. *neither can they,* 111 *them : which :* English Roman. Con-tents :—p. (1) " A " : (3) title : (5-15) Epistle dedicatory to Thomas Carleton ", signed " Tho: Vicars ": (17) " In Au-thorem & eius opera. Προσφώνησις ", a Latin poem : (19-22) " 'Ανακεφαλαίωσις : or Recapitulation of the Chiefe Passages in this Treatise ", a list of Contents : (23) quotation from Ennius : 1-123, the work : 123, a chronogram, 1624.

See Wood's *Ath. Oxon.,* ii. 424. The book was entered at Stationers' Hall to Will. Turner, 18 July 1623. The author, whose initials only occur in the book, was at this time bishop of Chichester : the editor Vicars had married the bishop's daughter. Sir Chr. Heydon's book was published in 1603 at Cambridge, and a second book by him on Astrology published in 1650 was followed by a reprint of the present work in 1651.

5. Flavel, John.   TRACTA-'TVS DE DE-'MONSTRATI-'ONE METHO-DICVS & PO-|LEMICVS, *quatuor | libris absolutus : | Antehæc in usum Iuuen-tutis | in Collegio* WADHAMI *| apud Oxonienses privatis | prælectionibus traditus,* | à | IOHANNE FLAVEL | Art. Mag. & ejusdem | Colleg;j Socio. [*woodcuts.*]

Impr. 42 : 1624 : 16°.

For the author and book see Wood's *Ath. Oxon.,* ii. 207, and 1619 F.   Only known at present from a titlepage in the Bagford collections at the British Museum (463. h. 3), but it is not likely to be rare.

6. France.   ARTICLES | [&c. precisely as 1623 F adding after REALME. :—] *Wherein, their iudgement touching the principall Contro-versies now on foote betwixt the Remonstrantes | and Contra-remonstrantes, is briefly declared.* | [then *woodcuts*, not device].

Impr. 39, &c. exactly as 1623 F.

This is a reissue of the sheets of 1623 F with part of the titlepage altered.   There is another issue of this reissue, *undated, with impr. 49 *a*, but no other change from the present edition of any kind.

7. Hayes, William.   THE | PARAGON | OF PERSIA ; | *OR* | THE LAVVYERS | *LOOKING-GLASSE.* | Opened in a sermon at S. MARIES | in Oxford, at the Assises, the | 7 day of Iuly, 1624. | *By* WILLIAM HAYES, *Master of Arts of* Magdalen Hall. | [two *mottos*, then *woodcut.*]

Impr. 45 : 1624 : 16°.

Only known at present from a titlepage in the Bagford collections in the British Museum (463. h. 3), but it is not likely to be rare.

8. Heylyn, Peter.   Microcosmus: the reference in Wood's *Ath. Oxon.,* iii. 557 to an edition of this year, is probably an error for 1625.

9. Oxford, University.   CAMDENI | INSIGNIA· |

Impr. 42 : 1624 : sm. 4° : pp. [76], signn. ( )² *c*, *cc*₁, *ccc*₂ A–F⁴ G² : sign. H 1ʳ beg. *In Camdenum* : Pica Roman. Contents :—( ) 1ʳ title : 1ᵛ " Donum Camdenianum ", his benefaction to the University : ( ) 2ʳ–2ᵛ, A 1ʳ–G 2ᵛ, the poems : *c* 1ʳ–4ᵛ " Oratio in memoriam . . . Gulielmi Camdeni . . . prolata per Zoucheum Townley ex Æde Christi, Oratorem publicum tunc temporis deputatum " : *cc* 1ʳ– *ccc* 1ᵛ, " Parentatio historica : sive Commemoratio vitæ et mortis V. C. Gulielmi Camdeni Clarentii, facta Oxoniæ in Scholâ Historicâ per Degoreum Whear Historiarum Prælectorem, ab eodem Camdeno ibidem constitutum ", 2 Dec. 1623 : *ccc* 1ᵛ–2ᵛ " Nuncius chronogrammaticus ", 3 Latin poems on Camden by Whear, introducing chronograms : A 1ʳ–G 2ᵛ, see above.

See Wood's *Ath. Oxon.,* ii. 348, *Fasti Oxon.,* i. 398.   Poems by members of the University of Oxford on the death of William Camden, which took place on 9 Nov. 1623.   Most are in Latin, but there are 10 Greek, with 5 anagrams, and 2 chronograms.   Whear's Oration contains many biographical details about Camden.

10. ———.   SCHOLA | MORALIS | PHILOSOPHIAE | *OXON.* | In funere WHITI pullata. | [*device.*]

Impr. 40: 1624: sm. 4°: pp. [2]+6
+ [8]: p. 3 beg. *White dato*: Pica &
Great Primer Roman. Contents:—p. (1)
title: (2) "Annua Whiti munificentia",
his bequests to the University, &c.: 1-6
poems: (1-8) "Oratio funebris habita
Oxoniae, Aprilis 22°, A° 1624, in laudem
Doctoris White ... per Guil. Price ...".

See Wood's *Ath. Oxon.*, ii. 352. Dr. Thomas White, founder of a Professorship of
Moral Philosophy, died 1 Mar. 162¾. The poems are all in Latin, except two in
Greek.

11. ***'P[rideaux], I[ohn].**　　ALLOQVIVM SERE-'NISSIMO REGI IACOBO |
WOODSTOCHLE HABITVM　24. *Augusti. Anno* 1624. | [the text follows.]

[Oxford, 1624?] sm. 4°: pp. [8], sign.
A¹: sign. A 2ʳ beg. *turbat quid dicam*:
Great Primer Roman. Contents:—sign.
A 1ʳ title: A 1ʳ-A 4ʳ, the speech, signed
"I. P. V. Ox." i.e. J. Prideaux, Vice-
cancellarius Oxon.

See Wood's *Ath. Oxon.*, iii. 267. The speech describes, among other things, the
recent architectural and public works in Oxford: and is reprinted in Prideaux's Perez-
Vzzah (1625 ?).

12. **Randol,** John.　　A | SERMON | PREACHT AT | Sᵗ MARIES IN |
OXFORD, the 5. of August: | 1624. Concerning the | *Kingdomes Peace.*
BY | IOHN RANDOL B: in D: of | *Brasen-nose* Colledge. | [two *mottos*:
then *woodcuts*.]

Impr. 50: 1624: sm. 4°: pp. [4]+33
+[3]: p. 11 beg. *especially if*: Pica
Roman. Contents: p. (1) title: (3-4)
dedication to lord "Davers" (i.e. Dan-
vers): 1-33, the sermon, on Mark iii. 24:
(2) "To the most criticall Reader" (altered by the use of smaller type to "To
other most criticall Readers"), an apology
for Errata, giving two examples.

See Wood's *Fasti Oxon.*, i. 415.

1625.

1. **Bedingfield,** Robert.　　A | SERMON | PREACHED AT | PAVLS
CROSSE | THE 24. OF OCTO-BER. 1624. | BY | ROBERT BEDINGFIELD Master |
of Arts, and Student of | *Christ-Church* in | Oxford. | [device: the
whole title is within lines.]

Impr. 52: 1625: sm. 4°: pp. [4]+43
+[1]: p. 11 beg. *ent euidence*: English
Roman. Contents: p. (1) title: (3-4)
dedication to Sir Thomas Richardson, the
author's uncle, dated "From my study
in Christ-Church in Oxford. Nouemb.
24." 1624: 1-43 the sermon, on Rom.
vi. 23: 43, "Errata".

See Wood's *Fasti Oxon.*, i. 457. The title and each page are within bounding lines.
The author gives as one of his reasons for printing the sermon, that it was very wet
when he delivered it, so that his auditors were few.

2. **Butler,** Charles.　　ΣΥΓΓΕΝΕΙΑ. | DE PROPINQVITATE | Matri-
monium impediente, | REGVLA. | *Quæ vna omnes quæstionis huius | diffi-
cultates facilè | expediat.* | [line] | Authore CAROLO BVTLER, Magd. | [*line,*
then *motto,* then *device.*]

Impr. 60: 1625: sm. 4°: pp. [4]+71
+[1]: p. 11 beg. *linea recta*: Great
Primer Roman. Contents:—p. (1) title:
(3-4) "Ad Lectorem": 1-71 the work.

See Wood's *Ath. Oxon.*, iii. 210.

3. **Carpenter,** Nathanael. GEOGRAPHY | DELINEATED | FORTH IN TWO | BOOKES. *CONTAINING THE SPHERICALL | AND TOPICALL PARTS | THEREOF.* | By NATHANAEL CARPENTER | Fellow of *Exeter Colledge* | in Oxford. | [*motto*: then *device*.]

Impr. 61 : 1625: sm. 4°: pp. [18] + 274 + [18] + 286 + [4] + 4 folded leaves, see below: pp. 11 beg. *Earth & Water,* 111 *Vorld may be,* also 11 *teration next.* 111 *monstrated in* : Pica Roman. Contents :— 3 title : (5–7) dedication to the earl of Pembroke : (9–15) "... contents of each chapter of the first booke ...": (17–18) "To my Booke", a poem : 1–274 the first book : (5) a titlepage :— "GEOGRAPHY | THE SECOND | BOOKE. | *CONTAINING THE GENERALL | Topicall, part thereof.* | By . . . [&c. exactly as first title, imprint and all, but different

motto] : (7–9) dedication to the earl of Montgomery : 11–18) "A table of the ... contents of the second booke ...": 1–286, the second book : 1) Apology for erratas and an omitted diagram : (2) "Errors . . .". There should be four diagrams on folded leaves, after pp. (8) "The Analysis of the first Booke"; 252 "A Table . . .": (18) "The Analysis of the seconde Booke": 228 "A Table of the Climates ...". The omitted diagram would have followed p. 62 of the second part.

See Wood's *Ath. Oxon.,* ii. 422, and 1635 C. The treatise is of the theory and principles of Geography, not of details like Heylyn's *Microcosmus.* The author maintains that the earth is the centre of the universe, the sun and planets revolving round it. There are many woodcut diagrams in the text.

4. **G., T.** AN | ANSWER | TO | VVITHERS | MOTTO. | *Without a Frontispice.* | WHEREIN, | Nec HABEO, Nec CAREO, Nec CVRO, | are neither approued, nor confuted : | but modestly controuled, | or qualified. | [*mottos,* a quaestio and responsio] | [two *lines.*]

Impr. 50 : 1625: (eights) 12°: pp. [96], signn. A–F: sign. B 1 beg. *whom Princes* : Pica Roman. Contents :—sign. A 1 title : A 2, "The Booke to the Reader" : A 2, "Virgilius de litera *Pythagorca*" : A 3–A 4 "To Master

Wither himselfe", signed "*T. G. Esquire*" : A 5–A 6 "To the Reader", signed as before : A 7–B 2, "The Introduction", in verse : B 3 F 6, The Answer, in three parts : F 7–8 [not seen].

Very scarce. George Wither's *Withers Motto, Nec habeo, nec Careo, nec Curo,* was published in 1621 and consists of reflexions on human affairs : this book is a poetical satire on those reflexions, and on the character of Wither. The author is unknown.

5. **Godwin,** Thomas. ROMANAE | HISTORIAE AN-|THOLOGIA RE-COG-|NITA ET AVCTA. | *AN* | ENGLISH EXPOSI-|TION OF THE ROMANE | Antiquities, wherein many Romane | and English Offices are paralleld, | *and divers obscure Phrases* | explained. | For the vse of ABINGDON Schoole. | [*line*] | *Reuised and enlarged by the Author.* | [*line*: then *woodcuts.*]

Impr. 53 : 1625: sm. 4°: pp. [8] + 276 + [28] : p. 11 beg. *malefactor, but,* 111 *ther, sometimes* : Pica Roman. Contents :—p. (3) title : 5–6, dedication to dr. John Young, dated "Abindoniae 14.

Calend. Decemb. . . . 1622 . . . Tho: Godwyn" : (7) "Benevolo lectori" : (8) "A short Table ... of euery Booke and Section" : 1–276, the work : (1–26) "Index rerum et verborum ...".

See 1614 G. This edition was printed in London, though published in Oxford : it was not entered at Stationer's Hall in 1624 or 1625.

6. **Heylyn,** Peter. ΜΙΚΡΟ῾ΚΟΣΜΟΣ. | A | LITTLE DESCRIP-|TION OF THE | GREAT WORLD. | *Augmented and reuised.* | [*line*] | By PETER HEYLYN. | [*line*: then *motto*: then *device.*]

Impr. 55 : 1625 : (eights) sm. 4° : pp. [16] + 812 + [2] + one leaf, see below : p. 11 beg. 1. *First then*, 711 *Captain ob-serving* : Pica Roman. Contents :—p. (1) title : (2-3) dedication to King Charles : (5-6) "To the Reader" : (7-8) "To my brother the Author", a poem by Edw. Heylyn : (9-11) "A Table of the principall countries, ..." : (12-16) "A Table of the principall things" : (16) "A computation of . . . forraine coynes . . ." : 1-812, (1), the work : (2) a correction of p. 148 and "Errata". Before p. 7 should come a narrow folded leaf, probably about 10 in. high by 5 in. wide, with "The Table of Climes", printed on one side only.

See 1621 H : Wood's *Ath. Oxon.*, iii. 557 ("1624").

7. **James,** Richard.   ANTI-POSSEVINVS, | *SIVE* | CONCIO | HABITA AD | Clerum in Academiâ Ox-|oniensi *Ann. Domini* | 1625. | [*line*] | *Authore* | RICHARDO IAMESIO Socio | *C. C. C. Vectensi.* | *line*, then *motto*, then *line*.]

Impr. 60 : 1625 : sm. 4° : pp. [6] + 25 + [3] : p. 11 beg. *praesertim cùm* : Eng-lish Roman. Contents :—p. (3) title : (5) "Ad librum suum", a Latin poem : 1-25 the Sermon, on 2 Tim. iv. 13.

See Wood's *Ath. Oxon.*, ii. 629. A singular sermon, more learned than theological. The title seems to be explained by pp. 20-21, where Antonio Possevino (*d.* 1611) is cited as planning a purgatio bibliothecarum in the interests of the Roman Catholic Church : to this James opposes his plea for freedom of research.

8. **James,** Thomas.   AN | EXPLANATION | OR | ENLARGING OF | the ten Articles in the Supplication of | Doctor IAMES, lately exhibi-|ted to the Clergy of | *England.* | OR | A manifest proofe that they are both reas-|onable and faisible within the time mentioned. | [*motto*, then *device.*]

Impr. 58 : 1625 : sm. 4° : pp. [2] + 36 + [2] : p. 11 beg. *Dowists doe make* : Pica Roman. Contents : p. (1) title : 1-36, the work.

See Wood's *Ath. Oxon.*, ii. 467. This is a reprint of the text of the *Humble . . . Request* below (except the last paragraph beginning "For the raising of the charges," which James probably saw to be unpractical), with the addition of comments, written in senile style but obviously by dr. James, and of great interest both for the biography of the author and the principles of criticism as applied to editing a text from MSS. These 26 "Theses or Rules concerning the Art Criticke" are, at p. 23, followed by examples. Dr. James paid two Dutchmen for transcription abroad at the rate of 20*s.* per quire, each quire taking them a week, and the hundred quires per year sufficing to keep two presses at work (p. 17). At p. 26 he explains that a critical remark by bp. Bilson first set him about compiling the *Ecloga Oxonio-Cantabrigiensis* (Lond. 1600).

9. *James,** dr. Thomas.   [woodcuts] | THE | HVMBLE | AND EARNEST | REQVEST OF THOMAS | IAMES, D^r OF DIVINI-|TY, AND SVBDEANE | of the Cathedrall Church | of *Welles*, to the *Church* | *of England*; for, and | in the behalfe of | Bookes touching Re-|ligion. | [the text of the work follows.]

No imprint or date, but Oxford, 1625 (perhaps 1624) (eight) 16° : pp. 15 + [1] : Great Primer English. Contents :— p. 1 title as above : 1-15, the request, signed "T. I. S. T. P. B. P. N." (i.e. Thomas James, Sanctae Theologiae Pro-fessor : for B. P. N. see note to 1599 R. : but the occurrence of the letters here without any text or motto favours the interpretation "Bono Publico Natus") : (1) a from of approbation of the scheme, signed by 17 leading men in Oxford.

Rare. See Wood's *Ath. Oxon.*, ii. 467. This (and still more the *Explanation* above, which see) is an interesting plea for the application of criticism to aid in restoring the texts of Fathers and Schoolmen which had been corrupted by Roman Catholic theologians. The date cannot be precisely ascertained: the titles of the approvers only confine it to 1624, 1625, or 1626: the *Explanation* alludes to it as "lately" issued: so that it is difficult to say whether 1624 or 1625 is the year of issue.

10. ———. A MANVDV-|CTION, OR INTRO-|DVCTION VNTO | DIVINITIE: | *CONTAINING* | A Confutation of Papists by Pa-|pists, throughout the important Articles | *of our Religion* ; *their testimonies taken* | either out of the *Indices Expurgatorii*, | or out of the *Fathers*, and ancient | *Records* ; | But especially the Manuscripts. | [*line*] | *By* THO. IAMES, *Doctor of Diuinitie, late* | Fellow of *New Colledge* in *Oxford*, and Sub-Deane | of the Cathedrall Church of Welles. | [*line*, then *note*, then *line*.]

Impr. 62 : 1625 : sm. 4° : pp. [8] + 136 + [8] : p. 11 beg. *The first Corollary*, 111 *onely titular*: Pica Roman. Contents:— p. (1) title : (3–6) dedication to the bp. of Lincoln, dated "Lond. 26 April, 1625": (7) "The points that are briefly handled in this Booke": (8) "Errata": 1–136, (1). the work : (2–3) "A Table of the Manuscript bookes vrged in this Booke": (4–8) "An Alphabeticall note of the Printed Bookes . . . here cited".

See Wood's *Ath. Oxon.*, ii. 467. The whole of this book was printed in London, not Oxford.

11. **King**, Henry, and John King. TWO | SERMONS. | VPON THE ACT | SVNDAY, BEING | the 10th of Iuly. | 1625. | Deliuered at St MARIES | in Oxford. | [*line*, then *motto*, then *device*.]

Impr. 56 : 1625 : sm. 4° : pp. [4] + 33 + [3] + 43 + [1] : p. 11 beg. *doe not your* : English Roman. Contents:—p. (1) title : (3) a half-title "David's Enlargement. The morning sermon on the Act Sunday : Preached by Henry King . . .": 1–33, the sermon, on Ps. xxxii. 5, (2) a half-title "David's Strait. The after-noones sermon . . . Deliuered by Iohn King . . .": 1–43, the sermon, on 2 Sam. xxiv. 14.

See Wood's *Ath. Oxon.*, ii. 632, iii. 840 respectively. Every page, including the title, is included within bounding lines.

12. **King**, dr. John. CENOTAPHIVM | IACOBI. | *Sive* | *LAVDATIO FVNEBRIS* | *PIÆ ET FOELICI MEMORIÆ* | *SERENISSIMI POTENTISSIMI-QVE* | IACOBI | Magnæ Britanniæ, Franciæ, *&* Hiberniæ | *Monarchæ dedicata, & pub-|licè recitata* | à IOHANNE KING Academiæ | Oxoniensis Oratore. | [chronogrammatical *motto* : then *line*.]

Impr. 53 : 1625 : sm. 4° : pp. [40], signn. A–E⁴: sign. D 1ʳ beg. *lire, quæ alioquin* : Great Primer Roman. Con-tents :—sign. A 2ʳ, title : A 3ʳ–E 3ʳ, the oration.

See Wood's *Ath. Oxon.*, ii. 632. At sign. D 2ʳ begins a list of the late king's literary works.

13. **Leslie**, Henry. A | SERMON | PREACHED | BEFORE HIS | MAIESTY at *Windsore*, | the 19. of *Iuly*. 1625. | By HENRIE LESLIE, one of his | MAIESTIES Chaplaines | in Ordinary | *line*, then 2 *mottos* with *line* between, then *woodcuts*.]

Impr. 56 : 1625 : sm. 4° : pp. [6] + 34 : p. 11 beg. *in the Parable* : English Roman. Contents :—p. (1) title : (3-4) dedication to James earl of Carlisle : (5) | "A Table of the Contents" : (6) "... Errours in the Print" : 1-34, the sermon, on Heb. iii. 8.

14. **Nettles,** Stephen. AN | ANSWER TO | THE IEVVISH | PART OF Mr SELDEN'S | HISTORY OF TITHES. | By STEPHEN NETTLES, | B. of Divinity | [*line* : then motto in Hebrew and English : then *device.*]

Impr. 58 *a* : 1625 : sm. 4° : pp. [12] + 189 + [3] : p. 11 beg. *giue him*, 111 *diuid-ing these* : English Roman. Contents :— p. (1) title : (3-5) dedication to dr. John Prideaux, dated "Lexden, May 4. 1625" : | (7-11) "The Preface" : 1-189, the work : (2) "... faults ..." due to absence of author and difficulty of the written copy.

See Wood's *Fasti Oxon.*, i. 416. Selden's *History of Tithes* was published in 1618. This treatise is a vindication of a public sermon on the subject which gave some offence. Hebrew Pica (unpointed) type is freely used in the book, for the first time. The title and every page are within bounding lines.

15. **Oxford,** University. EPITHALAMIA | OXONIENSIA | IN AVSPICA-TISSIMVM, | POTENTISSIMI MONARCHÆ | CAROLI, | *MAGNÆ BRITANNIÆ,* | *FRANCIÆ, ET HIBERNIÆ* | *Regis, &c. cum* HENRETTA MARIA, | *alterna memoriæ* HENRICI | *Magni Gallorum Regis* | *Filia, Connubium.* | [*device.*]

Impr. 53 : 1625 : sm. 4° : pp. [100], sign. ¶, A L⁴ M² : sign. B 1r beg. *Vir-tutis qui* : English Roman. Contents :— | sign. ¶ 1r title : ¶ 2r-4r 5 special Latin poems : A 1r-M 1v, the poems : M 2r "Ad Lectorem", a final poem.

The marriage of king Charles with Henrietta Maria was on 1 May 1625 at Paris and on 14 June at Canterbury. The poems are Latin, except 1 Hebrew and 7 Greek : not one is French. There are five anagrams and two chronograms.

16. ———. OXONIENSIS | ACADEMIAE | PARENTALIA. | *SACRATISSIMÆ MEMORIÆ* | potentissimi Monarchæ IACOBI, Magnæ | BRITANNIAE, FRANCIAE & | HIBERNIAE Regis, Fidei Orthodoxæ | defensoris cele-berrimi, &c. Dicata. | [*device.*]

Impr. 53 : 1625 : sm. 4° : pp. [96], sign. ¶¹, ¶¶² A-K⁴ L² : sign. B 1r beg. *Sacrificium* : English (except sign. G which is Great primer) Roman. Con- | tents :—sign. ¶ 2r title, ¶ 3r, poetical Latin dedication to king Charles : ¶ 3v-L 1v, the poems : L 2r "Conclusio ad Lectorem", a Latin poem.

Latin poems by members of the University on the death of king James i, which took place on 27 Mar. 1625 : all in Latin except 3 Hebrew and 2 Greek : there are 5 chronograms, an anagram, and one poem printed in a peculiar shape.

17. **Pemble,** William. Vindiciae fidei, or a treatise of iusti-fication by faith, wherein that point is fully cleared, and vindicated from the cauils of its aduersaries. Deliuered in certaine Lectures at Magdalen Hall in Oxford, By William Pemble ... and now published since his death for the publique benefit.

Impr. 59 : 1625 : sm. 4° : pp. [8] + 239 + [3].

Very rare. See Wood's *Ath. Oxon.*, ii. 331. The above title and details are from notes of a copy belonging to lord Robartes, seen by me 18 Nov. 1881.

18. **Prideaux**, dr. John.   Lectiones novem de totidem religionis capitibus . . .

A private copy was seen by me in 1881.

19. ———.   PEREZ-VZZAH : | *OR* | The Breach of Vzzah : | As it was deliuered in a Sermon before His | MAIESTY at *Woodstocke*, August | the 24. *Anno* 1624. | BY | IOHN PRIDEAUX, *Rector of Exeter Colledge,* | *His* MAIESTIE'S *Professor in Diuinity*, | *and at that time Vice-Chancellor of* | *the Vniuersity of* Oxford. | [*motto*, then *deuice*.]

Impr. 50: 1625: sm. 4°: pp. [4]+23 +[9]: p. 11 beg. *so often*: English Roman.   Contents :—p. (1) title : (3-4) dedication to James earl of Arran, dated "Oxford, Exeter Colledge, Octob. 22.

1624.": 1-23, the sermon, on 2 Sam. vi. 6 7: (2-7) "Alloquium serenissimo regi Jacobo Woodstochiæ habitum 24 Augusti. Anno 1624.", signed "I. P. V. Oxon.": (8-9) not seen.

See Wood's *Ath. Oxon.*, iii. 267, 1636 r, (*alloquium*) 1624 r.

20. ———.   A | SERMON | PREACHED ON | THE FIFTH OF OC-TOBER 1624 : AT THE | CONSECRATION OF | St IAMES CHAPPEL | IN *Exeter Colledge.* | BY | IOHN PRIDEAUX, *Rector of* Exeter Col-ledge, *His* MAIESTIES *Professor in* | *Diuinity, and at that time Vice-Chancellour of the Vniuersity of* Oxford. | [*motto*, then *woodcuts*.].

Impr. 50: 1625: sm. 4°: pp. [36], signn. ¶, A-C¹ D²: sign. B 1ʳ beg. *nell whether*: English Roman.   Contents :— sign. A 2ʳ, title : A 3ʳ-4ᵛ, Epistle dedi-

catory to dr. Geo. Hakewill, dated "Exeter Colledge. Novemb. 15". (1624): A 1ʳ-D 1ᵛ, the sermon, on Luke xix. 46: D 2, not seen.

Rare. See Wood's *Ath. Oxon.*, iii. 267. The Chapel of Exeter here concerned (which is not now standing) was built entirely at dr. Hakewill's expense, at a cost of about £1200. The preface to the sermon mentions many Exeter men of the time and, incidentally, that dr. Hakewill was a kinsman of sir Thomas Bodley. The sermon was reprinted at Oxford in 1636.

21. **Rawlinson**, John.   QVADRIGA | SALVTIS. | FOVRE | QVADRAGESIMAL, | OR LENT-SERMONS, PREACHED | at *WHITEHALL* : | BY | Io. RAWLINSON Doctor of Diuinity, | Principal of *Edmund-Hall* in *Oxford*, | and one of his MAIESTIES | Chaplaines in Ordinary. | [*deuice*.]

Impr. 57: 1625: sm. 4°: pp. [8]+26 +[4]+29+[3]+29+[3]+28+[2]: pp. 11 beg. *after, if at*: *Adonibezek, it*: *So*, *in like*, and *she wilbee*: English Roman. Contents :—p. (1) title: (3-5) dedication to Charles i, as Prince Charles: (7) half-title "The Dove-like Soule . . . Feb. 19. 1618. By I. R. . . .": 1-26, the sermon, on Ps. lv. 6: (3) half-title "Lex Talionis. . . . March 17. 1620. By I. R. . . .": 1-29, the sermon, on Judges i. 7: (2)

half-title "The Surprising of Heaven. . . . March 29. 1621. By I. R. . . .": 1-29, the sermon, on Matt. xi. 12: (2) half-title "The Bridegrome, and his Bride. . . . March 19. 1622 . . . By I. R. . . .": 1-28, the sermon, on Song of Solomon iv. 8: (1) "Faults escaped in some of the printed Copies . . ." beginning with "*Ser.* 1. P. 10. *Of the soule, as wings do the nakednes.* (omitted lin. 1". (in the copy seen these are corrected),

See Wood's *Ath. Oxon.*, ii. 506, and 1622 R. The title and every page have bounding lines.

22. **Taylor**, John, the Water-poet.   THE | FEAREFVLL | SVMMER: | OR | LONDONS | CALAMITY, | the countries courtesy, | and both their misery. | [*line*] | By IOHN TAYLOR | [*woodcuts.*]

Impr. 58 : 1625: (eights) 12°: pp. [32], signn. AB⁸: sign. B 1ʳ beg. *Although my pangs*: Pica Roman. Contents :— sign. A 1ʳ, title : A 2ʳ, dedication to sir John Millissent, in verse : A 2ᵛ "To the Printer", signed " Io. Taylor. Or. Coll.": A 3ᵛ "The Preface": A 4ʳ–B 2ʳ, the poem : B 3ʳ–B 6ᵛ " Against Swearing", in prose and verse : B 7ʳ–7ᵛ " My farewell to the famous Vniuersity of Oxford", in prose.

Rare. A poem on the plague at London in the summer of 1625. There are allusions to the author's stay in Oxford for some weeks and the small mortality there.

23. **Terry**, John.   THEOLOGICALL | LOGICKE : | OR | THE THIRD PART OF THE | TRYALL OF TRVTH : | Wherein is declared the excellency and æquity of the | Christian Faith, and that it is not withstood and resi-|sted ; but assisted and fortified by all the forces of right | reason, and by all the aide that artificiall Logicke can | yeeld. | *Against the heathenish Atheist, and the Romish Catholick, | whereof the one taketh exception against the Faith of | Christ in generall ; and the other against the doctrine | thereof, as it is professed in the Reformed Churches, as | being in their opinions absurd, and contrary to the cui-|dent and vndeniable grounds of reason.* | BY | IOHN TERRY Minister of the Word of | God at *Stocton.* | [*woodcuts.*]

Impr. 50: 1625: sm. 4°: pp. [2] + 229 + [1]: p. II beg. *O Lord, and, III party to whom*: Pica Roman. Contents :—p. (1) title : (2) 2 mottos: 1–4, dedication to the bp. of Bath and Wells : 5–11 "To the Christian Reader": 12–23 " The Quæstions that are handled in . . . this Treatise": 25–229, the work.

See Wood's *Ath. Oxon.,* ii. 410, and 1600 T, 1602 T.

24. **Wall**, dr. John.   THE | VVATERING | OF APOLLOS. | Deliuered in a Sermon at | Sᵗ MARIES in *Oxford* | the 8. of August | 1624. | *By* IOHN WALL *Do-|ctor in Divinity of* | Christ-Church. | [*motto*, then *woodcuts.*]

Impr. 59: 1625: (eights) 16°: pp. [64], signn. A–D⁸: sign. B 2ʳ beg. *and are mightie*: English Roman. Contents :—sign. A 1ʳ title : A 2ʳ, dedication to the bp. of Lincoln : A 3ʳ–A 6ᵛ the Epistle dedicatory to the same : A 7ʳ– D 6ᵛ, the sermon, on Acts xviii. 28.

See Wood's *Ath. Oxon.,* iii. 736. The author was chaplain to the bishop of Lincoln. Hebrew pointed type seems to be used for the first time at Oxford in this sermon, at sign. C 6ᵛ.

25. **Whear**, Degory.   DE | RATIONE | ET METHODO | Legendi Historias | *Dissertatio.* | Authore DEGOREO WHEAR | Pri. Hist. Præl. Pub. CAM-DENIANO apud | *Oxonienses.* | *Huic præmittitur eiusdem Authoris | Oratio Auspicalis habita, vbi Ca-|thedram Historicam primum ad-|scendit.* | [*woodcut.*]

Impr. 53 : 1625 : (fours) 12°: pp. [8] + 24 + [8] + 79 + [1] : pp. II beg. *horremus, domi* and *quam immensum*: Eng- lish Roman. Contents :—p. (1) title : (3–7) dedication to the earl of Pembroke, dated " Scrib. Oxoniæ 8 Kal. viiᵇʳⁱˢ,

1625 ": 1-24 " Oratio auspicalis habita | totius partes tractatarum indigitamenta ",
in Scholis publicis cùm primùm L. | a conspectus : 1-79, (1), the work, in
Annæi Flori interpretationem aggre- | 3 parts.
derer " : (1-3) " Rerum per dissertationis |

See Wood's *Ath. Oxon.*, iii. 217. The first edition was published in London in
1623, with a similar title, giving 12 July 1623 as the date of the Dissertation : the preface is dated 29 Sept. 1623 and the dedication is to William Camden, then alive, but
the Oratio is not prefixed. For other edd. see 1637 W, 1662.

1626.

1. Attonitus, Richardus, pseudonym. VERITAS ODIOSA. | FRAG-
MENTA VARIA | COLLOQVII | MACHIAVELLI ET MERCVRII. | 1626. | Ex
Schedis M. S. Richardi Attoniti Eboracensis Pro-|to-Cancellarij nuper
Classis | Anglicanæ. | [*two lines.*]

Impr. 67 : [1626?] : sm. 4° : pp. 30 | Roman. Contents :—p. 1 title : 3-30,
+[2]: p. 11 beg. *Chrestienté* : Pica | the work : (1-2) not seen.

Very rare. This is a curious production of a Dutch press, and appears to be a
vigorous defence of Barneveldt (*d.* 1619) and the Arminians against Maurice prince
of Orange and the Gomarists. Latin, French, Dutch and Italian are used, and the
whole piece abounds with lacunae. " Walter Map " in the imprint is of course the well-
known archdeacon of Oxford in the 12th cent., whose satires are still appreciated.

2. **Barnes**, Robert. A | SERMON | PREACHED AT | HENLY AT THE
VISI-|tation on the 27. of Aprill, | 1626. | *VPON THOSE WORDS OF* | *the*
9. *Psalme, Vers.* 16. | *The Lord is knowne to execute judgement.* |
[*woodcut.*]

Impr. 63 : 1626 : sm. 4° : pp. [8] + 30 | signed " Rob. Barnes ", " from my study
+[2]: p. 11 beg. *of Yorke* : English | at Greys this 4th of May, 1626 " : 1-30,
Roman. Contents :—p. (1) title : (3-8) | the sermon.
Epistle dedicatorie to sir Richard Blunt, |

See Wood's *Fasti Oxon.*, i. 339. The author was the son of Joseph Barnes the
printer, and a Fellow of Magdalen College : the dedication contains some biographical
matter, and the sermon some Henley affairs, such as ploughing on Easter Tuesday,
which the preacher laments.

3. **Bayley**, Thomas. THOMÆ BAYLÆI | MANINGFORDIENSIS | *Ec-*
clesiæ Pastoris. | DE | MERITO MORTIS CHRISTI, | ET MODO CONVERSIONIS. |
DIATRIBÆ DVÆ. | *PROVT AB IPSO IN SCHOLA* | *THEOLOGICA APVD OXONI-*
EN- | *ses publicè ad disputandum* | *propositæ fuerunt Maij.* 8. | *An. Dom.*
1621. | *Nec non Concio ejusdem ad* | *Clerum.* | APVD | *Eosdem habita in*
templo Beatæ Mariæ, | *Iulij* 5. *An. D.* 1622. | [*line.*]

Impr. 65 : 1626 : sm. 4° : pp. [12] + | christianum " : (12) the two quaestiones
63 + [1] : p. 11 beg. *per se quidem* : Great | debated in the Diatribae, with answers in
Primer Roman. Contents :—p. (3) title : | Latin verse : 1-25 the two diatribae :
(5-8) Epistola dedicatoria to sir Thomas | 27-63, the concio, on Jud. 11.
Coventry : (9-11) " Praefatio ad lectorem |

See Wood's *Ath. Oxon.*, iii. 633. The preface explains that the discourses were
printed in order to confute a charge of Arminianism.

K

4. **Cameron,** John.   AN | EXAMINATION | OF THOSE PLAVSI-'ble Appearances which seeme | most to commend the Romish | Church, and to preiudice | the Reformed. | *DISCOVERING THEM* | *to be but meere shifts, purposely in-'vented, to hinder an exact triall of do-'ctrine by the Scriptures.* | BY | Mr IOHN CAMERON. | *Englished out of French.* | [*woodcuts.*]

Impr. 59 : 1626 : sm. 4° : pp. [8] + 173 + [3] : p. 11 beg. *superiours. These,* III. *Chap. xxvii* : English Roman. Contents :—p. (1) title : (3-4) " To the Reader," unsigned, but by William Pinke the translator, see below : (5-8) " A Table of the Chapters" : 1-173 The Examination, in 41 chapters and a Con-clusion : (2) " Faults escaped in some copies," 6¼ lines of Errata.

See Wood's *Ath. Oxon.*, ii. 476, where Bliss adds a note from White Kennett's copy of the 1st ed. of the Athenæ (at i. 463) " William Pinke. He translated and published An Examination ... 1626. 4to. Ded. to the Master Wardens and Assistants of the Skinners Company. by W. P. [William Pinke] acknowledging his Engage-ments to the whole Company, and reverencing the Memory of that worthy Knight Sir James Lancaster." Neither the British Museum copy nor the two Bodleian copies contain the above dedication, the signatures of the preliminary matter being, on each leaf :—(blank), *2, **, (blank), forming one gathering of 4 leaves of a natural kind, though the double asterisk is odd. The original French bore the title " Traicté auquel sont examinez les preiugez de ceux de l'Eglise Romaine. Contre la Religion Reformee" (La Rochelle, 1617.) Cameron was a Scotchman, minister at Bordeaux and Professor of Theology at Saumur. The address to the reader apologises for using the word *prejudice* as a translation of the French *Preiugé*, which means a preconceit either good or bad : and says " I have not construed but translated."

5. **H[akewill],** G[eorge].   A | COMPARISON | BETVVEENE THE | DAYES OF PVRIM | and that of the *Powder treason* | for the better Con-tinuance of | the memory of it, and the | stirring vp of mens affe-|ctions to a more Zea-|lous observati-|on there of. | [*line*] | *Written by G. H. D. D.* | [*line.*]

Impr. 58 : 1626 : sm. 4° : pp. 36 : p. 11 beg. *more diuelish* : Great Primer Roman.   Contents :—p. 1, title, within arched border : 2, the text, Deut. xxxii. 26-28 : 3-36, the sermon.

See Wood's *Ath. Oxon*, iii. 255.

6. **Prideaux,** John.   CONCIO | HABITA OXONIÆ | ad Artium *Bacca-laureos* in | Die Cinerum Feb. 22°. | 1626. | PER | IOHANNEM PRIDEAVX S. S. Th. | *Professorem Regium, & P. T. ejusdem | Academiæ Vicecan-cellarium.* | [*motto,* then *device.*]

Impr. 60 (with " Excubebant ") : 1626 : sm. 4° : pp. viii + 40 : p. 11 beg. *latet ad* : Great Primer Roman.   Contents :—p. (3) title : (5-7) Latin dedication to Robert lord Dormer, dated " Exon: Coll: ex Musæo meo d. 8. Martij ... 1626" i.e. 162⅚ : 1-44 (" 40 "), the sermon, on 1 Sam. xiv. 26.

See Wood's *Ath. Oxon.,* iii. 273. The " P. T." of the title seems to be *Pro Tem-fore* : the use of 1626 for 1625 or 162⅚ is noticeable.

7. ——.   LECTIONES | DECEM. | DE TOTIDEM RELIGIONIS | Capitibus præcipuè hoc tempore con-|troversis prout publicè habebantur | Oxoniæ

in Vesperijs. | PER | IOHANNEM PRIDEAVX Exoniensis Collegij | Rectorem.
& S. Th. Professorem Regium. | *Editio secunda, priori emaculatior, &*
auctior. | [two *mottos*, then *device.*]

Impr. 60: 1626: sm. 4°: pp. [14] +
366: p. 11 beg. *& ult.*, 111 *mitia cele-*
bramus: Great Primer Roman. Contents :—p. (1) title: (3–7) Latin dedication to Charles prince of Wales: (9–11)
"Ad Lectorem": (12–14) "Rerum
Capita ... Quæstiones ...", 10 of each:
1–366, the 10 lectiones delivered in successive Comitia 1616–1625.

See Wood's *Ath. Oxon.*, iii. 267. I have not seen even any notice of the first
edition. These Lectiones are quite distinct from the Orationes below. See 1627 P.

8. ——.   ORATIONES | NOVEM INAVGV-'RALES, DE TOTIDEM | THEO-
LOGIÆ APICIBVS. | scitu non indignis, prout in promo-|tione Doctorum,
Oxoniæ | publicè proponebantur. | in Comitijs. | *Accedit ad Artium*
Baccalaureos, de Mosis | *Institutione Concio, pro more habita* | *in die*
Cinerum, An. 1616. | PER | IOHANNEM PRIDEAVX, | Exoniensis Collegij
Recto-|rem. & SS. Th. Professo-|rem Regium. | [two *mottos*, one in
Hebrew: then *woodcuts.*]

Impr. 64: 1626: sm. 4°: pp. [12] +
196 + 28: pp. 11 beg. *lia est terebrans,*
and *de vita Mosis*, 111 *randum. Verum*:
English Roman. Contents :—p. (1) title:
(3–7) Latin dedication to the earl of
Pembroke: (9–10) "Ad lectorem": (11)
"Rerum Capita": 1–196, the nine orations, delivered at successive Comitia
1616–22, 1624–5: 1–28, the Concio, on
Acts vii. 22.

See Wood's *Ath. Oxon.*, iii. 267. The names of the doctors are given for each
year.

9. **Reuter,** Adam.   DE | CONSILIO | TRACTATVS | *QVEM* | NOBILIS-
SIMO SVFFOLCIÆ | *Comiti consecrat* | ADAM REVTER | [*woodcut.*]

Impr. 53: 1626: sm. 4°: pp. [4] +
220 ["221", 129 being omitted] + [2]:
p. 11 beg. *sapientis principis*, 111 *Quo*
jure?: Pica Roman. Contents :—p. (1)
title: (3–4) Latin dedication to the duke
of Suffolk: 1–"221" the treatise.

See Wood's *Ath. Oxon.*, ii. 421.

10. **Wall,** John.   IACOBS | LADDER, | *OR* | *Christian advancement.* |
Deliuered in a Sermon at | *Newparke* in Glocester-|shire, the seat of the
right | Honourable the Lord | *Berkley*, this late heauy | visitation. | *By*
IOHN WALL *Doctour* in | *Divinity of Christ-Church* | *in Oxford.* | [*motto,*
then *line.*]

Impr. 66: 1626: (eights) 16°: pp.
[16] + 55 + [1]: p. 11 beg. *not mount as*:
Great Primer Roman. Contents :—p.
(3) title: (5) dedication to lady Eliz.
Berkley: (7–13) Epistle dedicatory to the
same: 1–55, the sermon, on 1 Pet. v. 6.

See Wood's *Ath. Oxon.*, iii. 734.

11. **Wower,** Jan.   "Joan. Wouveri ... pietas erga *Benefactores*
—Oxon. 1626."

So in the sale catalogue of the *Bibliotheca Gulstoniana* (bp. William Gulston's
books), Lond. 1688, 4°, p. 35, no. 290. But see 1628 W.

1627.

1. Felix, Marcus Minucius.   M. MINVCII | FELICIS | OCTAVIVS. |
[*woodcuts.*]

Impr. 74: 1627: (twelves) 16°: pp. [6] + 129 + [9]: p. 11 beg. *here, quàm in,* 111 *dicimus; non*: Pica Roman. Contents:—p. (1) title: (3-5) " Typographus lectori ": (6) quotation from Lactantius about Minucius Felix: 1-129, the work: (2) " Errata ".

See 1631 F, 1636 F, 1662, 1678.   The printer says that he has cleared this edition from the errors of Froben's.   I have seen a copy in which the type of pages 12 and 13 has changed places.   The work is an apology for Christianity.

2. Fell, dr. Samuel.   *PRIMITIÆ,* | SIVE | ORATIO | H^ABI^T^A OXON^I^AE | IN SCHOLA THEOLOGICA | *NONO NOVEMBRIS.* | ET | *CONCIO LATINA AD* | *BACCALAVREOS DIE* | *CINERVM.* | Per SAMVELEM FELL Præbendarium Ecclesiæ | Christi, & Publicum Professorem in Theo-|logiâ, pro Dominâ MARGARETA | *Comitissâ Richmondiæ.* | [*device.*]

Impr. 53: 1627: sm. 4°: pp. [2] + 17 + [1] + 18 + [2]: p. 11 beg. *quantulùm theologica*: English Roman. Contents:— p. (1) title: 1-17, the oration: (1) half title to the Concio: 1-18, the sermon on Col. ii. 8.

See Wood's *Ath. Oxon.,* iii. 243.   The (inaugural) oration contains some details about Fell's predecessor in the professorship, dr. Seb. Benefield: the two pieces would seem to have been delivered in 1626 and 1627.

3. H[akewill], G[eorge].   AN | APOLOGIE | OF THE POWER AND | PROVIDENCE OF GOD | IN THE GOVERNMENT | OF THE WORLD. | *OR* | AN EXAMINATION | AND CENSVRE OF THE | COMMON ERROUR TOVCHING | NATVRES PERPETVALL AND | VNIVERSALL DECAY, DIVI-|DED INTO FOVRE BOOKES: | *WHEREOF* | *The first treates of this pretended decay in generall, together with some prepa-|ratiues thereunto.* | *The second of the pretended decay of the Heauens and Elements, together with* | *that of the Elementary bodies, man only excepted.* | *The third of the pretended decay of mankinde in regard of age and duration, of* | *strength and stature, of arts and wits.* | *The fourth of this pretended decay in matter of manners, together with a large* | *proofe of the future consummation of the World from the testimony of the Gentiles, and the vses which we are to draw from the consideration thereof.* | By *G. H.* D. D. | [*motto,* then *device.*]

Impr. 58: 1627: (fours) fol.: pp. [36] + 473 + [5]: p. 11 beg. *Yet Phillip,* 111 *rable to their*: English Roman. Contents:—p. (1) title: (3-7) dedication to the University of Oxford, signed " G. H.": 9-19) " the Preface ": (20) " Errata ": (21-34) " The Contents . . .": (35) "of the value of the Roman sesterce . . . ": (36) quotation from Boethius, with English translation: 1-473, the work: (2-5) " A Revise," corrections of a few passages, &c.

The author was George Hakewill.   See Wood's *Ath. Oxon.,* iii. 256, where " Lond." is a mistake for " Oxford ": for other edd. see 1630 H, 1635 H.

4. **Heylyn**, Peter.   MIKPO΄KOΣMOΣ. | *A* | LITTLE DE-|SCRIPTION OF | THE GREAT WORLD. | The third Edition. Revised. | [*line*] | By PETER HEYLYN. | [*line*, then *motto*, then *woodcut*.]

Impr. 71 : 1627 : (eights) sm. 4° : pp. [20] + folded leaf + 807 + [5] : p. 11 beg. 1. *First then*, 501 *Scotland is by* : Pica Roman. Contents :—p. (1) title, within an arched border; (3-4) dedication to prince Charles : (5-6) "To the Reader" from the second ed. : (7-8) "To my brother the Author", a poem by Edw. Heylyn : (9-12) "A Table of the principall Coun-tries . . .": (13-14) "A table of the antient . . . nations . . .": (15-19) "A table of the most principall things . . .": (19) ". . . Forraine coynes . . .": 1-807, (1-2), the work : (3) "Errata". Before p. 7 should come a folded leaf, as in the 2nd ed. (1625).

See 1621 H, Wood's *Ath. Oxon.*, iii. 557. In the copy seen on p (2) at the end of the book, in the original printing of the English lines beginning "But whither goeth", l. 6 (beg. "Into safe") is before l. 4, making nonsense : and a corrected reprint of the whole 12 lines is pasted over the faulty original.

5. **Holyoke**, Francis.   DICTIONARIVM ETYMO-|LOGICVM LATINVM, ANTIQVIS-|simum & novissimum nunc demum infinitis | penè laboribus & continuis vigilijs com-|positum & absolutum à FRANCISCO | de Sacra Quercu. | That is, | *A Dictionarie declaring the originall and derivations of all words vsed* | in any Latine Authors, with the reason of their derivations and appella-¸tions; neuer any in this kinde extant before : the quantities of syllables, as | also the differences of those words, whose affinitie in signification | or otherwise, might cause a promiscuous and improper | vse : the pure and improper words gathered | into one Dictionarie, and distingui-|shed by this marke : †. | Wherevnto besides the hard and most vsefull words in Divinitie, Philosophie, | Physicke, and Logicke, are added many thousand other words out of | approued authours old and new, with their Greeke in more exactnesse then | ever was in *Calepine, Morelius,* or any other : and also the coines, | measures, weights, and Greeke Rootes, none of which | are extant in any Edition formerly | published. | *Herevnto is also annexed the proper names adorned with their Etymologies, illustrated,* | and explained, with Histories, Pro-verbes, Mythologies, &c. together with the Chronologie of | the persons, and the beginning of noted Citties, and plantation of sundry Coun-|tries, the Geography, and the names both ancient and new | of the most re-markable places, | *LASTLY RIDERS DICTIONARIE I THE ENGLISH* | before the latine compiled by RIDER, is augmented | with many hundreds of words, both out of the Law, | and out of the Latine, French, and other languages, | such as were and are with vs in common vse, | but never printed vntill now to the | perfecting of that worke. | Also the Romane Calender. | *By the great industrie and paines of* | FRANCIS HOLYOKE. |

Impr. 68 : 1627 : (eights) sm. 4° : pp. [1736], signn. ( )² A-Z, Aa-Zz, Aaa-Zzz, Aaaa-Eeee⁸, Ffff-Llll⁴, Mmmm², ( )⁴, A-Z, Aa-Ff⁸, Gg-Ii⁴ : signn. Bb 1ʳ beg. *Plin. l.* 4. 45. Bbb 1ʳ *Præcipuè, adu.,* B 1ʳ *A crafts mans,* Bb 1ʳ *Taken or drawne out* : Long Primer Roman. Contents :—sign. ( ) 1ʳ title within lines, 2ʳ "Ad Lectorem" signed "T. S. C. R." :, 2ʳ-2ᵛ, seven Latin poems on the book, one by Robert Burton : A 1ʳ-sss 1ʳ, the Latin-English lexicon : sss 1ᵛ, Holyoke's Latin dedica-tion to Clement Throckmorton " 20 [!] Cal. Mart. 1611 " : sss 2ʳ-Ffff 4ᵛ, "Dic-tionarium etymologicum propriorum no-minum" : Gggg 1ʳ-Mmmm 1ʳ, "Radices Græcæ linguæ . . . collectæ & compo-sitæ. Opera & studio T. W.", a short Greek-Latin lexicon : ( ) 1ʳ a title within lines :—"*RIDERS* | DICTIONARIE | COR-

RECTED AND | AVGMENTED WITH THE | ADDITION OF MANY HVN-|DRED WORDS NOT EXTANT | IN ANY FORMER EDI-TION. | HEREVNTO ARE ANNEXED | RIDERS CALENDER, AND CER-|TAINE TABLES EXPLAINING | *the names, weights and valuations of* | auncient and modern coynes, as | *also a table of the Hebrew, Greeke* | *& Latine measures reduced to our* | *English standard & assise.* | *WHEREVNTO IS JOYNED A DICTIO-* | *NARY* ETYMOLOGICALL, DERIVING | *each word from his proper fountaine, the first* | that ever was extant in that kind, with | many worthy castigations and addi-*tions, as will appeare in the title and epistle before it.* | [*line*] | BY | FRANCIS HOLIOKE | | [*line*]", then impr. 58 : ( ) 2ʳ–2ᵛ, dedication to lady Dudley by Holyoke: ( ) 3ʳ, Latin dedication to sir F. Walsingham, dated "Oxoniæ, Calend. Octob." by John Rider: ( ) 3ᵛ "To the Reader" dated "From Oxon. the xxx of September" by Rider: ( ) 4ʳ–4ᵛ, poems &c. by Rider, John Case (30 Sept. 1589) &c. : A–Ee 8ᵛ, "Bibliotheca Rideri scholastica", an English-Latin lexicon: Ff1ʳ–11h 3ʳ "Certaine generall heads of Birds, Colours, &c.", English-Latin: 11h 3ᵛ–4ʳ, a short English-Latin geographical dictionary: 11h 4ʳ–1i 4ᵛ, "Johannis Rideri Calendarium Romanum . . .", followed by lists of weights, measures, &c. and foreign coins, the last, signed "W. T. P."

Rare, see 1589 R. Of bp. Rider's double lexicon the first part at least (English-Latin) was published at Oxford in 1589. In 1606 Francis Holyoke supplied a Latin-English part (based on Rider's Index) and published both at London. Subsequent edd. of the two parts together are Lond. 1617, Lond. 1626 (ed. N. Gray), the present one Oxf. 1627, Lond. 1633 (called the 4th), Lond. 1640 (called the 5th), Lond. 1649, Lond. 1659 (acc. to Bohn's Lowndes, s. v. Rider, where however since 1637 is an error for 1627, this 1659 may be one for 1649), and, edited by Thomas Holyoke son of Francis, Lond. 1677.

6. James, dr. Thomas. *INDEX* | GENERALIS | LIBRORVM PROHI- | BITORVM à PONTIFI-|ciis, unà cum Editionibus | *expurgatis vel expur-*|gandis juxta seriem Li-|terarum & tripli-|cem classem. | *In usum Biblio-theca Bodleia- anæ, & Curatoribus eiusdem* | specialiter designatus | PER | THO. IAMES S. Theol. | D. Coll. B. Mariæ Winton | in Oxon. Vulgò Novi dicti | quondam Socium. | [*woodcuts.*]

Impr. 69 : 1627 : (twelves) 16° : pp. [144], sign. *, A–L.¹²: sign. B 1ʳ beg. *In Biblia*: Pica Roman. Contents :—* 1ʳ, "[*]ᵛ: 2ʳ, title: 3ʳ, Latin dedication to the Curators of the Bodleian, followed (4ʳ–6ᵛ) by an Epistola dedicatoria to them : 7ʳ–10ᵛ, Ad Lectorem : 11ʳ, Errata : A1–K5ᵛ, the work : K6ʳ–L10ᵛ, "Tabula", an index of authors : L11ʳ "Cautio".

See Wood's *Ath. Oxon.*, ii. 467. The intention of the book is the reverse of the aim of the *Indices Expurgatorii*, namely to give a select list of recommended books. Those which were in the Bodleian are marked with a star.

7. Pasor, Matthias. ORATIO | *PRO* | LINGVÆ ARABICÆ | *PROFES-SIONE, PVBLICE* | ad Academicos habita in | schola Theologica *Vni-*|*versitatis Oxoniensis* | xxv. Octob. | 1626. | à | MATTHIA PASORE, *Artium Magi-stro & non ita pridem Mathematum Pro-*|*fessore in Vniversitate* Haidelbergensi. | [two *mottos*, one Hebrew.]

Impr.60 : 1627 : (eights) 16° : pp. [34], signn. A–B⁴C²: sign. B 1ʳ beg. *mentariorum Rabbinnicorum*: English Roman. Contents :—sign. A 1ʳ, title: A 1ᵛ, "decretum Concilii Viennensis", see below, then device : 2ʳ–2ᵛ, dedication to the University of Oxford, in Latin, dated 5 Dec. 1626 : A 3ʳ–C 2ᵛ, the oration.

See Wood's *Ath. Oxon.*, iii. 445. The oration is of considerable interest for the history of Oriental studies at Oxford. It claims to be the first on the subject at Oxford, quotes the decree of the Council of Vienne 1311–12 that there ought to be instruction in Hebrew, Arabic and Chaldee at Oxford, and urges the fitness of the study in Oxford. Pasor was lecturer on Arabic only from 1626 to 1629. Some Arabic MSS. in the Bodleian are mentioned on sign. B7ʳ and B7ᵛ.

8. **Prideaux**, dr. John. In the *Catalogus . . . librorum . . . Richardi Davis bibliopolæ, pars quarta* (Lond. 1692, 4°) p. 10, no. 183 is " Joan. Prideaux Lectiones novem, Oxon. 1627." See 1626 P.

9. **Richardson**, Gabriel. [*woodcut*] | OF | THE STATE | OF EVROPE. | *XIIII. Bookes.* | CONTAINING THE HISTO-|RIE, AND RELATION OF THE | *MANY PROVINCES* | HEREOF. | *Continued out of approved Authours.* | BY | GABRIEL RICHARDSON BATCHELOVR | in Divinitie, and FELLOW of BRASEN-|NOSE *College in Oxford.* | [*device.*]

Impr. 70 : 1627 : (fours) fol. : pp. [4] + 18 + 67 + 37 + [1] + 14 + 13 + [1] + 50 + 23 + [1] + 11 + [1] + 74 + 26 + [2] + 11 + [1] + 68 + 29 + [1] + 64 + [2] : pp. 11 [bk. 1] beg. *Di ocesse with,* (bk. 6) *Arco-briga,* (bk. 10) *Berry. Bounded,* (bk. 11) *Vindomana* : English Roman. Contents :—p. (1) title ; (3-4) dedication to the bp. of Lincoln : 1—. . .64, the treatise in 14 books separately paged.

See Wood's *Ath. Oxon.,* iii. 38. The first four books contain Great Britain. The signatures begin again with the 10th and with the 11th book, but every book is separately paged. The matter is a mixture of history and geography.

10. **Smith**, Samuel. Wood (*Ath. Oxon.,* ii. 283) mentions an edition of the Aditus ad Logicam of this year : see 1617 S.

11. **Vicars**, Thomas. PVSILLVS GREX. | ΕΛΕΓΧΟΣ. | REFVTATIO | CVIVSDAM LIBELLI DE AM-|PLITVDINE REGNI COELESTIS | *SVB EMENTITO CAELII SECVNDI* | CVRIONIS NOMINE IN LV-|CEM EMISSI. | *Qua docetur ex Scripturis beatorum numerum majorem* | *non esse numero damnatorum, sed potius minorem.* | *Ad excutiendum securitatis veternum nostris homini-bus* | *potissimùm conscripta.* | *Authore* THOMA *de* VICARIIS *S. T. Bac. Pastore* | *Cockfieldiensi in agro quondam Australium Saxonum.* | [*two mottos,* then *woodcuts.*]

Impr. 72 : 1627 : sm. 4° : pp. 32 : p. 11 beg. *argumentaque* : English Roman. Contents :—p. 1, title : 2, " Ad Lectores Candidos " : 3-6, Latin letters between " Thom. Vicarsius " (" Gallager ", = of Cockfield) and John Goldsmith (" Gallinager " = of Henfield), and William Cox, canon of Chichester, one dated 7 Jan. 1622 or 1623 : 7-32, the discourse, on Luke xii. 32.

See Wood's *Ath. Oxon.,* ii. 443. The original treatise of Coelius Secundus Curio (an Italian, *d.* 1569) entitled " . . . De amplitudine beati regni Dei dialogi sive libri duo " was first published in 1554, and his contention that the number of the saved is greater than that of the lost is here refuted.

12. **Wake**, Isaac. REX PLATONICVS : | [&c. exactly as 1615 W, except that the colon in the first line is italic, not Roman, and " Quarta " for " Tertia ".]

Impr. 73: 1627: (twelves) 16º: pp. [8] + 238 + [18]: p. 11 beg. *mentum de-mississimo,* 111 *neri, vt quum*: Long Primer Roman. Contents:—p. (1) title: (3–7) dedication to prince Henry, as in 1st ed.: 1–236, the work: 237–238, (1), the Chancellor's letter with preface: (3) title "ORATIO | FVNEBRIS | habita in Tem-*plo beatæ Ma-|riæ Oxon.* | Ab ISAACO WAKE, | *PVBLICO ACA-|demiæ Oratore, Maij* | 25. An. 1607. quum | *mæsti Ox-onienses,* | *pijs manibus* IO-|HANNIS RAI-| NOLDI *paren-|tarent.* | " [woodcuts, then impr. 73]: (5–17) the oration.

See 1607 W. This fourth edition is a verbatim but not literatim reprint of the 3rd ed. (1615).

13. **Wall,** dr. John.   CHRIST IN | PROGRESSE. | DELIVERED IN A SER-|mon at *Shelford* in *Nottingham-|shire,* the seate of the right Honou-|rable the Lord STANHOPE. | *By* IOHN WALL *Doctour in Divini-|ty of Christ-Church in Oxford.* | [*motto,* then *woodcut.*]

Impr. 58: 1627: (eights) 12º: pp. [16] + 50 + [2]: p. 11 beg. *where the Lord*: Great Primer Roman. Contents:— (1–2) not seen: (3) title: (5) dedication to sir Henry Stanhope, son of lord Stan-hope: (7–13) "The Epistle dedicatory": (15–16) not seen: 1–50, the sermon, on Matth. xxi. 9.

See Wood's *Ath. Oxon.,* iii. 735.

1628.

1. [**Airay,** Christopher].   FASCICVLVS | PRÆCEPTORVM | *LOGICORVM IN* | *gratiam juventutis* A-|CADEMICÆ *compositus* | *& nunc primùm typis donatus.* | [*woodcuts.*]

Impr. 72: 1628: (eights) 16º: pp. [8] + 224: p. 11 beg. *co*: *vt, si,* 111 1. *Necessaria, cui*: Long Primer Roman. Contents:—p. (3) title: (5–6) "Typo-graphus benevolo Lectori . . .": (7) "Sphalmata . . .", errata: (8) "*Arbor Porphyriana*": 1–224, the work com-prising an "Introductio generalis . . ." and six books.

The first edition of Airay's Logic, see 1633 A, 1660. The preface explains that the author's name is omitted from modesty, and that several MSS. of the first three books have been compared and something added, as well as three more books.

2. Bodleian Library.   The entry in the "Catalogi . . . librorum . . . Richardi Davis . . . pars quarta," Lond. 1692, p. 29:—" 108. Catalogus Librorum in Bibliotheca Bodleiana—Oxon. 1628 " must be an error for 1620.

3. **Brerewood,** Edward   TRACTATVS | QVIDAM | LOGICI | DE | *PRÆDICABILIBVS,* | ET | *PRÆDICAMENTIS.* | *Ab eruditissimo Viro* ED-VARDO BREREWOOD | Artium Magistro, è Collegio *Ænei-Nasi,* olim con-scripti: | nunc verò ab erroribus (qui frequenti transcriptione irrepserant) vindicati, ad pristinum nitorem, na-|tivamq; puritatem diligentissimâ manuscripto-|rum collatione restituti, & in lucem editi, | *Per* T. S. *Art. Mag. & Collegij Ænei-Nasi Socium.* | [*line,* then *motto,* then *device.*]

Impr. 72 *b* : 1628 : sm. 4° : pp. [32] + single leaf + 472 : p. 11 beg. *genus & species*, 401 *les sit sanus* : Pica Roman. Contents :— p. (1) title : (3-8) epistola dedicatoria to sir Rich. Brook of Norton, signed "Thomas Sixesmith", "Oxonij, è Musæo meo, in Collegio Ænea-Nasensi, 13. Calend. Octob. 1628": (9-12) "Eru-dito Lectori . . .": (13-31) "Index sectionum quæstionumque . . .": a folded sm. folio leaf "Pag. 1" bearing an "Analysis" of logic, printed on one side only, perhaps not by Brerewood : 1-472, the ten treatises (pp. 63 64 are another folded leaf, printed in style similar to the former one, but "Sect. 17").

See Wood's *Ath. Oxon.*, ii. 140.   Brerewood died in 1613.

4. **Burton**, Robert.   [Engraved title :—] THE | ANATOMY OF MELANCHOLY. | *What it is, with all the kinds causes,* | *symptomes, prog-nostickes, & seuerall cures of it.* | In three Partitions, with their severall Sections, members & subsections, | Philosophically, Medicinally, | Historically, opened & cut up. | BY | *Democritus Junior.* | *With a Satyricall Preface, conducing* | *to the following Discourse.* | *The thirde Edition, corrected and* | *augmented by the Author.* | *motto* : see below.]

Impr. 70 : 1628 : (fours` folio : pp. [8?] + 77 + [11] + 646 (after 208 are two unnumbered leaves, and after 374 one) + [12] : p. 11 beg. *atq; auidè,* 501 *so they must* : English Roman.   Contents :—p. (1) engraved title : [(3-6) not seen, two leaves of verses?] (7) dedication to George lord Berkeley : 1-77 "Democritus Iunior to the reader" : (2) "Lectori malè feriato" : (4-7) "the Synopsis of the first partition" : (8-9) "Democritus Iunior ad librum suum", elegiacs : (10-11) "The Authors Abstract of Melancholy, διαλο-γικῶς", verses : 1-208, the first partition : (1-4) "The Synopsis of the second partition" : 209-374, the second partition : (1-2) "Analysis of the third partition" : 375-646, the third partition : (1-8) "The Table", an index : (9) "Errata sic corrigas" : (11) Impr. 75, between woodcuts.

See Wood's *Ath. Oxon.*, ii. 653, and 1621 B.   The author's name does not occur in the book.   The engraved title is divided into 12 parts, arranged in horizontal rows of three, but the rows are not of equal height : no. 1 (left top corner) is "Zelotipia," birds with river and trees : 2. "Democritus Abderites" by his garden, under a tree : 3. "Solitudo," deer &c. in a glade : 4. (second row) "Inamorato" a love-sick youth with suitable surroundings : 5. title, as above : 6. "Hypocondriacus" a king, sitting : 7. "Superstitiosus," a monk on his knees, telling his beads : 8. "Democritus Junior," half length, with arms, book, sphere and ladder (?) : 9. "Maniacus," chained : 10. "Borago," the plant : 11. Imprint, with "C: le ... Blon. fe :" the engraver : 12. "Helleborus," the plant.   This title is found in later editions, but in a comparatively worn state.

5. **Cameron**, John.   A | TRACT OF THE | SOVERAIGNE IVDGE | OF CONTROVERSIES | IN MATTERS OF | RELIGION. | [*line*] | By IOHN CAMERON Minister of the | Word of God, and Divinity Professour | in the Academie of *Montauban.* | [*line*] | *Translated into English by* IOHN | Vernevil. *M.A.* | [*motto,* and translation.]

Impr. 80 : 1628 : sm. 4° : pp. 48 : p. 11 beg. *constrayned first of all* : Pica Roman.   Contents :—p. 1, title : 3-4, dedication to sir Thomas Leigh, dated "from the publique Library in Oxford this 30 of Aug. 1628" : 5 6, "To the Reader" : 7-48, the treatise.

See Wood's *Ath. Oxon.*, iii. 222.   The author states that when he first came into England he "belonged unto" Sir Tho. Leigh and his grandfather of the same names. The "sovereign judge" of the treatise is declared to be "God speaking in the Scriptures."

6. **Carpenter**, Nathaniel.   *Achitophel: or, the Picture of a wicked Politician*, in 3 parts. Dubl. 1627, oct. Ox. 1628, qu.

So in Wood's *Ath. Oxon.*, ii. 422, where Wood relates that the Lond. 1629 ed. (and presumably all subsequent editions) is expurgated of passages supposed to reflect on Arminianism. See 1640 C. The British Museum, Bodleian, Advocates' Library at Edinburgh and the Library of Trinity College, Dublin, do not seem to possess a copy of either of the two first editions.

7. **C[asa]**, J[=Giovanni della].   ETHICA | IVVENILIS | *J. C.* | GALA-TEVS | Seu | De Morum Honestate & E-|legantia; Liber ex Italico | Latinus; | [*line*] | Ejusdem *J. W.* de Umbra | Variæ. | [*woodcuts.*]

Impr. 87 : 1628: (twelves) 16°: pp. [4] + 129 + [3]: p. 11 beg. *mo nobis bene,* III *prehendere, vel*: Pica Roman. Contents :—pp. (1-2), not seen: (3) title, within a double line: (4) second title

" Ethica Iuvenilis, seu Manuductorium ad laudabilem morum Concinnitatem . . .", and preface signed "G. W.": 1-129, the treatise: (2-3) not seen.

See 1630 C. The author was Giovanni della Casa, and the translator Nathan Chytraeus, whose initials occur on p. 1: but the copy seen had no trace of " J. W. de Umbra variæ," though the binding was original. There are many editions of the Italian and Latin forms of this treatise (see 1630 C and 1665), and some of an English translation. Pp. 1-128 of this edition were reissued as part of the 1665 edition.

8. **D[ickinson]**, W[illiam].   *MILKE* | FOR BABES. | *THE* | ENGLISH CATECHISME, | SET DOWNE IN THE | Common-Prayer Booke, breifly ex-|planed for the private vse of the | *Younger and more vnlearned sort of* | *his Parishioners of* Apleton, *in* | the County of Berks. | *.*.* | By W. D. | [two *mottos.*]

Impr. 85 : 1628: sm. 4°: pp. [8] + 39 + [1]: p. 11 beg. *sible resemblance*: Pica English and Roman. Contents :—

p. (1) title, (2) four " Errata ": 3-8 " To his parishioners . . ." of Appleton, a dedication and preface: 1-39 the work.

For the author see Wood's *Fasti Oxon.*, i. 389.

9. **Doughty**, John.   *A DISCOVRSE* | CONCERNING | THE ABSTRUSE-NESSE | of Divine Mysteries, together | *with our knowledge of them* | MAY I. 1627. | ANOTHER | *TOVCHING CHVRCH-* | Schismes but the Vnanimity | of Orthodox Professours | FEB. 17. 1628. | [*line*] | By *I. D.* Mr of Arts and Fellow of | *Merton Colledge in Oxford.* | [*line.*]

Impr. 84 : 1628 : sm. 4°: pp. [4] + 26 + 26 : pp. 11 beg. *for mans delight,* and *by discountenance*: English Roman. Contents :—p. (1) title, within a line :

(3-4) dedication to Dr. Brent, warden of Merton, signed " Iohn Doughty ": 1-26 the first sermon, on Rom. xii. 16 : 1-26 the second, on Rom. xvi. 17.

See Wood's *Ath. Oxon.*, iii. 977. The signatures run through the whole volume. All the pages of text are within a bounding line doubled at the top and outer side.

10. **Field**, dr. Richard.   OF | THE CHVRCH, | FIVE BOOKES. | BY | RICHARD FIELD DOCTOR | OF DIVINITY | AND SOME=TIMES DEANE OF | GLOCESTER. | [*line*] | *THE SECOND EDITION VERY MVCH AVG=* | *mented,*

in the thirde booke, and the Appendix to the same. | [*line, then device, then line.*]

Impr. 68 a : 1628 : (sixes) fol. : pp. [16] + 906 + [2] : p. 11 beg. *tators of dawngerous, 701 wrongs of the Court* : Pica Roman. Contents :—p. (1) title : (3-4) Epistle dedicatory to the duke of Buckingham, signed "Nathaniel Field", the author's son. (5-?) Epistle dedicatory to the archbp. of Canterbury, by Rich. Field : (9-15) "what things are handled in the bookes following" : (15) "Errata" : 1-28, the work, bk 1 : 29-46, bk 2 : 47-142, bk 3 : 183-342, "an Appendix..." : 343-402, bk 4 : 403, a title to book 5, and its appendix, with impr. 68 : 403-746, bk 5 : 747-906, the appendix : 1-? not seen.

See Wood's *Ath. Oxon.*, ii. 284. 1635 F. The first ed. (two different issues) was Lond. 1606 : 5th book, Lond. 1610). The author died in 1626. Three edd. or parts of edd. have been issued even in the 19th century. The signatures run completely through the book.

11. Godwin, Thomas.

ROMANÆ | HISTORIÆ | ANTHOLOGIA RECOGNITA ET | AVCTA. | *AN* | ENGLISH EXPOSITION | OF THE ROMAN ANTI-quities, wherein many Roman | & English offices are paralleld | *and divers obscure phrases* | *explained* | *For the use of* ABINGDON *Schools.* [*line*] | Newly revised and inlarged by the | *Author.* | [*line.*]

Impr. 70 : 1628 : sm. 4° : pp. [8] + 277 + [23] : p. 11 beg. *malefactor, but,* 201. *Cap. 8. De rapu* : Pica Roman. Contents :—p. (1) title, within an arched border : (3-4) dedication to dr. Young. 14 Cal. Dec 1622 : (5-?) "Benevolo lec-tori..." : (7) "A short table..." of contents : 1-277, the work : (1-23) "In-dex rerum et verborum".

See 1614 G.

12. Gumbleden, John.

GODS | GREAT MERCY TO MANKINDE IN *JESVS CHRIST.* | A | SERMON PREACHED AT Pauls Crosse. March 18 : being | *Palme Sunday.* 1626. | By IOHN GVMBLEDEN M^r of Artes. [*two mottos, then woodcut.*]

Impr. 81 : 1628 : sm. 4° : pp. [4] + 34 - [3] : p. 11 beg. *off he comes* : Pica Roman. Contents :—p. (1) title : (3-4) "To the Reader", dated "From my Study at Longworth in Berkshiere. Octob. 14. 1627" : 1-34, the sermon, on Is. liii. 6.

See Wood's *Ath. Oxon.* iii. 436.

13. Howson, John, bp. of Oxford.

ARTICLES | ECCLESIASTICALL | to be enquired of by the Church-wardens & | Sidesmen within the Dioces of Oxon: set forth | *by the authority of the Right Reverend Father* | *in God* IOHN *by the Divine providence* | *of God Lord Bishop of Oxon: Anno* | 1628. *Being the third yeare* | *from his Lordships* | *Visita-tion.* | [*woodcut.*] |

Impr. 82 : 1628 : sm. 4° : pp. [12], sign. A 1° 3° : sign. B 1° beg. *spected to concealc* : Pica English. Contents :— sign. A 1° title : A 1° "The Oath" : A 2°- B 3°. "Articles concerning the Clergie", &c.

14. Parre, bp. Richard.

CONCIO AD | CLERVM HABITA OXONIÆ IN |

Comitijs Iul. 12. 1625. | PER | RICH: PARRE. S.S. | *Theol. Bac. Coll. Aenei-'nasi Socium.* | [*woodcuts.*]

Impr. 72 *a* : 1628 : (eights) 16° : pp. [8] + 46 + [2] : p. 11 beg. *demùm sunt hæc* : English Roman. Contents :—p. (1) | title: (3–7) epistola dedicatoria to Thomas earl of Southampton : (8) "Errata" : 1–46, the sermon on Rev. iii. 4.

See Wood's *Ath. Oxon.*, iii. 345. The dedication states that Parre was chaplain to his patron the earl of Southampton.

15. **Parre**, bp. Richard.   THE | END OF THE | PERFECT MAN. | A | SERMON PREACHED AT | *the Buriall of the right Honourable Sir* | ROBERT SPENCER Knight | Baron SPENCER of *Wormeleighton,* | *Novemb.* 6. 1627. in *Braynton* | *Church in Nor-'thamptonshire,* | BY | RICHARD PARRE Bachelour in | Divinity, and late Fellow of Brasen-nose Col-|ledge in Oxford, now Rector of | *Ladbrook* in Warwickshire. | [*woodcuts.*]

Impr. 68 : 1628 : sm. 4° : pp. [8] + 29 + [7] : p. 11 beg. *hortation. As long* : Pica Roman. Contents :—p. (1) title : (3–6) epistle dedicatory to William lord Spencer of Wormleighton : (7–8) " The | Preface" : 1–29, the sermon on Ps. xxxvii. 37 : (2–6) seven poems, in English, Greek (one) and Latin (one) on lord Spencer's death, no doubt by Parre.

See Wood's *Ath. Oxon.*, iii. 345.

16. **Pemble**, William.   FIVE | GODLY, AND PRO-|fitable Sermons concerning | 1 *The slaverie of sinne.* | 2 The mischiefe of ignorance. | 3 The roote of Apostasie. | 4 The benefit of Gods service. | 5 The Christians loue. | *Preached in his life time in sundry places.* | By that late faithfull Minister of | *Christ* Mr WILLIAM | PEMBLE *of Mag-|dalen Hall in the Vni-|versity of Oxford.* |

Impr. 84 : 1628 : sm. 4° : pp. [4] + 24 + 72 + " 31 "–" 38 " + [4?] : pp. 11 beg. *and cast themselues,* and *tence* 2. *Thess* : pp. 33 beg. *as those Children,* and *his happyness* : Pica Roman. Contents :— p. (1) title, within arched border : (3–4) " To the Reader", signed by the editor | " Iohn Tombes " : 1–24 the first sermon, on John viii. 34 : 1–25, the second, on Hos. iv. 6 : 27–43, the third, on Heb. iii. 12–13 : 44–66, the fourth on Ex. xxxiv. 23–24 : 67–71, " 31 "–" 38 ", 1, the fifth, on Cant. ii. 16 : (3–4) not seen.

See Wood's *Ath. Oxon.*, ii. 331 (where " Lond." is an error for " Oxf.") and 1629, P. Pemble died in 1623. The editor was a pupil of Pemble (Wood's *Ath. Oxon.*, iii. 1062), and succeeded him in his lectureship at Magdalen hall. There is something curious about the printing of this volume: the pagination is peculiar, and sign. Ki{r} (p. " 31 ") has the running title of sermon 4 instead of 5: also the catchword on p. " 38 " is *haue* instead of *having,* and the next page differs in style of printing. The second edition shows each sermon with a separate pagination, but appears otherwise to be a verbatim reprint. The signatures of this first ed. begin again with the second sermon, and the first at least of the last two leaves bears no signature, though beginning a new sheet.

17. **Rudyerd**, sir Benjamin.   BENIAMIN RVDIERD | HIS SPEECH IN BEHALFE | OF THE CLERGIE, AND OF | *Parishes* miserably destitute of In-|struction, through want of | *Maintenance.* | CONFIRMED BY THE | Testimonies of Bishop IEWEL, | Master PERKINS, and Sir | HENRY SPELMAN. | [*line, motto, ine.*]

Impr. 76: 1628: sm. 4°: pp. [2]+ 14+[2]: p. 11 beg. *taine vnto him*: Pica Roman. Contents:—p. (1) title: 1–14, the speech.

See Wood's *Ath. Oxon.*, iii. 456. This tract is generally found without any title page (signn. A—B⁴ only): the London booksellers seem to have printed one for their own purposes, not deeming the title as it heads p. 1 ("Sir Beniamin Ruddierd's speach in behalfe of the Cleargy.") sufficient. Some early copies have the number of the first page central over the author's name, enclosed in brackets; but it was doubtless soon moved to the upper right hand corner, because in its original place it seemed to indicate a first *part* of the tract rather than simply the first page. This speech was reprinted at London in 1641.

18. **Sparke**, William. THE | MYSTERY | OF | GODLINESSE: | A | GENERALL DISCOVRSE | OF THE REASON THAT IS | IN CHRISTIAN RELIGION. | [*line*] | By WILLIAM SPARKE Divinity Rea=|der at *Magd: Coll:* in *Oxford* and Par=|son of *Blechly* in *Buckingham-shire.* | [*line*, then 2 *mottos.*]

Impr. 77: 1628: sm. 4°: pp. [16]+ 78+[2]+78+[2]: pp. 11 beg. *All the glory*, and *children, yee cannot*: English Roman. Contents:—p. (1) title: (3–5) dedication to George duke of Bucking-ham: (7–12) "The Preface to the Reader": (13–15) "The Contents": 1–78 "Booke I", in 3 chapters: 1–78 "Booke II", in 3 chapters: 78, imprint 78.

See Wood's *Ath. Oxon.*, ii. 495. The second book, which is distinct in pagination, signatures and colophon, seems to have been printed separately and even issued by itself.

19. **Tozer**, Henry. DIRECTIONS | *FOR* | A GODLY LIFE: | Especi-ally for Communi-|cating at the Lord's Table. | *Intended first for private vse*; | *now publish'd for the good of* | *those who desire the safty of* | *their owne soules, and* | *shall bee pleased to* | *make vse thereof.* | BY | H. TOZER Mr of Arts, and | Fellow of *Exceter* Col-|ledge in *Oxford.* | [*motto*: then *line.*]

Impr. 68: 1628: (twelves) 16°: pp. 198+[6]: p. 11 beg. *this I now*, 101 *Re-deemer liueth*: Pica Roman. Contents:— p. 1, title: 3–11, Epistle dedicatory to Lorenzo Cary son of viscount Falkland: 13–198, the directions: (1–3) "The Con-tents of each Chapter".

See Wood's *Ath. Oxon.*, iii. 274, and 1640 T. There were also Oxford edd. in 1671 (8th), 1680 (10th), but all editions seem to be uncommon.

20. **Vossius**, Gerardus Johannes. GERARDI IOH. VOSSII | *V. Cl.* | THESES THEOLOGICÆ | ET | HISTORICÆ, | *De varijs doctrinæ Christianæ Capitibus*; | Quas, aliquot abhinc annis, dispu-|tandas proposuit in | ACADEMIA LEIDENSI. | [*woodcut.*]

Impr. 83: 1628: (eights) sm. 4°: pp. [8]+680: p. 11 beg *illius de chao*, 501 *Nec meliorem*: Pica Roman. Contents:— p. (1) title: [pp. 3–4 are perhaps always torn out, as blank]: (5) Errata: (6–7) "Syllabus & Ordo Disputationum": 1 680, the forty disputations, each di-vided into theses.

See 1631 V. These Disputations were printed at Leiden in 1615, and the Hague in 1638. In the title the 1st, 2nd, 4th, 6th and 9th, as well as the first line of the Imprint "Bellositi Dobunorum," are in red ink. There are large paper copies of this work.

21. **Wall**, John.   *THE* | LION IN THE | LAMBE. | OR STRENGTH IN | *WEAKENES.* | DELIVERED IN A SER-|mon at *Shelford* in *Nottingham-|shire,* the seate of the right Ho-|nourable the Lord | STANHOPE. | By IOHN WALL. *Doctour in Divini-|ty of Christ-Church in* Oxford. | [*motto,* then *woodcut.*]

Impr. 86: 1628: (eights) 16°: pp. [16] + 55 + [1]: p. 11 beg. *was sinne wrought*: Great Primer Roman. Contents:—p. (3) title: (5, 7-15) dedication and epistle dedicatory to lady Katharine Stanhope: 1-55, the sermon, on Rev. vii. 10.

See Wood's *Ath. Oxon.,* iii. 735.

22. **Whear**, Degory.   DEGOREI | WHEARI | *PRAEL. HIST.* | CAMDENI-ANI. | *PIETAS erga BE-NEFACTORES* | continens, | *Parentationem His-toricam* | *Manibus Camdeni oblatam.* | *Dedicationem Imaginis Camde-|nianæ in Scholâ Historica.* | *Necnon* | *Epistolarum Eucharisticarum fascicu-|lum.* | [*line.*]

Impr. 72 *a*: 1628: (eights) 16°: pp. [8] + 48 + 133 + [3]: pp. 11 beg. *tutes tam chari*, and *incolumem. dabam,* 111 *Prædocto Guil. Smitho*: Pica Roman. Contents:—p. (1) title: (2) two mottos: (3 7) dedication to the University of Oxford: 1-19, "Parentatio historica, sive Commemoratio vitæ et mortis V.C. Guli elmi Camdeni Clarentii, facta Oxoniæ in Scholâ Historicâ statim à funere, Ann. 1623", a speech: 20 22, "Nuncius Chronogrammaticus, de obitu . . . Camdeni . . .", a poem with chronograms: 23-48, "Dedicatio imaginis Camdenianæ in Schola Historica, 12 Novemb. 1626," a speech, with more chronograms: 1, a half title "Epistolarum eucharisticharum fasciculus": 2, a motto: 3-5 dedication to dr. Benj. Rudierd, dated "Oxoniæ 6 Idus Apr. 1628", in Latin: 6-93. 56 letters from dr. Whear to friends, 1601-26, in Latin: 95, a title "[*woodcuts*] | DEGOREI | WHEARI | PRAELEC. | HISTOR.| *CAMDEN.* | *CHARISTERIA* | [*woodcuts*]" | impr. 69: 96, motto: 97-103, dedication to John Pym, dated "Oxon. . a.d. 5 Kal. Mai. 1628": 104-133, the Charisteria, letters by Whear to accompany presenta-tion copies of his *Methodus historica* (1625 W): 134 "Errata sic corrigenda...".

See Wood's *Ath. Oxon.,* iii. 219. The title of this work appears to explain an extraordinary entry in the *Bibliotheca Gulstoniana* (1688) p. 35 "Joan. Wouveri pietas erga Benefactores, Oxon. 1626"!

23. **White**, Antony.   TRVTH | AND ERROR | DISCOVERED | IN TWO SER-|MONS IN St MA-|ries in *Oxford.* | [*line*] | *By* ANTONY WHITE *Master of Arts | of Corpus Christi Colledge in Oxford.* | [*line,* then *woodcut.*]

Impr. 79: 1628: sm. 4°: pp. [4] + 59 + [1]: p. 11 beg. *in the superstitious*: English Roman. Contents:—p. (1) title: (3-4) dedication to sir Henry Neville: 1-30, the first sermon, on Prov. xxiii. 23, "Truth purchast": 31-59, the second, on James i. 16, "Error abandon'd".

See Wood's *Fasti Oxon.,* i. 347. Every printed page is within bounding lines, on the top and outer side double.

1629.

1. **Ames**, William.   BELLARMINVS | ENERVATVS, | à | GVILIELMO AMESIO | *S. S. Theologiæ Doctore in* | Academia Franckerana. | *In quatuor*

Tomos divisus: | *Ab Auctore recognitus, & multis* | *in locis auctus.* | Editio tertia. | [*woodcuts.*]

Impr. 88 : 1629 : 12° : pp. [24] + 283 + [5] + 288 + 299 + [5] + 230 : pp. 11 beg. *Canonem retulerunt,* and *Argumenta Bellarmini,* and *Bona opera,* and *nullam. Protest.* : Long Primer Roman. Contents:—p. (1) title : (3-5) dedication to the Belgian states : (6) " Ad Lectorem ": (7-12) " Index Controversiarum quæ hoc opere tractantur ": (13-23) " Index locorum Scripturæ . . . " : 1-283, tome 1 : (2) a title " Bellarminus enervatus, sive disputationes antibellarminianæ, in Illustri Frisiorum Academia, quæ est Franekeræ, publicè habitæ ; a Guilielmo Amesio Theologiæ Doctore. Tomus secundus. Ab Auctore recognitus & auctus ", with impr. 72 a : (4-5) dedication to Ernest Casimir count of Nassau, 20 Nov. 1625, in Latin : 1-288, tome 2 : 1, title, exactly as in vol. 2, with *tertius* for *secundus* : 3-4, dedication to senators of Friesland, 4 Kal. Apr. 1626 : 5-299, tome 3 : (2) title, exactly as in vol. 2 with *quartus* for *secundus* : (4-5) dedication to four curators of the University of Franeker, 3 Kal. Oct. 1626 : 1-230, tome 4.

This is a long controversial treatise against Bellarmine on the Calvinist side, and covers nearly the whole ground of theology. There are editions issued at Amsterdam in 1625-6, 1628 and 1638, and at London in 1632-33.

2. **Burges,** Cornelius.　　　BAPTISMALL. | *REGENERATION* | of Elect Infants, | Professed by the Church of | *England, according to the Scriptures,* | *the Primitiue Church, the pre-'sent Reformed Churches, and* | *many particular Di- vines apart.* | By COR: BVRGES, D^r of Divinity, and | one of his Maiesties Chaplaines | in Ordinary. | [two *mottos.*]

Impr. 91 : 1629 : sm. 4° : pp. [16] + 347 + [1] : p. 11 beg. *world with such* : Great Primer Roman. Contents :—p. (1) title, within arched border : (3-8) Epistle dedicatory to Francis earl of Bedford : (9-13) " To the Readers " : (14-15) " A Table of the severall Chapters . . . " : (16) " The principall Authors quoted . . . " . 1-347, the work : 347 " Errata ".

See Wood's *Ath. Oxon.,* iii. 684. The address " to the Reader " states that the book is " the summe of sundry Lectures deliuered in mine owne Charge " St. Magnus, London, and that some had accused him of altering what he had preached before publishing it.

3. **Burton,** Samuel, archdeacon of Gloucester.　　　*ARTICLES* | TO BE ENQVIRED OF | in the Generall Visitation of the | *Archdeacon* of the Diocesse of | GLOCESTER, | HOLDEN IN THE YEARE OF OVR | Lord God. 1629. In the fift yeare of the Reigne | of our most gracious Soueraigne Lord, | CHARLES, by the grace of | God, King of great Brit-|taine, France, and | *Ireland, Defender of* | *the Faith, &c.* | [*woodcut.*]

Impr. 93 : 1629 : sm. 4° : pp. [16], signn. A-B⁴ : sign. B 1ʳ beg. *Articles concerning Schoolmasters* : Pica English. Contents :—sign. A 1ʳ, title : A 1ᵛ " The Tenor of the Oath to be ministred to the Churchwardens and Sworne-men ", with a text : A 2ʳ-B 4ʳ, the Articles : B 4ʳ, note about Recusants and Communicants.

4. **Butler,** Charles.　　　ORATORIÆ | LIBRI DVO. | QVORVM | *Alter ejus Definitionem,* | *Alter Partitionem* | EXPLICAT : | *IN VSVM SCHOLARVM* | *recèns editi.* | [*line*] | Authore CAROLO BVTLERO, Magd. | [*line, then device.*]

Impr. 98 : 1629: sm. 4°: pp. [132], signn. ( )² A-Q⁴: sign. B 1ʳ beg. *clarant: vt cum* : Long Primer Roman. Contents :—sign. ( ) 1ʳ, title: 2ʳ "Lectori Benevolo . . .", dated "Wotton. 8. *Cal. Iul.* 1629", signed "C. B. M.": A 1ʳ–Q 4ᵛ, the work : Q 4ᵛ, "Monitio ad Lectorem", errata and corrigenda.

See 1633 B. For the author see Wood's *Ath. Oxon.*, iii. 209–10. The reference there to a *Rhetoricæ Libri duo* of this year is probably an error for *Oratoriæ Libri duo.* At sign. A 4ᵛ is a description of the various type in use, giving a series of Nonpareil, Breuier, (Long) Primier, Pique, English, Great Primier, Double Pique, Canon, with specimens of each.

5. **Catechism.**　　　Catechesis | RELIGIONIS | CHRISTIANÆ | QVÆ TRADITVR | in Ecclesijs & Scholis Ele=|ctoralis Palatinatus. | [*woodcut.*]

Impr. 72 : 1629: (twelves) 24°: pp. [6]+63+[3]: p. 11 beg. *est, Vnctus* : Long Primer Roman. Contents :—p. (1) title : (2) woodcuts and a text : (3–6) edict of Frederick Elector of the Rhine about the Catechism, 19 Jan. 156¾, in Latin : 1–49, the catechism : 50–63 "Precationes aliquot privatæ & publicæ".

An edition of the Heidelberg catechism.

6. **Chaloner,** dr. Edward.　　　SIX | SERMONS | NOW FIRST | PVB-LISHED, | *Preached by that learned and* | *worthy Divine* Edward | Chaloner *lately deceas'd,* Dʳ in | Divinity, sometimes Cha-|plaine in Ordinary to our | Soveraigne K. *Iames,* | and to his MAIESTY | that now is ; and late | Principall of *Al-\ban Hall* in | *Oxford.* | [*line*] | *Printed according to the Author's* | *coppies, written with his owne hand.* | [*line, then woodcuts.*]

Impr. 94 : 1629: sm. 4°: pp. [8]+150+[2]: p 11 beg. *arrow drawne,* III *and selfe-conceited* : Pica Roman. Contents :—p. (1) title, within arched border : (3–5) Epistle dedicatory to the Earl of Pembroke, signed "Ab. Sherman": (7–8) "The Titles and severall Texts...": 1–150, the six sermons, on Tit. i. 13, Matt. xx. 6, Rom. i. 21, Acts xxi. 14, Luke viii. 21, Gal. ii. 5: (1) "Errata".

See Wood's *Ath. Oxon.*, ii. 378. This is a second set of six sermons : one set having been issued by Chaloner himself (who died in 1625) at London in 1623, when a Fellow of All Souls.

7. **Corbet,** Richard, bp. of Oxford.　　　ARTICLES | TO BE ENQVIRED | OF WITHIN THE DIOCES | Of *Oxford,* in the first Visitation of | the Right Reverend Father in God, | *Richard,* Lord Bishop of | *Oxford.* | HELD | In the yeare of our Lord God 1629. in the fift yeare | of the Raigne of our most gratious Soveraigne Lord, | *Charles,* by the grace of God King of Great | *Brittaine, France,* and *Ireland,* | Defendor of the Faith &c : | [*device.*]

Impr. 85 *a* : 1629: sm. 4°: pp. [16], signn. A–B⁴: sign. B 1ʳ beg. *3. Whether any hath* : Pica English. Contents :— sign. A 1ʳ, title : A 1ᵛ–A 2ʳ, Directions, Oath &c. : A 2ᵛ–B 4ʳ, the Articles : B 4ᵛ, note about Recusants and Communicants.

8. **Heylyn,** Peter.　　　ΜΙΚΡΟ΄ ΚΟΣΜΟΣ. | *A* | LITTLE DE=|SCRIPTION OF | THE GREAT WORLD. | The fourth Edition. Revised. | [*line*] | *By* PETER HEYLYN. | [*line, then motto, then woodcut.*]

Impr. 100 : 1629 : (eights) sm. 4° : pp. [20] + 807 + folded leaf between pp. 6 and 7 + [5] : p. 11 beg. *1. First then there,* 711 *The chiefe riuers* : Pica Roman. Contents :—p. (1) title, within an arched border : (3-4) dedication to prince Charles : (5 6) "To the Reader" : (7-8) "To my brother the Author" : a poem signed "Edw. Heylyn" : (9-12) "A table of the principall Countries, Provinces, and Seas . . .": (13-14) "A table of the antient Tribes and Nations . . .": (15-19) "A table of the most principall things . . .": (20) "A computation of the forraine coynes herein mentioned . . .": 1-807, (1-2) the work : between pp. 6 and 7 is a tall narrow strip, about 14 × 5 in., bearing on one side "The table of climes."

A note in the All Souls copy shows that the book was on sale on 18 Aug. 1629.

9. **Oxford,** University.   [*woodcuts*] | STATVTA. | [and] CAROLVS R. | *Ordo siue series electionis Procuratorum* . . . | . . . | . . . *quotannis faciendae.* | [and] STATVTA.

Impr. 96 : 1629 : (one) obl. folio : pp. [2] : Pica Italic. Contents :—p. (1) in centre a title "Carolus R. . . . ." as above, below a metal engraving showing the cycle of Proctors : on left and right two strips of printed Statutes concerning Proctors, each headed "Statuta" and pasted to the central cycle : the imprint is at the lower right hand corner.

The central part of this broadsheet is entirely occupied with a steel or copper engraving representing ingeniously the Colleges which elect Proctors from 1629 to 1720 : in the centre are some general notes. This Caroline cycle is repeated after 23 years, commencing with 1629. The two strips of "Statuta" occur also separately, printed on a single sheet in two columns.

10. **Pemble,** William.   *DE* | SENSIBVS | INTERNIS. | TRACTATVS | GVLIELMI PEMBELI, | Aulæ Magdalensis in Aca-|demia Oxoniensi nuper | *alumni dignissimi.* | [*line*] | *Editio Posthuma.* | [*line*] | [*woodcut.*]

Impr. 101 : 1629 : (twelves) 16° : pp. [4] + 74 + [2] : p. 11 beg. *te. quá sensus* : Long Primer Roman. Contents :—p. (1) title : (3-4) "Lectori . . .": 1-74 the work : (1-2) not seen.

Probably edited by Richard Capel, who issued two of Pemble's treatises often bound up with this one (*De formarum (et Animæ) origine,* Lond. 1629, and *De (creatione et) providentia Dei,* Lond. 1631.

11. ——.   *FIVE* | GODLY, AND PRO-|fitable Sermons concerning. | 1 *The slaverie of sinne.* | 2 *The mischeife of ignorance.* | 3 *The roote of Apostasie.* | 4 *The benefit of Gods service.* | *The Christians loue.* | *Preached in his life time in sundry places.* | By that late faithfull Minister of Christ | Mr WILLIAM PEMBLE | *of Magdalen Hall in the* | *Vniversitie of* | *Oxford.* | The second Edition. |

Impr. 97 a : 1629 : (fours) 8° : [4] + 24 + 25 + [1] + 17 + [1] + 22 + 15 + [3] : pp. 11 beg. *and cast* and *tence 2. Thess.* and *ready to* and *Votaries vse* and *in praier* : Pica Roman. Contents :—p. (1) title within an arched border : (3-4) "To the Reader", signed by the editor "Iohn Tombes" : 1-24 (&c. as above, the un-numbered pages being blank, and the title of each part appearing only in the headline : the signatures run through the entire work) the Sermons, on John viii. 34, Hos. iv. 6, Heb. iii. 12, 23, Ex. xxxiv. 23-4, Song of Sol. ii. 16.

See 1628 P.

12. ——.   VINDICIÆ | *FIDEI,* | OR | A TREATISE | of Iustification by Faith, | *wherein the truth of that point* | *is fully cleared, and vindicated* |

from the cauills of it's | *Adversaries* | Deliuered at Magdalen Hall | in
Oxford; by WILLIAM | PEMBLE, Mᴿ of Arts. | The second Edition.
[*line*, then *motto*, then *line*.]

Impr. 97 : 1629 : sm. 4° : pp. [8]+
248 : p. 11 beg. *plainely*. *He*. 111 *some
time failes* : English Roman. Contents:—
p. (1) title, within arched border : (3-6)
dedication to Magdalen hall, Oxford,

dated " From Tewkeisbury this 9 of Iuly
1629", signed " Iohn Geree": (7-8)
"To the Christian Reader," signed
" Rich. Capel" : 1-248, the work.

See Wood's *Ath. Oxon.*. ii. 330, and 1625 P. The dedication contains some
account of the author by the editor. The preface is by the author's tutor, to whom
Pemble left these lectures, and gives the anecdote which Wood relates of Pemble's
death bed.

13. **Prideaux**, dr. John.   *TABVLÆ* | AD | GRAMMATICA | Græca
Introductoriæ. | IN QVIBVS | *Succinctè compingitur, brevissima, sed tamen
ex-|pedita, singularum partium orationis decli-|nabilium, Variandi ratio.* |
ACCESSIT | Vestibuli vice, ad eandem linguam παραίνεσις in gratiam |
tyronum, quibus vt convenit explicatiora evol-|vere, ita necesse est hæc
ipsa | ad vnguem tenere. | [*motto*, then *woodcut*.]

Impr. 92 : 1629 : sm. 4° : pp. [34],
signn. A-D⁴ E¹ : sign. B1ʳ beg. *profero
clarâ* : Pica Roman. Contents :—sign.
1ʳ, title : A2ʳ-A2ᵛ, dedication to dr.
Tho. Holland, dated " Exon. Colleg.

Ian. 1. 1607 ... Io. Prideaux ": A3ʳ-B3ᵛ
" ... Præfatio ": B4ʳ-D4ᵛ, the tables :
E1ʳ, "Conclusio ad Lectorem", and short
Latin poem.

See Wood's *Ath. Oxon.*, iii. 267; and 1607 P, of which this is a reprint.

14. ———.   TYROCINIVM | AD SYLLOGISMVM | Legitimum contexendum,
& | *captiosum dissuendum, ex-|peditissimum*. | IN QVO | *Ad formam ex-
pensa Syllogisticam perstringuntur* | *punctîm Sophismata, nec minus solidè,
quàm* | *vulgò fit, ratione materiæ*; | Excerptis ex optimis Authoribus
exemplis Græcolatinis, | vt majori cum voluptate & fructu, ex vtriusq;
lin-|guæ candidatis & legantur, & | intelligantur. | [*motto*, then *woodcut*.]

Impr. 92 : 1629 : sm. 4° : pp. [18],
signn. A², ( )¹, B¹, C² : sign. B1ʳ beg.
Sectio prima de : Pica and Long Primer
Roman. Contents :—sign. A1ʳ, title :
A2ʳ-( )ᵛ, dedication to Christianus son
of Hermannus Julius a Dane, and Gre-

gorius and Erricus sons of Petrus Julius,
signed "Johannes Prideaux ", "e Musæo
Oxonii . . . pridiè Solstitium Brumale
Exod 22. 21. *ADVenaM*, non *Contri-
stabis*."—1607: ( )ʳ 2 Latin poems :
B1ʳ C2ᵛ, the treatise.

See Wood's *Ath. Oxon.*, iii. 267. This piece though apparently separate is really
an integral part of the preceding piece, sign. E of the latter (two leaves) forming the
last leaf of that piece and the 3rd leaf of this! The dedication tells an anecdote of the
last moments of Offenius the tutor of the three dedicatees.

15. **Rainolds**, dr. John.   *THE OVERTHROW* | OF STAGE-PLAYES.
By the way of controversie betwixt | *D. Gager* and *D. Rainoldes,*
wherein all the | reasons that can be made for them are notably refu-|*ted ;
the obiections answered, and the case so cleared* | *and resolved, as that the
iudgement of any man,* | *that is not froward and perverse, may* | *easilie bee
satisfied.* | WHEREIN IS MANIFESTLY PRO-|ved, that it is not onely vnlawfull
to be an Actor, | *but a beholder of those vanities.* | *WHEREVNTO ARE
ADDED ALSO* | and annexed in the end certaine Latine Letters betwixt

the said *Maister Rainoldes,* and *Doct. Gentiles,* | Reader of the Civill Law in *Oxford,* con-|cerning the same matter. | *The second Edition.* | [*woodcut.*]

Impr. 89: 1629: sm. 4°: pp. [8] + 190 + [1]: p. 11 beg. *ture witnesseth it:* Pica Roman. Contents:—p. (1) title: (3–7) "The Printer to the Reader", from the first ed.: 1–27, Rainolds' Answer to Gager, 10 July 1592: 29–164, Rainolds second answer, 30 May 1593: 164 (misprinted "264") –190, four letters between Rainolds and Albericus Gentilis, 1593, in Latin.

See Wood's *Ath. Oxon.,* ii. 15 and 88 for this controversy. The first ed. of this work was issued in 1599, and included the letters: but the printer is not at present known. There are mentions of the connexion of the University of Oxford with play acting on pp. 143, 149.

16. **Salvianus,** st.   SANCTI | SALVIANI | MASSILIENSIS | PRESBYTERI *DE GVBERNATIONE* | *Dei, et de iusto præsentiq;* | ejus judicio ad S. SALO-|NIVM EPISCOPVM, | libri VIII. | *Eiusdem Epistolarum lib.* I. | TIMOTHEI NO-MINE | *ad Ecclesiam Catholic. lib.* IV. | Cum duplici indice | [*woodcuts.*]

Impr. 90: 1629: (twelves) 16°: pp. [16] + 512: p. 11 beg. *consulari, illis, 401 tamen quæ emant:* Long Primer Roman. Contents:—p. (3) title: (5–6) account of Salvianus, from Trithemius: (7–13) "Index rerum et verborum ...": (14–15) "Index locorum Scripturæ ...": 1–297, Salvianus de gubernatione Dei: 298–324, ejusdem Epistolae: 325–488, ejusdem ad Ecclesiam Catholicam: 489–512 "Annotationes aliquot in Salvian(um) ... Autore Ioanne Alexandro Brassicano".

See 1633 S.

17. **T., B.**   A | PRESERVATIVE, | TO KEEPE A PRO-|TESTANT FROM BECOMMING | *a Papist.* | *Herein these two sayings following* | *are ex-pounded.* | Thou art Peter, and vpon this rocke (or stone) | I will build my Church; *Mat. 16.* 18. | But I haue prayed for thee that thy faith faile | not; *Luk. 22. 32.* | *Herevnto is adioyned an admonition to* | English *Papists, that deny the* | *Popes Supremacy in* | *part or in whole.* | *By T. B.* | [*motto.*] |

Impr. 78: 1629: (eighths) 1.°: pp. [8] + 53 + [3]: p. 11 beg. *something doubtfull:* English Roman. Contents:— p. (1) title: (3–6) dedication to sir Thomas Roe, signed "*T. B.*", dated 12 Mar. 162¾: (7–8) "To the Reader", signed "*T. B.*": 1–53, the exposition.

The dedication states the author's obligations to sir T. Roe, and especially to sir William Killygrew.

18. **Truman,** Richard.   A | CHRISTIAN | *Memorandum,* | OR *Advertisement wherein is* | handled the Doctrine | of Reproofe. | WHAT IT IS, HOW WE MVST RE-|proue, How necessary it is: With Exhortations | and Arguments moving vs to the right | performance of that duty, and | Reproofe for neglecting | *Reproofe.* | By RICHARD TRVMAN *M*r *of Arts and* | *Minister of Gods word at* Dallington | *neere* Northampton. | [*motto.*]

Impr. 99: 1629: (eights) 16°: pp. [16] + 125 + [3]: p. 11 beg. *the Prophet, in iect malice:* English Roman. Contents:—p. (1) title: (3–10) Epistle dedicatory to William lord Spencer: (11–15) "To the Reader": 1–125, the work.

19. **Z[ouche]**, Richard.   ELEMENTA | Iurisprudentiæ, | *DEFINI-TIONIBVS*, | REGVLIS, ET SENTEN-tijs Selectioribus Iuris Ci- vilis Illustrata. | [*line*] | Autore *R. Z.* P. R. Oxon. | [*line*: then *device*.]

Impr. 95 : 1629 : (eights) 16° : pp. [16] + 277 + [3] : p. 11 beg. *runt, personæ*, 111 *ministratione offerunt* : Pica Roman.   Contents :—p. (1–2) not seen : (3) title, "cum Privilegio" : (5) dedication to lord Pembroke, signed "R. Z." : (7–9) "Iuventuti Magnæ Britanniæ Iuris Studiosæ", an epistle dedicatory, dated "ex Aulâ Alban: pridie Cal: Iun. 1629," but not signed : (11–16) a list of parts and sections : 1–277, the work, in 7 parts : 277, note by the author of a possible future volume completing this one.

See Wood's *Ath. Oxon.*, iii. 511, and 1636 Z.   There are editions of Leyden, 1652 and (acc. to Wood) Amst. 1681.   The "P. R." on the title of this and the 1636 edition is *Professor Regius*.

1630.

1. **Aleman**, Mateo.   THE ROGVE : | OR, | THE LIFE | OF GVZMAN | DE *ALFARACHE*. | WRITTEN IN SPANISH | by MATHEO ALEMAN, | *Seruant to his Catholike Majestie,* | *and borne in SEVILL.* | [*device*.]

Impr. 102 : 1630 : sixes (la. 8°) : pp. [36] + 267 + [17] + 357 + [3] : pp. 11 begg. *out reason*, and (*in punishment*, 111 *Chapter ii* and *great deale of* : Pica Roman. Contents :—p. (1) title, within two bounding lines : (3–6) dedication to sir John Strangwayes, in Spanish, signed "Don Diego Puede-Ser ; de Santa Maria Magdalena", i. e. James May-be or Mabbe, Fellow of Magdalen College, Oxford, the translator : (7 8) dedication by "Matheo Aleman" to "Don Francisco de Roias marquesse de Poza" in English : (9–13) three prefaces : (14–20) laudatory pieces on the book, chiefly in poetry, including one poem by Ben Johnson : (21 24) "A table of the Chapters and matter . . ." : (25–36) three lists or indexes : 1–267, the first book : (2) a titlepage "THE ROGVE : | [*line*] | OR, | THE SECOND PART OF THE LIFE | OF GVZMAN DE | ALFARACHE. | WRITTEN IN SPANISH | by MATHEO ALEMAN | *Seruant to his Catholike Majestie, and* | *borne in* SEVILL. | [*woodcuts*]" with impr. 103 : (4–7) the author's Preface to part 2, in English : (8–15) laudatory pieces, chiefly in verse : (16–17) "The Contents of the Second Part" : 1–357, the second part : (2 3) not seen.

For the translator see Wood's *Ath. Oxon.*, iii. 53.   This is a reprint, even to many of the mis-prints, of the London ed. of 1622 (also "1623") printed for Edw. Blount, who assigned his edition to R. Allot, for whom the Oxford edition was printed, on 1 Dec. 1628.   The only omission is the two lists of errata in the London issue.   The demand for this entertaining book was such that a third corrected edition was published by Allot in 1634.   The translator was secretary to sir John Digby whem Ambassador in Spain, and the first edition of the original Spanish is dated 1599 (1st part) and 1602 or 1603 (2nd part).   Each page (and margin) is enclosed within lines.

2. **B., E.**   THE | CVRSE OF SACRILEDGE. | PREACHED IN A PRIVATE PA-rish Church, the Sunday before | Michaelmas last. | *TO WHICH ARE ANNEXED* | *some certain Quære's, which are pertinent* | *to the vnmasking of our homebred* | *Church-Robbers.* | [*motto*, then "D. E. B.", then *woodcut*.]

Impr. 85*b* : 1630 : sm. 4° : pp. (8) + 38 + [6] : p. 11 beg. *the learned, That* : English Roman.   Contents :—(1–2) not seen : (3) title : (5–7) Preface signed "E. B.", p. 5 marked ¶ 2 : 1–38, the sermon on Mal. iii. 9 : (1) "A Post-script" signed "D. E. B." : (3–5) "A catalogue of . . . Quæres . . . submitted by the Author . . .".

A sermon on tithes, in defence of the system.

3. **Bayly**, rev. John.   TWO | SERMONS | THE ANGELL | *GVARDIAN.* | THE LIGHT | *ENLIGHTNING.* | PREACHED | BY IOHN BAYLY ONE OF | HIS MAIESTIES CHAP- LAINES, *GVARDIAN* | of Chrrists Hospitall in | *Ruthyn,* and sometimes | Fellow of *Exeter* | *Coll. Oxon.* | [*device.*]

Impr. 85: 1630: sm. 4°: pp. [4] + 17 + [3] + 14 + [2]: pp. 11 begg. *grannt that,* and *other; the*: English Roman. Contents :—p. (1) title : (3 4) dedication to his father Lewes Bayly bp. of Bangor, dated " *From my Chamber in Exon Coll. Novemb.* 6 . . . 1630": 1–17, the first sermon, on Ps. xxxiv. 7 : (2) a titlepage " THE LIGHT | *ENLIGHTNING.* | A | SER-MON | PREACHED " [&c., precisely as first title, except " Christs "], with device and impr. 85 : 1, dedication to John Prideaux rector of Exeter college : 3-14, the second sermon, on John i. 9.

See Wood's *Ath. Oxon.,* ii. 499 (where *Lond.* is an error for *Oxf.*. The second sermon is independent, in paging and title (not signatures), of the rest of the book. The author says these are his first printed works.

4. **Brerewood**, Edward.   A | LEARNED | TREATISE | *OF THE* | SABAOTH, | WRITTEN | By Mr EDWARD BREREWOOD, | Professor in *Gresham Colledge,* | LONDON· | TO Mr NICOLAS BYFIELD, | *Preacher in Chester.* | With Mr BYFIELDS answere and | Mr BREREWOODS | *REPLY.* |

Impr. 108: 1630: sm. 4°: pp. [4] + 101 + [3] : p. 11 beg. *by Moses,* 65 *heare, or see*: English Roman. Contents :—p. (1), title : (3) 3 texts : (4) " Faults " of the press : 1-55, the work, dated at end " May 16. 1611. At Gresham house in London ": 57, a title " Mr. | BYFIELDS | ANSVVERE, | WITH M^r | BREREVVOODS | REPLY. | [device, then impr. 108] : 59-60, " The Preface to M^r. Brerewoods reply ", signed " M^r. Brerm-woods " : 61-101, the Answer and Reply, in parallel columns, as far as possible.

See Wood's *Ath. Oxon.,* ii. 140, 325, and 1631 B, 1632 B.   The author died in Nov. 1613.   Richard Byfield, brother of Nicholas, who received Brerewood's treatise " a little before November " 1640, wrote a special confutation of it (Lond. 1631), and the controversy became general.

5. **Casa**, Giovanni della.   IO. *CASÆ V. CL.* | GALATEVS | SEV DE MORVM | HONESTATE, ET ELE-|GANTIA; LIBER EX | Italico Latinus, | *Inter-prete* | NATHANE CHYTRÆO, | cum ejusdem Notis, nuper additis. | *EIVSDEM CASÆ LIBEL-|lus de officijs inter potentiores,* | *&* *tenuiores amicos.* | [*woodcut.*]

Impr. 73 *a* : 1630: (eights) 12°: pp. [18] + 213 + [1] : p. 11 beg. *negotij dedit,* III *liq; philosopho?*) : Pica Roman. Contents :—p. (1) title : (2) " Lectori . . . Chytræus" : (3-5) dedication to Nicolaüs Casa by Chytraeus, " Rostochio Idib. Septemb....1577 ": (6-9) "Prooemium " to Nic. Casius by " Joannes Caselius ", " Rostochio iv Non. Maias . . . 1578 ": (9-13) a recommendation of the book, dated " Rostochij Idibus . . . sextilis . . . 1578 ": (14-18) " De tribus virtutibus cognatis..." signed "Ioannes Caselius": 1-103, the Galateus : 104-141, "Ioannis Casæ de Officiis inter potentiores et tenuiores amicos Liber": 142-213, " Na-thanis Chytræi Notæ in Galateum . . ." with a Prooemium to " Caspar von der Wenge ".

See 1628 C.   Even in 1892 an edition of Peterson's English translation of the *Galateo* (1576) was privately printed.

6. **Hakewill**, George.   AN | APOLOGIE | OR | DECLARATION | OF THE POWER AND | PROVIDENCE OF GOD IN THE | GOVERNMENT OF THE

WORLD. | CONSISTING IN | AN EXAMINATION AND | CENSVRE OF THE COMMON | ERROVR TOVCHING NATVRES PER=|PETVALL AND VNIVERSALL DECAY, | DIVIDED INTO FOVRE BOOKES. | *WHEREOF* | *The first treates* [&c. as 1627 H, dividing lines at *there-| vnto.* | *that of the* | *excepted.* | *strength and* | *wits.* | *proofe of the* | *vse which* | *thereof.* | : also "Heavens," "onely"] | [*line*] | By GEORGE HAKEWILL Doctor of | Divinity and Archdeacon of *Surrey.* | [*line*] | *The second Edition revised, and in sundry passages augmented by the Authour ;* | *with advertisements and tables newly annexed in the end of the booke,* | *an Index whereof is presented in the next page.* | [*motto.*] | There is also a London title, see below.]

Impr. 68 : 1630 : (sixes) la. 8° : pp. [40] + 523 + [69] : p. 11 beg. *you to Lucians,* 501 *some bodies which* : English Roman. Contents :—(2) "The argument of the Front[ispiece] and of the worke", printed in London : (3) engraved title, see below : (5) title : (6) "An Index of the advertisements and tables newly annexed ...": (7-11) dedication to the University of Oxford : (13-23) "The Preface": 25-38) "The Contents ...": (39) quotation from Boethius, with translation : 1-523, the work in 4 books : (2-42) "Advertisements to the learned reader occasioned by this second impression" : (43) "... the value of the Roman Sesterce" : (44-45) bp. Godwin's calculations of large numbers of sesterces : (46-60) "An alphabeticall table ..." (60-63) "A table of the authours quoted ..." : (64-67) "A table of the texts of scripture quoted ..." : (69) "Errata".

See Wood's *Ath. Oxon.*, 256 and 1627 H. The chief additions in this new edition are to be found in the "Advertisements", the fifth of which contains some complimentary letters about the first edition by archbp. Ussher and others. The engraved title measures $10\frac{3}{8} \times 6\frac{1}{2}$ in. and bears a London imprint, "London. Printed for Robert Allott, at the | Beare in Paules Churchyard. 1630", and six allegorical scenes surrounding a short title, beneath which are the arms and crest of the author. "T. Cecill sculp", probably in London.

7. **Hommius,** Festus.   LXX. | DISPVTATIO-|NES THEOLOGICÆ; | adversus | PONTIFICIOS : | Quibus omnes inter Evangelicos & | Pontificios Controversiæ continentur, & | excutiuntur : In gratiam SS. Theologiæ Stu- diosorum in Academiâ LEYDENSI pri-|*ratim institute, in* | *Collegio Anti=Bellarminiano,* | PRÆSIDE | FESTO HOMMIO, | Eccl. Lugdun. Pastore. | *Editio secunda ; adjectionibus in* | *margine locupletior.* | [*woodcuts.*]

Impr. 104 : 1630 : (eights) 16° : pp. [16] + 428 + [4] : p. 11 beg. *Mosen quidem,* III *stitutus est* : Long Primer Roman. Contents :—p. (1) title : (3 8) the author's dedication to Princes Maurice of Orange and Louis of Nassau, dated Leiden, 24 Aug. 1614 : (9-10) "Lectori Benevolo ...": (11-12) two complimentary poems : (13-16) "Index Disputationum ": 1-428, the work : (1-4) "Leges Collegii hujus Anti-Bellarminiani", with the names of the students. All in Latin : every printed page and margin are within bounding lines.

The first edition was issued at Leiden in 1614 : see 1639 H.

8. **Oxford,** University.   .[*woodcut*] | BRITANNIAE | NATALIS. | [*device.*]

Impr. 73 *a* : 1630 : sm. 4° : pp. [4] + 78 : p. 11 beg. *Crescito pacifici* : Pica Roman. Contents :—p. (1) title : (3) dedication to King Charles by the University of Oxford : (4), 1-78, the poems.

148 poems (4 Greek, 3 French, the rest Latin) addressed to the King by members of the University of Oxford on the birth of Charles ii on 29 May 1630 : a chronogram is on p. 43.

9. **Pemble,** William. A BRIEFE IN-|TRODVCTION | TO GEOGRAPHY | CONTAINING A | DESCRIPTION OF THE GROVNDS, AND GENERALL | PART THEREOF, VERY NE-|*cessary for young students in* | *that science.* | WRITTEN BY THAT LEARNED | *man,* M͏ͬ WILLIAM PEMBLE, *Master* | *of Arts, of Magdalen Hall in Oxford.* | [*device.*]

Impr. 84 *a* : 1630 : sm. 4° : pp. [4] + 64 + [2] : p. 12 beg. *The third rule* : Pica Roman. Contents :—p. (1) title : | (3) " To the Reader " by the editor : 1–64 the work.

See Wood's *Ath. Oxon.,* ii. 331. Pemble died in 1623 : but the treatise was reissued in 1669 according to Cole in Bliss's Wood's *Ath. Oxon.* and in 1685, both times at Oxford, as well as in the collected editions of Pemble's works (3rd ed. 1635 &c.) at London. There are several woodcut diagrams, but the whole book is occupied solely with what the author calls the general part of Geography, that is to say with the " nature, qualities, measure, with other general properties of the earth ", and not with a description of separate countries.

10. ———. " *A Sum of moral Philosophy.* Oxon. 1630 qu[arto]."

So in Wood's *Ath. Oxon.,* ii. 331, where 1630 may be an error for 1632.

11. **Pinke,** William. [two *lines*] | THE TRYALL OF | OVR SINCERE LOVE | TO CHRIST : | [*line*] | *By* W. PINKE, *late Fellow of Mag-*|*dalen Colledge in* OXFORD. | [*line,* then *motto,* then *device.*]

Impr. 106 : 1630 : sm. 4° : pp. [2] + 30 + [2] + 28 : pp. 11 begg. *custome or,* and *God, and while* : English Roman. Contents :—p. (1) title (every page has a | double headline : 1–30, a Sermon, on Eph. vi. 24 : 1–28 a second sermon on the same text.

See Wood's *Ath. Oxon.,* ii. 475, where the 1631 edition with four sermons is con-fused with this in which there seem to be only two. The 3rd ed. (Oxf. 1636) and 5th (Oxf. 1659) contain also four. Probably William Lyford, whose preface dated 7 July 1630 is prefixed to all other editions, edited this tentative issue also. The pagination and signatures are separate for the two sermons. Pinke died in 1629.

12. **Piscator,** Johannes. APHORISMI | DOCTRINÆ | CHRISTIANÆ | maximam partem ex In-|stitutione Calvini | *excerpti.* | SIVE | Loci COM-MVNES THEOLO-|gici, brevibus sententijs expositi. | *Per JOHAN: PISCA-*|*TOREM* | EDITIO VNDECIMA. | *Superioribus tum limatior, tum* | *locupletior.* | [*woodcut.*]

Impr. 105 : 1630 : (twelves) 24° : pp. [10] + 203 + [3] : p. 11 beg. *veteris testa-*|*menti,* iii *tarit a in filio* : Long Primer Roman. Contents :—p. (1) title : (2) " Ad Lectorem ", a preface to a new | edition signed " Philip: Ludovicus Pisca-tor ", the author's son, 1 May 1629 : (3–9) the author's preface to Beza : 1–203, the treatise : (1–2) " Index [28] locorum com-munium ".

Piscator (Fischer?) died in 1626, and the first edition of the *Aphorismi* appears to have been issued in 1592. This edition is often found bound with the Catechismus Oxf. 1629.

13. **Thornborough,** bp. John. THE | LAST WILL AND | TESTA-MENT OF IESVS | Christ, touching the blessed Sacrament | *of his body,* *and bloud, Signed, Sealed and* | *Delivered* to the vse of all faithfull Christi-|ans in the presence of many Witnesses, and | *proved in the*

Prerogatiue of the Church of | Christ, by Reverend Bishops, Learned Doctors, | *and Ancient Fathers of the same Church.* | Exemplified, copied out, and explained by the | *Reverend Father in God,* IOHN THORNBURGH, | *Bishop of Worcester.* | [*motto*: then *device.*]

Impr. 68 : 1630 : (fours) 8° : pp. [6] + 118 + [4] : p. 11 beg. *are to be,* 111 *would not haue* : English Roman. Contents :— p. (1) title : (3–5) dedication to (William) earl of Pembroke : 1–118, the work, a treatise on the Lord's Supper : (1–4) not seen.

See Wood's *Ath. Oxon.,* iii. 5 : the dedication gives some biographical details of the author.

14. **Widdowes,** Giles.   THE | SCHISMATICAL | *PVRITAN.* | *A* | SERMON PREACHED AT WIT-|NEY concerning the lawfulnesse of Church-| *Authority, for ordaining, and comman-|ding of Rites, and Ceremonies, to* | *beautifie the Church.* | By GILES WIDDOWES Rector of Sᵗ | Martins Church in Oxford. | [*motto,* then *woodcut.*]

Impr. 107 : 1630 : sm. 4° : pp. [48], signn. A–F¹ : sign. B1ʳ beg. *wee Confesse* : English Roman. Contents :—sign. A1ʳ title : A2ʳ A2ᵛ, dedication to Katharine duchess of Buckingham : A3ʳ–C3ᵛ " To the Puritan " : C4ʳ–F3ᵛ, the sermon, on 1 Cor. xiv. 40.

See Wood's *Ath. Oxon.,* iii. 179, and 1631 P & W ('2nd ed. of this Sermon), and also an answer to Prynne. The long preface contains an account of Puritans, in their ten subdivisions of Perfectists, Sermonists, Separatists, Anabaptists, Brownists, Loves-familists, Precisians, Sabbatarians, Anti-disciplinarians, Predestinatists.

1631.

1. **Acontius,** Jacobus.   STRATAGEMATVM | SATANÆ | *Libri Octo* | Quos | *IACOBVS ACONTIVS* | *Vir Summi iudicij nec mino'ris pietatis, annis abhinc penè,* | *primum edidit & Sereniss°* | *Reginæ ELIZABETHÆ* | *in-scripsit* | *Editio iterata & emendata* | [*motto.*]

Impr. 87 : 1631 : (eights) 16° : pp. [16] + 426 + [32] : p. 11 beg. *tur cupidi-tate,* 201 *nominis vir* : Pica Roman. Contents :—p. (1) title, engraved : (3) dedication to qu. Elizabeth by the author, in Latin : (5–16) "... Præfatio" : 1–426, the work in 8 books : (1–26) " Iacobus Acontius Iohanni Wolfio Tigurino ... " a letter on the method of preparing books, dated " Londini xii Kal. Decembr. MD.LXII " : (27–32) " Index rerum præcipuarum ... ".

The first edition was published at Bâle in 1565 and there are English translations (1648, &c.) : the sheets of this Oxford edition were reissued at Oxford in 1650 with a printed titlepage. The engraved title (4 1/16 × 2 3/8 in.) contains the title in the centre, and on each side figures of " Veritas " with a book, and " Charitas " with a bird : above is a figure " Religionis " (*sic*). Below are six figures of Sins and in their midst Satan rising from hell. The imprint is also engraved on the plate. From Brit. Mus. MS. Harl. 5901 fol. 73ʳ it would seem that Bagford saw some *printed* title stating that Turner was the printer : the engraved title only is in the copies seen.

2. **Bible,** Old Testament, Psalms.   THE | PSALMES | of | KING | DAVID | TRANSLATED | by | KING IAMES | *Cum Priuilegio Regiæ* | *Maies-talis.* |

Impr. (as colophon) 68 : (twelves) 16° : pp. [4] + 319 + [5] : p. 11 beg. *But whil'st,* III *19 My God* : Long Primer Roman. Contents :—p. (2) engraved plate of the royal Arms, supporters &c., and a proclamation of Charles i allowing the printing of the work, " Will: Marshall. sculpsit." : (3) engraved title, see below : 1–319, the work : (1) arms of the University and colophon imprint.

The titlepage shows the Book of Psalms sent down from heaven and received by David and James i. It is on one plate with the royal arms and proclamation, and is printed from metal.

3. **Bolton,** Robert. HELPES | TO | HVMILIATION. | [*line*] | *By R. B.* | [*line, motto, line, woodcuts.*]

Impr. 115 : 1631 : (twelves) 16mo : pp. [12] + 164 + [4] : p. 11 beg. *Some measure,* III *of nature* : Great Primer Roman. Contents :—p. (3) title : (5–12) "To the Reader", by the editor, giving the author's full name : 1–164, the work, a discourse on Acts ii. 37: (1) Michael Sparke's business mark.

See Wood's *Ath. Oxon.,* ii. 515. The preface states that this publication is by leave of the author though not undertaken by him, so it preceded his death on 17 Dec. 1631. Every page has double bounding lines at top and outer side margin. Spark must have sent his engraved business mark. chiefly a monogram of the letters of his names, to Oxford to be printed : see below, F.

4. **Brerewood,** Edward. A | LEARNED TREATISE | OF THE | SABBATH, | [&c. exactly as 1630 B, except no comma after " Brerewood " and " Byfield ", and " Reply." After " Reply.":—] *The second Edition diligently corrected.* | [*woodcut.*]

Impr. 108 : 1631 : sm. 4° : pp. [4] + 101 + [3] : p. 11 beg. *by Moses,* 65 beg. *heare, or see* : English Roman. Contents :—exactly as 1680 B, except p. (4) is blank, and " At Gresham . . . London" is omitted, as well as " M^r. Brerinwoods ".

See 1630 B, of which this is a corrected reprint : the editor in the interval discovered the difference between *Sabaoth* and *Sabbath,* and uses the latter only, in the first edition using the former only !

5. ——, TRACTATVS | QVIDAM LOGICI | DE | PRÆDICABILIBVS, | ET | PRÆDICAMENTIS | *Ab eruditissime Viro* EDVARDO | BREREWOOD, Artium Magistro, è Col-legio *Ænei-Nasi,* olim conscripti : nunc verò ab erroribus (qui frequenti transcriptione | irrepserant) vindicati, ad pristinum nitorem, nati-|vamque puritatem diligentissimâ manuscripto-|rum collatione restituti, & in lucem editi : | *Per* T. S. *Art. Mag. & Collegij* Ænei-Nasi *Socium.* | *Editio altera,* | In quâ accessêrunt duo ejusdem Authoris insignes | *Tractatus* ; prior de *Meteoris,* posterior de | *Oculo* : limâ, luceque donati : | *Per eundem* T. S. [*line,* then *motto,* then *woodcuts.*]

Impr. 109 : 1631 : (eights) 12° : pp. [32] + folded sheet + 431 + [3] + [next article, which see] : p. 11 beg. *Sol. Prædicabilia,* 401, *1 Respectu communis* : Long Primer Roman. Contents :—(1) title : (3–8) Epistola dedicatoria to lord Rich. Brooke of Norton, signed by the editor " Oxonij, e Musæo meo, in Collegio Ænea-Nasensi, 13 Calend. Oct. 1628 . . . Thomas Sixesmith" : (9–13) " Erudito lectori . . ." signed " T. S.": (14–31) " Index sectionum quæstionumque . . ." : 1–431, the work, pp. 58–59 being a folded leaf : (1–3) blank : for the rest see the next art.

See 1628 B, of which this is a reprint, with the two additional treatises. The next article is strictly part of the present work, but the signatures, pagination &c. being quite distinct the only sign of its secondary character is the omission of the name of the *place* in the imprint), it is here for convenience' sake treated separately : it is also more common to find it separate than to meet with the entire work.

6. —† ——. TRACTATVS DVO | *Quorum primus est* | DE METEORIS. | *Secundus* | DE OCVLO. | Quos scripsit olim eximius ille Philosophus | EDVARDVS BRIERVVOODVS : | *Restituit tandem, ab erroribus mendisq; Vin-*| *dicavit, & publici iuris fecit.* | T. S. | Art. Mag. & Colleg. *Ænea-Nasensis* | Socius. | [*woodcut.*]

Impr. 109: 1631: (eights) 12° : pp. [4] + 104 + [4] + 39 (p. 39 misprinted 63) + [1]: pp. 11 begg. *Sect. 11. In qua, Obliquæ, quibus* : Long Primer and (2nd part) Pica Roman. Contents :—p. (1) title : (3) dedication by Thomas Sixesmith the editor to Brasenose college.

Oxford : 1-83 De Meteoris, in 2 books *De Meteorologicus* and *De Cometis* : 84-104 "De Mari" : (1) "A" : (2-3) woodcut diagrams of the eye : (4) "Index . . ." to the following treatise : 1-63, De Oculo.

See preceding article, of which this is a part. Some woodcuts occur in the text.

7. **Burgersdicius,** Franco. IDEA | *PHILOSOPHIÆ* | TVM | NATVRALIS, | TVM | MORALIS, | *SIVE* | Epitome compendiosa vtrivsq; ex | Aristotele excerpta & Me-|thodicè disposita; | *A* | M. FRANC: BVRGERSDICIO | in Academia Lugduno-Batavâ, *Lo-gices & Ethices Professore ordinario.* | *Editio tertia prioribus emendatior.* |

Impr. 105 *a* : 1631: (twelves) 16mo : pp. [6] + 103 + [1] + (next article) : p. 11 beg. 2 *Natura est* : Pica Roman. Contents :—p. (1) title : (3-4) "Philosophiæ studiosis", signed "Franco Burgersdi-

cius" : (5-6) "Tituli et ordo disputationum . . ." Ideae Naturalis : 1-103, the Idea Philosophiae Naturalis : (1) blank : for the rest see next article.

The first edition of the Natural Philosophy was in 1622, and of the Moral in 1623, both at Leiden : both were again issued at the same place in 1626 and the Moral Philosophy again in 1629. The 4th ed. was in 1637 (Oxford), the next 1641 (Oxford), and others followed, but not at Oxford. The next art. is strictly part of this book, but is in form quite independent. Burgersdijck died in Feb. 1635 or 1636.

8. — ——. IDEA | *PHILGSOPHIÆ* | MORALIS, | Ex | ARISTOTELE maxima parte | excerpta, & methodice | *disposita.* | *A* | M. FRANCONE BVRGERSDICIO, in | Academiâ Lugduno Batavâ, | *Logices & Ethices Pro-*| *fessore Ordinario.* | Editio tertia. | *Plurimùm emendata & magnâ accessione* | *Locupletata.* | [*woodcuts.*]

Impr. 105 : 1631: (twelves) 16mo : pp. [4] + 342 : p. 11 beg. *natur ; altera,* 211 *dorem quærunt* : Pica Roman. Con-

tents :—p. (1) title : (3-4) "Index Capitum & titulorum . . ." : 1-342 the work.

See preceding article.

9. **Davenant,** Edward. ARTICLES | MINISTRED IN | THE FIRST VISITA-|TION OF THE RIGHT | Worshipfull Mr Doctor *Dave-|nant* Archdeacon of Barke shire | in the yeare of our Lord | God 1631. | [*device.*]

Impr. 82 : 1631: sm. 4° : pp. [4] + 16 : p. 11 beg. *the Church, and* : Pica English. Contents :—(1) title : (2) "The Oath of

the Church-wardens" : (3-4) "The Charge of the Church-wardens . . ." : 1-15, the 70 articles of enquiry.

10. **F., A.**   *The Saints Legacies*: | OR, | A COLLECTION | of cer-taine PROMISES | out of the word of God. | *Collected for private vse, but pub-|lished for the comfort of Gods people.* | BY *A. F.* | [*line, then mottos.*]

Impr. 116: 1631: (twelves) 16mo : pp. [24] + 203 + [21]: p. 11 beg. *thee with many*, 111 *steps shall not* : Great Primer Roman.   Contents :—(1) title : (3–6) " The Author to the Printer ", dated 4 Aug. 1630: (7–18) " To the Reader " : (19 23) " Rules to be observed in reading the Promises " : 1–203. the 105 Legacies : (2–4) a short conclusion : (6–17) " A table . . ." or index; (18) Michael Sparke's business mark.

The author complains of a pirated and imperfect edition, probably under another title, issued by Robert Swayne " now deceased " (printer at London, 1621–29). In C. S. Palmer's Catalogue of Books, pt. 10 (June 1878), no. 256, this book is attributed to Anthony Farindon, for whom see Wood's *Ath. Oxon.*, iii. 457.   Every page is within double lines at top and outside margin.   The original title was probably " Promises ", for the compositor of one side of the first sheet of the text placed that as part of the headline, while the compositor of the other side and of the rest of the work has, as the author suggests, the new title " Saints Legacies " or " Legacies ".

11. **Felix**, Marcus Minucius.   M. MINVCII | FELICIS | OCTAVIVS | [*line, then device.*]

Impr. 110: 1631: (twelves) 24mo : pp. [8] + 129 + [7] : p. 11 beg. *here; quàm*, 111 *dicimus ; non* : Pica Roman.   Contents :—(3) title : (5–7) " Typogra-phus lectori " : (8) passage from Lactan-tius : 1–129, the work.

See 1627 F, of which this is a reprint.

12. **Florus**, Lucius Annaeus.   L. IVLII FLORI | rerum à | ROMANIS | GESTARVM | LIBRI IV. | A IOHANNE STADIO *emendati.* | *Editio nova singulis Neotericis purgatior &* | *emendatior.* | *SEORSVM EXCVSVS* | IN EOS COM-MENTARIVS | IOAN. STADII, Historiæ & Ma-|theseos Lovanij Professoris primi : in | quo obscura in lucem proferuntur, omissa sup-|plentur, in-versa restituuntur, breviter denique, | quicquid in Romana Historia dignum est | observatione annotatur; vnà cum va-|riarum lectionum & castiga-|tionum rationibus. | [*device.*]

Impr. 117: 1631: (twelves) 16mo : pp. 137 + [1] + 319 + [35] : pp. 11 beg. *immortalium docuit* and *rum pleb.*, 301 *non potuit* (*petebat* : Long Primer Roman. Contents :—p. 1, title : 3–5, 2 compli-mentary Latin pieces : 7–137, the text of Florus : 1, a title :—" I. STADII | IN L. IVLII FLORI | HISTORIA-|RVM LIBROS   IV | COMMENTARII. | *Editio nova singu-lis Neotericis* | *purgatior & emendatior.* | [*device, then impr. 69*]: 3–16, " Ioannis Stadii . . . Præfatio " : 17–319, the com-mentary : (2–4) " Index capitum . . ." : (6–23) " Index nominum . . ." : (24–31) " Index posterior rerum . . ." : (31) two errata.

The first edition of Stadius's commentary was in 1567 at Antwerp : other Oxford ones were issued in 1638, 1661 and 1669.

13. **Gardyner**, Richard.   CONCIO | *AD* | CLERVM | HABITA | IN TEMPLO BEATÆ | MARIÆ *Oxon: Feb.* 14. | PER | RICHARDVM GARDYNER Sa: | Theol: Doct: & Eccles. Cath: | Christi Canonicum. | [*woodcut.*]

Impr. 118: 1631: sm. 4°: pp. [8]+24: p. 11 beg. *mit, & radosa*: Great Primer Roman. Contents:—(1-2) not seen: (3) title: (5-8) dedication to Laud, bp. of London, chancellor of the University: 1-24, the sermon, on 1 Tim. iv. 16.

See Wood's *Ath. Oxon.*, iii. 922: the dedication is of some autobiographical interest. One of the Bodleian copies of this sermon bears an autograph note of the author which shows that this book was issued not later than 16 March 163⅞.

14. **Godwin,** Thomas.   *ROMANÆ* | HISTORIAE | ANTHOLOGIA | [&c. exactly as 1628 G, and within a similar border.]

Impr. 75 a: 1631: sm. 4°: pp. [8]+277+[23]: [&c. exactly as 1628 G.]

See 1614 G: this is almost an exact reprint of the 1628 edition, with different imprint and date.

15. **Heylyn,** Peter.   ΜΙΚΡΟ΄ΚΟΣΜΟΣ | A | LITTLE | DE-SCRIPTION OF | THE GREAT WORLD. | The fifth Edition. | [*line*] | *By* PETER HEYLYN. | [*line, motto, device.*]

Impr. 119: 1631: (eights) sm. 4°: pp. [20]+807+[5]: p. 11 beg. *1. First then there*, 701 *dales, or l'indelici*: Pica Roman. Contents:—p. (1) title, within arched border: (3-4) dedication to "Prince Charles" as in 1621: (5-6) "To the Reader": (7-8) Poem "To my brother the Author" by Edw. Heylyn: (9-12) "A Table of the principal Countries...": (13-14) "A Table of the ancient Tribes ...": (15-19) "A Table of the most principall things...": (20) "A computation of ... forraine coyne...": 1-807, (1-2) the work: (4-5) not seen.

See 1621 H.

16. **Oxford,** University.   AD | magnificvm | Et Spectatissimum Virum Domi-|num IOHANNEM CIRENBERGIVM | PROCONSVLEM CIVITATIS | *GEDANENSIS.* | Ob acceptum Synodalium Epistolarum | *Concilij Basi-lensis* Αυτόγραφον *sigillo eiusdem in* | *plumbum impresso obsignatum, quod nobilissimus* | *Dominus* THOMAS ROE *Eques Auratus,* | *Serenissimi Magnæ Britanniæ Regis Legatus* | *ab eo sibi prius officiosè oblatum, Oxoniensi Bib-|liothecæ transmisit ac dono dedit.* | *CARMEN* | HONORARIVM. | [*line.*]

Impr. 73 a: 1631: sm. 4°: pp. [6]+17+[1]: p. 11 beg. *Nec calamus*: English Roman. Contents:—(1) title: (3-5) Latin preface to Johannes Cirenbergius by J. Rous: 1-17, complimentary poems.

Eight Latin poems by members of the University of Oxford to thank the proximate and immediate donors of MS. Roe 20, presented by Johann Cirenberg of Dantzig (Gedanum) to sir Thomas Roe on 28 Mar. 1630, and by him to the University as an addition to the Roe MSS. in Aug. 1630.

17. **Page,** William.   A | TREATISE | OR | IVSTIFICATION | OF BOWING AT | THE NAME OF | *IESVS.* | By way of Answere to an Appendix | *against it.* | TOGETHER WITH AN EXAMI-nation of such considerable reasons as are | made by Mr *Prinne* in a reply to | Mr *Widdowes* concerning | *the same argument.* | [*line*] | *By* WILLIAM PAGE *Bac. of Divinity* | *and Fellow of* All-Soules *Colledge* | *in* Oxford. | [*line, then 2 mottos.*]

Impr. 85 *a* : 1631 : sm. 4° : pp. [16] +
206 : p. 11 beg. *since the omission,* 101
lookes forward : English Roman. Contents :—(1) title : 3–15) dedication to
the University of Oxford : (16) Errata :
1–126, the treatise or " Answere " : 129,
a title :—" A | FVRTHER | IVSTIFICA-
TION | OF BOWING AT | THE NAME OF |
IESVS, | OR | AN EXAMINATION OF SVCH |
CONSIDERA· BLE REASONS AS ARE | made
by Mr. *Prinne* [&c., exactly as in the
main title, imprint and all, except that
the two mottos are different] " : 130–132
(misprinted 140–142) " To the Reader " :
133–206, the further answer.

See Wood's *Ath. Oxon.,* iii. 654, where Wood quotes two letters about this book,
one against it from the Archbishop of Canterbury's Secretary, one for it by Laud, which
show that the book was in course of printing in May–June 1631, but not yet published
on June 22.   The error of pagination on pp. 130–32 (" 140–42 ") was due to the prefatory matter of the second part being supposed by the compositor to follow the 3rd
leaf of what is now sheet s, instead of the 3rd leaf of sheet Q.

18. **Pareus,** David.   DAVIDIS PAREI | *Theologi Archipalatini.* |
IN | S. MATTHÆI | EVANGELIVM | COMMENTARIVS | Quo præter accuratam
textus Sacri Analysin, & Harmoniæ Evangelicæ collatio-'nem Orthodoxa
Fidei Christianæ capita à depravationibus IOHANNIS | MALDONATI Iesuitæ,
& aliorum, Perspicue & solide vindicantur. | Cui subiungitur . in duas S.

Petri Epistolas : | *Nec non* | IN ⎰IOEL, ⎱ | *Commentarius, tum cruditione*
                                  ⎰AMOS, ⎱
                                  ⎱HAGGAI : ⎰

tum perspicuitate celeberrimus. | [*device.*]

Impr. 113 : 1631 : (eights) sm. 4° :
pp. [12] + 800 + 120 : pp. 11 begg. *voluit,
Christi* and *eo : vnde patet,* 701 *catorum
nostrorum* : Pica Roman. Contents :—
p. (1) title : (3) " Ad Lectorem " by the
editor : (4–12), 1–800, Pareus on St.
Matthew : 1–48, on St. Peter : 49–78,
on Joel : 79–91, on Haggai : 92–120, on
Amos.

In 1622 the year of Pareus's death several of his treatises were publicly burnt at
Oxford, as opposed to the King's authority, including his commentary on the Romans.
Underlined words in the title are printed in red. The last 120 pages seem to have
been printed in London, not Oxford.

19. **Parsons,** Bartholomew.   DORCAS : | OR. | A PERFECT | PATTERNE
OF A | TRUE DISCIPLE. | A Sermon Preached by | *Bartholomew Parsons*
B. of Di-|vinity and Rector of *Ludger-|shall* in the County of *Wilts.*
[*line,* then 2 *mottos.*]

Impr. 68 : 1631 : sm. 4° : pp. [8] + 36 :
p. 11 beg. *ing out of*; Great Primer
Roman. Contents :—(1) title, within
arched border : (3–7) dedication to sir
Francis Pile, dated " From my house at
Collingborne April 1. 1631 " : 1–36, the
sermon, on Acts ix. 36.

See Wood's *Ath. Oxon.,* iii. 26.   The title and outer margin of each page are within
double lines.

20. **Pinke,** William.   *THE* | TRYALL | of a Christians syncere |
loue vnto Christ: | [*line*] | By Mr WILLIAM PINKE, Master | of Arts late
Fellow of Mag.|*dalen Colledge in* | OXFORD. | [*line, motto, woodcuts.*]

Impr. 84 *a* : 1631 : sm. 4° : pp. [8] + 29 + [3] + 30 + [2] + 28 + [2] + 25 + [1] : pp. 11 beg. *choisest mercies*, and *custome or*, and *God, and while*, and *yet doth not* : English Roman. Contents :—p. (1) title, within arched border; 3-8) dedication to lord George Digby, dated "Shirburn. Iul. 7. 1630", signed by the editor, William Lyford : 1-29, sermon on Luke xiv. 26 : 1-30, sermon on Eph. vi. 24, beg. *Not to mispend* : 1-28, sermon on Eph. vi. 24, beg. *I will not discourage* : (1-2) "To the Reader" signed "W. Lyford" : 1-25, pieces of a sermon on 1 Cor. xvi. 22.

See 1630 P, of which the 2nd and 3rd sermons here are reissues of the sheets ; the preface to the fourth explains that it is fragmentary. Every page has a double head-line, but the four sermons are separate in pagination and signatures. Pinke was one of lord Digby's " Readers " when the latter was at Magdalen.

21. **Powel,** Griffith. "Powel (G.) De Demonstratione . Oxon. 1631 ": "Analysis Aristot. lib. de Demonstratione a G. Powell . Oxon. 1631."

So in *Catalogus librorum Richardi Davis*, 1686, p. 94, no. 92 : and in *Catalogus librorum . . . in ædibus Thomæ Bowman*, 168⅞, sign. D1ᵛ, no. 15. The book is no doubt a reprint of 1594 P.

22. **Preston,** John. THREE | SERMONS | VPON THE SA⸗CRAMENT OF | THE LORDS | *SVPPER.* | *By the late Faithfull* | *and VVorthy Minister* | *of Iesus Christ* | IOHN PRESTON, | Dʳ in Divinity, Chaplaine in | Ordinary to his MAIESTY, Master of *Emanuel* Colledge | in Cambridge, and some- | times Preacher of | Lincolnes Inne. |

Impr. 120 : 1631 : sm. 4° : pp. [2] + 91 + [1] : p. 11 beg. *onely to be* : Pica Roman. Contents :—p. (1) title, within arched border : 1-91, the sermons, on 1 John v. 14.

For the author, see Wood's *Fasti Oxon.*, i. 333.

23. **Primerose,** James. ACADEMIA | MONSPELIENSIS | A IACOBO PRI-|MIROSIO *Monspe-|liensi* & *Oxoniensi* | Doctore descripta. | EIVSDEM LAVRVS | *MONSPELIACA.* | [*device.*]

Impr. 111 : 1631 : sm. 4° : pp. [8] + 38 + [2] : p. 11 beg. *tuenda, renam* : English Roman. Contents:—p. (1) title within arched border : (3-8), 1-2, dedi- cation to dr. Thomas Clayton regius professor of Medicine at Oxford : 3-38 the work : (1-2) not seen.

See Wood's *Fasti Oxon.*, i. 450. The work contains the Quaestiones and Theses by which Primerose obtained his doctor's degree in medicine at Montpellier 2 May 1617, beginning on 21 Jan. 161⅞ : also the first medical quaestio defended after his degree, on 21 Dec. 1617. The " Laurus " must refer to the dedication in which an interesting account of the University of Montpellier is given. The occasion of publishing this medical work so long after the time at which it was written, was no doubt the incorporation of dr. Primerose at Oxford in March 162⅔. In the Bliss sale (1858) a copy of this book was sold " with duplicate title-page containing a variation " which I have not seen.

24. **Sanderson,** Robert. LOGICÆ | ARTIS COM-|PENDIVM. | TERTIA HAC EDITI-|one recognitum, duplici | *Appendice auctum, & pub-|lici iuris factum.* | à ROB. SANDERSON Collegij | Lincolniensis in almâ | *Oxoniensi Socio.* | [*device.*]

Impr. 96: 1631: (eights) 16mo: pp. [8] + 239 + [1] + 124 + [4]: pp. 11 beg. *possint esse*, and *sed ij fere*, pp. 111 *mutatis terminis*, and *margine peculiari*: Pica Roman. Contents:—p. (1) title: (3-6) "Elenchus capitum . . .": (7) "Ad Lectorem": (8) "Errata . . .": 1-239 the work: 1-124. two appendixes, one "De usu Logicæ", one "Miscella": (1-4) not seen.

See 1615 S. There is a woodcut diagram at p. 149.

25. **Scheiblerus,** Christophorus. PHILOSOPHIA COMPENDIOSA SEV | PHILOSOPHIA | *Exhibens* | LOGICÆ, METAPHYSICÆ, | PHYSICÆ, GEOMETRIÆ, | ASTRONOMIÆ, OPTICÆ, | ETHICÆ, POLITICÆ, | ET OECONOMICÆ | COMPENDIVM METHODICVM, | *Cui* | *Addita est etiam* HEIZONIS BVSCHERI | *Arithmetica, in vsum Pedagogij Gisseni.* AVTORE | CHRISTOPHORO SCHEIBLERO, Logicæ ac | Metaphysicæ Professore. | *Editio quinta recognita, & multis mendis liberata.* | [*woodcuts.*] |

Impr. 121: 1631: 16mo.

At present I only know this book from a titlepage in the Bagford collections at the British Museum (463. b. 4, no. 981): but it is not likely to be really uncommon.

26. **Strada,** Firmianus. FAMIANI | STRADÆ | ROMANI | E SOCIETATE IESV. | *PROLVSIONES* | *ACADEMICÆ.* | Iuxta exemplar AVTHORIS recognitæ, | *atque suis* Indicibus *illustratæ.* | [*device.*] [the name of place and date are in red ink, as are also the words underlined in the above title.]

Impr. 72 c: 1631: (eights) 16º: pp. [8] + 331 + [29]: p. 11 beg. *bus, tam opportuna*, 301 *l'olo tuqu am*: Long Primer Roman. Contents:—p. (1) title: (3-7) dedication to Alexander card. Ursino: 1-331, the Prolusiones, in 3 books: (2-27) "Index rerum et verborum . . .": (28-29) "Index Prolusionum . . .".

The first edition was in 1617. The subjects are oratorical, poetical and historical.

27. **Vincentius,** Lirinensis. PEREGRINI, | *ID EST, VT VVLGO PERHIBETVR,* | VINCENTII LI-RINENSIS. *AD-*VERSVS PROPHA-NAS HÆRESES, | Commonitoria duo. | *Editio repurgata, cæteris purior & emendatior.* | *Huic adijcitur* AVGVSTINI | *liber* de Hæresibus. | [*woodcuts.*]

Impr. 112: 1631: (twelves) 24mo: pp. [12] + 274 + [2]: p. 11 beg. *nat. Quid si*: 201 *tibus quamlibet*: Pica Roman. Contents:—p. (1) "A": (5) title: (7-11) "Lectori . . .", a preface: 1-150, Vincentius's work: 151-269. Augustinus's work: 270-274, "Appendix trium hæresium", i. e. of Papists, Mohammedans, Anabaptists: (1) "Errata . . .".

Underlined words in the title above are printed in red, and also "Oxoniæ", and "1631." in the imprint.

28. **Vossius,** Gerardus Johannes. GERARDI IOANNIS VOSSI RHETORICES | CONTRACTÆ, | *SIVE* | PARTITIONVM | ORATORIARVM· | Libri V. | *Ex decreto Illustr. ac Pot.* HOLLANDIÆ, & | WEST-FRISIÆ DD. ORDINVM *in* | *vsum Scholarum ejusdem Pro-vinciæ excusi.* | Editio altera castigatior. | [*device.*]

Impr. 114: 1631: (twelves) 16mo: pp. [16]+559+[1]: p. 11 beg. *vel probatur*, 401 *Hoc est, somnum*: Pica Roman. Contents :—p. (1) title : (3–10 dedication to Beniaminus Auberius Maurerius Fonti- dangaeus, dated "Lugduni Bat. ꝏ IↃ c XXI. XII Kal. vii.*bris*": (11–15) "Series Capitum": (16) Complimentary Latin poem by Daniel Heinsius: 1–559, the work.

The first edition was presumably in 1621, but the ordinary bibliographies do not give the date, except one which gives 1606. Other Oxford editions were issued in 1655 and 1672, and several others in London and abroad.

29. ———. GERARDI IOH. VOSSII. | *V. CL.* | THESES THEOLOGICÆ | ET HISTORICÆ, | *De varijs doctrinæ Christianæ Capitibus* ; | Quas, aliquot abhinc annis, dispu-|tandas proposuit in | ACADEMIA LEIDENSI. | *Editio Iterata & Emendata.* | [*device.*]

Impr. 87 *a*: 1631: (eights) sm. 4°: pp. [8]+680: p. 11 beg. *illius de chao*, 501 *Nec meliorem*: Pica Roman. Contents :—p. (1) title, (3–4) "Typographus Lectori...": (5–6) "Syllabus & Ordo Disputationum ": (8) a Latin 6-line complimentary poem signed "Philalethes": 1–680, the forty dissertations.

See 1628 V: the printer confesses that this is an unauthorized reprint of the original edition, in consequence of the daily complaint of the rarity of the book : and says "Nactus itaque tandem amicorum ope istarum Thesium fasciculum (integrum vti spero,) ... sumpsi mihi fiduciam cum iterùm typis meis exprimendi". There is nothing in this to indicate that this is a reissue of the sheets of 1628 V, without even correction of the misprints: on the contrary the list of errata given in 1628 is omitted. The first eight pages only are printing of 1631. This edition appears to be quite rare, but perhaps only accidentally so, because copies have not found their way into public libraries; or possibly Vossius may have succeeded in stopping a pirated issue.

30. *W[alkington], T[homas]. THE | OPTICK...GLASSE | OF HV...MORS | OR | The touchstone of a golden | *temperature, or the Philosophers* | *stone to make a golden temper.* | Wherein the foure com-plections | *Sanguine. Cholericke, Phligmaticke, Melancholicke are suc-cinctly painted forth* | *and their externall intimates laid open* | *to the purblindeye of ignorance itselfe,* | *by which euery one may iudge,* | *of what complection he is, and* | *answerably learn what is* | *most sutable to his* | *nature.* | *by* T. W. *Master* | *of Artes* | [*motto.*]

Impr. 122: (eights) 12°: pp. [26]+168+[2]: p. 11 beg. *damagement both*, 111 *temperatures, this*: Pica Roman. Contents :—p. (2 engraving, see below : (3) engraved title, see below : (5–13), Epistle dedicatory to sir Justinian Lewin, dated "from my study in Saint *Johns* (Camb.) x Calend March. T. W.": 15–25 "To the Reader", signed "T. W.": (25–26) "The Titles and Contents of the severall Chapters...": 1–162, the work : 163–167, "The Close", a poem: 168, "Catastrophe Lectori", an English poem.

For the author, see Wood's *Fasti Oxon.*, i. 350. The proof of authorship is not clear, but the fact seems generally accepted, and Walkington was certainly a Fellow of St. John's College, Cambridge. The book has also been attributed to Tho. Wilbie and T. Wombwell, according to Bohn's Lowndes. This is a reprint of the 1607 London edition, re-printed at London in 1639 and 1663. Hitherto this Oxford edition has been generally regarded as the first, and the British Museum catalogue assigns it doubtfully to 1605. But it cannot be earlier than 1627 from the woodcuts used, and in that year first William Turner printed books by himself. And it cannot be later than 2 Aug. 1638 when Michael Sparke assigned this book to John Dawson with one of 1631 and one not earlier than 1631. Again, a comparison of 20 imprints of Michael Sparke between 1627 and 1638 raises a presumption that he did not use the expression "are to be sold by Michael Sparke at (or, dwelling at) the Blue Bible in Green

Arbour " (nor was he connected with Oxford printers) until 1632, and he uses no local description of the kind at all in his imprints till 1629. On the whole 1631 is a probable year for the issue of this book, and 1631–33 more likely than any earlier or later date.

The engraved title on steel (size of plate 5½ × 3½ in.) does not occur in the 1607 ed. and was doubtless made for this occasion : it was altered in the imprint and then used again in 1639 and 1663. On either side of the title is a graduate in cap and gown representing "CAMBRIDGE" and "OXFORD": together they hold upright what seems intended for an optic glass or touchstone, but presents the exact appearance of a half-closed umbrella. Facing the title and part of the plate is another engraving (plate 5½ × 3½ in., as the title) which a reference to pag. 77 l. 2 shows to represent the Temperaments or complexions, with concentric rings : at top are two small wholly fanciful engravings of "Oxford " and "Cambridge ", each 7/16 × 1 11/16 in.

31. **Widdowes,** Giles.   THE | LAWLESSE | KNEELESSE | SCHISMATICALL. | *PVRITAN.* | OR | A CONFVTATION | OF THE AVTHOR | OF AN *APPENDIX,* | concerning bowing at the | name of *Iesus.* | WRITTEN | by GILES WIDDOWES Rector of S^t | MARTINS Church in Oxford, | and late fellow of | *Oriell Colledge.* | [*motto.*]

Impr. 107: 1631 : sm. 4°: pp. [4] + 90 + [1]: p. 11 beg. *must bow. now:* Pica Roman.   Contents : –(1) title: (3–4) dedication to Endymion Porter : 1–11,

" To the true Protestant Reader ": 13–90, the treatise, in defence of bowing at the name of Jesus: 91, " Errata ".

See Wood's *Ath. Oxon.,* iii. 179, and 1630 W.   This is a reply to Prynne's attack on the latter work.

32. ——.   THE | SCHISMATICAL | *PVRITAN.* | [&c., exactly as 1630 W, except *Ceremoines* for *Ceremonies,* and after " Oxford " | *The second edition, Augmented.* |

Impr. 137: 1631: sm. 4°: pp. [48], signn. A–F⁴: sign. B1ᵛ beg. *wee confesse :* English Roman.   Contents :—sign. A1:

title : A2ʳ–A2ᵛ, dedication, as in 1st ed. : A3ʳ–C4ʳ " To the Puritan ": D1ʳ–F4ᵛ, the sermon, on 1 Cor. xiv. 40.

See 1630 W: the augmentation appears to be only in the Preface.

1632.

1. **Bancroft,** John, bp. of Oxford.   ARTICLES TO | BE ENQVIRED OF | WITHIN THE DIOCES | Of *Oxford,* in the first Visitati-|on of the Right Reverend Fa-|ther in GOD, *Iohn* Lord | Bishop of *Oxford.* | HELD | In the yeare of our Lord God 1632. in the eighth | yeare of the Raigne of our most gracious Soveraigne | Lord, *Charles,* by the grace of God King of | Great *Brittaine, France,* and *Ireland* | Defender of the Faith &c. | [*woodcut.*]

Impr. 93: 1632: sm. 4°: pp. [16], signn. A–B⁴: sign. B1ᵛ beg. 15 *Whether:* Pica English.   Contents :—sign. A1ʳ, title: A2ʳ–2ᵛ, Oath and Charge of the

Churchwardens, &c. : A3ʳ " Directions for making bills of Presentments for the Dioces . . .": A3ʳ–B3ʳ, the Articles: B3ʳ–3ᵛ, directions.

2. **Brerewood,** Edward.   A | SECOND TREATISE | *Of The* | SABBATH, | OR | AN EXPLICATION OF | the Fourth *Commaundement.* |

Written, | By Mr Edward Brerewood | professor in *Gresham Colledge* | in London. | [*woodcut.*]

Impr. 124: 1632: sm. 4°: pp. 50 + [2]: p. 11 beg. *cation ; so*: English Roman. Contents :—p. 1, title: 3–40, the treatise: 41–50 "Quæstio" about servants' Sunday work, in English.

See 1630 B, Wood's *Ath. Oxon.*, ed. Bliss, ii. 141.

3. **Burton**, Robert.   THE | ANATOMY OF | MELANCHOLY | [&c., exactly as 1628 B, being from the same plate with "thirde" altered to "fourth."]

Impr. 70: 1632: (fours) folio: pp. [10] + 78 + [6] + 722 (after 218 are two unnumbered leaves) + [10]: p. 11 beg. *Iudgement,* 601 *graphers, would*: English Roman. Contents :—(2) "The Argument of the Frontispeice": (3) engraved title, inserted: (5) dedication to lord Berkeley: (7–10) "Democritus Iunior ad Librum suum", English verse: 1–78, "Democritus Iunior to the Reader": (1) "Lectori malè feriato": (2) a Latin poem: (3–6) "The Synopsis of the first partition": 1–218, the first partition: (1–4) "The Synopsis of the second partition": 219–407, the second partition: 408–10, "Analysis of the third partition": 411–722, the third partition: (1–9) "The Table": (9) "Errata …": (10) Impr. 75, between woodcuts.

See Wood's *Ath. Oxon.*, ii. 653 and 1621 B. Ten of the divisions of the titlepage have now small numbers attached to them, arranged thus :—2, 1, 3 (top row): 4, title, 5: 6, 10, 7: 8, imprint, 9 (lowest row). This plate is described in the *Catalogue of Prints in the British Museum. Div.* i. *Satires*, vol. 1 (Lond. 1870), p. 79.

4. **Clement**, st., of Rome.   "Clementis ad Corinthios Epistola prior, Gr. et Lat. cum Notis P. Junii. 4*to. J. Lichfield*, 1632."

So in the *Catalogue of the second … portion* of dr. Philip Bliss's library, sold in Aug. 1858, p. 13, no. 150: but it is probably an error for 1633, although possibly some copies may have borne this date.

5. **Daye**, Lionel.   CONCIO | AD | CLERVM | HABITA | OXONII DIE | Martis post Comitia | *An: Dom:* 1609. | AVTHORE LIONELLO DAYE | tunc temporis Collegij | *Bailiolensis Socio.* | [*woodcut.*]

Impr. 73*a*: 1632: sm. 4°: pp. [4] + 33 + [3]: p. 11 beg. *quium oris*: English Roman. Contents :—p. (1) title: (3–4) "Amicis meis Oxoniensibus", dated "Ex ædibus meis Whichfordiensibus. Ian. 23. 1631": 1–33, the sermon, on Luke xxii. 31, in Latin.

See Wood's *Fasti Oxon.*, i. 326. The author says he now prints his old sermon, because it had been a great consolation to him, he having just lost his eldest son, a B.A. of Christ Church, by illness.

6. **Downinge**, Calybute.   A | DISCOVRSE | OF THE | STATE ECCLESIA-|STICALL OF THIS | *Kingdome, in relation to the Civill.* | Considered *vnder three* CONCLVSIONS. | With a DIGRESSION discussing | *some ordinary Exceptions against* | Ecclesiasticall Officers. | [line] | *By* C. D. | [*device.*]

Impr. 119: 1632: [the rest *absolutely* as 1633 D.: for that issue the title of this edition was torn off, and a new one substituted.]

7. **Ovid.** OVID'S | METAMORPHOSIS | ENGLISHED, | MYTHOLOGIZ'D, | *And* | Represented in Figures. | An Essay to the Translation | of VIRGIL'S ÆNEIS. | *By G. S.* |

Impr. 82*a* : 1632 : (fours) folio: pp. [20?] + 549 + 1, not counting 16 engravings: p. 11 beg. *Who o're so,* 401 (*a For Ione* : English Roman. Contents :— p. (1) title : (2) "The minde of the frontispecce . . ." : (3) an engraved titlepage, see description below : (5) dedication to prince Charles, signed "George Sandys" : (6-9) two panegyrics: (10-12) "to the Reader" : (13-16) "The Life of Ovid": (17-19) "Ovid defended" : (20) Latin poem : 1-531, the work, with notes : 532, "To the Reader": 533-49, the first Aeneid of Virgil in English verse : (1) "Errata". Each of the 15 bks. and the Life are preceded by a full-page engraving.

See Wood's *Ath. Oxon.*, iii. 100. The first and second editions were issued at London in 1626 and 1628: this is the third, and others followed but were not published at Oxford. The first five books had been issued by Sandys at least twice (2nd ed., Lond. 1621). The large engraved titlepage (9⅝ × 5¼ in.) is similar to the title of the 1626 London folio edition in general design, but different in detail. In the 1632 engraving the title (nearly as on the printed leaf, as far as "G. S.", with date only and no imprint) is on a sheet held by and between two figures of Amor and Sapientia, and on the lower edge of the sheet is "*Francisco Clein Inv: Salamon Sauery sculp:*". Other emblematic figures and some Latin sentences fill the page. The British Museum copy has the engraved title, but the copy presented by the translator in 1636 to the Bodleian has not. The book is singular in having no small woodcut ornaments.

8. **Pemble,** William. A | SVMME OF | MORALL | PHILOSOPHY | SVCCINCTLY | GATHERED, ELE-gantly Composed, | and Methodically | *handled,* | BY | THAT LEARNED SCHOLLER | AND WORTHY DIVINE | *WILLIAM PEMBLE* Mr of | Arts and late Commoner | of *Mag. Hall.* | [two *mottos.*]

Impr. 84*a* : 1632 : sm. 4° : pp. [4] + "82" ("56" occurs twice in the pagination) + [1] : p. 11 beg. *selues, that* : Pica Roman. Contents :—p. (1) title: (3) "To the Reader": (4) a logical division of Disciplines: 1-"82", the work: (1) "Index".

See Wood's *Ath. Oxon.*, ii. 331, and 1630 P. The book is an analysis, rather than a readable treatise.

9. **Sennertus,** Daniel. DANIELIS | SENNERTI | Vratislaviensis | *EPITOME* | NATURALIS | SCIENTLÆ | [*device*] | EDITIO TERTIA. | Auctior & Correctior. |

Impr. 123 : 1632 : (eights) 12° : pp. [16] + 632 + [22] : p. 11 beg. *Actiones voluntati,* 611 *suam sedem* : Pica Roman. Contents :—p. (1) title : (3-9) Epistola dedicatoria to Severinus Schattenus à Schattenhall, dated "Calend. April. . . . . 1618": (11-13) "Lectori candido . . .": (15-16) "Index librorum et capitum". 1-632, the work, in 8 books : (1-2) "Conclusio" : (3-20) index.

The first edition was presumably issued in 1618, the second at Wittenberg in 1624 : other Oxford editions came out in 1653 and 1664.

1633.

1. **A[iray],** C[hristopher]. FASCICVLVS | *PRAECEPTORVM* | LOGICORVM: | IN | *Gratiam juventutis* | Academicæ *compo-situs & typis donatus.* | *Editio altera limatior* | *operâ secundâ* | C. A. | [*line.*]

Impr. 69 : 1633 : (eights) 16° : pp. [8] + 224 : p. 11 beg. *nec genere*, 111, *t. Necessaria, cui* : Long Primer Roman. Contents :—(3) title, within an arched | border : (5–6) "Typographus Benevolo Lectori . . ." : (7) "Sphalmata . . .", errata : (8) "*Arbor Porphyriana*" : 1–224, the work.

This is a reprint of 1628 A, and appears to be rare, for Wood believed the 1660 edition to be the second.

2. *Articles.　　　ARTICLES | Given by | and delivered to the Church-wardens | to be considered and answered in his visitation | holden in the yeare of our Lord God | WHEREVNTO THE SAID | Church-wardens and sidemen are | vpon their oathes to answere | truly and particularly. | [*device*]. |

Impr. 68*b* : n. d. : sm. 4° : pp. [16], signn. A–B¹ : sign. B1ʳ beg. *Lords Prayer* : Pica English. Contents :—sign. A1ʳ, | title : A2ʳ, instructions and Oath : A3ʳ–B4ʳ, the articles.

This is a general undated form of Articles of Visitation apparently for a Bishop's or Archdeacon's use. The occurrence of a particular woodcut shows that this is the earliest year to which the printing can be assigned.

3. **Bacon,** sir Francis, Lord Verulam.　　　THE TWO | BOOKES OF | Sʳ FRANCIS BACON, | *OF* | THE PROFICIENCE | and Advancement of Learning, | DIVINE and HVMANE. | [*line.*] | *To the* KING. | [*line, then woodcut.*] |

Impr. 138 : 1633 : sm. 4° : pp. [2] + 335 + [1] : p. 11 beg. *he spoiled*, 201 *tage* | *in the race* : English Roman. Contents :— p. (1) title : 1–335, the work.

This is the 3rd edition, the previous ones being Lond. 1605, Lond. 1629 (from which latter the present edition is an almost lineatim reprint) ; no separate one in English was subsequently issued till this century : see 1640 B.

4. **Bartholinus,** Caspar.　　　*CASP. BARTHOLINI* | ENCHIRIDION | ETHICVM : | SEV | *EPITOME* | PHILOSOPHIÆ | MORALIS. | *Praecepta breviter & dilucidè, me-|thodóque novâ & facili expli-|cata exhibens* | Pro angustâ tyronum me-|moriâ | [*woodcut.*] |

Impr. 137 : 1633 : (twelves) 16° : pp. [72], signn. A–C¹² : sign. B1ʳ beg. *tudinis ; ut* : Long Primer Roman. Contents :— | sign. A1ʳ, title : A1ᵛ, dedication to prince Hulderic : A2ʳ–C10ʳ, the work : C11ʳ–C11ᵛ, "Index capitum . . .".

This was reprinted at Oxford in 1665 with Casa's Galateus.

5. ——.　　　*CASPARI BARTHOLINI* | *Philosophi & Medici* | ANATO-MICÆ | INSTITVTIONES | CORPORIS HVMANI | Vtriusque sexûs | His-TORIAM & DECLARATIO-|nem exhibentes, | Cum plurimis novis observa-tionibus | & opinionibus, | Nec non | *Illustriorum, quae in* ANTHROPO-|LOGIA *occurrunt controver-|siarum decisionibus.* | Cum indice Capitum & Rerum locupletissimo. | [*woodcut.*] |

Impr. 69 : 1633 : (twelves) 16° : pp. [24] + 417 + [51] : p. 11 beg. *nisi in*, 301 *ramos intercostales* : Long Primer Roman. Contents :—p. (1) title : (2) contents of | the work : (3–7) dedication to Oligerus Rosaecranzius, dated 18 Dec. 1610, in Latin : (8–17) "Ad Benevolum Lectorem meum . . .", dated as above : (18–24)

"Index capitum . . .": 1–417, the work consisting of a Proœmium, 4 libri and 4 libelli: (1–44) the index: (45–47)

"Admonitio Autoris ad Lectorem qui benignus" about a charge of plagiarism, dated "Hafniæ", 1 Sept. 1622.

The first edition was issued in 1611: this new one appears to be reprinted from the edition Goslariæ et Rostochii 1632.

6. Browne, Thomas.   [The British Museum Catalogue by an error states that there is a copy of Browne's *Copie of a Sermon* dated 1633: see 1634 B.]

7. **Burton**, William.   "*Laudatio funebris in Obitum Viri excellentiss. D. Thomæ Alleni.* Lond. 1632. Ox. 1633. qu."

So in Wood's *Ath. Oxon.*, ed. Bliss, iii. 439: the London edition of 1632 is known, but at present not the Oxford issue.

Butler, Charles.   The reference to a 1633 edition of the *Feminine Monarchie*, made in 1609 B, is an error.

8. **Butler**, Charles.   ORATORIÆ | LIBRI DVO: | QVORVM | *Alter ejus Definitionem,* | *Alter Partitionem* | EXPLICAT: | IN VSVM SCHOLARVM | *recèns editi.* | [line] | Authore CAROLO BVTLERO, *Magd.* | [line, then device.]

Impr. 69: 1633: sm. 4°: pp. [136], signn. A, A Q¹: sign. B1ʳ beg. *clarant; vt cùm*: Long Primer Roman. Contents :— A1ʳ, title : A2ʳ–A2ᵛ, dedication to Thomas lord Coventry, dated "Wotton, 5. *Idus Martii*, Ann. Dom. 1633. . . ." : A3ʳ, two complimentary Latin poems to the author by I. H. and S. W. : A3ᵛ–4ᵛ, "Lectori Benevolo . . ." as in 1629: A1ʳ–Q4ᵛ, the work: Q4ᵛ, "Monitio . . .", errata and corrigenda.

See Wood's *Ath. Oxon.*, iii. 210, 1629 B. This is a reprint of the 1629 edition, but the new dedication states that Butler's Rhetoric (see 1600 B) was used in the chief schools of the kingdom.

9. ——.   THE | ENGLISH | GRAMMAR, | OR | The Institution of Letters, Syl-lables, and Words, in the En-glish tongue. | *Whereunto is annexed* | An Index of Words Like and Unlike. | [line] | *By* | CHARLS BVTLER Magd. *Master of Arts.* | [line, then *motto*, then *device*.]

Impr. 125: 1633: sm. 4°: pp. [8] + 63 + [29] : p. 11 beg. *largᵉ sargᵉ*: Pica Roman and English. Contents :—p. (1) title within double lines : (3–8) "To the Reader", signed "Wotton Sept. 11. An. D. 1633. C. B. M.": (8) "Ad Authorem" a Latin poem by S. W.: 1–63, the grammar: (2–29) the index: (29) "The Printer to the Reader".

See Wood's *Ath. Oxon.*, iii. 210 where this edition is not mentioned, and 1634 B. This book, as well as the same author's *Feminine Monarchie or history of Bees* (see 1634 B), are printed in a peculiar phonetic manner. The system is of considerable interest for the history of phonetic reforms of spelling and of English pronunciation, but made no way in practical use. The preface asserts the superiority of English in generality, by which he means wide geographical extent of usage, but laments the uncertain correspondence of sound and spelling, and the labour of learning the language, these two defects being due both to the want of alphabetical characters for certain sounds, and to historical changes of pronunciation, to which some persons adapt the old spelling and some do not. The author supplies the characters wanted, and counsels strictly phonetic spelling with certain exceptions where letters not strictly sounded indicate idiom or derivation. Generally an aspirated letter is represented by a line drawn through the letter (đ, ꝥ, ǥ, but ɜ), and mute vowels by a substituted comma (as strang', tru', nam'ly) when not omitted (as qestion). Also conjoined double e and double o are used, but the exceptions to the phonetic spelling would be, among others, a serious objection to this system of compromise. In 1585 W. Bullokar published an edition of Æsop's Fables in English, in a somewhat similar style of orthography.

10. **Clemens**, Romanus. ΚΛΗΜΕΝΤΟΣ | ΠΡΟΣ ΚΟΡΙΝΘΙΟΥΣ | ΕΠΙΣΤΟΛΗ ΠΡΩΤΗ. | CLEMENTIS | AD CORINTHIOS | EPISTOLA PRIOR. | Ex laceris reliquijs vetustissimi exemplaris Biblio-|thecæ Regiæ eruit, lacunas explevit, Latinè ver-|tit, & notis brevioribus illustravit. | [*line*] | PATRICIVS IVNIVS *Pet. F. Scotobritannus,* | *Sereᵐᵒ Britanniarum Fr. & Hib. Regi* | CAROLO *à Bibliothecis.* | [*line,* then *motto.*]

Impr. 73 : 1633 : sm. 4°: pp. [24]+ 76 + [48] : p. 11 beg. τῶν ἁπάντων: English Roman. Contents:—p. (3) title: (5-8) dedication to the king: (9-19) "Veterum testimonia de Clemente ... ": (21-23) "Benevolo Lectori", dated "Oxonij pridie Cal: Nov. 1632": 1-76, the Epistle: (1-40) Latin notes: (41-47) "Fragmentum Epistolæ secundæ ex eodem MS.": (48) "παροράματα", errata.

See Wood's *Fasti Oxon.*, ed. Bliss, i. 308. Patrick Young was Library Keeper to the King's Library at St. James's Palace (now the Old Royal Library at the British Museum), and edited this book from the Alexandrine MS. of the Greek Bible. Red ink is used in the words underlined above, and for "Oxonii," and "Academiæ" in the imprint, and for all words in the text which are supplied by the editor, who calls it "Novum et inusitatum imprimendi genus". Some copies are on large paper, and some have an inserted leaf containing "Summa Privilegii", reserving rights of translation, reproduction and sale for ten years. This leaf is found before or after the dedication.

11. **Combachius**, Johannes. *IOH. COMBACHII,* | METAPHY-| SICORVM, | LIBRI DVO | *VNIVERSAM PRIMÆ* | *Philosophiæ doctrinam theoremati-|bus brevissimis comprehendentes, & | Commentariis necessariis illustrantes: stu-|diosis ejus disciplinæ per quam | utiles & fructuosi.* | EDITIO TERTIA | Prioribus editionibus auctior & | castigatior. | *Additus est cuilibet libro in fine Index | rerum & verborum locuples.* | [two *lines.*]

Impr. 69 : 1633 : 16mo.

At present only known from a titlepage in the Bagford Collections at the British Museum (463. h. 4, no. 1110), but it is not likely to be really rare. The 2nd edition seems to have been issued abroad in 1620, and a "3rd" in 1630, of which this is probably a reprint.

12. **Cyprianus**, S. S. CYPRIANVS | *DE* | BONO PATIENTIÆ | COL-LATVS CVM | *MS. OXONIENSIBVS,* | *EDITIS* | A IEREM. STEPHANO, | SS. Theol. Bac. cum | *spicilegio notarum.* | [*woodcuts.*]

Impr. 129a: 1633: (twelves) 16°: pp. [16] + 87 + [5]: p. 11 beg. *daret & divina*: English Roman. Contents :— p. (1) title, within line, double at top and bottom: (3-9) dedication to William Noye attorney general: (11-16) "... Argumentum libri ...": 1-57, the work: 59-87, "Annotationes in libellum S. Cypriani ...", with collations of four MSS.

See Wood's *Ath. Oxon.*, ed. Bliss, iii. 671. In 1632 Stephens had issued a similar edition of Cyprian De unitate ecclesiae.

13. **Downe**, rev. John.   *CERTAINE* | TREATISES | OF | THE LATE
REVEREND | and Learned Divine, Mr *Iohn* | *Downe*, Rector of the Church
of *Instow* | in *Devonshire*, Bachelour of Divi-nity, and sometimes Fellow
of *Ema-|nuell* Colledge in *Cambridge*. | *Published at the instance of his
friends*. | [*line*, then *motto*, then *line*, then *woodcut*.]

Impr. 126: 1633: sm. 4°: pp. [6] +
57 + [1] + 185 + [3] + 34 + [2] + 26 + [2]
+ 34 + [2] + 24 + [2] + 26 + [2] + 51 + [3]
+ 125 + [3] + 68: incipits, see below in
Contents: English Roman. Contents:—
(1) title, within arched border: (3) dedication by the publisher (dr. G. Hakewill)
to the bp. and clergy of the diocese of
Exeter: (4) "The Contents of these treatises", a list of titles: (5) a title "The
funerall sermon on behalfe of the anthor
of these ensuing workes, preached by
George Hakewill . . ." with impr. 128:
1-34, the sermon, on Dan. xii. 3: 55-57,
letter from bp. Joseph Hall, dated "Exon
Palace Mar. 22. 1631", to Hakewill
about the book: p. 11 beg. *Some there*:
(1) a title ". . . Two treatises 1 Concerning the force and efficacy of reading—2
Christs prayer for his Church", with impr.
128: 1-51, 1st treatise, on Acts xv. 21:
53-185, 2nd treatise, on John xvii. 1 &c.:
p. 11 beg. *ever bee a*, 101 *are communi-
cated*: (2) a title "A godlie discourse of
Selfe-deniall", with impr. 128: 1-34, the
sermon, on Luke ix. 23: p. 11 beg. *The*

Counsell: (1) a title "An apologie of the
iustice of God", with impr. 128: 1-26,
the sermon, on Gen. xviii. 25: p. 11 beg.
divine actions: (1) a title "An amulet
or preservative against the contempt of
the ministry", with impr. 128: 1-34,
the sermon, on Tit. ii. 15: p. 11 beg.
Ghost were: (1) a title "The dove-like
serpent", with impr. 128: 1-24, the sermon, on Matt. x. 16: p. 11 beg. *The deafe
care*: (1) a title "Subiection To the
higher powers", with impr. 128: 1-26
("27"), the sermon on Rom. xiii. 5: p. 11
beg. *Simply considered*: (1) a title "A
defence of the lavvfulnesse of lots in
gaming against the Arguments of N. N.",
with impr. 128: 1-51, the work: p. 11
beg. "shall haue these": (2) a title
"The Reall Presence of Transubstantia-
tion vnknowne to the Ancient Fathers",
with impr. 128: p. 11 beg. *grace of God*:
(2) "A defence of the former Answer
against the Reply of N. N.", with impr.
128: 1-68, the work: 68, a note to be
added to the first sermon: p. 11 beg.
stantiation? Nothing.

See Wood's *Fasti Oxon.*, i. 286, Dict. of Nat. Biogr., and 1635 D (for Hakewill see
Ath. Oxon., iii. 255). Downe was a nephew of bp. Jewel: educated at Emmanuel
college Cambridge, and incorporated at Oxford in 1600. He died in about 1631. The
signatures run through the entire work, with one break.

14. **Downinge**, Calybute.   A | DISCOVRSE | OF THE | STATE
ECCLESIA-|STICALL OF THIS | Kingdome, in relation to the Civill. | *Con-
sidered vnder three* CONCLUSIONS. | With a DIGRESSION, discussing | *some
ordinary Exceptions against* | Ecclesiasticall Officers. | [*line*] | *BY* C. D. |
[*line*, then *woodcut*.]

Impr. 119: 1633: sm. 4°: pp. [4] +
98 + [2]: p. 11 beg. *distinguished by*:
Pica Roman. Contents:—(1) title: (3)
dedication to William earl of Salisbury,

signed "Calybute Downinge": (4)
"Errata": 1-98, the work, in three
parts: the digression is on pp. 30-42:
(1-2) not seen.

See Wood's *Ath. Oxon.*, iii. 107 and 1632 D, 1634 D. Wood throws doubt on this
really being by Downinge. Downinge was chaplain to the earl of Salisbury.

15. Erasmus, Desiderius.   The Oxford 1663 edition of the
Moriae Encomium bears on its first titlepage the erroneous date 1633.

16. **Evans**, William.   A | TRANSLATION | of the Booke of |
NATURE, | into the Vse of | GRACE. | PERFORMED AND PRINCIPALLY | in-
tended for the benefit of those who | plead ignorance, or that they are

not Book-|*learned, or that they want teachers and* | *so thinke to excuse themselues* | *in their sinnes.* | [*line.*] | By WILLIAM EVANS, M^r of Arts of | St *Mary Hall in Oxford.* | [*line, then two mottos.*]

Impr. 127; 1633: sm. 4°: pp. [8] + 95 + [9]: p. 11 beg. *consumed away*: Pica Roman. Contents :—p. (1) title: (3–4) dedication to Thomas 2nd lord Coventry: (5–8) "To the Reader": 1–95, the work: (1) "Errata": (2–7) 76 "... heads of certaine doctrines ..." by way of index.

See Wood's *Fasti Oxon.*, i. 479. The dedication states that this is the author's first (and, as it seems, last) publication.

17. **Gerhardus**, Johannes.   IOH: GERHARDI | MEDITATIONES | *SACRÆ.* | EDITIO POSTREMA, | *prioribus emendatior.* | [*woodcut.*]

Impr. 129: 1633 : twelves (16°): pp. [2] + 238 + [4]: p. 11 beg. *tis ex templo*, 201 *hoc interpretare*: Long Primer Eng-lish. Contents :—p. (1) title, within lines : 1–238 ("235"), the Meditations: (2–3) "Index", a list of the 51 meditations.

The first edition was apparently in 1606 with 50 Meditations, and editions were issued in Latin in 1621, 1627, 1629, Lond. 1672, and later, and English translations in 1629 (by R. Winterton, printed at Cambridge) and later, even in 1840 (at Oxford).

18. **Godwyn**, Thomas.   ROMANÆ | HISTORIAE | ANTHOLOGIA | RECOGNITA ET | AVCTA. | AN | ENGLISH EXPOSITION | OF THE ROMAN ANTI-|quities, wherein many Roman and | English offices are paralleld | *and divers obscure phra-|ses explained.* | *For the vse of* ABINGDON *Schoole.* | [*line*] | Newly revised and inlarged by the | *Author* | [*line.*]

Impr. 141: 1633: (fours) sm. 4°: pp. [8] + 277 + [23]: p. 11 beg. *malefactor*, *but*, 111 *gainst another*: Pica Roman. Contents :—p. (1) title, within an arched border: (3–4) Latin dedication to dr. John Young, signed "Tho. Godwyn", dated "Abindoniæ 14 Calend. Decemb.... 1622": (5) "Benevolo Lectori ...": (7) "A short table shewing the Argument of every Booke and Section": 1–277, the work, in four books: (1–23) "Index rerum et verborum ...".

See 1614 G.

19. †**Grave**, Jean de.   [*line*] | THE | PATH-WAY TO | THE GATE OF | *TONGVES:* | BEING, | THE FIRST INSTRV-|CTION FOR LITTLE | CHIL-DREN. | With | A short manner to conjugue | the French Verbes. | *Ordered and made Latine, French and* | *English by* IEAN de GRAUE, | *Professour of the French Tongue* | *in the City of* | LONDON. | [*line.*]

Impr. 136: 1633: pp. [48], signn. A–C⁶: sign. B1ʳ beg. *discas oportet*: Long Primer Roman and English. Contents :— sign. A1ʳ title, within line: A2ʳ–A2ᵛ. intro-duction in Latin, English and French : A3ʳ–C6ᵛ, the work.

Very rare. The book consists of the names of the numbers, the Church Catechism, and the conjugation of French verbs, all in parallel Latin, English and French columns: and serves as an introduction to the English editions by John Anchoran (1631, 1633, 1637, 1639 or 1640, &c.) of J. A. Comenius's celebrated *Janua lingua-rum.* See 1634 S. The book is interesting as showing a connexion between William Turner the Oxford printer (1624–40) and the London printer of the same name (1623–35). The Stationers' Register (ed. Arber, iv. 334) records the transfer of all the Lon-don Turner's rights in this book and the *Clavis ad portam* (which was certainly printed by the Oxford Turner in 1634, see 1634 S) to Michael Sparke on 17 Mar. 163⅘. Neither of these books was registered at Stationers' Hall, and so probably this book as well as the *Clavis* was printed at Oxford, though the imprint, type and woodcuts are not by themselves decisive. Probably the two Turners are in fact identical, and the Oxford printing establishment, though founded a year later than the other (but as a bookseller's business not later than 161?), was the chief one. It is curious that under these circumstances Turner was allowed to be a member of the Stationers' Company, which was particularly jealous of provincial presses.

20. Gregorius, monk.   A | LETTER, | RELATING THE | Martyr-dome of KETABAN, Mother | of TEIMVRASES Prince of the | *GEORGIANS,* | *& withall* | A notable Imposture of the Iesuites | vpon that occasion: | SENT | From GREGORIVS Monke and | Priest, Agent for the Patriarke of | ANTIOCH *vnto the most* | *holy and learned* Abbot | SOPHRONIVS. | [*line*] | *Written first in Greeke, and now* | *done in English* | [*line.*]

Impr. 82: 1633: sm. 4°: pp. [6] + 23 + [3]: p. 11 beg. *Iberia: and:* Great Primer Roman. Contents:—p. (1) title: (3-6) "To the Reader", about the	Georgians, probably by the translator: 1-23, the letter, dated "Trapezunt May 16. *Ann.* 1626".

A rare tract. See Wood's *Fasti Oxon.,* ed. Bliss, i. 479. The incident related belongs to the year 1614, when the King of Persia put Ketaban to death for refusing to forsake Christianity. Some Jesuits are said to have dressed up a carcase as Keta-ban's, to have carried it to her son, and to have enjoyed much honour by the miracles which it wrought. Ultimately the real body arrived and the Jesuits were banished. The translator was Thomas Crosfield of Queen's College, Oxford: and the Letter was published in Greek and Latin (at London ?) in 1632.

21. Hakewill, George.   THE | VANITIE | OF | THE EYE. | First begun for the Com-|fort of a Gentlewoman berea-|ved of her sight, and since | upon occasion inlarged | and published for the | Common good. | BY GEORGE HAKEVVILL Ma-|ster of Arts, and Fellow of Exe-|ter Coll. in Oxford. | [*line*] | *The second Edition.* | [*line, then motto.*] |

Impr. 142: 1633: (twelves) 16°: pp. [6] + 173 + [1]: p. 11 beg. *ripping up,* 111 *as much of:* Pica Roman. Contents:— p. (1) title, within double bounding lines:	(3-6) "The Contents of the severall Chapters...": 1-173, the work in 31 chapters.

See 1608 II. This is really the 4th ed., not the 2nd.

22. Heylyn, Peter.   ΜΙΚΡΟ΄ΚΟΣΜΟΣ | (&c., precisely as 1631 II, except "sixth" for "fifth".)

Impr. 140: 1633: (eights) sm. 4°; pp. [20] + 808 (the last misprinted 807) + [4]: p. 11 beg. *1 First then there,* 701 *dales, or Vindelici:* Pica Roman. Con-	tents:—exactly as 1631 H, except "For-raine Coynes", and the necessary change of reference (only) to the last five pages.

See 1621 II: this edition is apparently an almost lineatim reprint of the 5th edition.

23. Holyday, Barten.   PHILOSOPHIÆ | POLITO-BARBARÆ | SPECI-MEN, | IN QUO | *De* ANIMA & *ejus* | HABITIBUS INTEL-LECTUALIBUS, | *Quæstiones aliquot,* | LIBRIS DVOBVS, | Illustrantur à [*line*] | BARTENIO HOLYDAY | [*line.*] |

Impr. 69: 1633: sm. 4°: pp. [12] + 189 + [3]: p. 11 beg. *piniones diversas*: Great Primer Roman. Contents:—p. 1, title, within arched border: (3–8) "Præfatio": (9–11) "Series rerum ...", a list of contents: 1–189, two books and an oration: (1) "Errata".

See Wood's *Ath. Oxon.*, iii. 522. These are exercises and speeches composed by Holyday in about 1617–21, when prælector of Rhetoric and Philosophy at Christ Church, Oxford, and concern the De Anima, Ethics and Rhetoric of Aristotle. What is considered to be the barbarous element in the Philosophy, is not clear.

24. **James**, dr. Richard.　　　CONCIO | HABITA AD | *CLERVM* | *OXONIENSEM* | *de Ecclesia.* | AVTHORE *RICHARDO* | *IAMESIO Vectensi*, Baccalaureo | Sacræ Th. Socio *CCC.* | [*line, motto, line, woodcut.*]

Impr. 130: 1633: sm. 4°: pp. [36], signn. A–D⁴ E²: sign. B1ʳ beg. *cum omnes*: English Roman. Contents:—sign. A1ʳ, title: A2ʳ–2ᵛ, dedication to sir Kenelm Digby: A3ʳ–E1ᵛ, the sermon, on Matth. xvi. 18.

See Wood's *Ath. Oxon.*, ii. 630. Some copies of this book have the remains of a torn titlepage, apparently a cancel leaf following the ordinary title.

25. **More**, sir Thomas.　　　EPISTOLA | THOMÆ MORI AD | *ACA-DEMIAM* | *OXON.* | Adjecta sunt quædam Poemata | in mortem | CLARISSIMI VIRI | ROBERTI COTTONI | & | THOMÆ ALLENI. | [*line, then motto, then line.*] |

Impr. 113a: 1633: sm. 4°: pp. [4] + 18 + [10]: p. 11 beg. *ei periti*: Great Primer Roman. Contents:—p. (1) title: (3–4) dedication to sir Kenelm Digby, signed "Rich. Iamesius", the editor: 1–17, the Letter, dated "Abingdoniæ ... 4° Kal. Aprilis": 18, "Nota magistri Briani Twyne" about the occasion of the letter: (1–7) three Latin poems and a Latin note by James on Cotton and Allen.

See Wood's *Ath. Oxon.*, i. 85, ii. 630. This is a rather uncommon book, containing a persuasive to the study of Greek, written in 1518, probably at the king's instigation. The opponents of the New Learning called themselves Trojans in opposition to the Grecians. The letter is reprinted by Hearne in his edition of Roper's Life of More (Oxf. 1716, 8°). Sir Robert Cotton died in 1631, and Thomas Allen of Gloucester hall in Oxford in 1632.

26. **Oxford**, University.　　　[two *lines*] | *Musarum Oxoniensium* | PRO | REGE SVO | *SOTERIA.* | [*Anagram*, &c., then *device.*]

Impr. 131: 1633: sm. 4°: pp. [72], signn. §, §§⁴, §§§², A, "BC", D–G¹, H⁴: sign. BC1ʳ beg. *Nec morbos*: English Roman. Contents:—sign. §1ʳ, title: §2ʳ–112ʳ, the poems: 112ᵛ, device and impr. 132.

The occasion of these verses seems to have been an illness of the King late in 1632. Most of the poems are Latin, but four are English and one Greek. One of the printers (W. Turner) contributes some Latin verses. An anagram occurs in the title, and a chronogram (1632) on E1ᵛ. There are curious variations in issues, and marks (see the register of signatures) of the difficulty of obtaining and marshalling in order these collections of separate poems. The early issues of sheet A on A3ʳ print "R. NEVVLIN S. T. B.", the later and common ones insert C. C. C. after the name, as also in A1ᵛ, A3ʳ (twice): so "Nov. C." is inserted on A4ᵛ, cf. A2ᵛ. An interesting copy is in the British Museum, being the one specially printed for the King's personal acceptance. The differences are that the book is on larger paper (the size even as bound and cut down being 7¾ × 6in.), and the title entirely reprinted. Every line of the title is in larger type and spread out laterally, except the anagram itself and imprint: also ll. 1 and 4 are roman, not italic, and ll. 3, 4, 6, 7 are printed *in gold*. In l. 6 the two V's are lower case Us, and in l. 7 Rex appears as REX. So too the device is altered, and it is amusing to see that the imprint, for fear of royal vengeance, is altered from the English " W. T." (William Turner) to the Latin " G. T."! This fact shows also that the *last* and not the first copy was struck off for the King, sheet A agreeing with this in being the later issue (see above).

27. ——.　　　SOLIS | BRITANNICI | *PERIGÆUM.* | SIVE | ITINERANTIS CAROLI | AVSPICATISSIMA | *PERIODVS.* | [two *lines.*]

Impr. 53 : 1633 : sm. 4°: pp. [100], signn. § A–C, DE, F–M¹ N²: sign. B1ʳ beg. Εἰς ἄλοχον : English Roman.　Con- | tents :—sign. §1ʳ title : §2ʳ–N2ʳ, the poems.

Poems by members of the University congratulating the King on his return from Scotland in Aug. 1633. The perigee of the sun or a planet is when it is nearest to the earth. Most of the poems are Latin, but six are Greek, sixteen at the end English, and one French. Three chronograms occur. One English poem is by John Lichfield the printer. There are some signs of an arrangement of the poems, those by great persons coming first, and the English last. Some copies of a later issue have an extra sheet after 1 (ii, four leaves) inserted, with more poems, which necessitated a re-arrangement of sheet K.

28. ——.　　　VITIS | CAROLINÆ | GEMMA ALTERA | *SIVE* | AVSPICA-TISSIMA | DVCIS EBORACENSIS | GENETHLIACA | *Decantata ad* | *VADA ISIDIS* | [two *lines.*]

Impr. 53 : 1633 : sm. 4°: pp. [88], signn. A–L¹, see below : sign. B1ʳ beg. *Te* | *pariter* : English Roman.　Contents :— sign. A1ʳ, title : A2ʳ–L3ᵛ, the poems.

These poems celebrate the birth of James ii on 15 Oct. 1633, and are as usual chiefly in Latin, but six in Greek, eighteen in English (an innovation) and one in French. There is a second issue, perhaps commoner than the first described above, with the following changes. In sheet H, sign. H1ᵛ l. 9 has *Conjugis alvus*, not *uxorius alvus* : H3ʳ begins with a *Greek* poem, the rest of sheet H is re-arranged and a new sheet h of four leaves is inserted. Also in sheet L a new poem by W. Dutton is inserted. The sheets not specified above are identical in the two issues.

29. **Parsons,** Bartholomew.　　　BOAZ | *AND* | RUTH | BLESSED : | OR | A SACRED CON-|TRACT HONOV-'red with a Solemne | *Benediction.* | BY | BARTHOLOMEW PARSONS B. of Divinity | and Rector of *Ludgershall* in the | County of *Willes.* | [two *mottos.*]

Impr. 134 : 1633 : sm. 4°: pp. [8] + 40 : p. 11 beg. *ever are blessed* : English Roman.　Contents :—p. (1) title : (3–7) | Epistle Dedicatorie to Peregrine Thistle-thwaite and Dorothy his wife : 1–40, the sermon, on Ruth iv. 11.

See Wood's *Ath. Oxon.,* ed. Bliss, iii. 26.　This sermon was to have been delivered at the wedding of Mr. Thistlethwaite, but some accident interposed, and it is here in an enlarged form.

30. **Pavonius,** Franciscus.　　　SUMMA | ETHICÆ : | *SIVE,* | INTRO-DVCTIO | IN ARISTOTELIS, | ET THEOLOGORVM | DOCTRINAM | Moralem. | CVM QVATVOR INDICIBVS, | *Vno Propositionum in libri initio ;* | *alio Aristotelico, tertio Tho-|mistico, quarto Rerum,* | in fine. | Auctore FRAN-CISCO PAVONIO | Catacensi Theologo Societatis JESV. | [*woodcut.*]

Impr. 139: 1633: (twelves) 16°: pp. [12] + 381 + [51]: p. 11 beg. *maximè*, 301 *justum debitum*: Long Primer Roman. Contents:—p. (1) title within double lines: (3-4) dedication to Mutius Vitellescus, dated 29 Sept. 1617: (5-12) "Index propositionum": 1-381, the work: (1-2) "Epilogus": (4-51) The four indexes.

The author was an Italian Jesuit, who died in 1637. The first edition of this work seems to have been issued at Lyons in 1620.

31. **Pemble**, William.   '*Enchiridion Oratorium*.   Ox. 1633 "qu." &c.'

So in Wood's *Ath. Oxon.*, ed. Bliss, ii. 331. There seems to be some mistake, since no such treatise was printed among Pemble's Collected Works: possibly Butler's work on Oratory above has been confused by Wood: but Watt mentions the work under *Pembelo* as well as *Pemble*, as if he had been independent of Wood.

32. **Potter**, Christopher.   WANT OF | CHARITIE, | Iustly charged, | ON ALL SVCH *ROMA-|nists*, as dare (without truth or | modesty affirme, that *Prote-|stancie destroyeth Salvation*. | In Answer to a late Po-|pish Pamphlet intituled | *Charity Mistaken &c.* | *By* CHRISTOPHER POTTER D.D. | Chaplaine to his Ma‸y in Ordina-|rie, and Provost of *Queenes* | *Colledge* in Oxford. |

Impr. 133: 1633: (eights) 12°: pp. [24] + 128 + 120: pp. 11 beg. *forbids to* and *struck her children*: English Roman. Contents:—p. (1) title, within double lines: (3-6) "The Epistle Dedicatory": (7-8) to the reader: (9-24) analysis of *Charity mistaken* and the answer, as a list of contents: 1-128, 1-120, "Answer to Charity mistaken", the work.

The work against which this was directed was written by a Jesuit named Matthias Wilson, who also employed the names of Nicholas Smith and, as in this case, Edward Knott, and was published in 1630. By Oct. 1634 this first edition was nearly sold out, and the author submitted a copy to archbp. Laud for his approval or correction, with a view to a second edition. Laud suggested the alteration of a few passages, and this was made part of the accusations against him at his trial (see Prynne's *Canterburies Doom*, Lond. 1646, p. 251). The second edition thus altered was printed at London in 1634.

33. **Reusner**, Nicolas.   NICOLAI REVSNERI LEORINI | IC. Comitis Palat. Cæs. | SYMBOLORVM | IMPERATORIORUM | Classis Prima. | *QVA SYM-|BOLA CONTINENTVR | Impp. ac Cæsarum Romanorum Italico-|rum, à C. Iulio Cæsare, usque ad | Constantinum Magnum.* | OPVS PHILOLOGICVM ET | Politicum, veréque Regium ac Impera-|torium: omnibus omnium ordinum, & cum | primis civilis sapientiæ studiosis lectu | futurum utile; ac jucundum. | *QVINTA EDITIO.* | [*device.*]

Impr. 137: 1633: (twelves) 16°: pp. [12] + 173 + [37] + 209 + [39] + 198 + [34]: pp. 11 beg. *Quod exemplo* and *honestam rem* and *Nam & secundum*: Long Primer Roman. Contents:—p. (1) title: (3-8) preface to Maximilian grand duke of Austria, dated 1 Oct. 1587: (9-11) poems on the work: 1-173 the Classis Prima: (1-23) indexes: (24) a title:— NICOLAI REUSNERI LEORINI | *Silesii*, | SYMBOLORVM | IMPERATORIORUM | Classis Secunda. | *QVA CONTINENTVR SYM-|BOLA | Impp. Cæsarúmque Romanorum-Græco-rum, à Fl. Constantino Magno, usque | ad Carolum Magnum, pri-|mum Cæsarem Germanicum.* | OPVS AVREVM ET VERE | Politicum, ac Regium. | [*device*, then impr. 137]: (26-33) preface to Ernest grand duke of Austria, dated 7 Oct. 1587: (33-36) poems on the work: 1-209, the Classis secunda: (1-24) indexes: (26) a title:—NICOLAI REUSNERI LEORINI | IC. Comitis Palat. Cæs. | SYMBOLORVM | IMPERATORIORUM |

Classis Tertia. | *QVA SYMBOLA CON-TINENTVR* | *Impp. Cæsarúmque Roman-orum-Ger-|manicorum: à Carolo Magno, pri- mo Cæs. Germanico, usque ad | Fer-dinandum II. Cæs. Austriacum* | OPUS JUCUNDISSIMÆ | Et utilissimæ lectionis. |

[*device*: then impr. 137] : (28-32) preface to Matthias grand duke of Austria, dated 15 Oct. 1587 : (33-39) poems on the work : 1-224 (224 misprinted 198), the Classis Tertia : (1 28) indexes : (29-34) not seen.

See 1638 R. This is a curious example of three parts of a volume being entirely independent of each other, there being no general titlepage, but yet being indissolubly welded together by the signatures, so that no part could be issued separately. The first edition seems to have been issued in 1587, the 4th at London in 1619. The plan of the work is to assign a motto to every emperor, and then to discuss the motto and character of the person together: so that in effect the book is largely a discussion of proverbs of the nature of Erasmus's *Adagia*.

34. Salvianus, S.   SANCTI | SALVIANI | MASSILIENSIS | *PRESBY-TERI*, | DE | GVBERNATIONE | Dei, & de justo præsentiq; | ejus judicio ad *S. Salonium* | Episcopum, *Lib.* VIII. | *Eiusdem Epistolarum Lib. I.* | TIMOTHEI NOMINE AD | *Ecclesiam Catholic.* Lib. IV. | Cum duplici indice. |

Impr. 129 *b* : 1633: 12mo: pp. [16] + 512 : p. 11 beg. *consulari*, 401 *tamen quæ* : Pica Roman. Contents :—p. (3) title within line, double at top and bottom : (5-6) Extract from Joh. Trithemius : (7-13) " Index rerum et verborum . . .":

(14-15) " Index locorum Scripturæ . . .": 1-297, De gubernatione Dei : 298-324, Epistolæ: 325-488, Ad ecclesiam catho-licam: 489-512 " Annotationes aliquot . . . autore Ioanne Alexandro Brassicano ".

See 1629 S, of which this is an almost exact reprint in larger type.

35. Sclater, William.   [*line*] | Vtriusque Epistolæ | AD CORIN-THIOS | EXPLICATIO | *ANALYTICA.* | VNÀ | CVM SCHOLIIS: | Authore *Gul. Sclatero* SS. Theol. Doctore, | Nunc tandem à Filio suo *Coll. Regalis* | in *Academia Cantabr.* Socio | in lucem edita. | [*line, motto, line, motto, woodcut.*]

Impr. 69 : 1633: sm. 4° : pp. [12] + 260: p. 11 beg. *testimonio*, 201 *operam nostram* : English Roman. Contents :— p. (1) title, within a line : (2-7) Epistola dedicatoria to dr. Edw. Kellett and mr.

George Goade, signed " Gulielmus Sclater " : (9-10) " Lectori . . .": (11) " Sphalmata . . .": 1-2, title repeated, see below: 3-154, the explanation of 1 Cor. : 155-260, do. of 2 Cor.

See Wood's *Ath. Oxon.*, iii. 228, but this author is not to be confused, as Wood points out, with William Slatyer the writer of *Palæ-Albion*. The dedication gives some autobiographical notes about the editor, whose tutor at Cambridge was mr. Goade. Strictly, it appears that there should be two titles as above (to be distin-guished by the first title having *ANALYTICA.* and ἄρτιος, the second *ANALYTICA*; and ἄρτιος): the second was printed as pp. 1-2, when no dedication or preface was intended ; and when the usual prefatory matter with the first title was printed, no doubt the second would be generally removed by the binder.

36. Sermonetta, cardinal, i.e. Enrico Gaetani.   INSTRVCTIONS | FOR YOVNG | GENTLEMEN; | OR | The instructions of | *Cardinall Sermonetta,* to | his Cousen PETRO | CAETANO, | AT | *HIS FIRST GOING* | into Flanders to the Duke | of *Parma*, to serue | PHILIP, King | *of Spaine.* |

Impr. 135: 1633: (twelves) 16°: pp. [8] + 122 + [2]: p. 11 beg. *Keepe letters,* 101 *dissimulatiõ*: Great Primer Roman. Contents:—p. (1) title, within a line | double except at bottom: (3-7) "The Printer to the Reader", with postscript: 1-122, the work: (1) "Errata".

The sheets of this were re-issued with a new titlepage at Oxford in 1644, and republished with other treatises in 1772, and perhaps oftener. The head-line throughout is "Instructions for young Noblemen": every page has double lines on the upper and outer margins.

37. **Smith**, Samuel.   Aditus ad Logicam.

Wood in his *Ath. Oxon.*, ed. Bliss (ii. 283) mentions an edition of this year, which would be the 7th: see 1617 S.

38. **T[ipping]**, W[illiam].   A | DISCOVRSE | *OF* | ETERNITIE | Collected and Composed for | *the Common good,* | [*line*] | By W. T. | [*line*, then *device*.] |

Impr. 134: 1633: sm. 4°: pp. [8] + 71 + [1]: p. 11 beg. *and everlasting*: English Roman. Contents:—p. (3) title: (5-7) "To the Christian Reader", signed | "VV. T.": (8) "The Contents . . .": 1-71, the work, in two books: 71, a prayer, and errata "in some copies".

See Wood's *Ath. Oxon.*, iii. 244. There was another (anonymous) edition Lond. 1646: the author was known after this book was issued as "Eternity Tipping".

39. **Tozer**, Henry.   A | CHRISTIAN | AMENDMENT | Delivered in a Sermon on New-]yeares day 1631. in St *Martines* | Church in *Oxford*, and | *now published*: | [*line*] | By H. TOZER M^r of Arts and Fellow of | *Exeter* Colledge in *Oxford*. | [*line*, two *mottos*, *woodcuts*.] |

Impr. 85 *a*: 1633: (eights) 12°: pp. [12] + 80 + [4]: p. 11 beg. *And these*: Great Primer Roman. Contents:—p. (1) | title: (3-11) Epistle dedicatory to sir Walter Pye, kt.: 1-80, the sermon, on 2 Cor. v. 17.

See Wood's *Ath. Oxon.*, iii. 274. Sir Walter Pye jun. had been Tozer's pupil when at Exeter college.

1634.

1. **A[llen?]**, J[ohn].   THE | YOVNGER | BROTHER HIS | APOLOGIE, | OR | *A FATHERS FREE POWER* | disputed, for the disposition of his Lands, | or other his Fortunes to his Sonne, Sonnes, | *or any one of them: as right Reason, the* | *Lawes of God and Nature, the Civill,* | *Canon, and Municipall Laws* | *of this Kingdome doe* | command. | [*motto*, then *woodcuts*.]

Impr. 126: 1634 [on title, 1624!]: sm. 4to: pp. [10] + 56 + [2]: p. 11 beg. *verse, with all*: English Roman. Contents:— p. (1) title: (3-7) The Epistle to the Reader, signed "J. A.": (8-10) "The | principall contents": 1-56, the work: (1) "Mantissa", a quotation from Salvianus, about anonymity: (2) a colophon, consisting of a motto, large device of the Arms of the University, and impr. 73 *b*.

This is a rare book, arguing against exclusive privileges of primogeniture, and for the right and in some cases duty of parents to disinherit the eldest son. Other editions were issued at Oxford in 1641 and 1671, but I do not find information about John Allen, nor the ground for ascribing the book to one of that name.   On the page preceding the colophon is this figure :— * I * M * * F * * A * M *   There is an account of the book in Oldys's *British Librarian* (1737), p. 210.

2. **Barclay,** John.   EVPHORMIONIS | LVSININI, | *Sive,* | IOANNIS | BARCLAII | *Partes quinq;.* | Satyricon bipartitum. L. 1 & 2. | Apologia pro se. L. 3 | Icon Animorum. L. 4. | Veritatis Lachrymæ. L. 5. | *Cum Clavi præfixa.* | [*line.*] | *Accessit* | Conspiratio Anglicana. | [*line,* then *woodcuts.*]

Impr. 143: 1634: (twelves) 16°: pp. [10] + 782 + [2]: p. 11 beg. *tibus allatus,* 801 *Illis autem*: Long Primer Roman. Contents :—p. (1) title : (3–5) dedication by "Euphormio" to James i : (6–10) "Clavis, nomina ignota . . . exponens": 1–156, part 1, as above : 157–310, part 2, dedicated to lord Salisbury : 311–357, part 3, dedicated to Charles Emmanuel I duke of Savoy, dated London, 1 Sept. 1610 : 358–553, part 4, dedicated to Louis xiii : 554–767, part 5. "Alitophili Veritatis Lachrymæ, sive Euphormionis Lusinini Continuatio", dedicated to Henry of Bourbon the Dauphin : 769–782, "Series patefacti divinitus parricidii, . . . in . . . Regem regnumque Britanniæ cogitati . . . Nonis ixbribus MDCV. Illo ipso Novembri scripta, nunc demum edita," the head-line is "Conspiratio Anglicana".

For John Barclay (*d.* 1621) see the Dict. of National Biography, and for the bibliography of this work Jules Dukas's book.   Part 1 was first issued in 1603, part 2 in 1607, part 3 in 1611, part 4 in 1614, part 5 in 1625.   The author is satirical on Jesuits and Puritans alike, as well as on individuals.

3. ——.   IOANNIS | BARCLAII | ARGENIS. | *Editio Novissima.* | CVM CLAVE, HOC | est: nominum propriorum eluci-|tione hactenus nondum | edita. | [*device.*]

Impr. 144: (twelves) 16°: pp. [30] + 705 + [9]: p. 11 beg. *sæva consilia,* 601 *sedente, regiam*: Long Primer Roman. Contents:—p. (1) title : (3–8) Epistola dedicatoria to Louis xiii, dated Rome 1 July 1621 : (9) a sentence : (10–29) "Discursus de autore Scripti, & judicium de nominibus Argenidæis", head line "Discursus in Argenidem": 1–676, the work in five books : 677–705, "Discursus . . . [headline "Clavis"] in Argenidem . . .": (1–2) "Tabula nominum fictorum . . .": (3–9) "Index . . .".

See last item.   The Argenis, which like the Satyricon is a political satire, was written and first published in 1621.   The first discursus must have been rather out of date in this edition, for it suggests that the satire was written by William Barclay, father of the author.   Argenis is a female character in the book, apparently representing the hope of the house of Valois.

4. **Blaxton,** John.   THE | ENGLISH | VSVRER ; | *OR* | VSVRY CONDEMNED, | *BY* | The most learned and famous Di-|uines of the Church of *England,* and Dedi-|cated to all his Maiesties Subiects, for | the stay of further increase | of the same. | [*line*] | Collected | By IOHN BLAXTON, Preacher of | God's Word at *Osmington,* in *Dorcet-shire.* | [*line,* then *motto,* then *line.*]

Impr. 148 : 1634 : sm. 4° : pp. [20] + 84 : p. 11 beg. *Chap.* 3. *The Testimony* : Pica Roman. Contents :—p. (2) "The Illustration" a poem on the frontispiece : (3) "The English Vsurer", the frontispiece, a picture with title and motto : (7) title : (9–12) "To the Reader" : (13) "A Table of the Contents" : (14) a list of authorities : (15–17) complimentary English poems by Josua Sylvester, Francis Quarles and (in Latin) John Garbrand of Oxford : (18–19) "To the Vsurer" : 1–82, the work : 83–84, poem by George Withers.

This book was printed in London by John Norton jun. (1633–39) for Francis Bowman in Oxford, and does not appear to have been entered in the Stationers' Hall Register. The frontispiece contains a woodcut representing a Usurer seated at his table, a small fiend behind his head, and on a label "I say I will haue all | both Vse & principall." On the reader's right are two pigs, one alive, one dead, with suitable labels. The size of the woodcut is $4\frac{5}{16} \times 5\frac{1}{4}$ in. See next entry.

5. ——, THE | ENGLISH | *USURER.* | OR, | USURY CONDEMNED, | *BY* | The most Learned, and famous | Divines of the Church of *England*, and | Dedicated to all his *Majesties* Subiects, | for the stay of further increase | *of the same.* | [line] | Collected | By IOHN BLAXTON, Preacher of | Gods Word at *Osmington*, in *Dorcetshire.* | [line] | *The second Impression, Corrected by the Authour* | [line, then the same motto as before, but no line following.]

Impr. 148 : 1634 : sm. 4° : pp. [16] + 80 : p. 11 beg. *vaine, if it* : Pica Roman. Contents (see above) :—p. (2) frontispiece : (3) "The Illustration" : (5) title : (7–10) "To the Reader" : (11) Table : (12) authorities : (13–14) three poems, as above : (15–16) "To the usurer" : 1–78, the work : 79–80, Withers' poem.

See last entry.

6. **Browne**, Thomas.   [*woodcut*] | THE | COPIE OF THE | Sermon preached before the | *Vniversitie at S. Maries in* | OXFORD, | *on Tuesday the* | XXIV. of Decem. 1633. | [*line*] | By THO. BROWNE, *One of the* Students *of Christ-Church.* | [*line*, then *woodcut.*]

Impr. 146 : 1634 : sm. 4° : pp. 53 + [3] : p. 11 beg. *Edward the Sixt* : Great Primer Roman. Contents :—p. 1, title : 3–53, the sermon, on Ps. cxxx. 4 : 53, impr. 85 *d.*

See Wood's *Ath. Oxon.*, ed. Bliss, iii. 1003. The Bidding Prayer, in an informal style, is intercalated at pp. 9–14, between the introductory part and the body of the sermon. See 1633 B : the British Museum "1633" copy is absolutely identical with the above issue except that instead of Impr. 146 with the date in Roman numerals, it has Impr. 82 *b* and "Anno 1634", the woodcut having been slightly shifted downwards in this issue.

7. **Butler**, Charles.   THE | ENGLISH | GRAMMAR, | OR | The Institution of Letters, Syl-|lables, and Words in the En-|glish tung. | *Wher'unto is annexed* | An Index of words Lik' and Unlik' | [*line*] | *By* | CHARLS BUTLER, Magd. *Master of Arts.* | [*motto, then device.*]

Impr. 125 : 1634 : sm. 4° : pp. [12] + 63 + [29] : p. 11 beg. *larg', sarg'* : Pica Roman. Contents :—p. (1) title, within double lin s : (3–4) dedication to prince Charles : (5–11) "To the Reader", dated "Wotton Sept. 1. An. D. 1633. C. B. M." : (12) "Ad Authorem" a Latin poem by S. W. : 1–63, the grammar : (2–29) the Index : (29) The Printer to the Reader.

See Wood's *Ath. Oxon.*, ed. Bliss, iii. 210, and 1633 B. The body of the work is a reissue of the sheets of the 1633 edition, but the title is reset, and the prefatory matter enlarged.

8. ———.   THE | *Feminin' Monarchi'*, | OR | THE HISTORI | OF BEE·S | SHEWING | *Their admirable Natur', and Propertis;* | *Their Generation and Colonis;* | *Their Government, Loyalti, Art, Industri;* | *Enimi's, VVars, Magnanimiti, &c.* | TOGETHER | With the right Order-ing of them from tim' to tim': | and the sweet Profit arising ther'of. | [*line*] | *Written out of Experienc'* | By | CHARLS BUTLER, *Magd.* | [*line, then motto.*]

Impr. 126: 1634: sm. 4°: pp. [16] + 182: p. 11 beg. *her, animamque*: Pica Roman. Contents:—p. (1) title: (2) en-graving of a hive, with verses: (3-4) dedication to the queen: (5-8) The pre-face, dated "Wotton. Mai 11. 1623": (8) The Printer to the reader, referring to Butler's English Grammar for the phonetic spelling used: (9-11) commendatory verses by George Wither (Latin and Eng-lish), and others: (12-16) The contents of the book: 1-182, the work in 10 chapters.

See Wood's *Ath. Oxon.*, ed. Bliss, iii. 209, and 1609 B, of which this is an enlarged edition: the preface is that of the 1623 edition. The peculiar spelling and type are part of Butler's system as elaborated in his English Grammar (see 1633 B). There are a few woodcuts, and music at pp. 78-81.

9. **Cosin**, Richard.   ECCLESIÆ ANGLICANAE | POLITEIA IN TABVLAS DIGESTA. | AVTHORE *RICHARDO COSIN* LEGVM | Doctore, olim Decano Curiæ de ARCVBVS, & | *Cancellario, seu Vicario Generali Reverendiss.* | Patris IOANNIS Archiepiscopi | *CANTVARIENSIS.* | [*woodcut.*]

Impr. 73: 1634: (twos) obl. 8°: pp. [64], signn. ( )², ( )², A-O²: sign. B1ʳ beg. *TAB. I. B*: Pica Roman. Contents:— sign. ( )1ʳ, title: ( )2ʳ-2ᵛ, Epistola dedicatoria to king James by "Tho. Crompton": ( )1ʳ "Ad Lectorum Moni-torium": ( )1ʳ-1ᵛ "Capita tabularum": ( )2, not seen: A1ʳ-O2ʳ, the tabulae.

For the editor (*d.* 1608) see Wood's *Fasti Oxon.*, ed. Bliss, i. 249. The author, a lawyer educated at Cambridge, died in 1597. The first edition, of which this is a reprint slightly different in arrangement, was published at London in 1604, fol.: the 3rd at the Hague in 1661: the 4th at Oxford in 1684, fol. These tables exhibit the whole status and administration of the Church of England in a synoptic form. The words underlined in the above title are in red ink, as well as *Oxoniæ*, and *anno salutis M.DC.XXIV.* in the imprint. The book is peculiar in form. The 1604 and 1684 editions may be called ordinary folios in shape: this one is made up of folio sheets (each containing two folio leaves) folded once and bound oblong, the intention being that the binder should cut through the line of folding at foot and bind the book as if of quarto size, each oblong leaf thus bound being again awkwardly folded once so as to lie within an ordinary quarto binding. In the present edition the original 16 tables are arranged to form 28, and are printed on one side of the leaf only.

10. **Downinge**, Calybute.   A | DISCOVRSE | OF THE | STATE ECCLESIA-|STICALL OF THIS | *Kingdome, in relation to the Civill.* | Con-*sidered under three* CONCLVSIONS. | With a DIGRESSION discussing | *some ordinary Exceptions concer-*|ning Ecclesiasticall Officers. | *By* C. D. | *The second Edition, revised and enlarged.* | [*device.*]

Impr. 147 : 1634 : sm. 4° : pp. [4] + 112 : p. 11 beg. *into factions* : Pica Roman. Contents :—p. (1) title, within double lines : (3) dedication to lord Salisbury, | signed "Calybute Downinge": 1–112, the work, the digression occupying pp. 31–44: 112, "Errata".

See Wood's *Ath. Oxon.*, ed. Bliss, iii. 107, and 1633 D.

11. Du Moulin, Pierre, *d.* 1658.

See *Smith*, Richard, below.

12. Fitz-Geffry, Charles.   THE BLESSED | BIRTH-DAY | CELEBRATED | *IN* | Some Pious Meditations, on the | ANGELS ANTHEM. | *Luke* 2. 14. | ALSO HOLY RAPTVRES | In contemplating of the most obscrue-|able Adjuncts about our Saviours | NATIVITIE. | [*line*] | By CHARLES FITZ-GEFFRY. | [*line*, then *motto.*]

Impr. 84 *b* : 1634 : sm. 4° : pp. [4] + 55 + [1] : p. 11 beg. *For such a* : English Roman. Contents :—p. (1) title : (3–4), | 35–6, Complimentary poems by Henry Beesley : 1–34, the Blessed Birthday : 37–55, the Raptures.

Rare. See Wood's *Ath. Oxon.*, ed. Bliss, ii. 607, and 1636 F. Grosart's edition of Fitz-Geffrey's poems reprints the 2nd edition (1636) with the passages different from it which occur in this 1st edition, and mentions a faulty 3rd edition of 1654.

13. Lucian.   CERTAINE SELECT | DIALOGVES | OF | LVCIAN : | *TOGETHER WITH* | *HIS TRVE HISTORIE,* | *Translated from the Greeke into English* | [*line*] | By Mr FRANCIS HICKS. | [*line*] | Whereunto is added the life of LVCIAN | gathered out of his owne Writings, with briefe | Notes and Illustrations upon each Dia-'logue and Booke, by *T. H.* M^r of Arts of | *Christ-Church* in *Oxford.* | [*woodcut.*]

Impr. 119 : 1634 : sm. 4° : pp. [16] + 196 + [2] : p. 11 beg. *Menippus. Thus* : Pica Roman. Contents :—p. (1) title, within double lines : (3–4) dedication to dr. Brian Duppa signed "Th. Hickes" : | (5–6) "To the honest and judicious reader" by 'T. H.': (7) Lucian's epigram on his own book, with English translation by 'T. H.': (9–15) Life of Lucian: 1–196, the work.

See Wood's *Ath. Oxon.*, ed. Bliss, ii. 491, 584. Francis Hickes died in 163⅝, and the Dialogues are edited by his son. They are Lucian's Περὶ τοῦ Ἐνυπνίου ἤτοι βίος Λουκιανοῦ, Ἰκαρομένιππος, Μένιππος, Ὄνειρος, Κατάπλους, Χάρων, Ἀληθὴς Ἱστορία, Τίμων, Συμπόσιον.

14. Mason, Francis.   THE | AVTHORITY | OF THE CHVRCH | in making Canons and | Constitutions concerning | *things indifferent.* | AND | THE OBEDIENCE | THERETO REQVIRED ; | with particular application | to the present estate of the | *Church of England.* | By FRAN. MASON Batchelor of Diuinity, | and sometime fellow of *Merton* | Colledge in *Oxford.* | The second edition Revised. | [*motto*, then *line*.]

Impr. 85 *c* : 1634 : sm. 4° : pp. [6] + 72 + [2] : p. 11 beg. *remooued* : *for* : Pica Roman. Contents :—p. (1) title : (3–6) | Epistle dedicatory to Richard archbp. of Canterbury, from the first edition : 1–72, the work, on 1 Cor. xiv. 40.

See Wood's *Ath. Oxon.*, ed. Bliss, ii. 306. The first edition was issued at London in 1607, being then enlarged from a sermon at Norwich delivered in 1605. The present edition was reprinted in 1705.

15. Mercurius Davidicus.   "Mercurius Davidicus, or a patterne | of Loyall Devotion" bears the date of 1634, but is clearly of 1643.

16. **Oxford,** University.   [*device*] | A PROCLAMATION, | ¶ For the well ordering of the Market in the Cittie of OXFORD, and for the | redresse of Abuses, in Weights and Measures, within the Precincts | of the VNIVERSITIE of *OXFORD.* |

Impr. (as colophon) 85 *e* : 1634 : la. 4° : | pp. [6] : p. (3) beg. *Said Victualls for* : | Great Primer Roman.   Contents :—pp. (1, 3, 5), the proclamation.

Rare.   This is a proclamation by the Chancellor of the University (archbp. Laud), see O. Ogle's History of the Oxford Market in the Oxford Historical Society's *Collectanea*, vol. 2.   The three leaves are separate, and printed on one side only.

17. ———,   CORPVS | STATVTORVM | VNIVERSITATIS | OXON. | SIVE | PANDECTES CONSTITVTIONVM | ACADEMICARVM, E LIBRIS PVBLICIS | ET REGESTIS VNIVERSITATIS | CONSARCINATVS. | [two *lines*, then *device*.]

Impr. 60 *a* : 1634 : fol. : pp. [264], signn. ( ), §, ¶, ¶¶, ¶¶¶, A–Z, Aa–Kk, a–z, aa–ee² : sign. Bi* beg. § 4. *De officio,* bi* *eisdem terminis* : Double (Small) Pica Roman.   Contents :—sign. ( )2*, title : §1*–2* "Præfatio ad Lectorem" : §2* | "Admonitio ad Lectorem de veteri Calendario omisso" : §2*, "Errata . . ." : ¶1*–¶¶¶2*, "Elenchus Titulorum . . ." : A1*–p1*, the Corpus, in 21 Tituli : p2*–aa2*, "Appendix Statutorum . . ." : bb1*–ee2*, "Statuta Aularia".

This is the early form of the Laudian Statutes.   Its history may be read in Wood's History of the University or in Griffiths and Shadwell's edition of the later (1636) form, published in 1888.   Briefly, certain Delegates, especially dr. Zouch and Bryan Twyne (who wrote the preface), completed their work, and the University sent up the Corpus to the Chancellor, archbp. Laud, in Aug. 1633.   He altered it and had it printed, and in July 1634 declared that the Corpus thus printed (the present work) should be the statutes under which the University should be governed for a year, Mich. 1634—Mich. 1635.   Finally in June 1636 the full and authentic code was formally approved, and additions from it were entered in the copies of the 1634 edition, the code not being printed as a whole or precisely until 1888.   In 1768 a new edition was printed with certain changes and additions, and the 1768 edition is still in progress, the successive statutes being still connected by paging with that issue.

A large part of the edition is on parchment, being presented in that form to the King, the chancellor of the University, each College, the Halls, and the Proctors.   Blank spaces are left in many places for additions.   Large paper copies are also found.   For Synopsises of the statutes, see 1635 O, 1638 O.

18. **Pinke,** William.   THE | TRYALL | of a Christians syncere | *loue vnto Christ.* | [*line*] | By M⸳ WILLIAM PINKE, Master | of Arts late Fellow of Mag-|*dalen Colledge in* | OXFORD. | [*line*, then *motto*] | The second Edition. | [*woodcuts.*] |

Impr. 97 *a* : 1634 : (twelves) 16° : pp. [16] + 51 + [1] + 60 + 56 + 66 [" 2 " misprinted " 46 "!] : pp. 11 beg. *whosoever he,* and *separated from,* and *head and eares,* and *those reasons I* : Pica Roman. Contents :—p. (1) title : (3–11) Epistle dedicatory to lord George Digby, signed | "William Lyford", the editor, "Shirburn. Inl. 7. 1630." : (12–16) "To the Reader" : 1–51, The discourse part 1, on 1 Cor. xvi. 22 : (1*, 1–60, part 2 on Eph. vi. 24 (beg. "Not to mispend") : 1–56, part 3 on the same text (beg. "I will not discourage ") : 1–66, part 4, on Luke xiv. 26.

For the author see Wood's *Ath. Oxon.,* ed. Bliss, ii. 475, and 1630 P, where a reference to this, the 2nd ed., is accidentally omitted.   This issue has four sermons and a slightly altered title.

19. Puteanus, Erycius.   ERYCI | PUTEANI | COMVS, | SIVE | PHAGESIPOSIA | CIMMERIA. | SOMNIVM. | [*device.*]

Impr. 121 *a* : 1634: (twelves) 16°: pp. [14] + 190: p. 11 beg. *accepto signo*: Pica Roman. Contents:—p. (1) title, within double lines : (3–9) Præfatio, to Christo- phorus Ettenius: (11–14) Latin poem by Daniel Heinsius on the book: 1–185, the work: 186–190, Latin elegy by Nic. Burgundus addressed to Puteanus.

A satire on the gluttony and other luxurious vices of the age, in the guise of a dream of what takes place among the utopian Cimmerii. The first edition was issued at Louvain in 1611: this may be the second in Latin. Puteanus died in 1646, having lived during most of his life at Louvain.

20. ——.   ERYCI PUTEANI | HISTORIÆ | INSVBRICÆ | libri VI. | Qui IRRUPTIONES BARBA-|RORUM in ITALIAM continent: | *Rerum ab Origine gentis ad O-|thonem M.* EPITOME. | [*device.*]

Impr. 69: 1634: (twelves) 16°: pp.[28] + 192 +[32]: p. 11 beg. *dinis venirent*: Pica Roman. Contents:—p. (1) title, within double lines: (3) dedication to Philip prince of Orange: (4–19) preface to the same, dated " Lovanii, in Arce, viii Kal. Septem. M.DC.XIV": (20–23) " Animaduersio ", including some errata : (24–27), complimentary pieces: (28) a quotation: 1–143. the work, consisting of a " Præfatiuncula " and 6 books: 144, explanation introducing the following piece: 145–150, " Irruptio Cimbrorum in Italiam, descripta a Floro lib. iii.": 151, note introducing the following piece : 152–170, " Additiuncula ex And. Alciati De formula R. Imperii libello ": 171–2, dedication of the Chronology to Floritius: 173–192, " Chronologia Insubrica " : (1–31) " Index rerum ".

This work describes the irruptions of the Barbarians into Italy till the year 973: the Insubrians lived in the district round Milan. The history seems to have been first issued in 1614, but Puteanus was Professor at Milan only from 1601 to 1606.

21. Ridley, sir Thomas.   A | VIEW OF | THE | CIVILE AND | ECCLESIASTI-|CALL LAW: | And wherein the Practice of them | *is streitned, and may be releeved* | within this Land. | *Written by* Sr THOMAS Ridley Knight, | and Doctor of the Civile Law. | *The second Edition, by* I. G. *Mr of Arts.* | [*device.*] |

Impr. 68 *c* : 1634: sm. 4°: pp. [12] + 277 +[27]: p. 11 beg. *also mad persons*, 201 *wrought by*: Pica Roman. Contents :—p. (1) title, within double lines : (3–6) " To the Reader ", signed " I. G.": (7–10) Epistle dedicatory to King James, signed by the author: (11–12) " To the Reader " by the author: 1–277, the work: (2–25) " an index of the principall Matters and Words . . .": (25) " Errata ".

See Wood's *Ath. Oxon.*, iii. 205, for the editor and book. The first edition was issued at London in 1607: the present one was edited by dr. John Gregory, who has added many notes and the index, the author having died in 1622 or 1628. The title in the copies seen (one on large paper given by the author) has been sewn or pasted in separately, an original titlepage having been torn out. Perhaps this was in order to secure proper printing in red ink, for the words underlined in the title above are in red ink, as are also in the imprint the words *Oxford, University : 1634.*, and *Cum Privilegio.* The next editions were issued at Oxford in 1662 and 1675 or 1676. This is the first Oxford book in which I have noticed Anglo-Saxon type (Pica, pp. 184, 193, in the notes).

22. Saltonstall, Wye.   CLAVIS | AD PORTAM, | OR | A KEY FITTED | to open the Gate of | Tongues. | WHEREIN YOV MAY | readily finde the

Latine and French for | any English word necessary for | all young
Schollers. | [*device.*]

Impr. 119: 1634: (eights) 12°: pp.
[96], signn. A–F⁸: sign B2ᵛ beg. *annals*:
Long Primer Roman. Contents:—sign.
A3ʳ, title: A4ʳ–5ʳ, dedication to the
schoolmasters of Great Britain, signed
"Wye Saltonstall": A6ʳ–6ᵛ, "Discipulis
... de usu huius Clavis ... præfatiuncula": A7ʳ–8ᵛ, five Latin and one English poem about the work, by Saltonstall:
B1ʳ–F7ᵛ, the work.

Rare. See Wood's *Ath. Oxon.*, ed. Bliss, ii. 676. This is an alphabetical index of
English words and phrases occurring in the 1058 sections found in Comenius's *Gate of
Tongues*, as edited for the second time in Latin, English and French, by John
Anchoran in 1633 (London). Earlier editions of Comenius's celebrated work were
published at Leutschau in 1631 (first edition), then at Leipzig (2nd edition) in 1632
(both as *Janua linguarum*), and (as *Porta linguarum trilinguis*) Anchoran's editions,
Lond. 1631, and 1632: the 3rd and 4th London Anchoran editions 1637 and 1639 or
1640 reprint Saltonstall's index, but it is noticeable that Saltonstall's five short Latin
introductory poems contain at least 18 false quantities, and that he was a commoner
of Queen's college without ever matriculating or taking his degree. See 1633 G.

23. **Smiglecius**, Martinus.   LOGICA | MARTINI | SMIGLECII SO-|
CIETATIS IESV, | S. THEOLOGIÆ | Doctoris, | *SELECTIS DISPUTATIONI- bus*
& quæstionibus illustrata, | Et in duos Tomos distributa: | *In qua* |
QVICQVID IN ARISTOTELICO | ORGANO VEL COGNITV NECESSARI-um, vel
obscuritate perplexum, tam clarè & per-|spicuè, quam solidè ac nervosè |
pertractatur. | *Cum Indice Rerum copioso.* | *AD* | Perillustrem ac Magnifi-
cum Dominum, | Dᵐ THOMAM ZAMOYSCIVM, &c. |

Impr. 145: 1634: (eights) sm. 4°:
pp. [16] + 761 + [35]: p. 11 beg. *Dico*
igitur, 501 *lis, posterior*: Long Primer
Roman. Contents:—p. (1) title: (3–6)
epistle dedicatory to Thomas Zamoyscius,
dated "Calissii [Kalisch] ... 15 Augusti
1616": (6) an imprimatur dated 24 June
1616: (7–16) "Index disputationum et
quæstionum ...": 1–761, the work in
two parts (the second part has a bastard
title, with no imprint, but date only):
(2–35) "Index rerum præcipuarum ...".

Reissued at Oxford in 1658. The first edition appeared in two volumes at Ingol-
stadt in 1618, the year of the death of the author, who was a Pole by birth. The
subject is treated in scholastic style by *quaestiones*.

24. **Smith**, rev. Richard, of Barnstaple.   MVNITION | AGAINST |
MANS MISERIE | AND | MORTALITIE. | A Treatise containing the | most
effectuall remedies a-|gainst the miserable state of | man in this life,
selected | out of the chiefest both | Humane and Divine | Authors. |
BY | RICHARD SMITH *Prea-|cher of Gods Word in* Bar-|staple *in* Devon-
shire. | [*line*] | *The third Edition.* | [*line*.]

Impr. 142: 1634: (twelves) 16°: pp.
[20] + 194 + [14] + 93 + [3]: pp. 11 beg.
kind. *A third,* and *unto fresh Rivers*:
Pica Roman. Contents:—p. (1) title,
within double lines: (3–14) Epistle dedicatory to lady Elizabeth Basset, dated
"Barstable ... 1609. Januarie 1 ...",
signed "Ricard Smyth": (15–16) "The
Contents ...": (17–20) "The sinners
counsell to his Soule", a poem: 1–194,
the work: (3) a title, within double
lines:—"HERACLITVS: | OR | MEDITA-
TIONS | *Vpon the vanitie and mi-|serie of*
humane life; | First written in French by |
that excellent Scholler and | admirable
divine *Peter Du* | *Moulin* Minister of the
sa-|cred Word in the reformed | Church
of Paris: | *And translated into English* |
by R. S. *Gentleman* | [two *lines*]", impr.
142: (5–8) Epistle dedicatory by the
translator to his father "S. F. S.": (9–14)
"The author's Epistle dedicatory to the
Lady Anne of Rohan....", signed "Peter
Du Moulin": 1–93, the work.

For the first work see 1612 S, of which this is a simple reprint. Twenty-seven Richard Smiths took their degree at Oxford between 1550 and 1609, and the author of this book has not yet been identified among them.

The second work, which is necessarily linked to the first by the signatures, though not covered by the titlepage, is a reprint of 1609 D. No doubt the reprinter of these works thought the two R. S.s identical, but they are in all probability not, the translator of Molinaeus being Robert Stafford.

25. **Tozer,** Henry.   CHRISTVS: | SIVE | *DICTA & FACTA* | CHRISTI: | Prout à quatuor Evangelistis | sparsim recitantur. | Collecta & Ordine disposita | ab | HENRICO TOZER, *A. M. &* | Exoniensis *Collegij in Academiâ* | Oxoniensi *Socio.* | [*woodcut.*]

Impr. 72 *a* : 1634: (eights) 12° : pp. [8] + 67 + [5] : p. 11 beg. *1. Excommunicationem* : Pica Roman. Contents :—p. (1) title, within double lines: (3-7) Epistola dedicatoria to Charles and Philip sons of the earl of Pembroke: 1-67, the work: (1) "Errata".

See Wood's *Ath. Oxon.*, ed. Bliss, iii. 274. The matter is arranged in a kind of logical order and disposed in divisions and subdivisions. Both the dedicatees matriculated at Exeter College in 1632.

26. **Zouche,** Richard.   DESCRIPTIO | IVRIS ET IVDICII | FEVDALIS, SE-|cundum Consuetudi-|nes *Mediolani* & | *Normanniæ.* | *PRO* | INTRO-DVCTIONE | AD STVDIVM | *IVRISPRVDENTIÆ* | *Anglicanæ.* | [*line*] | Autore R. Z. I. C. P. R. | *OXONIÆ.* | [*line.*]

Impr. 95 *a* : 1634: (eights) 16° : pp. [8] + 79 + [1] : p. 11 beg. *bes vel habebis* : Pica Roman. Contents :—p. (1) title : (3) dedication to archbp. Laud : (5-6) "Iuventuti academicæ Iurisprudentiæ studiosæ", "Dat. ex Aulâ Alban. Pridie Cal. Iunij 1634." : (7-8) list of divisions of the work : 1-79, the work : (1) note of a natural continuation of the book, in Latin.

See Wood's *Ath. Oxon.*, iii. 511 : the author was principal of St. Alban hall and, as the title indicates, Juris Civilis Professor Regius. Wood's reference to a 1636 S° edition of this book may be due to a confusion between it and the *Elementa Jurisprudentiae* by the same author.

1635.

1. **Bancroft,** John, bp. of Oxford.   ARTICLES | TO | BE ENQVIRED | OF WITHIN THE | Dioces of OXFORD, in the | second *Visitation* of the Right Re-|verend Father in God Iohn | Lord Bishop of OXFORD. | HELD | In the yeare of our LORD GOD 1635. in the | eleauenth yeare of the Raigne of our most gra-|cious Soveraigne Lord, CHARLES, by the grace | of GOD King of great *Brittaine, France,* and | *Ireland,* Defender of the Faith &c. | [*woodcut.*]

Impr. 152 : 1635 : sm. 4° : pp. [16], signn. A-B¹ : sign. B1ʳ beg. 15 *Whether hath* : Pica English. Contents :—sign. A1ʳ, title : A2ʳ, the oath : A2ᵛ, the charge : A3ʳ, directions : A3ᵛ-B3ʳ, the articles, in three divisions : B3ᵛ, directions about Recusants, &c.

2. **Carpenter,** Nathanael.   GEOGRAPHIE | DELINEATED FORTH | IN TWO | BOOKES. | CONTAINING | The Sphericall and Topicall parts

thereof, | By NATHANAEL CARPENTER, Fellow of | Exeter Colledge in Oxford. | [*line*] | THE SECOND EDITION CORRECTED. | [*line, then motto, then woodcut.*]

Impr. 149 : 1635 : (eights) sm. 4° : pp. [16] + 272 + [16] + 286 + [2] + 4 folded leaves, see below : pp. 11 beg. *Eearth & Water*, and *teration next*, 111 2. *The position*, and *monstrated in* : Pica Roman. Contents :—p. (1) title : (3–5) dedication, as in 1625 : (6–13) "... Contents of each Chapter of the first Booke ...": (15–16) "To my Booke", a poem : 1–272, the first book : (1–2) not seen : (3) a title :— GEOGRAPHIE | THE SECOND | BOOKE. |

CONTAINING | the generall Topicall | part thereof, | By NATHANAEL CARPEN-TER, Fellow of | Exeter Colledge in Oxford. | [*line*, then *motto*, then woodcut, and Impr. 149] " : (5–7) dedication, as in 1625 : (9–16) "A table of the ... Contents of the second Booke ...": 1–286, the second book : (1–2) not seen. There should be four tables as in the 1625 edition, and there are numerous woodcut diagrams in the text.

See Wood's *Ath. Oxon.*, ed. Bliss, ii. 422, and 1625 C. The signatures of the two parts are in a certain sense independent, but indicate essential connexion.

3. **Chaucer,** Geoffrey.   AMORVM | TROILI | *ET* | CRESEIDÆ | Libri duo priores | *Anglico-Latini.* | [*woodcut.*]

Impr. 95 *a* : 1635 : sm. 4° : pp. [28] + 105 + [8] + 160 ["159"] + [1] : p. 11 beg. 13. *Great rumor*, and 15. *With that they* : English Roman italic and Pica English. Contents :—p. (1) title, within arched border : (3–6) dedication to Patricius Junius (Patrick Young) the King's librarian, by sir Francis Kinaston : (7–8) not seen, probably blank : (9–12) " Candido Lectori Franciscus Kinaston ...", dated

" Ex Aulâ Albâ Regiâ [Whitehall] xiii Calendarum Decembris, . . . CIƆ Ɔ cxxxiiii" : (13–28) complimentary Latin and English poems : 2–105, the first book, Latin on the verso of each leaf, English on the recto : (2–7) dedication to John Rouse, Bodley's librarian, by Kinaston : 1–159 (" 21 " repeated after " 24 "), the second book.

See Wood's *Ath. Oxon.*, iii. 38. The Latin translation is in a singular rhythmical rhyming metre, essentially decasyllabic iambics, but with an extra unaccented syllable at end, and with certain licences in resolving a long syllable into two short. The rhymes are *ababbcc*. The first two lines for example are " Dolorem Troili duplicem narrare | Qui Priami Regis Trojæ fuit gnatus." This appears to be by far the earliest translation of any part of Chaucer into another language. Part of a commentary on the piece by sir F. Kinaston was printed in 1796. The English part is in black-letter, the Latin in italic Roman. One of the complimentary poems is in would-be Chaucerian style. The collation of this book is difficult : but probably it is this :—signn. A, †, *1, **2, ( )1, B–Z, Aa–Nn4 : †1–**2 is matter foisted in, which prevented the true fourth leaf of sign. A from forming, as it should, the first leaf of the Latin translation (pp. 1–2 of the 1st book). Accordingly one of two plans was adopted : either the 4th leaf of sign. A was torn off, and a new 4th leaf inserted where the translation begins (which seems to have been usually done, and which gives the collation above, assuming the existence at one time of an A4) : or the torn-off fourth leaf was itself awkwardly pasted on to sign. 2**.

4. **Downe,** John.   *A* | TREATISE | OF THE TRVE | NATVRE AND | *DEFINITION* | *of justifying faith*; | TOGETHER WITH A DEFENCE | of the same, against the Answere of | *N. Baxter.* | By IOHN DOWNE B. in Divinity, and some-|time *Fellow of* EMANVEL *C. in Cambridge.* | [*motto, with translation.*]

Impr. 126 : 1635 : sm. 4° : pp. [16] + 404 : p. 11 beg. *the Prince of,* 301 *that it was* : English Roman. Contents :—(p. 1)

title : (3–16) "To the Reader": 1–13, the treatise on justifying faith : 17–189, 'A defence of the former treatise . . .

against the answer of N. B.": 191, a title :—[two *lines*] | OF | THE FAITH | OF | INFANTS, | AND HOW THEY ARE | Iustified and Saued. | [*line*] | *By the late Reuerend and Learned Diuine* | *Master* Iohn Downe, *Bachelour of* | *Diuinity, and sometimes Fellow* ! *of Emanuell Col- | ledge* | *in Cambridge.* | [*woodcut,* then impr. 126]: 193 210, the treatise: 211, a title :—[*line*] | 211 | [*line*] | NOT CON- SENT | OF FATHERS | EVT | SCRIPTVRE | THE GROVND OF FAITH. | [*line*] | *Writ- ten by the occasion of a conference had* | *with* M. Bayly, *by the late Reuerend* | *and Learned Diuine, Master* Iohn | Downe, *Bachelour of Diuinity,* | *and sometimes Fellow of* | *Emanuell Colledge* | *in Cambridge.* | [*woodcut,* then impr. 126.]: 213-272, the treatise : 263-290, "Of sitting and kneeling at the Communion " : 291-296, " How S. Paul and S. Iames are to bee reconciled in the matter of Iustifi- cation " : 297-309, " . . . of the Creed . . . " : 310-315, " A short Catechisme " : 316-320, " Peccatum formaliter & propriè non esse infinitum, exercitatio aduersus N." : 321-325, "Of choice of meats and Abstinence " : 326-355, " An answer unto certaine reasons for Separation " : 356- 365, "Of vowes and specially that of vir- ginity " : 366-369, " A letter " of consola- tion : 371-376, " The blessed Virgin Mary is truly Deipara, the Mother of God " : 377-404, religious poems and translations in verse, including a translation of Mure- tus's Institution for Children.

See Wood's *Fasti Oxon.,* ed. Bliss, i. 287, where London is probably an error for Oxford : and 1633 D. This is a new set of treatises by Downe. The introduction to the first piece gives an amusing account of the controversy with Baxter.

5. **Downeham,** George. THE | CHRISTIANS | FREEDOME, | Wherein is fully expressed the | Doctrine of CHRISTIAN | LIBERTIE. | *By the R* *Reuerend Father in God,* | GEORGE DOWNEHAM, | *Doctor of Diuinity and* | *L. B. of Derry.* | [*woodcuts.*]

Impr. 154: 1635: (eights) 12°: pp. [8] + 156 + [4] + 80. and one folded leaf : pp. 11 begg. *of rightcousnesse,* and *In the new,* 101 *euen by :* English Roman. Con- tents :—p. (1) title, within double lines : (3-7) "To the ... Reader ...": 1-156, the work, in 26 sections : 1-23, 7 addi- tional sections : 25-76, "The necessity of handling the question concerning Chris- tian Libertie": 76-80, "A Prayer".

For the author see Wood's *Fasti Oxon.,* ed. Bliss, i. 255: see 1636 D. The words underlined in the above title are in red ink, as well as "Oxford," and "William Webb," in the imprint. A folded leaf should follow the introductory matter containing "The Table" of the 26 sections. The signatures show that pp. 1-24, 25-76 in the second part are genuine additions, but genuinely part of the book.

6. ——. THE CHRISTIANS FREEDOME | [&c., precisely as the pre- ceding article, except that " THE SECOND EDITION " is added as a new line after " *Derry.*"]

Impr. &c., precisely as the preceding article.
A simple reissue of the sheets of the first edition, room for the additional words on the title being found by slightly depressing the woodcuts. Perhaps the folded " table " was not issued with the second edition. Some copies have the date 1636.

7. **Fawkner,** Antony. THE | WIDDOWES | PETITION, | Delivered in a Sermon before the | Iudges at the Assises held at *Northampton,* | Iuly 25. 1633. by ANTONY | FAWKNER, Parson of *Saltry* | *All-Saints, alias Moygne* | in Huntingtonshire. | [*motto,* then *woodcut.*]

Impr. 150 : 1635 : sm. 4° : pp. [6] + 28 + [2] : p. 11 beg. *demand,* Πρυτανεία : English Roman. Contents : p. (1) title : (3–5) Epistle dedicatory to sir Lewis Wat- son, dated " Saltry All-Saints . . . Iuly 30. 1633 " : 1–28, the Sermon, on Luke xviii. 3.

See Wood's *Ath. Oxon.,* ed. Bliss, ii. 611. Sir L. Watson was the author's patron.

8. **Field,** dr. Richard.   OF THE | CHURCH, | FIVE BOOKES. | [*line*] | BY | RICHARD FIELD, DOCTOR OF | DIVINITY, AND SOMETIMES | *Deane of* GLOCESTER. | [*line*] | *THE THIRD EDITION.* | [*line,* then *device.*]

Impr. 68 : 1635 : (sixes) folio : pp. [16] + 956 + [2] : p. 11 beg. *tation of dangerous,* 701 *wrongs of the Court* : Pica Roman.   Contents :—*precisely* as 1628 F, omitting the Errata on p. (15).

See 1628 F, of which this appears to be a verbatim reprint.

9. **Hakewill,** George.   AN | APOLOGIE [&c., precisely as 1630 H, except in l. 11 of this 3rd edition, PER-, not PER⸱, in l. 12 PETUALL AND UNIVERSALL, in l. 13 SIX. not FOVRE : in l. 1 of the italic type, *preparatives,* and the line ends with *thereunto* : in l. 7 *testimonie, use,* and the line ends at *which we.* After l. 8 (*consideration thereof*) follows :—] *The fifth and sixth are spent in answering Objections made since the second impression.* [*line*] | By GEORGE HAKEWILL Doctour of | Divinitie and Archdeacon of *Surrey.* | [*line*] | *The third Edition revised, and in sundry passages and whole Sections augmented by* | *the Authour ; besides the addition of two entire bookes not formerly published.* | [*motto.*] [There is also a London title, see below.]

Impr. 68 : 1635 : (sixes) la. 8° : pp. [52] + 606 + [10] + 378 + [42] : pp. 11 beg. *dan. and Scaliger* and *dence doth worke,* 501 *of right* : English Roman. Contents :—(1–11), as 1630 H. except that p. (6) is blank : (13–22) "the preface" : (23) "An Advertisement to the Reader occasioned by this third impression " : (24–30) testimonies to the book and author : (31–45) "The contents . . . " : (46–49) about sesterces : (50) extract from Boethius, with translation : (51) "An index of the tables added . . . " : 1–606, the work, bks. 1–4 : (3–6) controversial letters of bp. G(odfrey) G(oodman) and dr. Hakewill : (7–8) two encouragements to the author : 1–378. the works, bks. 5–6 : (1–24) index to bks. 1–4 : (25–30) index to bks. 5–6 : (31–35) authors quoted : (36–42) texts quoted : (42) " Errata ".

See Wood's *Ath. Oxon.,* ed. Bliss, iii. 256, and 1627 H. The engraved title is identical with that of 1630 H, with the date altered. Books 5–6 appear in this edition for the first time, the former being chiefly directed against bp. Goodman's *Fall of man* (Lond. 1616) as reasserted at greater length in about 1630 by the author, whose arguments are printed in the course of this book.

10. **Laurence,** Thomas.   TWO | SERMONS· | THE FIRST | PREACHED AT St *MARIES* | in OXFORD Iuly 13. 1634. | being Act-Sunday. | THE SECOND, | IN THE CATHEDRALL | CHVRCH OF *SARVM.* AT THE | Visitation of the most Reverend | Father in God WILLIAM | Arch-Bishop of *Canter-bury.* | *May* 23. 1634. | [*line*] | By THOMAS LAVRENCE D^r of Divinity, and late Fellow of *Allsoules* Colledge, | and Chaplaine to his MAIESTY | *in* ORDINARY. | [*line.*]

Impr. 82: 1635: sm. 4°: pp. [4]+40 +34+[2]: pp. 11 begg. *condition of*, and *hast given them*: English Roman. Con- | tents :—p. (3) title, within double lines : 1–34, the first sermon, on Ex xx. 21 : 1–40, the second sermon on 1 Cor. i. 12.

See Wood's *Ath. Oxon.*, ed Bliss, iii. 438. The signatures would suggest that the Sermon on 1 Cor. i. 12 was the Act-Sermon, but all copies seem to be bound as above, and the prefixing of the Act Sermon may have been an after-thought. There is nothing in the sermons themselves to settle the point !

11. **Legh**, Edward. <u>SELECTED</u> | *AND* | CHOICE | OBSERVATIONS | concerning the | TWELVE FIRST | CÆSARS | EMPEROVRS of | <u>ROME.</u> | [*line*] | By EDWARD LEGH Master | of Arts of *Magdalen Hall* | in OXFORD. | [*line.*]

Impr. 154: 1635: (twelves) 16°: pp. [24]+209+[7]: p. 11 beg. *shew, as* : English Roman. Contents :—p. (9) title : (11–24) author's Epistle dedicatory to his | father Henry : 1–208, the observations : 209, " An aduertisement to the Reader ", not seen.

See Wood's *Ath. Oxon.*, ed. Bliss, iii. 927, where other editions are mentioned, some with extended range of subject. The words underlined in the above title are printed in red, as well as " Oxford " and " William Webb." in the imprint. The signatures of the prefatory matter are peculiar : as four blank leaves precede the title, these were neglected and the leaf following the title bears *2 instead of *6, no others having any printed signature.

12. **Montague**, bp. Richard. APPARATVS | AD ORIGINES | ECCLESIASTICAS· | COLLECTORE | [*line*] | R. MONTACVTIO. | [*line*, then *device.*]

Impr. 151: 1635: (fours) la. 8°: pp. [30]+393+[11]: p. 11 beg. *sponsum est*, 301 *vetus Anna*: Pica Roman. Con- tents :—p. (1) title, within border and | double lines: (3) dedication to the memory of James i : (5–29) " Præfatio ": 1–393, the work, in 11 Apparatuses: (1) " Errata ", a long list: (2–11) " Index ".

The author, a Cambridge man, though at this time bp. of Chichester (1628–38), signs the dedication as " R. M. humillimus Ecclesiæ Cicestrensis Minister ". This work discusses pre-Christian antiquities, as preparations (apparatus) to the Life of Christ which is the subject of the same author's *Origines Ecclesiastica* (tom. i, 2 parts, Lond. 1636, 1640). The underlined words in the above title are printed in red, as well as " Oxoniæ," in the imprint. A copy was presented by the author to Henry Spelman on 4 Sept. 1635.

13. *†**Oxford**, University. . . . ENCYCLOPÆDIA { Seu ORBIS LITERA= ACADEMIA OXONI= [*device*] RVM provt in florentissimâ iam et omnium planè celeberrimâ | ENSI singulis Terminis publicè in Scholis auditoribus proponuntur |

No imprint, but Oxford (?), 1635 (?): (one) la. 4°. Contents :—p. (1) the En- cyclopædia.

This is a fine sheet, engraved by " T. Cecill " on metal, 16¾×16½ in. In the upper part there is a dedication of " hæc Encyclopædia et Synopsis Statutorum " to archbp. Laud. A large series of concentric circular spaces fill the centre, each divided into a left hand and right hand half :—counting from the centre (a sun), (1) days of the week, (2) hours of the day, (3) subjects, (4) explanation of the next circle, (5) List of proper audience and books for each lecture : (6) explanation of the next circle, (7) lists of fines for absent professors and absent audience : in the four corners are notes, one of which supplies another title for the sheet, namely " Cyclus Prælectorum . . . ex

Corpore Statutorum depromptus et delineatus . . .". Some copies issued in 1638, see below) have a small printed label "Iovis" pasted over "Martis", or else the plate itself altered to "Iovis", in the note that Easter Term ends on the *Tuesday* before Pentecost, and a longer slip pasted at the foot containing a note about the teaching of Arabic and Medicine.

The chart is usually found folded and pasted in the 1638 edition of the abridged Statutes: but a copy in the University Archives is pasted *between* the two columns of the 1635 *Synopsis Statutorum*, which in combination with the dedication quoted above suggests that it was first issued in 1635, a natural year for it, when the interest in the new Code of Statutes was fresh. There is nothing to suggest that it was printed away from Oxford. The device in the title is a well-made representation of the University arms with the motto "Sapientiæ et felicitatis".

Thomas Crossfield of Queen's certainly edited the 1638 *Statuta selecta*, and may have issued the *Synopsis* (which is in his style), and possibly therefore the *Encyclopædia*. At any rate he took the plate of the *Encyclopædia* and used it in 1638. It is in his own copy of the *Statuta selecta* that the altered plate is found (see above); and the note about Arabic and Medicine is there in his own handwriting preceded by a ☞, just as in the printed slip.

14. ———.   *SYNOPSIS SEV EPITOME STATVTORVM,* | *Eorum præsertim, quæ Iuventuti Academ.* Oxon: *maximè* | *expedit pro Doctrinâ & Moribus habere cognita.* |

Impr. 153 : 1635 : (one) folio : pp. [2] : | Primer Roman. Contents :—p. (1) the 2nd col. beg. *Tempus ad Gradus* : Long | Synopsis, in two columns.

These are extracts from the newly printed Corpus Statutorum, for the use of junior members of the University, but the fuller edition in book form first issued in 1638 (which see,) was taken as the model for all succeeding issues. The title heads the first column, and the colophon ends the 2nd. See the preceding article, for possible authorship.

Persius.   The statement by Wood (*Ath. Oxon.*, ed. Bliss, iii. 523) that there is a 1635 *Oxford* edition of Barten Holyday's translation of Persius, which deceived Brüggemann, is erroneous : the edition referred to was printed at London.

15. **Rives,** John, archdeacon of Berks.   ARTICLES | MINISTRED IN | THE FIRST VISITA-|tion of the right worshipfull Mr | IOHN RIVES Batchelour of Law | Arch-deacon of the Arch-dea-|conry of *Berks*, in the yeare | of our Lord God | 1635. | [*woodcut.*]

Impr. 152 *a* : 1635 : sm. 4° : pp. [4] + | (3) the oath : (4) the charge : 1–18, the 18 + [2] : p. 11 beg. *Parishioners in* : | 77 articles : 18, a direction : (1–2) not Pica English. Contents :—p. (1) title : | seen.

16. **Rouse,** John.   APPENDIX | AD | CATALOGVM | LIBRORVM IN | BIBLIOTHECA | BODLEIANA, | QVI PRODIIT | Anno Domini 1620. | [*line*] | EDITIO SECVNDA | [*line*] | Recognita, & Authoribus plus minus CIƆIƆCIƆ locupletata. | [*device.*]

Impr. 73 : 1635 : sm. 4° : pp. [4] + 208 : | (3–4) "Bibliothecarius lectori" : 1–208, p. 11 beg. *App. Appianus Alexand.* : Long | the work. Primer Roman. Contents :—p. (1) title : |

See 1620 J. This is Rouse's new edition of the little Appendix to the 1620 edition of the Catalogue. The MSS. are still mixed with the printed books. The preface shows that Verneuil's book, see below in this year, could be regarded as a part of this work, though formally distinct. Rouse's name does not occur, but is necessarily inferred from the preface.

17. [Verneuil, John].   CATALOGVS | INTERPRETVM | S. SCRIPTVR.E, | IVXTA NVMERORVM ORDINEM, | QVO EXTANT IN | BIBLIOTHECA | BODLEIANA : | OLIM A D. IAMESIO | *Ju rsum Theologorum concinnatus, nunc verò* | *alterá ferè parte auctior redditus.* | Accessit elenchus Authorum, tam recentium quam Antiquorum, qui | in quatuor libros Sententiarum & *Th. Aquinatis* Summas, Item | in Euangelia Dominicalia totius anni, & de Casibus | conscientiæ ; nec non in Orationem Domi-|nicam, Symbolum Aposto-lorum, | & Decalogum scripserunt. | *Editio correcta, diu multùmq; de-siderata.* | [*device.*] |

Impr. 73 : 1635 : sm. 4° : pp. 55 + [1] : | Roman. Contents :—p. 3, title : 4, a p. 11 beg. *Rab. Maurus* : Long Primer | preface : 5-55, the work.

See Wood's *Ath. Oxon.*, ed. Bliss. iii. 222. This is an anonymous and much enlarged edition of pp. 163-179 of James's Bodleian Catalogue (Oxf. 1605): made by John Verneuil sub-librarian. The preface mentions a pirated edition of this book, made without the knowledge of the authorities of the Library, but no copy seems to be known. See *Rouse*, above in this year.

18. **Wake,** Isaac.   REX | *PLATONICVS :* | SIVE, | DE POTENTISSIMI | PRINCIPIS | IACOBI | BRITANNIARVM REGIS, | ad Illustrissimam Academiam | Oxoniensem, aduentu, | Aug. 27. Anno | M.DC.V. | *NARRATIO* | *Ab* Isaaco WAKE *Publico* | *Academiæ ejusdem Oratore, tunc* | *temporis conscripta, nunc ite-'rum in lucem edita, mul-'tis in locis auctior &* | *emendatior.* | EDITIO QVINTA. | [*line.*]

Impr. 151 : 1635 : (twelves) 16° : pp. | Templo Beatæ | *Mariæ Oxon.* | Ab
[8] + 239 + [17] : p. 11 beg. *tur. Ipsoque,* | ISAACO WAKE, Publico Academiæ Ora-;
201 *sed istæ* : Long Primer Roman. Con- | *tore ; Maij* 23. *An.* 1607. | quum mœsti
tents :—p. (1) title : (3-7) dedication as in | Oxonienses, | piis manibus IOHANNIS |
1st edition : 1-236, the work : 237-239, | RAINOLDI *parentarent.* | [*woodcut,* then
the Chancellor's letter with preface : (2) | Impr. 151.] : (4-16) the oration.
title :—ORATIO | FVNEBRIS | HABITA IN |

See 1607 W. This appears to be a reprint of the 4th edition.

1636.

1. **Articles.**   ARTICVLI | DE QVIBVS CONVENIT INTER | ARCHI-EPISCOPOS, | ET | EPISCOPOS VTRIVSQVE PROVINCIÆ, ET | Clerum vniversum in Synodo, Londini. An. | 1562. secundum computationem Ecclesiæ | Anglicanæ, ad tollendam opinionum dissentio-|nem, *& consensum in vera Reli-gione firmandum.* | *Æditi authoritate serenissimæ* REGINÆ. | ITEM | Liber quorundam Canonum | DISCIPLINÆ ECCLESIÆ | ANGLICANÆ. ANNO 1571. | 3. De Episcopis. | 5. De Decanis Ecclesiarum. | 8. De Archi-diaconis. | 9. De Cancellariis. &c. | 14 De Ædituis Ecclesiarum. | 19. De Concionatoribus. | 20. De Residentia. | 21. De Pluralitatibus. | 21. De Ludimagistris. | 22. De Patronis. &c. [the last five lines are printed in a parallel line with the first five, a line separating the two columns] | [*woodcuts* between two *lines.*]

Impr. 151: 1636: sm. 4°: pp. 24 + 23 +[1]: pp. 11 begg. *De prædestinatione, and gendis sacris*: English Roman. Contents:—p. 1, title: 3–24, the Articles: 24, "Confirmatio Articulorum": 1, half-title: 2, list of Canons: 3–23, the Canons: (1) "℈ Forma sententiæ excommunicationis."

2. **Barclay,** John.   IOANNIS | BARCLAII | POEMATVM | LIBRI DVO. | [*line*] | *Editio postrema aucta.* | [*line,* then *device.*]

Impr. 153: 1636: (twelves) 16°: pp. [14] + 100 + [2]: p. 11 beg. *Fregit, & Auroræ*: Long Primer Roman. Contents:— p. (1) title, within double lines: (3–6) dedication to prince (afterwards king) Charles, from the 1615 ed.: (7–12) a Latin poem in Charles's honour, *beg.* "Fama per attonitas": 1–33, the poems, bk. 1: 34, "Ad benevolum Lectorem": 35, a title:—"IOANNIS | BARCLAII | POEMATVM | LIBER II. | [*two lines,* then *woodcut,* then *two lines*]", with impr. 87 a: 37–66, the poems, bk. 2: 67–97 "Tumulus . . . Gustavi Adolphi . . ." a poem, by C. B.: 98–100, five short Latin poems, signed at end "H. G."

This appears to be a reprint of the 1615 (London) edition, with the addition of the poem on pp. 64–100. The signatures indicate that pp. 67–end are an addition to the original book, but a catchword on p. 66 shows that the two parts are not independent. Only these two (separate) editions of Barclay's Poems were published: the author died in 1621.

3. **Bushell,** Thomas.   THE | SEVERALL | SPEECHES AND | Songs, at the presentment of | Mr BVSHELLS ROCK | TO THE | QVEENES | Most Excellent Majesty. | *Aug.* 23, 1636. | HER HIGHNESSE | being Gratiously Pleased to | Honour the said ROCK, not | only with HER | ROYALL *Presence;* | BVT | COMMANDED THE SAME | to be called after her owne | *Princely name* | HENRETTA. | [*line.*]

Impr. 152: 1636: sm. 4°: pp. [12], signn. A⁴, B²: sign. B1ᵛ beg. *And returne*: Pica Roman. Contents:—sign. A1ʳ, title, within double lines and woodcuts: A2ʳ–B2ʳ, the speeches and songs.

Rare. See Wood's *Ath. Oxon.*, ed. Bliss, iii. 1010, where will be found an interesting account of Bushell's discovery of a peculiar rock at Enstone near Oxford, and of the ceremonies with which it was presented to the Queen. The speeches and songs, presented by a hermit, the author himself, Echo, &c., were set to music by Simon Ive (see sign. B2ᵛ).

4. **Carpenter,** Nathanael.   PHILOSOPHIA | LIBERA, | [&c., exactly as 1622 C, omitting a comma in ll. 5, 7, and with "nova", "Carpentario", "Collegii", and "| Editio tertia, correctior |"]

Impr. 159: 1636: [&c., precisely as 1622 C, except that the first leaf and the last two leaves have not been seen, p. 111 beg. *substantiali. At nullam,* and the title is within a line.

See Wood's *Ath. Oxon.*, ed. Bliss, ii. 421, and 1622 C, of which this is an almost exact reprint. Some copies bear the date 1637.

Downcham, George. See 1635 D.

5. **Felix,** Marcus Minucius.   M. MINVCII | FELICIS | OCTAVIVS. | [*device.*]

Impr. 69: 1636: (twelves) 24°: pp. [8] + 129 + [7]: p. 11 beg. *bere, quàm,* 111 *dicimus, non*: Pica Roman. Contents:— p. (3) title within two bounding lines, [&c. precisely as 1631 F.]

See 1627 F: this seems to be a reprint of 1631 F.

6. ——.   MINVCIVS | FELIX | His dialogne called | *OCTAVIVS.* | Containing a defence | of Christian | *religion.* | Translated by | RICHARD IAMES | of C. C. C. *OXON.* | [*woodcuts.*]

Impr. 155: 1636: (twelves) 24°: pp. [8] + 165 + [19]: p. 11 beg. *to heare both,* 111 *refuted Gods*: Pica Roman. Contents:—p. (1) title: (3-6) epistle dedicatory to lady Cotton: (7-8) "To the Reader": 1-165, the work: (2-12) three religious poems, "A Good Friday thought", " A Christmasse Caroll" (*beg.* "Since now the jolly season's by"), " A Hymn on Christs ascension".

Scarce. See Wood's *Ath. Oxon.*, ed. Bliss, ii. 630.

7. **Fitz-Geffry,** Charles.   THE BLESSED | BIRTH-DAY, | CELE-BRATED IN | some religious meditations | on the Angels Anthem. | LVC. 2. 14. | ALSO HOLY | TRANSPORTATIONS | in contemplating some of the | most obserueable adiuncts about | *our Saviours Nativity.* | Extracted for the most { Sacred Scriptures, part out of the { Ancient Fathers, { Christian Poets. } | And some moderne Approved Authors. | [*line*] | By CHARLES FITZ-GEFFRY. | [*line*] | The second Edition with Additions. |

Impr. 156: 1636: (eights) 12°: pp. [8] + 80: p. 11 beg. *If he in time*: English Roman. Contents :—p. (1) title, (3-5) "To the Devote Author . . ." a poem signed "Hen. Beesely *A.M. A.A.*": (7) Complimentary poem to the author by Steph. Haxby of Cambridge: 1-47, the Blessed Birthday, a poem: 48 "Votum Authoris ad Iesum . . .": 49-80, the Transportations, 16 poems.

See Wood's *Ath. Oxon.*, ed. Bliss, ii. 607. This is a reprint of the first edition, see 1634 F, with some additions and the omission of the poem before the second part. It is this second issue which Dr. Grosart reprinted in 1881 in Fitz-Geffrey's *Poems.*

8. **Florus,** Lucius Annaeus.   THE | ROMAN | Histories of LVCI=|VS IVLIVS FLORVS | *from the foundation* | *of* ROME, *till Cæsar* | AVGVSTVS, *for aboue* | DCC. *yeares, & from then=|ce to* TRAIAN *near* CC. | *yeares, divided by* Flor' | *into* IV *ages.* | *Translated into* | ENGLISH |

Impr. 161: 1636: (twelves) 16°: pp. [26] + 336: p. 11 beg. *wore, being,* 301 *more luckie*: Pica Roman. Contents :— (1-2) not seen: (3) engraved title, inserted: (5-10) Epistle dedicatory to George marquis of Buckingham, signed "Philanactophil": (11-19) "To the Reader": (20-24) "The preface of Lucius Florus": (25-26) not seen: 1-336, the Histories: 336 "The end of the foure Bookes of the Roman Histories . . . translated into English by E.M.B. Soli Deo gloria".

The translator of this work, which first appeared in English at London in 1618, was Edmund (Maria) Bolton. The present edition was printed in London but published at Oxford, and the title is the engraved one of 1618, by Simon Pass, displaying in the upper centre a Roman, in the lower centre the title, an eagle at top, and symbols and letterpress about, and altered in the imprint only. The collation assumes that a sheet of ten leaves could not be printed and that a blank leaf is needed before and after the prefatory matter: the title is on an inserted leaf. This edition was issued after the translator's death, and seems not to be entered in the London Stationers Company's Registers.

9. **Grotius,** Hugo.   DEFENSIO | FIDEI CATHOLICÆ | DE | SATIS-FACTIONE | CHRISTI, | *Adversus* | FAVSTVM SOCINVM | Senensem : | *Scripta*

ab | HVGONE GROTIO. | [*line*] | *Cum* Gerardi Iohannis Vossii | *ad judicium* Hermanni RA-|venspergeri *de hoc* | LIBRO. | RESPONSIONE. | [*line.*]

Impr. 153: 1636: (twelves) 16°: pp. [12] + 256 + [40] + 136: pp. II begg *Cruciatus*, and *hæc nostra*, III *Cap. vi*, and *tur, Paulus*: Pica and (2nd part) Long Primer Roman. Contents:—p. (1) title: (3-10) " Veritatis evangelicæ studiosis . . .", dated " *Lug. Batav.* in Collegio Theolog. Ill. DD. Ord. *Holl & Westf.* 8. *Kal. Sept.* An. Chri. cIↄ Iↄ cxvii. Ger. Ioannides Vossius, *Coll. Regens*": (11-12) "Lectori" by the unnamed editor: 1-219, the Defensio: 220-256 Testimonia veterum: (1-16) an index in order of contents: (17) a bastard title to the second part, with impr. 87 *a*, and date: (19-35) "Præfatio", signed "Ger. Ioannides Vossiun . . .": (37-40) "Lectori" by the editor: 1-136, the Responsio.

The two previous editions of Grotius's work were issued at Leyden in 1617, while Vossius's *Responsio* was published at the same place in 1618. Words underlined in the above title are in red ink, as are also "Oxoniæ," and " MDCXXXVI " in the imprint. N is omitted in the series of signatures.

10. **Heylyn**, Peter.   ΜΙΚΡΟΚΟΣΜΟΣ: | A | LITTLE | DESCRIPTION | OF THE GREAT | WORLD. | *The seventh Edition.* | [*line*] | By PETER HEYLYN. | [*line, motto, woodcut.*]

Impr. 158: 1636: (eights) sm. 4°: pp. [20] + 808 + [4]: p. II beg. 1. *First then*, 701 *dates, or Vindelici*: Pica Roman. Contents:—(precisely as 1633 H, except that the title is within double lines, instead of an arched border, and that every leaf has been seen.)

See 1621 H. This is a reprint, almost line for line, of 1633 H. The copy seen had a folded table of climes as in the 1625 edition, after p. 228.

11. [**Lily**, William].   A | Short Introduction | OF | GRAMMAR | GENERALLY | TO BE USED: | *Compiled and set forth for the bring-*|ing up of all those that intend to at-|taine to the knowledge of the | *Latine tongue.* | [*woodcut.*]

Impr. 68 *d*: 1636: (eights) 12°: pp. [74] + 130 + [36]: p. II beg. *comprehenderunt*, III *Sic Ovid*: Long Primer Roman and English. Contents:—p. (1), title: (2) royal arms, with " C.R.": (3-8) " ❋ To the Reader, &c.": (9) about letters: (10) two prayers: (11-70) a Latin grammar in English: (71-2) Latin poem by Will. Lily: (73) a title within a line and border: — " Brevissima | institutio, | *Seu* | Ratio Grammatices | cognoscendæ, ad omni-|um puerorum utilita-|tem præscripta: | *Quam solam Regia Majestas* | *in omnibus Scholis do-*|*cendam præcipit.* | [*line, woodcut. line*]", with impr. 72 *c*: (74) arms of the University, &c.: 1-130, a Latin grammar, syntax and prosody, in Latin: (1-30) "Omnium nominum . . . ac verborum interpretatio . . .": (31-3) four Latin poems, including graces: (34) woodcut picture of the tree of knowledge, and students gathering the fruit.

This is the first Latin grammar printed at Oxford since 1518, and is issued " Cum Privilegio." The grammar itself was already, in its Latin form, more than a hundred years old, and many editions of it had been printed. Other Oxford editions were issued at least in 1651, 1672-3, 1675, 1679, 1687, 1692, 1699, 1709, 1714, 1733. For William Lily see Wood's *Ath. Oxon.*, ed. Bliss, i. 32. The signatures connect the two parts of the book.

The importance of this issue is considerable. In consequence of disputes between John Lichfield and Turner, archbp. Laud's attention had been called to the state of printing at Oxford, and the absence of any such printing privileges as were possessed by Cambridge. A charter of privileges was accordingly obtained, dated 12 Nov. 1632, confirmed and amplified by another dated 13 March 1633. These allowed the University to print Bibles, Prayerbooks, Grammars, Almanacs, &c., which had till then been the monopolies of the London Stationers' Company and the University Press at

Cambridge. No Bibles or Prayerbooks were issued at Oxford till 1675, but this Grammar and three Almanacs (see 1637 B, C, and W.) raised the standard of revolt against monopoly. On 20 March 163⅜ the Stationers' Company agreed to pay the University £200 a year, if it would agree not to issue the classes of books in question, and no further difficulties arose till after the Restoration.

12. **Longinus**, Dionysius.   ΔΙΟΝΥΣΙΟΥ | ΛΟΓΓΙΝΟΥ | ΡΗΤΟΡΟΣ ΠΕΡΙ | ὕψους λόγου βιβλίον | DIONYSII LONGINI | Rhetoris | *Præstantissimi* | Liber | *De grandiloquentia sive* | *sublimi dicendi genere* | Latine redditus | ὑποθέσεσι συνοπτικαῖς | *et ad oram notationibus* | *aliquot illustratus* | [*line*] | *Edendum curavit et notarum* | *insuper auctarium adjunxit.* G. L. | [*line.*]

Impr. 112 *a*: 1636: (eights) 12°: pp. [42] + 176 + [2] + 117 + [1] and one folded plate: pp. 11 beg. ἐκ τοῦ φοβεροῦ, and *qui Geometriæ*: Pica Roman. Contents:— p. (3) engraved title, see below: (5–10) "Iuventuti Academicæ", signed "Gerardus Langbaine", the editor: (11–24) complimentary Latin pieces by Gabriel de Petra, the author of the Latin translation and notes, 1610, and others: (24–42) three Latin prefatory pieces, about Longinus: a folded oblong 16mo sheet bearing a Diagramma or synopsis of the subject: 1, extract from Suidas about Longinus: 2–161, the treatise in Greek and (on the verso of each leaf) Latin, with marginal notes: 162–176, 1–2 Σύνοψις, further notes: 1–117, (1) "Notarum auctarium" with a critical preface, and (on p. 20) an engraving: ending with a Latin poem on the death of Thomas "Wethereld" (Wetherell) of Queen's college Oxford.

See Wood's *Ath. Oxon.*, ed. Bliss, iii. 446, and 1638 L. The first part of this volume to the end of the Σύνοψις except Langbaine's preface, is a reprint of the 1612 (Geneva) edition by Gabriel de Petra: the notes are Langbaine's first published work. The engraved title by William Marshall is from a metal plate, displaying Hermes, an eagle, Phaethon, &c., round the title: and is an inserted leaf. Signatures o and P are run into one. The date on the title appears to be that of the engraving, but as it was altered in the 2nd edition, though the plate is practically identical, it may be taken as the date of the book also.

13. **Masque.**   THE | KING | *AND* | QVEENES | Entertainement at | *RICHMOND.* | AFTER | THEIR DEPARTVRE | from OXFORD: In a Masque, | presented by the most Illustrious | PRINCE, | *PRINCE* | CHARLES | Sept. 12. 1636. | *motto*, then *line*.]

Impr. 152: 1636: sm. 4°: pp. 31 + [1]: p. 11 beg. *Tom. Tellow*: Great Primer Roman. Contents:—p. 1, title, within a border of woodcuts between lines: 3, dedication to the queen: 5–30, the masque.

Rare. The introduction explains that the Masque was almost impromptu as concerns the speaking, the dances in which Prince Charles took a share being the important part. They were composed by Simon Hopper and the music by Charles Coleman. Most of the written part is in the Wiltshire dialect "because most of the interlocutors were *Wilshire* men."

14. **Oxford** University.   CORONAE | CAROLINÆ | QVADRATVRA. | SIVE | PERPETRANDI | *IMPERII* | CAROLINI | EX QVARTO PIGNORE | *FELICITER SVSCEPTO* | *Captatum Augurium.* | [*woodcut.*]

Impr. 151 *a*: 1636: sm. 4°: pp. [92], signn. a, aa⁴, aaa², aaaa, a–d⁴, e², A–C⁴, D², and a folded leaf: sign. b1ʳ beg. *Diva paris*, B1ʳ *From the wombs*: English Roman. Contents:—sign. a1ʳ, title: a2ʳ–e2ᵛ, Latin poems: A1ʳ–D1ᵛ, English poems to the queen: D2ʳ "The Printers vote", an English poem by Leonard Lichfield.

Poems by members of the University of Oxford on the birth of Princess Elizabeth,

28 Dec. 1635: in number about 142, of which 31 are English, 8 Greek, 2 Hebrew and 1 French. The number of English, and their separation from the rest is a mark of change. Most copies want the folded sheet (about 11×6 in.), which contains an engraved picture of a crown on a board supported at the four corners by a prince, two princesses and an infant in a cradle, all upon a large pedestal. Beneath are six Latin verses, beginning "Quam stabilis Quadrata," and then "Ita augustissimo Domino suo vovet humillima ancilla Acad. Oxon." Curiously the engraving cannot possibly be correct, since the place of prince James is taken by a female figure! Perhaps for this reason the plate was soon suppressed: it is certainly now very rarely found.

15. ———. FLOS | BRITANNICVS | VERIS NOVISSIMI | FILIOLA | CAROLO & MARJÆ | NATA | XVII MARTII Anno. | M.DC.XXXVI. | [*woodcut.*]

Impr. 151 *b*: 1636: sm. 4°: pp. [100], see below: p. (11) beg. *Non habeo*: English Roman. Contents:—p. (1) title, within a border of woodcuts: (3–100) the poems.

These are poems by members of the University of Oxford to celebrate the birth of the princess Anne, born 17 Mar. 163⅞ (died Dec. 1640). About two-thirds of the verses are to the king, chiefly in Latin (nine in Greek, one in Hebrew), the rest to the queen in English (two in French): there is one chronogram. The make-up of ordinary copies of the volume is extraordinary: there are no pages or signatures, but if A—O represent the sections the collation would be as follows, the figures in brackets indicating the mark affixed to the first page of some sections in the place where the pagination would naturally have been printed :—A¹, B¹, C¹ (1), D¹ (2), E¹ (3), F¹ (4), G¹ (6), H¹ (66: on 2nd leaf, 8). I¹ (5), K¹, L¹ (2), M¹, N¹ (1), O¹ (3)! The last page contains a poem by the printer, Leonard Lichfield. I have seen a copy in which a leaf following the title bore a printed Latin poem beginning "Quæ Te Mascula" referring to an emblem in diamond form displaying three lilies and two small and one large lion; which emblem occurs in a pen-and-ink drawing in the above copy on an inserted leaf preceding the title.

16. **Parsons**, Bartholomew. A | SERMON | PREACHED | AT | THE FVNERALL OF | Sʳ FRANCIS PILE Baronet, at | *Collingborne Kingstone* in the | County of *Wiltes*, on the 8. day of | *December*. 1635. | BY | BARTHOLOMEW PARSONS | *B.D.* and *Vicar* there. | [*two mottos,* then *woodcut.*]

Impr. 154: 1636: sm. 4°: pp. [4] + 39 + [1]: p. 11 beg. *there is a*: English Roman. Contents:—p. (1) title: (3–4) dedication to sir Francis Pile, "From Ludgershall. Dec. 17. 1635": 1–39, the sermon, on Is. lvii. 1–2.

See Wood's *Ath. Oxon.*, ed. Bliss, iii. 26. The dedication to the son shows that Parsons had known the father for 20 years.

17. **Pinke**, William. THE TRIALL OF | A | CHRISTIANS | SINCERE .LOVE | *VNTO CHRIST*. | By Mʳ WILLIAM PINKE, | Mʳ of Arts late Fellow of | Magdalen Colledge | in OXFORD. | [*motto*, then *line*] | THE THIRD EDITION. | [*line*, then *woodcuts*.]

Impr. 160: 1636: (twelves) 16°: pp. [16] + 54 + 127 + [1] + 62 + [4]: pp. 11 beg. *lat.* 3. 13, and *shrewd grudgings*, and *vnto you what*: Pica Roman. Contents:—p. (14) title: 3–11 Epistle dedicatory to lord Digby, dated "Shirburn. Iul. 7. 1630", by the editor William Lyford: (12–16) "To the reader" by W. Lyford: 1–54, sermon on 1 Cor. xvi. 22: 1–66, 67–127, two sermons on Eph. vi. 24: (1), 1–62, (1), sermon on Luke xiv. 26.

See Wood's *Ath. Oxon.*, ed. Bliss, ii. 475, and 1630 P.

18. **Prideaux,** John.   "*Twenty Sermons.* Oxon 1636 qu." [Bodl. 4to. P. 50. Th.]

So in Wood's *Ath. Oxon.*, ed. Bliss, iii. 268. There may have been a collected edition with some such title issued in 1636: but probably Wood refers to a collection without a general title, as contained in 4to P. 50 Th. (a reference added however to Wood's *Athenæ* by dr. Bliss). For a real titlepage to the collection of twenty sermons and for details of the separate sermons, all of which are dated 1636, see 1637 P.

19. **Wouwerus,** Joannes.   IOANNIS WOUWERI | DIES ÆSTIVA, | SIVE | DE VMBRA | PÆGNION. | Unà cum | IANI DOUSÆ F. *in ean-|dem Declamatione.* | [*line*] | *Editio postrema castigatior,* | *& adjectionibus in fine* | *locupletior.* | [*woodcut.*]

Impr. 153 *a*: 1636: (twelves) 16°: pp. [24] + 156 + [24]: p. 11 beg. *interpositionem,* III *riosos interemit*: Pica Roman. Contents:—p. (1) title, within double lines : (3–12) dedication to Hieronymus Voeglerus, dated "Ex arce Gottorpiana V. Kal. Augusti CIƆ IƆ CX. T. Joan. VVouwerus": (13–23) "... Prolegomena": 24 "Errata": 1–124. the work in 28 chapters: 124–154, Donsa's Declamatio : 154–156, Dousa's "In eandem rem Carmen": (1–4) "Index auctorum": (5–22) "Rerum memorabilium Index."

This appears to be a reprint of the first (1610) edition omitting the Elenchus Capitum and adding Dousa's Essay. The work is a fanciful treatment of the subject of shadow.

20. **Zouche,** Richard.   ELEMENTA | IVRISPRVDENTIÆ | DEFINITIONI-BVS, | Regulis, & sententiis selectioribus | *Iuris Civilis illustrata.* | *Quibus accessit* | DESCRIPTIO | IVRIS & IVDICII | TEMPORALIS | Secundum Consuetudines | *Feudales & Normannicas.* | *Nec non* | DESCRIPTIO | IVRIS & IVDICII | ECCLESIASTICI | SECVNDVM CANONES | & Constitutiones Anglicanas. | [*line*] | Autore R.Z. P.R. *Oxoniæ.* | [*line.*]

Impr. 157: 1636: sm. 4°: pp. [12] + 145 + [7] + 51 + [7] + 60 + [2]: pp. 11 beg. *pars secunda, pars secunda,* and *riæ ex fructibus*: Pica Roman. Contents:— p. (1) title, within double lines separated by woodcuts: (3–4) dedication to archbp. Laud, signed "Ric. Zouchæus": (5–7) "Iuventuti iurisprudentiæ studiosæ",dated "ex Aulâ Alban. Pridie Calend. Aug. 1636": (9–12) list of parts and sections of the book: 1–145 the work: (2) a title, within lines :—"DESCRIPTIO | IVRIS & IVDICII | TEMPORALIS | SECVNDVM CON-| SVETVDINES FEV-|*DALES ET* | *Normanni-cas*". | [*line, device, line,* and impr. 157]: (4–6) list of parts &c. : 1–51, the work : (2) a title, within lines :—DESCRIPTIO | *IVRIS & IVDICII* | ECCLESIASTICI | SECVNDVM CANONES | *& CONSTITVTIONES* | *Anglicanas.* [*line, device, line,* and impr. 157]: (4–7) list of parts, &c : 1–60, the work : (1) note of parts still wanting to the complete treatise, and "Errata".

See Wood's *Ath. Oxon.*, ed. Bliss, iii. 511. This is a reissue and enlargement of 1629 Z and 1634 Z, carrying the scheme further : it was completed in 1640 and 1650, and several parts have been reprinted. The signatures weld the three parts of the present volume into one.

*** The Almanacs by Booker and Wyberd, which bear 1637 on the titlepage, and are treated under that year, may have been issued late in 1636.

1637.

1. **Barlow**, bp. Thomas.   *PIETAS IN PATREM,* | OR | A FEW
TEARES VPON | THE LAMENTED DEATH OF | HIS MOST DEARE, AND LOVING |
Father RICHARD BARLOW, late of | *Langill* in *VVestmooreland,* who dyed
December 29 Ann. 1636. | [*line*] | *By* THOMAS BARLOW *Master of Arts,* |
Fellow of Queenes Coll. *in* Oxon: *and* | *eldest sonne of his deceased
father.* | [*line, motto, woodcut.*]

Impr. 119: 1637: sm. 4°: pp. [2] + 16
+ [2]: p. 11 beg. *To the sad:* Pica Roman.
Contents:—p. (1) title: (2) Τοῦ Παλλαδᾶ
εἰς Θάνατον, a four-line Greek epigram,
beg. Σῶμα πάθος ψυχῆς: 1–16, English
poems, five by T. Barlow, seven by relations and friends.

Rare. Barlow's second poem describes his dream of his father's death at the very
time of its occurrence, though he did not know of the illness. The impression was
strong enough to wake him.

2. **Bense**, Petrus.   ANALOGO-DIAPHORA, | SEU | Concordantia
Discrepans, | & Discrepantia Concordans | trium Linguarum, | *Gallicæ,
Italicæ, & Hispanicæ.* | Unde innotescat, quantum quæque à *Romanæ*
lin-|guæ, unde ortum duxere, idiomate deflexerit; | earum quoque ratio
& natura dilucidè & suc-|cinctè delineantur. | [*line*] | Operâ & studio |
PETRI BENSE *Parisini* apud | OXON: *has linguas profitentis.* | [*woodcut.*]

Impr. 98 : 1637: (eights) 12°: pp. [8]
+ 72: p. 11 beg. *quibuscumque:* Pica
Roman. Contents:—pp. (1–2) not seen :
(3) title: (5–8) dedication to the University of Oxford: 1–72, the work.

See Wood's *Ath. Oxon.,* ed. Bliss, ii. 624. This is not a formal grammar, but rather
a discussion of the resemblances and differences of the languages treated in points of
grammar and syntax.

3. **Booker**, John.   ALMANACK: | *Sivè* | Prognosticon Astro-
logicum, | & Diarium Meteorologicum, | *Vel* | Speculum Anni |
M. DC. XXXVII. | [*line*] | *Being the first after leap yeare.* | [*line*] |
Calculated for the Meridian of the | Honourable Citie of London. |
[*line*] | *Autore* Johanne Bookero *Astroph.* | [*line, motto, line.*]

Impr. 171 : 1637: (eights) 16°: pp.
(48), signn. A–C' : sign. B1ʳ beg. *Saturne
doth:* Long Primer Roman. Contents:—
sign. A1ʳ title, within border: A1ᵛ–A4ʳ,
preliminary notes : A4ᵛ–B8ʳ, the Almanac:
B8ᵛ–C8ᵛ, astrological notes and prognosti-
cations, with a chronogram.

John Booker was a prolific Almanac maker : his *Almanac and Prognostication* was
issued from 1631 to 1649: his *Celestial Observations* from 1651 to 1662, and the
Telescopium from 1659 to 1676, but the dates may be capable of extension, and as
Booker died in 1667, the *Telescopium* must have been carried on by a successor under
his name. Only this one issue was printed at Oxford, since the Stationers' Company
bought out the University's right of printing this and certain other kinds of book in
March 163⁹₆, see 1636 L, and *Booker, Wyberd* below. The underlined words in the
title are printed in red, as well as much of the woodcut border (which bears the signs
of the zodiac, the royal arms, and an open book), the words "Oxford," "to the famous

Universitie. 1637." in the imprint, and many words in the text. The same astrological woodcut occurs as in the Wyberd, but in a more injured state, showing that Wyberd had precedence in point of date. Booker's Almanac for 1636 was printed at Cambridge.

4. **Brerewood**, Edward.   TRACTATVS | QVIDAM LOGICI | DE | *PRÆDICABILIBVS*, | ET | PRÆDICAMENTIS | *Ab eruditissimo* EDVARDO BREREWOOD, | Artium Magistro, è Collegio *Ænei-Nasi,* olim | conscripti: nunc verò ab erroribus (qui frequenti | transcriptione irrepserant) vindicati, ad pristinum nito-|rem, nativámque puritatem diligentissimâ manu-| scriptorum collatione restituti, & in lucem editi: | *Per* T. S. *Art. Mag. & Collegij* Ænei-Nasi *Socium . Editio tertia,* | In quâ accesserunt duo ejusdem Authoris insignes | *Tractatus*; prior de *Meteoris,* posterior de | *Oculo:* limâ, lucéque donati: | *Per eundem* T. S. [*line, motto, woodcut.*]

Impr. 162: 1637: (eights) 12°: pp. [32] + folded sheet + 431 + [5] + 105 + [3] + 26: pp. 11 begg. *Sol. Prædicabilia,* and *Sect.* 11. *In qua* and 2. *In quo devehuntur*: Long Primer Roman. Contents: —[exactly as 1631 B to p. 431, except "ê" for "e", "Cal." for "Calend.": then:—] p. 2) a title:—" TRACTATVS DVO, | *Quorum primus est* | DE METEORIS. | *Secundus,* | DE OCVLO. | Quos scripsit olim eximius ille philosophus | EDVARDUS BREREWOODUS: | *Restituit tandem, ab erroribus mendisque* | *vindicavit, & publici juris fecit* | T.S. | Art. Mag. & Colleg. *Ænea-Nasensis* | Socius | [*woodcut*] | " with impr. 109, but no name of place: (4) dedication as 1631 B: 1–83, De Meteoris: 84–105, De Mari: (1–2) woodcut diagrams of the eye: (3) Index: 1–26, De Oculo.

See 1628 B, 1631 B (of which this is a reprint), Wood's *Ath. Oxon.,* ed. Bliss, ii. 140. The signatures connect the two divisions of this work.

5. **Burgersdicius**, Francon.   IDEA | PHILOSOPHIÆ | TUM | MORALIS, | TUM | NATURALIS: | SIVE | EPITOME COMPENDIOSA | utriusque ex *Aristotele* excerpta, | *& methodicè disposita*: | A | M. FRANC. BURGERSDICIO in | Academia *Lugduno-Batavâ,* Logices & | Ethices Professore ordinario. | *Editio quarta prioribus castigatior.* | [*line.*] |

Impr. 121: 1637: (twelves) 16°: pp. [4] + 332 + [6] + 101 + [1]: pp. 11 beg. *strictiore quâdam* and 2. *Natura est,* 211 *rem quærunt*: Pica Roman. Contents: — p. (1) title: (3–4) " Index Capitum & titulorum . . ." to the Idea Phil. Mor.: 1–332, the Idea Philosophiae Moralis: (1) title:—" FRANCONIS BVRGERSDICI | IDEA | PHILOSOPHIÆ | NATVRALIS: | SIVE | Methodus definitionum & controversiarum Physicarum. | *Editio postrema.*" [*woodcut,* then Impr. 121]: (3–4) " Philosophiæ Studiosis", signed " Franco Burgersdicius ": (5–6) " Tituli et Ordo disputationum ": 1–101, the Idea Philosophiae Naturalis.

See 1631 B, of which this is almost a reprint, the order of the two parts being reversed.

6. **Buridanus**, Johannes.   IOHANNIS | BVRIDANI | PHILOSOPHI | TRECENTIS RETRO | annis celeberrimi | QVÆSTIONES IN | DECEM LIBROS | *ETHICORVM* | ARISTOTELIS | AD NICOMACHVM. | [*device.*]

Impr. 168: 1637: (eights) sm. 4°: pp. [12] + 889 + [1]: p. 13 beg. *ad ea quæ,* 701 *alii prodesse*: Long Primer Roman. Contents:—p. (1) title, within double lines: (3–11) " Index quæstionum ": (12) " Typographus ad Lectores " and " Errata ": 1–889, the work in four books: 889, impr. 151.

This is perhaps the last separate edition of this work. Buridan, who lived in the fourteenth century, was a disciple of the English philosopher Occam.

7. **Bythner,** Victorinus.   TABVLA DIRECTORIA. | IN QVA | TOTVM
TO TEXNIKON LINGVÆ | Sanctæ, ad amussim delineatur. | QVAM | . . .
[2 lines] | D. HENRICO WOTTON | . . . [2 lines] | *inscribit Author* |
VICTORINVS BYTHNER. *P.* |

Impr. 98*a* : 1637 : la. 4", see below: | *vel Nomina* : English Roman. Contents,
pp. [6], see below : col. 1 beg. 1 *Verba* | see below.

See Wood's *Ath. Oxon.*, ed. Bliss, iii. 675. These are three rare sheets printed on
the recto only and intended to be pasted together, the two lower about 14 in. high by
18½ in. wide, the upper one about 7 × 18½ in. The two lower ones contain in five
columns a Hebrew grammar in nine divisions, the upper one "Chaldaismi & Syria-
cismi," between which is the title, and below them the preface " Lectori benevolo."
The colophon is at the end of the last column. The underlined words in the above
title are in red, as well as a few other words, including a chronogram.

8. **Carpenter,** Nathanael.   PHILOSOPHIA | LIBERA, | [&c.]: see
1636 C.

Clement of Rome.   References to a supposed edition of Clemens
Romanus in 1637, a reprint of the edition of 1633, are due to a confusion : the 1633 edition alone exists.

9. **Comenius,** Johannes Amos (Komensky).   CONATVVM | COMENI-
ANORVM | PRAELVDIA | EX BIBLIOTHECA *S. H.* | [*device.*]

Impr. 72 : 1637 : sm. 4" : pp. [6] + 52
+ [6] : p. 11 beg. *Tertiò, portento* : Pica
Roman. Contents :—p. (1) title : (3-4)
" Ad lectorem ", signed " Samuel Hart-
libius": (5)title :—" PORTA SAPIENTIAE |
RESERATA: | SIVE | PANSOPHIÆ CHRISTI-
ANÆ | SEMINARIVM. | Hoc est, | Nova,
compendiosa, & solida omnes Sci- | entias
& Artes, & quicquid manifesti vel oc-
culti | est, quod ingenio humano pene-
trare, solertiæ imitari, | linguæ eloqui
datur, breviùs, veriùs, meliùs, quàm | hac-
tenus, addiscendi Methodus. | [*line*] |
Auctore | Reverendo Clarissimóque Viro |
Domino *Iohanne Amoso Comenio.* | [*line,
2 mottos, woodcut.*]", with impr. 72*d*: (6)
a motto: 1-52, the work : (1-6 " Præ-
cipua Capita Didacticæ Magnæ, à Domino
Comenio elaboratæ . . ."

This is a kind of prospectus of the encyclopædic work on education which Comenius
was at the time contemplating, and although issued by Hartlib without the permission
of the author, partly in order to gather the opinions of scholars on the scheme, it was
not displeasing to Comenius, especially since some of his critics suggested a *Collegium
Pansophicum* to work out the details. This we learn from an appendix by Comenius
to the reprint of this Oxford edition in vol. i. of his *Opera didactica omnia* (Amst. 1657),
vol. i. col. 403, cf. 454.

10. **Cowper,** Thomas.   COWPER 1637. | AN | ALMANACK | for the
yeare of our | Lord 1637. | [*line*] | Being the first after leap-yeare. |
[*line*] | Together with some astrologicall rules | for the prediction of
weather for each | day in the yeare : with the principall High-wayes in
England and | *Wales.* | [*line*] | Referred to the famous Universitie and |
Citie of Oxford; but may indiffe-|rently serve for any other place within |
this Kingdome. | [*line*] | *By* THOMAS COWPER. | [*line, motto, line.*]

Impr. 68*d* : 12° : Pica Roman : title within a border of lines and woodcuts.

Very rare. Only known from a titlepage in Brit. Mus. MS. Harl. 5937, no. 140. See note under *Booker* above. The underlined words in the title above are printed in red ink, as well as "Oxford," and "the famous Universitie. 1637" in the imprint, and some words in the "Vulgar Notes" on the back of the title.

11. Deliciae deliciarum. DELITIÆ | DELITIARVM | SIVE | EPI-GRAMMATVM | optimis quibusq; hujus & no-|vissimi seculi poetis in amplissimâ | illâ Bibliothecâ | BODLEIANA, | Et penè omninò alibi ex-tantibus | ἀνθολογία, in unam corollam connexa | [*line*] | Operâ Ab. WRIGHT Art. Bac. | *& S. Ioan. Bapt. Coll. Socii.* | [*line*, then *motto.*]

Impr. 166: 1637: 12°: [16] + 247 + [1]: p. 11 beg. *Tale tamen,* 201 *De Virgilio*: Long Primer Roman. Contents: —p. (3) title: (5–8) dedication to dr. Will. Haywood, the editor's tutor: (9–11) "Lectori": (13–15) "Catalogus Auctorum": 1–247, the epigrams: 247. Errata.

See Wood's *Ath. Oxon.*, ed. Bliss, iv. 276. Wright took his M.A. degree on April 22, 1637. Unfortunately there is no indication of the source of each epigram, and almost all the authors are continental poets.

12. Fitz-Geffry, Charles. COMPASSION | TOWARDS CAPTIVES, | CHIEFLY | Toward our Brethren and Country-men | who are in miserable bondage | in BARBARIE. | *Vrged and pressed in three Sermons* | On HEB. 13. 3. | [*line*] | Preached in PLYMOVTH, in *October* 1636. | *By* CHARLES FITZ-GEFFRY. | [*line*] | *Whereunto are anexed* | An Epistle of St CYPRIAN concerning the Redemption | of the Bretheren from the bondage of *Barbarians*; | AND | *A passage concerning the benefits of Compassion, extracted* | out of St AMBROSE *his second booke of* Offices, Cap. 28. | [*motto.*]

Impr. 160 *a*: 1637: sm. 4°: pp. [12] + 50 + [10]: p. 11 beg. *heaven, but*: Pica Roman. Contents:—p. (1) title: (3–5) dedication to John Cause mayor of Plymouth, &c.: (7–12) "To the compassionate, that is, to the truly Christian Reader": 1–19, 21–35, 37–50, the three sermons: (1–4) the Cyprian: (5–7) the Ambrose.

See Wood's *Ath. Oxon.*, ed. Bliss, ii. 607.

13. Ironside, dr. Gilbert. SEVEN | QVESTIONS | OF THE | SABBATH | BRIEFLY DISPVTED, | after the manner of the | SCHOOLES. | Wherein such cases, and scruples, as are | *incident to this subject, are cleared, and resolved,* | [*line*] | By GILBERT IRONSIDE B.D. | [*line*, two *mottos, woodcuts.*]

Impr. 156 *a*: 1637: sm. 4°: pp. [24] + 297 + [3 : p. 11 beg. *may see,* 201 *speaks, were*: English Roman. Contents: —p. (1) title, within a line: (3–12) Epistle dedicatory to archbp. Laud: (13–18) "To the Reader": (19–23) "The severall Chapters with their Contents": 1–297, the work, in 31 chapters: (2) Note and "Errata."

See Wood's *Ath. Oxon.*, ed. Bliss, iii. 939. The note before the Errata shows that the author saw no proofs of his book for "the Authors coppy being not so legible as we could have wished, we were forc'd to transcribe it in his absence, and by this means these grosser escapes hapned."

14. Jackson, Thomas. DIVERSE | SERMONS, | WITH A SHORT | TREATISE | BEFITTING THESE | *PRESENT TIMES,* | Now first published |

BY | Thomas Iackson, D^r *in Divinity,* | *Chaplaine in ordinary* to his Majestie, | and President of *Corpus Christi Col-|ledge* in Oxford. | [*note,* then *woodcuts.*]

Impr. 152: 1637: sm. 4°: pp. [8] + 51 + [3] + 70 + [2] + 96 (but 29-34 are numbered 1-6) + [2]: pp. ll begg. *as no souldier,* and *whatsoever afflictions,* and *of his owne:* English Roman. Contents :— p. (3) title, within double lines: (5-6) dedication to prince Charles: 7-8) "Errata", with sub-titles: 1-25, 27-51, 2 sermons on 2 Chron. vi. 39-40: (2) a title: — "THREE | SERMONS | PREACHED | BEFORE THE | KING, | Vpon IER. 26. 19 ... [4 lines, then device and impr. 152]": 1-70, the sermons: (1) a title :—"A | TREATISE | CONCERNING | THE SIGNES OF | THE TIME, OR GODS | FOREWARN-INGS. | CONTAINING | The summe of some few Sermons delive-|red partly before the Kings Majesty partly | in the Towne of *New-Castle* | upon *Tine.* | *wood-cut,* then impr. 152]": 1-70, three discourses : 71, a title :—"A | SERMON | OR | POSTILL. | PREACHED IN *NEWE-* | *CASTLE* VPON *TINE* | The second *Sunday* in | *Advent* 1630. | [woodcut, then impr. 152]": 73-93, the sermon, on Luke xxi. 25 : 94-96, "A briefe Appendix . . ."

See Wood's *Ath. Oxon.,* ed. Bliss, ii 668. The signatures connect all the parts of this volume together. Every printed page is surrounded by double lines on the upper and outer margin, and a single line elsewhere.

15. **Parsons,** Bartholomew. HONOS | & ONVS Levitarum. | OR, | Tithes vindicated to the | Presbyters of the Gospel: | In a Sermon preached at an Archidiaco-|nall Visitation at *Marlebrough,* in the Diocese | of *Sarum,* on the 10. of October. 1636. | [*line*] | By *B. P.* | [*line,* 3 *mottos, line, device, line*].

Impr. 169: 1637: sm. 4°: pp. [8] + 31 + [1]: p. ll beg. *deny, but he* : Pica Roman. Contents :—p. (1) title : (3-7) Epistle dedicatory to Sir William Dod-dington "from the Rectory of *Ludgers-hall,* in the county of *Wiltes,* June 7, 1637.": 1-31, the sermon, on Deut. xxxiii. 11.

See Wood's *Ath. Oxon.,* ed. Bliss, iii. 26. In the copy seen the title is an inserted leaf, the first leaf having been torn out : perhaps this is accounted for by the title given by Wood " History of Tithes: or Tithes vindicated . . . .," and the running head line, which is still " The history of Tithes." Early copies may have this older title.

16. ———. " Sermon on Ephes. 6. 12, 13. Oxon. 1637. qu."

So in Wood's *Ath. Oxon.,* ed. Bliss, iii. 26 : but I have not met with a copy.

17. **Prideaux,** John. CERTAINE | SERMONS | PREACHED | By IOHN PRIDEAVX, Rector of | *Exeter Colledge, his* MAIESTIE'S *Pro-|fessor in Divinity in* OXFORD, *and* | Chaplaine *in Ordinary.* | [*device.*]

Impr. 152: 1637: (eights) sm. 4°: pp. [632], see below, signn. ( )^1 A-X^8, Y^1, Z. Aa-Rr^8, Ss^2: pp. ll begg. as below: English Roman. Contents :—sign. ( ) 1^r, title : i p. 1, a title, within double lines, as are all the succeeding titles :—" CHRISTS | COVNSELL FOR | ENDING LAVV | *CASES.* | AS IT HATH BEENE DELI- | VERED IN TWO SERMONS | vpon the fiue and twentieth verse of | *the fifth of Matthew.* | By IOHN PRIDEAVX, Doctor of | Divinity, *Regius Professor,* and Rector | of *Exeter Colledge.* [*motto, wood-cut,* and impr. 152 *b,* dated 1636]" : 3-4, dedication to Edmund Prideaux and his wife, dated " From Exeter Colledge in Oxford. October 12.": 5-31, 33-65, the sermons : then a blank page: p. ll beg. *Fall not* : ii. (pp. [6] + 39 + [1], p. ll beg. *it is reserued*) p. (1) a title " Ephesus backsliding : considered and applied to these times . . .", with impr. 152 *b,* 1636, an Act-sermon at St. Mary's, July 10, on Rev. ii. 4 : (3-6) dedication to dr. Laurence Bodley, Aug. 5 : 1-39, the sermon : iii. (pp. [2] + 27 + [1], p. ll beg. *in this point)* p. (1) a title " A Christians free-will offering . . .", with impr.

152 *b*, 1636, a Christmas sermon at Christ Church, on Ps. cx. 3: 1–27, the sermon: iv. (pp. [2] + 31 + [1], p. 11 beg. *with Pilate*) p. (1) a title " The first fruits of the Resurrection ..." with impr. 152 *b*, 1636, an Easter sermon at St. Peter's in the East, Oxford, on 1 Cor. xv. 20: 1–31, the sermon: v. (pp. [2] + 26, p. 11 beg. *abiects came*) p. (1) a title " Gowries Conspiracie ..." with impr. 152 *b*, a sermon at St. Mary's, Aug. 5: 1–26, the sermon, of some slight value for the history of the Gowrie plot, A. D. 1600: vi. (pp. [2] + 27 + [1], p. 11 beg. *Saint Augustine*), p. (1) a title " Higgaion & Selah: for the discovery of the powder-plot ..." with impr. 152 *b*, 1636, a sermon at St. Mary's on Nov. 5, on Ps. ix. 16: 1–27, the sermon: vii. (pp. [2] + 27 + [1], p. 11 beg. *murmured*) p. (1) a title " Hezekiah's sicknesse and recovery ...," with impr. 152 *b*, 1636, a sermon before the King at Woodstock, on 2 Chron. xxxii. 24: 1–27, the sermon: viii. (pp. [4] + 24 + [8], p. 11 beg. *springs, Schismatickes*) p. (1) a title " Perez-Vzzah, or The Breach of Vzzah ...," with impr. 152 *b*, 1636, a sermon before the King at Woodstock, 24 Aug. 1624, on 2 Sam. vi. 6–7: (3–4) dedication to James earl of Arran, dated 22 Oct. 1624: 1–24 (1), the sermon: (3–8) " Alloquium serenissimo regi Iacobo Woodstochiæ habitum 24. Augusti. Anno 1624": ix. (pp. [8] + 29 + [1], p. 11 beg. *acknowledge*) p. (1) a title " A sermon preached on the fift of October 1624, at the consecration of St James Chappell in Exeter Colledge ...", with impr. 152 *b*, 1636: (3–7) epistle dedicatory to dr. George Hakewill, dated Nov. 15: 1–29, the sermon on Luke xix. 46: x. (pp. 28, p. 11 beg. *which Iesus*) 1–28, a sermon on John vi. 14, without title, see below, but head line " The great Prophet's Advent": xi. (pp. [2] + 29 + [1], p. 11 beg. *Elenches*) p. (1) a title " Reverence to Rulers. A sermon preached at the Court ...", with impr. 152 *b*, 1636: 1–29, the sermon, on Acts xxiii. 5: xii. (pp. [2] + 22, p. 11 beg. *third a comfort*) p. (1) a title " The draught of the brooke. A sermon preached at the Court ...", with impr. 152 *b*, 1636: 1–22, the sermon, on Ps. cx. 7: xiii. (pp. [2] + 32, p. 11 beg. *a bit is*) p. (1) a title " Davids rejoycing for Christs Resurrection ...", an Easter sermon at St. Peter's in the East, on Ps. xvi. 10–11, with impr. 152 *b*, 1636: 1–32, the sermon: xiv. (pp. [2] + 27 + [1], p. 11 beg. *ther, There*) p. (1) a title " The Christians Expectation. A sermon preached at the Court ...", with impr. 152 *b*, 1636: 1–27, the sermon, on 2 Pet. iii. 13: xv. (pp. [2] + 26, p. 11 beg. *beyond wisdome*), p. (1) a title " Wisedomes Iustification. A sermon preached at the Court ...", with impr. 152 *b*, 1636: 1–26, the sermon, on Luke vii. 35: xvi. (pp. [2] + 24, p. 11 beg. *Gods appoyntment*) p. (1) a title " Heresies progresse. A sermon preached before the Court ...", with impr. 152 *b*, 1636: 1–24, the sermon, on 1 Cor. xi. 19: xvii. (pp. [2] + 27 + [1], p. 11 beg. *the world*) p. (1), a title " A Plot for preferment. A sermon preached at the Court ...", with impr. 152 *b*, 1636: 1–27, the sermon, on 1 Pet. v. 6: xviii. (pp. [2] + 27 + [1], p. 11 beg. *den lost*) p. (1) a title " The patronage of Angels. A sermon preached at the Court ...", with impr. 152 *b*, 1636: 1–27, the sermon, on Matth. xviii. 10: xix. (pp. [2] + 27 + [1], p. 11 beg. *Iohns conclusion*) p. (1) a title " Idolatrous Feasting. A sermon preached at the Court ...", with impr. 152 *b*, 1636: 1–27, the sermon, on 1 Cor. x. 7.

See Wood's *Ath. Oxon.*, ed. Bliss, iii. 265 for the author, and 1636 P. This is a collection of twenty sermons by dr. Prideaux from 1614, several preached before the king or court, and several preached at Oxford: those delivered at the consecration of Exeter College Chapel and about Gowrie's conspiracy being of considerable interest. All, except the second (which is grouped with the first) and the eleventh, have separate titlepages, and are often cited as separate editions, but the signatures run throughout the volume. Sign. Y consists of one leaf only, the other three having been obviously intended for a one-leaf title and two-leaf dedication of the sermon following (no. x in the above divisions, really the eleventh sermon), but apparently they were accidentally omitted. Some were already printed, those before printed at Oxford being nos. i (see 1615 P), ii (see 1614 P), and ix (see 1625 P): and nos. i–vii at least, were printed separately at London in 1621. Collections of these sermons are often found without the general title and in a confused order.

18. **Rous**, Francis.   *ARCHÆOLOGIÆ* | ATTICÆ | LIBRI TRES. | THREE BOOKES OF THE | ATTICK Antiquities. | CONTAINING | The description of the Citties glory, govern-|ment, division of the People, and Townes with-|in the *Athenian* Territories, their Religi-|on, Superstition, Sacrifices, account of | their Yeare, as also a full relation | of their

Iudicatories. | [*line*] | By Francis Rous Scholler of *Merton* | Colledge in *Oxon.* | [*line*: then *motto* from Aristides, in Greek and English.]

Impr. 160 *a*: 1637: sm. 4°: pp. [8] + 149 + [3]: p. 11 beg. *in height*, 101 *which standing*: Pica Roman.　Contents :—p. (1) title within a line : (3–6) Epistle dedicatory to Sir Nathaniel Brent, warden of　Merton College, Oxford, dated "From my study in Merton College, Iun. 9, 1637": (7) "To the Reader": (8) "Errata & inserenda": 1–149, the work in 3 bks. : (2–3) not seen.

See Wood's *Ath. Oxon.*, ed. Bliss, iii. 104.　This book, which passed through several editions at Oxford (1649, 1654, 1651, 1662, 1670, and 1675' and London (2nd ed. 1645. 9th ed. 1685), became a companion volume for school use to Godwin's *Roman Antiquities* (see 1614 G) and *Moses and Aaron* (Lond. 1625, &c.).

19. **Scheibler,** Christophorus.

Christophori | Scheibleri, | anteiac in Acade-|mia Gissena professoris, et | pædagogiarchæ, nunc | Tremonle | in Ecclesia Superinten-|dentis, & in Gymnasio Rectoris | metaphysica, | duobus libris | *Vniversum hujus scientiæ Systema comprehendens:* | opus tum omnium facul-|tatum : tum inprimis Philosophiæ & Theolo-|giæ Studiosis utile & necessarium. | præmissa est summaria metho-|dus, sive dispositio totius Scientiæ. | Et accessit Procœmium de usu Philosophiæ in Theolo-|gia, & prætensa ejus ad Theologiam contrarietate. | *Additi sunt singulis Libris* Indices *duo:* alter *Capitum generalium* | *Titulorum, & Articulorum in initio*: alter *rerum in fine.* | Quibus omnibus accessit Exercitationum auctarium, de selectis aliquibus Meta-|physicæ Capitibus.　Per *T. B. Art. Mag. & Coll Reg.* Oxon Socium. | [*line*] | editio ultima. | [*line*.]

Impr. 167 : 1637 : (eights) sm. 4° : pp. [24] + 21 + [3] + 472 + [48] + 456 + [34] + 186 + [2]: pp. 11 begg. *absolute*, and *Pererius,* and *voco. Æquivocum*, and *linquatur*: Long Primer Roman.　Contents :—p. (1) title within double lines : (3–6) Epistola dedicatoria to Ludwig, landgrave of Hesse, by Scheibler, dated Dec. 1616 : (7–11) "Lectori Philo-Metaphysico . . .", signed "Thomas Barlow . . .", the editor: (12–13) "Summaria Methodus . . ." : (14–24) "Index ad Librum primum . . .", in order of the chapters: 1–21 "Procœnium": (2) a titlepage to book one: 1–472,　bk. 1 : (1–30) "Index rerum alphabeticus": (31) a titlepage to book two : (33–36) Epistola dedicatoria to Philip, landgrave of Hesse, by Scheibler, dated March "1617": (37–48) "Index . . .", in order of the chapters : 1–456, book two: (1–26) "Index rerum alphabeticus . . .": (27) a titlepage "Exercitationes aliquot metaphysicæ, de Deo . . . per Thomam Barlow . . ." with impr. 69 : (29–31) "Lectori": (33–34) "Exercitationum . . . Syllabus": 1–186, six exercises: (1) errata.

Scheibler's *Metaphysica* was first issued in 1617, and reissued at Oxford in 1665, as well as often elsewhere.　Bp. Barlow edited it, and added the Exercitationes de Deo (see Wood's *Ath. Oxon.*, ed. Bliss, iv. 336), which were reissued in 1658.　The edition of 1638 is simply a reissue of the sheets of the 1637 edition, with different imprint and date on the first titlepage, and "Meta-" on the first titlepage altered to "Meta-."　Some woodcut diagrams occur in the Exercitationes : in which also the sections change from eights to fours.

20. ——.　　"157. Scheibleri (Chr.) Liber Commentariorum Topicorum—Oxon. 1637."

So in "Catalogi . . . librorum Richardi Davis bibliopolæ pars secunda" (1686), p. 75 among octavos.　Bagford (Brit. Mus. MS. Harl. 9501, fol. 76 ') also describes a copy : and it is probably not really rare, but has escaped the nets of the larger libraries.

21. **Stinton,** George.   A | SERMON | PREACHED IN | THE CATHEDRALL | Church of *Worcester* vp-|on Sunday Morning, | *Novemb.* 27. 1636. | IN | The time of PESTILENCE in o-|ther places of this Land, and now | in the time of the Visita-|tion of that *Citie*, with that | greivous Sicknesse; and | by reason of it. | By GEO. STINTON, | [*motto*, then *line*.]

Impr. 170: 1637: (eights) 16°: pp. 35 +[2]: p. 11 beg. *this consideration*: Pica Roman.   Contents:—p. 1, title, within a border of woodcuts: 3. dedication to Worcester: 4, the text, 1 Kings viii. 37-39: 1-35, the sermon.

See Wood's *Fasti Oxon.*, ed. Bliss, i. 406.

22. **Thesaurus,** Emmanuel.   REVERENDI PATRIS | EMANVELIS THESAVRI | E SOCIETATE IESV, | CÆSARES; | Et ejusdem varia carmina: | *Quibus accesserunt* | Nobilissimorum ORIENTIS | & OCCIDENTIS | Pontificum elogia, & | *varia opera Poëtica.* | Editio secunda emendatior, cum auctariolo. | [*woodcuts*, then *line*.]

Impr. 163: 1637: [4] + 151 +[1]: p. 11 beg. *Caligula. Nascitur*: 101 **Illius Panis*: Long Primer Roman.   Contents: —p. (1) title, within double lines: (3) Latin poem by George Herbert on Francis Bacon lord Verulam: (4) Latin epitaph on Gustavus Adolphus by Dan. Heinsius, with a chronogram: 1-38, the Cæsares: 39-151, "Ejusdem Carmina."

The first edition of this work by Emanuele Tesauro (*b.* 1581) was published in 1619 at Milan, and a third at the same place in 1643. Backer mentions doubts whether the author of this work is identical with the Jesuit who bore the same names. The book contains Latin epigrams on the Cæsars, and miscellaneous poems. The occurrence of Herbert's poem in the volume is singular. I have seen a copy in which the first line of the title contained " R. P." only, which probably indicates an early issue.

23. **V[erneuil],** I[ohn].   A | Nomenclator | of such Tracts and | Sermons as have beene | printed or translated into | English upon any place | of holy Scripture | [*woodcuts*, then *line*] | *Operâ, studio & impensis* | I. V. | [*line, woodcut, line*.]

Impr. 119: 1637: (twelves) 16°: pp. [156], signn. A-F¹² G⁶: sign. B1ʳ beg. *Ruth. Cap.* 4: Long Primer Roman.   Contents: —sign. A1ʳ, title: A2ʳ-3ᵛ " To the courteous and judicoius Reader," unsigned: A4ʳ-G5ʳ, the work; G⁶, not seen.

See Wood's *Ath. Oxon.*, ed. Bliss, iii. 222. The second edition of this work was issued, doubled in size, in 1642. The author was under-librarian at the Bodleian, and had compiled this list for private use: nearly all the books referred to in the work have their Bodleian references affixed, the arrangement being in the order of the books of the Bible, the Apocrypha being excluded. The fact that some of the books were not in the library "stirred up some well-wishers ... who deprived themselves to furnish this Place with some bookes that were wanting" (*Preface of 2nd edition*), among whom was Robert Burton.

24. **Whear,** Degory.   RELECTIONES | HYEMALES, | DE RATIONE | & Methodo legendi | *utrasq*; *Historias,* | CIVILES ET | ECCLESIASTICAS. | Quibus Historici probatissimi, non solùm | ordine quo sunt legendi catenatim recensentur, | sed doctorum etiam virorum de singulis judicia | subnectuntur. | *Nec non* | Vndè sig ulorum in Historia vel brevitas | dilatari, vel defectus suppleri, vel perplexitas | expediri; vel mutilationes deniq; temporum | injuriâ factæ resarciri possint, indicatur | [*line*] | à D. W. prælect. CAMDENIANO. | [*line*].

Impr. 164: 1637: (eights) 12°: pp. [32] + 285 + [5]: p. 11 beg. *dignos pronun-ciaret*, 201 *tiam minus*: Pica Roman. Contents:—p. (1) title, within a line: (3-10) dedication to the Vice-chancellor and Heads of Houses in the University of Oxford, dated " Ab aula Glocestrensi Kal. Iul. 1637 ", and signed " Degoreus Whear ": (11-32) " Relectionum Conspectus ": 1-20 " Antelogium," delivered 17 Oct. 1635: 21-285, the work, in three parts (45 + 5 + 7 sections).

See Wood's *Ath. Oxon.*, ed. Bliss, iii. 217 and 1625 W. This is really the 3rd edition. Some copies have impr. 165, instead of 164, omitting Forest's name.

25. **Wyberd**, John. synopsis | Anni Christi 1637. | *Sitè* | *Diarium Astronomicum, & Prog-*nosticon Astrologicum, & Me-*\teorologi-cum, ad annum primum* | *ab Intercalari.* 1637. | Contriving, besides the generall state of | the yeare, the daily disposition and inclination | of the aire, according to the severall positions | and configurations of the celestiall bodies. Also | the times of Conjunctions, greater and lesse; | and Aspects Lunar and mutuall. | Faithfully supputated according to Art, for the use | of those that are residing towards the end of the | 8 climate of the world; situate in the North-tem-\perate Zone: The Pole Artique surmounting the | Horizon 51 degrees 34 minutes. | [*line*] | *Per* Joannem Wyberdum. | Philophysicum, Astronomophilon. | [*line, motto, line.*]

Impr. 68 *d*: 1637: (eights) 16°: pp. [48], signn. A-C: sign. B1ʳ beg. *The Moone hath*: Long Primer Roman and English. Contents:—sign. A1ʳ, title, within a line and a border of woodcuts: A2ʳ-4ʳ prefatory notes, chronological and astrological: A4ᵛ-B8ʳ, the Calendar: B8ᵛ-C8ʳ, " A Prognostication " for each month.

Rare. This appears to be the first and last Almanac issued by Wyberd. See the note under *Booker*, above in this year. Besides the words underlined in the above title, the words " Oxford," and " famous Universitie. 1637.' in the imprint, are printed in red: as well as other words in the text of the book. There is an astrological woodcut of a man on sign. A 4ʳ.

1638.

1. **Achilles** Tatius. The Loves | of | clitophon | and | leucippe. | A most elegant History, written in | Greeke by Achilles Tatius: | And now Englished. | [*line, motto, line, woodcut, line.*]

Impr. 172: 1638: (eights) 12°: pp. [24] + 255 + [1]: p. 11 beg. *affaires, dis-traction*: English Roman. Contents:— p. (1) title: (2) verses " On the Frontispiece.": (3) an engraved title, see below : (5-6) " The Translator to the Reader ": (7-24) complimentary verses by friends of the translator, whose initials and Christian name are incidentally mentioned : 1-255, the book.

See Wood's *Fasti Oxon.*, ed. Bliss, i. 301. The translator of the Τὰ κατὰ Λευκίππην καὶ Κλειτοφῶντα was Anthony Hodges, of New College. Wood refers to an impression of this book in 1638 without the commendatory verses: this would be no doubt an early issue. The engraved title is a fine one by W. Marshall, in which the words of the ordinary title, with impr. 173, are on a shell held by two mermaids; behind is a storm-tossed ship with the two lovers on board and Cupid in the stern, with the city of " Alexandria " in the background. This title was probably intended to be printed on the second leaf of the first section: but as it is, the frontispiece is on an inserted leaf, and the true second leaf is torn out. This book seems to be still the only English translation of the romance, except that in Bohn's library.

2. **Bancroft**, John, bp. of Oxford.   ARTICLES | TO BE | ENQVIRED OF | WITHIN THE DIOCES OF | OXFORD, in the trienniall *Visi-|tation* of the Right Reverend Fa-|ther in God Iohn Lord Bi-|shop of OXFORD. | HELD | In the yeare of our LORD GOD 1638. in the | fourteenth yeare of the Reigne of our most | gracious Soveraign Lord, CHARLES | by the grace of GOD King of | great, *Brittaine France*, & | *Ireland*, Defender of | the Faith &c. | [*woodcut.*]

Impr. 152: 1638: sm. 4°: pp. [16], signn. A–B¹: sign. B1ʳ beg. *buried any:* Pica English. Contents:—p. sign. A1ʳ, | title: A2ʳ–A3ʳ, Oath, Charge and Direc-tions: A3ᵛ–B3ʳ, the Articles in two divi-sions: B3ᵛ, directions: B4, not seen.

3. **Burton**, Robert.   THE | Anatomy of | melancholy | [&c., exactly as 1628 B, being from the same plate with "fift" instead of "thirde," and different date.]

Impr. 70: 1638: (fours) folio: pp. [14] + 78 + [2] + 723 (after 218 are two unnumbered leaves) + [9]: pp. 11 beg. *judgement* and *in Germany*, 601 *sate up late:* English Roman. Contents:—ex-actly as in the 1632 edition, except that | the "Synopsis of the first partition" pre-cedes the poem "ad librum suum", the "analysis of the third partition" occupies pp. 399–401, and the partition extends to p. 723: while there is no colophon, there being no p. (10) at end.

See Wood's *Ath. Oxon.*, ed. Bliss, iii. 653 and 1621 B. There is a note before the *Errata* in which the author says that the book was begun to be printed not long before at Edinburgh "sed à typographis nostris illicò suppressa, Londini mox illorum cum venia protelata, Oxoniæ demum perfecta." Accordingly signn. A–X x are not Oxford printing, but presumably from Edinburgh type: at p. 347 begins Oxford printing, the prefatory matter being also Oxford work. It would appear that some Edinburgh printers began a reprint, that the Oxford printers interfered and suppressed it, that with their consent the part printed in Scotland was not destroyed but *protelata*, prolonged, given a further lease of life, at London, and finally brought to Oxford and completed. The woodcuts and details of printing point to the division being before p. 347. The signatures of the first sheet are *nil*, § 2, §, § 2, § 3, *nil* (l), not counting the engraved title which should occur between the first and second leaf.

4. **Bythner**, Victorinus.   [*line*] | לְשׁוֹן לִמּוּרִים | [*line*] | LINGUA ERUDITORUM. | *Hoc est*, | NOVA ET METHODICA | INSTITVTIO | Linguæ Sanctæ, | [*line*] | *Usui eorum* | Quibus *Fontes Israëlis* plenè | intelligere, & ex illis limpidissimas | aquas haurire, curæ cordique est, | accommo-data: | *.* | [*line*] | *Studio & Operâ* | VICTORINI BYTHNER. | [*line*.]

Impr. 183: 1638: (fours) 12°: pp. [8] + 224 + [2]: p. 11 beg. *discerpi*, 201 *locum ubi:* English Roman. Contents: —p. (1) title: (2) "Approbatio" by the Oxford Professor of Hebrew, and Impri-matur by the Vice-Chancellor: (3–4) Latin dedication to the dean and canons of Christ Church: (5) two Greek poems | on the book by Edw. Wirley, rector of St. Ebbe's, Oxford: (7) "Sceleton . . ." of the book, a plan of contents: (8) "Ad-monitio ad Lectorem": 1–224, the work in 11 chapters (120 rules), with an "Ap-pendix de Aramæismo . . .": (1) "Nomina authorum . . . ex quibus hæc Institutio est concinnata."

Rare. See Wood's *Ath. Oxon.*, ed. Bliss, iii. 675. This is the first edition, the second being published at Cambridge in 1645 (the author having moved thither when the Civil War broke out) and afterwards several times, separately or with the *Lyra Prophetica*, in London.   This is an advance on 1631 B.

5. **C[aussin]**, N[icolas].   *THE* | UNFORTUNATE | POLITIQUE, | First written in French | By C. N. | *Englished by* | G. P. | [*device.*]

Impr. 185 : 1638 : (eights) 16⁰ : pp. [8] + 218 + [4] : p. 11 beg. *rule, by,* 201 *selfe so* : English Roman.   Contents :— p. (1) title, within a border of woodcut ornaments : [3 7 "To the courteous and ingenious reader" : 1-218, the work, bearing as a second title "The Life of Herod."

This is a translation of the 4th book of the well-known *Cour Sainte* of Nicolas Caussin the Jesuit *d.* 1651 , entitled "De l'Impieté des Cours" or "Le Politique malheureux", omitting the first few words : and is in fact a biography of Herod the Great, with reflections on his conduct.   The translator gives no clue to his own name, but mentions the author as " the judicious and eloquent Caussinus."   The *Cour Sainte* (first issued in 1624) was translated as a whole into English in 1631 and into Italian, German, Spanish, and other languages, but this 4th part seems never to have been issued separately in French (in Italian 1634, &c.) : and this Oxford volume though not rare has escaped even the eye of Backer and his editor Sommervogel (1891), probably because concealed under initials.   Some copies have 1639 on the titlepage.

6. **Chillingworth**, William.   THE | RELIGION OF | PROTESTANTS | A SAFE VVAY | TO SALVATION. | OR | AN ANSVVER TO A | BOOKE ENTITLED | MERCY AND TRVTH, | Or, Charity maintain'd by | Catholiques, which pre-|tends to prove the | Contrary. | [*line*] | By WILLIAM CHILLINGWORTH Master | *of Arts of the University of* OXFORD. | [*line, motto, woodcuts.*]

Impr. 180 or 181 : 1638 : (fours) la. 8⁰ : pp. [32] + 413 + [3] : p. 11 beg. *vinced that they,* 411 *which remain* : English Roman.   Contents :—p. (1) title, within double lines : (3-7) epistle dedicatory to the king : (8) imprimatur by the Vice-chancellor and the two Theological Pro-fessors at Oxford, one dated 14 Oct. 1637 : (9-31) " The Preface to the author of Charity maintained [M. Wilson] with an answer to his pamphlet entituled a Direction to N. N." : 1-413, the book, which incorporates most of the text of the book answered : (1) Errata.

See Wood's *Ath. Oxon.*, ed. Bliss, iii. 91.   This book (which Wood erroneously states was issued in 1636, and which was republished in 1664, 1674, 1684, 1687, 1704, 1719, 1727, 1742, 1752, 1820, 1838, 1845, 1846), was the effect and cause of considerable controversy, Chillingworth having recently reverted from Roman Catholicism to Protestantism, and the form of the book being that of an answer to part 1 of M. Wilson's *Mercy and truth or Charity maintayn'd* (1634), itself an answer to Potter's *Want of Charity* (see 1633 P).   The controversy is well described in the Dict. of National Biography.   There was a suspicion that Wilson obtained advance copies of the sheets of this book as it went through the press, see Laud's History of the Chancellorship under the year, where are also given the archbishop's views about the advisability of Chillingworth answering the second part also of Wilson's book.   The present volume is headed " Part i." throughout.   The issue of this volume with an imprint showing that it was published in London is said to have some slight changes, but they are not easily to be found, and in general the two issues appear to be identical.   The description of the Errata and their cause shows that it was the custom, at least at Oxford, for authors to revise their proofs—which has been recently denied.

7. **C[roke]**, dr. Ch[arles].   A SAD | MEMORIALL | OF | HENRY CURWEN | ESQUIRE, THE MOST | WORTHY AND ONELY | CHILD OF Sʳ PATRICIUS | CURWEN Baronet of *War-*|*kington* in *Cum*|*berland,* | WHO WITH INFI-|NITE SORROW OF | all that knew him depar-|ted this life *August:* 21. | being Sunday: | 1636. | IN THE FOURTEENTH | yeare of

his age; and lyes in ¦terred in the Church of | *Amersham* in *Buc-*¦*king-* *hamshire.* | [*line.*]

Impr. 119: 1638: sm. 4°: pp. [8] + 32: p. 11 beg. *leeve that*: Great Primer Roman. Contents :—p. (1) title, within arched border: (3-4) dedication to sir Patricius and lady Curwen, signed "Ch. C.": (5) "The Author to the Reader": (7-8) not seen: 1-23, the sermon, on Job xiv. 2: 24-32, description of the funeral and copies of the verses upon the hearse.

Rare. See Wood's *Fasti Oxon.*, ed. Bliss, i. 424. Sir Patricius Curwen's son had been sent for tuition to the Rector of Amersham, dr. Croke, in whose house he died. The monument still exists at Amersham, and is described in Lipscomb's *Buckinghamshire*, iii. 169: the burial was on 23 Aug. 1636. The preface explains that "these papers have lien two years in Cumberland in a Manuscript, which privacie not satisfying the great affection of Noble Parents towards their deceased Son, they are now come to . . . view". The ten copies of verses are in Latin and English, the most considerable being "a Dialogue" in verse by Paul Solomeaux a Frenchman.

8. **Florus,** Lucius Julius.　　L. JULII FLORI | rerum à | ROMANIS | GESTARVM | LIBRI IV, | A JOHANNE STADIO *emendati.* | *Editio nova singulis Neotericis purgatior* | *& emendatior.* | SEORSUM EXCVSUS | IN EOS COMMENTARIUS | JOHAN: STADII, Historiæ & Ma-¦theseos Lovanii Professoris primi, | elaboratissimus: | Cui accesserunt Chronologicæ Doctiss: | CLAUD: SALMASII excerptiones. | Unà cum variis lectionibus ex notis *Gruteri,* | *Salmasii, Vineti,* & editionibus, colle-¦ctis; & cum hâc nostrâ collatis: | *Sub calce prodit* L. Ampelii *Liber Memorialis ex* | *Clariss: Salmasii bibliotheca petitus.* | Cum Indice Rerum & Verborum | uberrimo. | [two *lines.*]

Impr. 121: 1638: (twelves' 16°: pp. [4] + 137 + [1] + 319 + [123] + 31 + [1]: pp. 11 begg. *immortalium, rum pleb.,* *quem Carthaginienses*: Long Primer Roman. Contents :—p. (1) title: (3-4) "Typographus Lectori": 1, a title precisely as 1631 F, except that all V's are now U's, I's consonantal are J's, and ij's are ii's, and in ll. 7 8 "*purgatior* | *&* emendatior*", with impr. 72 *a*: 3-137, (1), 1-319, (1-35) are also precisely as in 1631 F, the titlepage on p. 2 differing slightly in minute points: (36-67) the Excerptiones, with Epilogus: (68-115) "Ad Florum variarum lectionum libel-lus": (116-123), 1-31 "Lucius Ampelius ex bibliotheca Cl. Salmasii", with preface.

This is a reprint of 1631 F, with additions shown on the titlepage. The underlined words are in red, as well as "Oxoniæ," in the imprint.

9. **Gardyner,** dr. Richard.　　A | SERMON | PREACH'D IN | THE CATHEDRALL | CHVRCH OF CHRIST | *IN OXFORD,* | On CHRISTMAS Day: | Wherein is defended the Catholique | Doctrine that Christ is True | God Truely Incarnate. | *AGAINST THE OLDE DE-*¦*cay'd Heresies newely* *Reviu'd in* | *these later Dayes.* | [*line*] | BY | RICHARD GARDYNER, D.D. And | *Canon* of the same *Church.* | [*line.*]

Impr. 175: 1638: sm. 4°: pp. [8] + 31 + [1]: p. 11 beg. *pable to save*: Great Primer Roman. Contents :—p. (3) title, within a line: (5-8) dedication to dr. Duppa dean of Ch. Ch.: 1-31, the sermon, on John i. 14.

See Wood's *Ath. Oxon.*, ed. Bliss, iii. 921.

10. ———.   *A SERMON* | PREACH'D | ON EASTER-DAY | AT OXFORD, IN SAINT | PETERS CHVRCH IN THE | EAST, the Accustomed place for the | REHEARSALL SERMON on | THAT DAY: | Wherein is prov'd the SONNE'S | Equality with the FATHER, the | *Deity of the Holy GHOST,* | AND | The Resurrection of the same Numericall Body, | *Against the old, and Recent Oppugners of* | *these* Sacred Verities. | [*line*] | BY | RICHARD GARDYNER, D.D. and Canon of | the Cathedrall Church of Christ in OXFORD. | [*line.*]

Impr. 174: 1638: sm. 4°: pp. [8] + 31 + [1]: p. 11 beg. *the vertue*: Great Primer Roman. Contents:—p. (1) title, within | a line: (3-7) Epistle dedicatory to dr. Richard Baylie: 1-31, the sermon, on Rom. viii. 11.

See Wood's *Ath. Oxon.*, ed. Bliss. iii. 921.

11. Godwyn, Thomas.   ROMANÆ | HISTORIAE | ANTHOLOGIA | [&c., exactly as 1633 G, except in line 9 "&" for "and," "use," and "inlarged by | *the Author*."]

Impr. 182: 1638: sm. 4°: [collation, contents &c. precisely as 1633 G, except | signature of dedication "Tho:" not "Tho."]

See 1614 G. This appears to be an absolute reprint of the 1633 edition.

12. Jackson, dr. Thomas.   A | TREATISE | OF THE CONSECRATION | OF THE SONNE OF | God to his everlasting | PRIESTHOOD. | AND | THE ACCOMPLISHMENT | of it by his glorious Resurrection | *and Ascension.* | BEING THE NINTH BOOK | of Commentaries upon the | Apostles CREED. | CONTINVED BY | THOMAS IACKSON Doctor in | Divinity, Chaplaine in ordinary to | his MAIESTY, and President of | C. C. C. in OXFORD. | [*line.*]

Impr. 180 a: 1638: sm. 4°: pp. [24] + 352 + [4]: p. 11 beg. *the wages*, 301 *10.36. This*: English Roman. Contents: —p. (1) title, within double lines: (3-7) Epistle dedicatory to the King: (9-11) | "To the Christian Reader": (13-22) "A table of the principall Arguments . . .", a list of contents: (23) "Errata": 1-352, (1-3), the treatise, in 43 chapters.

See Wood's *Ath. Oxon.*, ii. 667. Ten books of Jackson's Commentary on the Creed were published in 1613–1654, this being the 9th and the last issued in the author's lifetime, he dying in 1640. This part was published (according to Wood) in 1628 and 1633 in London, and now in Oxford. Every page is within lines.

13. Longinus, Dionysius.   ΔΙΟΝΥΣΙΟΥ | ΛΟΓΓΙΝΟΥ | [&c., from the same plate as 1636 L, except that a new line is added at end "Cum Indice", the imprint and date are altered, and at the foot outside the bounding line is "*editio Postrema.*"]

Impr. 87 a: 1638: [&c. precisely as 1636 L., except that the page following 117 bears in addition "Errata . . .", and a new "Index rerum et verborum" is appended on 14 pages (the last of which | adds "Imprimatur. *Ric. Baylie Vice-canc. Oxon.*"), and 4 blank pages follow: so that the collation is pp. [42] + 176 + [2] + 117 + [19] and one folded plate.]

See Wood's *Ath. Oxon.*, ed. Bliss, iii. 446. This is a reissue of the sheets of 1636 L with the changes noted above. Some copies omit the preface by Langbaine and with it the blank sheet before the inserted (engraved) title. Conversely there are copies of this edition with the 1636 title and no ornament at the back of the folded plate.

14. **Matthew**, archbp. Tobias.   PIISSIMI | ET | EMINENTISSIMI |
VIRI, D. TOBIÆ | MATTHÆI *Archiepis-|copi* olim *Eboracensis* | CONCIO APO-|
logetica adversus | Campianum. | [*motto,* then *woodcuts.*]

Impr. 176: 1638: (twelves) 16°: pp.
[10] + 86: p. 11 beg *ducens qui*: Pica
Roman.   Contents:—p. (1) title, within
a line doubled at the sides: (3) "Campiani

Calumnia . . . quam D. Tobias Matthæus
hac suâ Concione depellit": (4–9) Testimonia about the sermon and author: 1–
86, the sermon, on Deut. xxxii. 7.

See Wood's *Ath. Oxon.*, ed. Bliss, ii. 871, but the incident which was the occasion
of the sermon is related on col. 870. Matthew died on 29 Mar. 1628, and this sermon
was intended to disprove Campian's statement that Matthew practically confessed that
if one read and believed the fathers he would become a Papist. The sermon was
originally delivered at Oxford on 9 Oct. 1581, but this is certainly the first printed
edition.

15. **Oxford**, Christ Church.   DEATH REPEAL'D | BY A | THANKFVLL.
MEMORIALL | Sent from CHRIST-CHURCH | in OXFORD, | *CELEBRATING* |
THE NOBLE DESERTS OF | the Right Honourable, | PAVLE, | Late Lord
VIS-COUNT | BAYNING | of SUDBURY. | Who changed his Earthly Honours |
Iune the 11. 1638. | [*woodcuts.*]

Impr. 174: 1638: sm. 4°: pp. [4] +
50 ("42") + [2]: p. 11 beg. *We may
believe*: English Roman.   Contents:—

p. (1) title, within double lines: (3–4)
dedication to lady Penelope widow of
viscount Bayning: 1–"42", the poems.

See Wood's *Fasti Oxon.*, ed. Bliss, i. 468. These poems on lord Bayning's death
at Bentley hall in Essex are all by Christ Church men, 19 in English, 11 in Latin.
William Cartwright, Robert Burton, John Fell, Martin Llewellin and Jasper Mayne
are among the writers. Lord Bayning took his degree from Christ Church in 1633, but
was only 24 years old at his death, when the title became extinct.

16. **Oxford**, University.   *Musarum Oxoniensium* | CHARISTERIA |
PRO | SERENISSIMA | *REGINA* | MARIA, | RECENS | E NIXVS LABORIOSI |
discrimine receptâ. | [*woodcut.*]

Impr. 151 *b*: 1638: sm. 4°: pp. [88],
signn. A-D, DD, E, a-b, bb, c-d¹: sign.
B1ʳ beg. *Qui primos*: English Roman.

Contents:—sign. A1ʳ title, within double
lines: A2ʳ–d4ᵛ, poems.

These are verses to congratulate the Queen on her safe delivery and condole with
her for the loss of the infant princess, who seems to have lived only a few hours. The
reference is apparently to the birth of the princess Catherine (*b.* and *d.* 29 Jan. 1638),
but the ordinary pedigrees and histories seem not to notice this event. The poems are
in Latin and English, except three Greek and two French. The printer (Lichfield)
contributes a poem at the end. The signatures show the hasty method of printing.

17. ——.   STATVTA | *Selecta è Corpore* | *Statutorum* | VNIVERSI-
TATIS | OXON, | *Vt in promptu & ad ma-*|num sint, quæ magis ad usum, |
(*præcipuè Iuniorum*) | facere videntur: | [*line,* then *woodcut,* then *line.*]

Impr. 179: 1638: (eights) 16°: pp.
[8] + 213 + [15], and two folding plates:
p. 11 beg. *libros de Cælo*, 201 *non priùs*:
Pica Roman. Contents:—p. (3) title,
within a border: (5-7) "Admonitio ad
lectorem de veteri Calendario omisso",
with a table of "Non Dis." days: (8)

Explanation of symbols used: 1–197, the
statutes: 198-205, "Statuta Bibliothecæ
Bodleianæ . . . 1620": 207-213, "Em-
vomis: seu explanatio Iuramenti . . . ":
(2-3), not seen: (4-12) "Elenchus Ma-
teriarum": (14) "Errata . . . ".

This is the first edition of the selected Statutes, the beginning of a long series, and was compiled by Thomas Crossfield of Queen's College. Other editions were issued in 1661, and with the title "Parecbolæ" in 1671, 1674, 1682, 1693, 1705, 1710, 1721, 1729, 1740, 1756, 1771, 1784. 1794, 1808, 1815, 1820, 1828, 1830, 1835, 1838, 1840, 1841, 1842, 1843, 1845, 1846, and no doubt in some other years, especially after 1830: the book was in fact reprinted whenever the stock in hand was exhausted. Wharton's *Second Volume of the Remains of . . . William Laud . . .*, under the date, proves that it was issued in Jan. 163¾. A small folded sheet "Indiculus Statutorum", a plan of them arranged by subjects and bearing the signature A2, should follow the titlepage, and in some copies the large *Encyclopædia*, described in 1635 O, is inserted to face p. 16 or 20: but the book can hardly be pronounced imperfect, if this plate is wanting. The signatures of the prefatory matter are peculiar: the first two leaves (blank, and title) form a section of themselves, and also the next two, not counting the folded leaf, and this even in large paper copies. So too sign. *q* is divided into two sets of two and four leaves respectively! The 4th leaf of P is presumably blank and perhaps always torn off. The underlined words in the above title are printed in red, as well as " Excusa cum Licentiâ," and " pro Guil: Webb," in the imprint.

18. **Ranchinus**, Gulielmus.   A | REVIEW | OF THE | COVNCELL | OF | TRENT. | VVherein are contained the severall | nullities of it: With the many grievan-|ces and prejudices done by it to Christian | Kings and Princes: | As also to all Catholique Churches in the | World; and more particularly to the | GALLICANE Church. | [two *lines*] | First writ in *French* by a learned *Roman*-Catholique. | Now | *Translated into* English *by* G. L. | [two *lines* before, between and after a *motto* and *woodcut*.]

Impr. 177: 1638: (fours) la. 8°: pp. [28] + 388: p. 11 beg. *sider these*, 301 *to determine*: Pica Roman. Contents:— (1) title, within double line: (3–4) dedication to dr. Christopher Potter, by Gerard Langbaine the translator, dated " Queenes Colledge in Oxford April 12. 1638: (5– 10) "To the Reader" by the translator: (11–12) "An Advertisement to the Reader... " by the anonymous author: (13–26) "A summary of the Chapters ": (27) "Faults escaped ": 1–388, the work, in seven books.

See Wood's *Ath. Oxon.*, ed. Bliss, iii. 448. The author's name occurs in Langbaine's Preface. Ranchin's *Revision du Concil de Trente* was published anonymously in 1600.

19. **Randolph**, Thomas.   POEMS | WITH THE | MVSES | LOOKING-GLASSE: | AND | AMYNTAS· | [*line*] | By THOMAS RANDOLPH Master of Arts, | and late Fellow of *Trinity* Colledge in | *Cambridge.* | [*line*, then device.]

Impr. 174: 1638: sm. 4°: pp. [24] + 128 + [2] + 93 + [7] + 114: pp. 11 beg. *Went forth, shall see* and *For to be*: English Roman. Contents:—p. (1) title, within a line double at the sides: (3–24) poems on the author and book: 1–128, the poems: (1) a title :—" [*woodcut*] | THE MVSES | LOOKING-GLASSE. | [*line*] | By T. R. | [*line*, then *woodcut*] ", with impr. 184: 1–93. the play, in five acts: (2' a title :— "[two *lines*] | AMYNTAS | OR THE | IMPOSSIBLE DOVVRY. | A PASTORALL ACTED | before the KING & QUEENE | at *White-Hall.* | [*line*] | Written by THOMAS RANDOLPH. | [*line*, *motto*, *woodcut*] ", with impr. 184: (4) "Drammatis Personæ ": (6–7), 1–114, the play in five acts.

Rare. See Wood's *Ath. Oxon.*, ed. Bliss, i. 565, and the *Retrospective Review* vi. 61. The volume was posthumous (the author having died in March 163¾) and was edited by his brother Robert Randolph of Christ Church, Oxford. There are twelve sets of complimentary verses, in Latin and English, by the editor, Owen Feltham, and others. Editions of the poems and plays were published in 1640 (Oxford), 1643 (London), 1652 (London), 1664 (London) and 1668 (Oxford): both the last call themselves the 5th edition. The signatures run through the entire work.

20. Reusner, Nicolas.   NICOLAI REUSNERI LEORINI | IC. Comitis
Palat. Cæs. | SYMBOLORVM | IMPERATORIORUM | Classis Prima. | [&c.,
exactly as 1633 R, except "Impp:", "*Julio*", "OPUS PHILOLOGICUM,"
"utile," and "*SEXTA*" for "*QUINTA*"].

Impr. 137 : 1638: [&c. exactly as 1633 R, contents and all, except that the 3rd part contains 224 numbered pages, the last *not* being misprinted "198" as it is in the 5th edition : also the 3rd p. 11 begins "*Nam & secundùm*": the second and third titles differ slightly in small details. The number of unnumbered pages at the end of the 3rd part are 36, and the "34" in the collation of 1633 R is an error for 36: the four last leaves in each edition are blank.]

This is simply a verbatim reprint of 1633 R.

21. Scheiblerus, Christophorus.   . . . | METAPHYSICA | [precisely
as 1637 S, except as there noted].

Impr. 178: 1638 [&c. exactly as 1637 S, except as there noted].

This is a reissue of 1637 S.

22. Smiglecius, Martinus.   LOGICA | MARTINI | SMIGLECII | SO-
CIETATIS IESV | S: THEOLOGIÆ | DOCTORIS, | SELECTIS DISPVTATIO-|nibus &
quæstionibus illustrata, | ET IN DVOS TOMOS DISTRIBVTA : | In qua | Quic-
quid in *Aristotelico* organo vel | cognitu necessarium, vel obscuritate
perple-|xum, tam clarè & perspicuè, quàm so-|lidè ac nervosè pertractatur. |
| [*line*] | *Cum* INDICE *Rerum copioso.* | [*line*] | AD | Perillustrem ac Mag-
nificum Dominum, | Dᵐ THOMAM ZAMOYSCIUM, &c. |

Impr. 162*a*: 1638: (eights) sm. 4°: pp. [16] + 435 + [3] + "435" — "761" + [35]: p. 11 beg. *Dico igitur*, 701 *Non tamen*: Long Primer Roman. Contents: —p. (1) title, within double lines : (3-6) Epistola dedicatoria to Thomas Zamoyscius, dated "Calissii in Collegio Carne-coviano Societatis Jesu, 15. Augusti 1616 ": (6) "Approbatio R. P. Provincialis," 24 June 1616 : (7-11) "Index disputationum et quæstionum prima parte Contentarum ", a list : (12-16) "Index . . . partis secundæ": 1-435. "Pars prima logicæ . . .", disputations 1-11 : (2) a bastard title :—"Logicæ . . . pars altera . . .": 435—761, the second part, dispp. 12-18 : (2-35) "Index rerum præcipuarum . . .".

See 1634 S: this is a verbatim reprint of that edition.

23. Taylor, bp. Jeremy.   A | SERMON | PREACHED IN | SAINT
MARIES | Church in OXFORD. | Vpon the Anniversary of the | GUNPOWDER-
TREASON. | [*line*] | By IEREMY TAYLOR, Fellow of | *Allsoules Colledge in*
OXFORD. | [*line, motto, woodcut.*]

Impr. 180: 1638: sm. 4°: pp. [10] + 64: p. 11 beg. *third time*: English Roman. Contents: p. (1) title, within double lines : (3-10) dedication to archbp. Laud : 1-64, the sermon, on Luke ix. 54.

See Wood's *Ath. Oxon.*, ed. Bliss, iii. 787. This sermon, which seems to have been delivered on Nov. 5, 1638, dashed the hopes which the Roman Catholics seem to have entertained of the conversion of Taylor to their faith. Wood asserts (*ut supra*, 782) that "several things were put in[to the sermon] against the Papists by the then vice-chanc.", dr. Accepted Frewen. The sheets of this work were reissued as part of Taylor's *Treatises* (Lond. 1648).

24. *Thornburgh, Edward, archdeacon of Worcester.   ARTICLES

TO BE ENQVIRED | OF AND ANSWERED | unto by the Church-wardens and | Sworne-men within the *Arch-Dea-*|conrie of *Worcester* in the Visitation | of the Right worshipfull *Edward* | *Thornburgh* D^r of Divini-|ty Arch--| Deacon of | *Worcester.* | *Anno Domini* | [*line, woodcut, line.*]

Impr. 152: no date: sm. 4°: pp. [16], signn. A–B⁴: sign. B1ʳ beg. 16. *Hath your*: Pica English. Contents:—sign. A1ʳ, a form of summons to appear: A2ʳ, the title: A2ᵛ–3ʳ, Directions and Oath: A4ʳ–B4ᵛ, the 86 articles.

This is not dated, but the copy seen bore a summons to Stratford-on-Avon officials, filled up with the date 11 Apr. 1638. It could not be earlier than 1635 from the woodcut ornaments used and the printer, and is probably of the year 1638.

25. Valdés, Juan de. THE HUNDRED AND TEN | CONSIDERATIONS | of *SIGNIOR* | IOHN VALDESSO: | TREATING OF THOSE | things which are most profitable, most | necessary, and most perfect in our | Christian Profession. | WRITTEN IN SPANISH, | Brought out of Italy by *Vergerius,* and | first set forth in Italian at *Basil* by | *Cælius Secundus Curio,* | ANNO 1550. | Afterward translated into French, and Printed | at *Lions* 1563. and again at Paris 1565. | And now translated out of the Italian | Copy into English, with notes. | Whereunto is added an Epistle of the Authors, | or a Preface to his Divine Commentary | *upon the Romans.* | [*motto.*]

Impr. 180: 1638: sm. 4°: pp. [32] + 311 + [13]: p. 11 beg. *Consid. V,* 301 *the Heavens*: Pica Roman. Contents:—p. (1) title, within a line: (3–4) "The Publisher to the Reader": (5–13) "Brief notes relating to the dubious and offensive places . . .": (14–19) the preface of Curio (Basil. 1 May 1550): (20–28) "A Table of the . . . Considerations": (30) A "cen-sure" of the book, or imprimatur, by Thomas Jackson president of Corpus Christi College, Oxford : (31–2) "A copy of a letter written by Mr. George Herbert to his friend the Translator of this Book" dated "Bemmorton Sept. 29", 1637: 1–311,the Considerations: (1–11) the Epistle: (12) "Errata".

This translation of Juan de Valdés' work from the Italian is by Nicholas Ferrar of Little Gidding (*d.* 4 Dec. 1637), and it is interesting to find that there is a copy of this book in Little Gidding binding (Quaritch's General Catalogue of Books, vol. i. (1887), no. 5929: £4). There was an edition issued at Cambridge in 1646.

1639.

Bacon, sir Francis. Of the advancement and proficience of learning: see 1640 B.

1. Balzac, Jean Louis Guez de. A | COLLECTION | OF SOME MODERN | EPISTLES | *OF MONSIEVR* | DE BALZAC. | CAREFVLLY | TRANSLATED OUT | *OF FRENCH.* | [*line*] | *Being the Fourth and last Volume.* | [*line, motto, woodcuts.*]

Impr. 184: 1639: (eights) 12°: pp. [48] + 249 + [9]: p. 11 beg. *Let. III,* 201 *there is no*: Great Primer Roman. Contents:—p. (1) engraved title, see below: (3) title, within double lines: (5–11) "To the Reader", signed "F. B.", the printer F. Bowman: (13–15) "An advertisement of Mons. the King": (17–47) letters, a poem &c, see below: 1–249, the letters: (2–5) "A table of the letters".

The first three parts of Balzac's Letters were printed at London in 1634 (part 1, translated by William Tyrwhitt) and 1638 (parts 2 and 3, translated by sir Richard Baker). The present volume is a venture by the printer, who has prefixed some letters, papers, and a Latin poem all connected with the quarrel between Balzac and the Jesuit Franciscus Garassus, in which Louis xiii intervened as a conciliator. There is an engraved title by W. Marshall, in which kings and theologians do honour to Balzac, the title being " A new collection of Epistles of Mons : de Balzac, being the fourth and last volume. Newly translated", with impr. 192. The range of Balzac's letters is from 1631 to 1637.

2. **Bird,** John.　　GROUNDS OF | GRAMMER | PENNED AND | *PVBLISHED.* | [*line*] | By | IOHN BIRD Schoolemaster | *in the Citty of Gloecster.* | [*line,* Greek *motto, woodcuts.*]

Impr. 180 : 1639 : (eights) 16° : pp. [8] + 184 : p. 11 beg. *being the,* 101 *Adjectivall* : Long Primer Roman. Contents : —p. (1) title, within double lines : (3–5) dedication to archbp. Laud : (6-8) " To the Reader " : 1–184, the work.

See Wood's *Fasti Oxon.,* ed. Bliss, i. 411 ; but nothing seems to be known of the author at present. The book is a Latin grammar in English, for the use of which latter language the author excuses himself. The sheets of this work, omitting the prefatory matter and with a different style of title and imprint, were reissued at Oxford in 1641. The author divides grammar into Rudiment (grammar proper, divided into Elementary and Accidentary) and Regiment (syntax).

3. [**Cartwright,** William].　　THE | ROYALL | SLAVE. | *A* | Tragi-Comedy. | Presented to the King and Queene | by the Students of *Christ-Church* | in Oxford. *August* 30. 1636. | Presented since to both their Ma-|jesties at *Hampton-Court* by the | Kings Servants. | [two *lines.*]

Impr. 189 : 1639 : sm. 4° : pp. [68], signn. A-11⁴ 1² : sign. C1ʳ beg. *The grand contrivance* : Pica Roman. Contents :— sign. A1ʳ, title : A2ʳ, " The Prologue to the King and Queene " : A2ᵛ–3ʳ, " The Prologue to the Vniversity " : A3ᵛ, " The Prologue to their Majesties at Hampton-Court " : A4ʳ, " The Persons of the Play " : B1ʳ–H4ᵛ, the play : 11ʳ–2ʳ, three epilogues corresponding to the prologues.

See Wood's *Ath. Oxon.,* ed. Bliss, iii. 69, and 1640 C. Cartwright's poems and plays were published together in 1651, the author having died in 1643. The scene of this play is laid at Sardis. An account of the performance at Christ Church, at which the scenic arrangements seem to have been very elaborate, will be found in Wood's *Annals* under the year 1636.

4. **C**[aussin], N[icolas].　　The unfortunate politique : see 1638 C.

5. **Dugres,** Gabriel.　　DIALOGI | GALLICO-ANGLICO-LATINI. | PER | GABRIELEM DVGRES | LINGUAM GALLICAM IN | *ILLVSTRISSIMA ET* | FAMO-SISSIMA, OXONIENSI | ACADEMIA Edocentem. ' [*woodcut.*]

Impr. 186 : (eights) 12° : pp. [8] + 195 + [1] : p. 11 beg. *Commençons,* 101 *P. II fera* : Long Primer Roman. Contents :— p. (3) title, within a line : (5–7) French dedication to Charles prince of Wales : 1–195, the 22 dialogues in French, English (central in the page) and Latin.

See Wood's *Ath. Oxon.,* ed. Bliss, iii. 184. Dugres or Du Gres had already issued a French grammar at Cambridge in 1636, and new editions of his Dialogues, with rules of pronunciation and tables of verbs, were published at Oxford in 1652 and 1660.

6. **Foxle**, George.   THE | GROANES | OF THE | SPIRIT, | OR | THE | TRIALL. | of the Truth of | PRAYER. | [*motto, line, motto, line.*]

Impr. 187 or 188 : 1639 : (twelves) 16° : pp. [16] + 228 + [6] : p. 11 beg. *mired, but,* 101 *the sight* : English Roman. Contents :—p. (1) title, within border of woodcuts : (3–9) Epistle dedicatory "to the noble and much honoured Company of Hierusalem's Artillery", signed "George Foxle" : (10–14) "To the Reader", also signed : (15) " The contents . . . " : 1–228, the treatise.

A (George ?) Foxley is mentioned in Wood's *Ath. Oxon.*, ed. Bliss, iv. 137, as preaching in London in Jan. 164⅘. Copies of this treatise differ in the imprint, showing that it was published both at Leicester and Bristol. Each page is within lines, doubled at the top and outer side.

7. **Fromondus**, Libertus.   LIBERTI FROMONDI | S. TH. L. | *Collegii Falconis in Academia | Lovaniensi Philosophiæ Profes-soris Primarii* | METEOROLOGICORVM | LIBRI SEX. | [*device.*]

Impr. 190 : 1639 : (eights) 12° : pp. [16] + 505 + [23] : p. 11 beg. *nubem è Zona,* 401 *Multa generosa* : Long Primer Roman. Contents :—p. (1) " A " : (3) title : (5–10) dedication to Maximilian de Rassenghem, Lovanii, 1 Jan. 1627 : (11–15) " Ad Lectorem " : 1–505, the work, in 6 books : (2–8) " Index capitum et articulorum " in the order of the book : (10–22) " Index rerum memorabilium ", alphabetical.

This is a reprint of the 1627 or 1631 Antwerp edition, being itself the third. The scope of the work may be gathered from the definition of "Meteora" as being phenomena produced by vapour (rain, &c.), or by exhalation (fiery, as lightning and falling stars : or non-fiery, as winds), or by both (clouds). Fromondus lived from 1587 to 1654, chiefly at Louvain.

8. **Gardyner**, dr. Richard.   A | SERMON | CONCERNING | THE | EPIPHANY. | PREACHED AT THE | Cathedrall Church of Christ | in *Oxford.* | By RICHARD GARDYNER, D.D. | and *Canon* of the same | *Church.* | [*woodcut.*]

Impr. 193 : 1639 : sm. 4° : pp. [8] + 31 + [1] : p. 11 beg. *What right* : Great Primer Roman. Contents :—pp. (1–2), not seen : p. (3) title, within a border of woodcuts : (5–8) dedication to bp. John Bancroft : 1–31, the sermon, on Matth. ii. 2.

See Wood's *Ath. Oxon.*, ed. Bliss, iii. 921. The dedication mentions that the bishop had built the old palace at Cuddesdon, reformed the altars throughout his diocese, and suitably inscribed the Cathedral communion plate. Sign. A4ᵛ is paged 28 by error.

9. **Greaves**, Thomas (Gravius).   DE LINGVÆ | ARABICÆ | VTILITATE | ET PRÆSTANTIA | *Oratio* OXONII *habita* | Iul. 19. 1637. | A | THOMA GREAVES Coll. Corp. | *Christi Socio.* | Cum | Arabicam Lecturam à Reverendissimo | *Patre ac Domino* GVLIELMO | Archiepiscopo Cantuariensi & Academiæ | CANCELLARIO *Oxonij institutam* | loco absentis Professoris auspicaretur. | [*woodcut.*]

Impr. 151 : 1639 : sm. 4° : pp. [4] + 21 + [3] : p. 11 beg. *brarint. Innumera* : Great Primer Roman. Contents :—p. (1) title, within a line : (3) " Lectori . . . " : 1–21, the speech.

See Wood's *Ath. Oxon.*, ed. Bliss, iii. 1061. The speech mentions Laud's benefactions to the Bodleian. The absent professor was dr. Edward Pococke. Some copies have imprint 176.

10. **Grotius**, Hugo. De veritate religionis Christianæ.

Both in the 3rd and 4th part of Richard Davis's auction sale catalogue (3rd part (1688), p. 12, no. 550: 4th part (1692), p. 18, no. 323) an Oxford edition of 1639 is mentioned; as well as in Ersch and Gruber's Encyclopædia: but the edition itself is not in the greater libraries and ordinary bibliographies. The first edition was in Dutch in 1722, the Latin editions before 1639 were all published at Leyden in 1624, 1627, 1629, 1633 and 1637. There are Oxford editions of 1660 and 1662, as well as later.

11. **Heylyn**, Peter. ΜΙΚΡΟ΄ΚΟΣΜΟΣ | A | LITTLE DE-'SCRIPTION OF | THE GREAT WORLD. | [*line*] | *By* PETER HEYLYN. | [*line, motto, device.*]

Imp. 119: 1639: (eights) sm. 4°: pp. [20] + 808 + [4]: p. 11 beg. *1. First then, 701 duls, or l'indelici*: Pica Roman. Contents:—[as 1631 H, with a few minute differences of spelling or use of capitals, and a slight change of reference (only) to the last five pages.]

For the author and book see Wood's *Ath. Oxon.*, ed. Bliss, iii. 557: see also 1621 H. Some copies of this work have "1939" on the titlepage. There should be a folded leaf after p. 228 as in former editions.

12. **Hommius**, Festus. LXX. | dispvtatio-|nes theologicæ; | [&c., precisely as 1630 H, with "*tertia*" for "*secunda*", and the j in *adjectionibus* rightly italic.]

Impr. 72 *a*: 1639: [&c. exactly as 1630 H.]

This is a verbatim reprint of the 1630 edition.

13. **Hungerford**, sir Anthony. *THE* | ADVISE OF | A SONNE PRO-| FESSING THE RELI-'GION ESTABLISHED | in the present Church of Eng-|*land to his deare Mother a* | Roman Catholike. | *VVHEREVNTO IS ADDED* | THE MEMORIAL OF A FATHER | to his deare children, containing an | acknowledgement of God his great mercy, in | bringing him to the *Profession* of the true | *Religion, at this present established* | *in the Church of England.* | [*line*] BY | ANTH. HVNGERFORD of Blackbourton | in *Com. Oxon. KNIGHT.* | [*line.*]

Impr. 182: 1639: sm. 4°: pp. [2] + 62: p. 11 beg. *answer, that he*: English Roman. Contents:—p. (1) title, within a border of woodcuts: 1–38, the Advice: 39–40, a preface to the following piece, dated "From my house at Blackbourton this 7th of Aprill 1627": 41–62, the Memorial.

See Wood's *Ath. Oxon.*, ed. Bliss, ii. 411, where Wood says that the first part was written in about 1607, and that the writer died in June 1627: that Laud refused to license it for printing in 1635, because it was so strongly worded against Roman Catholicism, and that after this failure the son, sir Edward Hungerford, "got it to be printed at Oxon", with the Memorial.

14. **Jewell**, bp. John. APOLOGIA | ECCLESIÆ | ANGLICANÆ. | [*line*] | Auctore JOANNE JUELLO, | olim Episcopo Sarisburiensi. | [*line*] | Cum Versione Græca *J. S.* Bacc. in Art. | Coll. Mag. quondam Socii. | [*motto, then woodcut.*]

Impr. 153: 1639: (eights) 16°: pp. [12] + 331 + [1]: p. 11 beg. τῷ ἐξαιτεῖσθαι, 301 Θεῖος λόγος: Pica Roman. Contents:—p. (1) title: (3-4) Epistola P. Martyris, to Jewel: (5-11) the translator's dedication to dr. William Langton, president of Magdalen, signed "Joh. Smith": (1) a poor Greek epigram on this edition, signed "H. H.": 2-331, the work, Latin on the verso of each leaf, Greek on the recto.

See 1614 J: the first English and Latin editions were in 1562. It is odd that in the *Catalogus . . . librorum Richardi Davis . . . pars tertia* (1688) on p. 13 the date of this book is twice misprinted 1637.

15. **Kempis,** Thomas a.   THE | IMITATION | OF CHRIST, | *Divided into four Books.* | Written in Latin by | THOMAS à KEMPIS, | And the Translations of it | *Corrected & amended* | by W. P. | [*woodcut.*]

Impr. 156 *b*: 1639: (twelves) 16°: pp. [60] + 381 + [15]: p. 11 beg. *26. In their life, 301 not to be discussed*: Long Primer Roman. Contents:—p. (1) title, within double lines: (3-8) Epistle dedi- catory to Walter Curle, bp. of Winchester, signed "William Page": (9-60) "To the Christian reader" signed "W. P.": 1-381, the Imitation, in 4 books: (2-11) "A Table of the chapters . . .".

See Wood's *Ath. Oxon.,* ed. Bliss, iii. 655. This is the first Oxford edition of the *Imitation* and the only edition of dr. Page's revision. The reviser, who was the bp. of Winchester's chaplain, has removed such passages as would offend a Protestant. The preface is largely an exhortation to unity among the churches.

16. [**Mayne,** Jasper].   THE | CITYE MATCH. | *A* | COMOEDYE· | PRESENTED TO THE | KING and QVEENE | *AT WHITE-HALL.* | ACTED SINCE | AT BLACK-FRIERS BY HIS | MAIESTIES *Servants.* | [*motto,* then 2 *lines.*]

Impr. 180: 1639: (twos) la. 8°: pp. [6] + 64 + [2]: p. 11 beg. *Scena II*: Great Primer Roman. Contents:—p. (1) title, within double lines: (3) "To the reader": (4-5) two prologues: (6) "The Persons of the Play" &c.: 1-64, the play: (1-2) two epilogues.

See Wood's *Ath. Oxon.,* ed. Bliss, iii. 972. There are subsequent editions of the play in 1658 (Oxford) and 1659 (Oxford). The preface is depreciatory of the work, stating that it was at first written "out of obedience," and that it was only published in self-defence to avoid a threatened unauthorized issue in London.

17. **Prayer,** book of Common.   LIBER | PSALMORVM | ET PRECVM | in usum Ecclesiæ | *Cath. Christi* | OXON. | [*woodcut.*]

Impr. 151: 1639: (twelves) 16°: pp. 295 + [1]: p. 11 beg. *Cesset quæso,* 201 *Ac tradidit*: Long Primer Roman. Con- tents:—1, title, within double lines: 3- 283, the Psalter: 285-295, special prayers, as in 1615 P.

See 1615 P. It is noticeable that the University no longer prints the book of Common Prayer as a whole, but only the Psalter as found in that book, separately.

18. **Prideaux,** John.   TABVLÆ | AD | GRAMMATICA | GRÆCA INTRO- DVCTORIÆ. | IN QVIBVS | Succinctè compingitur, brevissima, sed | *tamen expedita, singularum partium orationis* | *declinabilium, Variandi ratio.* | ACCESSIT | Vestibuli vice, ad eandem linguam παραίνεσις in | gratiam tyronum, quibus ut convenit explica-|tiora evolvere, ita necesse est hæc ipsa | *ad unguem tenere.* | [*motto*] | EDITIO TERTIA. | [*woodcuts.*]

Impr. 191 : 1639 : sm. 4° : pp. [68], signn. A–F4,G2,H–I4 : sign. H1v beg. *profero clarâ*, F2v *15. Asserit A* : Pica Roman. Contents :—sign. A1r, title : A2r–A2v, dedication to dr. Tho. Holland, dated "Exon. Colleg. Ian. 1. 1607", and signed "Io. Prideaux" : A3r–B3v, preface as in the 1607 edition : B4r E1r, the work, "Conclusio", &c., as before : E2r, a title :—"TYROCINIVM | AD SYLLOGISMVM | Legitimum contexendum, & | *captiosum dissuendum, ex-|peditissimum.* | IN QVO | *Ad formam expensa Syllogisticam per-strin-|guntur punctìm Sophismata, nec minus solidè,* | *quàm vulgò fit, ratione materiæ*; | Excerptis ex optimis Autho-ribus exemplis Græco-latinis, | ut majori cum voluptate & fructu, ex utriusq; lin-|guæ candidatis & legantur, & | intelligan-tur. | [*motto*, then *woodcut*]" with impr. 157 : E3r–E4r, the dedication, as in the 1629 edition : E4v, two Latin poems : F1r–G2v, the treatise : H1r, a title :—"HEP-TADES | LOGICAE· | *SIVE* | MONITA AD AMPLIORES | Tractatus Introductoria. | [*motto*, then *device*]", with impr. 191 a : H2r–14v, the treatise.

See 1607 P, 1629 P, and Wood's *Ath. Oxon.*, ed. Bliss. iii. 267. The *Heptades* (seven divisions of Logic) seem to be here printed for the first time.

19. **Smith**, Samuel. ADITVS | AD | LOGICAM· | IN VSVM EORVM | qui primò ACADEMI-|AM Salutant. | [*line*] | *Autore* SAMVELE SMITH, | *Artium Magistro.* | [*line*] | *Editio quinta.* | [*woodcut.*]

Impr. 109 a : 1639 : (twelves) 16° : pp. [14] + 204 + [2] + 2 folded leaves : p. 11 beg. *Proximum est,* 111 *non au-tem* : Long Primer Roman. Contents :—p. (5) title : (7–11) "De nupera Lon-dinensi editione ad Lectorem Προτρεπτικός." : 1–204, the work in 3 books : (1) "Lectoribus . . ." : before pp. 33 and 43 should be folded tables of Substantia and Qualitas.

See 1617 S. The undated preface complains of a pirated London edition, which may be that of 1621.

20. **Tozer**, rev. Henry. CHRISTIAN | *WISDOME,* | OR | THE EX-CELLENCY | FAME AND RIGHT | MEANES OF | TRVE | WISDOME. | As it was briefly delivered in | a Sermon in St MARIES | Church in OXFORD, | *Noremb:* 11. 1638. | [*line*] | By H. TOZER B.D. Fellow | of Exeter Colledge. | [*line.*]

Impr. 152 : 1639 : (eights) 16° : pp. [8] + 107 + [1] : p. 11 beg. *The se-|cond Ge* | : Great Primer Roman. Contents :—p. 1, title, within double lines : 3–8, Epistle dedicatory to Robert (Kerr) earl of Ancrum : 1–107, the sermon, on 1 Kings x. 24.

See Wood's *Ath. Oxon.*, ed. Bliss, iii. 274.

21. **Wescombe**, Martin. FABVLÆ | PONTIFICIÆ | EVANGELICÆ | Veritatis radiis | *dissipatæ.* | [*line*] | *Autore* | MARTINO WESCOMBE | Artium Magistro in | *Academia celeberrima* | *Oxoniensi.* | [*line,* then *woodcuts.*]

Impr. 157 : 1639 : (eights) 16° : pp. [34] + 85 + [1] : p. 11 beg. *it, nec alicui* : English Roman. Contents :—p. (3) title, within double lines : (5–23) dedication to archbp. Laud : (25–33) "Ad candidum lectorem præfatio" : 1–85, the work, in five parts.

See Wood's *Ath. Oxon.*, ed. Bliss, ii. 675 : the author, according to the dedication, was a Franciscan at Toulouse, converted to Protestantism by Stephanus de Cursol, settled at Exeter and patronized by bp. Hall. In 163½ he became a member of Exeter College, and in 1639 incorporated at Cambridge : after which he is lost sight of, except that he is said to have been reconverted to Roman Catholicism, and to have gone abroad. The five "fabulæ" are "De universali Episcopo," "de infalli-bilitate papæ." "de Purgatorio," "de Transubstantiatione eucharistica," and "de Invocatione Sanctorum." Wescombe is a Somerset and Devon name.

1640.

1. **Bacon**, sir Francis, Viscount St. Alban's.   OF THE | ADVANCEMENT AND | PROFICIENCE OF LEARNING | or the | *PARTITIONS OF SCIENCES* | $\overline{\text{IX}}$ Bookes | *Written in Latin by the Most Eminent | Illustrious & Famous Lord | FRANCIS BACON | Baron of Verulam Vicont Sr Alban | Coun-silour of Estate and Lord | Chancellor of England.* | [*line*] | Interpreted | *by* GILBERT WATS. |

Impr. 194: 1640: (fours) la. 8°: pp. [36] + 60 + [14] + 479 ("477") + [21]: pp. 11 beg. *Nature, but,* and *on between,* 401 *hard and severe*: Great Primer Roman. Contents :—p. (1) engraved title, see below : (3-4) dedication to the king and the two universities, in Latin, by Wats : (5-8) dedication to prince Charles, signed "Gilbert Wats": (9-16) preface to the reader, by Wats : (17-22) "Testi-monies consecrate to . . . . Sr Francis Bacon . . . ": (23-24) Latin poem on the *Instauratio Magna* by George Herbert : (25-33) "Manes Verulamiani sive in obitum incomparabilis Francisci de Veru-lamio, &c. epicedia," 6 Latin poems, one by Thomas Randolph, &c. : (35-36) address by Bacon to each university, in parallel columns : 1-39, the author's pre-face : (41-42) "The generall argument of the IX. books" : (43-60) "The argu-ment of the chapters . . . ": (1-11) the general design of the *Instauratio Magna* : (13) a table of "the Emanation of sciences . . . ": 1-"477", the work in 9 books : (2-5) "A new world of sciences, or the Deficients", headings : (6-8) "The Index of Sacred Scriptures . . . ": (10-11) "The index of humane authors" : (12) "Errata", marginal corrections only : (13) "Lectori Academico . . .", intro-ducing what follows : (14-18) "Catalogus historiarum particularum . secundum capita" : (19) "Typographus Lectori" about what follows : (20) a Latin letter from the author to Trinity college Cam-bridge, *beg.* "Res omnes": (21) impr. 195, as a colophon.

See 1633 B. This is part 1 of the *Instauratio Magna,* and is an expansion of the two books of the *Advancement of Learning* first printed in 1605, which were enlarged in Latin to nine books, and published in 1623 (and 1635) by W. Rawley: here they are translated by G. Wats. Some copies have 1639 in the colophon. At pp. 266-69 are some woodcut facsimiles of cipher-alphabets, &c. The engraved titlepage by W. Marshall (9⅝ × 5⅜ in.) bears the title on a sheet suspended between two obelisks representing Oxford and Cambridge: above it are two globes and "INSTAVR.MAG.P.1.": below, a ship in full sail and the imprint: the whole is fully described in the British Museum *Catalogue of Prints and Drawings,* Div. 1, vol. 1 (1870), p. 116 (no. 153). Three out of the four British Museum copies have a portrait of Bacon, but the trans-lator's own copy in the Bodleian has not. The collation, being elaborate, is here appended :—(¶¹, ¶¶¹, ¶¶², ¶¶¶¹, A²B-C⁴: aa-gg⁴ hh²: †⁴, ††², †¹: A-Z, Aa-Zz, Aaa-Qqq⁴ Rrr²: pp. 351-2 are repeated in the numeration.

2. **Brerewood**, Edward.   TRACTATVS | ETHICI: | *SIVE* | COM-MENTARII | IN ALIQVOT ARI-|STOTELIS LIBROS | ad NICHOMACHIUM, | *De Moribus*: | A Celeberrimo Philosopho | EDVARDO BREREWOOD | Art. Mag. è Colleg. Ænea-|nasensi, olim conscripti: | Iam primùm ex authoris ipsius Autogra-|pho, summâ fide, nec minori curâ casti-|gati, & publici juris facti: | Per T. S. S. S. Theolog. Bacchalaureum, & | Colleg. Ænea-- nasens. apud *Oxon* Socium. | [*line.*]

Impr. 200 : 1640 : sm. 4° : pp. [16] + 245 + [3] : p. 11 beg. *De modo Doctrinæ,* 201 *tasia aliquando*: Long Primer Roman. Contents :—p. (1) title within double lines: (3–11) Epistola dedicatoria to James lord Strange, dated "Oxonii è Musæo meo in Collegio Ænea-nasensi, Nono Cal. Januarii 1639.", and signed "Thomas Sixesmith" : (13–16) "Index tractatuum, capitum, et quæstionum . . .": 1–245, the four treatises, on the first four books of the Ethics.

See Wood's *Ath. Oxon.,* ed. Bliss, ii. 141. The original MS. (finished 27 Oct. 1586) is now part of MS. Queen's coll. Oxford no. 218). The method of this commentary or rather analysis is scholastic and formal. The editor says that he rescued the original MS. from a "rurale musæum," when it was "pulvere situque squalidum, & tantum non sepultum.' The author died in 1613. It is curious that in Moss's *Manual of classical bibliography* (Lond., 1825, vol. i, p. 157) this book is called " Westerman, Commentaria in Ethica Aristotelis. Oxon. 4to. 1640," with a reference to Wood's *Ath. Oxon.,* ed. Bliss, ii. 141. The explanation is that *Westerman* heads the column in Wood's work, because the account of William Westerman follows Brerewood on that column: but the ascription deceived even so acute a bibliographer as the late professor Chandler in his List of editions of the Nicomachean Ethics (Oxf. 1878).

3. **Buridanus,** Johannes.   IOHANNIS | BVRIDANI | PHILOSOPHI | TRECENTIS RETRO | annis celeberrimi | QVÆSTIONES IN OCTO | LIBROS POLITICORVM | *ARISTOTELIS.* | VNA | CVM INDICE QVÆSTIONVM | Dubiorúm-que eisdem annexorum | locupletissimo. | [*woodcut.*]

Impr. 69 : 1640 : sm. 4° : pp. [4] + 431 + [16] : p. 11 beg. *quia unus homo,* 401 *crimini vitæ*: Long Primer Roman. Contents :—p. (1) title, within double lines : two epigrams, one by, and one to, Guillermus Baterel, the original editor : 1–431, the work : (1–15) index.

Baterel's annotated edition of Buridanus on the Politics was printed at least twice in the sixteenth century (1506 and 1526).

4. **Carpenter,** Nathaniel.   *ACHITOPHEL,* | OR | The Picture of a Wicked | POLITITIAN. | *Divided into three Parts.* | A TREATISE | Presented heretofore in three | Sermons to the Vniversity | of OXFORD and | *now Published.* | By NATH. CARPENTER | B. D. & Fellow of *Excet. Coll.* | in OXFORD. | [*line.*]

Impr. 193*a* : 1640 : (twelves) 24° : pp. [8] + 177 + [3] : p. 11 beg. *common equity,* 101 *next place* : Pica Roman. Contents : —p. (1) title, within a line : (3–8) dedica-tion to archbp. Ussher : 1–60, 61–125, 127–177, the three sermons, on 2 Sam. xvii. 23.

For an account of the earlier editions, see Wood's *Ath. Oxon.* ii., 422, and 1628 C. The present edition closely resembles the London ones of 1633 and 1638. Probably the " N. H." who edited the next article below, edited this also, Carpenter having died in 1628. The work is evidently intended to be read with a view to the political circumstances of the time, under the disguise of dealing with " a sacred tragedy " from Old Testament history.

5. ——.   CHORAZIN | AND | BETHSAIDA'S | VVoe, or warning-Peece. | A judicious and learned Sermon | On MATH. 11. V. 21. | Preached at St *Maries* in *Oxford,* by | that renowned and famous Divine, M^r | *Nathanael Carpenter,* Bachellor in | Divinity, sometime Fellow of | *Exeter* Colledge ; late Chap-laine to my Lords Grace | of *Ardmagh* in | *Ireland.* |

Impr. 193 *b* : 1640 : (twelves) 24° : pp. [8] + 95 + [1] : p. 11 beg. *were the Secretaries* : Pica Roman.   Contents : — (1) title : (3–8) Epistle dedicatory to dr. Thomas Winniffe, dean of St. Paul's, by " N.H." the editor : 1–95, the sermon.

See Wood's *Ath. Oxon.*, ed. Bliss, ii. 422. This is a reprint of the Lond. 1633 edition. The preface gives some valuable biographical notes about Carpenter, who died in 1628, and was the editor's tutor and " neere Affine" at Exeter college. It states with reference to the present book that " had not a kinsman's (Io. Ca.) friendly hand given it safe conduct over the Surges of the Ocean, in all likelyhood it had perished on the Netherland shores."

6. [**Cartwright,** William].   THE | ROYALL | SLAVE. | [&c., exactly as 1639 C, except that the hyphen in l. 7 is horizontal, that " *The second Edition*" is inserted between the two *lines*, and that after them is a *woodcut*.]

Impr. 189 : 1640 : sm. 4° : pp. [64], signn. A–H¹ : sign. C1ʳ beg. *Atos. I hope* : Pica Roman. Contents : — exactly as in 1639 C, except that the play only extends to 113ʳ, the three epilogues occupying 113ᵛ–114ᶜ.

See Wood's *Ath. Oxon.*, ed. Bliss, iii. 69, and 1639 C, of which this is a reprint.

7. [**Clain,** Johann Theodor].   HISTORIA BRITANNICA | *Hoc est,* | DE REBUS GESTIS | BRITANNIÆ | SEU | ANGLIÆ. | COMMENTARIOLI | TRES: | Nunc denuò excusi. | *QVIBVS ACCESSERVNT* | *præter generalem Angliæ descripti-|onem: Marginalia & Index* | *rerum copiosus.* | [*woodcuts.*]

Impr. 197 : 1640 : (twelves) 16° : pp. [12] + 220 + [44] : p. 11 beg. *fuisset. Brutus*, 201 *quam cogitatione* : Pica Roman. Contents : — p. (1) " A " between woodcuts : (5) title, within a line : (7–12) " Lectori . . . ", signed " M.H." : 1–7 " Angliæ descriptio generalis, ex Geographico Opusculo Johan. Büssenmecheri " : 9–61, 62–81, 82–220, the commentarioli : (1–44) " Index rerum et nominum memorabilium."

This is an anonymous history of Britain from the earliest times. The editor, M(atthew) H(unt), does not mention the fact, that an undated edition was printed at London by Henry Bynneman (who published from 1566 to 1587), with the title " De rebus gestis Britanniæ commentarioli tres. Ad Ornatissimum Virum M. Henricum Broncarem Armigerum E.S.", from which it has been conjectured that the author's initials were " E.S." The first words of the text are " Britannia est Insula natura triquetra." The name of Clain is given in the British Museum catalogue as the author of an Amberg edition of 1603, and in Thomas Thorpe's Catalogue of books (1851) p. 51 an edition printed at Hamburg in 1598 is mentioned under the same name, but I can find no account of the author, who probably lived at Amberg. Some have ascribed the book to John Clapham, who published an English *History of England* till the coming of the Saxons, in 1602 and 1606.

8. **Ferrand,** Jacques.   EPΩTOMANIA | OR | A TREATISE | Discoursing of the Essence, | Causes, Symptomes, Prog- | nosticks, and Cure of | LOVE, | OR | EROTIQVE | MELANCHOLY | [*line*] | *Written by* | IAMES FERRAND | Dʳ *of Physick.* | [*line*].

Impr. 160 *b* : 1640 : (eights) 16° : pp. [40] + 363 + [5] : p. 11 beg. *Poetesse was*, 301 *purpose, and* : Pica Roman. Contents : — p. (1) title, within a border between lines : (3–7) " The Author to the Reader " : (9–34) 8 English poems to the author and book by Oxford men, one by Martin Llewellin : (35–39) " A table of the chapters " : (39) " Errata " : 1–363, the work, in 39 chapters.

See Wood's *Ath. Oxon.*, ed. Bliss, iii. 350, where the translator from the French into English is stated to be Edmund Chilmead. The original French edition was published at Toulouse in 1612, under the title *Traité de l'essence et guérison de l'amour*, and at Paris in 1623 as *De la maladie d'amour, ou melancholie erotique*. If Robert Burton was acquainted with the first edition of this book, as he well may have been, there can be little doubt that he has taken or imitated the general method and treatment of the subject, in his *Anatomy of Melancholy*: but the French author is surpassed on his own ground. The research is greater and the felicities of language more numerous and striking in Burton, while the plan is also further and distinctively elaborated. There is no mention of Burton's book in the poems prefixed to this translation. The words underlined in the above title are printed in red, as well as " Oxford," and " sold by Edward Forrest , 1640." in the imprint.

9. **Fletcher**, John.   RVLE A WIFE | And have a Wife. | a comœdy | ACTED BY HIS | *Majesties Servants.* | [*line*] | Written by | JOHN FLETCHER | *Gent.* | [*line,* then *woodcut.*]

Impr. 180 : 1640 : sm. 4° : pp. [4] + 67 + [1] : p. 11 beg. *Only for present use* : Pica Roman.   Contents :—p. (1) title : (3) " Prologue" : 1–67, the play : (1) " Epilogue."

This was Fletcher's unaided composition, before the close of 1624, when it was twice performed at court. The underplot is said to be based on one of Cervantes' " Novelas Exemplares." See the *Dict. of Nat. Biogr.* under Fletcher, p. 307, col. 1. The present is the first edition, and the only quarto one.

10. ——.   The Tragœdy of | ROLLO | DUKE of Normandy. | ACTED BY HIS | *Majesties Servants.* | [*line*] | Written by | JOHN FLETCHER | *Gent.* | [*line,* then *woodcut.*]

Impr. 180 : 1640 : sm. 4° : pp. [2] + 73 + [1] : p. 11 beg. *But for you* : Pica Roman.   Contents :—p. (1) title : (2) " The Names of the Actors " : 1–73, the play.

The authorship of this play is doubtful. The first edition (Lond. 1639) was entitled " The Bloody Brother. A Tragedy. By *B. J. F.*" i.e. Ben Johnson and Fletcher?, and it was entered in the Stationers' Register on 4 Oct. 1639 as by " J. B." Massinger is also supposed to have had some share in it. See the *Dict. of Nat. Biogr.* under Fletcher, p. 308, col. 2.

11. **H**[arding], **S**[amuel], of Exeter college, Oxford.   SICILY | AND | NAPLES, | OR, THE | FATALL VNION· | A Tragœdy. | *By* | S. H. *A. B.* *è C. Ex:* [*line, motto,* two *lines.*]

Impr. 119 : 1640 : sm. 4° : pp. [12] + 96 : p. 11 beg. *Cass. If the varlets* : Pica Roman.   Contents :—p. (1) title : (2) " Dramatis Personæ" : (3) " To the Reader ", signed " P.P.", the editor : (4– 11) seven complimentary poems to the author, alluding to Shakespeare's, Ben Johnson's and Randolph's deaths : (12) Errata : 1–96, the play, with epilogue.

See Wood's *Ath. Oxon.*, ed. Bliss, iii. 31. The author died before 1650, not, as Foster's *Alumni Oxonienses* asserts, as late as 1699. The editor, who is known to be Philip Papillon of Exeter college, declares that the play is here printed without the author's knowledge and against his modesty. The lines relating to Shakespeare, which have perhaps only been reprinted in Pickering and Chatto's Catalogue of books, nos. 70–72 (June 1893), p. 15, are :—

> " But sad Melpomene . . .
> Hyes to pale Shakespeares urne, and from his tombe
> Takes up the bayes, and hither she is come."

12. **Jeanes,** Henry, of Hart hall, Oxford. A TREATISE | Concerning | A CHRISTIANS | CAREFULL AB-|stinence from all ap-|pearance of Evill: | Gathered | FOR THE MOST | part out of the Schoole-|men, and Casuists: | *Wherein* | *The Questions and Cases of* | *Conscience belonging unto the* | *difficult matter of Scandall* | *are briefly resolved:* | By HENRY JEANES, | M^r of Arts, lately of *Hart-|Hall* in OXON, and Rector of | he Church of *Beere-Cro-|combe* in *Somerset-shire.* | [*line.*]

Impr. 94*a*: 1640: 12°: pp. [4] + 151 + [1]: p. 11 beg. *onely from*: Pica Roman. Contents:—p. (1) title, within double lines: (3-4) dedication to Philip earl of Pembroke: 1-145, the discourse on "1 Thess. [v] 22": 147-151, "The Postscript to the Reader": (1) "Errata".

See Wood's *Ath. Oxon.*, iii. 591. This book appears to be rare, and was reprinted at Oxford in 1660.

13. **Oxford,** University. HORTI | CAROLINI | *ROSA ALTERA.* | [*device.*]

Impr. 151: 1640: sm. 4°: pp. [108], signn. ( )², *, **, A-E¹, F², *a-c¹,cc², d e¹* : sign. B1^r beg. *Iam meritò*, b1^r *Prethee forbeare*: English Roman & Italic. Contents:—( )1^r, title, within double lines: ( )2^r, poem dedicatory to the king, signed "Acad. Oxon.", in Latin: *1^r-F2^v, Latin poems: a1^r c4^r, English poems: c4^v "The Printer to their Maiesties", an English poem, signed "Leonard Lichfield."

These are verses to celebrate the birth of prince Henry, 8 July 1640 (*d.* 1660). Most are in Latin and English, but three in Greek, two in French, one in Hebrew. The signatures as usual show the difficulty of getting the poems sent in in time and arranged in proper order.

14. **Puteanus,** Erycius. ERYCI PUTEANI | AMOENITATVM | HUMANA-RVM | DIATRIBÆ DVÆ. | *PRIOR* | DE LACONISMO: | Ad Illustriss: & Excellentiss: | *Ducem Arscholanum.* | *ALTERA,* | THYRSI | PHILOTESII. | *SIVE* | Amor Laconissans: | Ad V. Nobilem & Prudentem, | Maxim. Plouuierium. | *Utraque elegantiis & acumini-|bus referta.* | [*two lines.*]

Impr. 198: 1640: (twelves) 16°: pp. [8] + 200 + [8]: p. 11 beg. *factus ita*, 101 *Laconismum*: English Roman. Contents: —p. (1) title, within a line: (3-7) "Lectori benevolo . . . ", signed "J. W" (estall): 1-116, 117 (misprinted 711)-195, the two diatribae: 196-200 "Sententiæ aliquot aculeatæ, è Seneca".

These are reprints of Diatribae 7 and 8 out of the entire set of twelve which form the *Amænitates.* The Thyrsi are short essays on *aculei*, which are pointed sentences on friendship and love. The editor (and printer) mentions the *Suada Attica* as "nuper excusa": see below.

15. ———. ERYCI PUTEANI | svada attica, | *SIVE* | ORATIONVM | SELECTARVM | SYNTAGMA. | *Item* PALÆSTRA *Bonæ Mentis,* | *prorsus inno-|vata.* | [*device.*]

Impr. 205: 1640: (eights) 16°: pp. [16] + 534 + [2 + ?]: p. 11 beg. *ego didi-cerim*, 501 *munerùmque*: Pica Roman. Contents:—p. (1) title: 3-10, dedication "Tribus ordinibus Brabantiæ", dated "Lovanii, in Arce, Kalendis Martiis M.DC.XV": 11-12, two quotations: 13 "Syllabus Orationum": (14) "Characterharum orationum": (15) a quotation: 1-419, the 22 orations: 419-421, two passages from Aulus Gellius: 421 "Typo-grapho lectori": 422-424, "Eryci Puteani paucul de morte": 425, a bastard title to the Palæstra: 427-429, "Ad lectorem", dated "Lovanii", XI. Kalend. Octobr. M.DC.XI.": 430-512, the Palæstra, 20 exercitationes &c.: 513-534, "Syllabus exercitationum" and short pieces, ending with " . . . Puteanus Lectori . . . ": (1-2) blank, the rest (if any) not seen.

There is no bibliography of the numerous works of Erycius Puteanus, but the *Suada Attica* was first published at Louvain in 1615, and the *Palæstra* in 1611. They contain orations and exercises delivered at Milan and Louvain. The *Palæstra Bonæ Mentis* is properly a hall at Louvain, where some of these were delivered, and in another sense a literary club which met there for debate, recitations and the like. See preceding article.

16. **Randolph,** Thomas.   POEMS, | With the MUSES | LOOKING--GLASSE, | AND | AMYNTAS· | [*line*] | By THO. RANDOLPH M.A. and late | Fellow of *Trinity* Col. in | *Cambridge.* | [*line.*] The second Edition Enlarged. | [*woodcuts.*]

Impr. 174: 1640: (eights) 16°: pp. [28] + 134 + [2] + 87 + [7] + 101 + [1]: pp. 11 beg. *Africk he loaths, High as the men,* and *For Mopsus*: Long Primer Roman. Contents :—p. (1) an engraved title, see below: (3) title, as above, within double lines : (5-26) twelve poems on the author and book: 1-134, the poems: (1) title of the Muses Looking-glass, almost as in 1638 R, with impr. 174: 1-87, (1), the play: (2) title of Amyntas, nearly as in 1638 R, but "By T.R.", with impr. 174: (4) "Dramatis Personæ": (6-7), 1-101, the play.

See Wood's *Ath. Oxon.*, ed. Bliss, i. 565, and 1638 R. The "enlargement" in this edition is not evident. The engraved title bears a bust of Randolph on a pedestal, with Philosophia and Poesis doing him honour, and a celestial sphere and Pegasus above. On the pedestal are the words "Poems by Tho : Randolph. The 2ᵈ Edition much Enlarged.", and below is impr. 196. Each of the three parts is separately paged, but the two plays are linked by the signatures, while the title alone connects the plays with the poems. The Cambridge 1640 edition of "The Jealous Lovers", a comedy by Randolph, is not infrequently found bound with this volume, but has no necessary connexion with it.

17. **R[ogers]**, H[ugh].   ΓΑΜΗΛΙΑ | On the happy marriage of the most | *accomplished paire,* | H. R. *Esq.* | And the vertuous *A. B.* | [*device.*] |

Impr. 202: 1640: sm. 4°: pp. [2] + 43 + [1]: p. 11 beg. *What beauty on*: Great Primer Italic and Roman. Con- tents :—p. (1) title, within double bound-ing lines except at foot (single line): 1-43, 19 poems, of which four are Latin.

Very rare. The only copy I have seen of this privately printed book is in the British Museum. The marriage (in 1640) was between Anne daughter of sir Edward Baynton, of Bromham (*d.* 1657), and Hugh Rogers esq. of Cannington. The poems are clearly by friends and relations of both parties, but are signed only with initials. A copy of the book was in the Heber sale (pt. viii, p. 49).

18. **Saints' Legacies.**   THE | SAINTS | LEGACIES, | OR | A COL-LECTION OF | CERTAINE PROMISES | OVT OF THE WORD | OF GOD. | Collected for private use, but | published for the comfort of | Gods people. | *Whereunto is now added the Saints* | *Support in times of trouble.* | THE 6. EDITION. |

Impr. 203: 1640: (twelves) 16°: pp. [36] + 157 + [5] + 31 + [23]: pp. 11 begg. *Though your*, and *soule, that*: English Roman. Contents :—pp. (1-4) not seen: (5) title, with border within lines : (7-24) dedication to all true Believers, by the editor: (25-32) "To the Reader": (33-35) "Rules to be observed in reading of promises": 1-157, the 105 legacies: (1- 2) "A postscript sent from the Authour": (4) a title within a line :—"AN | EPITOME OF | PROMISES | FOR THE | SAINTS SUP-PORT | IN TIME OF | TROVBLE. | [*line*] | *The sixth Edition.* | [*line, motto, line*]". with impr. 204: 1-31, 31 promises: (1-4) texts: (6-9) "A Postscript, to all true Beleevers": (10-18, 20-22) "Five Tables . . ." or indexes.

This is a rare and curious book : rare, inasmuch as no ordinary library catalogue or bibliography contains any mention of any edition or copy of it; and curious, as having its two parts—which are indissolubly joined by the signatures and sections—printed by the same printer for two different London publishers, R. Royston and S. Enderby. We must suppose these two to have ventured proportionate parts in the book.

19. **Sanderson**, Robert.   LOGICÆ | *ARTIS* | COMPENDIVM. | Editio Quarta. | [*line*] | Authore ROB. SANDERSON, | Coll. *Lincolniensis* in almâ | *Oxoniensi, quondam* | *Socio.* | [*line,* then *woodcuts.*]

Impr. 201 : 1640 : (eights) 16ᵃ: pp. [8] + 239 + [1] + . . . : p. 11 beg. *possint esse*, 201 *Cap. 21.*: Pica Roman. Contents :—pp. (1-2) not seen : (3) title, within a line : (5-8) "Elenchus capitum" : 1-239 the work, in three books : (the two Appendixes contain over 120 pages.)

Rare. See Wood's *Ath. Oxon.*, ed. Bliss, iii. 626, and 1615 S. The only copy I have seen, in Queen's College (Oxford) Library, is interleaved, and wants the two appendixes, which probably occupied the same number of pages as in the 1631 edition.

20. [**Snelling**, Thomas].   THIBALDVS | SIVE | *VINDICTÆ* | *INGENIVM.* | TRAGOEDIA. | [*line, motto, line, woodcut.*]

Impr. 157 : 1640 : (eights) 16°: pp. [24] + 80 : p. 11 beg. *Pro morte* : Pica Roman. Contents :—p. (1) title, with border between lines : (3-4) "Lectori" : (5-16) six complimentary Latin poems by St. John's College men : (17) "Dramatis Personæ" : (19-21) "Argumentum" : (23) "Errata . . . " : 1-80, the play.

For the author, see Wood's *Ath. Oxon.*, ed. Bliss, iii. 275. The sheets of this work were reissued in 1650 at London, with a new title *Pharamus, sive Libido vindex, Hispanica tragœdia*, but neither Wood nor his editors have been aware of this earlier edition. Both were anonymous, and the direct evidence for the authorship (which need not be doubted) is difficult to find. Bp. Barlow wrote the author's name on the title of his copy of *Pharamus.* The poems imply that the play had been written some years before 1640 : the author matriculated at St. John's College, Oxford, in June 1634.

21. **Tipping**, William.   "*A Return of Thankfulness for the unexpected Recovery out of a dangerous Sickness.* Oxon. 1640. Oct."

So in Wood's *Ath. Oxon.*, ed. Bliss, iii. 244.

22. **Tozer**, Henry.   DIRECTIONS | *FOR* | A GODLY LIFE : | ESPECIALLY FOR | Communicating at the | Lords Table. | *INTENDED FIRST FOR* | *private use ; now published for the* | *good of those who desire the safty* | *of* *their owne soules, and* | *shall be pleased to make* | *use thereof.* | By H. TOZER Mr of Arts, and | Fellow of *Exceter* Col-|ledge in *Oxford.* | *The fifth* *Edition.* | [*motto.*]

Impr. 199 : (twelves) 16°: pp. [10] + 195 + [11] : p. 11 beg. *Minister. 2*, 101 *was due* : Pica Roman. Contents :—p. (1) title, within line and border : (3-9) Epistle dedicatory, as in 1628 T : 1-195, the directions : (2-4) "The contents of each Chapter ".

For the author and book, but not this edition, see Wood's *Ath. Oxon.*, ed. Bliss, iii. 274 (and 1628 T). Each page is within a line, doubled at upper and outer margins.

23. ———.   " *Sermon on Joh.* 18. 3. Ox. 1640."

So in Wood's *Ath. Oxon.*, ed. Bliss, iii. 274.

24. **Twittee**, Thomas.   AD | CLERVM | PRO | FORMA CONCIO | HABITA IN TEMPLO | BEATÆ MARIÆ OXON: | MARTIJ 13. 1634. | [*line*] | PER THO: TWITTEE SANCTÆ | Theologiæ *Bac. è Coll. Oriell.* | [*line, motto.*] |

Impr. 157: 1640: sm. 4°: pp. [4] + 24: p. 11 beg. *men hi verè*: Great Primer Roman. Contents :—p. (1) title, within double lines: (3) dedication to dr. John Tolson provost of Oriel: 1–24, the sermon, on 1 Pet. iii. 8.

See Wood's *Fasti Oxon.*, ed. Bliss, i. 469. The dedication is of the modern kind, not an epistle dedicatory, and the printing is unusual, the first words of a paragraph being generally projections to the left, instead of indented.

25. **Z[ouche]**, R[ichard].   DESCRIPTIO | JURIS & JUDICII | MILI-TARIS | *AD QVAM LEGES QVÆ* | Rem Militarem, & Ordinem | *Persona-rum.* | NEC NON | JURIS & JUDICII | MARITIMI | AD QUAM QUÆ NAVI-| *GATIONEM ET* | Negotiationem Maritimam | *respiciunt, referuntur.* | [*line*] | Autore R. Z. P. R. *Oxoniæ.* | [*line.*]

Impr. 157: 1640: sm. 4°: pp. [8] + 36 + [4] + 40 + [4] : pp. 11 beg. *meris sunt*, and *quæsitum est*: Pica Roman. Contents :—p. (3) title, within double lines: (5–6) "Ad Lectorem", unsigned, but " Datum ex Aula Alb. Prid. Calend. April. 1640 " : (7–8) heads of chapters in divi-sion 1 : 1–36, the military division, in two parts: (1) a title, within double lines : " DESCRIPTIO | JURIS & JUDICII | MARI-TIMI | [&c., exactly as the main title, to its end, with woodcut and impr. 157: (3–4) heads of chapters in division 2 : 1–40, " De jure maritimo & de jure nautico " in two parts: (1) "Errata ".

See Wood's *Ath. Oxon.*, ed. Bliss, iii. 511. The signatures establish a connexion between the two divisions.

26. ———.   " *Descr. Juris & Judicii sacri; ad quam Leges, quæ ad Religionem & piam Causam respiciunt, referuntur.* Oxon. 1640. qu.*"

So in Wood's *Ath. Oxon.*, ed. Bliss, iii. 511, where it is stated that the De Jure Sacro, Militari and Maritimo, were issued together. In the Leyden reprint of 1652 the De jure sacro is rather shorter than the other two. It does not seem to have found its way into the Oxford or London libraries which have published their catalogues.

Periodical.

The *Quaestiones in Vesperiis* and *Quaestiones in Comitiis* (see Andrew Clark's *Register of the University of Oxford*, vol. ii. pt. i. [1887], p. 169) were often printed.

1602. The earliest I have seen are the theological "Quæstiones (Christo propitio) in Vesperijs discutiendæ, *Iul.* 10. 1602," followed by some belonging to the Comitia, and some Law *quaestiones* belonging to both, and by a specimen of dr. John King's treatment of his three *quaestiones*, in Latin verse: the whole forming a small sheet of 16 pages, with the last five blank.

1605. The *Quaestiones . . . in Comitiis . . . coram . . . Rege . . . Aug. . . .* 1605 were printed in folio sheet form, as was invariably the case in later years, occupying in this year four pages. Whether this issue was exceptional or not, is not clear.

1608. In this year at latest begins the series of ordinary folio sheets of *quaestiones*: of which examples have been seen for the years 1608, 1614, 1618, 1619, 1622, 1627, 1628, 1629, 1632, 1634, 1635, 1639, 1640, and intermittently until at least 1693.

SUPPLEMENT.

ADDITIONS AND CORRECTIONS IN CHRONOLOGICAL ORDER.

"1468"-84.

Pp. 1-4.   See pp. 237-62.   (App. A).

1483.

P. 3.   For the **Augustine** see p. 259.

P. 3.   *For* 3. ***Logic** *read* 3. ***'Logic.**

P. 3.   *For* 4. ***Lyndewoode** *read* 4. ***'Lyndewoode.**

1485.

P. 4.   **Alexander,** l. 3.
    For c²-c³ *read* c 2, c 3.

1486.

P. 4.   **Mirk,** last line.
    The first two leaves are in the Lambeth copy.

1517-19.

Pp. 5-7.   See pp. 263-65.   (App. B).

1518.

P. 7.   **Whittington,** l. 3.
    For protouatis *read* prothouatis.   Eleven copies are now known.

Pp. 8-9.   **Pliny and Lystrius.**

    Something can be added to the account.   The two original books in dispute are in the John Rylands (Spencer) Library at Manchester, and the *locus classicus* for their history is naturally in Dibdin's *Bibliotheca Spenceriana* (1814), ii. 271, iii. 411: where will be found a reproduction (in type) of the two titles and colophons.   Of the Pliny Dibdin states that one George Smith passed it on to Van Damme, from whom Askew bought it for fifteen guineas.   With respect to the Lystrius, it appears that the "Mr. Dent" who purchased it at the Askew sale was an agent or pseudonym of Mr. Alchorne.   The volume bears a manuscript note pretending to be from "i. Korsellis" at Haarlem in 1471, stating that the book came to him from his brother Frederick.

About 1513.

P. 11.   *Add:—*

    Syrretus, Antonius.   [Antonii Syrreti Formalitates de mente magistri Johannis Duns?] | Scoti ordinis fratrum minorum doctoris sub＊tilissimi cum nouis additionibus et con＊cordantijs magistri Mauritij de por＊tu hybernie in margine decora＊te et nouiter impresse : | [two Latin verses, then a woodcut of the Trinity with "Henricus Iacobi" and printer's mark at foot, then two more Latin verses] | ⟨Uenumdantur in vniuersitate Oxoniensi.   Sub | intersignio sanctissime Trinitatis ab Hen-| rico Jacobi bibliopole Londoniensis. |

This interesting title is found on a fragment of two leaves discovered by Mr. R. G. C. Procter in New College Library at Oxford, in Aug. 1891, and now marked "Auct.V. 16," fol. 3.   The verso of the title is occupied with a woodcut of the arms of Henry VIII, with supporters, two angels with scroll, &c.   The second leaf is marked A 2, and contains a dedication and certain definitions, all part of the Additiones Mauritii.   The book was no doubt printed in London, but sold in Oxford by Henricus Jacobi, who died in the latter city towards the end of 1514, intestate, see p. 273.   From an interesting account of Jacobi in *Bibliographica*, pt. I (1894), by Mr. E. G. Duff, it appears that Jacobi, after publishing in London from 1505 to 1512, came to Oxford in 1512 or 1513 (see pp. 95, 112 of the account).

This entry and that of 1506 should strictly be in a list by themselves, being neither "lost" nor "fictitious."

1585.

P. 14.   **Bilson, Thomas.**   *Add at end:—*

A curious account of an abortive effort on the part of Edmund Bollifant and three partners to produce a reprint of this book, will be found in Arber's *Transcript of the Stationers' Registers* II (1875), p. 793.

P. 17.   **Parsons,** Robert, (2nd entry, no. 6).   *Add at end:—*

An explanation of this reprint will be found in Arber's *Transcript of the Stationers' Registers* II (1875), p. 793 (a petition from N. Newton, E. Bollifant, and others, in the winter of 158⅘), from which it appears that John Wight, printer, of London, who had entered a copy of his edition of the book at Stationers' Hall on 28 Aug. 1584, sent his son to Oxford to buy up the whole of Barnes's reprint: which was done.   But Barnes promptly printed "two ympressions more," of which the present volume is no doubt one.   Possibly the preceding art. is the other re-impression, and Wight effectually suppressed the whole first edition.

1586.

P. 17.   *Insert:—*

Brasbridge, Thomas, of Magdalen college, Oxford.   QVÆSTI-| ONES IN OF-|FICIA M. T. | CICERONIS: | Compendiariam totius | *Opusculi Epitomen* | continentes. | [*woodcuts.*]

Impr. 5 : 1586: (eights) 12° : pp. [68], signn. A–D⁸ E²: sign. B 1ʳ beg. *rum alterum*: Pica Roman.   Contents:—sign. A 1ʳ, title within a border, A 2ʳ–2ᵛ, dedication to Laurence Humphrey, signed | "Thomas Brasbrigius," "Banburiæ, Idibus Nouembris, 1586": A 3ʳ–E 2 (printed E 3)ᵛ, the questions and answers: E 2ᵛ, two Latin lines signed "I. P. Iohannensis."

Very rare.   For the author, see Wood's *Ath. Oxon.*, ed. Bliss, i. 526.   The preface contains some autobiographical details.   There appear to be at least three editions of this work, 1586, 1592 (q. v.) and 1615 (q. v.), all printed at Oxford.

1589.

P. 28.   **Skelton, John.**

Lord Spencer's copy is of course now in the John Rylands Library at Manchester.

1591.

P. 31. **Tacitus.** *Add at end:—*

On 25 May 1591 a patent was issued to Richard Wright of Oxford and his assigns to print Tacitus's *History* in English, during his lifetime (Patent Rolls, 33 Eliz. pt. 17, mentioned in Arber's *Transcript of the Stationers' Registers* II (1875), p. 16). The metal engraving of a Roman Camp reappears in R. Grenewey's translation of the *Annals* of Tacitus (Lond. 1598, 1604, 1622).

1592.

P. 32. **Barlaamus,** last line but one.

For author *read* editor. Another presentation copy has been seen, also without device.

P. 32. **Brasbridge.**

See 1586 in this Supplement.

P. 33. **Elizabeth.**

There is a perfect copy of this rare pamphlet in the great Gloucestershire collections at Chestal, Dursley, in the possession of the Phelps family, kindly pointed out to me by F. A. Hyett, Esq. The title is:—SPEECHES | DELIVERED TO | HER MAIESTIE THIS | LAST PROGRESSE, AT THE | Right Honorable the Lady RVSSELS, at | Bissam, the Right Honorable the Lorde | CHANDOS at Sudley, at the Right | Honorable the Lord NORRIS, at | Ricorte. | [*device.*] On the verso of the title is a preface "To the Reader" signed by "I. B." the printer.

P. 33. **Gager** (no. 7).

The author of the *Bellum Grammaticale* was Andreas Guarna.

P. 34. **Gager** (no. 8). l. 4 (not l. 3).

For 1591 *read* 1592.

1593.

P. 35. After no. 4 *add:—*

Oxford, New College.   Ex donatione Magistri Fran-|cisci Bettes LL. D: Socij huius Col-|*legij. Anno Domini. 1593.*

This is a book label, found in Spiegelius's *Lexicon Juris Civilis,* 1549 (Oo. xii. 5), and perhaps in other volumes in New College Library at Oxford. The words are within a border of woodcuts, the outside measurement of the printed border being $1\frac{12}{16} \times 3\frac{3}{16}$ in.

1594.

P. 36. **Beacon.**

P. 1 bears "¶ j", and is therefore not wholly blank.

P. 37. **Powel** (no. 5). *Add at end:—*

See 1631 P.

1597.

P. 42. **Agatharchides.**

Professor Bywater has pointed out that the extracts from Agatharchides and Memnon are from an earlier printed edition of them, and not directly from Photius's *Bibliotheca,* which was first printed in 1601. Had the matter been taken from a MS. of Photius, the editor would no doubt have claimed the honour, whereas he claims credit only for the new translation into Latin.

P. 42. *After* **Agatharchides** *add* :—

Brett, Richard, of Lincoln College. Theses Mᵣⁱ BRET respondentis in Comitiis. | Oxon. 1597. | [text follows, as below.]

A single sheet, 8½ in. high by 6 broad, printed on both sides, containing three theses. The first is *Politia Ecclesiæ Anglicanæ cum iure divino non pugnat*, followed by short Latin, Greek, and Hebrew poems. The second is followed by Latin, "Caldaica," and "Syriea" poems, the last being written in MS. The third is followed by Latin, Arabic, and Æthiopic poems, the last two being filled in in MS. The Hebrew is in Pica type. For Brett, see Wood's *Ath. Oxon.* ii. 611 : he took the degree of Bachelor of Divinity on 6 June, 1597.

P. 43. *After* **King** *add* :—

Oxford, University. "Qvaestiones sex, totidem praelectionibvs, in schola Theologica, Oxoniae, pro Forma, Habitis, Discvssae, Et Disceptatae Anno 1597."

So in the Catalogue of W. H. Holyoak, 75 Humberstone Gate, Leicester, "March 1888," no. 10 : the copy was sold on Jan. 3, 1890 to the rev. Shaw Urmstone of Manchester.

1598.

P. 44. *After* **Butler** *add* :—

Butler, Charles. RHETORICÆ | LIBRI DVO. | QVORVM | *Prior de Tropis & Figuris,* | *Posterior de Voce & Gestu* | PRAECIPIT. | IN VSVM SCHOLA-rum accuratiùs editi. | *.* *.* | *.* | [*motto, then woodcuts.*]

Impr. 11: 1598: (eights) 16°: pp. [112], signn. ❦ A-F⁸ G¹: sign. H1ʳ beg. *sus, vivus*: Pica Roman. Contents :— sign. ❦1ᵛ, title: ❦2ʳ–3ʳ Epistola dedica- | toria to lord Thomas Egerton, dated "Oxon. 16. Calend. Decemb. [16 Nov.], 1598": ❦3ᵛ–4ᵛ, "Ad Lectorem": A1ʳ– G3ʳ, the work: G4 I have not seen.

Very rare : the only copy at present known is in Corpus Christi Library at Oxford. Even Wood (*Ath. Oxon.*, iii. 210) had not seen this first edition, since he implies that the date is 1600. See 1600 B, 1618 B, 1629 B.

1598 and 1599.

Pp. 44, 46.

The article **Lomazzo** has been inserted under 1599 instead of 1598, the proper year.

1599.

P. 47. **Richard.**

With respect to the letters "B. P. N.", see also 1625 J.

1603.

P. 55. **Davies.** *Add at end* :—

Ingleby, in his *Shakespeare's Centurie of Prayse* (2nd ed., 1879), points out a Shakespearean allusion on p. 215 of this work.

1606.

P. 65. **Oxford**, l. 1.

For .4 *read* 4.

1608.

P. 71. **Panke.** *Add at end:—*
See 1613 P, in this Supplement.

1610.

P. 78. **Rainolds,** top line of page.
For Ath. Oxon. ii. 15 *read Ath. Oxon.* ii. 15 and 193.

1612.

Pp. 82, 85.
The articles **Rawlinson** and **Reinolds** are out of their place at the latter reference, and should be on p. 82.

P. 85. **Smyth,** Richard. *Add at end:—*
The third edition was issued in 1634; see 1634 S.

1613.

P. 86. **Answer.**
This is of course by Richard Parkes, as is noted in the first edition (p. 59; 1604,
no. 7). "1604 A" is twice an error for "1604 P."

P. 89. **Colmore,** l. 3.
For SAACTPAVL *read* SANCTPAVL.

P. 92. **Oxford,** Univ. (Justa Funebria), l. 6.
The type is English Roman.

P. 92. Ibid. l. 11.
For preceding art. *read* art. no. 19.

P. 92. *After* **Oxford,** no. 21, *insert:—*

 Panke, John. THE FALL OF BABEL. | By the confusion of
Tongues, directly proouing against the | Papistes of this, and former
ages; that a view of their writings | and Bookes, being taken, it cannot
be discerned by any | man liuing, what they would say, or how be
vnder-'stood, in the question of the sacrifice of the Masse, | the Reall
presence or Transubstantiation; | but in explaning their mindes, they
fall | vpon such tearmes, as the Prote-|stants vse and allow. | FVRTHER. |
In the question of the Popes Supremacie is shewed, how they | *abuse an*
authoritie of the auncient Father S. Cyprian, a Canon of | the 1. Niceene
counsell, and the Ecclesiasticall historie of Socrates, and Sozomen: And
lastly is set downe a briefe of the succession | of Popes in the sea of
Rome, for these 1600. yeares togea-'ther: what diuersitie there is in their
accompt, what | heresies, schismes, and intrusions there hath been in
that sea, deliuered in opposition against their | Tables, wherewith now

adayes they are | very busie, and other thinges dis-|couered against them. | *By* IOHN PANKE. | [*motto*, then *woodcut.*]

Impr. 29 *a* : 1613 : sm. 4° : the rest as 1608 P.

The titlepage was not printed at Oxford, the woodcut being unknown there : the* rest is a reissue of the sheets of 1608 P. This edition has been erroneously dated 1623 in the British Museum *Catalogue of books . . . to the year* 1640.

P. 95.   Smith, l. 5.

For 1684. S. *read* 1617 S.

1614.

P. 95.   Benefield.

The date of the imprint should be 1614, not 1613.

Pp. 97, 100.   N., S. (no. 9).

This article should be headed S., N., and should follow no. 15 on p. 100.

P. 99.   Rainolds, l. 8.

For Pica English *read* Pica Roman.

1615.

P. 101.   Brasbridge.   *Add at end :—*

See 1586 in this Supplement.

1618.

P. 110.   Sanderson, last line.

For ii. 626 *read* iii. 626.

1619.

P. 111.   Flavel, l. 9.

For Long Primer English *read* Long Primer Roman.

1620.

P. 114.   James, l. 16.

For Procomium *read* Prooemium.

1621.

P. 115.   Burton.

An edition of the *Anatomy of Melancholy* has been issued in 1893, in which the editor claims to have verified most of Burton's quotations. See also 1640 F (Ferrand).

1622.

P. 116.   Carpenter, last line of page.

For CARPNETARIO *read* CARPENTARIO.

P. 118.   Oxford.

The date of the book (1622) has been accidentally omitted.

P. 118.   Rawlinson, l. 4.

For 1662 *read* 162½.

1623.

P. 119. **Panke.**

 The words " See 1613 P " are a reference to 1613 in this Supplement.

1625.

P. 123. **Carpenter, l. 7.**

 For Water *read* Water.

P. 126. **Pemble.**

 A reference to the 2nd edition, 1629, should have been inserted.

1628.

P. 138. **Casa.** The J. W. (de Umbra) is no doubt J. Wouverus.

1629.

P. 144. **Butler, ll. 5–7.**

 For the sentence The reference . . . *Oratoriæ Libri duo, read* The reference to a *Rhetorica* of this year is to a London edition of the *Rhetorica* and *Oratoria* together.

1630.

P. 150. **Hakewill, l. 2.**

 For PER₂|PETVALL *read* PER₂||PETVALL.

P. 150. **Ibid. l. 22.**

 For *Ath. Oxon.*, 256 read *Ath. Oxon.* iii. 256.

P. 151. **Pemble, l. 6.**

 For Impr. 84 *b read* Impr. 84 *a*.

P. 151. **Pinke.** *Add at end*:—

 See 1634 P (2nd ed.)

P. 151. *Insert*:—

 Stanley, Henry.   [*device*] | APPENDIX | AD LIBROS OMNES TAM | VETERIS QVAM NOVI TESTAMENTI. | HENRICVS [*device*] STANLEY | OXONIÆ. | M.DC.XXX. |

 Impr. as above: 1630: folio: pp. [2   *Appendix*: Pica (?) Roman. Contents:— + " 529 "–" 540 "]: pp. 529–40 begg.   p. (1) title : 529–40, tables, see below.

 This set of seven leaves is apparently an experiment to be used for indexing sermons or comments under the verse of the Bible to which they refer. They are blank tables in the form " Versus 1 [2, 3. &c. to 18] *Vid.* L. P. L. " six times and then " *Vid.* P. L. " Eighteen verses are on each page, and references to L(iber) P agina) L(inea) were intended to be filled in. No Latin Bible of folio size of 1629, '30 or '31 seems to exist, so probably this was intended to be bound up with some earlier edition. The only copy known is in the British Museum in MS. Harl. 5932, fol. 45 (Bagford's collections), and no doubt the intended publication was abandoned.

1631.

P. 153. **Bible, top line.**

 The date of imprint (1631) has been accidentally omitted.

P. 155. **F., A. (Saints Legacies).** *Add at end* :—

 See 1640 S.

P. 153. **Felix,** l. 1.
For Felix *read* Felix.

P. 155. Ibid. ll. 4–5.
bere ; quam *should be italic.*

P. 158. **Powel.** A copy of the work has now been seen, as follows :—
Powel, Griffin.   ANALYSIS | ANALYTICO-RVM POSTERIORVM | SIVE
LIBRORVM ARISTO-telis de Demonstratione, | in qua singula capita per |
quæstiones & responsi-nes perspicuè ex-ponuntur : | *adhibitis* | QVIBVSDAM
SCHOLIIS, | ex optimis quibusq; interpreti-bus desumptis, opera & studio
G. | POWEL *Oxoniensis confecta* | & *edita in vsum iuniorum.* | *Editio
secunda.* | [*woodcut.*]

Impr. 143 *a*: 1631: (eights) 12°: pp.
[16] + 241 + [3]: p. 11 beg. *Analysis
cap.* 2, 201 *strationis Medium*: Pica
Roman. Contents :—pp. (1–2) not seen:
(3) title: (5–7) dedication to the earl of
Essex, dated " Ex Collegio Iesu oxoniæ
Tertio Calend: Martij . . . Griffinus
Powel": (8–14) " Ad Lectorem Academicum, and " Prolegomena": (15–16)
not seen: 1–241, the Analysis: (2–3) not
seen.

See in body of text (1631 P).

1632.

P. 161. **Widdowes,** no. 32, l. 4.
For Impr. 137 *read* Impr. 107.

1633.

P. 168. **Gerhardus,** l. 5.
For Long Primer English *read* Long Primer Roman.

P. 172. **Reusner,** l. 9 (only).
In the collation *for 198 read* 224, with the last page misprinted 198: and *for*
34 *read* 36, making the necessary correction in the List of Contents.

1634.

P. 175. **Allen,** 2nd line of page.
It is the Bodleian Catalogue which ascribes the book to John Allen.

P. 175. **Barclay,** no. 3.
The date of the imprint (1634) has been accidentally omitted.

1635.

P. 183. **Chaucer,** l. 6.
In English Roman Italic *the word* Roman *is superfluous.*

P. 183. Ibid. last line.
For sign. 2** *read* sign. **2.

1636.

P. 189. **Carpenter.**

At the end of the technical description a] should be added.

P. 194. **Prideaux, l. 5.**

For 40° P. 50 Th. *read* 4° P. 50 Th.

1637.

P. 197. **Cowper.**

The date of the imprint (1637) is accidentally omitted.

P. 200. **Prideaux,** halfway down.

After Christ's Resurrection . . ." *add* with impr. 152 *b.*

1638.

P. 204. **Burton, l. 5 from end.**

Perhaps *protelata* is rather "continued," although there is no sign of London printing.

P. 209. **Oxford**—Statuta. *Add :—*

A copy of the Statuta Selecta has been seen in which opposite p. 20, instead of the *Encyclopædia* is found an undated folio folded broadside entitled :—SPECULUM | ACADEMICUM : | Quadratura Circuli, | Sive | *Cyclus Prælectorum* in Schema redactus .... This table gives a note of the day of the week, hour, professor, audience and fines, and bears at the foot " Pag. 20.", showing that it was intended for (at least some part of) this edition of the Statuta. In the last line copies vary between " Vesp." (as it should be) and " vesp."

1639.

P. 212. **Dugres.**

The date of the imprint (1639) is accidentally omitted.

P. 214. **Grotius,** 3rd line from end.

For 1722 *read* 1622.

1640.

P. 223. **Saints Legacies.** *Add at end :—*

The first edition of this book is described in 1631 F, so the note of its rarity must be modified.

In Arber's *Transcript of the Stationers' Registers* there is a record that this book under the title " A Collection of Certaine Promisis out of the Word of God " was entered by Robert Swayne on 21 June 1629, and that Swayne's widow (?) Martha transferred her rights in " the Promises or Saintes legacy " to Richard Royston on 6 Feb. 163½.

P. 223. **Tozer.**

The date of the imprint (1640) is accidentally omitted.

LIST OF UNDATED BOOKS

(WITH A REFERENCE TO THE YEAR UNDER WHICH THEY
ARE CATALOGUED).

Alexander: see 1485.

Angelus, Christophorus: see 1618.

Articles: see 1633.

Augustine: see 1483.

Cicero: see 1480.

France—Articles: see 1624.

Godwin, F., bp. of Llandaff: see 1603.

Hampole: see 1483.

Howson, John, bp. of Oxford: see 1622.

Hutchins, Robert: see 1617.

James, Thomas: Humble Request: see 1625.

Jesuits Pater Noster: see 1611.

Laet, Jaspar: see 1518.

Latin Grammar: see 1481, 1483.

Logic: see 1483.

Lyndewoode, Will.: see 1483.

Oxford, Merton College: see 1623.

—— University: Encyclopædia: see 1635.

—— —— Orders for the Market: see 1602, 1606.

Philosophy: de Philosophia: see 1586.

Shepery, John: see 1586.

Terence: see 1483.

Thornborough, John, bp. of Bristol: see 1605.

Thornburgh, Edw.: see 1639.

W., R.: Merry jests: see 1617.

W(alkington), T(homas): see 1631.

APPENDIX A.

The Fifteenth Century Press.

(Supplementary to, and corrective of, pp. 1-4.)

THE Oxford Press of the fifteenth century is a peculiarly interesting one. At present fifteen works are known to belong to it, ranging in date from "1468" (1478?) to 1486 (1489?). Not only is its origin quite independent, so far as is known, of Caxton's printing, not only are new products of the press still from time to time discovered, but the battle which has been waged about the date of its establishment has made the "1468" book a veritable typographical battleground, and in Henry Bradshaw's opinion a touchstone of intellectual acumen.

In the first place some details of the various books will be given: then an account of the type and presswork: and lastly a description of each book supplementary to, and corrective of, that contained on pp. 1-4.

DETAILS OF THE EARLY OXFORD PRESS.

No.	Date.	Place Named.	Printer Named.	Type Used.	Short Title.	Paper and Make-up.				Composition.		
						Size by folding.	Size by make-up.	Size by appearance.	Copies on vellum known.	Signatures.	No. of pages.†	Size of printed page.*
1	" 1468," Dec. 17	Oxonia	——	1	Jerome	double	eights	sm. 4°	o	a, b, &c.	84	$4\frac{3}{4} \times 2\frac{3}{4}$
2	1479	Oxonia (or -ae, plural)	——	1	Aretinus	double	eights	sm. 4°	o	a, b, &c.	348	$4\frac{3}{4} \times 2\frac{3}{4}$
3	14⁷⁹⁄₈₀ (?), Mar. 14.	Oxonia	——	1	Ægidius	double	eights	sm. 4°	o	a, b, &c.	48	$4\frac{3}{4} \times 2\frac{3}{4}$
4	[1480 ?]	——	——	2	Cicero	double	sixes	sm. 4°	o	a, b, &c.	60	$5\frac{1}{2} \times 3\frac{1}{2}$
5	[1481 ?]	——	——	2	Latin Grammar	double	?	sm. 4°	o	a, b, &c.	—	$5\frac{5}{16} \times 3\frac{7}{16}$
6	1481, Oct. 11	Alma universitas Oxon.	Theodoricus Rood de Colonia	2, 3	Ales	single	eights	folio	+	a, b, &c.; A, B, &c.	480	$7\frac{1}{2} \times 4\frac{3}{4}$
7	1482, July 31	——	——	2, 3	Latteburius	single	eights	folio	+	a, b, &c.; A, B, &c.	584	$7\frac{7}{8} \times 4\frac{7}{8}$
8	[1483 ?]	——	——	4, 5, 6	Anwykyll, with Vulgaria (two editions)	double	eights	sm. 4°	o	a, b, &c.	244	$4\frac{5}{8}-5\frac{3}{16} \times 3\frac{1}{2}-4\frac{3}{16}$
9	[1483 ?]	——	——	4, 5, 6	Augustine	double	eight	sm. 4°	o	a	16	$4\frac{1}{2} \times 2\frac{15}{16}$
10	[1483 ?]	——	——	4, 6	Hampole	double	sixes	sm. 4°	o	a, b, &c.	128	$5\frac{7}{16} \times 3\frac{3}{8}$
11	[1483 ?]	——	——	4, 6	Logic	double	sixes	sm. 4°	o	A, B, &c.; Aa, Bb, &c.	328	$5\frac{3}{8} \times 3\frac{3}{8}$
12	[1483 ?]	——	——	3, 4, 5, 6	Lyndewoode	single	eights & sixes	folio	+	a, b, &c.; A, B, &c.; aa, bb, &c.	732	$10\frac{1}{2} \times 6\frac{1}{8}-\frac{3}{8}$
13	1485	Alma universitas Oxoniac	{ Teodericus Rood de Colonia, and Thomas Hunte Anglicus }	3, 5	Phalaris	double	eights	sm. 4°	o	a, b, &c.	136	$4\frac{7}{8} \times 2\frac{7}{8}$
14	[1485 ?]	——	——	4, 5, 7	Textus Alexandri	?	?	sm. 4°	o	a, b, &c.	—	$5\frac{5}{16} \times 3\frac{3}{16}$
15	148⁶⁄₇ [?]	——	——	5, 7	Festial	single	eights & sixes	folio	o	a, b, &c.	348	$7\frac{3}{16} \times 4\frac{11}{16}$

† None is paged : nor are there catchwords.

* Exclusive of headline, signatures, and marginal notes.

DETAILS OF THE EARLY OXFORD PRESS (continued).

No.	Short Title.	Columns in a page.	Lines in a column.	Printing begins on signature.	Page even at side.	Headlines.	Marginal printing.	Paragraphs set back.	Space left for caps.	Directors.	Punctuation. . : , ? ()	Pages at a time	Spaced.	Red ink used.	Borders.	Woodcuts in text.	Woodcut caps.
				COMPOSITION (continued).								PRINTING.			ILLUSTRATIONS.		
1	Jerome	1	25	a 1	usually	o	o	+	+	once	+ + o o o	1	o	o	o	o	o
2	Aretinus	1	25	a 2	+	o	o	+	+	once, in one copy	+ + o o o	2	o	o	o	o	o
3	Ægidius	1	25	a 2	+	o	o	+	+	o	+ + o + o	2	o	+	o	o	o
4	Cicero	1	19	a 2?	+	o	o	o?	?	?	+ +(/) + +	2?	+	o	o	o	o
5	Latin Grammar	1	27	?	+	o	o	+	o	o	+ o o ? ?	?	o	o	o	o	o
6	Ales	2	38	a 2	+	o	o	+	+	o	+ o o o o	2	o	o	+	o	o
7	Latteburius	2	40	a 2	+	+	+	+	+	o	+ o o o o	2	o	o	+	o	o
8	Auwykyll, with Vulgaria (two editions)	1	22 ?	?	+	o	o	+	+	once	+ o o o o	2?	o	o	o	o	o
9	Augustine	1	26 ?	a 2	+	o	o	o	+	o	+ + o o o	?	o	o	o	o	o
10	Hampole	1	31	a 2	+	o	o	o	+	o	+ o o o o	4?	o	o	o	o	o
11	Logic	1	31	a 2	+	o	o	+	+	+	+ o o o o	4?	o	o	o	+	o
12	Lyndewoode	2	46 or 60	a 2 (a 1^v)	+	+	o	o	+	o	+ o o o o	?	o	o	o	o	o
13	Phalaris	1	21	a 1^v	+	o	o	o	+	o	+ o o o o	2	o	o	o	o	o
14	Textus Alexandri	1	—	?	+	o	o	?	?	o	+ o o o o	?	o	o	o	o	o
15	Festial	2	33	a 1^v	+	o	o	+	o	o	+ o o o o	?	o	o	o	+	+

Owners of Copies.

No.	British Museum.	Bodleian.	Cambridge University Library.	John Rylands Library.	Oxford Colleges, &c.	Cambridge Colleges.	Other owners of copies.	Total of copies.
1 Jerome	1	1*	1	1	3	0	Huth Library, Earl of Pembroke, Sir H. Dryden, Paris, America.	12
2 Aretinus . . .	1	1*	0	1	0*	0	Norwich Cathedral, Earl of Pembroke, Chetham Library, Lord Ashburnham.	7
3 Ægidius . . .	0	1	0	1	1	0		3
4 Cicero	0	0*	0	0	0*	0		0
5 Latin Grammar .	0*	0	0	0	0	0		0
6 Ales	1*	1*	2*	1	8*	0*	Durham and Lincoln Cathedrals, Dulwich College.	16
7 Latteburius . .	1*	1*	2	1	3*	2*	Lambeth, Westminster, Stonyhurst, Brussels, T. E. Cooke, Esq.	15
8 Anwykyll, with Vulgaria . . .	½	1½	½*	½	0	0*		(3)
9 Hampole . . .	0	0	2	1	0	0*		3
10 Logic	0	0*	0*	0	2	0*		2
11 Lyndewoode . .	3	1*	2	1	3	4	Edinburgh (Advocates' Library), Durham Cathedral, Glasgow, Paris, E. G. Duff, Esq., Lord Crawford.	20
12 Augustine . .	1	0	0	0	0	0		1
13 Phalaris . . .	0	0*	0	1	2*	0*		3
14 Textus Alexandri	0	0	0	0	0	0*		0
15 Festial	0*	1½	0	1	0*	0	Lambeth.	3½
Totals	8½	9	9⅚	9½	22	6	24	88½
Different books .	6½	8	5⅚	9½				

The finest set is undoubtedly possessed by the John Rylands Library at Manchester.

* With fragments of the book, independently of copies.

THE TYPE AND PRESS-WORK.

Seven kinds of type were used, the use of which can be seen on p. 238. Facsimiles of all of them are given in plates II–V.

These obviously divide the books into three groups. In the first group of three ("1468"–14$\frac{79}{80}$) only type no. 1 is used. In the second group of four (1480–82, Theodoric Rood) only types 2–3 are found. In the last group consisting of eight (1483–148$\frac{9}{?}$, T. Rood and Thomas Hunte) only types 4–7 are used, except that the peculiar black initial type (no. 3) is occasionally still used.

The press was of course a wooden hand-screw one, which was at first employed to print one page at a time (Jerome), but after the first book two pages and perhaps later four were struck off together. The earliest printing press of which we have an engraving is as late as 1$\frac{1}{5}\frac{2}{6}\frac{3}{6}$ (see an article in *Bibliographica*, 1894, no. 2), but there was great conservatism in detail, and from the early engravings and such researches as those which Blades, De Vinne, Talbot Reed, and others have made, we know many of the details of working in the earliest days.

Type 1.   "1468"–14$\frac{79}{80}$.

Character:—Cologne black.

Body:—English, nearly (10 lines = 1$\frac{13}{40}$ in. In modern English 10 lines = 1$\frac{7}{8}$ in.).

Used in the Jerome, Aretinus and Aegidius, with no other.

The "upper case" (to use a modern expression) consisted of at least 16 divisions, G, J, K, L, T, U, W, X, Y, Z not being used, and P seldom in the Jerome, H being there used for both H and P. This misuse is not found in the other two books. On the other hand there are two forms of C, E, N, and Q, both probably mixed in the same division. Q is in the Jerome almost always ℺ (a peculiarity found in some ornamental MSS., from the convenience of extending the tail into the margin), in the Aretinus and Aegidius always Q: the letter is however identical in all three books, but being on a square body it is in the Jerome turned one quarter round.

The "lower case" consisted of at least 121 divisions. Of the simple unmodified letters k and z are wanting, and except in the Jerome j (but ij is found in all, colligated). There are two forms of p, r, and three of s, the two p's and r's being used indiscriminately, but the two s's (final) and the ſ (initial and medial) having their proper use. Of colligated or modified letters there are at least eighty-three, and of other symbols eleven (for -et, &, con-, -us [two], id est, full stop, colon, ?). Of these 121 about 95 are common to all three. The signs of progress are as follows:—

In the Jerome, contrasted with the other two, Q is except in two places ℺, H is generally used as P, and I have not elsewhere noticed b, or j used by itself. On the other hand in the two others, and not in the Jerome, are found an extra short t in which the perpendicular stroke hardly appears at all above the horizontal line, and eleven new forms, including fe, ff, and pp in colligation. The Q and P are rightly used, always.

So too in the Jerome and Aretinus compared with the Aegidius we find that q is printed too high up, being in fact an inverted b, or, more accurately, an inverted broken h occasionally used for b. In the Jerome this is almost always the case, in the Aretinus as often as not, in the Aegidius hardly ever. It may be accidental that B and H and three minor modified letters are not found in the short Aegidius, that w (in wlt = vult) is only found in the Jerome, ꝉ (= id est) only in the Aretinus : but the occurrence of ſ (= ?) and of printing in red ink *only* in the Aegidius, is not insignificant.

The relative order of the three may therefore be assumed to be as above indicated.

Origin of the type.

It may be taken as certain that as Caxton's type is based on Bruges models, so the first Oxford type is ultimately derived from Cologne. Ulric Zel began printing there at least as early as 1466, and the general resemblance to his letters is clear. The likeness is still nearer when we follow Zel's influence on Arnold ther Hoernen (Cologne, from 1470), Richard Paffroet of Cologne (Deventer, from 1477), and especially a little-known Cologne printer named Gerard ten Raem de Bercka, whose only dated book is of 1478. John of Westphalia (Alost and Louvain, from 1473) and Jacobus de Breda, a successor of Paffroet at Deventer, also supply similarities. In the case of Gerard we actually find, besides a close general similarity, the same misuse of H as P. Unfortunately no works printed by him, except the dated *Modus Confitendi* and an undated *Aesopus*, are at present known, so that it must not be assumed that 1478 is his earliest or only date.

It is at present also unsafe to assume that Theodoricus Rood of Cologne who printed at Oxford in 1481–85 was the first Oxford printer, or ever used type no. 1.

Type 2 (1480?–1482).

Character :—Narrow Dutch Black.

Body :—English, nearly (10 lines = just less than 2 in.).

Used in the Cicero (1480?: by itself), Latin Grammar (1481?: by itself), Ales (1481 : chiefly, but with no. 3), and Latteburius (1482 : chiefly, but with no. 3).

The "upper case" consisted of 22 letters (J, K, U, W omitted).

The "lower case" consisted of at least 131 divisions. Of the simple letters j only occurs in colligation with i (as ij), and there are two forms of r, s (s, ſ) and y. There are about 93 colligated or modified letters.

Unfortunately it is very difficult to institute a close comparison of the use of letters, so as to establish a proper order of the books, in consequence of the fragmentary state of the Milo and the Latin Grammar. The Milo can be clearly separated from the rest: the type is *spaced*, so that 10 lines = between $2\frac{9}{16}$ and $2\frac{3}{4}$ in., and (), ſ (= ?), | (= comma) are found in it alone. In fact, but for the closest resemblance of actual type, the Milo would have to be regarded as printed elsewhere: and it cannot yet be said to be quite certainly printed at Oxford.   The Ales and Latteburius are hardly to be distinguished in the use of type, but I have observed w only in the Latteburius and Grammar.

The origin of the type is probably to be looked for near Cologne, from whence came Theodoricus Rood, the avowed printer of the Ales, and where a Theodoricus, who may probably be identified with Rood, printed in 1485-6 in a type smaller than, but similar to, the present one.   The narrow stilted look of the letters and the semicircular sweep in front of the A are noticeable features.   Henry Bradshaw detected a similarity between this type and that of Arnold ther Hoernen at Cologne.

Type 3 (1481–1485).

Character:—Heading and initial Black, a large special type.

Body:—2-line English, nearly (10 lines = 4 in. —, 10 lines of 2-line English = $3\frac{3}{4}$ in. +).

Used only in the Ales (1481) and Latteburius (1482) (for the beginnings of chapters), in the Lyndewoode (1483?: head lines) and the Phalaris (1485: one line).

The type is too sparsely used to enable us to describe the extent of the fount: but F, G, J, j, K, k, v, W, w, X, Y, Z, z are not found; I and g have two forms each; s, f are found; V is only used for the number five; and nine modified or conjoined letters occur.   The peculiarity of the letters is a slipped or detached upper corner in B, L, N, which is found in 1506 in Quentell's printing at Cologne, and may be compared with a smaller form used by Jean Veldener at Culenburg in 1484.

Type 4 (1483?–1485?).

Character:—Small Dutch Black.

Body:—Pica, nearly (10 lines = $1\frac{11}{16}$ + in., 10 lines in Pica = $1\frac{13}{16}$ – in.).

This is the small type of the Anwykyll and Lyndewoode (both 1483?), the ordinary type of the Hampole, Logic, and Augustine (all 1483?), and the small type of the Lyndewoode (1483?), and is used in the Textus Alexandri (1485?).   It is in many details similar to type 2, but may be readily distinguished by the o being broad and round in type 4, instead of narrow and oval as in type 2.   There are two forms of S in type 4, and only one in type 2.   The capitals are identical with those of type 6.

The fount consisted of 25 capitals (J, V, W wanting, but two forms of D, S), 27 small letters (z wanting, but r, s double) and at least 95 modified or conjoined letters, in all not less than 147 types.   Seven of the last class appear to be peculiar to the Logic, which may therefore be the latest of the group.

Type 5 (1483–148?).

Character:—Small Caxtonian Black.

Body:—Great Primer, nearly (10 lines = $2\frac{5}{16}$ in., 10 lines of Great Primer = $2\frac{3}{8}$ in.).

This is the larger type of the Anwykyll, the largest but one (ordinary large) of the Lyndewoode, the largest of the Augustine (all 1483?), the ordinary one of the Phalaris (1485), is used in the Textus Alexandri (1485?), and is the small type of the Festial (1486). The capitals are identical with those of type 7.

There are 19 capitals (J, K, V, W, X, Y, Z wanting) and 28 small letters (j, z wanting, but d, g, r, s double), and at least 44 modified or conjoined letters, five of which seem to be peculiar to the Festial, as is also the use of k. In all there were not less than 91 types.

Type 6 (1483?).

Character :—Large Dutch Black, a Church type going with no. 4.

Body :—Pica, nearly (as no. 4).

This is the larger type of the Hampole, the larger type (two half lines only) of the Logic, the larger type imbedded in the small type of the Lyndewoode, the intermediate type (one line) in the Augustine, and occurs in the Anwykyll (all 1483?). The capitals are identical with those of type 4.

There are 22 capitals (J, K, V, W, Z wanting, but S double), 24 small letters (j, k, w, z wanting, but r, s double), and at least 16 modified or conjoined letters, in all not less than 62 types. Eight of the modified letters appear to be peculiar to the Hampole.

Type 7 (1485?–148?).

Character :—Large Caxtonian Black, a Church type going with no. 5.

Body :—Great Primer, nearly (as no. 5).

This is used in the Textus Alexandri (1485?) and is the large type of the Festial (148?). The capitals are identical with those of type 5.

To judge from the Festial, there are 18 capitals (J, K, R, V, W, X, Y, Z not being used), 24 small letters (k, w, y, z not found, but r, s double), and at least 9 modified letters, 51 in all.

WATERMARKS.

At present the study of watermarks has not reached a stage at which they are able to contribute scientific proofs of high importance, nor will any proof be ever deducible from them except the earliest possible occurrence of an undated issue, although probabilities of concurrent printing may be arrived at. Only some plain facts, therefore, will be stated with respect to their occurrence in the early Oxford books.

If we take the first group (the Jerome, Aretinus and Aegidius), we find no less than 26, out of a total of 50. The Rufinus has seven (two shared with the others, one shared with the Aretinus only, one shared with the Latteburius, and three peculiar to itself). The Aretinus has 22, most of which are found in the later groups, but eight are peculiar to itself. The Aegidius has two only, common to the group.

In the second group (Cicero, Ales, Latteburius, Latin Grammar) there appear to be 28, of which four are common to all the groups, one is shared only with group one, seven only with group three, and sixteen are peculiar.

In the third group 38 occur, four of which are common to all the groups, nine are shared with the first alone, seven with the second alone, and eighteen are peculiar.

SEPARATE BOOKS.

1. **Jerome** ("1468," see p. 1).

The treatise of Tyrannius Rufinus on the Apostles' Creed, here ascribed to St. Jerome, was undoubtedly the first product of the Oxford press. It bears the date of 17 December, 1468, as the day on which the printing was finished. The colophon is clearly printed and bears no mark of haste, nor does it show the smallest trace of alteration in any of the copies seen by the present writer. Saturday is a reasonable day on which to conclude a work. A facsimile of the colophon is given in plate II.

Unfortunately for the peace of the bibliographer two spectres have haunted this book, one of which "pulveris exigui jactu" has been laid, but the other is not yet gone, although there is a prospect of ultimate eviction.

1. The Corsellis forgery.

In 1664 Richard Atkyns, a Gloucestershire gentleman of some position, and educated at Balliol, issued a book, the title of which sets forth with unusual clearness the object of the volume :—"The Original and Growth of Printing : Collected Out of History, and the *Records* of this Kingdome. Wherein is also Demonstrated, That Printing appertaineth to the *Prerogative Royal*; and is a Flower of the *Crown* of *England.* By Richard Atkyns, *Esq* : " (London, printed by John Streater, for the Author, MDCLXIV : quarto : pp. [12]+24). Atkyns's object was to recommend himself to Charles II's attention by proving that printing was a royal privilege : and for this it was very desirable that there should be evidence of the introduction of the art into England under royal protection. The testimony of Stowe—corroborated by Howell—that " William Caxton of London, Mercer," introduced it in 1471, was unsuitable. Atkyns, however, came upon a copy of the " 1468 " Oxford book, and " the same most worthy Person who trusted me with the aforesaid Book, did also present me with the Copy of a Record and Manuscript in *Lambeth-*House, heretofore in his Custody, belonging to the See (and not to any particular Arch-Bishop of *Canterbury*) ; the substance whereof was this (though I hope, for publique satisfaction, the Record it self, in its due time, will appear)." Then ensues the following story :—

> *Thomas Bourchier*, Arch-Bishop of *Canterbury*, moved the then King (*Hen.* the 6th) to use all possible means for procuring a Printing-Mold (for so 'twas there called) to be brought into this Kingdom ; the King (a good Man, and

much given to Works of this Nature) readily hearkned to the Motion; and taking private Advice, how to effect His Defign, concluded it could not be brought about without great Secrecy, and a confiderable Sum of Money given to fuch Perfon or Perfons, as would draw off fome of the Work-men from *Harlein* in *Holland*, where *John Cuthenberg* had newly invented it, and was himfelf perfonally at Work: 'Twas refolv'd, that lefs then one Thoufand Marks would not produce the defir'd Effect: Towards which Sum, the faid Arch-Bifhop prefented the King with Three Hundred Marks. The Money being now prepared, the Management of the Defign was committed to Mr. *Robert Turnour*, who then was of the Roabs to the King, and a Perfon moft in Favour with Him, of any of his Condition: Mr. *Turnour* took to his Affiftance Mr. *Caxton*, a Citizen of good Abilities, who Trading much into *Holland*, might be a Creditable Pretence, as well for his going, as ftay in the *Low Countries*: Mr. *Turnour* was in Difguife (his Beard and Hair fhaven quite off) but Mr. *Caxton* appeared known and publique. They having received the faid Sum of One Thoufand Marks, went firft to *Amfterdam*, then to *Leyden*, not daring to enter *Harlein* it felf; for the Town was very jealous, having imprifoned and apprehended divers Perfons, who came from other Parts for the fame purpofe: They ftaid till they had fpent the whole One Thoufand Marks in Gifts and Expences: So as the King was fain to fend Five Hundred Marks more, Mr. *Turnour* having written to the King, that he had almoft done his Work; a Bargain (as he faid) being ftruck betwixt him and two *Hollanders*, for bringing off one of the Work men, who fhould fufficiently difcover and teach this New Art: At laft, with much ado, they got off one of the Under-Workmen, whofe Name was *Frederick Corfells* (or rather *Corfellis*), who late one Night ftole from his Fellows in Difguife, into a Veffel prepared before for that purpofe; and fo the Wind (favouring the Defign) brought him fafe to *London*.

'Twas not thought fo prudent, to fet him on Work at *London*, (but by the Arch-Bifhops meanes, who had been Vice-Chancellor, and afterwards Chancellor of the Univerfity of *Oxon*) *Corfellis* was carryed with a Guard to *Oxon*; which Guard conftantly watch'd, to prevent *Corfellis* from any poffible Efcape, till he had made good his Promife, in teaching how to Print: So that at *Oxford* Printing was firft fet up in *England*, which was before there was any Printing-Prefs, or Printer, in *France, Spain, Italy*, or *Germany*, (except the City of *Mentz*) which claimes Seniority, as to Printing, even of *Harlein* it felf, calling her City, *Urbem Maguntinam Artis Tipographiæ Inventricem primam*, though 'tis known to be otherwife, that City gaining that Art by the Brother of one of the Workmen of *Harlein*, who had learnt it at Home of his Brother, and after fet up for himfelf at *Mentz*.

This Prefs at *Oxon* was at leaft ten years before there was any Printing in *Europe* (except at *Harlein*, and *Mentz*) where alfo it was but new born. This Prefs at *Oxford*, was afterwards found inconvenient, to be the fole Printing-place of *England*, as being too far from *London*, and the Sea: Whereupon the King fet up a Prefs at St. *Albans*, and another in the Abby of *Weftminfter*, where they Printed feveral Bookes of Divinity and Phyfick, (for the King, for Reafons beft known to himfelf and Council) permitted then no Law-Books to be Printed; nor did any Printer exercife that ART, but onely fuch as were the Kings fworn Servants; the King himfelf having the Price and Emolument for Printing Books.

Printing thus brought into *England*, was moft Gracioufly received by the King, and moft cordially entertained by the Church, the Printers having the Honour to be fworn the King's Servants, and the Favour to Lodge in the very Bofome of the Church; as in *Weftminfter*, St. *Albans*, *Oxon*, &c.

As no one believes in this story it is not worth while to do more than to point out that no corroboration of it has ever been found, (much less the original record difcovered), that Henry VI was deposed 4 March 146$\frac{9}{0}$, and that the type shows no resemblance to that of Haarlem. Nor does the rest of the book concern us. The tale, however, in the absence of contradiction, obtained some vogue, so that we find for instance in Layer Marney church in Essex some such inscription as the following "Præ-

missus, non amissus, Nicolas Corsellis Armiger Dominus hujus manerii
hic requiescit, hâc vitâ ad meliorem commigratus Anno D 1674 Die
Octobris 19º.

> Artem typographi miratam Belgicus Anglis
> Corsellis docuit, Regis prece munere victus.
> Hic fuit extremis mercator cognitus Indis :
> Incola jam cælis, virtus sua famaque vivent.

Johannes Corsellis ejus Executor & Consanguineus hoc monumentum
posuit." The Corsellis family came from Flanders in the 17th century.
There is no question that this clumsy forgery of Atkyns has had its effect
in befogging the subject to which it relates, and has predisposed critics to
suspect the date of the first Oxford book.

II. The disputed date, "1468."

The first who threw doubt on the recorded date of the Jerome was
Conyers Middleton in his *Dissertation on the origin of Printing* published
in 1735, and since then the opinion that 1468 is an error for 1478 (an
x having dropped out of " MCCCCLXXVIII ") has steadily gained ground
with the advance of critical methods, until authorities like Bradshaw
and Blades and Duff have come to regard the question as settled. The
only two separate and formal defences of the date (not counting inciden-
tal passages in books) are a MS. in the Guildhall Library in London, in
a volume of Stukeley's *Palæographia Britannica* marked B. 2. 1, perhaps
written in about 1770, and S. W. Singer's *Some Account of the book printed at
Oxford in MCCCCLXVIII* (London, 1812, 50 copies for private distribution),
a work which the author subsequently called in as far as he was able. In
the former the arguments are of a general character, such as that if, as
Middleton asserted, the King had not leisure to attend to such matters
during Civil War, the archbishop *had*, and that Caxton's silence counts
for nothing in the general obscurity which surrounds the earliest printing
presses. The Corsellis story is accepted. Singer is more scientific, as
befits the later date, and adduces several of the technical arguments which
may still be used.

It is now time to state the present aspect of the dispute, and to ascer-
tain how far the date " 1468 " is not only dubious but untenable. The
arguments against the date may be stated in presumed order of their
cogency, with the remarks on the other side which they severally suggest.

1. *The presence of Signatures.*

The Jerome presents to our eyes the ordinary signatures to which we
are accustomed in fifteenth-century books, that is to say the marks a j, a ij,
a iij, a iiij on the recto of each of the four leaves which form the first half
of the sections of eight leaves (sixteen pages) of which the book is generally
composed. These are placed just below the last letters of the printed
page, close under them. Now the earliest known book with a date in
which signatures elsewhere occur in this developed form is an *Expositio
Decalogi*, by Johannes Nider, printed at Cologne by Koelhoff in 1472, the
next being a Cologne book by F. de Platea in 1474. The argument is
that it is extremely unlikely that an isolated printer in a provincial town

in England should make such a discovery and advance, and that the next similar book should be a German one four years later[1].

What may be called the common ground of the discussion on this point is well explained in Blades's *Books in Chains* (Lond. 1892), pp. 85-122, in a paper on Signatures. He shows that the idea of signatures in manuscripts is as old as books themselves, but that in manuscripts the marks, being in writing and intended for the binder's eye alone, were naturally, as a rule, at the foot or corner of the page, and often cut off in the process of binding. When printing came in, the obvious difficulty was to print marks so far from the rest of the printed page as to be cut off in binding. This difficulty was met in two ways : either the signatures were *written in* at the extreme foot (from 1462 ?), or the signatures were stamped on by hand with single types (from 1473 ?). Some printers, however, did manage by care to print signatures far from the text (1474 on ?). Ultimately in a single case in 1472 and with increasing frequency from 1474 printers found that the essential ugliness of printed signatures close to the page was counterbalanced by the utility and convenience of the change, and our modern system was begun.

Now, it must be constantly remembered that the entire weight of disproof lies with those who dispute the printed date. This is why it is simply amusing to read Blades's sage words on the subject of this 1472 book with normal printed signatures. He is pledged to renounce the Oxford date, but he finds it awkward that there *is* an isolated book of 1472 in precisely the same category—with the same want of precedent, the same absence of imitators, the same forlorn appearance. Observe how he deals with it (p. 116 of the book above cited) :—" This is a puzzling book, for it is at least two years earlier than any other book so signed. In this city, too. [i.e. Lübeck[2]] many works were issued with MS. signatures with a later date than this. It is dangerous to assert that a book is wrongly dated because you cannot make it fit into a bibliographical theory ; but I feel inclined, from the general aspect of the book, to date it as 1482, rather than 1472." And yet a very high authority on typography assures me that the book is *undoubtedly* of 1472! What then prevents the tentative and isolated experiment of Cologne from having a similar tentative and isolated forerunner, even at Oxford? We may remember too that in the infancy of printing it was common to detect errors as the book went through the press, and often the printer himself corrected an error with his pen, as in the colophon of the Aegidius (see p. 1). Or a reader would do the same. But it is believed that in no copy of the Jerome is there any attempt to correct or even throw suspicion on the date. There is the date, plain and detailed, and it is allowable to wait for scientific proof before it is abandoned. *A priori* considerations have force, but they are liable to sudden overthrow.

Clearly the consideration of signatures alone cannot avail to disprove the date of the Jerome. But much more remains.

---

[1] As these pages pass through the press I am informed by Mr. E. G. Duff that Lord Crawford possesses an edition of Horace's Opuscula printed in " 1470" with signatures.

[2] Blades was under the erroneous impression that Koelhoff printed at Lübeck, instead of Cologne : where also books with manuscript signatures occur later than 1472.

2. *Signs of progress.*

It is said that, if we consider the interval between 1468 and 1479, we shall reasonably expect definite signs of progress. On the contrary, the first three Oxford books are printed with the same type, with similar signatures, with the same sized page and the same number of lines in a column. " In fact," says Blades in the *Antiquary*, vol. iii, no. 13, Jan. 1881, in an article on *The First Printing Press at Oxford*, " if a leaf of one was extracted and inserted in another it would, typographically, excite no remark." *Natura nihil facit per saltum*, and we are accustomed to apply the idea of evolution and development to every art and trade. It is asserted also that there is no other case of the cessation of a press for over ten years. But cessation of printing for such a time is not unknown. No book was produced at Bamberg between 1462 and 1480, or at Caen between 1480 and 1500, or at Brussels between 1484 and 1500, or at Haarlem for some years after 1486, or at Saragossa after 1475 till 1485? Moreover the only early printing known at Tavistock is two books in 1525 and 1534. The *same type* and *identical woodcuts* are found in the two, with an interval of nine years. And where there is cessation, it is obvious that we may be content with fewer signs of advance when work is resumed at the same press with the same type, than if the activity had been continuous, or if the instruments were changed.

But this question of progress is a plain issue. Are there no signs of advance in the two later books compared with the earlier one?

The first book often has an unevenness at the right-hand edge of a column (in 28 pages out of 84). In the other two it is always perfectly even [1]. Again, the Jerome starts printing on sign. a 1, whereas the other two start with a blank leaf, the printing beginning on a 2. Again, in the Jerome there is a peculiar misuse of the capitals H and Q (see p. 241), not found in the following books. And lastly, to omit smaller matters, there is the decided and important fact that whereas in the Jerome each page was printed separately, in the Aegidius and Aretinus two pages were printed at a time.

3. *The Type.*

Of the palmary arguments against the date, one still remains. The first Oxford type presents a remarkable similarity to that used by Gerard ten Raem de Bercka (see p. 242), and his only dated book at present known is of 1478. There is certainly a real connexion between the two founts, but we know so extremely little of this printer that it is at present unsafe to base any conclusion on his work. The typographical genealogy of the early printers of the Netherlands and Germany has not yet been fully drawn out, and of the 1478 *Modus Confitendi* (Hain 11455), which is here in question, only two copies *with the date* are known, one in the John Rylands (Spencer) library at Manchester and one on the continent. On this point we shall doubtless know more in time, but at present we are bound to suspend our judgment.

---

[1] In 1467 Ulric Zel of Cologne (see p. 242) was unacquainted with the setting-rule, which made evenness easy: he adopted it in 1468-9, but Colard Mansion at Bruges not till 1478 (Blades, *Books in Chains*, p. 128).

There are two subsidiary considerations left. One is that mistakes of date in colophons are not uncommon. An edition of Aeneas Sylvius's *Epistolae* (Cologne, printed by Koelhoff) is dated MCCCCLXVIII, which is stated to be an error for 1478, and an *Opusculum de componendis versibus* by Mataratius, printed at Venice, is also believed to be erroneously dated 1468 for 1478. Caxton's edition of Gower's *Confessio Amantis* is dated 1493 instead of 1483. I have noticed the following additional errors affecting dates before 1501:—720 for 1720, 1061 for 1601, 1099 for 1499, 1334 for 1734, 1400 for 1490 or 1500, 1444 for 1494, 1461 for 1471, 1461 for 1641, 1462 for 1472, 1472 for 1482.

There is no doubt therefore that a mistake of date in an early book has many parallels, and so far the improbability of it happening in other books is diminished. At the same time one would expect the first printers in a place of learning to be careful enough, even if an initial blunder of this magnitude were committed, to correct it in some copies before issue. It is of course conceivable that the date was deliberately falsified, to avoid expected unpleasant consequences of being found *flagrante delicto*, but this hypothesis may be left to be dealt with when some one maintains it.

5. *Books bound with the Jerome.*

There remains a consideration of some weight. Until this century it was common to bind together several books (not merely pamphlets) in one volume. What books have been found in the same binding with the "1468" volume? Four copies of the Jerome are, or are known to have been, bound with several other treatises (see p. 252). One is bound with (and before) the Aretinus of 1479, and it is interesting that though a few leaves of modern paper now separate them there is an offset of the first page of the Aretinus on the last page of the Jerome, showing that the Aretinus was bound with the Jerome before the former was entirely dry. No conclusion however about the date of the Jerome can be drawn from this, and whatever presumption of synchronism might be raised is removed by the fact that the well defined stains at the end of the Jerome and beginning of the Aretinus do *not* run from the one to the other. A second copy was bound with seven others, only two of which are dated, 1478 and (the Oxford Aegidius) 1479 : one of the undated is about 1485 (Perottus). A third copy was bound with four preceding treatises, of which the only dated one was the first, the Oxford Aegidius of 1479. A fourth has five pieces with it, the first two of which are of about 1480, the Jerome is third, the fourth is of 1485, the fifth is undated, and the last is of 1486 or 1487.

Clearly we are on very unsafe ground when we base any conclusion on these companion treatises, and our hesitation is not lessened when we notice that the only copy of the *Vulgaria Terentii* (Oxf., not later than 1483) which is bound with other treatises, occurs after books dated 1488 and 1486, the rest being without a date.

6. *First printing in Europe.*

The following list of places and dates will show how far it is likely, if we turn from facts to probabilities, that Oxford should have started printing in 1468. Only the first two towns of each country are given, with the exception of England: and the claim of Oxford is purposely ignored.

1. Germany (Mainz, not after 1454: Strassburg, before 1460: Cologne began not later than 1466).
2. Italy (Subiaco, 1465: Rome, 1467).
3. Switzerland (Basel, not after 1468: Beromünster, 1470).
4. France (Paris, 1470: Lyon, not after 1473).
5. Netherlands (Utrecht, about 1471–3: Alost, 1473).
6. Austro-Hungary (Buda-Pesth, 1473: Trient, 1475).
7. Spain (Valencia, 1474: Saragossa, 1475).
8. England (Westminster, 1477: Oxford, 1478: St. Alban's, 1480 [1479?]: London, 1480).
9. Denmark (Odensee, 1482: Schleswig, 1486).
10. Sweden (Stockholm, 1483: Wadsten, 1495).
11. Portugal (Lisbon, 1489: Leiria, 1492).
12. Montenegro (Cettinje, 1494).

It is hoped that the above summary statement of the arguments for and against the date of the Jerome will serve to make the present position of the question clear. What general conclusion can be arrived at before further facts are discovered? Caxton, who began to print in England in 1477, nowhere claims to have introduced printing into England. Is it still conceivable that Oxford preceded Westminster by nine years? The answer is that it is still conceivable, but not probable. The ground has been slowly and surely giving way beneath the defenders of the Oxford date, in proportion to the advance of our knowledge of early printing, and all that can be said is that it has not yet entirely slipped away. All the new contributions to the argument and all the chief bibliographers are against it, while no fresh defending forces are in sight. But it is still allowable to assert that the destructive arguments, even if we admit their cumulative cogency, do not at the present time amount to proof.

In the venerable building at the north-east corner of St. Mary's Church at Oxford—the old House of Congregation, which, though once the cradle of the University,

Nunc situs informis premit et deserta vetustas—

there is still a single tenant, feebly holding his ground and refusing to be evicted. He wears the form of King Alfred and bears a legend beneath, telling us boldly that he founded the University[1]. The clamour of disputation never reaches that silent room, the changes of centuries have disregarded it, and it remains the one place where a belief which cast

[1] AELFREDVS . | LEGVM . ANGLIAE . | ACADEMIAE . OXON . | CONDITOR .

a lustre of royalty over early Oxford, and to this day gives primacy to one of the oldest colleges, is still maintained without contradiction. The figure neither utters nor listens to argument: it asserts and chooses to assert. But the spirit of the age is at the door: St. Mary's is swathed in scaffolding: the sounds of trowel and saw penetrate through the dim glass and the cobwebs, and all things become new. It is probable that the opening years of the twentieth century will see the age-worn bust of Alfred and the copy of the Oxford Jerome in the University archives consigned to a common flame as Impostors in an age of light.

Copies known.

1. British Museum. Perfect. Given by the Earl of Oxford on 10 Mar. 1722 to James West, at whose sale in 1773 it probably passed to M. C. Tutet: then in the King's Library, which passed in 1829 to the British Museum, where it bore the mark 8. D. 5; now 167. b. 26.

2. Bodleian. Wanting e 10, a blank leaf. One page (b 7ᵛ) is printed askew, in this copy only. Owned in 1582 by William Wright: then Bp. Juxon's, who gave it on 31 July 1657 to Bp. Barlow, among whose books it passed to the Bodleian in 1693: where it has been successively marked A. 19. 6 Linc., Auct. Q. 1. 5. 18, Auct. Q. 1. 6. 12 and Auct. R. supra 13.

3. All Souls College, Oxford. Wanting a 4, a 5. Given by Benj. Buckler in 1756: bound in the 18th cent. with the Aretinus (see p. 253). Marked XX. 10. 1, now LL. 10. 17

4. Oriel College, Oxford. Perfect. Originally this was bound 4th in a volume containing Augustinus de dignitate sacerdotum: Meditationes Bernardi: Exempla Scripturae, Paris, 1478: the Jerome: Comm. Petri de Osoma in symbolum Quicunque vult, Paris: the Aegidius, Oxf. 1479: Ars bene moriendi: and Hugonis Speculum ecclesiae. Owned by Edmund Lyster in the 16th cent. The present binding is of the 18th century: but there are old manuscript signatures throughout the volume.

5. Oxford University Archives. Perfect. Owned by John Rhodes in 1664: given by Moses Pit, a London bookseller, 31 Jan. 1672. Bound with the *Casus breves* of Johannes Andreas (n. d.).

6. Cambridge University Library. Wanting e 10, a blank leaf. This copy has a painting of St. Jerome, a coloured capital and border, &c., and a coat of arms. It bears a George I bookplate dated 1713. Marked C. 5. 1, and now AB. 5. 18.

7. John Rylands Library, Manchester. Perfect. Bought for the Spencer Library for £150: bound by C. Lewis: marked 17320, or E. 237: transferred to Manchester with the whole Spencer Library.

8. The Huth Library.

9. The Earl of Pembroke's Library.

10. Sir Henry Dryden's Library. Wanting e 10, a blank leaf. In original binding, part of a volume containing Joh. Sulp. Verulanus de Octo partibus orationis: Aug. Senensis de loquendi regulis: the Jerome: Alb. de Ferrariis de horis canonicis, 1485: Kamintus on the pestilence: and two leaves of a Prognostication of 1486 or 1487.

11. Paris National Library. Bought by Lord Blandford in Feb. 1812 for £91: in the White Knights sale sold for £28.

12. A copy recently sold to an American. Perfect. It was originally in an Oxford contemporary binding with the Oxford Aegidius, 1479: Mich. de Hungaria's Tredecim Sermones: "Oxoniensis cuiusdam exercitationes": Adelard of Bath's Quaestt. naturales: the Jerome was last. Owned by A. Hilton in the 15th cent.

In 1862 a copy in F. S. Ellis's catalogue (p. 14, no. 957) was priced £110.

Fragments:—Leaves a 2, a 7, a 8, b 4, c 1, c 3, e 3, c 6–8 are in the Bodleian.

2. **Aretinus** (1479, see p. 1).

The reasons for placing this book second are given above at pp. 241–2 : if they are regarded as sufficient, we must take "1479" in the Aegidius as what we should call 1480, which is in agreement with the ordinary usage of the time and which gains a slight probability, in that the printing would have been finished on a Sunday, if the year were taken as 147$\frac{9}{80}$. All copies are poorly printed. It was quite fitting that the first book printed at Oxford should be theological and the second the Nicomachean Ethics of Aristotle.

Copies known.

1. British Museum. Wanting a 1, a blank leaf. In this copy alone there is a director for the large O of *Omnis* on b 1ʳ. Owned by Will. Davis in 1792 : then in the Grenville Library : marked "7. p. 115. 1," S. D. 5, 163. B. 2, G. 7930, and now C. 2. a. 7. Bound with it is a manuscript translation into Latin of Aristotle's *Œconomica* and *Politics*, dedicated to Humphrey Duke of Gloucester.

2. Bodleian. Perfect. In this copy at o 2ʳ and o 2ᵛ is a *c̃* printed in the margin, apparently meaning "cancel," since the recto is printed askew. Manuscript notes show that the book, which is in contemporary binding, was at first in the hands of an Oxford student (?) who received pittance from the Prior of Oseney. Then "Codex Michaelis Canni." Owned by John Selden, among whose books it came to the Library in 1659. Marked 8° A. 17 Art. Seld., Auct. Q. 1. 5. 17, Auct. R. supr. 8, and now S. Selden c. 2.

3. All Souls College, Oxford. Perfect. Bound with the Jerome (see p. 252).

4. Norwich Cathedral Library.

5. John Rylands Library, Manchester. Imperfect, wanting a 1, a blank leaf. Made up out of two copies, the Alchorne and the Freeling. Bound by C. Lewis : marked 15969 or G. 237 : transferred as the Jerome.

6. The Earl of Pembroke's Library.

7. Chetham Library at Manchester. Wants a 1 and two leaves in sign. k.

8. Lord Ashburnham.

Anthony Askew possessed a copy (Sale catal. 1775, no. 998, sold for £3 3s. to Dent), and an imperfect one occurred in the Bright sale in 1845 (no. 180), and fetched £5 15s.

Fragments:—The Bodleian possesses fragments comprising l 3, l 6–8, v 3, v 6, v 7, v 8 : Queen's College, Oxford, possesses m 8, with some variations of reading : and i 4 was in 1888 in the possession of F. J. H. Jenkinson, Esq., at Cambridge.

3. **Aegidius** (14$\frac{79}{80}$?, see p. 1).

In this work the colophon is printed in red, the only instance of colour printing in the early Oxford press. The book is for some reason rarer than the two which precede. It is noticeable that in every known copy the bad grammar of the printed colophon was corrected in red ink before it left the office.

Copies known.

1. Bodleian. Perfect. Owned by Robert Burton, the author of the *Anatomy of Melancholy*, in 1601. Originally bound first in a volume also containing De

viginti preceptis elegantiarum, Bois-le-duc, 1487: Perotti grammatica: Bona-
venturae Soliloquium.   Marked 4° A. 28 Th., then Auct. Q. 1. 5. 16, then
separately bound as Auct. R. supra 4.

2. Oriel College Library.   Perfect.   See the Jerome, no. 4.

3. John Rylands Library, Manchester.   Wanting a 1 and e 8, blank leaves and a 8.
Purchased by Lord Spencer: once part of the volume containing the Jerome
no. 12.

A copy was in the Harleian Library (Catal. vol. 3, no. 6674).

4. Cicero, Pro Milone (1480?, see p. 2).

This is a puzzling book.   The type so closely resembles Oxford type
that every bibliographer has accepted it provisionally as identical.   Yet
it exhibits spaced type, it uses / for a comma (both points unique in
Oxford printing), and the sections are made up in sixes.   It is also by
many years the first classic printed in England, the next being a Terence
in 1497.   The volume probably consisted of a—e in sixes, allowing
a leaf blank at the beginning: perhaps section e was in eight.   The first
half of each section bears signatures.   The book was clearly made up of
half quarto sheets, three to each section.   Mr. Blades was of opinion that
the type was more worn than that of the Ales: and Mr. E. G. Duff thinks
that the spacing and other peculiarities point to a later date than 1480.

Fragments known:—b 3-4, c 3-4 are in the Bodleian (Auct. R. supra 3), having been
presented by Sir William H. Cope in 1872.   They were fly leaves in a volume
containing five treatises dated from 1491 to 1505, probably bound in Oxford
for William Cope (d. 1513) who lived near Banbury.   Also c 1-2, 5-6 are in
Merton College Library, Oxford, among some loose printed fragments.

5. Latin Grammar (1481?, see p. 2).

This is only known from two leaves in the British Museum, acquired
in 1872 or late in 1871, which were found in the binding of a book,
which in the sixteenth cent. belonged to Nicholas Browere.   It is
a Latin grammar in English, the examples of which connect its composition with Oxford (e.g. "I goo to grammer att Oxforde Incumbo
grammatice Oxonij." "Y go to Oxforde Eo Oxonium vel ad Oxonium."
From letters in the *Athenaeum*, 4 and 11 Nov. 1871, and notes in the
book, it appears that the author might be John Anwykyll (see p. 257)
and that it is probably not by Holt or Stanbridge.   The chain lines run
across the page: but it is at present impossible to say whether the sections
were in sixes or eights.   Marked C. 33. i. 10.

6. Ales (1481, see p. 2).

The woodcut border which is found in some copies of the Ales and
Latteburius is the earliest found in English printing, though Caxton uses
woodcut engravings in the text (for the first time) in the same year.   It
consists of birds and flowers grouped on long winding stems, the four
pieces which form the border measuring in all not less than $11\frac{1}{4} + 7\frac{3}{4}$ in.
(no quite intact copy is known, the binder's ruthless knife invariably
removing a portion).   A full-size reproduction of it is given in E. G.
Duff's *Facsimiles of English types* (Lond. 1895).

Copies known.

1. British Museum. Without border. Wanting a 4, a 5. Re-bound lately, but with the original sides. Owned by William Wodebrigge, sub-prior of Butleigh, co. Suffolk : then by John Warner : then by Cranmer : then by lord Lumley. In the Old Royal Library : once 520. 9. 12, now C. 38. g. 1.

2. Bodleian. Without border. Perfect : in original Oxford binding, plain sides. Owned by Roger Balkwell in the 15th cent. Marked A. 5. 4 Art., then C. 7. 15 Art., now Auct. R. supra 10.

3. Oxford—Balliol.

4. Oxford—Brasenose. Without border. On vellum. Imperfect, wanting 13 leaves. In contemporary Oxford binding, with stamped sides. Owned by — Claxton and Patrick Grante.

5, 6. Oxford—Magdalen. Two copies, one imperfect, both with border. In J. E. T. Rogers's *History of Prices* is a note that Magdalen purchased a copy of this book in 1481 for 33s. 4d.

7. Oxford—New College.

8. Oxford—St. John's (*not* in Oriel, as has been stated).

9. Oxford—Trinity.

10. Oxford—Worcester. Without border. Imperfect, wanting a i (blank), k 2, y 3. Given to Gloucester Hall by Clement Barksdale.

11. Cambridge University Library. With border in three places, a 2, h 1, z 1. Perfect. Marked I*. 9. 15.

12. Do. Without border. Wanting a 1 (blank). Marked AB. 10. 9 : with George I's bookplate.

13. John Rylands Library, Manchester. With border in three places, a 2, h 1 and z 1. Wanting three leaves, a 1, g 6, y 8, all blank. Marked D. 237, E. 237, 19944, in the Spencer Library.

14. Durham Cathedral Library. Without border.

15. Dulwich College Library : bound with Lettou's edition of Ant. Andreae, 1480.

16. Lincoln Cathedral Library.

Fragments : —In the Bodleian r 6 and parts of C 1, E 6 : in Merton College, Oxford, two leaves (one is i 7) : in Corpus Christi College Oxford, part of one leaf : in the Cambridge University Library, parts of E 1 and other fragments : in the British Museum (MS. Harl. 5929, no. 36 : last leaf with colophon and date) : at Trinity College, Cambridge.

7. **Latteburius** (1482, see p. 2).

Some copies of this work also bear the engraved border noticed on p. 254. Some copies have a distinct variation on sign. " k k " (= K) 7ᵛ, thus

liū super capitulum s'm trenorū Ihe, *or*
liū sup capitulū secūdū trenorū Ihe.

Clearly the type was altered because s'm is a fair contraction when meaning "according to," but not properly used when meaning "second." See plate III.

Copies known.

1. British Museum. With border. Perfect. In the original stamped leather binding. Owned by Simon Foderby in the 15th century : by Christopher Viscount

Castlecomer, and W. F. (?) Hunter, 1824. Marked 1215. k. 1, 1215. k. 6, 45. b. 30. 135, now C. 37. h. 10.

2. Bodleian. With border. Perfect. Owned by John Cuthbertson, priest, and Robert Bonwick. Marked L. 1. 3 Th., L. 7. 2 Th., Auct. Q. 1. 2. 8, now Auct. R. supra 11.

3. Oxford—All Souls. Without border. On vellum. Perfect, except that part of O 6 (blank) is gone. Given by Richard Gavent, formerly Fellow of the College. The binding is contemporary Oxford stamped leather. This copy is remarkable from the fact that four names, apparently of parchment-sellers, occur as signing certain leaves: on 54 leaves (representing 108) F. H.: on 31, Hawkyns or Haukins: on 8, Alison: on 3, J. Alexander (Alysaunder): probably some other signings are cut off. A comparison of two sets of similar markings in other books almost establishes the fact that these names do not represent revisers of the printing, but simply the owners of the parchment. Sometimes "8 ff," and once "8 ff alison," occur, showing that the pieces were sold in bundles of eight (?). Marked P. 2. 18, then QQ. 8. 11.

4. Oxford—Corpus Christi College. With border. Wanting almost all of a 1, L 8, O 6 (blank leaves). In contemporary binding. Marked X. P. iv. 4, then Δ. 18. 3.

5. Oxford—New College.

6, 7. Cambridge University Library. Both with border. One perfect (E. 4. 1), in contemporary binding of stamped leather. Given by Albanus Butler to Richard Butler, rector of Aston-le-Walls (co. Northants) 23 June 1603. The other, AB. 7. 27, only wants a 1 (blank leaf); with a George I bookplate.

8. Cambridge—Jesus College. With border.

9. Cambridge—Trinity College. Perfect (?). Marked vi^d. 8. 9 (described in Sinker's *Catalogue*, 1876).

10. John Rylands Library at Manchester. With border. Wanting only a 1 (blank leaf). Owned by "Henri Joliff." Marked 16741 or E. 237.

11. Lambeth Library.

12. Westminster Chapter Library. On vellum.

13. Stonyhurst Library. Wanting only three blank leaves.

14. T. Etherington Cooke, Esq., residing in Glasgow. Perfect. With border. In original binding.

15. Brussels Library.

Copies occurred in the Sams sale (185-, £17 5s., one leaf in manuscript): Bateman sale (1893: lot 1176): Payne and Foss (1848: art. 3120, £8 8s.): Gardiner sale (£9 12s.): Towneley sale (1883, with border, wanting O 6, and also L 1 and L 8, II 3 and II 6 occurring in their stead: this copy was in Quaritch's Rough List, 99. no. 572, Sept. 1889, £32 10s.): B. H. Bright sale 1845, lot 3364 (£7 7s., with another book).

Fragments known:—Lord Robartes (on vellum, part of one leaf, O 3); Trinity College, Cambridge; Queen's College, Oxford (on vellum: I 3, I 5, B 4, B 5, kk 5, kk 6); King's College, Cambridge; Emmanuel College, Cambridge (on vellum, two half-leaves, in q. 4. 62); Wadham College, Oxford (f 2, f 3, f 6, f 7); British Museum (one leaf, i 8, in 618. l. 18, and one leaf on vellum in Harl. MS. 5977, fol. 44); S. Sandars, Esq. (one leaf); New College, Oxford (four leaves, II 2, II 7. g 3. p 4: and on vellum four leaves, D 2-3, &c.); Bodleian (I 3, I 5, kk 2, kk 7, M 2, b 2-5; C 7-8 on vellum); Brasenose College, Oxford (on vellum, I 6); Corpus Christi College, Oxford (four leaves: and two leaves on vellum).

8. **Anwykyll** (1483?, see p. 3).

Four of the chief English grammarians of the 16th century were connected with Magdalen College Grammar School at Oxford. The first master was John Anwykyll (1481?–87); the first usher and second master was John Stanbridge (1481?–88, 1488–94, *d.* 1510); John Holte, the author of the *Lac Puerorum*, was master; and Robert Whittington was Stanbridge's pupil at the school. Dean Colet, William Lily and Cardinal Wolsey were also members of Magdalen (see Bloxam's *Register of Magdalen College*, iii., ad init.). Of the Latin Grammar in Latin which is now before us and has been assigned with probability by Bradshaw to Anwykyll, no complete copy is known, but it was reprinted at Deventer in 1489. The *Vulgaria Terentii* occurs also separately, and consists of sentences from Terence with English translation.

There appear to be two different editions of this Grammar (not Vulgaria), for it can be shown that the Cambridge fragments are not of the same edition as the Bodleian book. Not only, for instance, are the contents of sign. h 3 in each entirely different, but the signatures themselves are in different type, and in the Corpus (Cambridge) fragment the signature is n 3, and yet it belongs to the Compendium and not the Vulgaria. The height of the printed page also varies considerably, and the width of the Vulgaria pages is less than that of the Grammar. The subject needs further investigation.

Parts known.

1. London—British Museum. Vulgaria Terentii only, with written date at end 5 Jan. 150⅞. Marked C. 33. i. 3.

2. Oxford—Bodleian. A fragment containing signn. fg⁶hk⁶lm⁸ and (Vulgaria) n–q⁶. Sign. i probably contained the Tertia pars grammaticae. With the Condover Hall (Cholmondeley) bookplate: bought by the Bodleian from Quaritch in 1892: in whose Rough List, no. 124, May 1892, it is priced £100. Now marked Inc. e. E 2 $\frac{14^{*3}}{1}$.

3. Oxford—Bodleian. The Vulgaria only, bound first in a volume containing also P. P. Vergerii de ingenuis moribus liber (Louvain, Joh. de Westphalia, n. d.), and Adelardi Quaestiones (n. pl. or d.). The following interesting inscription is in it:—" 1483. Frater Johannes grene emit hunc librum Oxoñ de elemosinis amicorum suorum." In plain 15th cent. binding. Owned also by Henry Strathyn at Bedford, John Uncle, Robert Hunter (all 16th cent.). Bought by the Bodleian at the T. Thomson sale Jan. 1866 (lot 1068) for £36. Marked Auct. R. supra 2.

4. Cambridge—University Library. The Vulgaria only. Bound originally in a volume containing Perotti Erudimenta Grammatices (Par. 1488); Opusculum quintupertitum grammaticale (Gouda, 1486); Ars Epistolandi Jac. P(ublicii) n. pl. or d.); the Vulgaria; Matheoli Perusini tractatus de memoria (n. pl. or d.). Marked AB. 5. 16. 4.

5. John Rylands Library, Manchester. The Vulgaria only.

Small Fragments known:—Cambridge University Library (two leaves, h 3, and [without sign.] the beginning of the 3rd part): Trinity College Library, Cambridge (one leaf, d 1, of the same edition as the University Library fragments). Photographs of these fragments are in the Bodleian. The Rev. W. D. Macray states in his *Annals of the Bodleian* (2nd ed., 1890, p. 159, *note*) that Bradshaw found two leaves at Corpus and two at St. John's both Cambridge), but these really belong to the Alexander (p. 260). Four leaves are in the library of Lord Dillon at Ditchley, Oxfordshire, discovered by Mr. Macray in 1867.

9. **Hampole** (1483?, see p. 3).

This work by Richard Rolle of Hampole (*d.* 1349) was also printed at Paris in 1510 and at Cologne in 1536. Noticed in J. Ph. Berjeau's *Bibliophile*, no. 24 (Dec. 1863), p. 146.

Copies known.

1. Cambridge University Library. Wants a 1 and l 4 (both blank : AB. 4. 31, with a George I bookplate).
2.   Do.   Do.   Wants l 4 (II* 9. 51. 5).
3. John Rylands Library, Manchester, purchased in 1893 from the Cambridge University Library. Wants almost all a 1 (F* 5. 26. 3, when at Cambridge).

Fragments:—Some leaves from the Babington sale (1889) are in the Library of St. John's College, Cambridge.

10. **Logic** (1483?, see p. 3).

There is a Registrum cartarum at the end of this book, on sign. D d 8^r. Diagrams are on A 4^r, A 5^v, B 6^v, cf. c c 2^r.

Copies known.

1. New College, Oxford. Wanting nearly all a 1 (blank leaf). Owned by John Utting. Marked Auct. V. 2. 18.
2. Merton College, Oxford. Wanting a 1 (blank), B 3, B 4. Marked D. 6. 13 Art., D. 8. 17 Art., then 19. E. 18.

Fragments:—Bodleian (one leaf, Q 2: marked Auct. K. supra 16) : Cambridge University Library : Trinity College, Cambridge (one leaf, 26 half leaves) : St. John's College, Cambridge (O 1, O 2, O 5, O 6) : Lambeth Library (four leaves).

11. **Lyndewoode** (1483?, see p. 3).

This contains a large wood engraving (on sign. a 1^v) of Jacobus de Voragine writing the Golden Legend, seated at his desk beneath a canopy; on each side are two trees, the foliage of which, as in the Festial, is represented by nearly horizontal lines in rude style. Size 4$\frac{3}{8}$ × 7$\frac{3}{4}$ in., to outer bounding lines. See plate IV.

Copies known.

1. British Museum. Wanting aa 1 and either S 10 or (the second) aa 1 (both blank). Marked 497. i. 1, then C. 37. l. 2. In this copy f 1, f 2, f 7, f 8, all g, h and i, k 1, k 2 have been re-set, compared with the other two, which are probably the earlier issue. As a test, in this copy the catchword on sign. f 1^r is under *quamuis*, but in nos. 2 and 3 under *glosa*, as is usual.
2. British Museum. Wanting S 10 (blank); and a duplicate of f 3, f 6 is placed after t 3. Owned by Tho. Chandler, dean of Hereford March 1482½ to 1490, then by James Scudamour, who gave it to Richard Tomson in 1595. Marked 711. i. 15, and 41. 11. 6. 164: now C. 37. l. 7. The sides of the binding are old stamped leather.

3. British Museum. Wanting a 1, R 1, R 8, cc 3, cc 6, and all dd. Owned by Nicholas Peir(ce?), John Harrison (?), and William Graves who gave it to the Museum. Marked 497. i. 2.

4. Oxford, Bodleian. Perfect. In original binding of stamped leather, re-backed. Marked L. 4. 8 Jur., then Auct. Q. 1. 1. 4, then Auct. R. supra 12, now Inc. b. E 2. $\frac{1488}{1}$

5. Oxford, All Souls. Perfect. Marked A. 1. 29, C. 3. 12, D. 11. 12, now I. 11. 10. Owned by Thomas Windsor in 1634, and bp. Nathaniel Crewe.

6. Oxford, New College. ("Auct. V. 12".)

7. Oxford, Queen's College.

8. Cambridge University Library. Wanting aa 1 (nearly all), y 4, y 5. With a George I bookplate, 1715. Marked B. 1. 5, now AB 1. 19.

9. ———— 2nd copy. Wanting A 2, S. 10, dd 1, dd 10. Marked L. 3. 38, now Q. 2. 14.

10. Cambridge, Clare College.

11. Cambridge, Corpus Christi College.

12. Cambridge, King's College.

13. Cambridge, St. John's College. On vellum.

14. John Rylands Library, Manchester: bought from the late Rev. J. E. Millard by Lord Spencer. Wanting a 1, S 10, aa 1, dd 10. This had been in the Savile sale (1862), lot 497.

15. Edinburgh, Advocates' Library.

16. Durham Cathedral Library.

17. Glasgow, Free Church College Library.

18. E. Gordon Duff, Esq.: bought at a London sale for £12 15s.: wanting a 1, S 10, aa 1.

19. Lord Crawford.

20. National Library at Paris. On vellum.

A copy occurred in the Bateman sale (1893), lot 1190.

Fragments known:—Bodleian (part of D 2: marked Auct. R. supra 17: now Inc. c. E 7. 1); Jesus College, Oxford (part of a leaf of index): Mr. E. G. Duff possesses a Valerius Maximus of 1519, in a Cambridge binding (about 1520), the boards of which are entirely made up of the Oxford Lyndewoode; from the Hailstone Library.

☞ The following book was discovered since sheet B was printed off.

12. Augustine (1483?).

Augustine, St. [Sign. a 2ʳ:—] Excitatio fidelis anime ad ele=mosinam faciendam A beato Aus|gustino conscripta.

[Oxford, about 1483]: (eight sm. 4°: pp. [16], sign. a: sign. a 3ʳ beg. *Non enim*. Contents:—sign. a 2–a 8ʳ, the sermon.

This piece of Oxford printing was discovered in the spring of 1891 in the British Museum. It was originally bound with Gerson's De modo vivendi (Joh. de Westphalia, n. d.), the Cordiale de quattuor novissimis (Delft, 1482). Albertanus de arte loquendi, 1484, Adelardi Quæstiones naturales, and the Historia septem sapientum. Marked 702. d. 34, now C. 38. f. 37: it had been part of lot 4912 in the Colbert sale. A fac-simile is given in E. G. Duff's *Early printed books* (Lond. 1893).

13. Phalaris (1485, see p. 4).

The computation of the date by Olympiads is very uncommon, in early printed books : it is however the most ancient classical method. Each Olympiad is a period of four years, and the first is computed to have commenced in July, B. C. 776 : so that July A. D. 1 corresponded with the beginning of Olympiad 195. The computation ceased for practical purposes in A. D. 395, and the present revival is of an artificial kind, in which the expression "every fifth year," which by a Greek could be applied to an Olympiad ($\Pi\epsilon\nu\tau\alpha\epsilon\tau\eta\rho\iota\varsigma$), was taken in its ordinary sense and used for computation. Thus "in the 297th Olympiad from the birth of Christ" was in the present book taken to represent ($297 \times 5 =$) A. D. 1485. A similar use is found in the 1472 (Venice) edition of the Epigrams of Ausonius[1]. But the 1494 (Parma) edition of the Declamations of Quintilian contains a futile attempt to use the ancient method, for it was printed "Olympiade quingentesima sexagesima octaua qui est annus a salute christiana M.cccc.xciiii quinto non. Iul.", whereas it would properly have been 1493. And M. A. Giry (*Manuel de Diplomatique*, 1894, p. 96) records an unintelligible attempt to use this computation in a deed of 1102.

Copies known.

1. Oxford, Corpus Christi College. Perfect. Owned by John Lacy, and Herbert Randolph (1724). Marked X P. 3. 12, then Δ. 1. 14.

2. Oxford, Wadham College.

3. John Rylands Library, Manchester. Perfect. Marked in the Spencer Library S. 5. 3, and 15835 (G. 237).

Fragments :—Bodleian (parts of i 4, i 6, now Auct. R. supra 9) : Corpus Christi College, Oxford (parts of l 2 and l 7): St. John's College Library, Oxford (one leaf) : Trin. Coll. Camb. (one leaf of sign. d) : Westminster Abbey Library (four leaves of sign. k).

14. Alexander (1485?, see p. 4).

There are editions of the Textus Alexandri by Pynson in 1505, 1513, 1516 and by Wynkin de Worde, 1503.

Fragments known :—St. John's College, Cambridge (c 2 and c 3 [?]) : Corpus Christi College, Cambridge (two leaves, n 3 and one unsigned ; probably part of the Alexander).

15. Festiall ($148\frac{6}{7}$, see p. 4).

Printed in "1486," "on the day aftir Seint Edward the kyng": which would seem to be March 19, $148\frac{6}{7}$. This book is distinguished by the occurrence of many woodcut engravings, and by the use of a woodcut capital G (52 times). This latter is the only woodcut letter used in the early Oxford Press (see Bradshaw in the *Communications* of the Cambridge Antiquarian Society, iii. 136). In the same paper (p. 138) Bradshaw suggests that the eleven large cuts were perhaps intended for

---

[1] "A nativitate Christi ducentesimae nonagesimae quintae Olympiadis anno. II. VII. Idus Decembres," = 7 Dec. 1472.

an edition of the Golden Legend, and that the five smaller ones belong to a lost Oxford Primer on Horae. The text is nearer to that of Caxton's second issue (1491) than of his first (1483). The two sets of woodcuts are as follows :—

Larger kind (general size, about $4\frac{1}{2} \times 4\frac{1}{2} - 5\frac{1}{2}$ in.).

1. ( ) 1ʳ. Woodcut of the Crucifixion, laid sideways.
2. ( ) 1ᵛ. Woodcut of St. Christopher bearing Christ, beneath a canopy.
3. h 5ᵛ. Bishop under canopy, with two trees (facsimile in Dibdin's *Ædes Althorpianæ*).
4. i 5ᵛ. Martyrdom of St. Thomas.
5. k 7ʳ. Stoning of St. Stephen (facsimile in Dibdin).
6. l 2ʳ. St. John the Evangelist (?) with cup and palm-branch, between two figures.
7. l 6ʳ. Murder of the Innocents.
8. l 8ᵛ. Murder of Thomas a Becket.
9. m 5ᵛ. The Circumcision.
10. n 6ʳ. The Conversion of St. Paul.
11. o 7ᵛ. The Annunciation.

Smaller kind (general size, about $2\frac{1}{4} \times 1\frac{1}{2}$ in.).

12. c 4ᵛ. Crucifixion.
    d 8ᵛ. Space for woodcut.
    e 2ᵛ.   Do. ?
13. e 3ʳ. Pentecost.
    e 5ʳ.   Do., the same woodcut.
14. f 2ᵛ. The Trinity.
15. h 1ʳ. St. Andrew with his cross, with a book and trees.
16. h 1ʳ. St. Andrew with his cross.

The prints are rude in execution, the foliage of trees being generally indicated simply by horizontal lines (as in a French *Ortus Sanitatis* of about 1485). The shoes, sword-scabbards, and the like are often entirely black, showing that the cuts were intended to be coloured by hand. They appear to be entirely unknown elsewhere. See plate V.

Copies known.

1. Bodleian. Imperfect. Wanting all ( ), c 3, c 4, g 4, k 4, k 5, o 4, o 5, r 5, s 3, s 4, s 5, s 6, z 1, z 3, z 4. Marked Auct. R. supra 5. The variations of signn. h and i show that this is a later issue than no. 2. Owned by William Little.

2. Bodleian. Imperfect. Wanting all ( ), a–f, g 1, g 2, h 1, i 6, k 1-3, k 6-8, l 3, l 6, l 8, o 3, p 6, r 4-6, t 1, t 6, x 1, x 2, x 7, x 8, y, z: but y 2, y 5 are inserted from Hearne's fragments. This was William Herbert's copy: no. 730 in the Utterson sale 1852, where it was bought by the Bodleian for £6 10s.: marked Auct. R. supra 7.

3. John Rylands Library, Manchester. Wanting a 1, a 2 (supplied in manuscript), z 4. Owned by Ratcliffe sale, no. 1430, £3 2s.), then Alchorne, then Johnes. No. 15409 (E. 237) in the Spencer Library. Dibdin's collation is very faulty. Signn. h, i are of the later kind.

4. Lambeth Library. Wants z 4 (blank). The variations in signn. h, i are of the later
   type. Once archbp. Tenison's copy. Marked once lxiii. 1. 19, now 38. 2. 23. f.

A copy occurred for sale in Rodd's 1831 catalogue, priced £6 6s.

Fragments:—British Museum (one leaf, y 3, in MS. Harl. 5919, no. 139): Wadham
   College, Oxford (1½ leaves): Brasenose College, Oxford (several leaves): parts
   of two leaves (q 6 and another) were offered by A. Iredale, bookseller of
   Torquay (catal. 31, Oct. 1887, no. 1) for 21s.

The Printing Press at Oxford ceases its work suddenly in 148$\frac{9}{?}$, and
there is no reason for this stop at present known. The printing at
St. Alban's ceased at about the same time. It has been suggested that
Rood left Oxford for Cologne, where a Theodericus printed books in 1485
and 1486 in a type similar to that of the Ales and Latteburius. In this case
Hunt may have continued for a short time alone, and then relinquished
the work.

APPENDIX B.

𝕿𝖍𝖊 𝕰𝖆𝖗𝖑𝖞 𝕾𝖎𝖝𝖙𝖊𝖊𝖓𝖙𝖍 𝕮𝖊𝖓𝖙𝖚𝖗𝖞 𝕻𝖗𝖊𝖘𝖘.

(Supplementary to, and corrective of, pp. 5-7.)

FROM December 1517 to February " 1519 " ($15\frac{19}{20}$?) a printing press is found in work at Oxford in St. John's Street near Merton College, connected in 1518 with the name of Johannes Scolar and in the last book with the name of Carolus Kyrfoth. Both of these appear to be foreigners, but nothing certain has yet been discovered about them or the causes of the establishment and cessation of the press[1]. In 1524 none of these names occurs among the inhabitants of Oxford paying taxes (Oxf. Hist. Soc., *City Documents*, ed. by J. E. T. Rogers, 1891, p. 5): nor are they otherwise known in Oxford as booksellers or stationers. Although Scolar uses the arms of the University (their earliest occurrence in print), yet the Registers of the University almost entirely ignore the fact that for the second time the greatest literary invention since speech and writing were known, was silently at work in its midst. Three of the books were however issued " Cum Privilegio." It is peculiar that whereas theology claimed a fair proportion of the first press, it is entirely absent from the second; grammar, logic, arithmetic, natural science, and the Ethics of Aristotle being alone represented, except that one broadside consists of a Prognostication, which Dorne's lists in 1520 show to have been a popular form of literature in Oxford at that time. All are in small quarto, and similar in the types used, namely an English and Brevier black-letter, with a Great Primer for titles. Not only at Oxford but also at Cambridge, York, Tavistock, and Abingdon, in all of which there was an early 16th cent. press, printing entirely ceases for nearly the central forty years of that century.

1. **Burley** on Aristotle (1517, see p. 5).

Copies known.

Oxford—Bodleian.

Oxford—St. John's College.

> The titlepage is reproduced in plate VI. The Royal Arms on the penultimate page of this treatise, and also in the 1518 Burley's *Principia*, are a wood engraving which belonged to Winkin de Worde, as I am informed by Mr. E. G. Duff.

[1] In 1528 we find a John Scolar, probably identical with the Oxford printer, printing a Breviary at Abingdon near Oxford for the use of the Abbey.

2. **Dedicus** (1518, May, see p. 6).

On the title is the woodcut mark of John Scolar engraved in Berjeau's *Printers' Marks* (Lond. 1866) no. 81, and his *Bookworm* (Lond. 1868), no. 32, p. 126: see also the *Corrections and Additions* to Chandler's Catalogue of editions of Aristotle's Ethics (Oxf. 1868), p. 7.

Copies known.

London—British Museum, bought at the Crawford sale, 1891, lot 932. The last leaf with colophon is also in MS. Harl. 5929, fol. 41.

Oxford—Corpus Christi College, wanting titlepage.

Oxford—Jesus College (two copies).

Cambridge—University Library: which has also a fragment containing the greater part of pp. 1–12, 14–17.

Edinburgh—University Library (wants 4 leaves, sign. I 3–6).

King's Norton Parish Library.

A copy was in the Inglis sale, 1826.

3. **De Luce** (1518, June 5: see p. 6).

Copies known.

Oxford—Bodleian.

Oxford—Jesus College.

Cambridge—University Library.

4. **Burley's** Principia (1518, June 7: see p. 5).

Copies known.

Oxford—Bodleian.

Oxford—Jesus College.

Cambridge—University Library, wanting D 4.

The titlepage is reproduced in plate VII. See note on the 1517 Burley, p. 263.

5. **Whittington** (1518, June 27: see p. 7, where in l. 3 *protouatis* is a misprint for *prothouatis*. The square brackets in the title may now be removed).

Copies known.

Oxford—Bodleian (imperfect).

Oxford—Jesus College.

Cambridge—University Library.

Cambridge—Pembroke College (six copies).

John Rylands Library.

Ham House.

6. **Laet** (1518?: see p. 6).

The title is now known to be " Prenostica " simply. The parts known are (1) from the Cambridge copy, from the top a head line and 34 lines, from the bottom 33 lines of small type and 5 of larger type : (2) from the Oxford copy, 22 lines from the top, and 22–24 from the bottom. At present the intervening space, which must be small, is unknown. The type is $8\frac{1}{4}$ in. broad, and red ink is used.

Copies known.

Oxford—Corpus Christi College (28 fragments of the upper and lower parts).

Cambridge—University Library (two fragments).

7. **Compotus** (1519 : see p. 7).

Beneath the title is a woodcut, $5\frac{3}{4} \times 4\frac{3}{4}$ in., representing a master at his desk, with a birch in his left hand and a book in his right : above him and on each side are other volumes, and before him five students on a bench with their books. Two windows are in the background. On A 2r is a diagram of the open hand ($5 \times 3\frac{5}{8}$ in.), for purposes of computation : and different diagrams of the hand or part of it are on A 2v, A 4r, A 4v.

Copy known.

Cambridge—University Library.

DETAILS OF THE EARLY SIXTEENTH CENTURY PRESS.

No.	Book.	Date.	Printer Named.	Place Named.
1	Burley on Aristotle	1517 Dec. 4	———	Academia Oxonie
2	Dedicus	1518 May 15	J. Scolar*	Celeberrima Universitas Oxoniensis (St. John's St.)
3	De Luce	1518 June 5	J. Scolar*	Do. Do.
4	Burley's Principia	1518 June 7	J. Scolar*	Do. Do.
5	Whittington	1518 June 27	J. Scolar	Oxonia
6	Laet (1518?)	———	———	Celeberrima Oxoniensis Academia
7	Compotus	"1519" Feb. 5	C. Kyrfoth	Celeberrima Universitas Oxoniensis (St. John's St.)

* With privilege.

No.	Book.	Pages.	Lines in Page.	Large Capitals.	Head Line	Woodcuts.
1	Burley on Aristotle	20	55	+	o	Oxf. & Royal Arms
2	Dedicus	152 (foliated)	56	+	+	Do. Do.
3	De Luce	16	55-6	+	+	Do. & Magi
4	Burley's Principia	16	57	o	+	Do. & Royal Arms & Scholar
5	Whittington	20	59	o	+	Do. & Scholar
6	Laet (1518?)	[broadside :	no	complete	copy	known]
7	Compotus	16	31-2	o	+	Do. & Scholars & Hands

APPENDIX C.

A CHRONOLOGICAL LIST OF PERSONS AND PROCEEDINGS CON-
NECTED WITH BOOK-PRODUCTION AT OXFORD,
A.D. 1180–1640.

THREE districts in Oxford are associated with the early production of books.

One is Bookbinders Bridge, which is still standing, namely the bridge which as one starts from close under the Castle in Titmouse Lane towards St. Thomas's Church, crosses the second piece of water. The bridge was on the limits of Oseney Abbey and the neighbouring tenements were largely occupied by binders who worked for the Abbey. See Clark's edition of Wood's *History of the City*, i. 433.

Schidyard St., now Oriel St., is said to imply by its name that it was the locus schediasticorum, the place of writers on *schedae* or sheets of paper. Certainly with St. John Baptist St. (now Merton St.) and Cat St., it was a great centre for scribes, illuminators, bookbinders, and the like. See Clark's Wood, as above, i. 139, 175, 184.

Also Cheney Lane, earlier St. Mildred's Lane, and now Market St., was largely tenanted by the same class. See Clark's Wood, i. 72.

The stationarius (or virgifer) of the University was regularly appointed (see Clark's *Register of the University*, vol. ii, pt. 1, p. 261), and was generally employed to value the books of a scholar after death or sequestration.

But these general facts require to be supplemented by the details which follow: with respect to which it must be remembered that many persons combined several of the trades here recorded, and that, for instance, the earliest printers always bound the books they produced.

[*Chief Authorities*:—

Coxe. = Catalogus codicum MSS. qui in collegiis aulisque Oxoniensibus hodie adservantur. Confecit H. O. Coxe. (Oxf. 1852.)

Kirchhoff, Albrecht: Die Handschriftenhändler des Mittelalters. Zweite Ausgabe. (Leipz. 1853), pp. 132, 136.

Magd. = Notes from the muniments of St. Mary Magdalen College, Oxford, by the rev. W. D. Macray. (Oxf. 1882.)

Oxf. City Doc. = Oxford City Documents, 1268–1665, edited by J. E. Thorold Rogers. (Oxf. Hist. Soc. vol. xviii, 1891.)

Twyne. = Brian Twyne's manuscript collections in the Oxford University archives.

Oxf. Univ. Archives—Wills. = An Index to Wills proved in the Court of the Chancellor of the University of Oxford, by John Griffiths. (Oxf. 1862.)]

(SCRIBES, ILLUMINATORS, BOOKBINDERS, STATIONERS AND BOOKSELLERS,
PARCHMENT-MAKERS, PRINTERS.)

Not later than 1180 :—

Peter, illuminator (Deed of Elias Bradfoth, in Oxf. Univ. Archives).

Ralph, illuminator (do.).

William, illuminator (do.).

Thomas, scribe ("scriptor") (do.).

Reginald, parchment-maker (do.).

Roger, parchment-maker (do.).

c. 1190–1200. John, "illuminator", in St. Mary's [1] parish (Magd.).

c. 1190–1200. Roger, "pergamenarius", in St. Mary's parish (Magd.).

1190–1215. Peter, illuminator, in St. Mary's parish (Magd.).

c. 1210–20 (?) Augustine, bookbinder, in St. Peter's-in-the-East parish (Magd.).

1212, Nov. A, scribe ("Explicit opus manuum mearum, quod compleui ego frater A subdiaconus sancte Frideswide seruientium minimus, anno ... M⁰ CC⁰ ... xii⁰ ... anno conuersionis mee vij⁰ ... " : Paris, Bibl. Nat. MS. fonds Français 24766).

In the first half of the 13th cent. occurs as a witness Reginald, bookbinder, in an old deed in the Oxford Univ. archives between Will. Burgey, and Nicholas "serviens Universitatis", in one of the mayoralties of Petrus filius Toraldi. (Twyne I, p. 52.)

c. 1232–40. John, illuminator, St. Peter's (Magd.).

c. 1232–40. Walter, bookbinder, St. Peter's (Magd.).

1237–8. Walter de Ensham, illuminator, St. Mary's (Magd.).

1240–57. Roger, scribe, ("exemplarius", alias "Saumplarier",) apparently dead in 1276 : St. Peter's (Magd.).

c. 1240–90. Simon Scoticus, parchment-maker ("parcamenarius") in Cattestrete, St. Peter's (Magd.).

1242. Robert de Derbi, illuminator, in Cattestrete, St. Peter's (Magd.).

About the middle of the 13th cent. the following names occur in Twyne's transcript of a St. Frideswide record—a deed between Petrus filius Toraldi and Adam filius Hugonis Ruffi about land in the parish of St. Mary the Virgin :—Robert, illuminator ; Simon, parchment-maker ; and as witnesses, Thomas, scribe ; Peter, parchment-maker (Twyne XXIII, p. 69).

1251–2. Stephen, parchment-maker ("percamenarius"), in Cattestrete, St. Peter's (Magd.).

1252–3. William, scribe ("le Samplarier"), St. Peter's (Magd.).

1252–90. Stephen, bookbinder, St. Peter's (Magd.).

1264–84. William de Pikerynge, bookbinder, ("laminator"), died before 1308 : found both in St. Mary's and St. Peter's deeds : probably

---

[1] "St. Mary's" and "St. Peter's", without qualification, are throughout this Appendix used for the parishes of St. Mary the Virgin and St. Peter-in-the-East.

the same as William the bookbinder of Oxford, the motto on whose seal in 1275 was " Vivite innocue ; lumen adest" (Magd.).

1266. Hugh, illuminator, St. Mary's (Magd.).

1266–78. Symon and Yon, bookbinders, St. Peter's (Magd.).

1267. Reginald, illuminator, St. Peter's (Magd.).

1268–90. Martin, scribe ("Exemplarius" alias "le Saumplarier") : dead in 1298 : St. Peter's (Magd.).

1290. In this year it is agreed between the University and City that "Pergamenarii, Luminatores, Scriptores" were in the jurisdiction of the Chancellor of the University (*Munimenta Academica*, ed. Anstey, p. 52).

Before 1304. Geoffrey, illuminator ("alluminator"), St. Mary's (Magd.).

1308. Robert, notary and stationer in Cattestrete : St. Mary's (Magd.).

In the first quarter of the 14th cent. William of Nottingham wrote MSS. Merton Coll. 158, 166, 168, 169, 170 at Oxford (Coxe : see Little's *Grey Friars in Oxford*, 1892, pp. 165–6).

134$\frac{0}{1}$, Feb. Adam, bookbinder, occurs incidentally as holding a tenement in Schidyerd way (now Oriel St.), in the Bodleian Oxford charter no. 125* (Turner's Catal., p. 307). This tenement he left to the altar of St. Thomas the Martyr in St. Mary the Virgin's church in 1349 (Wood's *City*, ed. A. Clark, ii. 22, from a copy of the will).

1341. Symon Faunt and John Faunt, bookbinders, St. Mary's (Magd.).

1342. In this year a MS. of William of Ockham's Summa Logices now at Bâle (F. ii. 25 according to A. G. Little's *Grey Friars in Oxford*, p. 226 : see Sir Tho. Phillipps's Catalogue of MSS. at Bâle, p. 7) was written at Oxford.

1344. John Joye, illuminator ("lumnour"), of Cattestrete : St. Peter's (Magd.).

1345. In this year the Chancellor of the University was acknowledged to have jurisdiction over "quattuor stationarios ad hujusmodi officium per ... Universitatem admissos et pro tempore admittendos ac Universitati juratos vel jurandos, necnon in omnes et singulos scriptores scholaribus in scriptorum officio servientes" (*Munimenta Academica*, ed. Anstey, p. 150, cf. 176 ; Wood's *Annals*, ed. Gutch, i. 441).

1349. In I. B. De Rossi's *Codices Palatini Latini bibliothecae Vaticanae descripti* (1886) in MS. no. 377 "adnotatur emptio codicis ' pro duobus Florenis cum dimidio Anno domini M⁰.CCC⁰.XL⁰ nono in ciuitate oxoniensi.' "

XIVth cent.　Roger, stationer (Oxf. Univ. Archives, box F, no 24).

,, 　　,, 　　Adam de Walton, parchment maker (*ibid.*, box F, no. 26).

,, 　　,, 　　William, bookbinder (*ibid.*, box F, no. 28).

c. 1350. MS. New College 134 was written at Oxford in about A.D. 1350 (Coxe).

In the 14th cent. in an undated deed in the Oxf. Univ. Archives between John Pilat and Walter "filius Paulini de Eynsham"

about land in St. Mary's parish, the following occur as witnesses :
—Ralph, Robert, James, illuminators ; Walter, Augustine, Adam,
bookbinders ("liurs") ; Simon. parchment-maker (Twyne XXIII,
p. 103 ; cf. Bodl. MS. Wood D. 2, p. 489).

1353. Thomas Hamme, bookseller (" Vetus quoddam inventarium de
bonis Thomæ Hamme bibliopolæ et stationarii ut videtur anno
domini 1353," once in the Oxf. Univ. Archives, box K, no. 2 ;
but this most interesting document is noted by Gerard Langbaine
as having been stolen during the Civil War (MS. Twyne I, 278).

1355. Richard Lynne, stationer (" stacionarius Universitatis Oxun.")
(Coxe): Richard the stationer occurs in Lent 1358 (Boase's
Registrum Oxoniense, 1st ed., p. xi).

1364. MS. New College 173 was written at Oxford in this year (Coxe).

1370. Robert, bookbinder, St. Mary's (Magd.): Robert Bokebinder
and Agnes his wife occur in 1377 (?) and 1380 (Oxf. City Doc.,
pp. 41, 47).

137¾, Jan. 27. At this date "Quia, propter excessivam multitudinem vendentium libros Oxoniæ Universitati minime juratorum, plerique
codices magni valoris ad partes exteras deferuntur" the University decreed that no booksellers except the sworn stationers or
their deputies should sell any book exceeding half a mark in value.
(Anstey's *Munimenta Academica*, p. 233 : see Appendix D. I,
below, p. 281).

1377? John, parchment-maker ("Parchemenor"), Holywell (Oxf. City
Doc., p. 52).

1377? Richard, parchment-maker ("Parchemenor"), Holywell (Oxf.
City Doc., p. 52).

1377? Roger Somervyle, stationer, St. Peter's (Oxf. City Doc., p. 52).

1380. MS. Corpus Christi College (Oxford) 151 was written at Oxford
in this year (Coxe).

1380. Roger, illuminator ("lymenour"), St. Mary's (Oxf. City Doc.,
p. 41).

1380. John Madesdon, illuminator ("limenour"), St. Mary's (Oxf. City
Doc., p. 41).

1380. William, illuminator (" Lymenour"), St. Mary's (Oxf. City Doc.,
p. 41).

1380. John Hyrys, parchment-maker ("Parchemener") (Oxf. City Doc.,
p. 41).

1380. Richard, parchment-maker (" Parchemener ") (Oxf. City Doc.,
p. 43).

1380. Edward, parchment-maker ("Parchemener ") (Oxf. City Doc.,
p. 44).

1380. John Langeport, once stationer (" quondam stationarius "), north-
east ward (Oxf. City Doc., p. 22).

1393. In Florence MS. Laurentian, bibl. S. Crucis, plut. xvii Sin., cod. x.
"Explicit compilatio quaedam . . . scripta per me F[ratrem]

I[acobum] Fey de Florentia Ordinis Fratrum Minorum in Conventu Oxoniae anno Domini mcccxciii, die . . . [xi Martii]" (Bandini's Catalogue, A. G. Little's *Grey Friars in Oxford*, p. 252).

1393. John Brother, illuminator (" limnator "), St. Mary's (Magd.).

1403. John Brown, stationer, sold MS. Merton College 130 in this year, (Coxe), cf. MS. New College 104 : see A.D. 1440.

1410. In the record of a tax levied on the University in this year occur the names of William and Roger, illuminators ; Richard, senior and junior, parchment-makers ; and Thomas and Robert, scribes (Twyne IV, p. 70).

1411. The University enacts that as the duties of the University stationers are laborious and anxious every one on graduation shall give clothes to one of the stationers (*Munimenta Academica*, ed. Anstey, p. 253).

1419. See under 1490.

1423. " Finit Menon Platonis [Latine] scriptus per Fredericum Naghel de Trajecto anno Domini mcccc.xxiij . . . in alma Universitate Oxoniensi " (MS. Corpus Christi College, Oxford, no. 243 : Coxe).

1424. " Guilermus Secomps venditor librorum " may possibly be an Oxford bookseller in this year (see Coxe's account of MS. Lincoln College Latin 14).

142½. John Dolle, bookbinder : see under 1453.

First half of 15th cent.   In Bodl. MS. e Mus. 155, p. 507 (written perhaps in the first half of the 15th cent.) " Explicit liber 3us de consideracione 4te essencie secundum Rogerum Bacon correctus et scriptus per Johannem Cokkes manibus suis propriis Oxon."

1426. John Wake, illuminator (" lymner "), St. Mary's (Magd.) : he appears as a surety in 1434 (Univ. Register Aaa, fol. 1).

1427. " Explicit conflatus Francisci de Maronis finitus per manus Nicolai de Bodelswerdia anno Domini 1427 . . . tum temporis Oxoniæ studentis " (MS. Merton College 133 : Coxe).   A similar inscription dated 1429 is in MS. Oriel College 70 (Coxe).   Kirchhoff mentions Nicolas de Frisia alias de Bolswerdia as a bookseller in 1427–31.

1430. " Explicit conflatus Francisci de Mayronis . . . finitus et completus anno Domini 1430 . . . per manus Johannis Jacobi Spaen de Amsterdamis, tunc temporis Oxonie studentis " (MS. Magd. Coll., Oxf., 103 : Coxe).

1434. John Clerk (Clericus) occurs as a stationer in this year and 1438 (Univ. Register Aaa, foll. 4*, 11).

c. 1436. " Stephanus ligator librorum de Oxonia " occurs at about this date in Cambr. Univ. MS. Dd. xiv. 2, fol. 139 (information from T. W. Jackson, M.A.).

1439. John Godsond occurs as a stationer (Oxf. Univ. Archives, Aaa, fol. 15ᵛ): he has a dispute in the same year with John Coneley a "lymner," his assistant (Anstey's *Munimenta Academica,* pp. 550–1): in 1458 he is paid for chaining some Exeter College books (Boase's *Reg. Exon.,* 1st ed., p. 21).

1440. John Brown, stationer, in this year (cited by Heyner) may be the same as the one noted under 1403.

1440. John More, stationer, occurs frequently: in 1440 he or a person of his name sells MS. Lincoln College, Latin 109, probably in Oxford (Coxe): on 7 Nov. 1444 he is mentioned in Anstey's *Munimenta Academica,* p. 741: in Apr. 1445 he values books in Oxford (*ibid.,* p. 544): also in 1447–48 (*ibid.,* pp. 565, 579, cf. 741) mentioned in the Treasurer's accounts at Oriel, 1451–65: on 12 Apr. 1454 or '55 he sold MS. Magd. Coll. (Oxf.) 4 in Oxford (Coxe): in 1457 he values Exeter College books (Boase's *Reg. Exon.,* 1st ed., p. lxviii): on 21 Oct. 1457 he sold MS. Magd. Coll. (Oxf.) 134 in Oxford ("Mare," in Coxe). A John More was living in 1460–61 and 1468–9 on the east side of Cat Street, probably in Lady Hall = Great St. Mary's Entry, according to the St. Mary the Virgin church accounts preserved in the Bodleian (Oxford Rolls 13 &c.). He was also a binder (Oriel accounts).

1445. John Coneley, illuminator: see 1439: he is bound to work for Godsond for one year from 8 Nov. 1445 for 4 marks and 10 shillings.

1446. "Thomas Bokebynder de Catys-street" was imprisoned by the Chancellor for saying that the mayor and townsfolk were not under oath to respect the rights of the University (Anstey, *Munimenta Academica,* p. 556).

1448. William Bedewyne, illuminator ("lymnour"), "late of Oxford," St. Peter's (Magd.).

XVth cent. Willelmus Sengleton wrote MS. New College 127 (Coxe): he may be the Will. Singleton who was admitted B.A. in 156⁹⁄₁₀ (*Register of the Univ.,* vol. i., ed. Boase, p. 265).

XVth cent. "Expliciunt Questiones . . . scripte per Johannem de Almania sive de Kasterle, in usum . . . Thome Grace. illic [sc. at Oxford] in artibus graduati," in MS. Magd. Coll. (Oxf.) 162 (Coxe).

1450–64. In these years Willelmus Salomon "Leonensis diocesis" wrote the works of Hugo de Sancto Caro or Hugo Viennensis in Oxford for Roger Keys, who in 14⁶³⁄₆₄ presented them to Exeter College, where they are now MSS. 51–68 (Coxe).

1452. "Johannes Bokebyndere Oxoniæ" occurs in the will of dr. Richard Browne (Anstey's *Munimenta Academica,* p. 648).

1453. John Delle or Dolle, stationer, mentioned (*Register of the Univ.,* vol. i., ed. Boase, p. 20, "Delle"): and in 1454 (Anstey's *Munimenta Academica,* p. 741, "Dolle"). In 1454 his name occurs in Bodleian Oxford Charters 491 (Turner's Catal., p. 351). He may be the same as John Dolle, bookbinder, who lived in Cat Street in 142½ (Boase's *Reg. Exon.,* 1894, p. 295).

1453. John Reynbold, a German, agreed at Oxford to write out three books of Duns Scotus on the Sentences (Bodl. MS. Ballard 46, fol. 70). He wrote several MSS. now at Balliol and Merton between 1451 and 1464.

1459. June 17. Will. Bokebynder occurs as a witness in Oxford, when MS. Merton Coll. 135 was given to the College (Coxe). In the same year he is mentioned in Oxford Univ. Archives. box F, no. 28.

1467. British Museum MS. Royal 6 D II once bore the following interesting inscription, before it was re-bound, " Iste liber ligatus erat Oxonii, in Catstrete, ad instantiam Reverendi Domini Thome Wybarun in sacra Theologia Bacalarii Monachi Roffensis. Anno Domini 1467 " (see Casley's *Catalogue of the Manuscripts of the King's Library* (1734), Dibdin's *Bibliographical Decameron* (1817), ii. 449: the volume contains the Letters of St. Jerome, and had been given to Rochester by Benedict, bp. of Rochester, *d.* 1226).

" 1468 "–148$\frac{4}{5}$. Oxford printing, see Appendix A.

1473. Thomas Hunt, "universitatis Oxonie stacionarius," sold Brit. Mus. MS. Burney 11 (a Latin Bible) in this year (see the Catalogue, printed in 1840). In 1477 and 1479 he was living in Haberdasher hall in the parish of St. Mary the Virgin (Bodl. MS. Wood F. 15. a collection of Oseney rentals: Wood's "Thomas Howle, stacioniar," of Haberdasher hall in 1477 in Bodl. MS. Wood D. 2, p. 587. from the above MS., is a mis-reading by Wood for Honte, i. e. Hunte). In 1483 he appears as agreeing to sell certain books in Oxford at fixed prices (the list, which is on a paper now forming a fly-leaf of a French translation of Livy (Paris, 1486) now in the Bodleian, is printed in the publications of the Oxf. Hist. Soc. vol. v. (*Collectanea*, I), pp. 74, 141–3). In all probability he is the same Thomas Hunt who in 1485 printed the *Phalaridis Epistolae* at Oxford in conjunction with Theodoric Rood (see pp. 4, 238).

1481–85. Theodoric Rood, printed at Oxford (see pp. 2, 4, 238).

1482. F. H., — Hawkins, J. Alexander (Alison) occur as parchment-sellers: see p. 256.

1490. William Vavasour, scribe. MS. Corpus Christi Coll. (Oxf.) 228 was written "per manum fratris Wyllelmi Vavysur," "Oxonie anno 1490" (the date and word "Oxonie" might possibly refer to the time and place of the "determinationes physicæ": but) MS. Corpus 227 was "scriptus per me fratrem Wyllelmum. studentem Oxonie anno . . . 1419 [1491]" and "per manum fratris Wyllelmi Vavysur ejusdem ordinis [sc. fratrum Minorum] . . . 1491."

1501. Sebastian Actors, bookseller of St. Mary the Virgin's parish. Record of a grant of administration after his decease, 23 April 1501 (Oxf. Univ. Archives—Wills).

1501. Christopher Coke, stationer. A similar record with inventory, 13 Dec. 1501 (*ibid.*).

150$\frac{2}{3}$. William Lesquier, bookseller. A similar record, 1 Feb. 150$\frac{2}{3}$ (*ibid.*).

1506. Georgius Castellanus, bookseller (?): see p. 11.

1514. Henricus Jacobi. On Dec. 11, 1514 administration of the effects of Henricus Jacobi, deceased, was granted (Oxf. Univ. Archives). Two imperfect leaves of an edition of the *Formalitates de mente magistri Johannis Duns Scoti* by Antonius Syrretus were found in New College Library at Oxford by R. G. C. Proctor, Esq., the first of which bears the words "Venundantur in vniuersitate Oxoniensi sub intersignio sanctissime Trinitatis ab Henrico Jacobi bibliopole Londoniensis." See p. 228.

1518. John Scolar and (15$\frac{18}{20}$) Carolus Kyrfoth, printers, see pp. 5–7, 263.

1521. John Dorne, bookseller. His day-ledger, showing what books he sold and at what prices, from 19 Jan.–23 Dec. 1520, is MS. Corpus Christi College, Oxford, no. 131; this and two leaves of a similar day-book of about 1518–19, found in a binding in the same College library, are printed in the Oxford Historical Society's *Collectanea* volume, no. 1 (pp. 78–139) and 2 (pp. 457–62), where also it is shown that Dorne, who was certainly "a Dutchman," and as such paid with others an alien tax at Oxford in 1524 (see Rogers's *Oxford City Documents*, Oxf. Hist. Soc. xviii, 1891, p. 56, as Johan Thorn), may be the Johannes Dorn who printed at Brunswick in 1507–9. An *Opus Insolubilium* printed by Treveris was to be sold "apud I. T.", which Mr. E. G. Duff thinks is probably I. Thorne.

1524. William Howberghe (Howbert or Hubbert), Douchman (Dutchman: he resigned his office as Stationer 11 Oct. 1532, see Boase's *Reg. Oxon.*, p. 171). Gerard Pylegreme, Douchman (his will is extant at Oxford, dated 7 Feb. "1537": Oxf. Univ. Archives). Balthasar Churchyard, Douchman. Harry Renkens, Douchman. All these pay taxes as Dorne above, in 1524, in the capacity of Stationers or Booksellers. Richard Alcoke, bell-ringer, Margarete Page, Rose Cater, Henry Mancipull, and "Sir Person" are possible additions to this list.

About 1525. Gressop, bookbinder. In Bodl. MS. Rawl. G. 47 (N. C. 14778) there is a note that the volume, which had been presented to All Souls Library by bp. Goldwell, was "resarcitus per Gressopum": the date must be about 1525.

1531, Oct. A commission from the bp. of Lincoln to search the booksellers' stalls at St. Frideswide's fair for heretical books (Brit. Mus. MS. Lansdowne 938).

1532. David Pratt, B.A., of Cambridge, is stationer from 10 March 153$\frac{2}{3}$ to Oct. 1536 (Boase's *Reg. Oxon.*, p. 171).

1534. A patent is issued to Cambridge (where printing had been exercised from 1521 to 1522) allowing the University to have three licensed stationers and printers or sellers of books, and authority to print books is granted to the Chancellor and three Doctors. No similar patent was issued to Oxford.

1552. Henry Mylward, stationer (Boase's *Reg. Oxon.*, p. xx). He retired on 11 Apr. 1597 from old age (Clark's *Register*, i. 262, where it is suggested that his name appears as Miller in 157$\frac{5}{6}$, living in

St. Mary's Parish). In 1583 (July 12) Beef Hall was leased to him (Oxf. Univ. Archives, box O, no. 10. cf. A. no. 14).

1554, Nov. 14. Herman Evans admitted stationer, but pronounced "contumax" in Oct. 1563 (Clark's *Register*, i. 261).

1556, Aug. 11. Nicholas Wayte, admitted bookseller (Clark, i. 321).

———————— Richard Walles, do. (Clark, *ibid.*).

—— Aug. 12. James à Wood, adm. parchment-seller (Clark, i. 322).

1564, Sept. 30. Thomas Wadloffe, adm. parchment-seller (Clark, *ibid.*).

1566, June 20. "Garbrande Harkes," bookseller, licensed to sell wine (Clark, i. 323).

156⅞, Jan. 27. Conrad Myller, adm. bookseller (Clark, i. 321): licensed to sell ale in St. Mary's parish, 16 Sept. 1572: living in 158⅔ (Clark, i. 325).

1567, Apr. 3. Gilbert Burnet, alias Cornyshe, adm. parchment-seller (Clark, i. 326).

1570, June 28. Nicholas Clyfton, adm. bookseller (Clark, i. 321).

—— Oct. 6. Christopher Cavye, do. (*ibid.*): in 1574 the Chancellor recommended that he should have a monopoly of second-hand books, since he was in difficulties (*ibid.*).

157⅞, Mar. 21. William Spyre, of St. Mary's parish, adm. bookseller on the Chancellor's recommendation. Still bookseller in 1590 (*ibid.*), and stationer in 1617 and 1619 (Clark, i. 321, 343). Probably the same as Will "Spewe" of the Company of Stationers (C. R. Rivington, *Stationers' Company*, 1883, p. 27). Died before 20 Nov. 1636 (Oxf. Univ. Archives—Wills).

1573, Sept. 8. **Joseph Barnes**, adm. bookseller (*ibid.*). He was licensed to sell wine from Oct. 1575 to at least Oct. 1596. He was sole printer to the University from 1585 to 1617, resigned on 12 Feb. 161⅞, and died in 1618, being buried in St. Mary's on Dec. 17 in that year. He lived (and printed) in a house at the west end of St. Mary's, now St. Mary's Entry (see *Letters from the Bodleian*, ii. 428).

1573, Sept. 8. Robert Cave, adm. bookseller (Clark, i. 321): still a bookseller in 1693 (fragm. in C. C. C., Oxf., Library from M. XX. 11).

1573, Dec. 5. Richard Garbrand, or Harks, adm. bookseller: still bookseller in 1599 (MS. Wood D. 3, p. 281, cf. 286, where it is stated that he was churchwarden of St. Mary's in 1569); he died before 31 Jan. 160⅔ (Clark, i. 323, compared with Griffiths' *Index of Oxford Wills*).

1574, Mar. 25. Dominique Pinart, adm. bookseller (Clark, *ibid.*): in 1583 he occurs as a bookbinder (Oxf. Univ. Archives, Reg. Y. 99); still bookseller in 161⅞ (Clark, i. 321). Died before 18 Feb. 162⅟₂ (Oxf. Univ. Archives—Wills).

1574. John Gore occurs as an Oxford bookseller in a lease summarized in MS. Wood D. 3, p. 281, and lived in or near Cat St.

1577. Apr. 24. Humphrey Archer, adm. bookseller (Clark, i. 321). Administration was granted after his death on 13 Feb. 158¾ (Oxf. Univ. Archives).

1577. Rowland Jenckes or Jenkes, a bookbinder, was condemned at the Assizes at Oxford for sedition (Wood's *History and Antiquities of the University of Oxford*, ed. Gutch, ii. (1796), p. 188 : and Webster's *Treatise of Witchcraft*, p. 245, quoted by Bagford in Brit. Mus. MS. Harl. 5901, fol. 62).

1583. Carre occurs as a bookbinder (Oxf. Univ. Archives, Reg. Y. 99).

1584. Aug. 15. £100 is lent by the University to Joseph Barnes with which to set up a press, to be repaid in six years (*ibid.* Reg. L. 10, fol. 287, cf. 246). In Oct. 1592 the money had not been repaid.

1585. For printers and publishers from 1585–1640, see also p. 311.

158⅚, Jan. 10. A Committee of Convocation at Oxford appointed to consider *De libris imprimendis* (Oxf. Univ. Archives, Reg. L. 10, fol. 283).

1586, June 23. An Ordinance of the Star Chamber allows only two presses outside London, one at Oxford and one at Cambridge, and only one apprentice to each press (printed in full in Arber's *Transcript*, ii. 807).

1588. In about this year occurs an Inventory of the goods of John Pigot, scrivener, implying his previous death (Oxf. Univ. Archives—Wills).

1590, Nov. 27. Robert Foxon, adm. bookseller (Clark, i. 321): but on 7 Mar. 159⅚ an Inventory of his goods was taken, implying previous death (Oxf. Univ. Archives—Wills).

————————Thomas Middleton, adm. bookseller (Clark, *ibid.*): he died before 28 March 1604 (Oxf. Univ. Archives—Wills).

———————— Francis Peirce, do. (*ibid.*): still bookseller in 161⅚ (Clark, i. 521): died before 4 Jan. 162⅔ (Oxf. Univ. Archives—Wills).

———————— Stephen Wilson, do. (*ibid.*): in 1591 he is a bookbinder also (Clark, i. 342).

1591, May 25. A patent was granted to Richard Wright of Oxford and his assigns to print Tacitus's *History* in English, for life. (Patent Roll 33 Eliz., part 17, Arber's *Transcript*, ii. 16). This partly explains the peculiarity noticed in 1591, no. 5 (p. 31. above): clearly it was printed nominally by Barnes, but published in London and perhaps in part printed there. Wright appears as belonging to both cities.

159¾, Feb. 21. Thomas Gowre resigns the office of parchment seller and is succeeded by William Jennings (Fenninge?) (Clark, i. 522).

1594, Sept. 3. John Barnes, son of Joseph Barnes, is apprenticed to Rich. Watkins of St. Paul's Churchyard, London, for seven years from Mich. 1594 (Arber's *Transcript*, ii. 195: see the same work under date 7 June, 1602, &c.).

1596, May 21. Application was made to Convocation for a licence to Joseph Barnes to have a monopoly of printing inedited Greek and Latin books (Oxf. Univ. Archives, Reg. Ma., p. 15).

1597, Apr. 11. Lancelot Waistiell or Waystayle adm. stationer of the University: he resigned in 1608.

159⁸/₉, Mar. 16. John Crosley adm. bookseller (Clark, i. 321): stationer in 1611 (Clark, i. 342): died before 12 Feb. 161⅔ (Oxf. Univ. Archives—Wills, where he is described as a citizen of London).

160⁰/₁. Robert Billingsley occurs as a bookseller (Clark, i. 342): also bookbinder: he died before 17 Nov. 1606 (Oxf. Univ. Archives—Wills).

1603. The Stationers Company in London obtain a monopoly of printing Primers, Psalms and Almanacs.

1608, Apr. 18. Denis Edmonds adm. stationer.

1609. Nicholas Smith, bookbinder, died before 9 Aug. 1609 (Oxf. Univ. Archives—Wills): his wife Anne was Rob. Billingsley's widow.

1609, Oct. 24. John Garbrand alias Herks, bookseller, was licensed to sell wine (Clark, i. 323): he died before 29 Sept. 1617 (*ibid.*), and after 21 Mar. 161⁶/₇ (Clark, i. 321).

1609, Oct. 20. William Davies occurs as stationer (Clark, i. 342): still such in 1615 and 1621 and 1637 (Clark, i. 343–4): bookseller in March, 161⁶/₇ (Clark, i. 321).

16⁰⁹/₁₀, Mar. 13. A tenement in St. Mary's parish was leased to John Adams, stationer (Oxf. Univ. Archives, box A, no. 23): he was a bookbinder from 1610 to 1620 (Magd. college deeds, cf. Clark, i. 343). In 1637, July 20, a house just North of the Schools Quadrangle was "lately" in the tenure of John Adams, bookbinder (Agreement between Magdalen and the University in Reg. R. 24, fol. 149ʳ). For his printing, see pp. 308, 312.

1610, Dec. Henry Blewet or Bluett occurs as a bookseller in St Mary's parish (Clark, i. 321): still such in 161⁶/₇ (*ibid.*): died before 3 Jan. 163²/₃ ("bookbinder": Oxf. Univ. Archives—Wills).

1611. Sampson Stronge alias Starkey, limner, died before 30 Mar. 1611 (Oxf. Univ. Archives—Wills).

161⅚, Jan. 2. Robert Nixon alias Waie occurs as a bookseller (Clark, i. 343): and in 161⁶/₇ (i. 321).

161⁶/₇, Feb. 12. William Wrench becomes a University printer, until 19 Jan. 161⅞: see p. 311.

—— John Lichfield, do.: see p. 311: created Inferior Bedel 20 Mar. 161⁶/₇: resigned his offices Jan. 163⁴/₅.

161⁶/₇, Mar. 21. Richard Wylcocks is bookseller (Clark, i. 321, *bis*).

———— William Turner, do. (*ibid.*): is University printer from 1624 to 164½: see p. 312. In 1639 he was found to have abstracted in 1634 the Savile Greek type "under the pretence of printing a Greek Chronologer (one Malala)": and by Feb. 13, 163$\frac{7}{8}$ had brought them back (Wharton's *Remains of Laud*, ii. 174).

161$\frac{5}{6}$, Mar. 21. Edward Forrest is bookseller (Clark, i. 321).

——— William Toldervey, do. (*ibid.*).

——— John Westall, do. (*ibid.*) : he occurs as binding for the Bodleian in 1636–7 (Macray's *Annals*, 2nd ed., p. 77).

161$\frac{6}{7}$, Jan. 19. James Short do. : see p. 312.

1617, May 16. Roger Barnes, adm. bookseller (Clark, i. 321) : see 1626, below.

——— June 10. William Wildgoose, do. (*ibid.*).

——— June 11. John Allam, do. (*ibid.*).

The two latter with Christopher Barker, William Johnson and John Chambers were reprimanded on 23 May, 1617, for setting up as booksellers without the Vice-Chancellor's leave (*ibid.*).

1619, July 30. Edward Miles occurs as bookseller (Clark, i. 343) : he was Clerk of the University, and died before 1 May, 1637 (Oxf. Univ. Archives—Wills).

162$\frac{0}{1}$, Jan. 6. Richard Parne adm. parchment seller, in place of Henry Dochin, dead, who had succeeded John Cooke (Clark, i. 322).

1623, Apr. Thomas Huggins occurs as stationer (Clark, i. 343), also in 1627 (of St. Mary's parish) and 1634 (*ibid.* and 344).

162$\frac{5}{6}$. William Webbe occurs as stationer (Clark. i. 343). See p. 312. Still stationer in 163$\frac{2}{3}$ (*ibid.* 344), and binder to the Bodleian (Macray's *Annals*, 2nd ed., p. 77 : died in 1652).

1626, June 18. Roger Barnes and John his son occur as bookbinders (Clark, i. 343), John is still bookbinder in 1630 (*ibid.*) and 1636–7, (Macray's *Annals of the Bodleian*, 2nd ed., p. 77). Roger died before 30 Nov. 1631 (of All Saints parish, bookbinder and stationer : Oxf. Univ. Archives—Wills).

1629, June 16. The University of Cambridge begs the loan of the Greek matrixes given to Oxford by sir Henry Savile : the request was granted on June 30 on Laud's recommendation, and the matrixes returned 24 June, 1631. The year in which Savile's famous " silver " Greek type (with which the *Chrysostom* of 1610–13 was printed at Eton) came to Oxford is not at present ascertainable.

1631. From the fine of £300 inflicted on the printer of the Wicked Bible of this year a fount of Greek type was purchased by Laud (not before 1634) for printing in London, Oxford or Cambridge, as the editors of the books might prefer. As a fact the printing took place in London, from 1637 on.

1632, Nov. 12. The first charter to Oxford allowing printing : printed in App D. II., p. 281 : confirmed and amplified, 13 March, 163$\frac{2}{3}$ (p. 283). Laud in a letter to the University mentions King and Motteshead as two printers the University might well appoint out of the three allowed.

1635. Leonard Lichfield succeeded his father John, as University printer: died in 1657.

1636. Tit. xviii, sect. 5 of the Statutes of the University is framed " De Typographis Universitatis ": printed in App. D. V., p. 287. The Architypographus is here first mentioned.

1636. John Haviland of London is stated to have a press at London, Oxford and Cambridge (Arber's *Transcript*, iii. 704).

1636-37. — Seale occurs as binding for the Bodleian (Macray's *Annals*, 2nd ed., p. 77).

—— — Bott, do. (*ibid.*).

163⁶⁄₇, Mar. 12. See p. 285 (agreement between the University and the Stationers' Company).

1637, July 11. A severe decree of Star-Chamber is issued, restricting printing, but allowing the rights of Oxford : printed in Arber's *Transcript*, iv. 528.

1637. In this year Laud, who had in every way facilitated the acquisition of good Oriental and other type by the University, was able to write to the Vice-Chancellor (on May 5) " You are now upon a very good way towards the setting up of a learned Press."

1637, Oct. 14. The will of Hugh Jones of St. Mary Magdalen parish, printer (apprentice ?), was proved (Oxf. Univ. Archives—Wills).

1638, Apr. 12. The will of John Wilmot, stationer, was proved (*ibid.*).

1639. See under 161⁶⁄₉ (Turner).

1639, Aug. 12. Agreement with the Stationers' Company: see p. 287.

The following booksellers of Oxford are at present only known from their imprints :—

> Jackson, Simon, 1618.
> Cripps, Henry, 1620-39.
> Peerse, Elias, 1625-39.
> Curteyne, Henry, 1625-40.
> Butler, Thomas, 1628.
> Bowman, Francis, 1634-40.
> Allam, Thomas, 1636-39.
> Godwin, Joseph, 1637-39.
> Robinson, Thomas, 1639-40.
> Hunt, Matthew, 1639-40.
> Young, Robert, 1640.

[London booksellers who published for Oxford printers are here omitted: see pp. 311-3.]

[The following discussion of the authorship of the *Praise of Music* (1586, no. 10) is referred to on p. 20 as occurring in Appendix C, and is therefore here inserted.]

The Praise of Music (1586).

This work is probably not by John Case, although constantly attributed to him. The facts of the matter may be stated as follows.

The book is strictly anonymous: all that can be gathered directly from it is that the author was himself an enthusiastic musician. though not necessarily of eminence; that he was a well-read scholar. as well in the Fathers as in the Classics, and that his style and method point to a man of imaginative mind, young in years, and with considerable elegance of thought and expression. The printer writes a dedication to Sir Walter Raleigh, alluding to the book as "an Orphan of one of Lady Musickes children." This can only be meant to convey the impression that the author was dead: on the other hand the treatise can only have been composed recently from the allusions to the controversy about Church music: in fact the author was undoubtedly a Protestant in Elizabeth's reign, who approved of elaborate music in Churches. within certain common-sense limits.

In 1588 John Case published at Oxford an "Apologia Musices" written in Latin, and maintaining nearly the same view about Church music as the book before us, to which Case makes no allusion. Case was elected scholar of St. John's College, Oxford, in 1564 ; and in 1568 fellow. "But so it was," says Wood (*Ath. Ox.*, ed. Bliss, i. 685), "that being Popishly affected he left his fellowship and married [in 1574] and . . . read logic and philosophy to young men (mostly of the R. C. religion) in a private house in St. Mary Magd. parish."

The external evidence about the authorship in question may be put as follows. In favour of Case is the important fact that Thomas Watson the poet in a sonnet to Case does certainly seem to allude to the English as well as the Latin treatise. Most of the expressions may, and more than one must, apply to the *Apologia*, but the allusion to Marsyas can only refer to the " Praise," which indeed is mentioned by name, " Mr. John Case . . . his learned booke lately made in the prayes of Musick." Again, the fact that the *Apologia* nowhere alludes to the former poem is itself an argument that they were not independent of each other, while supposing that Case was partly ashamed of so light and poetical a production and desired to be judged rather by a more philosophical work. such as the Latin treatise, we can understand a desire to ignore the former. To this may be added that such considerations as the above were sufficient to convince critics like Dr. Farmer, Mr. Joseph Haslewood and Dr. Bliss, as well as almost all others who have considered the point. Against such a conclusion the following points may be urged. Antony à Wood, who wrote lives of all Oxford writers up to his own time, and who was born in 1632, will not even suggest that Case was the author, but on the contrary declares that in all his searches he could never discover who wrote the book. Richard Heber seems also to have argued against Case's connexion. With respect to Watson's testimony it must be remembered that he had left the University some years before either book was published, and that it is quite possible that he wrote his sonnet with both books before him and with little on which to form a judgment except an obvious similarity of subject and point of view. Some catalogues are said to have credited the printer with the authorship, and Lowndes ascribes it to Barnaby Barnes!

The internal evidence is against the common authorship of the two books. The style of E.[1] is light, poetical and imaginative, with numerous digressions, apologized for and repeated : that of L. is more staid and so to speak scholastic ; the sentences and thoughts fall into a logical form which are natural to Case. The latter passes by the mythological part of the history of Music, the former finds it in accordance with his taste. Both authors are learned: in E. the references to the Fathers are as numerous as those from any other source : in L. the references to secular authors predominate. Both draw from common sources, such as the *Theatrum vitae humanae* of Beyerlinck and the classical authors : but in the longest quotation common to both, one from Ornithoparchus's *Micrologus* (E. pp. 39–40 : L. pref.), a treatise on singing and music (afterwards, in 1609, translated into English), in which the imaginary descent of Concentus and Accentus from Sonus is given, they differ materially in one point of the account : nor are the explanations of the kinds and effects of the Greek styles of music entirely in accord. So too there are expressions peculiar to each book which could hardly have been absent from the other, had the authors been the same person (as in E. allusions to Mercury's three parts of music ; the Roman college of minstrels ; three causes of music, pleasure, grief and enthusiasm : in L. to inanimate nature moved by music, Homer as a minstrel, the idea that strings from wolves'and sheep's guts would not harmonize together, bees not having ears, modern musicians). But lastly the personality of the authors is different. Both indeed take up the same general point of view, that music is lawful in a Church, and both entirely neglect the *science* of music though they profess to be ardent musicians : but in E. there is a distinct purpose to oppose the attempt to exclude all mixed and " exquisite " music from the public services : the author writes to his equals for the purpose of interesting and convincing them : in L. we see the dialectician addressing those trained in the schools and accustomed to the subtle distinctions and formalities of scholastic logic, and also the teacher of youth, indulging in moral and didactic reflexions (pp. 53–55). Once more, Case, according to Wood, was known before 1574 to have proclivities towards the Roman Catholic religion, and accordingly in L. we find no word of blame addressed to that Church, the nearest approach being a note of triumph over the defeat of the Armada on the last page. Could he then have written, as the author of E., the following expressions, all used in contempt, " in the time of popery " (p. 129), " popish church Musicke (ibid.), " the hypocriticall Monkes and Friers sang their seuen canonicall houres " (p. 133), " rotten rythmes of popery and superstitious inuocation or praying vnto Saints doth not giue greater cause of vomit to any man than to my selfe " (p. 136)?

The author of the " Praise of Musicke " may one day be discovered, but he will probably be found to be some other than Dr. John Case.

---

[1] E., the English *Praise of Musicke* : L., the Latin *Apologia musices.*

APPENDIX D.

I.

(Statute to prevent the removal of valuable books from
Oxford, A.D. 1373: from *Munimenta Academica*, ed. by
F. Anstey (Rolls Series) 1868, i. 233: with *œ* altered to *ae*.)

Quia, propter excessivam multitudinem vendentium libros,
Oxoniae Universitati minime juratorum, plerique codices magni
valoris ad partes exteras deferuntur, veri domini librorum
eorumdem exquisitis coloribus seducuntur, a stationariis Universitatis praedictae lucrum consuetum subtrahitur, in Universitatis dedecus non modicum, gravamen et jacturam, habita
primitus de praemissis deliberatione sufficienti, per congre-
gationem Regentium antiquam consuetudinem in hac parte
renovare volentium *extitit ordinatum*, quod de caetero nullus
librorum venditor, publicis stationariis duntaxat exceptis, seu
ab eis legitime deputatis, aliquem librum alienum seu proprium
vendat excedentem pretium dimidiae marcae, infra jurisdictio-
nem domini Cancellarii Universitatis praefatae, sub poenis
inferius annotatis; *videlicet* quod, si quis legitime convictus
fuerit super transgressione hujus ordinationis, prima vice incar-
ceretur, et, in secunda vice et transgressione, solvat dimidiam
marcam Universitatis usibus applicandam, tertia vero convictus
abjuret officium sive artem venditionis hujusmodi infra limites
superius expressatos.

Facta est autem haec ordinatio vicesimo septimo die mensis
Januarii, anno Domini millesimo trecentesimo septuagesimo
tertio.

II.

1632, Nov. 12.

(Letters patent from Charles I granting to the University three printers
and booksellers with privileges. Printed from the original in the Oxford
University Archives.)

Carolus Dei gratia Anglie Scotie Francie et Hibernie Rex fidei defensor
&c. **Omnibus** ad quos presentes litere pervenerint salutem **Sciatis** quod

nos de gratia nostra speciali ac ex certa scientia et mero motu nostris dedimus et concessimus Ac per presentes pro nobis heredibus et Successoribus nostris damus et concedimus dilectis nobis in Christo Cancellario Magistris et Scholaribus Vniversitatis nostre Oxon licenciam quod ipsi et Successores sui per scripta comuni eorum Sigillo munita de tempore in tempus tres Typographos librorum Impressores et Bibliopolas tam de alienigenis et extra obedientiam nostram heredum et Successorum nostrorum ortis vel oriundis quam de Indigenis infra eandem obedientiam natis vel nascendis infra Septum vel Ambitum eiusdem Vniversitatis residentes et inhabitantes tam conductivas quam proprias Domos habentes vel tenentes designare poterint et constituere quorum singuli omnimodos libros seu Codices publice non prohibitos editos vel edendos et librorum exemplar Cancellarii eiusdem Vniversitatis vel eius vices gerentis ac trium Doctorum quorum vnus ad minus Sacre Theologie existat Professor quibus per eosdem Cancellarium magistros et Scholares facultas facta fuerit libros examinandi Judicio approbandos ibidem imprimere excudere ac Typis mandare ac tam libros et Codices illos quam alios vbicunque sive infra Dominia nostra heredum vel successorum nostrorum seu extra eadem impressos vel excusos ac vt prefertur approbatos tam in eadem vniversitate quam alibi vendicioni exponere vendere et distrahere quocies voluerint valeant et possint Quibus quidem Typographis librorum Impressoribus ac Bibliopolis et singulis eorum tam presentibus quam futuris ad omnia premissa licite et impune agendi licentiam similiter damus et concedimus per presentes. **Ac** pro nobis heredibus et Successoribus nostris vlterius volumus et concedimus quod huiusmodi Typographi librorum Impressores et Bibliopole eciam extra obedienciam nostram heredum vel Successorum nostrorum orti vel oriundi et eorum singuli quamdiu infra ambitum vniversitatis predicte moram traxerint et negocio antedicto sint intendentes in omnibus et per omnia tanquam fideles Subditi et ligei nostri infra Regnum Anglie oriundi reputentur habeantur et tractentur et singulis libertatibus liberis consuetudinibus legibus et privilegiis vti et gaudere valeant libere et quiete provt aliquis fidelis Subditus et ligeus noster heredum vel Successorum nostrorum infra Regnum Anglie ortus vel oriundus vti et gaudere debeat et ad quotas onera Consuetudines vel Imposiciones quascunque aliter aut alio modo quam ceteri fideles Subditi et ligei nostri heredum vel Successorum nostrorum infra Regnum Anglie orti vel oriundi Solvenda vel contribuenda nullus eorum arctetur vel compellatur Statutis de Alienigenis antehac editis seu Statutis vel Provisionibus quibusvis aliis in contrarium non obstantibus **Proviso** tamen quod iidem Typographi librorum Impressores et Bibliopole et singuli eorum extra obedienciam nostram heredum vel Successorum nostrorum oriundi omnia et omnimoda Custumas et Subsidia et alia debita et onera pro rebus et merchandizis suis extra Regnum Anglie traducendis vel in idem Regnum inducendis vt alienigene solvere teneantur et legibus Regni nostri Anglie sint obedientes **Eo quod** expressa mencio de vero valore annuo vel de certitudine premissorum sive eorum alicuius aut de aliis Donis sive Concessionibus per nos seu per aliquem Progenitorum sive Predecessorum nostrorum prefatis Cancellario Magistris et Scholaribus ante hec tempora facta in presentibus minime facta existit aut aliquo Statuto Actu Ordinacione Provisione Proclamacione sive Restriccione in contrarium inde antehac habitis factis editis ordinatis sive provisis aut aliqua

alia re causa vel materia quacunque in aliquo non obstante **In Cuius** rei
testimonium has literas nostras fieri fecimus Patentes **Teste** me ipso apud
Westmonasterium Duodecimo die Novembris Anno regni nostri octavo.

per breve de privato Sigillo.   Wolseley.

III.

163¾, March 13.

(Letters patent from Charles I. confirming the charter of 12 Nov. 1632,
and further allowing each printer to have two presses and two apprentices,
forbidding unauthorized reprints for 21 years.   Printed from the original
in the Oxford University Archives.)

Carolus Dei gratia Anglie Scocie Francie et hibernie Rex fidei Defensor
&c. **Omnibus** ad quos presentes litere pervenerint salutem **Inspeximus**
quasdam literas nostras Patentes magno Sigillo nostro Anglie Sigillatas
Quarum tenor sequitur in hec verba Carolus dei gracia ... [&c., as above,
dated 12 Nov. 1632, ending] ... Anno regni nostri Octavo **Sciatis** quod nos
de gracia nostra speciali ac ex certa scientia et mero motu nostris predictas
literas Patentes et singula in eisdem contenta tam predictis Cancellario
Magistris et Scholaribus quam Typographis librorum Impressoribus et
Bibliopolis sub forma in eisdem literis Patentibus specificata designandis
et constituendis tam presentibus quam futuris concedimus et confirmamus
Volentes quod eorum singuli libertatibus et privilegiis in eisdem contentis
plenarie gaudeant et vtantur **Volumus** eciam et pro nobis heredibus et
Successoribus nostris concedimus eisdem Cancellario Magistris et Scholaribus et Successoribus suis et Bibliopolis librorum Impressoribus et Typographis in vniversitate predicta designandis et constituendis vt predictum
est dum moram trahunt et residentes sunt infra septum vel ambitum eiusdem
vniversitatis quod liceat eorum cuilibet duo Prela seu Impressoria infra pre-
cincta predicta habere et occupare eisque vti in omnibus suis necessariis
Decreto in Curia Camere Stellate Anno regni Domine Elizabethe nuper
Regine Anglie vicesimo octavo [17 Nov. 1585–16 Nov. 1586] seu decreto
quovis alio in contrarium in aliquo non obstante **Et** quod quilibet dictorum
Typographorum librorum Impressorum et Bibliopolarum duos Apprenticios
ad sibi deserviendum in arte et misterio predicto capere et conducere valeat
Statutis in huiusmodi casu editis et provisis in aliquo non obstantibus **Ac**
vt Magistri et Scholares eiusdem vniversitatis librorum exemplaria idiomatis
diversi tam vernaculi quam peregrini in Bibliothecis in eadem Vniversitate
hactenus latencia divulgare ac libros Concionum exemplaria et tractatus de
novo componere et edere in religionis Christiane ac bonarum literarum et
Artium incrementum incitentur Dictique Typographi et librorum Impressores labores et sumptus huiusmodi exemplaria ac libros typis mandandi et
imprimendi subeant libencius **Sciatis** vlterius quod nos de vberiori gracia
nostra speciali et ex certa scientia et mero motu nostris concessimus dictis
Cancellario Magistris et Scholaribus et Successoribus suis ac Typographis
et librorum Impressoribus infra septum vel ambitum Vniversitatis predicte

pro tempore existentibus residentibus tam presentibus quam futuris in forma predicta designandis et constituendis Et tenore presencium pro nobis heredibus et Successoribus nostris volumus et concedimus quod quocies predictorum Typographorum seu librorum Impressorum quispiam exemplaria librorum Idiomatis cuiuscunque vernaculi vel peregrini ex Bibliotheca quavis infra Vniversitatem predictam desumpta preantea non excusa vel impressa Dummodo huiusmodi Exemplaria sub forma in predictis literis Patentibus specificata divulgari approbentur Typis mandare vel imprimere quod non liceat alicui cuiuscunque status vel condicionis infra Terminum viginti et vnius Annorum proximorum post huiusmodi exemplarium primam impressionem absque speciali licencia Cancellarii Magistrorum et Scholarium predictorum in scriptis prehabita imprimere seu reimprimere aut ab aliis imprimi seu reimprimi facere aut impressa aut reimpressa vendere venalia habere edere vel evulgare seu clam vel palam distrahere infra Diciones nobis vbicunque subiectas **Ac** de vberiori gracia nostra speciali ac ex certa scientia et mero motu nostris pro nobis heredibus et Successoribus nostris concessimus dictis Cancellario Magistris et Scholaribus et Successoribus suis ac Typographis et librorum Impressoribus infra septum vel ambitum vniversitatis predicte pro tempore existentibus residentibus tam presentibus quam futuris in forma predicta designandis et constituendis **Et volumus** tenore presencium quod quociescunque predictorum Typographorum vel librorum Impressorum quispiam Conciones tractatus vel libros per Magistrorum seu Scholarium predictorum quempiam de novo componendos et edendos Dummodo huiusmodi Conciones tractatus et libri vt prefertur approbentur Typis mandare vel imprimere quod non liceat alicui cuiuscunque status vel Condicionis infra decem Annos proximos post huiusmodi Concionum tractatuum vel librorum primam impressionem absque speciali licencia Cancellarii Magistrorum et Scholarium predictorum in scriptis prehabita imprimere seu reimprimere aut ab aliis imprimi seu reimprimi facere aut impressos vel reimpressos vendere venales habere edere vel evulgare seu clam vel palam distrahere infra Diciones nostras Typographis Bibliopolis librorum Impressoribus aliisque vniversis cuiuscunque Status vel Condicionis existant infra Diciones nostras vbicunque constitutis strictius inhibentes ne quis eorum infra seperatos Terminos decem Annorum et viginti et vnius Annorum proximorum post huiusmodi exemplarium Concionum tractatuum seu librorum primam Impressionem preter Typographos vel librorum Impressores in Vniversitate predicta vt predictum designandos et constituendos infra Diciones nostras imprimere seu reimprimere aut ab aliis imprimi seu reimprimi facere aut impressos vel reimpressos vendere venales habere edere vel evulgare seu clam vel palam infra Dominia nostra distrahere inducere vel importare sine licentia dictorum Cancellarii Magistrorum et Scholarium in Scriptis prius habita presumat sub pena Confiscacionis librorum huiusmodi preter Arbitrar, in mandata nostra contemnentes infligenda **Ac** eisdem Cancellario Magistris et Scholaribus damus et concedimus potestatem in locis quibusvis infra Dominia nostra in quibus iusta fuerit suspicionis causa libros excusos vel distractos contra tenorem Mandati nostri abscondi vel custodiri per seipsos vel Deputatos suos pacis Custode Constabulario vel Decennario eis asciociato scrutari et disquirere ac libros huiusmodi repertos capere ad loca publica ad vsum nostrum deferre ibidem remansuros quovsque vlterius in

ea parte ordinatum fuerit **Mandantes** insuper vniversis et singulis vice-
comitibus Custodibus pacis Maioribus Balliuis Constabulariis Decennariis
Prepositis et Ministris quocies ex parte predictorum Cancellarii Magistrorum
et Scholarium fuerint requisiti quod eis auxiliantes sint consulentes et pre-
sidio assistentes. **Eo quod** expressa mencio de vero valore annuo vel de
certitudine premissorum siue eorum alicuius aut de aliis Donis siue Concessionibus per nos seu per aliquem Progenitorum siue Predecessorum
nostrorum prefatis Cancellario Magistris et Scholaribus ante hec tempora
facta in presentibus minime facta existit aut aliquo Statuto Actu Ordinacione
Provisione Proclamacione siue Restriccione in contrarium inde antehac
habito facto edito ordinato siue proviso aut aliqua alia re causa vel materia
quacunque in aliquo non obstante **In Cuius** rei testimonium has literas
nostras fieri fecimus Patentes **Teste** me ipso apud Westmonasterium Tertio-
decimo die Marcii Anno regni nostri Octavo

per Breve de privato Sigillo   Wolseley
(with the Seal attached).

IV.

163⁷, March 12..

(An Indenture between the University of Oxford and the Stationers'
Company, by which the former releases to the latter all its rights of
printing Bibles &c. for the term of three years from 16 Feb. 163⁷. for
the sum of £200 yearly. Printed from the original in the University
Archives.)

This Indenture made the Twentieth Day of March Anno Domini 1636
And in the Twelueth yeare of the Raigne of our soueraigne Lord Charles by
the grace of God of England Scotland France and Ireland King Defender
of the faith &c. **Betweene** the Chancellor Masters and Schollers of the
vniuersity of Oxford of the one part And the Master and Keepers or
Wardens and Communaltie of the Art or Mistery of Stationers of the Citty
of London of the other part **Whereas** by an Order made at whitehall the
Ninth Day of March in the yeare of our Lord god 1635 by the Kings most
excellent Maiestie and the right honorable the Lords and others of his
highnes priuie Councell it is recyted that there had thentofore risen Diverse
Debates and Controuersies betweene the vniuersitie of Cambridge and the
Printers there And the Kings Printer and the Company of Stacioners in
London for the printing of Diuers Bookes in regard of a Charter for printing
graunted to the vniuersitie of Cambridge 26° Hen. 8⁰ And that the same
Controuersies and Contentions vpon seuerall Refferences from his Maiestie
had byn setled by two Orders The one of the Tenth of December 1623 The
other of the Sixteenth of Aprill 1629 And that in regard his Maiestie of his
equall indulgence and grace to the vniuersitie of Oxford had graunted the
like Charter for printing to the said vniuersitie of Oxford as was formerly
graunted to the vniuersity of Cambridge It was that day ordered by the
Board according to the Kings expresse pleasure declared That the vniuersitie

of Oxford and their Printers should for the time to Come enioy the benifitt of all the Articles and Clauses in the said Orders of the Tenth of December 1623 And of the Sixteenth of Aprill 1629 As by the same Order made the said Ninth day of March relacion being therevnto had appeareth **Now this Indenture witnesseth** that the Chancellor Masters and Schollers of the said vniuersitie of Oxford for divers good Causes and Consideracions them therevnto moveing **Haue** given and graunted And by these presents doe give and graunt vnto the said Master and Keepers or Wardens and Comunaltie their Successors and assignes full power License Libertie and authority to print and Cause to be Imprinted Al and euery such and such number of Bibles and other Bookes and things whatsoeuer now or heretofore vsed to be printed by the Kings Maiesties Printer And alsoe Lilies Grammers As the said Chancellors Masters and Schollers or their Printer or Printers of the said vniuersitie may might Could or ought to print or Comprint or cause to be Comprinted or imprinted by force or vertue of the said Three seuerall Orders before mencioned or any of them **To haue and to hould** the said power License Libertie and authoritie vnto the said Master and Keepers or Wardens and Comunalty and their Successors and Assignes from the Sixteenth Day of February last past for and During the Terme of Three yeares fully to be Compleat and ended **At vpon and vnder** the yearely Rent or Summe of Two hundred Poundes of Currant English money Payable at the Feasts of the Annunciacion of the Blessed Ladie St Marie the Virgin and of St Michaell Tharchangell by euen and equall porcions The first payment thereof to begin and to be made at and vpon the Fiue and Twentieth Day of this instant month of March or within Fifteene Dayes after either or any of the said Feasts or Dayes of payment **And the said** Chancellor Masters and Schollers doe for themselues and their Successors Couenant graunt and agree to and with the said Master and Keepers or Wardens and Comunaltie and their Successors and Assignes by these presents That neither the printers of the said vniuersitie of Oxford nor any of them nor any person or persons whatsoeuer by or vpon any License or authoritie deriued or to be deriued from or given or graunted by the said Chauncellor Masters and Schollers other then the said Master and Keepers or Wardens and Communalty their Successors and Assignes shall or will at any tyme or tymes hereafter within or During the said Terme of Three yeares print or Comprint or Cause permit or suffer to be imprinted or Comprinted any Booke Bookes or parcell of Booke Bookes Copies or things whatsoeuer in the said Orders or any or either of them mencioned or which they the said Chancellor Masters and Schollers or their Printers may or might print or Comprint by force or vertue of the said Orders or any or either of them **And the said** Master and Keepers or Wardens and Comunaltie doe for themselues and their Successors Couenaunt graunt and agree to and with the said Chancellor Masters and Schollers and their Successors by these presents That they the said Master and Keepers or Wardens and Comunaltie and their Successors shall and will well and truely pay the said Two hundred pound in manner and forme and at the daies and tymes before lymited and expressed for the payment thereof vnto the said Chancellor Masters and Schollers **And lastly** it is mutually Couenanted graunted and promised by and betweene the said parties to these presents

and their successors respectively That vpon and at the tyme of the Expiration
of the said Terme of Three yeares They and either of them shall and will
renue Continue and then make and Conclude such and the like amicable
Composicion and agreement And vpon such termes rates and proposicions
as are herein Conteyned and expressed for soe long tyme after and vntill it
shall be reasonably agreed on both parts to relinquish the same **In witnes**
whereof to the one part of these present Indentures remayning with the said
Master and Keepers or wardens and Comunalty of the said Art or mistery
of Stacioners of the saide Citty of London The said Chancellor Masters and
Schollers of the said vniuersity of Oxford haue sett their Comon seale And
to the other parte of these present Indentures remayning with the said
Chancellor Masters and Schollers of the said vniuersitie of Oxford The said
Master and Keepers or wardens and Comunaltie of the said Art or mistery
of Stacioners of the said Citty of London haue sett their Comon seale The
Day and yeares first aboue written

Delivered as the Deede of the Stationers of London for the vse of the
Chancellors M^rs and Schollers of the Vniversitie of Oxford 31° Martij
1637.   By the Warden of the sayd Companie in the presence of ˜

John French
John Thimble
G. Locksmyth

[with a fragment of the seal]

[With this Indenture is an agreement of the same date that if more
than £200 a year be agreed to be paid to the University of Cambridge
for a similar suspension of rights a correspondingly increased sum will
be paid to the University of Oxford.]

A precisely similar indenture and agreement dated 12 Aug. 1639
renew the deeds of 1636 for a second term of three years from 17 Feb.
16³⁹⁄₄₀, under the same conditions.

V.

(Tit. xviii, Sect. v. of the Laudian Statutes of the University, 1636,
printed from Griffiths' and Shadwell's edition, Oxford, 1888 ; with ae for
æ.   It would appear that no Architypographus was appointed till 1658.)

DE TYPOGRAPHIS UNIVERSITATIS.

Cum Sereniss. REX CAROLUS eius nominis Primus, pro eo affectu quo
Literas ac Literatos fovet, Privilegia Universitatis, quoad rem Typographicam
nimis antehac arctata, mirum in modum amplificaverit : ne Clementiss.
Regis indulgentia sordidi ac illiberales Artifices ad privatum suum quaestum
abutantur : Statutum est, quod nullus Typographus in posterum his Privilegiis aut titulo Typographi Universitatis nostrae gaudebit, nisi qui in

Admissione sua singulis Statutis et Ordinationibus circa regimen Typographorum, per Domum Convocationis factis, vel in posterum edendis, se submiserit.

Quoniam vero in re Typographica usu compertum est, Mechanicos hosce Artifices (lucri sui compendium cum dispendio operis plerumque sectantes) Calligraphiae seu Operis decori et elegantiae minime studere, sed opera quaeque rudia ac inemendata in publicam lucem extrudere; Idcirco praesenti Statuto cautum .esto, quod publicae Universitatis Typographiae, instruendae in Domo aliqua huic usui specialiter deputata, praeficiatur Architypographus unus, Vir Graecis Latinisque literis probe instructus, et in studiis Philologicis versatissimus: Cuius munus erit, Operis Typographicis ibidem praeesse; materiam sive supellectilem typographicam (Chartam scilicet, Praela, Typos, et alia huius Opificii instrumenta) ut sint in suo quaeque genere lectissima providere. In Operibus e publica Universitatis Typographia prodeuntibus, Typorum modulum, Chartae qualitatem, Marginum mensuram praescribere; Correctorum errata emendare; et alia quaecunque, ad Operis ornatum et perfectionem spectantia, sedulo curare. Cui muneri quo alacrius et liberius vacet, (praeter certam portionem lucri e libris impressis provenientis, ipsi posthaec, pro ratione symbolae quam ad publicae Typographiae peculium seu sortem communem contulerit, assignandam ab iis qui a Domo Convocationis ad ordinanda Statuta Typographica delegandi erunt,) Officium superioris Bedelli in Iure Civili, (utpote reliquis minus negotiosum,) quandocunque primum quoquo modo vacaverit, perpetuo in posterum annectendum fore praesenti Statuto cautum esto.

APPENDIX E.

WOODCUT ORNAMENTS, TYPE, ETC.

A. *Woodcut and Metal Ornaments.* 1585–1640.

OF these there are two classes, the first large and used for the centre of titlepages or with conspicuous colophons (these I term *Devises*), the other smaller ornaments, used for borders, or to mark the beginning or end of a chapter, or generally for decorative purposes: these I call *Woodcuts*. The descriptions which follow are not intended to be fuller than is sufficient to distinguish the more important. The measurements (as always) are the least possible, and not the full size of the plate or block.

I. *Devices.*

Of these there are, in the period under review, fourteen :—

A. $3\frac{1}{8} \times 2\frac{7}{8}$ in. On a shield the arms of the University (with motto SAPIEN|TIAE : | ET. | FELI|CITA|TIS. |), within a border bearing ACADE⁼|MIA. | OXONI⁼|ENSIS. | At the corners are two females and two satyrs.

Used in 1585-93, 1597–1600, and at intervals till 1635, but not from 1625 to 1633.

B. $1\frac{7}{8} \times 1\frac{1}{2}$ in. A metal engraving. In centre the arms of the University, with $\frac{\text{SA}|\text{et}}{\text{PI}|\text{Fe}}$, within a ribbon bearing ACADEMIA OXONIENSIS. Above and on each side and below are female figures with emblems and scrolls, and underneath all IOSEPH' BARNESIUS.

Used only in 1591. (Barne and Tacitus.)

B*a*. $1\frac{11}{16} \times 1\frac{3}{4}$ in. A wood engraving from B, omitting Barnes's name: the motto is $\frac{\text{SA}|\text{et}}{\text{PI}|\text{F}}$: and there are other small changes.

Used in 1627-8, 1630-33, 1635-7, 1640.

C. $1\frac{1}{4} \times 1\frac{5}{16}$ in. An ornamental shield, with the arms of the University, the legend being $\frac{\text{SA FE}}{\text{PI}|\text{LI}}$: at the sides AC: and OX. There is a defect (a short line omitted) $\frac{}{\text{ET}|\text{CI}}$ on one shoulder, which serves to distinguish it from H.

Used at intervals from 1592 to 1638.

There is a counterfeit of this used in London printing of at least 1616 and 1624 : see pp. 106, 120, and H, below.

D. $1\frac{7}{16} +$ in. squ. A nine-spoked wheel with two mottos "Omnia subiacent vicissi-tudini," and "Sola virtus cadere non potest."

Used in 1592-3, 1620, 1629.

U

E. $1\frac{1}{4} \times 1\frac{1}{16}$ in. An ornamental shield with the Royal Arms, and at the sides E: and R.

Used in 1594.

F. $1\frac{6}{16} \times 1\frac{6}{16}$ in. An ornamental shield with the arms of New College between two W's (William of Wykeham).

Used in 1598, 1605.

G. $1\frac{3}{4}$ in. squ. A circular watch-face, with "Donec dies est . Iohan: 9.4", and figures : for John Day of Oriel.

Used in 1614–5, 1620.

H. $1\frac{6}{16} \times 1\frac{3}{4}$. Similar to C, but slightly larger. Perhaps a London counterfeit.

Used in 1616 and 1624.

I. $2\frac{1}{4} + 1\frac{11}{16}$ in. In centre the arms of the University on a white shield with

SAP | FEL

IEN | ICIT , and round it a band with ACADE|MIA. | OXONIᵃ|ENSIS. At the corners

TIA | ATIS

are two winged figures, a rose and a thistle.

Used in 1628, and at intervals till 1637, by Turner only.

J. $2\frac{5}{8} \times 2\frac{7}{8}$ in. An Agnus Dei ; beneath it "IOH : I : 26" and "ECCE AGN' | DEI ", a text round it.

Used in 1628.

K. $1\frac{7}{16} \times 1\frac{3}{4}$. The arms of the University, with the motto

SAP | ·ET
IENC | FELI
TIA | CIT
   | ATE

, and round

it ACADEMIA. | OXONIESIS, a cherub above.

Used in 1630–4, 1636–8, 1640 : in and after 1634 the ATE is altered to ATIS.

L. $2\frac{1}{2} \times 2\frac{3}{8}$ in. The arms of Great Britain and Ireland, crowned, with "C.", "R." at sides of crown.

Used in 1636.

M. $4\frac{1}{2} \times 3\frac{3}{4}$. A Tree of Knowledge, boys plucking fruit, &c.

Used in 1636 (Lily's Grammar).

II. *Woodcuts.*

These are 142 in number (not counting *plain* woodcut capitals), of which 32 were used by Barnes. Most of these passed on to his successors, who augmented them. In 1627 the two University printers printed separately, and John Lichfield took the larger number for himself, a few being used in common. It would be idle to print a complete list of these, but the writer has full notes of the occurrence of all that are found in each book. Twelve are alphabets, fifteen frames within which any capital could be placed, and four are arched borders.

B. *Type.*

The following table exhibits the use made of different type by Oxford printers 1585–1640, but applies only to the chief type of the body of the work. Thus Pica Greek is the chief type of a book in 1591 at earliest, but it is found occasionally in 1587, and Long Primer Greek in 1585. So too Great Primer Greek is used in 1624, 9. And Hebrew type is used sporadically from 1596 on (Long Primer, Pica and English, pointed and unpointed : see 1596, 8 & 9 ; 1601, 2 ; 1602, 3 ; &c.)

OXFORD TYPE.

Type	1585	1590	1595	1600	1605	1610	1615	1620	1625	1630	1635	1640
English:												
1 Long Primer			2								½	½ ½
2 Pica	2 6 2 2 1	1 1 1 4	1 1 1 1 2		2 2 1	1	1	1	1	1½ 2	1 1½ 2½	2
3 Great Primer							1	1				
Roman:												
4 Minion	1											
5 Brevier		½ 1	1		1							
6 Long Primer	2 1 1	½ 1 1 2	½	1	1	1 1	1 1 1 1	2 1 2 1 2 1	2 1 5½ 2	4½ 1 6½ 4	4 2 7½ 3 7 3	
7 Pica	2 3 3 3	1 2½ 1½ 2	1 1 3 1 5½	5 2 3 5 6 3½ 1	4 2	3 7½ 7 6 1 2 4 4	1 3 2 5 2½ 7 1		12½ 6½ 5	15½ 3 4½ 12 3 9½ 10 5 4 14		7
8 English			1 2	1 1 7 3 1 8½ 6 9 7 4 6 1 16 16 5 5 3 4			1 2 2 4	2 12 3 5	5 3 7	6 4 12 2 6 5 4 10 3 3		8
9 Great Primer		½ 2 1		1		1		1 1	1½ 2 5	1 1 6	3 2 1 3 5 2½	9
10 Double Pica											1	
Italic:												
11 Long Primer		1				1						
12 Pica	2 3 1 1	½ 2	2 ½ ½			1				1		
13 English											½	½
14 Great Primer												1
Greek:												
15 Long Primer	1	½										
16 Pica		1 1½ 1	2			1	1					

The above table has reference only to the chief type of the body of the book.

	1585	1590	1595	1600	1605	1610	1615	1620	1625	1630	1635	1640
Number of books or pieces printed at Oxford	7 16 9 7 5	5 7 11 7 7	4 8 11 6 7	5 3 12 11 10	13 8 10 17 7	7 2 24 26 17	16 6 9 7 8	5 6 9 5 8	24 9 14 22	19 14 32	9 34 21 16 18	24 23 20 26
Average		8	7		10		12		12		21	

The ordinary size (*now*) of the type used in the Oxford Press from 1585 to 1640 is as follows, see p. 144 (1629, no. 4):—

	Name.	*Lines in one foot.*
Nonpareil	. . . .	. 144
Minion	. . . .	. 120
Brevier	. . . .	about 110
Long Primer	. . . .	. 90
Pica	. . . .	. 72
English	. . . .	. 64
Great Primer	. . . .	. 51
Double Pica (which is double "*small* Pica")	. . . .	. 41
Canon	. . . .	. 20

The old measures make the type of all these very slightly smaller than the above measurements.

C. *Notanda.*

It is curious to observe the small points which break the smooth course of ordinary printing in these earlier times, some of them marking progress, some a perturbation in the office, some stupidity. The following are random notes of some bibliographical interest.

1. The change of use in the case of *u* and *v* (*Vniuersity* being the old spelling, and *University* the new) may be remarked in progress in 1589, no. 5, and is practically completed by 1610. But a capital U is not found at all in the period dealt with, its place being in a few cases supplied by a large lower-case u.

2. For "at Oxford" the common Latin is *Oxoniæ*, but *Oxonii* occurs sporadically. *Bellositi Dobunorum* occurs in 1628: and *Rhydychen* (in Welsh books) in 1595, 1600.

3. In 1588 (no. 8) we first find an Oxford *édition de luxe*.

4. The state of the office is shown by 1595, no. 4 (small stock of type); 1601, no. 2 (Hebrew words sometimes transliterated, sometimes in Hebrew type: yet in 1603, no. 2, there is a complaint of the want of Hebrew type!); 1625, no. 16 (one sheet in different type); 1628, no. 16 (carelessness).

5. Red ink is found in $14\frac{78}{88}$, 1628, 1631, 1633 and thereafter; and gold-printing in 1633.

6. Curiosities of workmanship will be found in 1629, no. 14; 1631, nos. 10, 17; 1633, nos. 26, 33; 1634, no. 9; 1635, no. 3; 1636, no. 15 (signatures); 1638, nos. 3, 17 (do. ; 1640. no. 24: and eccentricity on the author's part in 1631, no. 29; 1633, no. 9 (phonetic spelling): 1635, no. 10. In 1613 no. 29 (Rainolds) on the first two pages of each section the headline is "prophecy", but on every other page it is "prophecie". 1634 no. 17 (Statuta is a true folio, in every sense in which the word is used.

7. The number of books or editions issued at Oxford is roughly as follows :— 15th cent., 15 : early 16th cent., 7 : 1585-1600, 125 : 1601–1620, 230 : 1621-1640, 370 : total, about 750. In the 17th cent. about 2700 were issued : in the 18th, about 2100 : in the first three quarters of the 19th, about 6500. The number from "1468" to 1900 may be estimated as likely to be about 16000.

8. Of the Oxford books issued from "1468" to 1640, the British Museum contains less than 70 per cent., and the Bodleian about 80 per cent. The following calculation is not far from the truth :—

Oxford books in Brit. Mus. and Bodl.	about	450
,, ,, in Brit. Mus. only	,,	50
,, ,, in Bodl. only	,,	150
,, ,, in neither library	,,	100
	Total	750

APPENDIX F.

IMPRINTS.

LISTS AND TABLES OF OXFORD IMPRINTS, 1585–1640.

THE following tables and lists explain themselves. They give a detailed picture of the mutual relations of Oxford and London printers and publishers, and the development of the Oxford book trade. It will be noticed how the archaisms (*Imprinted at Oxford by*, or *At Oxford, printed by*, &c.) are gradually worn off, with the rhetorical descriptions (such as *celeberrimæ Academiæ typographus*), and the use of colophons.

In some cases we find fictitious imprints, as in 1602, nos. 5, 11, 1611 (see impr. 7*a*). 1612 (impr. 7), 1613 (impr. 32), 1616 (impr. 35), 1626 (impr. 67). The number of books with no printer's or publisher's name is small (see impr. 107, and Appendix, p. 151 (Stanley)), and of *books* with no imprint at all there are very few instances, see 1586, 12 ; 1602, 8 and 9 ; 1603, 5 ; 1606, 5 ; 1622, 6 ; 1625. 9 ; 1635, 13.

In the list which follows the spelling is modernized, the form alone is exact.

1585.

(*Joseph Barnes*, 1585–1617.)

1. Oxoniæ, ex officina typographica Josephi Barnesii celeberrimæ Academiæ Oxoniensis typographi.
>>>> 1585 (also as a colophon).

1 *a*. (Omitting *typographica* and *Oxoniensis*).
>>>> 1589, 1591.

2. At Oxford, printed by Joseph Barnes, printer to the University.
>>>> 1585–6, 1592–4, 1598, 1603, 1606–9, 1615–16.

2 *a*. ... printer to that famous University.
>>>> 1585, 1594.

2 *b*. ... printer to the famous University.
>>>> 1586.

2 *c*. Omitting " at."
>>>> 1603.

3. Oxoniæ, ex ædibus Josephi Barnes.
        1585.

4. Imprinted [or Printed] at Oxford [or Oxenford] by Joseph Barnes, printer to the
        University.
            1585 (also as colophon), 1586, 1591, 1599, 1615.

   4 *a*. Adding "famous" before "University".
        1585.

1586.

5. Oxoniæ (or -ii`, ex officina typographica Josephi Barnesii.
        1586-7, 1590, 1592, 1597, 1608.

   5 *a*. Omitting *typographica*.
        1596, 1598.

   5 *b*. With *typographica* the last word.
        1598.

6. At Oxford, printed by Joseph Barnes, and are to be sold in Paul's Churchyard at
        the sign of the Tiger's head.
            1586-9, 1591-2, 1595.

   6 *a*. . . . at the Tiger's head.
        1587.

   6 *b*. Imprinted at Oxford by Joseph Barnes, and are to be sold in Paul's Church-
        yard at the sign of the Tiger's head.
        1588-9.

7. At Oxford, printed by Joseph Barnes.
        1586, 1594, 1603-4, 1607-9, 1610-12 [once as a fictitious imprint],
            1613-15.

   7 *a*. Printed at Oxford, by Joseph Barnes.
            1588, 1592, 1597, 1599, 1605, 1608-10, 1611 (a false imprint), 1613-15.

   7 *b*. Oxford, printed by Joseph Barnes.
        1608.

8. Excndebat Josephus Barnesins typographus Oxoniensis.
        [1586].

9. Oxoniæ, ex officina Josephi Barnesii, et veneunt in cœmeterio Paulino sub signo
        capitis Tigerini.
        1586.

9*. Impressas en Oxford por Ioseph Barnes, en el año de salud M.D.L.XXXVI.
        1586.

1587.

10. Oxoniæ, typis Iosephi Barnesii.
        1587.

11. Oxonii (or -iæ), excndebat Iosephus Barnesius.
        1587-88, 1590, 1592-96, 1598-99, 1601-17.

   11 *a*. With *Oxoniæ* last.
        1599.

1589.

12. Printed by Joseph Barnes, printer . . . are to be sold at the Tiger's head i . . .
        1589.

1590.

13. Oxonii, excudebat Josephus Barnesius celeberrimæ Academiæ Typographus.
1590.

13 *a.* Omitting Oxonii, and adding *Oxoniensis* after *Academiæ.*
1592.

13 *b.* With " Oxoniæ ", and " almæ " for " celeberrimæ."
1602–3.

13 *c.* With " Oxoniæ," and omitting " celeberrimæ."
1615, 1617.

1591.

(*Richard Wright,* of London, 1591.)

14. Printed at Oxford, by Joseph Barnes, for Richard Wright. Cum Privilegio.
1591.

15. Oxoniæ. In officinâ Josephi Barnesii.
1591.

1592.

16 Oxoniæ, excudebat Josephus Barnesius, væneunt cum Oxoniæ, tum ad caput Tigridis ad Divi Pauli Londinensium.
1592.

1595.

17. Joseph Barnes ai printiodd yn Rhydychen.
1595.

1596.

18. Oxoniæ, apud Josephum Barnesium.
1596, 1605.

19. At Oxford, printed by Joseph Barnes, and are to be sold in Paul's Churchyard at the sign of the Bible.
1596, 1600–1.

19 *a.* Printed at Oxford, by Joseph Barnes, and are to be sold in Paul's Churchyard at the sign of the Bible.
1597, 1599, 1600.

20. Oxoniæ, ex officina typographica Iosephi Barnesii, et veneunt Londini in Cœmeterio D. Pauli, ad insigne Bibliæ (or *Bibl.*).
1596–7.

1598.

21. Printed at Oxford, by Joseph Barnes, for R. H. [i.e. Richard Haydocke].
1598.

1602.

(*John Barnes*, of London, 1602–16.)

22. Oxford, printed by Joseph Barnes, and are to be sold by John Barnes at the Turk's Head in Fleet Street [London].
1602.

23. At Oxford, printed by Joseph Barnes, and are to be sold in Fleet Street [London] at the sign of the Turk's Head, by John Barnes.
1602 (Powel: *fictitious imprint*): 1602–3.

24. At Oxford, by Joseph Barnes, printer to the University.
1602 (Higins: *fictitious imprint*): 1602.

1603.

(*Simon Waterson*, of London, 1603–6.)

25. At Oxford, printed by Joseph Barnes, and are to be sold in Paul's Churchyard [London] at the signe of the Crown, by Simon Waterson.
1603–5.

25 *a*. Printed at Oxford, by Joseph Barnes . . . [&c. as above.]
1604–6.

1605.

26. Oxoniæ, excudebat Jos. Barnesius, prostant Londini apud Simonem Waterson in Cæmeterio Ædis Paulinæ.
1605.

27. At Oxford ¶ Printed by Joseph Barnes, and are to be sold by John Barnes, dwelling without Newgate [London] by S. Sepulchre's Church, at the signe of Paris.
1605.

1606.

28. Oxoniæ, excudebat Josephus Barnesius, & veneunt Londini apud Simonem Watersonum in cœmeterio Paulino ad signum Coronæ.
1606.

1612.

29. At Oxford, printed by Joseph Barnes, and are to be sold by John Barnes, dwelling near Holborn Conduit [London].
1612–13 (also *fictitious*).

29 *a*. Printed at Oxford, by Joseph Barnes, and are to be sold by John Barnes, dwelling near Holborn Conduit.
1613 (also *fictitious*).

30. Printed at Oxford, for John Barnes, dwelling near Holborn Conduit.
1612.

1613.

31. Oxoniæ. excudebat Josephus Barnesius, & Londini væneunt apud Johannem Barnesium propè aquæductum Holborniensem.
1613.

32. At Oxford, printed for John Barnes, and are to be sold near Holborn Conduit.
1613 (*fictitious*).

1614.

33. At Oxford, printed by Joseph Barnes, and are to be sold by John Barnes, over
against St. Pulcher's Church.
1614.

1616.

34. Oxford, printed by Joseph Barnes, for John Barnes.
1616 (*perh. fictitious*).

35. Oxford, printed by Joseph Barnes, for John Barnes, dwelling in Hosier Lane, near
Smithfield.
1616 (*fictitious*).

1617.

(*John Lichfield*, 1617–35. *William Wrench*, 1617.)

36. At Oxford, printed by John Lichfield and William Wrench, printers to the famous
University.
1617.

37. Oxoniæ, excudebant Johannes Lichfield et Gulielmus Wrench.
1617 (*excudebat* once, in *Jacobi Ara*).

38. At Oxford, printed by John Lichfield and William Wrench.
1617.

1618.

(*James Short*, 1618–24.)

39. At Oxford, printed by John Lichfield and James Short, printers to the famous
University.
1618–19: (without "At") 1620: (with "At") 1621–24.

40. Oxoniæ (or -ii), excudebant Johannes Lichfield et Jacobus Short.
1618–22, 1624.

(*Simon Jackson*, 1618.)

41. Oxoniæ, excudebant Johannes Lichfield et Jacobus Short, propter Simonem
Jackson.
1618.

1619.

42. Oxoniæ, excudebant Johannes Lichfield et Jacobus Short, Academiæ typographi.
1619-20, 1623-24.

42 *a.* Adding *Oxoniensis* after *Academiæ*.
1622.

(*William Spier*, 1619.)

43. At Oxford, printed by John Lichfield and James Short, for William Spier.
1619.

44. Printed at Oxford, by John Lichfield and James Short, printers to the University.
1619.

44 *a.* With "At Oxford" first.

45. At Oxford, printed by John Lichfield and James Short.
1619, 1622, 1624.

1620.

(*Henry Cripps*, 1620-39. *John Pyper*, of London, 1620.)

46. Oxford, printed by John Lichfield and James Short, for Henry Cripps, and are to
be sold by John Pyper in Paules Churchyard, at the sign of the Cross Keys.
1620.

47. Oxoniæ, excudebant I. L. & I. S. Academiæ Typographi.
1620, 1623.

48. At Oxford, printed by John Lichfield and James Short, for Henry Cripps.
1620-21, 1623-24.

1622.

(*William Davis*, bookseller, 1622-40.)

49. At Oxford, printed by John Lichfield and James Short, for William Davis,
bookseller.
1622.

49 *a.* (Omitting " bookseller ").
1624 (!).

1624.

(*William Turner*, 1624-40.)

50. Oxford, printed by John Lichfield and William Turner.
1624-5.

(*W. Jaggard*, of London, 1624.)

51. London, printed by W. Jaggard, for W. Turner of Oxford.
1624.

1625.

52. Oxford, printed by John Lichfield and William Turner, for Henry Cripps.
   1625.

53. Oxoniæ, excudebant Johannes Lichfield et Guilielmus Turner.
   1625-27 (Gulielmus), 1633 (Guliel.).

54. Printed for Henry Cripps of Oxford.
   1625 (*pr. in London*).

(*Thomas Huggins*, 1625-36.)

55. Oxford, printed by John Lichfield and William Turner, and are to be sold by W. Turner and T. Huggins.
   1625.

56. Oxford, printed by I. L. and W. T. for William Turner.
   1625.

(*Elias Peerse*, 1625-39.)

57. Oxford, printed by John Lichfield and William Turner, printers to the famous University, for Elias Peerse.
   1625.

58. Oxford, printed by John Lichfield and William Turner, printers to the famous University.
   1625-27.

   58 a. With *At* Oxford.
   1625.

(*Edward Forrest*, 1625-40.)

59. Oxford, printed by John Lichfield and William Turner, for Edward Forrest.
   1625-26.

60. Oxoniæ, excudebant Johannes Lichfield et Guilielmus Turner, Academiæ typographi.
   1625-27.

   60 a. Adding *celeberrimæ* before *Academiæ*.
   1634.

61. Oxford, printed by John Lichfield and William Turner, printers to the famous University, for Henry Cripps.
   1625.

(*Henry Curteyne*, 1625-40.)

62. Imprinted for Henry Cripps and Henry Curteyne at Oxford.
   1625 (*pr. in London*).

1626.

63. Oxford, Printed by J. L. and W. T.
   1626.

64. Oxoniæ, excudebant Johannes Lichfield & Guilielmus Turner, impensis Guilielmi Turner.
   1626.

65. Oxoniæ, excudebant J. L. & W. T., impensis Thomæ Huggins.
　　　1626.

66. Oxford, printed by John Lichfield and William Turner for Wi. Turner, Th.
　　Huggins. and Ed. Forrest.
　　　1626.

(Walter Map, pseudonym, 1626.)

67. Oxonii apud Gualtherum Mapes, Academiae Bidellum [PRINTED IN HOLLAND].
　　　1626.

1627.

68. Oxford, printed by William Turner, printer to the famous University.
　　　　1627-28, 1630; 1631; 1635.

　　68 *a*. With " At Oxford, imprinted . . . "
　　　　1628.

　　68 *b*. With " At Oxford printed . . . "
　　　　1633 or later.

　　68 *c*. Omitting *famous*, and adding *Cum Privilegio*.
　　　　1634.

　　68 *d*. Adding *Cum Privilegio*.
　　　　1636-37.

69. Oxoniæ, excudebat Guilielmus Turner.
　　　　1627-28 (with " Oxon."), 1631, 1633 (with " Oxonii "), 1633, 1634 (with
　　　　　　" Oxonii "), 1636 (" Oxonii" and " G. Turner "), 1637, 1640.

70. Oxford, printed for Henry Cripps [by L. Lichfield].
　　　　1627-28, 1632, 1638.

71. Oxford, printed by I. L. and W. T., for William Turner and Thomas Huggins.
　　　　1627.

72. Oxoniæ, excudebat Guilielmus Turner, Academiæ Typographus.
　　　　1627-1629, 1637.

　　72 *a*. Adding *celeberrimæ* before *Academiæ*.
　　　　1628-29, 1634, 1639 with Oxonii.

　　72 *b*. Adding *cum Privilegio*.
　　　　1628.

　　72 *c*. Adding *celeberrimæ* after *Academiæ*.
　　　　1631.

　　72 *d*. With " Oxoniæ ex officina Guilielmi Turneri, Academiæ typographi."
　　　　1637.

73. Oxoniæ, excudebat Johannes Lichfield, Academiæ Typographus.
　　　　1627, 1633 (with Oxonii), 1634-35.

　　73 *a*. Adding *alma* before *Academiæ*.
　　　　1630-32.

　　73 *b*. Adding *florentissima* before *Academiæ*.
　　　　1634 (as colophon).

74. Oxoniæ, impensis Thomæ Huggins & Henrici Curteyn [by W. Turner].
　　　　1627.

1628.

75. Oxford, printed by John Lichfield, printer to the famous University, for Henry Cripps.
>1628 (colophon), 1632 (colophon).

75 *a*. Prefixing *At*.
>1631.

(*Philemon Stephens*, of London, 1628.)
(*Christopher Meredith*, of London, 1628.)

76. Printed at Oxford, 1628. And are to be sold by Ph. Stephens and Ch. Meredith at the Golden Lion in Paul's Churchyard.
>1628.

(*William Webbe*, 1628–39.)

77. Oxford, printed [by John Lichfield] for William Webb.
>1628.

78. Oxford, printed by John Lichfield, printer to the famous University, for William Webb.
>1628–29.

79. Oxford, printed by John Lichfield, printer to the famous University, for Henry Curteyne.
>1628.

80. Oxford, printed by William Turner, printer to the famous University, and are to be sold by Henry Curteine.
>1628.

81. At Oxford, printed by John Lichfield, printer to the University, and are to be sold by William Web.
>1628.

82. Oxford, printed by John Lichfield.
>1628, 1631, 1633, 1635.

82 *a*. Imprinted at Oxford by John Lichfield. Cum privilegio.
>1632.

83. Bellositi Dobunorum, excudebat W. T., impensis W. W.
>1628.

84. Oxford (or, At Oxford), printed by John Lichfield, printer to the famous University, and are to be sold by Edward Forrest.
>1628.

84 *a*. Oxford, printed by John Lichfield, printer to the famous University, for Edward Forrest.
>1630–32.

84 *b*. As 84, omitting *famous*.
>1634[1].

85. At Oxford, printed by John Lichfield, printer to the famous University.
>1628, 1630.

85 *a*. (Omitting " At ").
>1629, 1631, 1633.

---

[1] The references to impr. 84 *b* in 1630-32 are errors for 84 *a*.

    85 *b.* (With "that" for "the").
        1630.

    85 *c.* As 85 *a*, with "Cum Privilegio."
        1634.

    85 *d.* As 85, omitting "At" and "famous," and putting "imprinted" for "printed."
        1634 (as colophon).

    85 *e.* As 85, except "Printed at Oxford," and omitting "famous."
        1634 (as colophon).

(*Thomas Butler*, 1628.)

86. Oxford, printed by John Lichfield, printer to the University, and are to be sold by Thomas Butler.
    1628.

87. Oxoniæ (or, Oxonii), impensis Gulielmi Webb bibliopolæ [by L. Lichfield ?].
    1628, 1631.

    87 *a.* Omitting *bibliopolæ*.
        1631, 1636, 1638.

1629.

(*Robert Allott*, of London, 1629–33.)

88. Oxoniæ, excudebat Guilielmus Turner, & veneunt per Robertum Allott, Londinensem, in Cœmiterio Pauli.
    1629.

89. At Oxford, printed by John Lichfield, printer to the famous University, for E. Forrest and W. Webbe.
    1629.

90. Oxoniæ, excudebat Guilielmus Turner, Academiæ typographus, impensis Henrici Curteyne.
    1629.

91. Oxford, printed by I. L. for Henry Curteyne
    1629.

92. Oxoniæ, recudebat Johannes Lichfield, et væneunt apud Eliam Pearse.
    1629.

93. Oxford, printed by I. L.
    1629, 1632.

94. At Oxford, printed by W. Turner for Henry Curteyne.
    1629.

    94 *a.* Omitting "At".
        1640.

95. Oxoniæ, excudebat Johannes Lichfield.   Cum privilegio.
    1629.

    95 *a.* Omitting *cum privilegio*.
        1634–35.

96. Oxoniæ, excudebat Johannes Lichfield, impensis Guilielmi Davis.
    1629, 1631.

97. At Oxford, printed by John Lichfield, printer to the University, for Edward
Forrest.
1629.

97 *a.* Adding "famous" before *University.*
1629-34.

98. Oxoniæ, excudebat Guilielmus Turner, impensis authoris.
1629, 1637.

98 *a.* Adding "cum licentia & permissu."
1637.

(*Henry Seale*, of London, 1629.)

99. Oxford, printed by John Lichfield, Printer to the University, and are to be sold in
Paul's Churchyard at the sign of the Tiger's Head by Henry Seale.
1629.

100. Oxford, printed by W. T. for William Turner and Thomas Huggins.
1629.

101. Oxoniæ, excudebat J. Lichfield, impensis Edvardi Forrest.
1629.

1630 [1].

102. Oxford, printed by William Turner, for Robert Allot, and are to be sold in
Paul's Churchyard.
1630.

103. Printed by W. T. for Robert Allot.
1630 (a 2nd title).

104. Oxoniæ, impensis Guilielmi Turner, celeberrimæ Academiæ typographi.
1630.

105. Oxoniæ, typis Joh. Lichfield, impensis Hen. Curteine.
1630-31.

105 *a.* Substituting "excudebat" for "typis".
1631.

106. Oxford, printed by William Turner for Edward Forrest.
1630.

107. Printed at Oxford for the Author [by Leonard Lichfield].
1630-31.

108. At Oxford, printed by John Lichfield, printer to the famous University, for
Thomas Huggins.
1630-31.

1631.

100. Oxoniæ, excudebat Guilielmus Turner, propriis impensis.
1631, 1637 (in secondary title the name of place is omitted in both years).

109 *a.* With ipsius impensis; and "Cum Privilegio" added.
1639.

---

[1] "*Oxoniæ*" simply is found on an *Appendix* by Hen. Stanley, 1630, but is not a genuine
imprint (see p. 233).

110. Oxoniæ, excudebat Gnilielmus Turner Academiæ celeberrimæ typographus, impensis Thomæ Huggins.
　　　1631.

111. Oxoniæ, apud Johannem Lichfield Academiæ typographum pro Gulielmo Webb.
　　　1631.

112. Oxoniæ, excudebat G. T. Academiæ celeberrimæ typographus, impensis Guilielmi Webb.
　　　1631.

　　112 *a.* Oxonij excud. G. T. Academiæ Typographus impensis Guil. Webb. Biblio-
　　　[*engraved*: -*poliæ* is omitted.]
　　　1636.

113. Oxoniæ, excudebat Johannes Lichfield, almæ Academiæ typographus, impensis Thomæ Huggins.
　　　1631.

　　113 *a.* Omitting *almæ.*
　　　1633.

114. Oxoniæ, pro Guiliel(mo) Turner et Th(oma) Huggins [by W. Turner].
　　　1631.

(*Michael Spark*, of London, 1631.)

115. Oxford, printed by William Turner, for Michael Sparke, dwelling in Greene Arbor [London].
　　　1631.

116. Oxford, printed by William Turner for Michael Sparke.
　　　1631.

117. Oxoniæ, excudebat W. T., impensis Ed. Forrest & Hen. Curteyne.
　　　1631.

118. Oxoniæ, excudebat Jo. Lichfield, impensis Guil. Davis, & Ed. Forrest.
　　　1631.

119. Oxford, printed by William Turner.
　　　1631-34, 1637-40.

120. Oxford, printed for William Turner, and Henry Curteyn, and are to be sold in Greene Arbor at the sign of the Blew Bible by Mich. Sparkes [by W. Turner].
　　　1631.

121. Oxoniæ, excudebat Guilielmus Turner, impensis Henrici Curteyne.
　　　1631, 1637 (with Oxonii), 1638.

　　121 *a.* With " Cum Privilegio ".
　　　1634 (Oxonii).

122. Oxford, printed by W. T. and are to be sold by M. S[parke] at the Blew Bible in Greene Arbor [London].
　　　1631 (engraved).

　　See 143 *a.*

1632.

123. Oxoniæ, excudebat Johannes Lichfield, impensis Henrici Cripps.　Cum Privilegio.
　　　1632.

124. At Oxford, printed by John Lichfield, and are to be sold by Thomas Huggins.
  1632.

1633.

125. Oxford, printed by William Turner, for the author [C. Butler].
  1633-34.

126. Oxford, printed by John Lichfield for Edward Forrest.
  1633-35.

127. Oxford, printed by John Lichfield printer to the University, and are to be sold by Thomas Huggins.
  1633.

128. Oxford, printed by J. L. for E. F. (on second title).
  1633.

129. Oxoniæ, apud Johannem Lichfield, Academiæ typographum, impensis Henrici Curteyne. Cum privilegio.
  1633.

  129 a. Omitting "cum privilegio".
    1633.

  129 b. With Excudebat Johannes . . . typographus, and omitting "Cum privilegio".
    1633.

130. Oxoniæ, excudebat Johannes Lichfield Academiæ typographus, et veneunt apud Thomam Huggins.
  1633.

131. Oxoniæ, excudebant I. L. W. T. (G. T.).
  1633.

132. Oxoniæ, excudebant I. L. G. T. celeberrimæ Academiæ Typographi.
  1633 (as colophon).

(*John Clarke*, of London, 1633-38.)

133. Oxford, printed by the Printers to the University, and are to be sold by John Clarke under S. Peter's Church in Corne-hill.
  1633.

134. Oxford, printed by John Lichfield for William Webb.
  1633.

135. Oxford, printed by John Lichfield for Thomas Huggins. Cum privilegio.
  1633.

136. Printed by William Turner.
  1633.

137. Oxonii, apud Guilielmum Turner. [The reference to this impr. in 1631 is an error for 107.]
    1633, 1638.

138. Oxford, printed by I. L. printer to the University, for Thomas Huggins. With permission of B. Fisher.
  1633.

139. Oxonii, sumptibus Guilielmi Turner.
    1633.

140. Oxford, printed for William Turner and Robert Allott.
    1633.

141. Oxford, printed by John Lichfield for Henry Cripps.
    1633.

142. Oxford, printed for William Turner [by W. Turner].
    1633-34.

1634.

143. Oxoniæ, excudebat I. L., impensis Henrici Cripps.   Cum privilegio.
    1634.

   143 *a.* Omitting "Cum privilegio".
    1631 (Appendix C).

144. Oxoniæ, excudebat I. L., impensis Thomæ Huggins.   Cum privilegio.
    1634.

145. Oxonii, excudebat I. L., impensis H. Crypps, E. Forrest, & H. Curteyne.   Cum Privilegio.
    1634.

146. At Oxford, printed by John Lichfield, and are to be sold by William Webbe.
    1634.

147. Oxford, printed by William Turner, and are to be sold by Ed. Forrest.
    1634.

(*John Norton*, of London, 1634.   *Francis Bowman*, 1634-40.)

148. London, printed by John Norton, and are to be sold by Francis Bowman in Oxford.
    1634.

1635.

149. Oxford, printed by John Lichfield for Henry Cripps, and are to be sold by Henry Curteyne.
    1635.

150. Oxford, printed by John Lichfield, and are to be sold by Elias Peerse, at his Shoppe in St. Maries Church-yard.
    1635.

(*Leonard Lichfield*, 1635-40.)

151. Oxoniæ, excudebat Leonardus Lichfield, Academiæ typographus.
    1635-37, 1639-40: in 1639 with "Oxonii."
      1640.

   151 *a.* Adding *celeberrimæ* before *Academiæ*.
    1636.

   151 *b.* Oxoniæ, typis Leonardi Lichfield, Academiæ typographi.
    1636, 1638.

152. Oxford, printed by Leonard Lichfield.
1635–39.

152 *a.* Prefixing *At.*
1635.

152 *b.* With "imprinted" for "printed".
1636–37.

153 Oxonii, excudebat Gulielmus Turner, impensis Gulielmi Webb.
1635–36, 1639 : in 1636 "Oxoniae."

153 *a.* With "G." for "Gulielmus," and "Guilielmi Webb."
1636.

154. Oxford, printed by Leonard Lichfield for William Webb.
1635–36.

1636.

155. Oxford, printed by Leonard Lichfield for Thomas Huggins.
1636.

156. Oxford, imprinted by Leonard Lichfield, printer to the University, and are to be
sold by Edward Forrest.
1636.

156 *a.* With "Printed," and "famous University."
1637.

156 *b.* As 156 *a* with "for" instead of "and are to be sold by."
1639.

157. Oxoniæ, excudebat Leonardus Lichfield.
1636, 1639, 1640.

158. Oxford, printed by William Turner, and are to be sold at the Black Bear in Paul's
Churchyard.
1636.

(*Thomas Allam,* 1636–39.)

159. Oxoniæ, excudebat Leonardus Lichfield, impensis Thomæ Allam.
1636–37.

160. At Oxford, printed by Leonard Lichfield, for Edward Forrest.
1636.

160 *a.* Omitting "At".
1637.

160 *b.* As 160 *a* with "and are to be sold by."
1640.

(*R. Bishop,* of London, 1636.)

161. London, printed by R. Bishop, and are to be sold by Fr. Bowman, in Oxford.
1636.

1637.

(*John Willimot,* or *Wilmot,* 1637–38.)

162. Oxoniæ, excudebat Guilielmus Turner, & veneunt apud Hen. Cripps, Ed. Forrest,
Hen. Curteyne, & John Willimot.
1637 (secondary title omits name of place).

162 *a*. " pro" for " & veneunt apud."
　　1638.

163. Oxoniæ, excudebat L. Lichfield, impensis Gulielmi Webb bibliopolæ.
　　1637.

164. Oxoniæ, excudebat L. Lichfield, impensis Ed. Forrest & H. Curteyne.
　　1637.

165. Oxoniæ, excudebat L. Lichfield, impensis H. Curteyne.
　　1637.

166. Oxoniæ, excudebat Leonardus Lichfield, impensis Gulielmi Webb.
　　1637.

(*J. Adams*, 1637.　*Joseph Godwin*, 1637–39.)

167. Oxoniæ, excudebat Guilielmus Turner pro J. Adams, & veneunt apud Joseph Godwin.
　　1637.

168. Oxoniæ, excudebat L. L., impensis Hen. Cripps, Ed. Forrest, Hen. Curteyne, & Ioh. Wilmot.
　　1637.

169. Oxford, printed by William Turner for William Webb.
　　1637.

170. Oxford, printed by L. Lichfield, for H. C. printer to the University. (Neither Cripps nor Curteyne were printers to the University, so probably there is some error.)
　　1637.

(*W. Harris*, of London, 1637.)

171. Oxford, printed by William Turner, printer to the famous University. 1637. And are to be sold at London by W. Harris in Colman Street.
　　1637.

1638.

(*John Allam*, 1638.)

172. Oxford, printed by William Turner for John Allam.
　　1638.

173. Oxford, imprinted for John Allam [by W. Turner].
　　1638.

174. Oxford, printed by Leonard Lichfield, printer to the University, for Francis Bowman.
　　1638, 1640.

175. Oxford, printed by Leonard Lichfield, printer to the University, for William Davis.
　　1638.

176. Oxoniæ, excudebat Leonardus Lichfield, impensis Ed. Forrest.
　　1638, 1639 (with Oxonii).

177. Oxford, printed by William Turner, printer to the famous University, for W. T[urner], Edw. Forrest and Will. Web.
　　1638.

(*John Westall*, 1638-40.)

178. Oxoniæ, excudebat Guil. Turner, pro Joh. Westall, Tho. Allam & Jos. Godwin.
1638.

179. Excusa cum Licentiâ, typis Guil: Turner typographi Universitatis, pro Guil:
Webb.
1638.

180. Oxford, printed by Leonard Lichfield, printer to the University.
1638-40.

180 *a.* Adding *famous* before *University.*
1638.

181. Oxford, printed by Leonard Lichfield, and are to be sold by John Clarke under
St. Peter's Church in Cornhill.
1638.

182. Oxford, printed by Leonard Lichfield for Henry Crypps.
1638, 1639.

183. Oxoniæ, typis Guil: Turner, impensis authoris (V. Bythner).
1638.

184. Oxford, printed by Leonard Lichfield, for Francis Bowman.
1638-39.

185. Oxford, printed by L. Lichfield for Joseph Godwin.
1638-39.

1639.

186. Oxoniæ, excudebat Leonardus Lichfield, impensis authoris (G. Dugres).
1639.

(*John Allen*, of Leicester, 1639.)

187. Oxford, printed by Leonard Lichfield, and are to be sold by John Allen in
" Leicester ".
1639.

(*Thomas Thomas*, of Bristol, 1639.)

188. Oxford, printed by Leonard Lichfield, and are to be sold by Tho. Thomas in
Bristol.
1639.

(*Thomas Robinson*, 1639-40.)

189. Oxford, printed by William Turner for Thomas Robinson.
1639-40.

190. Oxoniæ, excudebat Guilielmus Turner, impensis Hen. Crips.
1639.

191. Oxoniæ, excudebat Leonardus Lichfield, impensis Eliæ Pearse & Tho. Allam.
1639.

191 *a.* Simply reversing the order of the two publishers.
1639.

192. Oxford, printed for F. Bowman, stationer [by L. Lichfield].
    1639.

(*Matthew Hunt*, 1639–40.)

193. Oxford, printed by Leonard Lichfield, and are to be sold by Matthew Hunt.
    1639.

    193 *a*. " For " instead of "and are to be sold by."
    1640.

    193 *b*. As 193 *a*, beginning " Printed at Oxford by."
    1640.

1640.

(*Robert Young*, 1640.)

194. Oxford, printed by Leon: Lichfield, printer to the University, for Rob: Young
    & Ed. Forrest.
    1640.

195. Excudebat Oxonii Leonardus Lichfield primarius Academiæ typographus, im-
    pensis Roberti Young & Edvardi Forrest.
    1640.

196. Printed [at] Oxford for Francis Bowman [by L. Lichfield].
    1640 (engraved title).

197. Oxoniæ, excudebat Leonard. Lichfield, impensis Matthiæ Hunt.
    1640.

198. Oxoniæ, excudebat Guiliel. Turner, impensis Joh. Westall.
    1640.

199. Oxford, printed for Leonard Lichfield.
    1640.

200. Oxoniæ, excudebat Guilielmus Turner, impensis Edvardi Forrest.
    1640.

201. Oxoniæ, excudebat Leonardus Lichfield impensis Guliel. Davis.
    1640.

202. Oxford, printed by L. L.
    1640.

(*Richard Royston*, of London, 1640.)

203. Oxford, printed by Leonard Lichfield, for Richard Royston, in Ivy Lane.
    1640.

(*Samuel Enderby*, of London, 1640.)

204. Oxford, printed by Leon. Lichfield, for Samuel Enderby.
    1640.

205. Oxoniæ, excudebat Guilielmus Turner, impensis Tho. Robinson.
    1640.

OXFORD PRINTERS AND PUBLISHERS.

PRINTER —, in combination ⊤;   PUBLISHER ○, in combination ⊙;   L = London.

[The printers' names are in small capitals: the names following each printer, in roman type and with a — preceding, are of publishers for whom the printer worked.]

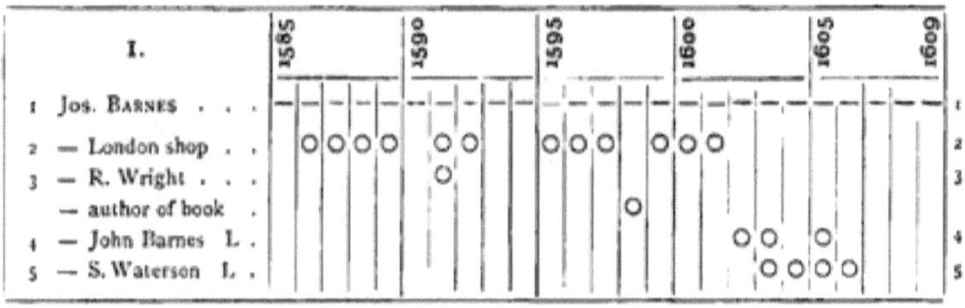

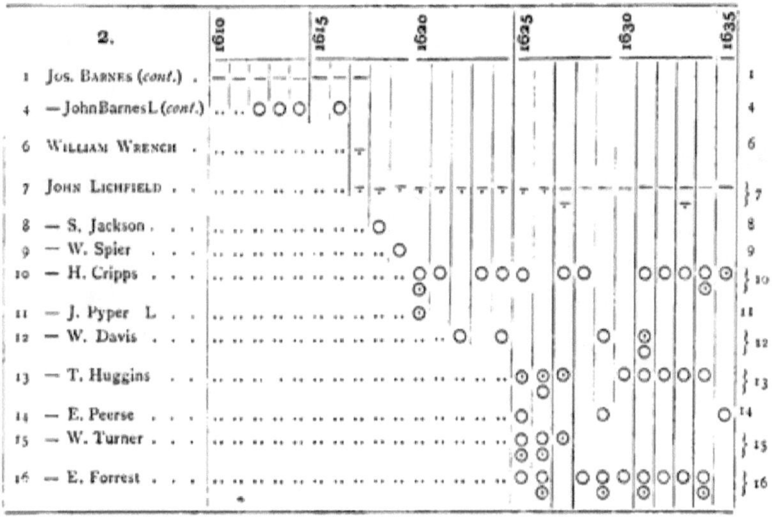

I.

		1585	1590	1595	1600	1605	1609
1	Jos. BARNES . . .						
2	— London shop . .						
3	— R. Wright . . .						
	— author of book .						
4	— John Barnes L .						
5	— S. Waterson L .						

2.

		1610	1615	1620	1625	1630	1635
1	Jos. BARNES (*cont.*) .						
4	—John Barnes L (*cont.*)						
6	WILLIAM WRENCH .						
7	JOHN LICHFIELD . .						
8	— S. Jackson . . .						
9	— W. Spier . . .						
10	— H. Cripps . . .						
11	— J. Pyper L . .						
12	— W. Davis . . .						
13	— T. Huggins . .						
14	— E. Peerse . . .						
15	— W. Turner . . .						
16	— E. Forrest . . .						

OXFORD PRINTERS AND PUBLISHERS (*continued*).

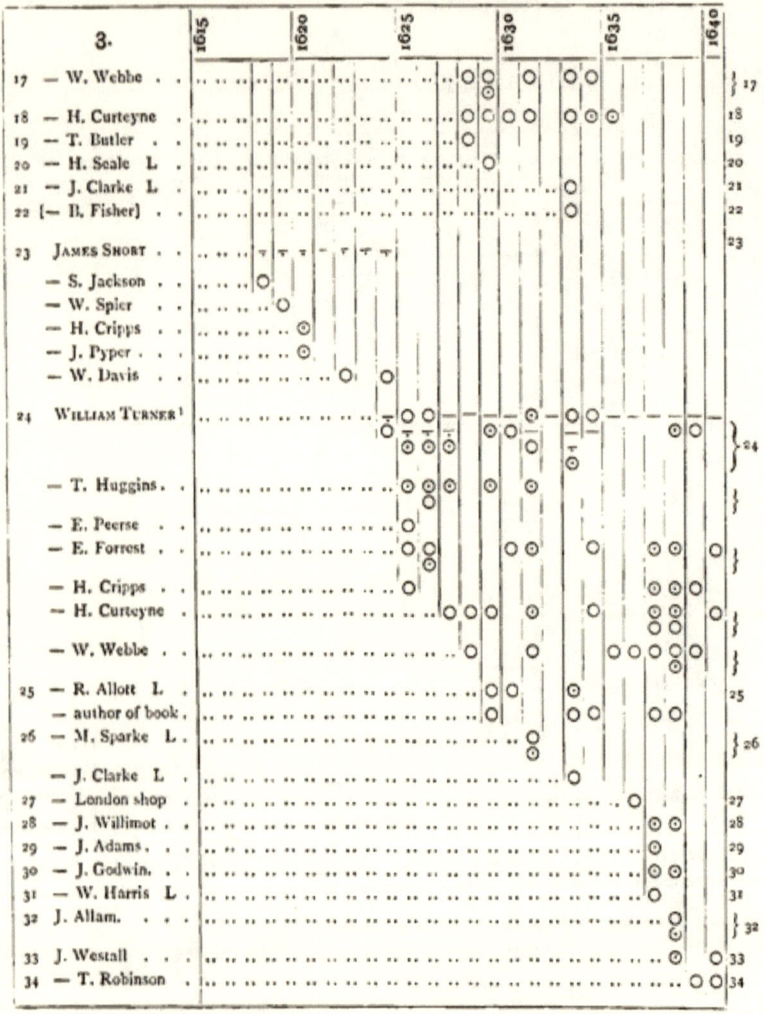

	3.	1615	1620	1625	1630	1635	1640	
17	— W. Webbe							17
18	— H. Curteyne							18
19	— T. Butler							19
20	— H. Seale L							20
21	— J. Clarke L							21
22	[— B. Fisher]							22
23	JAMES SHORT							23
	— S. Jackson							
	— W. Spier							
	— H. Cripps							
	— J. Pyper							
	— W. Davis							
24	WILLIAM TURNER [1]							24
	— T. Huggins							
	— E. Peerse							
	— E. Forrest							
	— H. Cripps							
	— H. Curteyne							
	— W. Webbe							
25	— R. Allott L							25
	— author of book							
26	— M. Sparke L							26
	— J. Clarke L							
27	— London shop							27
28	— J. Willimot							28
29	— J. Adams							29
30	— J. Godwin							30
31	— W. Harris L							31
32	J. Allam							32
33	J. Westall							33
34	— T. Robinson							34

[1] W. Jaggard printed in London for Turner in Oxford in 1624.

OXFORD PRINTERS AND PUBLISHERS (*continued*).

4.

		1635				1640	
35	LEONARD LICHFIELD					○	35
	— W. Webbe	○	○	○			
	— T. Huggins		○				
	— E. Forrest		○	◉	○	○	◉
36	— T. Allam		○	○		◉	36
	— H. Curteyne			○			
	— H. Cripps			◉	○	○	
	— J. Willimot (or Wilmot)			◉			
37	— F. Bowman				○	○	○	37
	— W. Davis				○		○
	— J. Clarke				○		
	— J. Godwin				○	○	
	— author of book					○	
38	— J. Allen of Leicester					○	38
39	— T. Thomas of Bristol					○	39
	— E. Peerse					◉	
40	— M. Hunt					○	○	40
41	— R. Young						◉	41
42	— R. Royston L						○	42
43	— S. Enderby L						○	43

5.

PUBLISHERS, WITH NO OXFORD PRINTER'S NAME.

		1625		1630		1635		1640
	H. Cripps [London[1] or with Lichfield]	◉ ○	○ ○		○		○	
	H. Curteyne [London or with Turner]	◉	◉					
	'W. Mapes'	○						
	T. Huggins [with Turner]	◉		◉				
44	P. Stephens	◉						
45	C. Meredith	◉						
	W. Webbe [with Lichfield]	○		○		○	○	
	author of book [do.]		○ ○					
	F. Bowman[2] [London or with Lichfield]				○	○		○ ○
	J. Allam [with Turner]						○	

[1] *i. e.* the *printer* was either a London man (as in 1625) or, if at Oxford, Lichfield (as in 1627-8, 1632, 1638).

[2] John Norton printed in London for Bowman in Oxford, 1634.
R. Bishop   „   „   „   „   1636.

INDEX

Brett, Richard. Symeon's Lives of Stt. John and Luke, ed. by R. Brett in Greek and Latin. 1597 S.
— Theses magistri Bret, respondentis in Comitiis Oxon. 1597, p. 230.
— Iconum sacrarum decas, authore R. B. 1603 B.
Bridegroom and his Bride, 1625. *See* Rawlinson, John.
Bridges, John, bp. of Oxford. Articles at his visitation, 1604. 1604 B.
Bridgwater, John. Concertatio eccl. Catholicae per Joannem Aquepontanum (1594), mentioned. 1594 L.
Brierwood, Edward. *See* Brerewood, Edward.
Bright Sale, mentioned, pp. 253, 256.
Bristol. Latin oration at Bristol by J. Sprint 16 Apr. 1587. 1587 S.
— mentioned. 1639 F.
Bristol, earl of. *See* Digby, George and John.
Britain, Great. Dedication to the schoolmasters of Great Britain, in Latin. 1634 S.
British Museum. *See* London—British Museum.
Broad, Thomas. Dialogue between a Jew and a Christian (on Sunday). 1621 B.
— Three questions answered (on Sunday observance). 1621 B.
Bromley, sir Thomas, lord chancellor of England. Dedication to him, 1585. 1586 C.
Broncar, Henricus, mentioned. 1640 C.
Brooke, sir Richard, of Norton. Dedication to him. 1628 B, 1631 B, 1637 B.
Brother, John, illuminator, mentioned, p. 270.
Browere, Nicholas, mentioned, p. 254.
Brown, John, stationer, mentioned, pp. 270, 271.
Browne, Thomas. The copy of the University sermon, 24 Dec. 1633 (on Ps. cxxx. 4). 1634 B.
Bruges, Giles, lord Chandos, mentioned. 1592 E.
Brunus, Leonardus, of Arezzo. Latin translation of Aristotle's Nicomachean Ethics, by Leonardus Arretinus. 1479 A, p. 253.
— a supposed edition of 1498, p. 10.
Brussels. The Library mentioned, p. 256.
Buckhurst, lord. *See* Dorset, earl of.
Buckingham, duke of, *d.* 1629. *See* Villiers, George.
Buckingham, Katharine, duchess of. Dedication to her. 1630 W, 1631 W.
Buckler, Benjamin, mentioned, p. 252.
Budden, dr. John. Gulielmi ... Waynfleti ... vita obitusque. 1602 B.

Büssenmecherus, Johannes. Extract from a book by him, in Latin. 1640 C.
Bullokar, W., mentioned. 1633 B.
Bunny, Edmund. Treatise tending to pacification [accompanying a revised edition of R. Parsons' Christian exercise]. 1585 P (*bis*).
— Account by him of his connexion with Parsons's Resolution or Directory. 1610 B.
— Of divorce for adultery and marrying again. 1610 B, 1613 B.
Bunny, Francis. Answer to a popish libel intituled "a Petition to the Bishops." 1607 B.
Burgersdicius, Franco. Idea Philosophiae tum Naturalis, tum Moralis, ed. 3ᵃ. 1631 B.
— Idea Philosophiae tum Moralis, tum Naturalis, ed. 4ᵃ. 1637 B.
Burges, Cornelius. Baptismal regeneration of elect infants. 1629 B.
Burgundus, Nicolaüs. Latin poem on Puteanus's Comus. 1634 P.
Burhill, Robert. Edited a sermon by bp. Smith, 1602. 1602 S.
— Invitatorius panegyricus. 1603 O.
— In controversiam inter Johannem Howsonum et Thomam Pyum tractatus. 1606 B.
— De potestate regia et usurpatione papali. 1613 B.
Buridanus, Johannes. Error for Walter Burley, mentioned, p. 10.
— Quaestiones in octo libros Politicorum Aristotelis. 1640 B.
Burley, Walter. Latin commentary on the Posterior Analytics of Aristotle. 1517 B, p. 263.
— — "1512," p. 11.
— De materia et forma (principia). 1518 B, p. 264.
— — "1500," p. 10.
— De relativis (principia). 1518 B, p. 264.
Burmannus, Petrus, Secundus. Letter of his, mentioned, p. 9.
Burnet, alias Cornish, Gilbert, parchment-seller, mentioned, p. 274.
Burton, Robert, mentioned. 1599 R, 1627 H, 1637 V, 1638 O.
— Anatomy of Melancholy. 1621 B, 1624 B, 1628 B, 1632 B, 1638 B. *See* p. 232.
— Note on the connexion between Ferrand's Ἐρωτομανία and Burton's *Anatomy of Melancholy.* 1640 F.
Burton, Samuel, archdeacon of Gloucester. Articles to be enquired of in his Visitation, 1629. 1629 B.
Burton, William. Laudatio funebris in obitum Thomae Alleni. 1633 B.

and Cornwall, with an answer.
1605 H.

Hyrys, John, parchment-seller, mentioned, p. 269.

I.

I., T., 1599, 1625. *See* James, Thomas.

I., W. Translated the *Jesuit's Pater Noster* from the French. 1611 J.

Idylls. *See* Henry, prince, 1612.

Ieronimus. *See* Jerome, st.

Ilium in Italiam. *See* Sansbury, John.

Illuminators, &c., in Oxford, pp. 267–78.

Imitation of Christ. *See* Kempis, Thomas à

Imprimaturs. *See* 1638 C.

In controversiam ... *See* Burhill, Robert, 1606.

Index Expurgatorius. Index generalis librorum prohibitorum a Pontificiis, per T. James. 1627 J.

Indulgence. Indulgence of " Oxf. 1489," mentioned, p. 9.

Ingleby, C. M., mentioned. p. 230.

Inglis sale. 1826, mentioned. 1589 S, p. 264.

Ingmethorp, Thomas. Sermon. 1598 I.

Innocent iii, pope. Indulgence of 1489 or 1499 by him, mentioned, p. 10.

Instructions for young gentlemen. *See* Sermonetta, card.

Insubrica historia. *See* Puteanus, Erycius.

Iredale, A., bookseller of Torquay, mentioned. p. 262.

Ireland. Proverb about Tuesday being unfortunate to Irish. 1612 D.

Ironside, dr. Gilbert. Seven questions of the Sabbath briefly disputed. 1637 I.

Isocrates. Πρὸς Δημόνικον, πρὸς Νικοκλέα, Νικόκλης. *See under* 1586 C.

— In Isocratis Busiridem praefatio, per Joh. Prideaux. 1607 P, 1629 P, 1639 P.

Italian. *See* Bense, Petrus; Petrucci, Lodovico.

— Grammar or introduction to the Italian tongue, by J. Sanford. 1605 S.

— Italian poems. 1606 O, 1613 O.

Italicus, Peregrinus, de Lugo. Principia seu introductiones, Lond. 1506, mentioned, p. 10.

Ive, Simon, musical composer, mentioned. 1636 B.

J.

J., S., 1614. *See under* S., N.

Jackson, Henry, of C.C.C., Oxford. Edited Hooker's sermon on Justification. 1612 H.

— Edited Wyclif's Wicket. 1612 W.

— Probably edited several of Hooker's smaller treatises. 1612 H.

Jackson, Henry, of C.C.C., Oxford. Translated Benefield on Amos into Latin (1614–15). 1613 B.

— Edited two sermons of dr. Hooker. 1614 H.

— Mentioned as editor of Rainold's Orationes. 1614 R.

Jackson, Simon, bookseller, mentioned, pp. 278, 297, 311, 312.

Jackson, Thomas, pres. of Corpus Christi college, Oxford. Two sermons. 1617 J.

— Diverse sermons. 1637 J.

— Treatise of the consecration of the Son of God. 1638 J.

— His judgement on Valdés' *Considerations.* 1638 V.

Jacobi, Henricus, bookseller of London, mentioned, pp. 228, 273.

Jacobus de Voragine, mentioned, p. 258.

Jaggard, William, bookseller of London, mentioned, pp. 298, 312.

James, illuminator, mentioned, p. 269.

James i, king. Dedications, &c., to him, 1603 B, D, O (*bis*), W, 1604 O, 1605 D, K, T, 1608 S, 1613 P. 1619 O, 1621 D, 1634 B, C, R, 1635 M.

— Ad Jacobum carmen, per G. Carleton. 1603 C.

— Academiae Oxoniensis pietas erga Jacobum regem. 1603 O.

— Oration to him in the Tower of London, 12 March 160?, by W. Hubbocke, in Latin and English, with dedication to the king. 1604 H.

— Musa hospitalis Ecclesiae Christi Oxon. (poems to greet the king, &c.). 1605 O.

— Rex Platonicus, sive de adventu Regis ad academiam Oxoniensem, 27 Aug. 1605; narratio ab Is. Wake. 1607 W (*bis*), 1615 W, 1627 W, 1635 W. 1663 W.

— mentioned. 1613 B.

— His Apologie for the Oath of Allegiance, mentioned. 1613 D.

— Jacobi ara congratulatory poems by the University of Oxford, on his return from Scotland). 1617 O.

— Sermon by J. Rawlinson on the king's "inauguration." 24 March. 1615; dedicated also to the king. 1619 R.

— Mandate about preaching (1622) mentioned. 1622 H.

— Latin speech to him by dr. J. Prideaux. 24 Aug. 1624. 1624 P.

— Cenotaphium Jacobi (a funeral oration by dr. John King, with a list of the king's works, &c.). 1625 K.

— Oxoniensis academiae Parentalia memoriae Jacobi dicata. 1625 O.

OXFORD *(continued)*:
St. John's Coll.
 MSS. mentioned. 1610 J.
 Complimentary Latin verses by St.
    John's men. 1640 S.
 Mentioned, pp. 255, 260, 263.
St. Mary the Virgin, parish.
 Oratio funebris habita ab I. Wake in
    templo B. Mariae, 25 Maii 1607.
    1607 W, 1615 W, 1627 W,
    635 W.
 Dedication to the parish. 1612 D.
 Mention of mr. Day's first sermon as
    vicar, 1609. 1612 D.
Trinity College.
 Decretum de gratiis collegio rependen-
    dis. 1602 O.
 Mentioned, p. 255.
University.
 Agreement that parchment-sellers,
    illuminators and scribes were in the
    jurisdiction of the University, A.D.
    1290, p. 268.
 — a similar acknowledgment about
    stationers, A.D. 1345, *ibid.*
 Valuable books only to be sold by the
    authorized stationers, A.D. 1374,
    pp. 269, 281.
 Statute about stationers receiving
    clothes from graduates, 1411, p. 270.
 Compotus manualis ad usum Oxonien-
    sium. 1519 C.
 Said to have instituted the keeping of
    Nov. 17 as the Queen's Day, in
    1569 (?). 1601 H; cf. 1602 H.
 State alluded to. 1587 P.
 Petition to Convocation (1590) about
    Case's Sphaera civitatis, mentioned.
    1588 C.
 Sanford's Εὐκτικὰ εἰδύλλια on occasion
    of Queen Elizabeth's visit to Ox-
    ford, &c., 1592. 1592 S.
 Dedications to it. 1592 B ("the
    gentlemen of Oxford"), 1604 S,
    1608 C, R, 1610 B (preface), 1619 M,
    1627 H, P, 1628 W, 1631 P, 1637
    B, W (the Vice-chancellor and Heads
    of Houses), 1640 B (the two Univer-
    sities).
 Quaestiones &c. in Schola Theologica,
    1597, p. 230.
 Theses R. Brett in Comitiis, 1597,
    p. 230.
 Account of conferment of D.D. degree.
    1599 H.
 De manuscriptis Oxoniensibus [list of
    authors, an appendix to T. James's
    edition of Richard de Bury's Philo-
    biblon]. 1599 R.
 Chancellor's Orders for the Market
    (undated). 1602 O.
 Answer of the University to the Petition

OXFORD *(continued)*:
 of Ministers desiring reformation of
    the Church. 1603 O (4 issues, one
    undated), 1604 O.
 Funebre officium in memoriam Elisa-
    bethae reginae. 1603 O.
 Academiae Oxoniensis pietas erga
    Jacobum regem (poems). 1603 O.
 Rex Platonicus, sive de adventu Jacobi
    Regis ad academiam Oxoniensem,
    27 Aug. 1605, narratio ab Is. Wake.
    1607 W (*bis*), 1615 W, 1627 W,
    1635 W, 1663 W.
 Orders of the Chancellor for the Market.
    1606 O.
 Theses for D.C.L. degree. 1608. 1608 C.
 Ilium in Italiam (engravings of Univer-
    sity and college arms, with poems).
    1608 S.
 Reference to the Act of 1608. 1609 H.
 Theological praelections by S. Benefield,
    in Latin. 1610 B.
 Allusion to the subject of Evangelical
    Counsels at Oxford (1609?). 1610 P.
 Account of a stay in Oxford 1610–13,
    by L. Petrucci: in Ital. and Latin
    verse. 1613 P.
 Testimonials given to C. Angelus, 1610
    and 1618. 1618 A.
 Sir George St. Paul's benefaction to
    the New Schools (about 1612 ?).
    1613 C.
 Case of a commoner of Corpus Christi
    college not matriculated. 1613 C.
 Epithalamia sive lusus Palatini in
    nuptias Frederici et Elizabethae.
    (Verses by Oxford men.) 1613 O.
 Thesis at the Act. 1613, quoted.
    1613 P.
 Justa funebria Ptolemaei Oxoniensis
    Latin verses on sir Thomas Bodley,
    by members of the University).
    1613 O.
 Carmina funebria in obitum Georgii de
    Sancto Paulo (perhaps by members
    of the University). 1614 S.
 Allusion to lord Paget's benefactions
    to the Margaret Professor of Divinity.
    1615 B.
 Jacobi ara (congratulatory poems to
    James i). 1617 O.
 Funebria sacra memoriae Annae reginae
    dicata (Latin poems). 1619 O.
 Clerk of the University mentioned
    Edward Miles, about 1620–30),
    p. 277.
 Thomae Baylaei diatribae duae in
    Schola Theologica Oxon., 1621.
    1626 B.
 Form of Latin oath to be taken by all
    graduates (in favour of Passive
    Obedience). 1622 O.

P.

Papillon, Philip. Edited Harding's Sicily and Naples, as 'P. P.' 1640 H.

Papistogelastes, 1614. *See* S., N.

Paragon of Persia. *See* Hayes, William.

Parallelus Torti. *See* Eudaemon-Johannes, Andreas.

Pararuades (= Errata) 1621 T.

Parchment-sellers, &c., in Oxford, pp. 267-78.

Parentalia, 1625. *See* Oxford—Univ.

Parentatio historica. *See* Whear, Degory.

Pareus, David, mentioned. 1622 O, 1631 P.

— Commentarius in SS. Matthaeum, Petrum, et in Joelem, Amos, Haggaeum. 1631 P.

Paris. The National Library mentioned, pp. 252, 259.

Parkes, Richard. His *Apologie* referred to. 1604 A.

— A brief answer unto certain objections against the descension of Christ into hell. (anon.) 1604 A, 1613 A.

— mentioned, p. 230.

Parkhurst, bp. John, mentioned 1586 S.

Parne, Richard, parchment-seller, mentioned, p. 277.

Parre, bp. Richard. Burial sermon on lord Spencer, 1627, on Ps. xxxvii. 37. 1628 P.

— Sermon on Rev. iii. 4. 1628 P.

Parry, David. Reprint of two of his prefaces in the 1587 ed. of Ursinus's Catechism. 1600 U.

— Two discourses of Ursinus, translated by Parry. 1600 U.

Parry, Henry, bp. of Gloucester. Ursinus's Summe of Christian religion, tr. by H. Parrie. 1587 U, 1589 U, 1591 U, 1595 U, 1601 U.

— Concio de victoria Christiana, in Apoc. iii. 21. 1593 P, 1594 P.

— Summa colloquii J. Rainoldi cum J. Harto (1583), H. Parraeo interprete 1610 R.

Parsons, Bartholomew. Dorcas, a sermon (on Acts ix. 36). 1631 P.

— Sermon on Boaz and Ruth (Ruth iv. 11). 1633 P.

— Funeral sermon on sir F. Pile, on Is. lvii. 2. 1636 P.

— Honos et onus Levitarum, on Tithes vindicated. By B. P. 1637 P.

— Sermon on Eph. vi. 12-13. 1637 P.

Parsons, Robert, the Jesuit. Book of Christian exercise appertaining to Resolution. By R. P. [i.e. R. Parsons]. 1585 P (*bis*).

— Christian Directory, mentioned. 1585 P.

— mentioned, 1608 J.

— 'R. P.'s *Resolution* or *Directory* mentioned. 1610 B.

Parsons, Robert, the Jesuit. Life of Parsons, by dr. James. 1612 J.

— mentioned, p. 228.

Pasor, Matthias. Oratio pro linguae Arabicae professione, 1626. 1627 P.

Pass, Simon, engraver. Titlepage by him. 1636 F.

Passive Obedience. *See* Dunster, John, 1610.

— Decretum Universitatis Oxoniensis in favour of Passive Obedience, 1622 O.

Pater Noster. *See* Lord's Prayer.

Path to piety. *See* Hinde, William.

Patten, William. *See* Waynflete, William.

Pavonius, Franciscus. Summa Ethicae. 1633 P.

Payne and Foss, messrs., booksellers, mentioned, p. 256.

Peerse, Elias, bookseller, mentioned, pp. 278, 299, 311, 312, 313.

Peirce, Frances, bookseller, mentioned, p. 275.

Peirce, Nicholas, mentioned, p. 259.

Pembelus, Guilielmus. *See* Pemble, William.

Pemble, William. Vindiciae fidei or a treatise of justification by faith. 1625 P, 1629 P.

— Five sermons. 1628 P.

— — 2nd ed. 1629 P.

— De sensibus internis tractatus. Guil. Pembeli. 1629 P.

— Brief introduction to Geography. 1630 P.

— Sum of moral philosophy. 1630 P, 1632 P.

— Enchiridion Oratorium (?). 1633 P.

Pembroke, earl of. *See* Herbert, George R. C., Henry, Philip, William.

Pembroke, Mary countess of. The Countess of Pembroke's Love (with a dedication to her), by Nicholas Breton. 1592 B.

Penry, John. Exhortation unto Wales, 1588, mentioned. 1587 P.

— Supplication on behalfe of Wales. 1587 P.

— View of publike wants within Wales, 1588, mentioned. 1587 P.

Peregrinus. *See* Vincentius Lirinensis.

Peregrinus, de Lugo. *See* Italicus, Peregrinus, de Lugo.

Periam sir William (?), mentioned, 1614 P.

Perkins, rev. William. An answer to mr. William Perkins, by John Higins. 1602 H (*bis*).

— mentioned. 1628 R.

Perrot, sir James. Discovery of discontented minds. 1596 P.

— The first part of the consideration of humane condition. By I. P[errot]. 1600 P.

Persius, Satires tr. into English by B.
Holyday. 2nd impression. 1616 P.
Person, sir ?), mentioned, p. 273.
Peter, illuminator, mentioned, p. 267
(*bis*).
Peter, parchment-seller, mentioned. p.
267.
Petition. Petition to the Bishops,
Preachers, and Gospellers (1606?),
mentioned. 1607 B.
Petra, Gabriel de. Edited Longinus De
grandiloquentia, 1612. 1636 L.
Petre, John, lord Petre of Writtle. Threni
Exoniensium in obitum Johannis
filii Guilielmi Petrei. 1613 O.
Petre, William, lord Petre of Writtle, *d.*
1637. Dedication to him. 1613 O.
Petrucci, Lodovico. Raccolta d' alcune
rime. Farrago poematum (&c.).
1613 P.
Phaedra. *See* Shepery, John.
Phalaris. The letters of Phalaris trans-
lated into Latin by Franciscus
Arctinus. 1485 P, p. 260.
Pharamus. *See* Snelling, Thomas.
Phelps family, mentioned, p. 229.
Phetiplacius, Richardus, &c. *See* Feti-
place, Richard, &c.
Philalethes, interlocutor. 1619 B.
— Poem signed 'Philalethes.' 1631 V.
Philanactophil, pseudonym. *See* Bolton,
Edmund (Maria).
Philip, prince of Orange. Dedication to
him. 1634 P.
Philip iii, king of Spain. The Jesuit's
Pater Noster given to Philip iii, king
of Spain. 1611 J.
Philobiblon *See* Richard de Bury.
Philosophia libera. *See* Carpenter, Na-
thaniel.
Philosophy. *See* Bartholinus, Caspar.
— *See* Burgersdicius, Franco.
— *See* Combachius, Johannes.
— *See* Holyday, Barten.
— *See* Pavonius, Franciscus.
— *See* Pemble, William.
— *See* Scheiblerus, Christophorus.
— De philosophia, Panathenaicae duae
in Comitiis Oxonii habitae (1585 &
1586) (possibly by Tho. Savile).
1586 P.
Phonetic spelling. *See* 1633 B, 1634 B.
Photius. His *Bibliotheca* mentioned.
1597 A.
Pickering, William de. *See* William de
Pickering.
Pictorius, Georgius, mentioned. 1609 B.
Pie, Thomas, 1586. *See* Pye, Thomas.
Piers, John, archbp. of York. Dedica-
tion to him. 1587 P.
— Funeral sermon on him by J. King,
1594. 1597 K, 1599 K, 1600 K.

Pietas erga benefactores. *See* Whear,
Degory ; Wower, Jan.
Pigot, John, scrivener. Mentioned. p.
275.
Pile, sir Francis, bart., *d.* 1635. Dedication to him. 1631 P.
— Funeral sermon on him, by B. Parsons.
1636 P.
Pile, sir Francis, *d.* 1649. Dedication to
him. 1636 P.
Pilgrim, Gerard, stationer, mentioned. p.
273.
Pilgrimage to Paradise *See* Breton,
Nicholas.
Pinart, Dominique, bookseller, mentioned,
p. 274.
Pinke, William. Translated and published (as ' W. P.') Cameron's Examination of the Romish Church.
1626 C.
— The trial of our sincere love to Christ
(2 sermons : ed. by W. Lyford).
1630 P.
— — 2nd ed. 1631 P.
— — 3rd ed. 1636 P.
— The trial of a Christian's sincere love
unto Christ, 2nd ed. (4 sermons).
1634 P.
Pinner, Charles. Sermon on 1 Tim. iv.
16. 1596 P.
— Sermon on 1 Pet. ii. 17. 1597 P.
— Sermon on 1 Tim. iv. 8. 1597 P.
Piper, John, bookseller, of London. men-
tioned, pp. 298, 311, 312.
Piscator, Johannes [Fischer ?] Aphorismi
doctrinae Christianae, 11a editio.
1630 P.
Piscator, Philippus Ludovicus. Preface
by him. 1630 P.
Pit, Moses, mentioned, p. 252.
Pitt, Thomas. *See* Pye, Thomas.
Plays. *See* Cartwright, William.
— *See* Fletcher, John.
— *See* Gager, William.
— *See* Harding, S.
— *See* Mayne, Jasper.
— *See* Randolph, Thomas.
— *See* Snelling, Thomas.
— The overthrow of stage plays, by dr.
John Rainolds. 2nd ed. 1629 R.
Pliny the younger. Plinii Epistolae
" Oxon. 1469 ", with forged imprint,
pp. 8, 9, 227.
Plouvierius, Maximus, mentioned. 1640 P.
Plummer, rev. Charles, mentioned. 1592
S.
Plutarch. Περὶ παίδων ἀγωγῆς. *See
under* 1586 C.
— De morbis animi et corporis in Latin).
1614 R.
— De utilitate ex hostibus capienda (in
Latin). 1614 R.

Plymouth. *See* Fitz-Geffry, Charles.
Pococke, dr. Edward, mentioned. 1639 G.
Polybius, mentioned. 1591 T.
Popery. *See* Rome.
Popham, sir John, of Littlecote. Sermon
　before him, by C. Pinner. 1597 P.
Porter, Endymion. Dedication to him.
　1631 W.
Portu Hiberniae, Mauritius de. *See* Mau-
　ritius de Portu Hiberniae.
Possevinus. Antonius, d. 1611, mentioned.
　1614 R.
— Anti-Possevinus, a sermon by Rich.
　James. 1625 J.
Pots, Richard, of Virginia. Extracts
　from his writings. 1612 S.
Potter, bp. Barnabas. The baronet's
　burial (sermon on sir Edw. Seymour .
　1613 P.
Potter, dr. Christopher. Want of charity
　justly charged on Romanists. 1633 P.
— mentioned. 1638 C
— Dedication to him. 1638 R.
Powel, David, mentioned. 1602 P.
Powel, Gabriel. Positions concerning
　Usury. 1602 P.
— Prodromus, a logical resolution of
　Rom. cap. 1. 1602 P.
— — (the same in Latin: dubious).
　1615 P.
— Consideration of the papists' reasons
　for toleration of popery. 1604 P.
Powel, Griffinus. *See* Powell, Griffith.
Powell, Griffith. Analysis Analyticorum
　Posteriorum Aristotelis, operâ and
　studio G. P. 1594 P.
— False date of a book by him. men-
　tioned. 1594 P.
— Analysis librorum Aristotelis de
　Sophisticis Elenchis, per G. P. 1598
　P.
— — a supposed edition of 1564 men-
　tioned, p. 13.
— Analysis librorum Aristotelis de De-
　monstratione. 1631 P.
Powell, Nathaniel, of Virginia. Extracts
　from his writings. 1612 S.
Powell, Thomas. Sermon. 1613 P.
Powhatan. Picture of him. 1612 S.
Poza, don Francisco de Roias marquesse
　de. Dedication to him. 1630 A.
P. R. *See* R., P.
Praenostica, 1518. *See* Laet, Jaspar.
Praise of Music, 1586. *See* Music.
Pratt, David, stationer. mentioned, p. 273.
Prayer, Book of Common. Reasons for
　refusal of subscription to the Book
　of Common Prayer, with an answer
　by T. Hutton. 1605 H.
— Liber precum publicarum in usum
　ecclesiae Cathedralis Christi Oxon.
　1615 P, 1639 P.

Prayers. *See* Winchester.
— Precationes aliquot privatae et publi-
　cae. 1629 C.
Preachers. Letter from the archbp. of
　Canterbury (about preachers). 1622
　A.
Preaching, 1622. *See* Howson, John.
Preces. *See* Prayers.
Prejudice, préjugé. Note on the use of
　the words. 1626 C.
Prenostica, 1518. *See* Laet. Jaspar.
Presse, Simon. Sermon at Eggington.
　1596. 1597 P.
Preston, dr. John. Three sermons on the
　Lord's Supper. 1631 P.
Price, dr. Daniel. Sermon, on Is. ii. 3.
　1608 P.
— Sermon, on Matt. xiii. 45–6. 1608 P.
— Sermon, on Rev. ii. 26. 1608 P.
— The defence of Truth against the
　Triumph of Truth by H. Leech.
　1610 P.
— Act sermon. 1613 P.
— Spiritual odours to the memory of
　prince Henry in four sermons.
　1613 P.
— Prince Henry his first anniversary.
　1613 P.
— Prince Henry his second anniversary.
　1614 P.
Price, Henry. Poem to N. Breton.
　1592 B.
— Epicedium in obitum Henrici comitis
　Derbeiensis. 1593 G.
Price, Sampson. Sermon. 1614 P.
Price, prof. William. Oratio funebris in
　laudem Tho. White. 1624 O.
Prideaux, Edmund. Dedication to him
　and his wife. 1637 P.
Prideaux, dr. John. rector of Exeter Col-
　lege, Oxford. Tabulae ad grammatica
　Graeca introductoriae : et ad eandem
　linguam παραίρεσις. 1607 P, 1608 P,
　1629 P, 1639 P.
— Castigatio Andreae Eudaemon-Johan-
　nis. 1614 P.
— Ephesus backsliding, a sermon. 1614
　P, 1636 P.
— Dedications to him. 1615 M, 1619
　B, 1625 N, 1630 B.
— Two Sermons on Matt. v. 25. 1615 P,
　1636 P.
— Alloquium regi Jacobo Woodstochiæ
　habitum 24 Aug. 1624; signed
　"I. P." 1624 P, 1625 P.
— Perez-Vzzah, a sermon, on 2 Sam. vi.
　6–7. 1625 P.
— Sermon at the consecration of Exeter
　college chapel, 1624. 1625 P, 1636 P.
— Concio ad Artium baccalaureos (1 Sam.
　xiv. 26). 1626 P.
— Lectiones decem prout publicè habe-

THE END

Oxford

PRINTED AT THE CLARENDON PRESS

BY HORACE HART, PRINTER TO THE UNIVERSITY

racionis assignet Si inquam hec secundū
tradicionis supra exposite regulam con
sequantur aduertimus deprecemur vt
nobis et omnibus qui hoc audiunt conce
dat dominus fide quam suscepimus custo
dia cursu consumato expectare iusticie
repositam coronam : et inueniri inter eos
qui resurgunt in vitam eternam·liberari
vero a confusione et obprobrio eterno ·
per cristum dominum nostrum per quem
ē deo patri omnipotēti cū spiritu sancto
gloria et imperium in secula seculorum
amen .

Explicit exposicio sancti Jerōnimi in
simbolo apostolorum ad papam lauren̄
cium Impressa Oxonie Et finita An
no domini · M · cccc · lxviij · xvij·die
decembris ·

JERONIMUS. OXFORD. "1468"

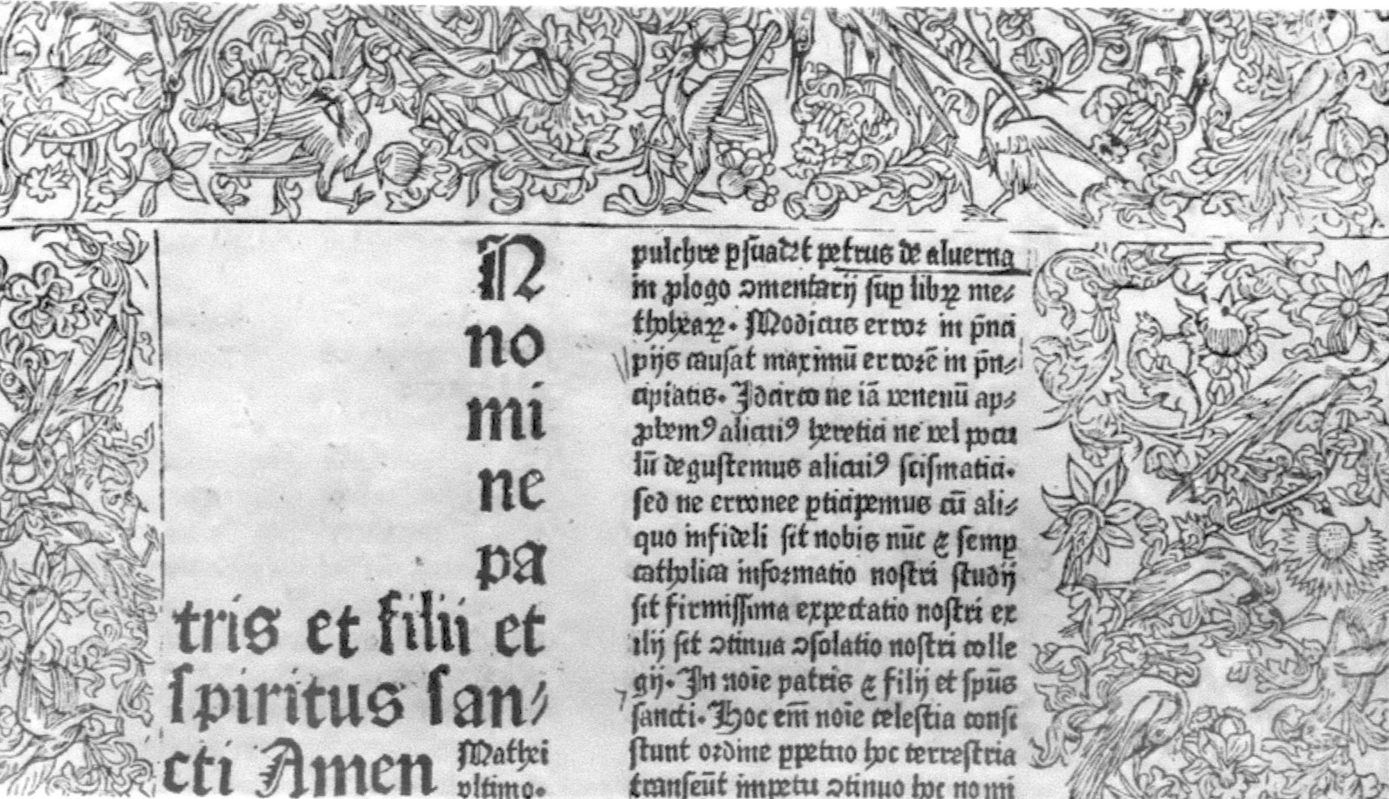

In nomine pa
tris et filii et
spiritus san
cti Amen Mathei vltimo.

pulchꝛe pſuadet petrus de aluerna
in ꝓlogo ꝯmentarij ſup libꝝ me-
tholeaꝝ· Modicus erroꝛ in ꝓncí
pijs cauſat maximū erroꝛē in pn-
cipatis· Idcirco ne iā venenū ap-
ꝓtem9 alicui9 heretici ne vel poꝛu-
lū deguſtemus alicui9 ſciſmatia-
ſed ne erꝛonee ptícipemus cū aliquo infideli ſit nobis nūc ꝯ ſemp
catholica infoꝛmatio noſtrí ſtudij
ſit firmiſſima expectatio noſtri ex
ilij ſít ꝯtínua ꝯſolatio noſtri colle
gij· In noíe patris ꝯ filij et ſpūs
ſancti· Hoc ēm noíe celeſtia conſi
ſtunt oꝛdine ꝑpetuo hoc terreſtria
tranſeūt impetu ꝯtinuo hoc no mí

tione ecclesie parochialis obtinet z capellā
hūs tñ z ochialia iura parochialia q
i qbus ofistāt nota plenius p Joan. ex oz
rochijs super Rubrica z tetigi supra hoc c.
ñ.c.i.d.ecclesijs pochialibus Alb anti
quus scz p spadū xl.annorū ad mīnus cum
ordīnatione episcopi a primdpio xvi.q.i.qs
in aunctis vbi patet cp ad solum episcopum
spectat constituere ecclesiam vel capellam pa
rochialem Quibus instituitur aliquis
vt primus auratus eiuschem licet dependeat
talis capella ab ecclesia suprioti vt notatur
xvi.q.i.c.plures in primdpio p Arch. Alas
tes namiqz capelle pñt prescribere decias z ta
lia iura spūalia otra matricem ecclesiā de pa
stripc.c.ex transmissa sui aut in tali capella ñ
sit institutus z pprtuus auratus pprtuus sed
remotiuus ad libitum prelati maioris eccle
sie zt michilomimus in casu talis capella has
here iura parochialia videliat ex osuetudine p

Int in quoli z
bet decanatu .
Duo vel tres vi
ri deū habentes
Boculis qui er
cessus publicos
prelatorum et aliorum clerico z
rum ad mandatum Archiepis
copi vel eius officialis ipsos de
nūcient .

Int in quolibet Hec
est ostitutio Edmūdi Ar
chiepi z fadt ad terdā par
tem Rubrice scz denūciacio
mibus Decanatus scilicet
rurali. Dña vel tres su

of god or and pyste of the
holy goste the whiche ye
ue vs grace to be fedde of
hym here in oure leuyng
that we may haue the blys
se that neuer shal haue en
de Amen.

In die sancte tri nitatis

GOod men and
wymmen thys
day ys an highe
and a solempne feste in
holy churche for it is of
the hooly Trinite For
as holy churche at wyt-
sont yde makith mencion
how the hooly goste co-
me on to cristus disciples
Now at this tyme is ma
de mencion of all iij. per
sones that is for to say.
Pater filius et spi
ritus Fadyr and sone
and holy goste thre per
sones and one god in tri
nite whe re for we be boun
de to doo all the reueren
ce and worshippe that
we can or may to this ho
ly trinite Also ye shall
vnderstonde whye howe
and what the cause that
this feste was ordeyned
A tis hooly feste was

VI

Tractatus expositorius / super libros poste-
riorū Arestotilis: preclarissimi philisophi
Walteri Burlei artium liberalium
et trium philosophiarū magistri meritissimi: ac in sacra
theologia doctoris perspi
cacissimi planissimiqȝ
suis posteris Oroniensibus admodum vtilis incipit feli-
citer cum summa diligentia.
recognitus.

Scire aūt opiamur. ꝛc. Qr scire ē finis ōnis
tionȝ ad hoc vt bn ordiem' ea q̄ sūt ōnī totīꝰ ops pcognosce finē. ideo
phōs hic in isto capło primo diffinit scire dicens siīplr scire ꝛ nō so-
phistico mō opinia mur vnūquodꝛ cum cām rei cognoscimꝰ ꝓpter quam

VII

¶ Tractatꝰ pbꝛeuis de materia ⁊ foꝛma: Mgꞓi Walteri Burlei doctoꝛis planissimi

¶ Aliud perbꝛeue cōpendiū de relatiuis e=
iusdem doctoꝛis vtile tamen admodum
nouellis logicis.